CW00672760

This is number one hundred and twenty-six in the
second numbered series of the
Miegunyah Volumes
made possible by the
Miegunyah Fund
established by bequests
under the wills of
Sir Russell and Lady Grimwade.

'Miegunyah' was the home of
Mab and Russell Grimwade
from 1911 to 1955.

MALCOLM FRASER

The Political Memoirs

MALCOLM FRASER

The Political Memoirs

MALCOLM FRASER
and MARGARET SIMONS

THE MIEGUNYAH PRESS
An imprint of Melbourne University Publishing Limited
187 Grattan Street, Carlton, Victoria 3053, Australia
mup-info@unimelb.edu.au
www.mup.com.au

First published 2010

Printed in Australia by Griffin Press, SA

National Library of Australia Cataloguing-in-Publication entry
Simons, Margaret, 1960–
Malcolm Fraser: The Political Memoirs / Margaret Simons, Malcolm Fraser.

9780522855791 (hbk.)

Includes index.
Bibliography.

Fraser, Malcolm, 1930–
Prime ministers—Australia—Biography.
Australia—Politics and government—1945–1965.

Other authors/contributors:
Fraser, Malcolm, 1930–

994.06092

This project has been assisted by the Australian Government through the Australia Council, its principal arts funding and advisory body.

Contents

List of Illustrations

Abbreviations of sources

AWM Australian War Memorial

NAA National Archives of Australia

UMA University of Melbourne Archives

A Note from the Narrator

This book is part memoir and part authorised biography. It is Malcolm Fraser's book, yet also the product of a collaboration between him and me, Margaret Simons. Doing it this way was Fraser's choice. He wanted somebody else involved, and more than just a ghost writer. He wanted to expose his record to a questioning if not a critical eye. 'I don't think there is any point in a book that is mere self-justification', he said when we first met. He wanted to be questioned. This, together with research and organising the material, was my role. I am the narrator or, if you like, the curator of this account of Fraser's life and work. After this note I will disappear behind the material.

It seemed to me and to the publisher, Louise Adler, that this book should be written in the first person, since it was conceived as a memoir. Fraser firmly vetoed that idea. 'Is there any way that it can be in the first person without me having to say "I, I, I" all the time?' he said, giving a little self-mocking grimace to each repetition of the word 'I'.

He was told there was not: that saying 'I' was what first person meant.

'Well, I don't want to say "I, I, I".'

That is where my job began. My voice was to intercede between the 'I' and the reader. Yet there were times when Fraser wanted to speak for himself and in his own voice—particularly on politics and policy. The third person, fortunately, both avoids the 'I, I, I' and is flexible enough to allow for the Fraser that emerged in our interviews sometimes to speak directly to the reader.

At that first meeting, before I had agreed to take on the project, I asked Fraser if there were limits to what he would talk about. Would he, for example, talk frankly about the dismissal of the Whitlam government? He said that he was bored with that and it was much less important than some of the other things there were to talk about. Then he said, in tones of mild surprise, 'You know, some people I work with now on human rights say they used to hate me back then'.

I said, 'Perhaps you killed their dreams'.

He went long-faced in the way that only Malcolm Fraser can, and replied, 'They were dreams that had to die'.

I think that was the moment in which I decided to take on the project.

Later, I teased Fraser that he wanted to write a memoir yet by his own admission hated talking about himself ('Absolutely loathe it', he agreed) and, even at the age of seventy-nine, preferred to think about the present and the future rather than the past. 'Well, the future is so much more interesting', he said. The past was of interest only to the extent that it illuminated the present and offered lessons for the future.

Fraser has never written his own account of the key events of his career. Nor has he read the accounts of others. He has not read, for example, the memoirs of Sir John Kerr or Gough Whitlam, or the books written by political journalists about the way in which he came to power and the impact of his prime ministership. Nor would he have collaborated in the writing of this account but for the fact that he wanted a book that spoke from his experience to the present and the future. He wanted more than a memoir. His motivation for collaborating with this book has been to talk about the continuing importance of the values that have shaped his life and his career. These values are what he sees as the core of liberalism. They are simply stated: respect for the individual, a commitment to individual liberty under the law and the principle that the strong should protect the weak. The story of how they play out, how they are frustrated, how they occasionally triumph and why they must be safeguarded is largely what this book is about.

From his earliest political speeches Fraser eschewed rigid ideologies or counsels of human perfection. Liberalism was pragmatic, he said, and flexible. This was what distinguished it from competing schemes of political thought. Liberalism would play out in different ways depending on the times and the people concerned, but the values at the core did not alter. It is this conception of liberalism that has motivated him to collaborate in this book. 'It's quite possible to talk about these things without saying that I always lived up to them', he said at an early stage in the project.

So how did we proceed? I interviewed Fraser on roughly a weekly basis for more than a year. Sometimes we met in his office in Collins Street, Melbourne, with its sweeping city views. We were often interrupted by the telephone. It quickly became clear to me that Fraser was still at the centre of a vast network and still involved, sometimes explicitly but much more often behind the scenes, in politics and public life. He spoke to Kevin Rudd in the lead-up to the 2007 federal election. He was one of those who persuaded Liberal Opposition Leader Brendan Nelson to take part in the apology to the stolen generations in the early days of the Rudd government. At the same time, sometimes in back-to-back phone calls, he lobbied the Minister for Aboriginal Affairs, Jenny Macklin, on the politics of preparing for that apology. Later he was in contact with his former staffer David Kemp, now President of the Victorian Liberal Party, over the reforms needed to revive the party. Again and again I saw him make phone calls to the most senior in the land on all sides of politics. Sometimes the calls were prompted by the topics of our conversations. At other times he was simply busy—still—with the affairs of the nation, and our interviews had to give way. He was nearly always put through straightaway or received a return call in minutes. Once, he was making a call to the Prime Minister's office, and was told that the person he was after was in a meeting. 'Well, it's Malcolm Fraser here' he began. The person on the other end of the line immediately decided that the target of the call was available after all. Fraser covered the mouthpiece and gave me an arch smile. 'The games people play', he said. All this was a telling insight into the continued power of Malcolm Fraser: partly the aura of having held the prime ministership, partly the standing of the man himself.

Other interviews were conducted at his Mornington Peninsula home. His dogs sat on our feet, pinched the biscuits Tamie had given us and punctuated our talk with their snuffles and demands for attention. Sometimes the recordings include sudden interjections from Fraser: 'Go away; you are being a damn nuisance'. Fortunately he was only sometimes talking to me.

Because of his bad back—a legacy of lifting 180-pound bags of superphosphate on the farm years ago—Fraser would sit erect in a high, hard-backed chair, while I sat below him on the couch or across the desk, surrounded by papers and notes. He often laughed, but rarely relaxed. There were no-go areas to do with his personal life and, most of all, his children. Some of our interviews were tough. Sometimes the questions made him angry. There were also times when he was visibly moved; once was when he was talking about his childhood and the frustrations of his parents' policy of children being seen and not heard. In his view, it is this, and the extraordinary solitude of his early years, that are to blame—if that is the word—for what others see as aloofness, and he describes as shyness. These things are also, surely, among the reasons for his extraordinary self-sufficiency. He spoke about how his grandchildren had been raised differently. 'For a long while I just didn't want to speak to anyone. I'd been told children should be seen and not heard. Children were not meant to say anything. Tell that to my grandchildren. They never stop chattering. Hamish comes in, he's the youngest, and says, "Grandad, I've got a joke. Come on. I'm making it up!" They are never going to be diffident! They are never going to be shy.' His voice cracked. He paused and went on. 'Today's kids get up at school from a very young age and say what happened over the weekend and whatever. The whole idea is that people express themselves. I think I was brought up in an environment where people were told not to express themselves. But the other part of that was people thought you couldn't hear. They thought that adults could talk about you and you wouldn't understand. Yet you understood absolutely what was being said and then, you know, they would realise that you understood and they'd start spelling the word. I can remember saying to my parents, "What are you spelling it for, because I can spell just as well as you and I know exactly what you are saying". They just didn't want me to understand.'

There was a moment of silence. Then Fraser coughed and said, 'Well. There you are'.

I came to understand his thick reserve—possessed by all the Frasers I met—as inseparable from his sense of dignity. The reserve and the reluctance to talk about himself were constant challenges for an interviewer wanting to bring a sense of the man to his readers. Yet in the end I came to like him for it. There may be other ways of maintaining personal dignity in the midst of public life, but this has been his.

Another time Fraser was moved was when we were talking about the Vietnam War. During his time as Army Minister, administering conscription, a member of his electorate attacked him in the bar of the Henty Hotel in Portland because his son's marble had been drawn in the lottery, and he was off to the war. 'I tried to explain why, but there is nothing you can say to persuade a parent that that's a good thing, especially when he was a good solid Labor man.' Nine months later Fraser was in the same bar and the man attacked him again, because his son had gone and married 'one of them women'—a Vietnamese—and was bringing her home. But the next time Fraser was in the bar, the man came up and wanted to buy him a beer, saying, 'That girl, she's the best thing that ever happened to our family'. Fraser said, 'So she would have known that she had a very hostile father-in-law, coming to Australia to that hostility. But she brought him round. Can you imagine …' Fraser stopped speaking. There was a long silence. We looked at each other. Then, once again, he broke it with a cough and the words 'Well. There you are'.

As well as conducting the interviews, I spent time digging in the archives in both Melbourne and Canberra, finding records of who Fraser was and what he thought many years ago, when the Cold War was raging and the Soviet threat seemed immense and imminent in a visceral way that is difficult to understand today. There was also work in discovering the ways in which the narrative of the Fraser government, as revealed by the archives, differs from that put about by his political enemies—not least his enemies within the Liberal Party. At the end of this work it seemed clear to me that the Fraser government is one of the most misunderstood and misrepresented governments in our history. Part of Fraser's motives for collaborating in this account is to correct the record—but repeatedly he declined to rely on his memory alone. He would proceed only when he knew the documentary proof was available. Although Fraser often protested in our interviews that his memory for details was poor, it became common for him to say something that seemed doubtful to me, only to be proved correct when I found it independently confirmed by the archival record.

In time I came to agree with Fraser: there were many more important things to talk about in this book than the dismissal, even though that is a topic that has its place and shall not be avoided. 'If the headlines when this book comes out are "New Information about the Dismissal", then in my view we will have failed', said Fraser. Success, to him, meant discussion about liberal ideals and how they should play out in present-day Australia. He wanted to talk, as always, about policy, about how to run a government and a country, and about the things that really matter in politics and public life. David Kemp, who was closer to Fraser than anyone other than family during his years as Prime Minister, told me that in his opinion Fraser was the most idealistic Prime Minister Australia has ever had, and probably the one most focussed on policy. Fraser believes, said Kemp, in 'will with a capital W'—in the efficacy of political leadership, in activism, in pushing through.

Fraser is not a man who easily makes stories of his life. In this, I think, he is unlike most of us, who shape our lives in the telling. Fraser is reluctant or perhaps even unable to do this. Shaping the story, curating the material, was my job. Our interactions were not always easy. There were topics that he had to be persuaded to talk about. There are certainly things in this book that Fraser would not have mentioned or explored left to himself. Nevertheless, it is his book, his story, and there is nothing between these covers that he has not authorised.

Fraser does not lack a sense of theme and meaning. The speech everyone remembers him by, the one in which he said that life was not meant to be easy, he wrote himself.[1] This was in 1971, at a time when his political career appeared to be wrecked. It seemed to him impossible that he would ever become this country's leader. In the popular imagination the 'Life wasn't meant to be easy' line has been reduced to a joke, or a jibe, given that Fraser was born comparatively wealthy. Yet in its original context the line is powerful and moving—the conclusion to a discussion of liberalism and the history of nations, and what a nation needs from its people. The full sentence reads: 'There is within me some part of the metaphysic, and thus I would add that life is not meant to be easy'.

The metaphysic? Fraser is not religious, and yet thinks religion is a necessary thing—that if it did not exist it would have to be quickly invented. People need a sense of higher purpose. 'I would probably like to be less logical and, you know, really to be able to believe there is a god, whether it is Allah, or the Christian god, or some other … But I think I studied too much philosophy. You can never know.' And yet he acknowledges a liking for inspirational preaching and words that soar, thoughts that inspire. He acknowledges a sense of higher purpose—a spiritual sense. I suggested to him once that he was an idealist. He paused, patted a dog, then said, 'Well, that is what it has all been about, really'.

Prelude

In the wet autumn of 1949, Malcolm Fraser left home for a month-long trip through New South Wales with his friend Gavin Casey. Fraser was just out of school, not yet nineteen. He was a tall young man—all arms and legs—and plagued by shyness. He had been in the debating society at school but had not acquitted himself well. When called to speak, he would find that without realising it he had torn up his notes in the agony of waiting, his hands needing something to do. He would stand up, say a very few words, and sit down again. Now, in a few weeks, he would be leaving for Oxford University. Although he was only dimly aware of it, he was on the brink of his intellectual and emotional awakening.

At Oxford he would first be made to feel small—aware of how little his education and background had prepared him for wrestling with the big and urgent ideas of his time. Then he would discover that this, the time in which he was coming to adulthood, was one for hope and for great things. The world war was over and a new machinery of international affairs was being constructed. At Oxford it seemed that humankind might at last find new and better ways of organising itself. Fraser would return to Australia determined to do more with his life than just farming.

But now, in March 1949, he was still emerging from boyhood. On his trip round New South Wales he kept a journal.[1] Reading through it today, it seems he was almost consciously trying on his adult self for size. There is, in the day-by-day entries, the mixture of pragmatism and idealism that came to characterise the mature man. He was a farmer's son. He had an eye for productivity and detail. He had strong opinions. He noted the pay rate for grape-pickers at Mildura (fourteen shillings and sixpence a tin), the quality of the livestock in the farms they visited and the number of sheep per acre. He also reflected on history and on the nature of his country. He tried to capture the beauty of the landscape and how it moved him.

He was itching for independence. He was happy to go to Oxford because it was on the other side of the world; he would have resisted going to Melbourne University. After experiencing school mostly as restriction, he wanted freedom. He was the product of an early childhood quite extraordinary for its isolation, solitude and lack of conversation. In his family, children were not consulted. Always, the adults seemed to be having conversations about him just out of his hearing. The likelihood was that, like most farmers' sons, he would live at home at least until marriage. 'You had no control over your life', he remembers. 'I thought I needed, at some stage, to be in an environment where I was making my own decisions. Being halfway round the world put you more in that sort of environment than if you are near home.'

Fraser and Casey set out in a farm truck along roads that were more dirt than bitumen. On the first day, they passed from the timbered, park-like country around Fraser's home farm of Nareen in Victoria's Western District on to the red plains of the Wimmera and then on to the Mallee, where the road rose and fell over apparently endless successions of sand dunes, and every paddock seemed to contain the ruined remains of a farm house. Fraser wrote in his journal:

> For the first time I saw what much of Australia was really like ... Erosion, nature's dreaded weapon, in these dry lands is painfully evident. Paddocks laid bare by the plough have been blasted by the wind and rain but still the farmers sow their wheat and reap the harvest that can never be sure and safe. It was in these dry but rich wheat lands of Australia that the soldier settlers, after World War I,

> strived for a living. For some the struggle was too great and the Mallee scrub reclaimed the farms as her own. But others, endowed with dogged courage and fortitude, have grown to love the Mallee and the hard healthy life which it means.

Coming into Mildura, they swam in the Murray River at Lock 11, and toured the orchards and packing sheds. Fraser reflected on the 'truly remarkable' wonders of the irrigation settlement. Then on to Broken Hill through salt bush and sand.

> Travelling in the half light, with the freshening wind stirring up dust storms all along the road, and with the sinking sun lighting up the red dust all round the sky produced a strange atmosphere of solitude. Soon, as the sun sank beneath the western sky, the lightning from the approaching storm lit up the horizon ... The almost savage beauty and allure of the country impressed itself upon us and we could easily see that any man who spent a few years here would never leave it for the closer settled areas.

They had arranged to stay with landholders along the route. Near Broken Hill they stayed with the White family of Willow Point Station, arriving in the early hours and sleeping in the cabin of the truck until daylight. Here, Fraser noted, the land could support reliably only one sheep to every 20 acres: 'Many people ran one sheep to 10 acres, but Mr White said their land was going backwards and that they ran into much trouble during droughts'.

In the evenings, White told them stories about the Aboriginals of the area. 'One in particular', Fraser wrote, 'stuck in my memory'. There had been an Aboriginal called Nanya. In 1860 he had gone with his two 'gins' into the waterless country to the west, hoping to avoid capture and imprisonment in a reservation. The tribe increased to twenty members. They lived on water from the roots of shrubs and trees, and whatever game they could kill. Then, in 1896, a half-caste discovered their tracks and gave them up. They were rounded up and sent to a reserve. 'But Nanya's spirit, which had been so strong and courageous when he was wandering in his arid hunting ground, broke in captivity and very soon he died.'

The next day, the boys toured the mines of Broken Hill, Fraser noting the value of the equipment and the impact of the handsome bonuses paid to miners on the prices charged in town. 'New buildings cost about two and a half times Melbourne prices.' They were delayed for three days because the roads to Bourke were impassable due to the rain. Then they set off again, camped near Wilcannia, got bogged and were pulled out by a passing truck. Fraser took a photo of a flock of emus. On again to Cobar and Nyngan, where Fraser noted that kangaroos and emus were rare. 'This is a typical example where a young country has, through neglect and indifference, allowed her native fauna to be ruthlessly hunted and killed. Present game laws are still inadequate and do not prevent wasteful killing.'

They spent two days helping to crutch sheep, then went on to Dubbo, where Fraser noted the rainfall statistics and the quality of the aerodrome. They helped on another station, sowing barley and treating ewes for blowfly, and went to a dance in the evening. On once more, getting bogged again, stopping for truck repairs in Coolah, then passing in the pitch of night along the dangerous track through the Abercrombie Ranges. 'On one side the mountains reared up to their majestic heights, while on the other the road seemed to fall away into an impenetrable abyss.'

Then there was more crutching of fly-blown sheep on a property near Bathurst, before heading on to the 'much-publicised but confusing and scattered Canberra'. Fraser was not impressed. He liked the War Memorial, but as for the rest: 'This city was planned to be a great metropolis and consequently everything was planned on a grand scale. Unfortunately there is little to encourage anyone to go there unless one is a civil servant or a politician. Therefore the great Canberra is not, and will not be'. He visited Parliament House:

'None of it was very impressive. In fact the House of Representatives looked rather shabby'. Just six years later, Fraser would enter that shabby chamber once again as its youngest member. Twenty years after that he would dominate it as Prime Minister.

But for now he turned for home, down the Hume Highway to Melbourne, then back to Nareen. It was time to pack for Oxford. He wrote on the last page in his journal:

> All my life I will have memories of calm nights beneath the sky, of waking before dawn to see the sun rise in the east and of driving over the lonely bush roads with dust eddying all round. The deformed Mallee scrub and the ghost farms, the great plains and the endless sand hills, the majestic mountains, the beautiful valleys and pleasant hills. All these are part of Australia and part of my memories. Among them I will find my home.

Part 1

Being Heard

1

Roots

For most of Fraser's political career, his opponents have found it easy to think that they know him because of his background. He has been aware of having to fight the stereotype. 'Western District. Melbourne Grammar. Oxford University. They think they know who you are', he says, but childhoods and families are never so simple, and Malcolm Fraser's certainly were not. Was it a happy childhood? 'Mostly', he says. 'Not always.'

Fraser was born on 21 May 1930, during the Great Depression. He was raised at Balpool-Nyang, a remote property on the Edward River in the New South Wales Riverina. On these low-lying alluvial plains looped by ancient water courses, Fraser had a childhood extraordinary for its beauty, silence and isolation. Deniliquin was two hours' drive away along black soil roads. If there was rain, it was impossible to get through. The trip involved crossing the river on a punt. Melbourne was eleven hours' drive. When the river flooded the family were cut off. The property was a mixture of a red-gum forest, flood plains and big grazing paddocks. Old photo albums show the forest in flood, and the family picnicking under a hard sun, perched on a levy bank built to stop the homestead from flooding. Una Fraser, Malcolm's mother, wore a twin-set for the camera. The children—Malcolm and his elder sister, Lorri—were in overalls or dungarees, all gap teeth and dust.

Other photos show supplies being brought up the Edward River and eagles flapping helplessly after being caught in traps. 'They took the lambs, you see', says Fraser. There were sawmillers at work in the forest, sweaty and muscled, their saws powered by steam engines. Amid all this is Fraser as a long-limbed little boy, on horseback or messing around in his homemade wooden dinghy on the river with his pet galah on his shoulder. From the age of seven or eight, Fraser would disappear all day into the forest on horseback. 'When I was ten or eleven, my parents told me I should never ride in the forest, but I'd been riding into it for at least two years, just by myself and a long way in. I always felt I knew exactly where home was, and if I hadn't, my horse would have. I could have just dropped the reins and the horse would have found its way home, but I never had to do that, because I knew where I was going.' He was in his element, confident and free. He had a rifle that he would carry along the river bank, and he learned to make the sounds of crows, so they would come close enough to be shot. Crows were the enemy. They gouged out the eyes of the lambs. Fraser remembers his pride on the day he shot five of them.

Fraser loved this property and his life there, but Balpool-Nyang became one of the first big losses in his life. Speaking about the loss still moves him to tears. His parents decided to sell when he was thirteen years old and away at school. He hadn't even known that the property was on the market. He was devastated. 'Kids weren't consulted in those days. I was told after the event. They knew I would have said "no". You accepted things as a child. They weren't all good things; you just accepted them. You had no control over your life, and at school, masters and mistresses told you what to do. At home your parents told you what to do.' His parents, worn down by the Depression years and successions of droughts and floods, had decided to move to the Western District of Victoria, an area with reliable rainfall. They bought Nareen, the property Fraser owned throughout his prime ministership and with which he is most often identified, although he no longer lives there. Sometime shortly after the sale of Balpool-Nyang, Fraser wrote the following words in a photo album:

> These are pictures of our Nyang. Droughts made us sell-out but forever will the memory of Nyang be strong within me. Nareen will never quite take its place. There are a few pictures of Nyang and a few pictures of Mum and Dad there. They remind me of every aspect of life on the station that I shall never forget.[1]

His only sibling, big sister Lorraine, or Lorri, was three and a half years older. At the age of six—when Malcolm was not yet three—she was sent away to boarding school. This was because, according to their mother, she was 'uncontrollable' and leading young Malcolm astray. Fraser remembers, 'She was a rebellious child'.

'And you weren't?'

'I was more accepting. Yes.'

Lorri Fraser, now Lorri Whiting, went on to be a significant abstract artist. She moved to Italy and has lived there ever since. Today she has a strong affection for her little brother, but few fond memories of her childhood. She remembers injustice, and emotional distance. When she was one year old, before Malcolm was born, her parents went to Europe for several months, leaving her with her grandparents. When her mother, Una, was in her last days, she wrote to Lorri apologising for the breach and hurt between them, and attributing the fact that they had never bonded to that early separation.

Years before, when interviewed about her famous son, Una contrasted the temperaments of her two children.[2] Malcolm, she said, was an easy child, 'perfectly normal and pleasant'. She claimed to have an almost telepathic connection with him. Lorri, on the other hand, was always having tantrums.

From Lorri's perspective, Malcolm was undoubtedly the favourite child—something that lasted well into their adult life. Both mother and father doted on him. Yet despite this and the fact that she was inevitably jealous of him, the two children were quite close. 'I think Malcolm was always aware that what happened to me was unjust.' Being the favoured one, she comments, can be as big a burden as being the second runner. She doesn't rule out the possibility that this early experience is part of what formed Malcolm and his abiding preoccupation with justice.

Once Lorri had gone to boarding school, there were no other children around. Malcolm had a succession of governesses, but none of them stayed long. Meanwhile, his parents did not believe in engaging children in conversation. Children were to be seen and not heard. And, yet the young boy was curious. Una remembered that as a child Malcolm was always wanting to be included. 'He always wanted to know what you were talking about. I would be talking to Neville and suddenly he would say, "What are you saying?"' Fraser, on the other hand, remembers the frustration of never being allowed to speak, and being told that there were some things children should not be thinking about at all. 'There were few conversations. I suppose I remember the ones informing me of what was going to happen to me. There were very few of what you would call real conversations.' Meanwhile, he half-overheard conversations about the Depression, and later the war. He also remembers conversations about Catholics, how they were not to be trusted. 'I would ask, "What's the problem? What's the matter with Catholics?"

'"Well, they are different. They are not Australians; they owe their loyalty to the Pope."

'You would never get people explaining what they thought and why they thought it. Such things were not discussed with children, but if my sister had wanted to marry a Catholic, my father would have just cut the traces. He really would have. He felt very strongly. On other things he was very reasonable, but this was a common prejudice at the time.'

Fraser attributes his father's attitude to Prime Minister Billy Hughes and the conscription referendum during World War I.

Hughes made the referendum an attack on Catholics, and Irish Catholics in particular, accusing them of being disloyal. 'My father would have believed everything Billy Hughes said', says Fraser. 'So did most of the men in the trenches in World War I.' Hughes's actions in encouraging sectarianism, says Fraser today, were the worst of any Prime Minister in Australian history. They could have led to armed conflict, he believes, had there not been a settlement of the Irish question in 1922. The scars lasted for fifty years.

Fraser has several times made the comparison between his father's generation's anti-Catholicism and the things that are said in present-day Australia about Muslims. Today, anti-Catholic prejudices look silly; it is hard to understand the hatred and suspicion that inspired them. So too, he says, will future Australians look back on the prejudice against Muslims as silly and ignorant. Reflecting on the reasons for his father's prejudice was to guide him during his own prime ministership. Racism is always present in society, ready to be stirred up, but political leadership can make a difference.

The Depression made its impact on Fraser's childhood. Although there is no doubt that his family was privileged, they were land-rich and comparatively cash-poor. Privacy was at a premium in the house, because the manager and his family had moved in, to save money. The half-overheard conversations from which the young Malcolm was excluded were often about money. There was a pervasive sense of trouble and worry. Cars had to be downgraded. The historic Toorak homestead of Norla, from which his grandfather, Sir Simon Fraser, had stirred up Victorian politics, had to be sold. One of Fraser's earliest memories is of it being demolished.

Back at Balpool-Nyang, it was either drought or flood. For years in a row lambs were killed at birth to save the ewes' strength. Willow trees around the homestead were cut down to provide feed for horses. Meanwhile the house, built by Malcolm's father after his marriage, moved as the alluvial soil of the plains shifted under the concrete blocks, and created enormous cracks in most rooms. When dust storms came it was hard to see from one side of the house to the other. Swaggies walked the roads looking for work and marking the gates of properties with secret signs which indicated to their fellows whether or not they could expect a friendly reception. Fraser does not know what the sign read on the gate at Balpool-Nyang. He remembers the 1938 drought in which his father, desperate to sell sheep, rang a battery-hen farm that was boiling up carcasses for feed. 'They had so many offers, they weren't taking any more. They said, "Well, we don't really need them … but if you pay the freight we'll accept delivery".' Fraser remembers his father laying off workers, and them pleading to be allowed to stay on, willing to work only for food. Fraser's father wouldn't consent. The unions, he said, would not allow it. They would make it the basis of a future claim.

Fraser's parents were always glad to get away from the hardship. Money worries were constant, but the family was hardly poor. For six weeks every summer they would go to Portsea on holiday, and trips to Melbourne were frequent. Asked what kind of people his parents were, Fraser says, 'They were very much part of the scene. Part of all the clubs you are meant to be part of'. They were, in fact, enmeshed in the Victorian establishment.

* * *

Balpool-Nyang had come into the family as part of the legacy of Fraser's paternal grandfather, Sir Simon Fraser.[3] The historical record favours winners, and Sir Simon was certainly one of those. Today, those who know about this side of Malcolm Fraser's background tend to see him through the prism of Sir Simon and his position at the centre of the squattocracy. Sir Simon was a wealthy and powerful self-made man, and one of the people who helped to form the nation of Australia. Although he died before Malcolm was born, his legacy, both of wealth and social position, determined much of his grandson's childhood.

Simon Fraser was a Canadian Scot, born in 1832 in the little fishing village of Pictou, Nova Scotia, the son of a farmer and flour mill owner who had migrated from Inverness. He arrived in Australia in 1853, at the age of twenty-one, one of thousands in search of their fortune on the goldfields. Soon after he arrived in Bendigo, he realised that most miners were doomed to leave the goldfields broke and defeated. He set up as a grocer, selling potatoes. After a few years, recognising that the gold could not last for ever, he moved to a shop in Elizabeth Street, Melbourne, from where he sold produce and horses. He soon moved into contracting for roads, bridges and railways; this was how he acquired his wealth. A few years later, he was in Queensland taking advantage of the wide open country to become a squatter. He formed the Squatting Investment Company with others, and bought properties all over the west of the state and down into New South Wales, including Balpool-Nyang. One of these was to play a particularly important part in Australian history. Aware that artesian water had been discovered in France and having seen springs on Australian properties, in 1886 Fraser began to bore on the station of Thurulgoona, about 30 miles from Cunnamulla, and found water. It was the beginning of artesian bores in Australia and the transformation of the inland.[4] Today, this is one of the few aspects of his family history to which Malcolm Fraser pays conscious tribute. He has given the name 'Thurulgoona' to his present home, on Victoria's Mornington Peninsula. Sir Simon's portrait hangs in the study.

Simon Fraser entered politics in 1874 as member for the Echuca-based seat of Rodney in the Victorian Legislative Assembly. He was married twice. His first wife was Margaret Bolger, who bore him two daughters before dying in 1880. Sir Simon's obituary in *The Bulletin* suggested that Bolger was a Catholic, and that this marriage was the root of his vehement anti-Catholicism.[5] Whatever the reason, sectarianism was one of his less noble legacies: he was intensely involved in the sectarian divides of the day. He was a leading member of the Protestant fraternal organisation the Orange Movement, and he often pushed the Protestant cause in parliament. He was also a prominent Mason—Grand Master of the Grand Lodge of Port Phillip. His second marriage, in 1885, was to Anna Bertha Collins, daughter of another Queensland pioneer and squatter, John Collins. Anna bore Simon three sons. Malcolm Fraser's father, John Neville (always known as Neville), was the youngest, born in 1890.

The historical record doesn't favour women, but Anna Fraser seems to have been a remarkable woman who used her position as wife to one of the country's leading men to push her own list of charities and causes. As well as being one of the best known charity workers of her time, she was a member of the Free Kindergarten Union of Victoria, a key progressive organisation dedicated to training teachers with a particular emphasis on providing high-quality early-childhood education to disadvantaged families. The wife of Prime Minister Alfred Deakin was the president. Anna was also on the council of the state branch of the Victoria League, which was established to encourage friendship between people of the Commonwealth and to promote migration from Commonwealth countries to Australia. She belonged as well to the Alexandra Club, a theoretically non-political organisation that provided rooms and facilities for ladies in the city; in fact, it was a centre of female power, including in its membership the wives of many of the country's most powerful men.[6]

After their wedding, Simon and Anna moved into Norla in the heart of Toorak. The gardens were used for fetes and fundraising for Anna's preoccupations. Fraser re-entered politics; he had a couple of unsuccessful contests before becoming a member of the Legislative Council for the South Yarra province. In September 1889, the weekly magazine *Table Talk* described him as 'enormously rich' and as controlling the policy of the *Evening Standard* newspaper, of which he was a large shareholder and director.[7] He was also a friend of David Syme, the proprietor of *The Age* newspaper. The two men shared a belief in free trade, but fell out when Syme switched sides to become a protectionist. Syme banned Fraser from the editorial columns of the paper; Fraser retorted by publishing his speeches as paid advertisements.

Fraser was a federalist. He was active in the earliest meetings held to discuss the creation of Australia, and helped to organise the Australian Federal Convention of 1897, which led to the drafting of the constitution and the creation of the Australian nation. Before that, he had been a representative at a conference of the various governments of the British Empire held in Ottawa in 1894. With the arrival of Federation he ran for the Senate, and topped the state poll. In 1906 he stood for re-election as an anti-socialist. He was knighted in 1918, shortly before his death of bronchitis at the age of eighty-seven. His obituary in *The Age* described him as 'a lovable personality' who was 'held in high esteem by many who are bitterly opposed to his political views. He was intensely patriotic in sentiment'. *The Bulletin* was less reverent to members of the squattocracy; it described Fraser as 'a hard shell politician' but nevertheless commented that he had served his adopted country 'better than most old identities who die rich' and that he was 'a good Australian in most respects'.[8]

Sir Simon Fraser left his children not only a political legacy, but extensive landholdings and the very best connections. By the time of his death he had worked with almost all of the families who were to shape Victorian politics. He knew the Baillieus and was close friends with Hubert Ralph Hamer, the father of the future Victorian Premier Dick Hamer. The next generation of these families remained entwined with the Frasers. The Squatting Investment Company that Sir Simon had co-founded had among its directors Richard Casey, whose son, also Richard but more commonly known as Dick, was a close friend of the Frasers and one of the most influential Liberal politicians of the Menzies era. From 1965, he was Governor-General. The Casey family was central to the Frasers. Malcolm's sister, Lorri, married Bertram (Bertie) Whiting, who had been aide-de-camp to Dick Casey during the latter's time as Governor of Bengal during World War II. It was Dick Casey's nephew, Gavin, who later accompanied Malcolm on his trip around New South Wales before he left Australia for Oxford.

This was the heritage to which Malcolm's parents, Neville and Una, owed their social position. Families, though, have two sides, and there was another aspect to Malcolm's family history that was barely spoken of.

Malcolm knew that there was never any money on his mother's side of the family. He met his maternal grandfather, Louis Arnold Woolf, just once. There is a photo of the old man standing stiffly alongside Lorri, a chubby Malcolm and some other children, in front of a seesaw. Another shows him sitting awkwardly on the ground with his grandchildren.[9] Woolf died in 1938, when Malcolm was seven years old. Lorri remembers knowing that there was something unusual—and therefore desperately interesting—about him. 'I knew that Louis Arnold Woolf was not a name like John or Simon or Fraser or Casey or all the other names of our respectable bunch.' But she could never find out much about him.

Woolf was at least part Jewish. This fact was kept from Malcolm until he was an adult. He remembers at Melbourne Grammar School needing to have it explained to him what a Jew was, and why the Jewish students didn't go to chapel. 'I was extraordinarily ignorant. I really was.' An obituary of Una Fraser written by her friend, the art critic Philip Jones, said, 'Her wide culture and questioning far ranging mind stem no doubt from her partly Jewish background. It seems a pity she obscured rather than celebrated this rich heritage'.[10]

Woolf was also a politician, though not a successful one. He seems to have been an intense idealist, as well as, according to Una's recollections, a dilettante interested in literature and a Shakespearian scholar. 'I well remember him shutting himself in our "den" and declaiming with much gusto speeches from *Othello* and *Hamlet*.' Although Una was alive throughout Fraser's career, she never discussed her father's history with him—though she did mention his political work in a letter she wrote for her grandchildren before her death. Fraser did not know the details of Woolf's career until the facts were discovered as part of the research for this book.

Louis Woolf had been born in New Zealand, the son of a Jewish father who had emigrated from South Africa, and Esther Reuben.[11]

Una believed that her grandmother was not Jewish, but the name suggests that the Jewish heritage may have been on both sides of the family.[12] Woolf never knew his father—he died of consumption two months before he was born. Later, his mother took him to Australia and remarried. Woolf did not get on with his stepfather, and he left home at an early age. He became an accountant. In 1895 he married Amy May Booth, one of thirteen children and a third-generation Australian. Her grandparents and parents had arrived in Sydney in 1849 and had settled in Ulladulla, on the south coast, where they opened a store and travellers' inn. Booth's father, John, went into property development, establishing the private town of Milton—named because of his admiration for Milton's *Paradise Lost*. He went on to become an investor and speculator, and in time a produce merchant in Sussex Street, Sydney. There, he met the Hordern family, who ran the famous Emporium department store, known as 'the Empo', which employed more than four thousand people. Booth's elder sister, Jane Maria, married into the Hordern family. Her son became Sir Samuel Hordern—one of the richest and most prominent Australians of his time.[13] There was little difference in age between Amy and her nieces and nephews, and she spent much of her childhood in the Hordern household, part of the family.

Amy Booth's marriage to Woolf carried her away from the centre of the colonial establishment and towards the edge of things. Woolf had lost most of his money in the 1890s crash; he had to start again. Amy and Louis's first daughter, Enid, was born in Sydney in 1896, but by the next year the family had moved to the small new colony of Swan River and the township of Perth. They knew nobody. Amy was desperately lonely, but Woolf apparently did well, setting up as an accountant in the centre of town. The 1890s was a formative decade for Western Australia. Thanks to gold discoveries at Kalgoorlie and Coolgardie, the population of Perth more than tripled in the decade, but by 1901 it was still home to only 27 000 people. In this small pond, Woolf was prominent, and his ambitions were not confined to accountancy. Like Simon Fraser, he became caught up in discussions about the creation of a new nation. He was both a federalist and a free trader. In the elections for the first Senate, in 1901, he ran as a candidate endorsed by the Australian Free-Trade and Liberal Association, one of the many organisations that were precursors to Menzies's Liberal Party.

Throughout February and March 1901 the *Perth Morning Herald* reported on Woolf's public meetings and addresses.[14] They were at first well attended and well received. Woolf seems to have been a serious and passionate speaker; his lectures were wide-ranging and packed with detail. He was in favour of a white Australia, and argued that free trade was the 'only democratic policy'. To begin with, he was greeted with cheers, but the positive reception didn't last. A *Herald* editorial made a criticism of him that is reminiscent of some that were later made of his grandson: 'Mr Woolf is, perhaps, one of the best authorities on financial questions in the state, and a sound and reliable man in every way, but his platform style is not effective. If he had personal magnetism together with knowledge, his chances of election would be all the greater'.[15]

The editorial was prescient. On the day of the election, Woolf received just 409 votes, coming fifth-last out of sixteen candidates. Surviving records give an indication of some of the prejudices he had to deal with and of his own suppression of his racial background. A collection of sketches of well-known Western Australians published in 1905 contains this implicitly racist contribution about Woolf:

> One of the leading accountants in town. He neither affirms nor denies he is a Jew. A familiar figure in town. Tall and round-shouldered, he strides along the street with head well ahead of him, hands clenching and opening, muttering as he goes. He is making a political speech to himself. In imagination he is on a public platform, being cheered to the echo by enthusiastic crowds. The reality was different. He stumped the country when seeking election to the first federal parliament. Wherever he went he was received with eloquent silence. No one threw vegetables, probably because they felt sorry for such a hopelessly

> impossible candidate. He does not know how he appears to other people, so this may do him a lot of good.[16]

In 1908, Woolf left for London, 'owing to medical advice that he should seek a change of scene and climate'. A dinner was held to farewell him, and it seems he had lost none of his fire. He gave a speech on liberalism which, in its passion and cadence, was apparently uncannily similar to some that were later given by his grandson Malcolm Fraser. The *Perth Morning Herald* paraphrased his words:

> The National Liberal League claimed that they were not only national but also liberal. What they had done in the past should be sufficient to prove that they desired the people to rule and not any faction. They asked all shades of political thought and all grades of social influence to join their ranks.[17]

Woolf returned to Perth after about a year and continued to be listed as an accountant until the year before his death, in 1938, of tuberculosis in a private hospital in the Blue Mountains. The balance of his estate was just under £700—a small amount even for the times.[18] Amy Woolf was in touch with Malcolm Fraser's family until her death, in a private hospital in Melbourne, in 1960. Fraser remembers her as an old woman, living in Cleveland Mansions in East Melbourne. She came to lunch with the family sometimes. His mother visited her, but he did not know her well.

⋆ ⋆ ⋆

Malcolm Fraser's parents, Neville Fraser and Una Woolf, met at a party on the battleship *Repulse* when Una was visiting her Hordern cousins in Sydney in 1924. The couple were married three years later at St Mark's Church of England, Darling Point. The Horderns seem to have clubbed together to make the day a success. Lady

Hordern lent Una a veil; Hordern cousins were the bridesmaids; and the reception was held at the Hordern family home.

Neville Fraser was twelve years older than Una. Educated at Melbourne Grammar, Trinity College at Melbourne University and then studying law at Magdalen College, Oxford, he had been in the thick of World War I, fighting at the Somme, Messines Ridge and Ypres. His war diaries survive as a record of the tedium and horror. Neville recorded the smell of rotting flesh alongside his success (and otherwise) at card games.[19] After the war, he seems never to have seriously considered practising law. He was, according to Malcolm Fraser, 'not a highly intellectual man'. He served on the local shire council at Wakool for eight years and was president for two. He was interested in politics, largely because of his father's example and his friendship with Dick Casey. According to Una, he toyed with the idea of a broader political career but never wanted to put in the hard work of getting pre-selected and campaigning.

In the early years of their marriage Una and Neville travelled through Europe, including the trip during which they left behind the one-year-old Lorri. As the Depression began to bite, Neville was forced to make managing Balpool his first priority. Una seems never to have warmed to life in the remote bush. 'Locusts and mice. Dogs. Drought. Floods. We had the lot.'

If Neville Fraser had trouble recovering from the horrors of World War I, he never confided this to his son. Certainly, though, he understood others who were not coping so well. Malcolm remembers some shearers arriving by boat after being lost in the flooded red-gum forest for days. They were half-starved. The first thing Neville did was fetch a bottle of brandy for the shearers' cook. 'The cook had been in the war and he was one of those people who couldn't really handle it. He was probably quite a good shearers' cook but he needed the grog to get by, and being stuck three days on the boat would have been really tough for him. My father knew that.' Fraser remembers another occasion on which his father refused to buy him a toy steam engine, because it was made in Germany.

Neville Fraser was a natural extrovert. Una once described him as 'peppery, like old Sir Simon', with very fixed ideas for which he would argue aggressively. 'Kind and generous to a degree with a lively mind and a great zest for life ... That he was a complex and unpredictable character was evident as I was not always very clever in understanding what his reaction or point of view would be.' In the early years, father and son seem to have been devoted to each other. Family movies show Neville ruffling Malcolm's hair. Una Fraser said that Malcolm was inseparable from his father, that as a very young child he was always 'perfectly happy' as long as he could be with him. Yet it seems to have been a relationship almost devoid of conversation. Fraser remembers it as being mainly about being taught how to do practical things, and play sport. 'Oh, being taught to shoot, taught to ride. He was a very good bowler; he wouldn't teach me to bowl because he hadn't enjoyed bowling: he wished he had been a great batsman! So he tried to make me into a great batsman.' He failed. Fraser enjoyed playing cricket for fun and later liked tennis as well, but never excelled at sport. Years later, when he was first contesting an election, he was forced to correct newspaper reports suggesting that he had great prowess.

> Sir,
>
> In the course of the recent federal election campaign statements have been made in the Melbourne press with regard to my football activities past and future. Three statements have been quoted as having been made by me. All are untrue. I did not say I played Australian Rules football for Melbourne Grammar or rugger for Oxford University. No local team in the Western District has ever approached me to play football. The only position that I would be qualified to fill on a football field would be that of goal post.[20]

As Fraser grew older, his relationship with his father became strained. Una said that Neville had trouble accepting that his son had grown up and had his own ideas. This continued into Fraser's early days in politics, when he was fighting the state government over issues like wool sales at Portland, and making enemies, including some among the family connections. Dick Hamer asked Neville to try to make Fraser back off. Neville, Una said, was 'worried sick'. The son did not bow to the father, although at this time they were all living at close quarters on Nareen.

Neville and Una's marriage was by all accounts a happy one, although they seem to have been very different people. Una told her friends that if she hadn't married she would have been a concert pianist or an actress. Even at Balpool she played the piano. She had acted in Repertory Theatre in Perth and had been educated with an emphasis on music and French. She is remembered as a reserved, highly intelligent and striking woman. Lorri recalls the family atmosphere as quite cool. 'It always seemed to me that we were very distant with each other', she says. Una's granddaughter Phoebe Fraser remembers Una as loving but 'not the kind of grandma who gets down on the floor and plays with you'.

According to her friend Philip Jones, Una flowered intellectually and culturally after she was widowed, in 1962. Based in her large South Yarra apartment she pursued her interests in the arts, entertained often and collected the work of some of the main figurative artists of the day as well as building one of the finest private collections of eighteenth-century English and Irish glass in Australia.[21] During this period, Una would say to those who inquired that her daughter's rebelliousness was because of her 'artistic temperament', and that perhaps she hadn't understood this when she was younger. Lorri, in turn, remembers little support from her parents for her artistic career, and sometimes what she took to be hostility from her father. Today, Lorri's work hangs prominently in Malcolm Fraser's Melbourne office and in his home.

There is plenty in Malcolm Fraser's family history to suggest that public life and politics might be his destiny, but little to explain his abiding concerns with human rights, equality and anti-racism.

His parents were more than caught up in the common prejudices of their time. So where does Fraser's anti-racism come from? He dismisses the rumours, spread by political colleagues, about South African neighbours whom he didn't like. 'I don't know. Perhaps it is innate', he says, and tells a story about Simon Fraser that he first heard from Labor politician Clyde Cameron, who discovered it when researching union history. In 1886, David Temple, the first secretary of the Australasian Shearers' Union, visited Balpool-Nyang to try to sign up members. Simon introduced him to the men, and told them that he belonged to associations and clubs to protect his interests, and if he had only his labour to sell then he would belong to a trade union. As a result, the Balpool-Nyang sheds were the first in the country to be unionised. Fraser's comment: 'That shows a concern for the idea of a fair go, at least'. His maternal grandfather, Louis Woolf, also seems to have been, in his way, a radical, and passionate about social justice. So too, within the limited roles available to women at the time, was his grandmother Anna Fraser.

* * *

Fraser's early years were haunted by the abiding fear of every parent at the time: polio. For a short while he went to a day school in Toorak, but the city air and pining for Balpool-Nyang meant he was regularly ill, developing the weak chest that has plagued him throughout his adult life. When he was eight he was found to be running a temperature at school, and was packed off home amid some drama. It wasn't polio, but something almost as bad: he was perilously ill with pneumonia. There were no antibiotics, and he nearly died. He remembers lying in bed and hearing a whispered conversation with a doctor in which his parents were discussing whether or not he would survive. This is one of his most powerful memories of being shut out of conversation. 'Lying there, you don't really know what is happening and they are having a consultation with your GP in the corner of the room, and then you realise that you are very ill indeed.'

The illness was a landmark. It brought to an end his life of freedom at the centre of the family. Once he had recovered it was thought important to send him away for his health. His parents chose Tudor House in the New South Wales highlands, known for its clean air. As usual, Fraser was not consulted about the move or included in discussions about it. He was simply told. Almost twenty years earlier, another Anglican boy with a weak chest—Patrick White, who went on to be Australia's best known author—had been sent there for similar reasons. White, a coddled child, experienced Tudor House as a place of freedom.[22] Not much had changed when Fraser went there, but for him the experience was one of restriction. Today, the ethos at Tudor House is the same as it was in Fraser's and White's days. The school advertises itself as being one where:

> The boys are encouraged to do the things once taken for granted—to climb trees, to ride bikes, to fall over and to get up, to make mistakes, to get dirty, to camp and to grow gardens. [23]

Fraser began at Tudor House in 1940 and was there until December 1943, when he was thirteen years old. It was a rough-and-tumble life. The freedom was extraordinary by the standards of most schools. Fraser was allowed to take his rifle, though it was kept under lock and key. After lessons he was able to go wandering across the 170 acres of school grounds by foot and on bike. But Fraser nevertheless felt restricted: at home he had been so free; now he was regimented and told what to do. In retrospect, he thinks it was a good school, but at the time he was sometimes content, and sometimes miserable. He felt 'dumped' by his family. With the coming of World War II his father had enlisted again. His mother was mostly in Melbourne, which meant that when the other boys were visited at weekends Fraser was most often on his own. Una later described this situation as something that 'has never ceased to sadden me'.[24] Fraser's letters home sounded cheery enough, but they were punctuated frequently by 'I am longing to see you'.[25] His parents did visit when they could, but it was difficult due to wartime restrictions on travel, and he didn't see anything like as much of them as he would have liked. 'I accepted that you had to go to school and my parents continued to tell me that it's the best years of your life. I said, "Well, I just don't believe that". They said everyone had to go to school. I said I'd sooner stay at Balpool.'

For the first time he was with plenty of boys his own age, but it was, he says, 'too late. The die was cast. I had been solitary for too long so I was still in part self-contained or reserved or whatever. I don't think anything really was going to alter that'. He had some friends, but did not make them easily. School work, though, was never a problem. He was seldom first in the class, but nearly always in the top three or four.

War talk, and the impression of imminent threat, hung about everything. During school holidays Fraser would overhear conversations. 'I can remember going into the room and my mother had women in for lunch or bridge, or something or other, and they were saying, "When they come, will people be safer in the countryside or in the cities?" I said, "What do you mean?" I didn't read newspapers. I knew the war was on but the last thing you were told was that Australia might be occupied. But adults of that time really thought it was going to be. They couldn't see what would stop the Japanese.' As usual, the young Fraser asked for more information but was told that it was not something for children to worry about.

Back at school, though, the boys were set to digging trenches in the grounds. Even then Fraser thought this stupid. 'If the Japanese were going to arrive, what in the hell good would those trenches be?' In 1942, when Japanese aircraft bombed the port of Darwin, the children were taught what to do in an air raid. Fraser thought it was a waste of time, but a few months later Japanese midget submarines entered Sydney Harbour and sank a ferry boat, killing nineteen people, and preparations at Tudor House began to seem slightly less ridiculous. One of Fraser's favourite teachers left overnight because he was a conscientious objector and about to be named as such:

the school was worried for its reputation. Other younger masters disappeared to join the fighting and were replaced by older ones, sometimes brought out of retirement.

Fraser's school reports suggest that his masters recognised his leadership potential, but also his tendency to walk alone. In 1943, his final year, the headmaster said, 'There are still signs of that aloofness and peremptory manner which formerly prevented him from having a really positive influence in house, but there has been a decided improvement in this respect'. Other masters referred to 'an apparent aloofness, due probably to shyness'.[26] Una, writing in 1980, remembered that her son's standards had always been high.

> Anything that fell short of them in dealing with his friends found him inclined to intolerance, something he has had to come to terms with through time and experience and [he is] now less likely to judge harshly, although a friend who let him down he might find hard to forgive.[27]

In 1942, Fraser was asked in class to write a poem in the fashion of Rupert Brooke's 'The Great Lover'. The result was published in the school newsletter.

> These I Have Loved
>
> The touch of tools once more as I ply chisel and hammer,
> The smell of the eucalyptus tree as I worked under its shadow,
> Sweet music of oars as they dip into the water and out again,
> Ah! The steady patter of rain on the windows once more,
> To feel the hard crust of bread and taste many tasted foods,
> The firm kick of a gun as I go shooting along the river.
> To rock to the sway of a horse as I canter over the plains,
> To tread the firm ground of the hills as the sun lifts his fiery mane up into the sky,

> To go for an early-morning swim in the fresh blue sea,
> To watch the eagles as they circle high above the treetops,
> Huge cross cut saws as they eat their way through the timber,
> The clatter of machinery as it weaves some new invention of man's progress,
> The glory of the silver-tipped clouds in their mad race through the sky,
> The chatter of birds as they fly through the trees,
> Last of all, wind rustling through the treetops, and swaying the branches in its arms.[28]

In his letters home, Fraser asked constantly about Balpool-Nyang and the impact of the drought, as well as being keen to keep up the supply of sweets and chocolates.

> Would you try to get an Easter egg like ones you once got about a year ago, they are chocolate on the outside, inside that there is some white muck for white of egg inside that is some yellow muck for the yellow part of the egg. Will you send one or two of those described above and one or two different ones. I hope you have not got scarlet fever yet.[29]

In his last year at the school—1943—it rained. Ironically, it was the death knell for Balpool-Nyang, because for the first time in many years the property looked green enough to fetch a good price at sale. Fraser was told by letter that the sale had gone through; it was the first he had heard about it. Today, after decades of bruising public life, he still describes the day he received the letter as the worst of his life. He is clearly upset when he talks about it, and his wife, Tamie, says that he is almost always moved to tears when the subject comes up.

Yet it seems that Fraser had already, at the age of thirteen, acquired a formidable reserve, even with his parents. The letter he wrote to them gave away nothing of his pain.

> I was awfully sorry to hear that Nyang was to be sold. But I know that it is for the best and seeing that you have lost so much in it. Don't worry about the hols, something will turn up. If it is to be sold I would like to see it again before it is handed over.[30]

He didn't see the property again. Balpool was sold, walk-in walk-out. The ponies, the equipment, the house and furniture—all of it went. There was a period of some months before Fraser's parents bought Nareen. When they did, Fraser was hugely relieved. They would still be in the country, not shackled to Melbourne. He could have a pony again. But, 'Second time around is never quite the same, no matter how long you have been there'. Even white Australians, Fraser remarks, can have powerful roots in country. His are in the Riverina. For a long while, the Western District was merely where he lived.

Fraser may have been an accepting child—less rebellious than his sister—but by the time he was due to start secondary school he was digging in his heels about some things. He was determined not to be a boarder, because it would have meant even more regimentation. In truth, although his mother would have preferred him to board, there wasn't any great pressure for him to do so because his parents owned a flat in Alcaston House, at the top end of Collins Street. It was tiny, but they managed to rent an extra room elsewhere in the building to use as Fraser's bedroom. Melbourne Grammar was a natural choice: Neville had been there. But Fraser said he would have chosen it in any case over the only other school considered appropriate—Geelong Grammar. He had heard that Melbourne Grammar had a broader social mix, and that was what he wanted.

Fraser's conflicts with his father began at this time, at first over sport. He stopped playing cricket, despite Neville's urgings. 'I know I disappointed him in that, but I just didn't want to, or I wanted to do other things. Even then, I just wanted to do my own thing. Tennis was a different matter; I liked playing tennis. If Father had taught me to be a bowler, then perhaps. He was a very, very good bowler indeed … but anyway, he didn't. It was a difficult psychology. If you're a batsman, you make one mistake and you're done: you can't make it up. In tennis, if you make one mistake, you can make it up in the next couple of shots. If you are a bowler, getting bashed around the ground, you can get him out next ball. But a batsman—I didn't like the psychology of that.'

He was content at Melbourne Grammar, but never academically stretched. 'The school was quite good at looking after the duller kids and trying to get them a decent job. But it was never challenging.' He was in the debating society but, thanks to his nerves, rarely made a speech of more than a minute or two. In any case, the debate reached no great heights. 'No, no way. I mean, they tried to debate public issues, but I think there was so little understanding that it was almost farcical.'

There was another, almost submerged, theme to this period in Fraser's life. Sometimes, when he was home at Nareen, he was aware that his father was doing something mysterious. If they were out driving they sometimes would take a circuitous route. They would be checking up on something, and there were half-overheard conversations about who was reliable, who could be trusted and who was loyal. Fraser became aware that his father was involved in a clandestine anti-communist organisation. He barely remembers how he knew this; it was never spoken about openly. He does know that Neville would make reports to someone called Herring, and that other family friends were involved as well, 'All very honourable people'.[31]

Fraser remembers a background fear among his family and friends that there would be a communist push in Australia. This threat seemed real in a way that is difficult to imagine or recreate in modern-day Australia, but the people who were involved were not fools. This was the era in which the phrase 'the Cold War' was entering the popular lexicon. Only a few years before, communist waterside workers had refused to load ships in Sydney because, until Germany attacked Russia, they would not cooperate with the war effort. Now the future of Europe seemed in the balance, as

Russia and the Allies carved up their zones of influence. In 1948, the blockade of Berlin began. At the same time, within Australia there were politicians who were communist sympathisers, and many intellectuals and unionists who saw much to admire in Russia. Fraser remembers: 'A lot of people believed that there would be a communist push, and that they should go out against it. They were frightened of some of the politicians who were travelling to Russia, travelling to Moscow and doing this and doing that'.

There was a number of anti-communist groups operating in Australia at the time, several of which are known to have been active in the Western District of Victoria. The best known was the Association, founded in the late 1940s. Members of the Association believed that the British system was being sabotaged by communism. The Association's aims and beliefs included loyalty to the Crown and the Commonwealth, the upholding of the Australian constitution and freedom to join any political party that shared these aims. Its main goal was to organise the civilian population to meet any emergencies caused by a communist uprising.[32] Neville's friend Dick Casey had connections with the Association and a lifelong interest in intelligence, security and anti-communism. Among other things, Casey is known to have acted as an intermediary between the Association, Robert Menzies and the anti-communist industrial groups associated with Bob Santamaria, who, in turn, was later to form a long-term friendship with Malcolm Fraser, and to become one of the people he looked to for advice.

As a teenager and young man, Fraser came to understand that the threat from communism was real and urgent, and that his father and his father's friends did not trust the political process to protect the country. Courageous and honourable people might have to take matters into their own hands. Neville would have coffee with people and 'see what they thought about this or that. He might send a telegram afterwards to somebody reporting on their attitude to communism, and on who would stand up, who wouldn't, who was too frightened, who would accept anything and not fight'.

How does Fraser feel about all this now?

'I feel sad that people felt they had to do it. I knew about three people who were involved. They were all among the most honourable people I've ever met.'

Anti-communism was a driving force in the early years of Fraser's political career, but one of the many ways in which father and son were different was that as an adult, Malcolm Fraser had profound faith in the ability of the political system to combat the threat, at least internally. He believed in proper process. He also believed, though, in activism, and in people of good will taking a lead, confronting threat and if necessary defying convention.

* * *

During the Depression there had been doubts about whether Fraser would go to Oxford. It seemed the family might not be able to afford to send him in his father's footsteps. But thanks to the postwar recovery and the move to Nareen, the family fortunes had recovered, and he knew he would be off. But what to study? Lorri had long since made her rebellion explicit, and had taken her own path. She remembers that at the age of thirteen she made a conscious decision never to pass another exam at school. She fulfilled her ambition, except for once, and that was an accident. Instead of going to university, while her brother finished secondary school she was studying sculpture at technical college, mixing with left-wing friends and courting with Bertie Whiting, a poet. The two of them tried to earn money by bee-keeping for a while, living in a caravan. She became and remained what she describes as 'a soft leftie'. When she was at home she would have long and acrimonious arguments with Neville.

Bob Southey, later a Liberal Party Federal President, had just returned from Magdalen College at Oxford. Neville knew Southey and invited him home for a chat with Malcolm. Southey extolled the benefits of the subjects he had been studying: philosophy, politics and economics. He told Fraser that they would help him to understand what was going on in the world. Fraser was sold. The course was recognised as being a fitting preparation for a political career, but Fraser claims to have had no clear idea of what he wanted to do at the time. Politics was in the background thanks to grandfather Simon Fraser and the family friendship with the Caseys, but at that stage all Fraser knew was that he wanted to be something more than only a farmer. Throughout his school years he had studied conscientiously and achieved creditably, and yet not a single master had caught his imagination, opened his mind to possibility or suggested how he might use his talents and his growing sense of a need for men such as himself to act in the world. 'There was nothing, really, intellectually speaking, before Oxford', he says. By the time he reached the end of school, he was more than restless.

2

Learning to Think

Among Malcolm Fraser's personal papers in the University of Melbourne archives is a box of exercise books and foolscap paper covered in his characteristic cursive. These are the records of the work he did at Oxford as he read his way through the set books and acquainted himself with the great thinkers of his own day and of the centuries preceding. His handwriting became untidier as he aged. The notes he made as Prime Minister on the bottom of memorandums are barely legible to those not used to his scrawl. He would mark a paragraph with a heavy vertical line, and add a single word or phrase: 'Get an answer' or 'Yes' or 'No'. But back then, before he turned twenty, his handwriting was a matter of square capital letters, abundant verticals and generous loops.[1]

He was methodical in his learning. He would read with an exercise book open by his side and meticulously summarise the material on the right-hand page. On the facing page he made comments and notes to himself. Thus he worked through Bertrand Russell's *Theory of Knowledge* and *Problems of Philosophy*, and the questions of what it is possible to know and how we can claim to know it. 'But for introspection we could never imagine the minds of others', Fraser wrote to himself on one left-hand page. As Russell teased out the question of whether, indeed, it is possible to know anything at all, Fraser wrote in his notes: 'This process is a nonsense', and later a word that might be 'rot' or 'rats', and, later still, 'I doubt this'. As Russell asserted that not all knowledge is logical, and that some things, such as the knowledge that happiness is better than misery, are a given and independent of logic, Fraser wrote: 'Doubt this again. Russell bungles and confuses logic and maths that are deductive systems with ethics, which is, I think, purely sociological'. His notes continue with the notion of innate knowledge being given short shrift. 'Wrong', he wrote, and 'All a muddle'. Today he remembers, 'What we studied was very much involved in the search for knowledge. Is there any absolute truth? Indeed, is there an absolute? What is the source of everything? If you look at all the modern philosophers, there was metaphysical assumption at the very core of everything that they were doing. If you take a metaphysical core, you can construct anything you like, because you can't prove it or disprove it … And all the muddle you can get in. "I think therefore I am", said Descartes. But how do you know you are thinking? You may only believe you are thinking. But that doesn't mean you exist, just that you believe. And so on, and on and on'.

Fraser preferred John Locke, and his *An Essay Concerning Human Understanding*. Locke said there is no innate knowledge: the mind is 'white paper, void of all characters'. How then does it come by 'that vast store which the busy and boundless fancy of man has painted on it with endless variety? Whence has it all the materials of reason and knowledge?' Locke answered the question with one word: experience. From observation and reason, said Locke, come all our understanding. The individual is central, and the freedom to think and reason is at the core of what it means to be human. Governments are legitimate so long as natural rights are respected. If they become tyrannical, citizens are justified in overthrowing them.

In his slow and careful manner, Fraser read his way through the works of Thomas Hobbes and Jean-Jacques Rousseau. He came to Niccolò Machiavelli's *The Prince*. 'Avoid being despised and hated', advised the author; 'have gravity and fortitude'. From Jean-Jacques Rousseau, Fraser noted the idea that 'Man is born free but everywhere he is in chains'. All of the thinkers that Fraser liked, even Descartes, with his 'I think therefore I am', placed the individual, and individual freedom, at the heart of things. This was a message that spoke to Fraser, the self-sufficient, solitary boy. He had learned, as a child, to rely on himself and his own judgement. Ever since, he had wanted freedom. Oxford provided the intellectual framework for his instincts, and made them more than matters of individual preference. They were universal imperatives. Years later, Fraser summed up what he had learned.

> If the human being is to be central, empiricism, pragmatism, basic common decency would seem to require such a commitment be universal. And thus the assertion of human rights and freedom is fundamental to any person who claims to be liberal. It is liberalism's supreme contribution to human thought and human progress ... Those who look for a perfect system of government are unlikely to find it. Those who look to general rules that can apply in all circumstances will be misled. Good government is essentially pragmatic. Decisions need to be guided by philosophy but based on empirical evidence. Government is not about a deductive system; it is inductive, based on circumstances and facts as they emerge. There are no formulas that can make government easy.[2]

Fraser also read the leading economic textbooks of the day. In his essays he considered whether there was an optimum size for a firm appropriate to each industry, and whether political parties were a necessary part of the machinery of democracy. On the latter question, Fraser thought not. He wrote: 'I would go so far as to say that [political parties] are the remnants of past regimes, that they are totally unsuited to democracy and a constant danger to its survival'. He decried the 'subordination of individuality to the machine'.

The politics, philosophy and economics course had, when first introduced in 1920, been known as Modern Greats. This title captured an idea that was at the time novel: that studying the ancients of Classical Greece and Rome was no longer as relevant for those entering public life as a knowledge of the innovative thinkers of modern times. Fraser was told in his first week that philosophy was important because it would teach him how to reason, politics would acquaint him with the different methods that humans had used to govern themselves and solve their problems, and economics was valuable because, in the modern world, most of politics was concerned with it, and it provided the analytical framework for thinking through social phenomena. 'We were told, "You might think it's three separate subjects, but it's not. It will come together sometime in the second year". And it did. You saw the relevance of it all, even of symbolic logic. You saw how you could cut the crap, how you could tell if someone had a totally phoney argument.' Modern Greats was part of the search for new ways of thinking that followed a generation of England's finest young men being cut to ribbons in World War I. New solutions were needed. The course in which Fraser was enrolled was woven around modernity and idealism—themes that had only swelled in the wake of yet another bloody war.

Later, Fraser described those postwar years as the beginning of a new age of enlightenment. In the years prior to his arrival at Oxford, in 1949, the United Nations, the World Bank and the International Monetary Fund had been established. The year before he arrived, the Universal Declaration of Human Rights had been adopted by the United Nations, and during his time at Oxford countries all over the world were negotiating conventions to give the declaration legal force. All these mechanisms were, as Fraser said later, 'designed to establish a fairer and a more peaceful world. Colonialism would be outlawed. People would look after their own affairs. The techniques of modern economics gave hope to governments worldwide that unemployment could be banished'.[3]

* * *

Fraser was at the intellectual heart of Europe, and, for the first time since his early childhood, he felt free. 'There were rules, sure, but I thought I'd escaped something, and it was a very exciting and optimistic time.' As is traditional at Oxford and Cambridge universities, Fraser's chief identification was with his college, Magdalen, rather than with the university as a whole. Like most undergraduates he lived in college and had a scout—a manservant—who was not backward in ticking off the students if they made too much mess. Fraser had his own bedroom and living room in one of the more modern parts of the college. He had a washbasin in his room and shared a bathroom. Magdalen was an ancient and beautiful institution, but even here there was only limited shelter from the hardships of postwar Britain. In many practical ways, life was grim. Meals were held in the dining hall. Rationing applied. There was little meat, other than fowl of some kind. 'It certainly wasn't chicken. It was both fowl and foul', remembers Fraser. The Magdalen rowing team had to be fed whale meat to give them enough protein for training. 'For about three days people envied them the meat. Then at the end of the week there were members of the team trying to get out of rowing so they didn't have to eat any more whale. It was probably a bit better than boarding school. You could order a drink if you wanted to.' Fraser familiarised himself with Audit ale, 'so thick you could eat it', and watched the dons at the high table, each with their own little carafe of wine, 'to make sure that they all got equal shares and nobody hogged it'.

Under the Oxford college system, Fraser's principal intellectual relationship was with his college tutor, and in this he was fortunate. His tutor was Thomas Dewar Weldon, known to everyone as Harry, a key figure at Oxford. Weldon had served in World War I, in which he was wounded and decorated. Like Fraser's father, he had been in the Royal Field Artillery. The war marked Weldon deeply; his colleagues claimed that he never fully recovered emotionally. A tall man with a military bearing, he was antagonistic to some of the more traditional Oxford dons, including CS Lewis, who described Weldon as the most hard-boiled atheist he had ever known. He devoted himself to his students, always available to them with a glass of whisky or wine and a preparedness to discuss both the course material and the wider world. *The Oxford Dictionary of National Biography* says of Weldon that he 'did not suffer fools gladly and he was intolerant of lazy thinking; yet he could also be a loyal friend. This combination of qualities helped win the respect of his peers'.[4] To Fraser, Weldon was an exemplar of energetic, thoughtful pragmatism. Weldon convinced the young Australian that philosophy was important, and a practical pursuit.

Weldon was, according to his biographers, responsible not only for forming the Modern Greats curriculum, but also for transforming Magdalen from an easy-going place in which wealth and family position were key selection criteria to an academic meritocracy. He was propelled to make Magdalen a centre for the type of modern thought that would lead mankind to a better future. Thus, the Magdalen that Fraser entered was a very different, and much more demanding, institution from the one his father had known before World War I.[5]

Weldon was known for his work on logic. Rather than searching for ultimate truth, he was interested in clarity and clear thinking. His first book, published four years before Fraser was at Oxford, was an introduction to Immanuel Kant. When Fraser arrived, Weldon was re-establishing himself after having his career interrupted by war once again. He had been the personal assistant of Air Vice-Marshal Arthur Harris of Bomber Command, involved in justifying to sceptical politicians Harris's strategy of bombing German cities. Replying to the accusation of terrorism, Weldon had explained the attacks by arguing that they aimed to shorten the war and thus reduce the number of human lives lost. In later years, after a whisky or two, and too many 'logic-chopping tutorials', Weldon would ask students to nominate how many human lives they thought Cologne Cathedral was worth.[6]

During his first year at Oxford, Fraser had to work hard at understanding and getting to grips with the tides of thought that made up his course of politics, philosophy and economics. After being near the top of his class throughout his school career, now he felt that he knew nothing—about either the course material or the state of the world. At Oxford, thrown into the deep end of modernist thought, he was a relatively untutored colonial boy. Nor did his family's social position mean much here. He was an outsider, and he was green. His fellow undergraduates were more sophisticated and knowledgeable in every way. Fraser remembers, 'They would have understood apartheid. I said, "What's apartheid?" Apartheid wouldn't have been written up much in Australian newspapers, and I didn't read newspapers in those days. I probably would have argued, if I said anything at all, that the policy is equal but separate development. If it is equal development, what is wrong with that? That shows you how much I knew. But people around Oxford University had been condemning it. There was a South African—he just didn't want to go home. Pressure compelled him to go home. He just felt appalled at what was being done in 1948 and 1949'. In fear of failure and humiliation, Fraser set about catching up.

To begin with, Weldon was simply terrifying. At their first meeting, when Fraser's bags were barely unpacked, Weldon thrust at him a copy of John Maynard Keynes's *General Theory of Employment, Interest and Money*. 'Write a 2000-word essay on this by next Friday', he said. Fraser had never heard of Keynes. He went to the library and began to struggle with the book. He felt as though he were illiterate. 'What did the terms mean, the marginal productivity of capital? Somebody with my sort of education knew nothing about this.' He wrote 2000 words. 'The worst rubbish I ever wrote—absolute crap. Absolutely pathetic drivel.' He doesn't remember Weldon's response. Probably, Fraser reflects, the task was designed to sort the geniuses from those who needed more work. He understood only too well that he fell into the latter category.

There were others who marked Fraser. One was the leading liberal thinker Isaiah Berlin. Fraser remembers Berlin 'putting his head on one side and talking nineteen to the dozen' as he taught them modern logic. Another was the philosopher Gilbert Ryle, who was credited with restoring Oxford to a leading place in philosophy. His book *Concept of Mind* was one of the texts that Fraser meticulously noted. Ryle was against metaphysical assumptions, and Fraser agreed with him. In one of his essays, Fraser wrote:

> I must from the start deny the existence of the mind as distinct from the body. I will admit no hidden entity. As Ryle puts it, there is no machine within the machine … If a machine makes a mistake we say it has gone wrong and fetch the mechanic. To a person we are much more likely to say 'Have another try'.

In the same essay, Fraser rejected the notion of determinism, because without free will, he said, 'morality also goes out the door'. In a marginal note in his exercise books he asked himself, 'Is there anything to be said for metaphysics? The idea that God exists is a nonsense'. This attitude—what CS Lewis might have called 'hard-boiled atheism'—did not persist. Fraser continued to reject metaphysical assumptions as a foundation for human reasoning, law or politics, yet embraced 'something of the metaphysic' as the core of his motivation in public life. 'There is no point talking about it, because you can't prove it', he says. And yet were it not for that 'something of the metaphysic', he would not have entered politics. 'I suppose I would have entered a commercial career and tried to make as much money as a number of my contemporaries have done.'[7]

It was the work of Keynes that in many ways topped and tailed Fraser's experience at Oxford. He not only got to grips with Keynes; he came to regard him as one of the main reasons for the optimistic spirit of the times. Keynes justified the belief that mankind could solve its problems. 'He was a man who gave hope. He gave encouragement. You could build a better world. You didn't have to live in this miserable, wretched world.' Among Fraser's university essays and notes there is a draft of a speech about Keynes. It is not clear when it was written, though there is a reference at the beginning to a forthcoming political event that may have been the 1950 election. It begins:

> JM Keynes has had a profound influence on your life and mine. He was not like Churchill or Disraeli: a man whose actions appear in the headlines of national papers. His work, though, is no less important and was accomplished quietly. The main result of his teaching brings untold benefits to every man and woman irrespective of nationality. I want to remind you of the world into which he was born and to show you how he rid that world of one important and ever-present fear.

The fear to which Fraser referred was economic depression. The speech went on to sketch Keynes's life story. It explained the importance of the gold standard in governing the wealth of nations—how gold flows in and out of a country to pay the difference between imports and exports.

> If England found that the goods were not selling abroad she would soon have to export gold. Through the central Bank of England and the trading banks, gold was closely bound to the internal credit position of industry and commerce. This meant that a persistent gold drain resulted in tighter credit conditions and in low wage rates ... This system was thought to be unchanging and self-governing.

It had, Fraser wrote, worked well until World War I, but since then had become unfeasible and, in any case, 'the system was always bad', because the level of domestic employment depended directly upon the external trade balance. 'Slumps and depressions were an accepted part of the unchanging order of things.'

Into this stepped Keynes, having gained experience and reputation in India. Lloyd George called on him to join the Treasury at the beginning of World War I. Keynes saw that the gold standard was unworkable and began to lobby for its abolition and for the establishment of an international financial body. He went to Versailles as part of the team negotiating peace. Fraser wrote that Keynes, among others, had been opposed to the Australian Prime Minister Billy Hughes, who was advocating that Germany be punished for what it had done. Hughes wanted vengeance. Keynes rose above such base motives: he wanted a generous peace. Vengeance won out. Horrified at the terms extracted from Germany, convinced that they would lead to more trouble, Keynes resigned from the Treasury in protest and wrote his book *The Economic Consequences of the War*. 'Time', wrote Fraser, 'proved Keynes right', and not only about Versailles. By the mid 1920s it was clear that the gold standard was no longer working. Fraser wrote: 'For the first time practice had shown that the traditional dislike of devaluation together with the semi-religious attachment for the gold standard had resulted in great domestic trouble caused by the inherent incapacity of the system'.

The Depression came. In the middle of it, Keynes published his *General Theory*, the book Fraser had so struggled with in his first week at Oxford. Now he wrote:

> The book revolutionised economic thinking and government financial policies ... The cruelty of the gold standard ... was finally exposed. The book showed how governments could control the economic activity of a country through the budget and central bank finance. For the first time economic equilibrium was regarded as something that men could achieve by skilful manipulation of these tools. The automatic fatality of the gold standard that guaranteed a slump about once every eleven years was gone.

The result of Keynes's work, Fraser concluded, was that:

> Men no longer throw up their hands in despair at inflation and depression. They set to work to do something about it, before the disease becomes painful. And this is Keynes's great achievement. Before him we did not think there was

> anything we could do about it ... It is for us now with hope and with reason to make full use of the knowledge Keynes left behind him. We have the technical knowledge to keep the economy on a level keel and our success depends on how skilful we become in allying the economic answers with what is politically expedient.

Fraser does not remember writing this speech. He is sure he did not deliver it. He says he never made a speech of any significance until his pre-selection address after his return to Australia. He attended the Oxford Union, the famous debating society where would-be politicians cut their teeth, yet never dreamed of giving a speech there himself. 'I was an undergraduate and I had been brought up in a world that said that children should be seen and not heard and not interfere in the affairs of people who are senior and whatever. Now we live with an egalitarian approach to life. My grandson, in a restaurant, from the age of about three, would go around from table to table and ask people, "What do you do? Where are you from?" Even as an undergraduate I would have shrivelled to death from fear before I could do anything like that.' But Fraser recognises the sentiments of the speech, and fifty-five years of political experience have not dimmed his enthusiasm for Keynes. Today he describes him as 'by far the best economist of the last century. I also think he has been the most maligned and misunderstood economist of the last century'.

This is an enthusiasm that will surprise those who remember Fraser's prime ministership in terms of razor gangs and cuts to government spending—the beginning of the fashion for small government. Keynes's contribution to economic thought was about the importance of interventionist government. He advocated the use of government spending to mitigate the adverse effects of recessions and depressions. For most of the last forty years, Keynes has been out of fashion; instead, it is his antagonists—Friedrich Hayek and Milton Friedman—with their philosophy of small government and unrestrained market forces, who have carried the age. Only with the global economic crisis that began in 2008 has Keynes's name been mentioned again with approval. Fraser was always an admirer.

Fraser remembers arguing during his prime ministership with his speechwriter David Kemp. Kemp wanted Fraser to say something disparaging about Keynes and Fraser didn't want to. Fraser gave way to Kemp, and regrets it. 'On the day, it was just a fight I didn't want to spend energy on.' Keynes, says Fraser, was misunderstood. He was writing in the teeth of the Depression. Increased government spending was the appropriate prescription for the times. 'If he had been writing for the 1960s or 1970s, he would have been writing in quite different ways. He would then have said, "This is a time for a government to spend less money, and all those governments that are spending more money are causing inflation and not safeguarding their economies. They are adding to the boom". I think that economic rationalists had to destroy what there was before they could get people to fully embrace the world that now exists, and so, you know, it became a slur to say "That is Keynesian economics" when the government borrowed money. Well, Keynes was advocating that people should borrow money in the 1930s, when there was massive unemployment, massive unused resources, massive depression. He would not have recommended that for the governments in Europe in the 1960s and 1970s who were spending far too much money, borrowed money, and running up huge deficits. That was regarded as Keynesian economics, but it wasn't Keynesian economics. He would have opposed that absolutely. It was easier just to say that it was Keynesian economics because they wanted to destroy Keynes.'

* * *

There is a convention among archivists that the order of archival papers not be disturbed more than is necessary for their preservation. The way in which a donor kept their papers might seem haphazard, but is usually idiosyncratic, revealing of connections apparent in no other way. So it is that the archival box containing Fraser's university notes and essays also contains the notes for the speech that saw him launch his political career and obtain pre-selection for the seat of Wannon in the year after his return to Australia. This speech is of a piece with his Oxford studies.

Fraser's adult political development began at Oxford. There, his intellect was awakened, as was his idealism; Oxford set him on his course. 'There was nothing before Oxford, really', he says. What Oxford taught him, he says, was 'how to think'. Yet although he was profoundly marked by Oxford, he did not leave much mark upon it. In later years, Australian journalists made the trip to Magdalen in search of details on Prime Minister Fraser. Oxford dons struggled to remember him. Harry Woodley, the head porter at Magdalen during Fraser's time there, remembered him as 'fairly reserved, not what I'd call a good mixer ... He was a very pleasant chap, but I couldn't imagine him on the hustings'.[8] The journalists made the obvious comparison with another Oxford man, Bob Hawke, who was well remembered, as much for his partying and drinking exploits as for his academic brilliance.

Fraser, on the other hand, was a fascinated and engaged spectator at Oxford, rather than a participant. He admired his tutors, but did not develop strong personal relationships with them. He had no mentors. He was still, in many ways, locked within himself. As he travelled silently from lecture to lecture, and from tutorial to tutorial, thinking his thoughts and writing his essays, Fraser began to see his shyness not as strength, but as weakness—even a curse. He was ashamed of it, and viewed it as something that was fitting and necessary for a man such as himself to overcome. He had no idea how this might be done. Yet the draft of his undelivered speech on Keynes shows that he had things to say, and wanted to say them.

Socially he was less inhibited. Never the life of the party, he nevertheless was part of a tight-knit group of about eight fellow undergraduates, and together they would kick back in the comfortable lounge rooms of Magdalen and talk 'about the affairs of the day, about nonsense, about lectures'. They went drinking together at the Eastgate Hotel opposite the college, and on one occasion Fraser drank so much at a restaurant that he had to be carried home.

One of Fraser's best friends was a scholarship boy, Nicholas Browne-Wilkinson, who went on to become head of the Privy Council and Vice-Chancellor of the High Court. It was Browne-Wilkinson who, in 1999, delivered the watershed judgement concerning Augustus Pinochet, the Chilean dictator charged with crimes against humanity—one of the most important events in the history of international law. Another friend was a brilliant law student, Colin Forbes, who mystified Fraser by committing suicide shortly after leaving university. 'He had so much going for him', says Fraser. 'What drives people to that?' John Turner, future Prime Minister of Canada, was also part of the group, and Fraser kept in touch with him throughout both of their political careers. Also a friend was Raymond Bonham-Carter, son of the political activist Violet Bonham-Carter, who was in turn the daughter of Prime Minister Asquith. Raymond Bonham-Carter became a leading banker and figure in British public affairs, as well as the father of the actress Helena Bonham-Carter.

This small group was not part of the elite at Oxford. With the exception of Bonham-Carter, they were neither the richest nor the best connected, yet clearly they included some of the most able. Fraser, the boy from down under, lacked some of the social connections of his friends. He remembers Bonham-Carter being surprised when he turned up, courtesy of some of his London-based cousins, at one of the prestigious 'coming out' parties that served as a marriage market among the English upper classes. 'He didn't mean to be offensive. He just was surprised that I had the connections to get there.'

In his second year at Oxford, Fraser fell in love. This is one of the things he will not talk about. 'No, I'm not going down that track.' Some of the story, though, is already on the public record in a previous biography.[9] The woman was Anne Reid, an Australian whom he met at a party in London. For a while, it seemed that both the Fraser children might be destined to marry poets. Lorri was with Bertie Whiting, and Malcolm was pursuing Reid, who also wrote poetry. Reid was an idealist, and a romantic. It was she who ended the affair with Fraser, and it apparently caused him great pain. She went on to marry the historian Geoffrey Fairbairn, who was one of the few academics who supported the Liberal government's prosecution of the Vietnam War. As Anne Fairbairn, she advocated poetry as a 'universal language' that could bind people from different cultures—particularly from Australia and the Arab world. In 1998 she was awarded an Order of Australia for services to literature and international relations.

At the end of Fraser's second year, thanks to his parents' generosity, he was able to buy his first car—a Jowett Javelin. That summer he and three of his friends took it for a trip around Europe. Money was tight, and the budget was a total of twenty-two pounds and ten pence for three weeks, including car fare, tickets, petrol and food. There was nothing left for accommodation, which alarmed Fraser's English friends. He proposed that they sleep out under the stars, as people did when travelling in Australia, and so they slept in the open when it was fine and in the car when it rained. They went for a week without a bath, and ate raw rolled oats for breakfast because they swelled in the stomach and stopped them from feeling hungry.

This was the social climate in which Fraser came to intellectual adulthood. He was surrounded by big intellects, big ideas and lively idealism. He was in every sense awakened.

* * *

In Fraser's final year at Oxford, he found another thinker who shared his hunger for activism, and his idealism. Arnold Toynbee was a fashionable historian at the time. He made headlines with his immense comparative history of the world—twelve volumes in all—in which he suggested that human affairs can be analysed in terms of universal rhythms of rise, flowering and decline. 'I only read the two-volume digest', says Fraser. 'That was enough.' Toynbee drew on myths and metaphors as much as on hard historical fact to reject determinist ideas of history. His was a sweeping and inspiring analysis, based not on nation-states alone but on civilisations, including religious groupings. It was possible, he said, for civilisations and empires to shape their own destinies. All civilisations are faced with threats and challenges; how they respond determines whether they triumph or fail. 'Civilisations die from suicide, not by murder', Toynbee wrote. Civilisations have to change, to grow, or they will die. Thus, conservatism is the way of death. It is essential to be progressive and active. Keynes and Toynbee seemed to Fraser to go together. Man was the master of his own destiny. 'I was probably attracted to Toynbee's theory because it was hopeful. Nothing was inevitable: you could take control', he says. Fraser was to return to Toynbee's ideas repeatedly in his early political speeches. Before he left Oxford he was already thinking about the ways in which Toynbee's model applied to Australia.

Also at Oxford was the historian AJP Taylor. Fraser went to his lectures even though he did not need to for his course. Everyone knew that Taylor was writing a book. 'If a man was writing a book, I thought you should go and hear him speak. If the book was already written, then you could just read the book.' Taylor was exactly the kind of intellectual Fraser had been taught to suspect. He was a former communist, but Fraser found him a free thinker rather than an ideologue. In his lectures, he offered a view of foreign policy and of communism that challenged Fraser's predispositions. 'I remember making quite a study of the Korean War, because of what Taylor was saying', he says. By the time he had finished his study, Fraser in many ways agreed with Taylor's views: 'I respected his independence of mind, his rejection of the slavish orthodoxy of some Marxist thought; and he argued well and his views had substance'. But Fraser did not agree with all of Taylor's analysis. It was, he noted, the United Nations, part of the new machinery of international hope, that had asked the Western nations to go to the defence of South Korea. It was not US imperialism. The Korean

War was part of a larger conflict, in which two civilisations, the West and Communism, were trying to determine the future of the world. The name for this conflict was on everyone's lips: the Cold War. In Oxford, people spoke mostly of the battle over Europe. In Australia, Fraser knew, the frontier was South-East Asia. This was Australia's challenge: the challenge that Fraser had been pondering in the light of Toynbee's ideas.

Meanwhile Britain under Labour was establishing the welfare state and nationalising industry while still recovering from World War II. Outside the beautiful walls of Magdalen College, with its landmark tower and its deer park, the country looked grim. In London there were dilapidated, unpainted buildings. It took most of the decade to repair bomb damage in the major cities. The people were shabbily dressed. There were few cars on the road, and because of postwar balance of payment problems, the best British goods went for export. Many kinds of food were still rationed. On the one hand, the British working class was probably better off than ever before: rationing at least meant that nobody went hungry. On the other hand, the country was bankrupt and drab. This was the Britain that inspired George Orwell's *1984*—a place where government control was total. In Australia, the fear, both familiar to Fraser from childhood and newly threatening, was that the countries of South-East Asia would 'go communist'. In England, the question was how far the Labour government would push socialism.

What did communism mean to the young Fraser? It was the opposing philosophy to liberalism. It was the challenge to human reason. It meant: 'Complete lack of personal freedom. Complete government control. Total government domination by the state of all the individuals in the state. No political freedom, no individual freedom. I believe the state should survive to protect the rights of individuals, but in my mind communism saw the individual's purpose as being to serve the state. That was the reverse of what it ought to be. If you are really trying to define the ultimate objective of communism, it would be that the state would own production, distribution and everything. It would own everything, which means it would own the people as well'. The difference between socialism and communism, he understood, was that socialism could be established by democratic means, whereas communism was imposed by force. He was against both because they put the state ahead of the individual. But it was communism that Fraser feared. There could be no doubt, watching events in Europe and South-East Asia, that the Soviet Union was outward-looking and aggressive.

Yet at Oxford Fraser had learned to be optimistic and pragmatic. 'The end of the war, victory in the Pacific, carried with it the message that human beings could sort things out, could resolve their differences. And the United States and Russia were talking, even though Russia was saying that communism must thrive and therefore the United States must fall. The United States didn't sit back and say, "We won't talk until you acknowledge our right to exist".'

Fraser now draws a comparison with the present day, and the refusal of the West to negotiate with its opponents. 'Western policies have again made it so easy for the terrorists. For some time the West had been urging and encouraging democratic elections, not only in Palestine but throughout the Middle East. When Hamas won the free and fair democratic election, that should have been predictable to anyone with knowledge of Palestine. It would have been possible to say to Hamas, "From our point of view your attitudes and policies must change, but you have won a democratic election; therefore, we will talk, we will negotiate". Little by little it may have been possible to find areas of agreement. Instead, the United States and others refused to talk to Hamas and cut off aid. They forced Hamas back to the weapons that it had known from the beginning: to violence, to warfare. In the process of reneging on their own principles, the West gave the terrorists a major weapon; democracy would only be acceptable if it gave the result the West wanted.' Always, Fraser says, one should keep talking. This is the essence of diplomacy and of pragmatism—of managing human affairs through reason, not ideology.

* * *

Academically, Fraser did not do particularly well at Oxford. His results slipped in his final year. Why was this, given his intense engagement with the ideas that underpinned the curriculum? Fraser makes no excuses: 'I didn't work hard enough. It was my own fault, I think. I worked very hard in the first year, because I wasn't sure that I could master anything or everything, and by the end of the second term you had to do exams which decided whether you stayed in the place or didn't stay in the place. Well, I got through that quite well, and in the second year I probably worked reasonably hard, and in the third year I worked less hard'. Another problem was the verbal examination, designed to see whether a candidate should transfer to a higher degree. 'I don't think I handled that very well. I thought the questioner was asking me questions which I'd covered in the written papers, and so instead of going through it again, I said on a couple of occasions, "Well, I thought I'd answered that adequately in the written papers", where clearly he was wanting more.' Fraser was still locked in himself.

Others have suggested that the reasons for his ordinary results might include the pain of his relationship with Anne Reid.[10] Fraser's mother remembered that there was a time when her son was homesick, and talked of abandoning his course and coming home.[11] Whatever the reason, Fraser graduated in 1952 with a third-class degree, about halfway down the field of 228 students who took their degrees that year.

More significant than his result, though, was the impact that Oxford had had on him. There was no one moment in which it became clear to him that he wanted a political career. Rather, he was 'caught up in the notion that it was a time for hope. A time for doing things. I was caught up in the belief that a better world should be built. That was part of what these different people and lecturers were trying to do. Harry Weldon at one point in a tutorial was asked, "What's the line?" He said, "There is no line; you've got to work it out for yourself. All we can do is to try to help your thought processes. Try to think clearly". They were trying to teach people to think, because that was what was needed in this new world'. But what could he, Fraser, do in the world if he could not speak, and engage, and persuade? Politics had always been there. 'Perhaps I began to think at this stage that politics might be combined with farming, which of course you can't really do. If you want to achieve anything in politics it is all-consuming.' The one clear thought he had was that while he was happy to return to Nareen and help his father on the farm, this was not all that he wanted to do. There had to be more; he had to reach out. He had to speak, and take his place.

Another eighteen months of study, and he could have had a law degree. Some of his friends suggested he should do two years of national service. 'I can remember somebody in particular wanting me to join the 60th Rifles.' But Fraser felt in his heart that if he didn't return home now, he might never do so. He had few friends from school. 'I was getting to the stage that most of the friends I had were in England. I thought that if I had all my friends in England and none in Australia, it would be hard to leave, and I didn't want to get into that position.' He had never been in any doubt about where his future lay. He had grown up. He wanted to go home.

3

The Candidate Must Have a Voice

Malcolm Fraser is used to strangers approaching him in shops and in the street to tell him that he looks extraordinarily like a former Australian Prime Minister. 'Yes, people have said that to me before', he replies archly. He finds this slightly less surprising than the times when he is recognised, and by people who were not born when he led the country. 'A while ago I took the grandchildren into a place that I hate, McDonald's. They wanted a Big Mac. I took them in and there were not many people, but there was a young girl, about eighteen, mopping the floor. She said, "You are Malcolm Fraser", and I said, "Yes".' Over the French fries and soft drinks, she congratulated him on a speech he had made criticising the Howard government's record on human rights. In particular, he had criticised the treatment of asylum seekers and the new legislation aimed at countering terrorism. Fraser had recalled the Liberal Party that he had joined more than forty years previously. He had said that Menzies had intended the Liberal Party to be one of

> progressive ideas, a forward-looking party, willing to make experiments ... a party that believes fervently in the rule of law, in higher education accessible to all able students,

> in a government accepting national obligations and a vision for the future, a party that slowly abolished the White Australia policy and broadened Australia to a more open, multicultural society. It was a party of hope and of vision.[1]

Now he wondered if he could remain a Liberal. 'The party has become a party of fear and reaction. It is conservative and not liberal. It has not led in positive directions; it has allowed and, some would say, promoted race and religion to be part of today's agenda. I find it unrecognisable as liberal.' Fraser had detailed the ways in which the terrorism legislation offended liberal ideals. The onus of proof of guilt was effectively reversed. People could be arrested without being told why, and for knowing something that they didn't know they knew. Journalists would not be able to report that such people had been arrested without themselves being jailed. Personal freedom had never been so eroded by an Australian government, he said. This was a law that one would expect in tyrannical countries and not in Australia.

Now this young woman in McDonald's was congratulating him on his inflammatory words. 'Stick it to 'em, stick it to 'em!' she said, and he thanked her, and she went on mopping the floor. 'She was obviously someone who was interested in public policy and who read newspapers. And there she was cleaning McDonald's with a big mop. Perhaps she was a university student making a bit of money. They do all kinds of things these days.'

Such encounters make Fraser wonder how and whether it is possible to describe the Australia of the 1950s—the country to which he returned after Oxford—to a new generation. How does one convey that the present day is not the first time that Australia and the Western world have faced a threat to freedom? Fraser knows that much of the rhetoric of those times, including the speeches he made, seems shrill today, even foolish. How to help young people to understand the political imperatives of the time? How, even, to convey the ordinary physical realities of an Australia that was so much poorer in material possessions, in which skinny children were more common than the well fed, in which there was no such thing as McDonald's, or fast food, and in which an apple could still be a treat for a child? How to talk of a country in which only a small number of privileged young people went to university, and for most adults hard physical labour was necessary for almost any kind of security, let alone advancement? The divisions in society were harsher then, and harder to overcome. Is it possible for a new generation to understand what it meant to be born in the Depression to parents scarred by world war, and to come to adulthood at a time when almost everyone older than oneself had made wartime sacrifices for the country?

The present-day world has fears enough for its time, but Australia in the 1950s was also strung between fear and hope. Another war, this time with the Soviet Union, seemed likely and perhaps inevitable, and who knew how many Australians would be loyal to the cause? There were communists in the country's main trade unions. There were politicians with sympathies towards Moscow. Among Australia's intellectuals and in the unions there were many who thought it inevitable and desirable that socialism would become the natural order. Only a few years before, Labor had tried to nationalise the nation's banks, and this was still its policy.

The rights and wrongs of the past can seem crystal-clear, but when one stands in the present and looks forwards, the road is always covered in mist. So how much of what Fraser did and said back then was right, and necessary, and would make sense to that young woman mopping the floor? And how much was wrong? How should a liberal democracy defend itself against those devoted to its violent overthrow, and what are the limits of political freedom?

Fraser was a modernist. He wanted reform. He wanted what today would be called social justice. He did not want socialism. He returned to the Western District of Victoria in the winter of 1952, aged twenty-two. His social position and his inheritance were givens. He need have made no effort to become the owner and manager of Nareen in his father's stead. But he wanted to do more than this. Within weeks of arriving he had decided that he would not refer to himself as a grazier or a pastoralist; those words carried too many innuendos of class and privilege. Instead, he gave his occupation on forms as 'primary producer', and continued to describe himself in this way from then on, in election pamphlets and even on his marriage certificate.

Beyond the Western District the dominant ideological themes of the time were communism and socialism, and what they meant for Australia and the Western world. The Korean War had not yet ended. Australian armed forces were part of the coalition resisting communist insurrection in Malaya. In Europe, the Berlin airlift, in which the US and British governments had countered a Soviet blockade by flying in food and the necessities of life to west Berlin, had ended just three years earlier, but had confirmed the division of Berlin, and Germany, into two units. Communism seemed on the move everywhere, and the threat was both internal and external. It was to become Fraser's primary concern.

The society that Fraser re-entered was sharply stratified. In the nearby town of Hamilton, the graziers drank at the Hamilton Club, while the working men and agricultural labourers drank in the front bar of the local pubs. It was us and them, but the graziers and the landholders could not assume that their views held sway. They were outnumbered, and this was a democracy.

The federal seat of Wannon, in which Nareen was located, was held by Labor and had been for all but three of the previous twelve years. Stretching from the Mallee to the sea, from the South Australian border to the eastern edge of the Grampians, Wannon was the second-largest electorate in the state, and one of the most diverse. The region's roads were still mainly unsealed, and it was five hours' drive from the centre of Wannon to Melbourne, but there was no sheltering from change, progress and threat. Almost every rural industry was represented in the electorate. In the south-west, the little town of Portland was being developed by a cooperative as a major deepwater port that could serve all of central Victoria and much of South Australia. This offered vast possibilities, but also challenges. Over the next few years, its advancement would become a threat to the vested interests that gathered around Melbourne and Geelong. Advocacy for Portland was one of the first political battles for the young Fraser.

In the southern districts of the electorate around the coast, and in the east, the Catholic Church was dominant, with the population largely of Irish descent and Labor voters by habit and class loyalty. In the farming areas, the squattocracy was offset by soldier settlers who had struggled hard to make a living from their blocks. Mechanisation was only just beginning to affect agriculture. The big farms still relied on small armies of agricultural labourers. In the main towns, there were woollen mills and butter factories. One of the region's fastest growing businesses was the clothing manufacturer Fletcher Jones, based in Warrnambool. Its founder had converted the business into one largely owned by its workers after being influenced by the Japanese labour activist Toyohiko Kagawa, who proposed cooperative economic systems as an alternative to capitalism.

Even for the well-off in Wannon, life was indescribably different from what it is today. Nareen had no washing machine; instead, there was a scrubbing board. There was no refrigerator, but a Coolgardie meat safe—a cupboard with mesh doors and a damp cloth draped into a tray of water to keep meat cool through evaporation. Before Fraser had left for Oxford, the house had relied on batteries for electricity, which meant lights were always being turned off to save power. While he was away, his father had bought a diesel generator that started automatically when the first light was switched on. 'You waited about twenty-five seconds after you had turned the light on before you would get light. Then everyone would say, "You turned the light on? Quick, turn some more lights on!" because you didn't want the engine running with too light a load.' The rural parts of the Western District were not connected to mains electricity until the early 1960s.

Fraser could hardly have felt further away from Oxford, yet he was enormously happy to be home. The country—its smells and colours—still moved him. He was back in the ute, driving in clouds of dust, and on horseback. He was crutching sheep and spreading fertiliser. But now he had a sense of mission: there had to be more. His childhood and his education had left him with a disposition towards activism, now underpinned by an intellectual appreciation of liberalism. Two contradictory impulses drove him: the child who had been told that he should be seen and not heard, and the young adult who had a determination, even a compulsion, to make a difference, but had yet to find either the confidence or the voice.

Fraser is apt to describe his entry into politics as an accident, 'or at least the timing was, anyway'. Yet in hindsight it seems clear that something of the kind was bound to happen. Within weeks of arriving home he was thinking about politics. He went to meetings of the Young Liberals in Hamilton, and there met the organiser for the electorate of Wannon Brian Cowling. The electorate was held by Labor's Don McLeod, a sixty-year-old World War I veteran and soldier settler who was well liked and hard-working, but not a high political achiever. The Liberal Party candidate was Dan Mackinnon, who had held the seat briefly, between 1949 and 1951, during the one period in recent history when Labor had lost the numbers. Wannon had always been a struggle for the Liberals. It was by no means a blue-ribbon seat. Mackinnon, having battled it out for years, was now considering running for the more easily winnable marginal neighbouring seat of Corangamite, in which he lived. That would leave the Liberal candidacy for Wannon vacant. There would have to be pre-selection. Even before Mackinnon made his intentions clear, Fraser was on the move. Cowling suggested to him that he should stand for pre-selection. He wouldn't win, of course—he was too young and not well known—but showing an interest would stand him in good stead if he was interested in a political career later in life.

A few miles up the road from Nareen lived Claude Austin, a family friend, local councillor and leading member of the Coleraine branch of the Liberal Party. Austin was an unusual man—anything but hidebound and conservative. He had turned his attention to national affairs after returning from World War II. He was, Fraser recalls, 'large and bluff, generally sucking on a pipe'. He was also a nature lover, and what these days would be called an ardent conservationist. He and his wife had been leading clients of the famous Australian garden designer Edna Walling, who had sculpted them a naturalistic garden at their homestead. Austin was also one of the prominent bird watchers of his time. Now, in the spring of 1952, Austin took a phone call from Malcolm Fraser. His young neighbour told him he was thinking of going into politics, and would like his advice. Austin invited Fraser around that afternoon, then turned to his wife and told her what the call had been about. She was staggered. Young Fraser was so shy and awkward; she could not imagine anyone less likely to be a politician.[2]

Austin, meanwhile, was thinking hard. The conventional view was that if Mackinnon moved on, he would be replaced by the former senator Magnus Cormack, who lived in Portland and who had been State President of the party. Austin, though, was no fan of Cormack. He thought him arrogant and dismissive, and he didn't like his views. Yet there was no reason to think the raw and awkward Fraser would do instead, or that he was the man who could wrest the seat from Labor. Fraser had not grown up in the district, and had been away at school or at Oxford for most of the time since the family moved into the area. Nevertheless, when Fraser arrived, Austin heard him out, then asked him how hard he was prepared to work. Whatever Fraser said, it convinced Austin. He told Fraser that he would have next to no chance of winning the pre-selection battle; privately, though, he had decided to help him.

Running for the Liberal Party seemed to Fraser like the only choice, but this was not, or not only, because of the legacy of Simon Fraser: it was because he wanted to join a party that aspired to represent everyone. 'Some people might have thought the Country Party would be more natural for me, since I was a farmer and all that. But I never wanted to be part of that party. I didn't want to represent sectional interests. I thought politics should be broader than that. And I thought whatever I had learned from Keynes was totally consistent with the sort of liberalism which Menzies was on about. He was espousing a mixed economy, and his idea of liberalism was never conservative. He was a progressive. Menzies deliberately rejected the British title "conservative". He never used the word "conservative" in the Australian context.'

A month or two later, Mackinnon announced that he would indeed be moving on. Fraser entered the contest with no great expectations, but, typically, once he was in he thought, 'To hell with it! No point throwing your hat into the ring and not trying to win. So I started to work at it'. There were to be three candidates for pre-selection: Fraser, Cormack and a Hamilton electrician, GH Robinson. The first challenge for Fraser was to become known. Cowling organised for him and the other candidates to speak at every Liberal Party branch. Fraser made very little impression—not a good speaker, and still too shy to be able to connect—but at least those attending got to know his face, and he was making it clear that he was prepared to work hard.

The convention at which delegates from Wannon Liberal Party branches selected their candidate was held on 11 November 1953—not the last time that Remembrance Day was a significant date in Fraser's career. He had sweated over a pre-selection speech; the initial typescript had been five pages long.[3] There was much in the first draft that would have annoyed Liberals whose notions of the party were conservatism and the defence of business interests. Fraser had begun with an exposition of his 'ideas on the respective roles of liberalism and of socialism'. He said he was not against progressive ideas: the Labor parties of England and Australia had carried on the tradition of the nineteenth-century Gladstonian liberals, 'a tradition of social reform, fair rents, factory laws and pensions, rather than one of socialism ... Few of us would deny that many great and humane reforms have come from the left side of politics'. But since the war, he said, there had been a change in the temper of the Labor parties of the two countries. The source and inspiration for their social reforms had dried up, and therefore:

> They had turned to the central core of their platform, the nationalisation of the means of production, distribution and exchange, to which we are bitterly opposed. They chose their time well, especially in England, for there the ravages and havoc of war had left a vast majority of the people ready for a change, and the change offered was socialism.

Fraser spent several pages talking about the Atlee government in England, and its nationalisation of coal, electricity, railways, road transport, iron, steel and the Bank of England. Even here Fraser was not uniformly opposed. In accord with what he had learned at Oxford, he adopted the stance of a utilitarian. 'There are only two standards of criticism of government action: does it make more people happier and does it make things run more efficiently.' Railways, coal and electricity, he said, probably ran as well under government control as in private hands, but, 'The effect of nationalisation on road transport has been disastrous'. The workers had been betrayed, because they were no better off and the boss was still remote and harsh: 'Their god has proved false and at the moment they have no other god to follow'. The search for new ideas meant that there was a danger that the Labor governments would 'go off the deep end and into communism'.

This, Fraser said, was a testing time for liberalism. Too often, liberalism had relied upon a negative: opposition to socialism. Liberals had also sometimes been conservative. Such policies 'in these critical years can only bring disaster'. Liberalism, said Fraser, was not a formula, like socialism, but a way of life.

> A liberal crusade must take the philosophy and belief in liberalism to everyone, and crusaders must remember that converts can only be made by the example of their own actions ... I want to play some part in this. I am young

> and would like nothing better than to devote a lifetime to this end.

But even as he sweated over this first draft, Fraser had realised, with some anxiety, that it wouldn't do: it read like one of his university essays. He needed a different voice, and, although the thought made his mouth dry, he knew that the last thing he should do was read from the typescript. 'That would be the same as throwing in the towel.' So he began to work on his public speaking. He stood at one end of Claude Austin's corridor, with Austin at the other, and practised projecting his voice. Austin would throw in interjections and insults to get him used to dealing with them. By the night of the pre-selection, Fraser had not a typescript but five pages of notes scrawled in his idiosyncratic longhand, each line running slightly uphill from left to right and with the word 'socialism' abbreviated to a snake-like 's'.

Nearly one hundred delegates from throughout Wannon gathered in the Hamilton Temperance Hall to hear the three candidates. Fraser drove from Nareen through flooded countryside, such a bundle of nerves that he wasn't sure he would be able to speak at all. Cormack went first. When he finished, he strode out of the hall, went around the back and threw up. Fraser reflected that he wasn't the only one who was nervous. Then he was on. He told the delegates:

> There are two reasons I want to stand for this seat. Ever since I can remember I have thought the socialist theory an unhappy one, and in these last few years we have all been given cogent arguments against socialism. It is the universality of the theory which leads to its application in inappropriate cases that does the harm.

He referred to the Atlee government in postwar England and used the phrase 'He has worshipped a false god and has no other god to follow' in referring to the English worker. The Labor Party in Australia would assuredly drive towards nationalisation if it were given the power, he said.

> I bitterly oppose socialism, but hatred of a doctrine is not enough to drive me into a lifelong career; there must be the other side. I could not enter this fight versus socialism if I did not love Australia, if I did not think she had a great industrial as well as agricultural future … It is not the greatness of this country in terms of power, productivity and population but in terms of individual people, the people I work with at home and the people I meet and see in Casterton. Each man from the street cleaner to the industrialist behind a rich desk has an equal right to a full and happy life. Each one has an equal right to go his own way unhampered so long as he does not harm our precious social framework. My wish that men may continue to enjoy this right is the real reason that urges me to enter a lifelong fight versus socialism, and I feel that this fight is worthwhile because of the unique and individual characteristics that I find in every person.

The speech made a favourable impression. Fraser's nerves showed through, but seemed to work in his favour. Cormack had given a more highly polished presentation, but Fraser's words seemed to come from the heart. Cormack was well known, but had made enemies in the Western District. Fraser had the merit of freshness.

There was an attempt by Cormack's supporters to unsettle Fraser by asking him a question about the limits of the liberal ideal. What did he think, for example, of the new anti-trust laws in the United States, designed to restrict monopolies and cartels? Fraser's Oxford training got him through. He had studied and written essays on this very topic. He had no problem with the idea that monopolies and cartels should be restrained. He says today, 'If the natural order of something is to be a monopoly, then it is better in government hands than in private hands. Then you can supervise and challenge what is happening. If it is a private monopoly then you need anti-trust laws and all sorts of regulation, and that gets very awkward. Look at Telstra'.

Late that night, Una and Neville Fraser took a call from their son. He was the new Liberal candidate for Wannon. Neville was flabbergasted. Nobody had thought that Fraser would win; indeed, he was not meant to win. The crucial factor had been the branches, and the Liberal Party local delegates' ability to make their own decisions. Had the party organisation intervened, Fraser wouldn't have had a chance.

The next day's newspapers, reporting his success, said he was one of the youngest men ever to stand for an Australian parliament. In the following months, newspapers described him as a Liberal Party 'baby', though noted that he was a big infant. Almost every article about him reported his height: 6 feet and 5 inches.[4]

* * *

The 1954 federal election, the first that Fraser contested, was one of the pivot points of Australian history. Robert Menzies almost lost to Labor, led by Dr Bert Evatt. The Labor Party received 50.1 per cent of the first preference vote, but the votes were in the wrong places, and Labor did not win a majority of seats. A few hundred votes going the other way in the right seats would have reversed the result. Had Labor won, the party split of 1955 which led to the creation of the Catholic-dominated anti-communist Democratic Labor Party would almost certainly not have happened. Had the Democratic Labor Party never existed, the long period of Menzies-led Liberal–Country Party dominance might not have happened, or at least would have played out differently. It is hard to conceive how different Australian history might have been.

The Labor Party and the union movement were at this time emerging from a battle for their souls. In the postwar years, the Communist Party had come close to taking over the Australian trade union movement. In 1945, communists had won 40 per cent of the votes at the Australian Council of Trade Unions congress in Sydney. The battle against communist influence had been dominated by the

Catholic political activist Bob Santamaria, one of the most influential figures in recent Australian history. With the backing of Archbishop Daniel Mannix and sections of the Catholic Church, Santamaria had founded the Catholic Social Studies Movement, generally known simply as 'the Movement'. This was a semi-clandestine organisation with the aim of inserting Catholic social and moral values into all sides of politics. As the communists grew in influence, the main focus of the Movement became countering their rise within the Labor movement. To do this, it recruited, infiltrated and backed Catholic activists to oppose communists in the unions. By the mid 1950s, the anti-communist Industrial Groups, or the 'Groupers', as they were known, had been largely successful: union after union had come under their domination. In all this, Santamaria had been supported by senior figures within the Labor Party, including Evatt himself. In the lead-up to the 1954 election, Evatt had met Santamaria to discuss methods of countering communist influence. Santamaria later claimed that Evatt had even asked him to write his policy speech for the election.[5] It is clear that Evatt anticipated an alliance with the anti-communist Groupers, had he gained power. As Prime Minister, he would have needed their support. The Labor Party had avoided becoming an ideological prisoner of the Moscow-dominated Communist Party, and was stronger as a result. At the time of the election, Labor was in power in all states except South Australia, and most commentators predicted a Labor win over Menzies.

Even in its success, though, the Movement had been sowing the seeds of its defeat. Having largely countered communism, the Movement broadened its focus and ambitions, taking on Labor figures who were not communists but were not sufficiently sympathetic to the Movement's aims. At the same time, Santamaria held seminars to try to present traditions of labour thought alternative to that of communism.[6] But Santamaria had influence in both political parties: while he was dealing with Evatt, he also had a direct line of communication with Menzies. The conduit was the Fraser family's friend Dick Casey.[7]

Despite the family connection, Fraser was not fully aware of the behind-the-scenes aspects of the fight against communism, but it was clear to him that Wannon, as a marginal seat, was a significant battleground in what was expected to be a cliffhanger election. Menzies was vulnerable. Inflation was running high, due to a wool boom. To try to bring it under control, Menzies had increased taxation and legislated for a quarter of growers' wool cheques to be put into a reserve. It was, as Menzies later remarked, 'the most unpopular budget in modern political history', and in 1953 the polls showed the government's stocks at the lowest point ever.[8] The Liberal Party stood on its record of development, but, from its point of view, communism and fear of communism were the dominant issues. A leaflet distributed throughout Wannon read: 'You know that Menzies's secret ballots gave unionists the power to get rid of the Reds. Don't give the Reds a second chance. Vote Liberal on May 29'. Another pamphlet gave the 'ABC of Achievement' for the Menzies government: 'A' was the secret ballot for union elections, a record low in strikes, increased production and increased prosperity; 'B' was more homes built, more coal won, rural production encouraged and rationing ended; 'C' was record savings, workable health services, strengthened defences and 'prestige abroad restored'. Labor was given a contrasting 'ABC of Failure', the main failings being described as opposition to secret ballots, endless strikes, appeasement of the Reds and 'socialism run riot'.[9]

Fraser believed that talking about the threat of communism was not enough to counter it. As he had said in his pre-selection speech, he believed it was necessary to set a personal example and offer a positive alternative. In an electorate like Wannon, remote from the centres of power, the candidate needed to be a conduit between electors and government. Fraser had promised to devote himself full-time to the job, and now he almost lived in his car, driving over dirt roads to every corner of the electorate. It was hard work, but it had its benefits: somehow the nerves, the shyness, began to be conquered. It was not so much that they weren't there, but that they could not be allowed to matter. 'A lot of it was just repetition', he remembers. 'You drive from one place to another, one time after another, and you see people, hundreds of people sometimes, in a day. And you say, "I'm Malcolm Fraser. I just wanted you to know who I am: I am the Liberal candidate for Wannon. I'm not here to talk about politics and I don't need to know who you are voting for or against. If you want ask me any questions, I will try to answer them. If I can't answer them, I'll get you the answers and talk to you later". And if they responded and said, "Come and have a cup of tea", or wanted to talk about this or that, I'd talk about whatever they wanted to talk about. That was the door-opener. By the time you'd said that twenty times a day, and sometimes been invited in and sometimes had the door slammed on you, well, you sort of get over worrying about yourself so much.'

Claude Austin gave him some good advice: 'Whatever you do, do not be seen at the Hamilton Club'. Fraser remembers, 'For a long while townspeople would find it very difficult if not impossible to get into the Hamilton Club. That changed, but when I started off in politics it was a reality. It was made worse by the fact that in those days not everyone had cars, and well-off people would drink too much in the Hamilton Club and then the youngsters, kids with more money and property than sense, would go and scream around the town drunk. Hoons, we'd call them these days. You only need one of those stories to really give the whole place a bad name, and you didn't want to be part of it. I didn't go into the Hamilton Club until twenty-five years later, when it didn't matter any more'. Instead, he went into the public bars of hotels all over the electorate. 'I wouldn't go into the saloon bar. If you go into the saloon bar you are tagged as thinking yourself a cut above.' He found that once he was in the public bar, and talk was lubricated with a few beers, his upper-class background didn't seem to matter so much. 'Once you get to know people, and they get to know you, then you are generally just accepted for what you are … I tried to disabuse people of their ideas about the Liberal Party. And in that, some of my worst enemies were my colleagues in the party. I was trying to convince people that it was a party for everyone and not an upper-class party or a wealthy party. And sometimes people would look at other Liberals and, well, it didn't help.' His family, fortunately, were not frequenters of the Hamilton Club, and were politically savvy enough to understand the 'problem' of their social position in the election context. They might have been members of all the 'right' clubs in Melbourne, but at home and in Hamilton they were careful. 'They understood the impediment', says Fraser.

Meanwhile, Fraser was finding powerful new ways to be heard. Early in the new year he had sought and gained a weekly spot on the local radio stations 3HA in Hamilton and 3YB in Warrnambool. He began giving short Sunday-night addresses to the electorate under the title *Our Australia*. With few breaks, Fraser gave these addresses to the electorate from the time of his pre-selection, in 1954, until his retirement from parliament, in 1983. They form a digest of Fraser's developing political philosophy and a fair catalogue of the history of Wannon. To begin with, each talk took Fraser hours to record, on reel-to-reel tapes. Everything in the home had to stop. Tamie Fraser remembers that in the early years of their marriage, the recording would take place on the kitchen table, and the timer on the oven going off would mean the whole thing had to be started again. Fraser sweated over the early addresses, drafting and redrafting, listening to his recording and redoing it if it didn't sound exactly right. 'I couldn't stand the sound of my own voice', he says today. He wanted the talks to be predicated on the assumption that electors were intelligent and interested in politics, and that they had a stake in the result of disputes and debates. He consciously adopted the tone that he had learned from his tutors and lecturers in Oxford. In all his time there, including in the first year, when he was very clearly at sea, none of the brilliant people from whom he was learning had ever talked down to him or made him feel that they regarded themselves as his intellectual superiors, 'although they very clearly were'. Now he began to address the people he wanted to represent.

The text of the radio talks was mailed to every local newspaper. Most ran them in full, or reported them as news stories. These were the days before television, when families gathered around the wireless in the evenings. Fraser's talks became the stuff of conversation all over the electorate. It became commonplace for people to approach him to argue over what he had said. Partly, Fraser was introducing the people of Wannon to the ideas he had learned at Oxford. He was bringing something of the modernist perspective home, in the hope that it would take root under the big skies of the Western District. He was also a farm boy, and a practical man. One week he would talk about myxomatosis and new methods for killing rabbits; another week he would describe a new kind of cradle used for treating sheep's feet and keeping them free of footrot; and in between, he would expand on his 'vision of Australia'—which was the title of his very first radio talk, on 24 January 1954. This first public address is not a speech that sits easily with the present-day Fraser. It is full of the common rhetoric of the time—the threat from the North and the peril of the Asian masses to the Australian way of life. Fraser began by recounting the riches of Australia and the sacrifices of men in war, before turning to the threat.

> In the last twenty-five years, the Asian races have asserted their own nationalism against influence from the Western countries. French armed forces are in difficulties in Indochina, where one million men have been fighting ceaselessly in the war against Viet Minh rebel or communist forces. Indonesians have done their utmost to take over their country, while it is only in the last twelve months that the British have cleared large areas of Malaya from communist terrorisation. Australia is faced with a double peril from the North, brought about by the teaming millions in these Asian lands. A thousand million living on a pannikin of rice a day: how much better some of them could do with Australia in their hands. These people are learning Western ways, and their recently aroused nationalism has been

> harnessed to the communist cause. Whether or not they have absorbed the communist doctrine, they are backed by the might of Russia. Their danger to us is very great. We have a land vast in size and empty of people. We cannot rely on America to defend us forever.[10]

Most expressions of the 'yellow peril' during Fraser's time included latent racism. Was it there in Fraser's talk as well? Doubtless there were listeners who heard it that way, but from Fraser's point of view his 'vision of Australia' has to be considered in the context of other speeches. It was not race but communism that he was worried about. Fraser saw Australia through the prism of Toynbee's theories on the rise and fall of civilisations, predicated on the ways in which nations responded to challenge and threat. He saw South-East Asia as the main testing ground for Western liberalism; but this was about methods of government, not about race.

In the early 1960s, several of Fraser's radio talks were used to tell his electorate about the countries to the north, their inhabitants' customs and habits, and their importance to Australia. In 1962, he gave his listeners an account of the visit to Canberra by the king and queen of Thailand. Fraser said that the Thais had 'a long tradition of freedom' and that the royal visit

> should bring home to Australians that we are part of South-East Asia, and must live with South-East Asia. I wish more Australians when they go for their holidays abroad could perhaps travel to the countries of South-East Asia and learn something of the habits and customs of the people.[11]

He argued that Australia should be a 'bridge' between Asia and the West.

The second radio talk had a more pragmatic title: 'Beef from the North'. It was about the best way of transporting cattle from the Kimberleys to southern abattoirs—by air or road. The following week his topic was wages, and how they should be set fairly. In this, he returned to his Oxford theme of the cruelty of the gold standard when it meant that deteriorations in foreign exchange must be reflected in unemployment. He repeated the utilitarian sentiment of his pre-selection speech: 'The first consideration of any government must be the prosperity and happiness of its own people'. The following week he returned to the communist threat, and spelled out its nature in a talk titled 'A Comparison of Governments'. He broadcast over the vast miles of Wannon:

> In relating one government to another, three types must be considered. There is our own democratic government which allows free expression of the will of the people. There are regimes that rely solely on force to defend themselves both within and without. And most dangerously there are regimes, like Russian communism, which secure support for their rule by whipping up the fanaticism of their people for some cause. In this case the cause is domination of the world by the proletariat.

The danger of communism, he said, was that it offered 'a false answer to all the world's problems, and for this reason can attract the support of people who are too lazy to recognise the real value in life for themselves'. In Russian communism the 'fanatical belief' in the destiny of the proletariat had taken the place of religion.

> Belief in such things, if it really grips a nation, whether it be right or wrong, is extraordinarily dangerous. We have seen how Hitler making the German people believe in their destiny as a ruling race led to a vast war. It was the belief of nearly every German that he should dominate the people of other countries that led to his whole-hearted support for Nazi Germany. It could be the belief of every communist in the inevitability of their revolution that may lead to the final step: actual war against the democracies.

For Fraser, communism was analogous to fanatical religion. He was still Weldon's student, and suspicious of the metaphysic.

He believed, with Locke, that the core of human knowledge and progress lay not in metaphysics but in experience and rationality. He told the electorate of Wannon: 'The truth and real democratic way of life cannot be expressed in one catch-phrase or sentence, as can the essence of communism. It must be lived and experienced so that through time we will learn tolerance, sympathy and good will to all men'.[12]

For the following week's radio talk Fraser turned to an exercise in imaginative writing, anticipating the imminent visit of the Queen to Wannon—the first time a reigning monarch had visited Australia.

> The people of Wannon are anxious and expectant. It is bright and warm. A perfect summer's day ... Then a welcoming cry is heard from the outskirts which is drowned by many voices as the people see the royal car and in it Her Gracious Majesty Queen Elizabeth II. The Queen smiles and royally waves ...

He quickly moved on from imaginative description to stating why the Queen was important.

> In this small figure is embodied the strength and happiness of the British peoples ... The people see in her the manifestation of the British heritage, a tradition of freedom and of fairness which has been defended and enhanced from generation to generation ... They see in her the victory of generosity, kindness and charity ... It shows the pattern of a great Commonwealth of Nations ... In each and every one of these lands, men and women are part of the British heritage which makes possible life without fear, and freedom from want.

Only 'eternal vigilance against dangers both within and without' made the Queen's visit possible and guaranteed that she would be able to come again.[13]

The next month Fraser spoke on 'A Great Fear Buried': economic depression. He told the people of Wannon about Keynes, the International Monetary Fund and the wonderful 'knowledge' of how to prevent recession and depression. Two weeks later, he talked about footrot. He followed that up with an extraordinary address on the place of women, telling his listeners that in his travels around Wannon housewives often claimed to know nothing of politics. They told him he should speak to their husbands. This wasn't good enough, said Fraser. In the eyes of the law, women took equal place 'as people with feelings and emotions common to every person'. Fraser gave the women of Wannon some examples to think about. He quoted John Stuart Mill. He told them that Madam Pandit Nehru had just been elected as President of the United Nations' General Council, presiding over an assembly of sixty nations. He talked about Florence Nightingale and the suffragettes, and reminded them that Australia was one of the first countries in the world to give women the vote. Finally, he talked about the Queen and the 'second Elizabethan age'. Women's advice was 'not only desirable but necessary' in every area of life, Fraser said. In voting, 'Each one of us, every man and every woman, must think and give his or her judgement carefully'.[14] It is hard to imagine what the housewives of Wannon made of this lecture, delivered by a young man not yet turned twenty-four. In the following week he spoke about jobs, and in the following about US beef imports.

On 6 April 1954, Menzies called the election for 29 May. It was the latest possible date. As is the way with governments in trouble, Menzies had delayed for as long as he could. Now the battle was on; but Fraser's tone in his radio addresses hardly altered. His next topic was 'Men for Australia', in which he advocated increased migration.

> The quality of the migrants we get depends upon the future Australia holds for them ... If we accept them as Australians in every way then our new people will feel at

> home and will write back to the Old World encouraging others to come here ... If these things are done we cannot fail to keep Australia free and happy, but if we don't use the resources nature has given us in this land then other races will overshadow us.[15]

Two days after Fraser broadcast the talk, one of the most significant events in the political history of Australia took place. On 13 April Menzies announced to parliament that a Russian spy, Vladimir Petrov, had been operating in Australia and had defected to the West. This news, greeted with shock and fear around the nation, seemed to give substance to the fear of communism. Menzies announced a royal commission into Soviet espionage, and said Petrov was happy to help because 'He no longer believes'.[16] The move for the commission was supported by the Labor Party.

In the following week, there were violent anti-communist demonstrations at Sydney airport as Petrov's wife, Evdokia, was escorted by KGB agents to her aircraft and then, when the plane landed at Darwin, was seized by Northern Territory police. The photos of Evdokia being roughly handled by the KGB agents became some of the best remembered Australian images of the 1950s, although in Wannon the issue was hardly mentioned.

Whole books have been written about the Petrov affair, and whether or not Menzies manipulated the timing of the announcement to help his election prospects. In fact, Menzies issued a directive to all Liberal candidates telling them that because the matter was being investigated by the royal commission it should not be allowed to become party-political: they were not to refer to Petrov in an election context.[17] Fraser, like all other candidates, received and obeyed the directive. So it was that on 18 April, just five days after the announcement about Petrov, Fraser was talking about a far more prosaic threat: plagues of rabbits, and the use of myxomatosis to combat them.

The seriousness with which Menzies took the directive was emphasised when the Country Party politician Artie Fadden travelled to Hamilton to speak in Fraser's support. Fraser recalls Fadden telling the crowd that the inquiry into Petrov was not a political matter, and that Menzies didn't want it discussed; but he urged voters to consider: 'Who would you want to implement the report when it comes out?' The next day, Fadden took a call from a furious Menzies. 'He told him he was never to do anything like that ever again.'

Fraser's radio talks were causing a stir within the party. One day in mid May, when he was door-knocking in the tiny town of Edenhope in the western Wimmera, he received a message from the State President of the Liberal Party, JM Anderson, demanding that he drop everything and go to Melbourne. When he got there—six hours' drive on dirt roads—he was asked to explain why he had been making statements without approval. Fraser recalls, 'I said I was the candidate and I had to have a voice'. He was reprimanded, but when he reported the incident to Claude Austin the matter was taken to the electorate finance committee, and a curt message was sent back to party headquarters. If state headquarters wanted to talk to the candidate, they would have to do it through the Wannon campaign committee. 'So in the end it was the State President who was rebuked by an independent Wannon. That independence of mind was important from then on. I always knew if I could get Wannon's support for what I was doing and so long as I could justify what I had done, then that was enough.'

The radio addresses continued. Fraser talked about industrial arbitration: Australia's 'own invention' and one of the things of which the country should be proud.

> We must remember that nobody in the wide world had ever heard of such a thing as a basic wage until our Commonwealth Arbitration Court invented it. We must remember that it was the Arbitration Court that awarded first the 48-, then the 44-, and now the 40-hour week. We must remember that it was the Arbitration Court that put the prosperity pound onto the basic wage, which was rightly paid with no complaint and no protest.[18]

Then he was back to footrot and myxomatosis. His last talk before the election was a catalogue of the Menzies government's record: the secret ballot had made it possible 'for every decent unionist to have his say in his union affairs'; the government had cooperated with the unions, and this had isolated the extremists; taxation had been reduced; a comprehensive health plan had been introduced; pensions had been increased. 'Never before has a government gone to the polls with such a record as that of this last Liberal–Country Party government of ours.'[19]

It was clear that the battle for Wannon would be close. The city-based media began to pay attention to the young farmer who was running against the established Labor man. The Melbourne *Sun* reported during the campaign that 'The local Australian Labor Party members are taking Mr Fraser very seriously. They complain mildly that the Australian Labor Party central executive is not taking him seriously enough and is not giving them enough financial support'.[20] Labor had had some bad luck: its candidate, Don McLeod, had been ill for more than half of the campaign, first with flu and then hospitalised with pneumonia. Meanwhile, Fraser had been everywhere, and was backed up by some big guns. Menzies as well as Fadden had visited the electorate and addressed large meetings.

It was nearly a week after the election before the result in Wannon was known. The headline in *The Argus* was 'All Eyes on Wannon', and it was right. Reporters made their way out west to interview the man who was expected to be both 'the youngest, and the tallest man ever elected to an Australian parliament'.[21] The *Sun* published an article about the young Fraser, illustrated with a picture of him leaning against a bench in a leather jacket, elastic-sided boots and working trousers, under the heading 'Youngest Ever?'

> He looks like Sir Edmund Hillary, 6 feet and 5 inches, lean and rugged, with a wave of long brown hair that tends to flap down over his forehead ... Next time you are in the public gallery of the House of Representatives, look along

> the rows of government back benches and you'll probably see him.

The article went on, suggestively, 'Mr Fraser, an Oxford graduate in the Modern Greats ... is neither married nor engaged'. Where once there had been shyness and awkwardness, Fraser was now described as 'quietly proud but singularly composed ... Mr Fraser's speech reflects his Oxford training. It's subdued and precise but not synthetically English. He's the friendly, informal, outdoor type, his face suntanned by weeks of campaigning'. Fraser did not smoke, had covered more than twelve thousand miles through Wannon, and, if he won, promised to tour the electorate completely at least three times a year. Each tour would take about three weeks.[22]

The article and its picture made their way to a farmhouse in the neighbouring electorate of Corangamite, where they were seen by a young woman who had only recently left boarding school. Tamara Beggs was not particularly interested in politics, and had never heard of Malcolm Fraser. Seeing the picture of the young Edmund Hillary lookalike, she read the article then flipped the page impatiently. Running for parliament when you are only twenty-four? The man must be a complete fool and a bore, she decided. Two and a half years later, she would marry him.

In the meantime, with the election result still not known, *The Argus* editorialised under the headline 'A Young Man Brings a Hope'.

> The vigour and success of 24-year-old Malcolm Fraser's fight for the Wannon federal seat stimulates hope that politics will soon cease to be the almost exclusive preserve of aging gentlemen who wish to spend the evening of their lives in profitable comfort, while they listen to their arteries clogging.

The article quoted Fraser as saying that he wanted to live to see twenty to thirty million people living in Australia. 'There he declares the foresight and measures the responsibility of today's youth ...

Old men may dream dreams, and young men may see visions. And who can say that parliament is not better off for a vision now and then?'[23]

It was not to be. Labor's McLeod won the seat by just seventeen votes: an extraordinary result. In his final address, Fraser told the electorate that he would be back: he would contest the seat again; and in the meantime would keep travelling, trying to meet as many of them as possible.

The closeness of the result meant that Fraser had no trouble in regaining pre-selection in August 1955. He resumed his weekly radio talks. The first was delivered from Warrnambool, where he was studying the problems of the dairy industry.

In the months following Menzies's narrow win, almost everything about the political landscape changed. Rather than being within reach of government, Labor all but self-destructed. Evatt had expected to win in 1954. Now he was in deep trouble in his own party, and with himself. He was convinced that the revelations about Petrov had been orchestrated to give substance to the Liberals' claims about the communist threat. Most other commentators thought that the Petrov issue had hardly bitten in 1954; its impact was felt later, in 1955. The commentators blamed Evatt himself for his defeat. In the last weeks of the campaign he had made extravagant promises without clearing them with his own executive. Menzies had been able to pick him apart with ease for economic irresponsibility. Most disastrous of all for Labor, the Petrov Royal Commission was underway, and members of Evatt's personal staff had been named as having connections with the Soviet embassy. Evatt insisted on appearing before the commission in September 1954, and made such outlandish and unfounded accusations that the judges terminated his leave to appear.

The role of Bob Santamaria and the Movement was no longer a well-kept secret. Their actions within the union movement were being talked about openly. In the months after the election, Santamaria became aware of growing hostility from Evatt, while elements in the

Catholic Church were also backing away from him. On 5 October 1954, Evatt called a press conference and turned savagely on the Industrial Groups, the Movement and Santamaria, in the process fanning an old and dangerous flame—anti-Catholic sectarianism. Once again, Catholics were said to be involved in clandestine movements, not to be trusted, owing their loyalty elsewhere. Evatt's attack took many loyal Labor Party members by surprise. They had been proud of their role in combating communist influence.

The Australian Labor Party split had begun and by the end of the year had spread throughout Australia. Anti-communist Labor members eventually became the Catholic-dominated Democratic Labor Party, an ally of the Liberal and Country parties, withholding votes and preferences from Labor as a bargaining weapon in the hope of forcing the party to reform itself. The split kept Labor out of power for another seventeen years. One of the beneficiaries of this was Malcolm Fraser: the Catholic votes in his electorate went mainly to the Democratic Labor Party, and the preferences flowed to him.

Not surprisingly, Menzies capitalised on the Labor Party's troubles by calling an early election for 10 December 1955. In the meantime, Fraser had continued to campaign ever since his narrow defeat the year before. 'It was just hard work. I just travelled around there, went to all the little places where no candidate or member had ever been, and I drank in the pubs. I think my record was going into about fourteen or fifteen pubs a day, and I'm glad we didn't have today's drink-driving laws, because I wouldn't have qualified at any point.' Fraser was now on the state executive of the party. In his speech after being confirmed as candidate, he had described Evatt as 'a great threat' and referred to his 'strange ways'. Only liberalism offered hope and vision, he said.[24]

In his weekly radio address, Fraser told the electorate that he had three main reasons for wanting to enter politics:

> Faith in Australians as a proud, strong and independent people; belief in the future of this country as a secure home for ourselves and our children; and knowledge that there is

> a vital job to be done through our political institutions that cannot end while we maintain our unchallengeable belief in British democracy. The things we often take for granted, the four freedoms—of speech, of worship, freedom from want, and from fear—and equality of all men before the law, are not enjoyed by all the peoples of the world. They will remain ours only while we are prepared to work and fight for them. It is my wish to play a part in the great work that is going on and that must continue. I was too young to fight in the war, but I am not too young now to fight and work for my faith and belief in Australia.

He also spoke on the need for continued immigration. Only with many more new Australians could the country develop. Most migrants were eager to settle and learn Australian ways. 'We could often make this easier for them by remembering that their background and upbringing were often in many ways different from our own.'[25]

He spoke frequently on the hopes for the Portland harbour. Soon, all petrol brought into the region would be coming through Portland. All that was needed, Fraser said, was for the wool firms to open up a wool sales centre. 'If I get into parliament I am going to fight for Portland as Victoria's third port', Fraser said.

In October 1955, he talked about party politics, how people cursed it, because of the risk that the machine would impose its will on the individual. Only a few years before, Fraser had argued exactly this case in a university essay, but now he said that parties were necessary for stable government and effective opposition. Nevertheless, 'Electors must still expect [members of parliament] to remain responsible to their own conscience ... The party system only becomes an evil if the so-called machine completely dominates the individual members of the party'.

In May 1955, the European communist states had signed the Warsaw Pact. In November, the Soviet Union confirmed to the world that it had exploded a hydrogen bomb. It was no longer possible to deny the Soviet Union's expansionist ambitions. Just days afterwards, Fraser told the electorate of Wannon that Russia had held out a 'bowl of roses' to the Western powers, but it had withered 'and only the thorns remain'. For a time it had appeared that Russia wanted to live peacefully alongside the West, but,

> For communists, there is no peaceful co-existence ... It is true that in Russia an ordinary citizen may enter a church, but it is also true that once a citizen is taken into the party, the House of God is denied him. A Russian communist is not allowed to be a Christian. Perverted and twisted though it is, communism is his religion.

As for Evatt: 'I know Dr Evatt says he is not pro-communist, and I am prepared to accept his word on this, but if he is not pro-communist surely he should do something to fight communists instead of apathetically watching them entrench themselves in Australia once more'. Evatt had killed the industrial groups that fought communism and had not replaced them with anything else, said Fraser. Meanwhile, Australian Labor Party men were going into unions on joint tickets with communists.

The big swing to Fraser in the 1954 election meant that he would probably have won in 1955 in any case. Thanks to the split, he won in a landslide. He was helped by the fact that McLeod was not contesting the seat. The new Labor candidate was Roy Cundy, a local farmer. Terence Callander, a baker from Harrow, was representing the Anti-Communist Labor Party, which was shortly to become the Democratic Labor Party.

Nationally, in 1955 there was a swing of more than 5 per cent away from the Australian Labor Party, and most of that was picked up by the Anti-Communist Labor Party, which nevertheless won no seats. Menzies had a clear victory: seventy-five seats to the Australian Labor Party's forty-seven.

Wannon had fallen decisively to the Liberal and Country Party (as the Victorian division of the Liberal Party was called at the time), and has never since been held by Labor. Fraser increased his majorities at every election until his retirement from parliament, in 1983. He was helped by Democratic Labor Party preferences and by the Country Party's never running a candidate against him, but over time those issues became academic; he was safe in the seat in his own right.

★ ★ ★

The year that Malcolm Fraser came to parliament as its youngest member marked the high-water point of the struggle within Australia against communism; but this is a judgement that is possible only in retrospect: it was not clear at the time.[26] In the short term, the departure of the anti-communists from the Labor Party created opportunities for the communists, and broad alliances were formed between them and Labor, including combined tickets for union officeholders. Nevertheless, it is now possible to see that 1955 was a turning point. In February 1956, just a few months after Fraser entered parliament, the Soviet leader Nikita Khrushchev denounced Joseph Stalin as a brutal despot in a sensational speech to the twentieth congress of the Communist Party. The world heard from the Soviets themselves about the assassinations of political rivals, the prison camps and the repression. The 'de-Stalinisation' at the heart of the Soviet Union raised hopes across Eastern Europe that Soviet-style communism could be reformed, that more freedom might be possible. In October, the Hungarian people rose up against Soviet rule, but weeks later they were overrun by Soviet tanks, and the Hungarian leaders, who had planned to take the country out of the Warsaw Pact, were executed. The pattern was repeated across Europe throughout the decade that followed, most notably when the Prague Spring—another attempt to reform the Soviet communist model—was brutally suppressed in 1968. The Soviet Union was aggressive, imperialist and expansionist. Fraser saw no reason to doubt that the communist threat was real.

Domestically, the strains on the Australian Communist Party eventually ended it as a significant political force. Its leadership tried to suppress and deny Khrushchev's revelations at first, but the truth was out, and many who had supported the Soviet Union throughout World War II underwent a crisis of faith and conscience. Significant numbers of party members, including the intellectual leadership, left in protest when it backed the Soviet invasion of Hungary. The party retained influence in trade unions and in left-wing movements, but contested few state or federal elections. In the 1960s, it was split between Maoists and those loyal to the Soviet Union. A new phase began, in which the party distanced itself from Stalinism. It opposed the invasion of Czechoslovakia in 1968, and split again between those still loyal to Moscow and those seeking a non-Stalinist form of socialism. Thus, the Australian Communist Party entered a long period of decline that culminated in its winding up in 1991.

Today, Fraser thinks it significant and a sign of hope that the communist influence within Australia was combated not through suppression but through the political process. Certainly, there was surveillance of communists, and oppression. The Hope royal commission, which later reported to Fraser's government, found that the Australian Security Intelligence Organisation had become so politicised, and so preoccupied with finding communists within Australia, that it had ignored the very real possibility that it had itself been infiltrated by Soviet agents. However, communism was not outlawed; people could not be jailed merely for their political beliefs. Yet there had been a time, before Fraser entered parliament, when a different course seemed likely. In 1950, in fulfilment of an election promise, the Menzies government had moved to outlaw membership of the Communist Party. The Communist Party Dissolution Bill was one of the most draconian ever introduced into an Australian parliament—at least until the Howard government's anti-terrorism legislation. The Bill gave power to the government to publicly declare any citizen a communist and to bar them from holding office in a range of public organisations, including trade unions. Any organisations that were suspected of being affiliated with the Communist Party would be dissolved. Anyone who carried on the work of the party after it was declared illegal would be jailed for five years. Because of the difficulty of identifying a communist, the law essentially allowed for someone to be accused of a crime against the Commonwealth on very little evidence; the traditional legal stance of 'innocent until proven guilty' would be reversed. If someone was accused of being a communist, they were guilty unless they could prove otherwise. The law had popular support to begin with: Roy Morgan ran a public opinion poll in June 1950 which reported that 80 per cent supported the banning of the Communist Party. Demonising communists appeared to be a vote winner.

The Bill had a stormy passage through parliament, but, in the wake of the Korean War, it was passed. It was straightaway challenged in the High Court. The ensuing constitutional battle had little to do with human rights or freedom of speech: it rested on whether the Commonwealth had the power to pass such laws. The government argued that the Communist Party was a threat to national defence, but the High Court held that the defence of Australia was not under so great a threat as to justify the banning of a political party. Not satisfied, the Menzies government called a referendum, seeking to change the constitution to give it the power necessary to legislate. The referendum was narrowly defeated after an enormously vigorous campaign by Evatt and the Labor Party. The Menzies government had not succeeded in convincing the Australian people that communism was a threat sufficient to justify the undermining of their civil rights.

Fraser had been overseas, at Oxford, during these events, and only broadly aware of them. In the years after his entry to parliament, he was to become one of the government's most vehement anti-communists, an ardent 'Cold Warrior'. Well into his prime ministership he remained suspicious of the Soviet Union, long after others were talking détente. It was this that caused people to think of him as a right-winger, and to overlook first the youthful, then the middle-aged, liberal idealism.

In recent times, Fraser has said that Evatt was right—very right indeed—to oppose and campaign against the Communist Party

Dissolution Bill. 'He won, rightly. It was much to his credit; it said a great deal about principle and his readiness to support principles. Where do we see such courage today, such determination? Perhaps that is why bad policy has assumed a dominance in certain areas.'[27] But would the Fraser of the early 1950s, so fearful of communism and so critical of Evatt, have been on Evatt's side, or Menzies's? Today he likes to think he would have been with Evatt. He also thinks that Menzies never had his heart in the legislation. He bases this view on his study of history, and his discussions with Menzies in later years. It is a view quite out of kilter with that of most historians. Fraser says, 'Look at the kind of campaign that Evatt ran against the legislation compared to the campaign Menzies ran for it. Menzies spoke very seldom, very little. He was a real believer in the rule of law, and a real liberal. But there was a strong anti-communist element within the Liberal Party. There was a number of senior, important ex-servicemen around who would have had this view, and they would have been pushing him. On my reading of Menzies's character, he wouldn't have liked this legislation, though he was wily enough politically to use it, I guess'. Fraser says that Menzies had been scarred by being 'dumped' by the United Australia Party after his first term as Prime Minister, between 1939 and 1941. The legacy, Fraser says, was that Menzies developed 'a sort of caution and weariness about factionalism, even though the Liberal Party was a different creature, and one which, really, he had created. Even though after 1949 he was in a strong position, I think he probably felt that it would be buying too big an argument with the party not to be seen to act against the communists'.

There is support for Fraser's view. In his autobiography, Bob Santamaria recorded that he had advised Menzies, through Dick Casey, against the legislation. He thought it was a counter-productive and 'useless' ritual that would split the opposition to communism and undermine the campaign to isolate them. Santamaria's advice on this was rejected. He later wrote that Menzies had been motivated partly by pressure to be seen to 'do something' and partly by his own concern that if there were another war, communist trade unionists might be 'treacherous'.[28] Fraser says today, 'On the one hand, thinking oneself back into that era, you can see why banning the Communist Party seemed necessary to some, but, on the other hand, it goes directly against liberal philosophy. It goes against the rule of law; it goes against free speech; it goes against all sorts of things'. There are parallels, he agrees, with the legislation that the Howard government introduced that banned terrorist organisations. Communists might have been committed to violent revolution; is that the same as terrorism? 'I think there is a difference, but I am not sure I can define it in the clearest terms.' In any case, banning organisations is not the best way to deal with the threat, he says. If someone is planning an act of violence, there are already laws available to deal with that.

It is difficult for the present-day Fraser to think himself back to those times. Would he really have put liberal values first, had he been part of the Menzies government at the time of the attempts to ban the Communist Party? He believes so. He believed in the political process; his Oxford training had taught him that the way to win the battle of ideas was to talk, to argue and to lead by example. Everything he was doing in trying to enter politics was an expression of those beliefs. His Oxford education and his own temperament had led him to a belief in activism, in the need to face threats full-on, to use one's experience and intelligence. He also knew that, in the battles of history, civilisations had prospered through free thought, example and action. Suppressing threats was a kind of running away.

* * *

Fraser delivered his maiden speech in parliament on 22 February 1956. He was nervous, of course. Menzies was a distant and unapproachable figure. Even Dick Casey, the family friend, seemed impossibly senior and remote. Fraser was not only the youngest member of parliament at the time, but also one of the minority who had never served his country in time of war. He was the first of a new generation.

He remained nervous for many years whenever giving a major speech. 'Menzies sometimes sat in the back if I was making a speech, and he would say, "I think I make you nervous".

'I would say, "You do".

'He would say, "Why?"

'I didn't say why. He was the great, powerful, senior person. What was a miniscule member of parliament doing? I always had that feeling. Be seen and not heard. But I had to be heard! Those sorts of feelings don't exist in today's world. Everyone knows that they have a right to have their say. I had to learn that sense of entitlement.'

Fraser's childhood had given him extraordinary self-sufficiency, extraordinary shyness and, paradoxically, a strong desire to be heard. 'The candidate must have a voice', he had told the State President of the Liberal Party. His maiden speech was like a digest of the addresses he had already given on the radio to his electorate. Like those remarkable talks to the people of Wannon, it included a combination of the views of a farmer and those of a pragmatist, an idealist, a modernist and a Cold Warrior. He repeated his hope of living to see twenty-five million people in Australia.

> Then we shall be able to look the world in the face far more boldly and play a more effective part in the maintenance of world peace and freedom. Then, we shall not be independent, but we shall be far less dependent on outside help in times of national emergency.

He spoke of the development of his own electorate as a cause for hope that Australia could support more people. 'Three blades of grass have been made to grow where formerly there was only one. Three and four sheep are being carried to the acre on land that formerly carried only half a sheep.' He talked about the new harbour at Portland. He concluded:

> I was too young to fight in the last war, and I owe a debt of gratitude to those who fought in World War I, as well as in World War II. But I am not too young now to fight for my

> faith and belief in the future of this great nation, in which the individual is, and always shall remain, supreme. I have spoken tonight of power and the prosecution of state and federal works. I have spoken of increased population. But all these things will mean nothing if one thing is ever forgotten—that the individual happiness of each citizen is, and must remain for ever, the first thought of our national leaders.[29]

Fraser sat down. How did he feel? 'Exhausted.'

The candidate had found his voice. Nobody would ever again succeed in telling Malcolm Fraser to be seen and not heard. Many people over the years would have done well to understand that.

4

Love, Danger and Privilege

Malcolm Fraser had found the woman he wanted to marry.

Watching the two of them together now, after more than fifty years of marriage, it is possible to see the way they have grown together, and the push and pull of their partnership. In their daily domestic conversation there are the robust exchanges of equals. They are a tight partnership, neither subservient to the other. They stand up to each other, and look after each other—him insisting on her having flu injections before flying to help out their daughter, who is struggling with sick children. She, for many years now, easing the way for him at social occasions with the stock of anecdotes and niceties that have seen them through public life. She has mitigated the awkwardness and shyness that have never left him. On the day that it was her turn to be interviewed for this book, she sent him out to do the grocery shopping so she could talk about him in peace. He came back too early, and was sent out again. 'I am saying very nice things about you', she told him tartly as he left. He ducked his head back around the door. 'Why can't you do that when I'm here?' he said, and went out, green shopping bags under his arm, laughing.

Does he know all the ways that she helps him? 'Oh, I don't suppose so', she says. 'I mean, you don't go around in a marriage saying "Do you realise what I did for you there, and there, and there?"'

There have been very few big decisions over the years—political or personal—in which her opinion hasn't been heard. 'It has been a great trial for him', she says jokingly. Fraser gives her more credit. 'I am determined that Tamie is not to be a cipher in this book', he says. She has been central. He adds, with some feeling, 'She is a strong woman'. Tamie, on the other hand, would be just as happy to disappear from these pages. 'It really should not be about me, and I don't see that you need all that stuff. People don't need to know who I really am.' What remains here is the result of that battle between them.

Tamara Margaret Beggs, known as Tamie or Tam to her family, was born in 1936, the eldest child of an established and well-off Western District family. When she talks about the training and the attitudes that carried her through political life, she talks first about her parents, and their notions of duty. Unlike her husband, as a child Tamie was always encouraged to speak her mind. Yet like him, she was shy. 'People one on one don't scare me at all. People en masse scare me to death.' Thanks to her mother, she understood this as her failing, to be put aside and overcome if she was not to be the worst of things—a bore. The tenets of the family values were strong, and were clearly and frequently stated. Tamie internalised them. First, one should be loyal to one's family. Second, one should contribute to one's community. After that, there was loyalty to one's country.

Tamie was educated first by governesses, then by correspondence, then sent to board at the Geelong Church of England Girls' Grammar School, the Hermitage, at the age of nine. It is Fraser who fills in the details of Tamie's school life; Tamie herself volunteers little. She says she regarded boarding school as something 'to be endured'. Academically, 'I did well enough when I worked hard, but nothing special'. Reading an early draft of this chapter, Fraser is somewhere between amused and annoyed at her self-effacement. 'She is not telling you the whole story.' He flicks across the desk a sheet on which her achievements are listed. 'What she isn't telling you is that she is every bit as much of a leader as I am.' Tamie was a school prefect and house prefect, school house captain, music captain, sports captain, tennis captain and baseball captain. She won a prize for being the girl who contributed most to the school in work, sport and 'general leadership'. She had an astonishingly successful school career: she virtually ran the place. Her academic results were a reflection of the fact that between all her other responsibilities, she barely had time to study—yet, here too, she did creditably.

When Tamie graduated from the Hermitage, her mother wanted to send her to finishing school in Melbourne, but she couldn't think of anything worse. She begged to be allowed to go home. There, she helped to run the house, 'did farmy stuff' and became a leader in the district Red Cross—a role she has maintained ever since.

Tamie's parents were members of the Liberal Party, but not active. They did not live in Wannon, but in the neighbouring electorate of Corangamite. Nevertheless, the closeness of the 1954 Wannon result piqued local interest and was the subject of conversation even in the Beggses' house, where politics was rarely discussed. Then Tamie heard Fraser on the radio, giving his weekly addresses. This was a novelty. The notion of 'current events' did not really exist in those days. It was not until the 1960s, and television and current events shows on the ABC, that the idea of politics being beamed into people's living rooms took hold. She listened, but she still thought him 'dopey ... superficial little thing that I was'.

They finally met at a New Year's Eve party. Tamie was nineteen years old, and he was twenty-five. The year 1955 was ending. Fraser had just been elected, but had yet to attend his first session of parliament. A few weeks previously he had been to his first party meeting and, with ten other new Liberal members of parliament, had been briefed by the government whip Hubert Opperman. The other members of the class of 1955 were to be both rivals and companions in the years ahead. They included Fred Chaney (senior), who became a friend; Peter Howson, later to be Australia's first Minister for the Environment; Bill Snedden, a future leader of the party; and Jim Killen, later Minister for Defence and one of parliament's most flamboyant and well-liked members, but for Fraser a sparring partner. Fraser was excited by the prospects before him, and was trying to work out what to say in his maiden speech.

Trying to chat to Tamara Beggs, Fraser asked whether she would be going to the meeting of the local Liberal Party branch in a few weeks' time. She reacted with horror: nothing would induce her to do something like that! Later, he asked her if she would join the Young Liberals. She told him she certainly would not. Why not? 'Because I think they're all goops', she said.

Neither of them will talk in detail about their courting; it is personal. One thing they shared was an understanding of communism as a complete subjugation of the will of the individual to the collective. Like Fraser, Tamie was instinctively revolted by the notion.

Their engagement was announced in May 1956, and made the front page of the Melbourne *Sun*, with a photo of the smiling couple and a story that led on the main things that journalists thought they knew about Fraser at the time—that he was both the youngest and the tallest member of parliament.[1] They were married just seven months later, on 9 December, in the tiny weatherboard Anglican church in the town of Willaura, near Tamie's home. Fraser wore a top hat, she conventional white. Pictures of that day show the country in summer, dry paddocks the backdrop to white dresses, coat tails and bouquets. This was a happy occasion—two notable local families coming together. Perhaps only the groom would have given a thought to the state of the world. Yet as they posed for photos, on the verge of their many years together, Malcolm and Tamie shared a view that the world was in danger, and that the threat could not be ignored.

The wedding had been held, unconventionally, on a Sunday, because the day before had seen the closing ceremony of the Melbourne Olympics. These were already being called the 'friendly games', but in fact they had been a microcosm of world tensions. Six countries had boycotted the games amid international tensions over the second Egyptian–Israeli conflict in the Sinai, violence in North Africa and the Franco-British naval involvement in the Suez crisis. The Soviet and Hungarian water polo teams had come to blows in the swimming pool—the legacy of the brutal Soviet repression of the Hungarian resistance just months before. Following the Melbourne games, forty-five Hungarians defected to the West.

Fraser and Tamie went off for a brief honeymoon. When they came back, Fraser lost his voice to laryngitis, which meant that Tamie had to stand in for him at her first public occasion—a naturalisation ceremony in the Wimmera town of Edenhope. Some of the people receiving Australian citizenship that day were from Hungary. Citizenship ceremonies were a relatively new phenomenon. One of Fraser's first official duties as member for Wannon had been to conduct one in Portland; he had spoken there about the vast act of courage involved in immigration, and the huge possibilities of development in Australia's north, sharing again his dream of seeing twenty-five million people in Australia. 'Unique and moving' was how the local paper had described the ceremony.[2] This time, Tamie had to fill in for him. They worked together on her speech. She remembers, 'I talked about how painful it was to live in Hungary and how in Australia you're free, that we are a free country. Everyone was nearly in tears at this point and then I managed to talk about the high standard of living in this country, except I said "the high standard of loving" by mistake. I stopped. I was just back from my honeymoon! And I said, "Oh, my husband wrote this". Well, of course, everyone broke down and howled with laughter. And there I was, this little twenty year old trying to be statesmanlike. Anyway, they were very kind'.

Somewhere in this period, Tamie asked Fraser what his ultimate ambition was in politics. He told her he would like to be Minister for Defence. Nothing was more important, he said, than the defence of Australia; he feared for the future. In the year since he had been elected to parliament, there had been a shift in Fraser's thinking. The young man who had arrived home from Oxford so full of hope for the world was more troubled, now, than optimistic. Even as he became a husband and then, very shortly afterwards, a father, his view of the world outside his domestic sphere was darkening. The shadow that had fallen over Europe was now cast over South-East Asia. On 7 April 1954, as Fraser had been driving the length and breadth of Wannon as he contested his first election, President Eisenhower of the United States had coined the domino metaphor:

> You have a row of dominoes set up. You knock over the first one, and ... the last one ... will go over very quickly. So you could have the beginning of disintegration ... the loss of Indochina, of Burma, of Thailand, of the Peninsula and Indonesia ... you are talking really about millions and millions and millions of people.[3]

Parliament sat for the first time after the 1955 election at the beginning of 1956. *The Age* newspaper's Canberra correspondent reported that for the first time in many years, Labor newcomers to parliament were showing a degree of ability that their counterparts would find hard to match. Chief among the promising newcomers was Jim Cairns, Member for Yarra, who had won his seat thanks to the previous member leaving the party to join the Anti-Communist Labor Party. Cairns, *The Age* noted, 'is slight in figure with keen features and seemed to make an impression from the first day'. He had had a distinguished academic career, and Menzies had already 'singled him out as an opponent worthy of note'.[4] Fraser also gained this impression. When Cairns was due to make a speech, Menzies would make a point of being present. Very few other members received the same treatment.

Evatt was still leader of the Labor Party, but it was clear that there was a number of men who could soon replace him. Already on the opposition benches when Fraser arrived was the former shearer Clyde Cameron, who, as the dominant figure in the Australian Workers' Union, had been one of the most energetic opponents of

Santamaria's Groupers. Cameron and Fraser were politically opposed, yet over the years grazier and shearer struck up an understanding and a mutual respect. Gough Whitlam, fourteen years Fraser's senior, had been in parliament since 1952, and was already acknowledged as one of the House's best speakers, and one of the few who could hold his own against Menzies. Whitlam impressed Fraser. 'He was an eloquent speaker, and a man of vision. I don't think I was awed by him in any way. If I was, it was an emotion I had to hide even from myself. I thought, and I still think, that Gough is an extraordinary mixture. He is certainly a folk hero; he had some grand ideas; he has a sense of Australian identity. I don't think he's got any idea of how to manage anything, no idea how to manage other people and no concerns for their sensitivity. And he thought economics was totally irrelevant.'

Turning his attention to the government, *The Age* correspondent singled out two newcomers 'most likely to make their way' among the ambitious men who won their seats in 1955. They were Fraser and Fred Chaney.

> Mr Fraser, at twenty-five, is the youngest member of the present parliament, but looks older than his years. He is 6 feet 4 inches tall and a first-class speaker, with a wide range of knowledge. His work-hardened hands do not suggest the academic, but he is an Oxford graduate in philosophy, politics and economics.

Despite the correspondent's opinion, it was to be ten years before Fraser became a minister. He was passed over several times. 'I would have loved to have been in the Menzies ministry. I think it is probably best that I wasn't. Quite a number of people make failures of themselves by getting promoted too quickly. They don't know enough, haven't enough experience.' For those first few years Fraser took stock, worked out how to operate within the party system, while being determined not to suborn his will to the machine. 'Well, of course I felt intimidated, but I also felt you were a member of parliament and you were there to do a job and you were there to speak your mind. That after all was what the Liberal Party was all about.' The promising young men who had entered parliament in 1955 were jockeying for position, trying to get noticed, but Fraser did not attach his star to any one person or faction. This was partly out of shyness, and partly deliberate. 'I wanted to remain free, which is just a part of me, I guess.' In the first two years, when opportunities to speak in parliament were rare, Fraser used some of his speeches to criticise areas of policy for which the future leader Harold Holt was responsible. Yet it was Holt who first made Fraser a minister—not Menzies. 'I don't think Harold held it against me in any way.'

So what did Fraser learn during those ten years? It was mainly about how to get on with people. 'You might know what you are talking about, but you have to work with other people. You certainly don't always get your own way. Most people have something valuable to say. You have to learn that all the wisdom isn't in your head and not even necessarily on your side of politics.'

Not all of the people alongside him on the government benches impressed him. Mentally, he found himself measuring them against a personal yardstick. Would he want them in his electorate, as part of his battle to turn Wannon from a marginal to a safe seat? He couldn't imagine many of his colleagues impressing the soldier settlers, the shearers or the factory workers. The ones he would want in his electorate were those who could relate to ordinary working people. They were Menzies himself; the former Prime Minister and now Treasurer Artie Fadden, who was known for his ability to get royally drunk, yet turn up to work sharp as a tack the next morning; 'Black Jack' John McEwen, who was shortly to replace Fadden as Country Party leader and Deputy Prime Minister; the Minister for Defence South Australian Philip McBride; the fiery Anti-Communist Shane Paltridge, then Minister for Transport; and of course the old family friend Dick Casey, then Minister for External Affairs and seen by some as a possible successor to Menzies. Fraser remembers, 'They were down-to-earth people. Many of the others I really wanted to keep away'.

Menzies himself was close to a deity in Fraser's mind at first. As a backbencher, though, he had little to do with him. 'I could always get to see him if I wanted to within a couple of days, but I didn't ask too often.' After Menzies had retired, they became much closer. Fraser would visit the old man and seek his advice. But over time he became more measured in his judgement. 'I liked Menzies. He was a great man and when judged against the standards of his time he was a true liberal. Look at what he achieved. The end of the White Australia policy began in his time, but it was formally ended afterwards. His policies on education and universities were really advanced for the time. He was the one who made the Commonwealth the major funder of and responsible for universities. He forced the Americans to adopt the ANZUS treaty. Then you look at the health service, and at the scholarships scheme for universities, and living allowances for poor families. Menzies was an extraordinarily clear thinker, and he was a very good speaker, obviously. But I think if you read his speeches afterwards, there wasn't all that much in them. He never tried to have all that much in them because he wanted to give an audience two or three points. He wouldn't do it in twenty. Evatt's speeches sounded terrible to listen to, but if you read them, they often came out better.' Fraser came to think of Menzies as a cautious man, sometimes unduly cautious. Menzies, unlike Fraser, was not always an activist.

Meanwhile, Fraser soon became known for speeches that had a lot more than one or two points in them—speeches that were dense with ideas, and bristling with argument. One of the first of these was given in March 1956, during a debate on international affairs. Somewhere between Oxford and Canberra, Fraser had lost his raw hope for the world. 'The dreams of the postwar world', he told parliament, 'have largely been abortive'. He talked again of Keynes, and his insistence that rich nations—those who were always 'creditors' in world trade—recognise their obligation to poor nations, or the 'debtors' of the world. A nation that was always in credit was not playing its part in international trade. Keynes's ideas, said Fraser, were not being honoured. The United States was not fulfilling its obligations, the International Monetary Fund and the World Bank were not fully achieving their roles; and across the world trade barriers were being increased rather than lowered. This kept the poor nations of the world in debt. If the problems of world trade and global poverty were not solved, the Soviets and communism would take advantage of the resentment in poor nations, and freedom would be imperilled. Fraser said:

> I believe that we are destined to a long struggle between the ideas of East and West, that we shall reach a static position only when Russian militarism ceases its attitude to the world, or after a great struggle on our part to maintain our independence. This is partly due to the limited success of the United Nations.

But Fraser was still an idealist, still seeking new ways forwards. In this speech, he gave first voice to ideas that became a major theme of his political career: the role of the British Commonwealth of Nations. 'Although our fathers may not like it, the fact is that the British Empire is passing out of existence and in its place is coming something which will be far more enduring and beneficial to world peace—the British Commonwealth of Nations.' The death of the British Empire, Fraser said, meant that Australia had pursued a more independent policy, as evidenced by the ANZUS treaty and its participation in the newly established Southeast Asian Treaty Organization, a collaboration of nations formed in 1954 to combat communism. In this new world there was a unique and important task for Australia.

> Through our geographical position in relation to the countries to our north, Australia can be the bridge between the divisions of opinion which inevitably arise between England and America ... Australia can also be the bridge,

> and this is vital to our continued independence, between the white and the coloured races. The way in which we help the nations to our immediate north, some towards self-government and others towards achieving their own aims and building up their own economies, will do a great deal towards accomplishing this object.

In all this work, he went on, the Commonwealth could play its part, and even be an example to the United Nations.[5]

Fraser did not, in this speech or in others given at around the same time, anticipate victory over communism. Rather, he envisaged a state of static division, in which the two ways of organising governments—democratic and communist—would co-exist. But this was possible only if the Soviets ceased aggression, and only if the West stood firm.

In these early speeches, and consistently thereafter, Fraser was at heart a free trader, but also a sceptic about the rest of the world's commitment to free trade. He says today, 'I believed that if you could develop a free trade world you would probably be better off, but I always had a view that Australia would put itself at risk if we abolished all protection for manufacturing industry while we were denied access to the major affluent markets for agricultural produce'. He describes those who characterise him as protectionist as 'inaccurate'. He includes in this his old friend Fred Chaney, who spoke in January 2009 at the National Archives when cabinet documents from 1978 were released. Fraser says, 'The real trade issue in today's world is the hypocrisy of the wealthy countries, espousing free trade but denying access to their markets for the natural produce of most of the world's poor countries'. In a world where powerful nations have protection, Australia has to be pragmatic. During his prime ministership, Fraser made a common cause between Australia and Third World countries who were also trying to sell agricultural produce to protectionist rich countries.

Just a few months after his speech on international affairs, Fraser tested his party's tolerance towards a new, and very young, member of parliament. He made two speeches criticising the government's economic management, and in particular its explanation for inflation, which was caused, he said, not by personal consumption, as the government had claimed, but by the rapid pace of development. It was vital for Australia to maintain development and immigration, but these needed to be kept in check. Short-term measures were being proposed when what was needed were fundamental structural solutions and the boosting of the level of exports. 'Although some people may not like the thought that we have a managed economy, since we have it, let us make the best job of it that we possibly can', he said. He proposed reducing immigration for a while, 'not as a permanent measure, but as a policy to be followed for two, three or perhaps four years, during which time we must try, by every means in our power, to persuade and encourage secondary industries to export'.[6]

In other speeches that year, the practical farmer showed through. He lectured his colleagues on the most beneficial quantities of superphosphate to be used on pasture. He spoke several times on the Commonwealth Scientific and Industrial Research Organisation (CSIRO), and its importance to farmers and to national development. Fraser could always talk with intimate knowledge about what was needed to produce food from the land.

* * *

By 1957, after one year in parliament and as a newly married man, it was time for Fraser to make a home for himself. He made some significant choices. When Fraser's parents had decided, against his will, to leave the Riverina and move to the Western District, they had done so because they longed, in the wake of the Depression and drought, for reliable rainfall. Making the drive from the Riverina to the Western District in 2008, again amid drought and looming recession, it is easy to understand their decision. Balpool-Nyang, on the southern edge of the great flatness of the Hay Plains, is wild, hard country. The colours are grey and red. The depleted Edward

River loops through like pea-green soup. The slightest breeze kicks up a dust storm. The scrub has tenaciousness. To Fraser as a boy, this country represented wildness, and freedom. To his parents, it was worry, hardship and isolation.

To travel south is to journey into settled certainties. Once you cross the Murray, the country grows greener with every passing kilometre, until, west of the Grampians, you reach the rolling green hills of the Western District. Here, Europeans are more confidently established. The homes of the original settlers in Victoria still stand. Nareen is one of the gracious and privileged places that define the district.

Nareen was a country seat, a centre of the relationships of country life. Today, the cook at Nareen can count more than seventy years during which her family has been on the payroll. Her father worked for Neville Fraser, and she cooked for Fraser and Tamie throughout his prime ministership, helping to entertain the world leaders who visited, as well as providing morning smoko for the jackaroos and shearers. She remembers the young Fraser and his elder sister arriving at Nareen for the first time. She remembers watching the different personalities of the siblings develop. Lorri rejected Nareen and all it represented, eventually being bought out of the family inheritance; Fraser stayed, but redefined that inheritance.

Nareen is a beautiful place. The homestead is long, low and white. High-ceilinged rooms open off a long central corridor, with the formal living rooms looking out over a smooth green lawn to clipped hedges, camellias and gardens of European bulbs. At the back there is a tennis court, the focus of Sunday social lunches. Behind it is a constellation of smaller houses, garages and equipment sheds. Among them is the wool shed, just a stone's throw from what the jackaroos still call 'the big house'.

Now it was time for Malcolm and Tamie to make their own home. They built a new house on Nareen within shouting distance of the old homestead, choosing Guilford Bell, a cutting-edge modernist architect, to design it. Bell was known for reinterpreting the Australian homestead tradition. The house he designed for the

Frasers was long and low, with a veranda front and rear, like the main house, but unquestionably modern and for its time quite radical. Instead of the formal spaces of the old homestead, there were big windows and light-filled rooms designed for a free-flowing family life. The old house looked out over meticulously maintained lawn and hedges; the new house had 'old' Nareen at its back, and looked out over paddocks and to the hills beyond. As a young man, Malcolm Fraser was looking out and beyond. He did not fear communism because of the disruption to class and privilege, but because of its threat to freedom. He wanted social mobility, better access to education, more equality. He wanted to be a liberal both abroad and at home.

The old house and all Nareen represented were part of Fraser. Throughout the turbulent years ahead, during which the family made homes in Canberra and Melbourne, Nareen was always the true home and sanctuary. Tamie remembers walking through the door a hundred times when everyone was under pressure, and 'The house would just embrace and comfort you'. Nareen is, as its present owner comments, the sort of place that 'might make a young man feel that he had the wind behind him'. And of course it did. Independence of mind was always a luxury Fraser could afford. But Nareen and what it represented also gave him an impediment to overcome: he had to convince people who had previously voted Labor to back him, not once but many times. He remembers, 'If I wanted to achieve anything, I had to look after the base. Otherwise, I could have been out at the next election, and what is the point of that?' Since his first campaign, he had deliberately toured the electorate in a beaten up old Holden ute. 'By the end of my time in politics, it wouldn't have mattered what I drove, because they knew me, but in the early days it was important to signal that I really did want to represent ordinary people, that I could understand what life was like for them.'

But the hours spent on the ute's bench seats, together with the legacy of farm work, were beginning to take their toll: Fraser's back gave out. He spent much of his second year in parliament wearing a metal brace, almost like a cage. Zara and Harold Holt wrote to him recommending that he consult Zara's physiotherapist, a White Russian immigrant with innovative methods, rather than wearing 'that awful brace'.[7]

Fraser and Tamie decided they would live in Canberra for the whole of the time that parliament was sitting, rather than constantly travelling between Wannon and the capital. Given the precariousness of Fraser's seat, this was regarded by his colleagues as a suicidal decision. Tamie remembers people trying to persuade her to talk Fraser out of it. But Fraser explained the decision to the electorate in one of his radio addresses. By staying in Canberra, he said, he would have regular access to the departments and be better able to represent their interests and take up their concerns. Also, he would have access to the Parliamentary Library, and so be able to do research that would help him to help the nation.

Between parliamentary sittings, he threw himself into electoral work. When his Labor predecessor had handed over the electorate correspondence there had been only about three items. In his campaigning, Fraser had repeatedly told the people of Wannon that it was the job of a member of parliament to represent the electorate to the government. He had encouraged people to write to him with any problem at all. 'If any elector has a problem, I will always be available to discuss that problem', he had said at the declaration of his victory in 1955, and he repeated the pledge many times in his radio addresses and in newspaper columns and letters to the editor.[8]

The electorate took him at his word. Today the Fraser archive includes about 33 metres of boxes filled with his electoral correspondence. If stacked in one column on their sides, the boxes would be the same height as a ten-storey building. There are letters on everything from international affairs to the height of the philatelic sales counter at the Hamilton post office. Perhaps one-third of the letters concerns simple matters of services. (Should anyone ever wish to write a history of the postal service in the Western District of Victoria, or the telephone exchanges, or roads, they could do worse than start with the Fraser archive.) Initially with only one staff member, Fraser devised a system for dealing with the letters. He would follow up any matter, whether it was state or federal. There is a form of words that recurs in his replies, letter after letter. 'Thank you for writing to me ... I have [done so and so] ... If I don't hear within a few weeks I will write to you again.' And he did. If he hadn't heard back from ministers or departments within three weeks, he would follow up and write back to the elector to let them know that he had done so. Matters were not allowed to drop. Fraser says, 'In those days, many of my electors had left school at twelve and thirteen. A lot of people didn't know how to find their way around a government department'. Soon Fraser found people taking him up on his promise to help them in other ways: he was asked to intercede between farmers and their lawyers, and between farmers and banks. He took to posting out bulletins of relevant information on government measures to community groups. Businessmen were on the mailing list, and so were nearly all community organisations; clergymen received summarised information on social security measures in the budget, for example. By the time Fraser left parliament, his constituents had forgotten there was ever a time when they did not receive such information. Fraser says, 'What people might have taken as being just a political act initially they came to regard as a service'.

Meanwhile, Fraser and Tamie were learning how to live together, and she was beginning to appreciate what she had let herself in for. They made, in the early days, some 'terrible mistakes', she says. One winter's night early in their marriage, they drove 100 miles to attend a Returned and Services League function. Fraser went in, then came out and told her he had made a mistake: it was a men-only function. Tamie remembers, 'I could have gone in and insisted, but it would have spoiled their evening completely and embarrassed him horribly, so I sat in the car and read the owner's handbook for three hours in the dark. Oh, God, it was a bad evening ... And after that we had a talk, and made a little agreement never ever to do that again. And I never went anywhere after that without a book. Not for the whole of our life together'.

When they moved to Canberra for the first parliamentary sitting after their marriage, it seemed to Tamie that the whole city was full of grey, bald men. Everyone was much older than her. It was crushingly lonely; she spent her twenty-first birthday, in February 1957, wandering around the Australian War Memorial in tears.

Later that year, Larry Anthony, the member for the New South Wales seat of Richmond, died suddenly, and his son, Doug Anthony, was elected in his place. Doug was just six months older than Fraser, and the two men arranged a social occasion with their wives. By now, Tamie was pregnant. Nervous, she tried to squeeze herself into an elegant dinner dress. 'I squeezed and shoved trying to do up the zip, but it was hopeless.' In those days, maternity gear was the antithesis of elegance, but, for the first time, she was forced to wear her maternity outfit. They had arranged to meet the other couple at the top of the steps in Parliament House. When they got there, Margot Anthony was in exactly the same maternity outfit. The two women went through pregnancy together, keeping each other company while the men were otherwise occupied. Tamie had her first child, Mark, three days after Margot gave birth, in February 1958. Doug Anthony became one of Fraser's strongest personal and political friends, and the friendship was forged and maintained by the women as much as by the men.

For Fraser, friendships were always few. Partly, this was the legacy of his early, isolated school days. 'Nothing was going to change me all that much, I'm afraid.' Partly, it was politics, and the realities of working closely and under pressure with people who, in between times, lived far away. 'Politics is not a business where you make a great many friends. I mean, you have your family, you've got acquaintances, you've got people you trust, you've got people you work with, some of whom you trust and some of whom you don't trust ... It leaves you very little time to make friends that you go fishing with, or shooting with, or play bridge with.'

Fraser was not the kind of father who changed nappies. 'He tried once. We had to wash the bedspread afterwards', Tamie remembers. He would come home late at night, sometimes wanting to talk, and because time together was so limited she would put everything aside to sit and listen, and they would talk over the politics of the day. Tamie was the domestic support, but no doormat. She had not been brought up to think of herself as an adjunct to somebody else's life. She learned to appreciate the way her husband argued. She regarded him as a shrewd judge of people—of what motivated them and of how far they could be pushed. 'The worrying thing is, he is a very great respecter of your parameters. You know, he's quite good at reading you, and finding your limit, your buttons, and pushing you right to the very limit. But when you're there, at the edge of yourself, he recognises that and backs off. I've seen him do it with the kids. If you believe in something so fiercely that you defend and defend and defend it, and that's what you believe and he's not going to change your mind, well, then he'll look at it and see maybe he's made a mistake. And I find that quite wonderful and interesting. He has done it in politics all the time. It's how he works out his own thoughts. But it also means he reads people very well. People don't see that in him, but it is true.' Over the years she saw this ability play out repeatedly: in the events leading to the dismissal, in his reading both of his own senators and of the Governor-General Sir John Kerr, and later, during his prime ministership, in his negotiations with world leaders, including Margaret Thatcher over Rhodesia.

One of the few personal friends Fraser did make during his first years in Canberra was the member of parliament Frank Timson, who took pity on the awkward young Fraser after he had had a particularly rough week at the hands of his ambitious colleagues. Timson suggested they go fly-fishing together. Fraser said he only fished with lead lines in the bay, but after rustling up equipment—including a rod that Fraser still keeps—and a hasty lesson in casting on the lawns of Parliament House, they headed off for the weekend at Eucumbene. The dam water was rising fast over fresh ground, and the trout were growing magnificently. Fraser hooked two—the largest over 7 pounds. He wandered over to Timson. 'Did you get a bite?' said Timson. Fraser was straight-faced, unaware of whether the fish he had caught were a respectable size or not. He took off his jacket and tipped the fish onto the ground. It was the largest wild fish he was ever to catch. 'The fish had been hooked, but so was I.' He and Tamie have since fished all over the world. For Fraser, the long days in beautiful places were a return to the freedom of his early childhood; they also became a way to connect with people. Sadly, though, Timson was not his friend for long: he died in 1960.

In 1957, the year that Fraser and Tamie moved to Canberra, Fraser's first major speech was in support of the Japanese Free Trade Agreement, which had been negotiated by Jack McEwen, amid controversy. People on both sides of politics feared the impact of Japanese imports on Australian manufacturing. As well, there was still powerful resentment over World War II. Today, Fraser regards McEwen as one of the most underrated politicians of his time. 'He had a sense of vision. He thought about the future and was courageous enough to work for it, even at enormous political risk to himself and his party. He went to cabinet to get authority to negotiate and, after a very long discussion, he got authority, but Menzies said to him, "Right, Jack, you've got authority to negotiate, but in your name". McEwen was going to carry the can if it went wrong.'

Fraser remembers the subsequent party room discussion. 'People started getting up, saying, "We don't need this; we've got our great and powerful friends, traditional allies: they will always look out for us". Probably three or four or five or six people spoke, and it was gathering momentum. Well, McEwen never lost his temper unless it was deliberate, to make a point. He was a very controlled person. He jumped to his feet and banged the table hard and said, "And that's just the bloody trouble: our great and powerful friends won't allow us to sell this and this and this. Britain tells us they are not going to go into the common market, but they *are* going to go into the common market and then they will be adding to the list of things they won't buy. This and this and this. And the Americans won't let us sell this". And then he started naming people. "If you want me to go into your electorate and tell them that your farmers are going to be broke because you opposed the trade deal that would have given them the market for their product, then I will do it! And you will lose the election—you, not me. You will lose!" He went around three or four, mostly his own people, and there wasn't a word against the trade treaty after that, because they all knew it was true. Menzies would never have made a speech like that. He was too cautious. But McEwen recognised the reality of the world. Australia just had to get access to affluent markets.'

Fraser needed no urging to get the point. This was, after all, part of what he had been saying about trade the previous year. In his speech supporting the agreement, Fraser said that the idea of free world trade had been born in the postwar years and 'has been dying slowly ever since ... It is only natural with these conditions of world trade that the government should seek ways and means of assuring markets for our products so that we can sell what we produce'.[9]

Many people had told Fraser, in the wake of his decision to spend parliamentary sitting times in Canberra, that he would be a 'oncer', and would not retain his seat. As the 1958 election approached, Fraser fell ill. His health was never robust: his back always gave him trouble, and his chest, weak since the pneumonia, often let him down. Now he fell even more seriously ill, with hepatitis. He went to bed for a couple of weeks, then tried to get up to campaign, collapsed, and was ordered back to bed. It was to be more than a year before he felt fully well again. Meanwhile, he was furious with frustration, and, 'I am sure I drove Tamie completely mad'. Fraser announced his illness in his radio address to the electorate, and said he would be making even more use of radio, as well as giving twelve talks around the electorate, in which he would

> hope to cover nearly every aspect of government policy, both past and future ... If there are any particular questions on any item of policy which I may or may not

> have mentioned, I urge you to contact me at my home in Nareen. I will be only too happy to try to get an answer to you before the date of the election.[10]

Meanwhile, cabinet ministers spoke on his behalf in the major centres. 'Dick Casey went down to speak for me in Warrnambool. I wasn't able to campaign or do anything; I was trying to get fit and get Dick to understand something about the dairy industry in Warrnambool. I think he talked about something else.' Fraser was coming to an independent view of this old family friend: 'He was an honourable man, but perhaps not all that interested in the dairy industry'.

When the figures went up, Fraser had increased his majority. Nationally, this was the election in which the full effects of the Australian Labor Party split were felt. In Wannon, Democratic Labor Party voters followed the how-to-vote card more closely than in 1955, and Fraser won more than 90 per cent of their preferences.

His standing increased by his win, Fraser made a wide-ranging speech in parliament, in which he touched upon foreign affairs. The issue was whether India should remain in the Commonwealth, even though it had decided that it would no longer have Queen Elizabeth as its monarch or recognise the Crown. Fraser said, 'I regret India's decision … as much as any other person in this place', but argued that India should remain in the Commonwealth. He made a point that he repeated many times in the following years: that there were more black people in the British Commonwealth than white, and that this was a strength and an opportunity. 'By promoting respect for the views of others, the British Commonwealth, with its greatly diverse membership, sets the United Nations a good example.'

He went on to talk about disarmament, and how important it was that any agreements made with the Soviets be properly supervised and accountable. Then he turned to domestic matters, and criticised education policy for emphasising scientists at the expense of philosophers. This was the year that Sputnik I had been launched, and the Soviets looked like winning the space race; but Fraser said philosophy was probably more important than technology.

> We must remember the important study of the art of learning to live together. This is not a science but a study and an art. Many of the world's major problems have arisen in recent years because our scientific knowledge of methods of destruction has completely outrun our knowledge of the art of living and of how to get along together ... A satellite moving around the skies does nothing towards adding one jot to the sum of human happiness, but studies of ways of living can add very greatly to that sum.

Once again, Fraser repeated his assertion, so apparently at odds with the 'life wasn't meant to be easy' statement of his middle years: 'The only real purpose of life is human happiness'.[11]

A few weeks later, he was on his feet talking about defence. In an echo of his earlier statement to Tamie when she asked about his ultimate ambitions, he said, 'Adequate defence for Australia is fundamental to our existence as a civilised people. Nothing is more important than the defence of this country'. He responded to Clyde Cameron's suggestion that Labor would cut the defence budget to £100 million with a surge of rhetoric: 'If there are any people in Australia who object to the sum of £200 million being used each year as an insurance for the future security of our people, they do not deserve to enjoy the advantages and benefits of being Australians'.[12] Later that year, Fraser criticised Labor for suggesting that because of the atom bomb, all conflict must be avoided. 'We cannot deny the use of force in all circumstances, because our freedom is something that we must preserve. We must not be afraid of force when force is absolutely necessary and when it is just and right.'[13]

From Fraser's point of view, the shadows over Asia were lengthening, and there was a new threat on his horizon—communist China. In May 1959, in a radio address to his electorate, he talked about China's invasion of Tibet following a revolt against Chinese interference in religious life. Australia hadn't paid enough attention to what was happening in the Himalayas, Fraser told the farmers and labourers of Wannon. The Tibetan rebellion had been 'nothing more or less than a struggle for freedom'. He likened Tibet to the Soviet invasion of Hungary three years before. 'It is a reminder to every democratic country that the benefits of freedom can only be maintained by constant initiative and effort.'[14]

A few weeks earlier, in another radio address, Fraser had lamented to his electors that Australians knew so little of Asia. He had learned nothing about Asia at school, he said, and he doubted that things had changed. But Australia, of all Western countries, should look at Asia

> from the point of view of an Asian, because if our customs, our manners and our skins are Western, our geographic position is Asian and this makes us Asians. Quite certainly, our fate is ultimately bound up with events in this part of the world ... When communism is mentioned, Australians generally shrug their shoulders, saying, 'Oh, that's boloney; it would never happen here'. But would we take the same attitude if every country between Darwin and Peking was under communist control?

Australians had to help the emergent democracies of South-East Asia, and come to understand their attitudes and problems. 'One day our survival may depend on it.'[15]

At the same time as painting this 'big picture', Fraser was also bothering his fellows in the party room by making speeches about birds. 'Some of my colleagues thought that my interest in this was really odd.' He was in some ways repaying a political debt: Claude Austin, the ornithologist and Wannon Liberal Party power broker who had backed Fraser for pre-selection, had been in his ear. Austin was using a new word: conservation. 'Claude was convinced that it was going to be very much an issue in the future, but it wasn't really then ... He was right, of course.' Fraser was campaigning, at Austin's behest, for a ban on the export of Australian native birds.

Three-quarters of the birds exported died en route, he told the electors of Wannon in a radio address.[16] Some species were captured in such numbers that their existence was endangered. Fraser was successful: the trade was banned.

A few years later, again at Austin's instigation, Fraser was invited to join a group of enthusiasts, chief among them the CSIRO scientist Francis Noble Ratcliffe, to form the Australian Conservation Foundation. His main role was to persuade the Treasurer Harold Holt to grant the organisation tax exemption. Once again, he was successful. This was the beginning of Fraser's activism as a conservationist. He is not, and never has been, a 'deep green', believing in preservation for its own sake. Human beings are the measure and the focus of his concern. 'The environment is there to be managed', he says. National parks should not be 'locked up' but should be available to be enjoyed. But it is in management that he thinks the present generation is failing. 'Where is the scheme to replumb our cities to separate grey water from drinking water? Sure it would be a big national project, but it would be do-able, if we started now. Where is the vision?'

It was also in 1959 that the first evidence of Fraser's abhorrence of racism—one of the abiding concerns of his public career—appeared on the public record. In September he chose Papua and New Guinea as the topic of one of his radio addresses to the electorate. The Minister for Territories, Paul Hasluck, had been criticised for moving the territory too quickly to independence, and Fraser defended him.

> There is no intention, nor will there ever be any intention, of developing New Guinea for a few thousand whites, some of whom regard themselves as a superior type of animal. White people are welcomed in New Guinea if they are of the right kind. The sort of white person who is a hangover from old colonial days and who thinks that a packet of cigarettes is sufficient wages for a week's work would do much better to stay away … So far as New

> Guinea is concerned, Australians must remember that the eyes of all South-East Asia and of the United Nations are watching what we are doing. There may be many who expect, or even hope, that we will fall in the kind of error that has been made in South Africa.[17]

Fraser's next mention of South Africa was in a radio address in April 1960, following an event that had shocked the world: South Africa had allowed its police force in the township of Sharpeville to fire on demonstrators who were protesting against apartheid laws. Sixty-seven Africans had been killed, and more than one hundred and eighty wounded. More than seventeen hundred people were arrested, and in the days following the government banned the two main groups opposing apartheid: the African National Congress and the Pan-African Congress. Like many others, Fraser was shocked and revolted. How could this be happening in a Commonwealth country? What should be done in response? Menzies's view, both at the time and long afterwards, was that apartheid was an internal matter for South Africa. No matter what the outside world thought, there was no justification for interfering. But, over the weeks following Sharpeville, Fraser's views developed differently. In his April radio address, he asked why the Sharpeville massacre had aroused a greater degree of indignation than other atrocities, such as those in communist countries: the brutal repressions in Tibet and Hungary. He concluded that it was because apartheid was itself abhorrent, and South Africa had

> pursued this policy without regard for human suffering and for the human feelings of a great number of coloured people in their country. It seems quite clear that they have been doing all in their power to deny the coloured peoples of the Dominion of South Africa the normal political liberties which we of British heritage place so dear. It seems also that the policy of apartheid stems from a false belief that one people are more important than another.

Apartheid was anathema, Fraser said, and a bad example of how to handle 'undeveloped peoples'. Again, he contrasted apartheid to the way in which Australia was handling Papua New Guinea.[18]

Two weeks later he returned to the topic. People had been suggesting that South Africa should be expelled from the Commonwealth. Fraser thought this a 'rash' proposition. The Commonwealth was the only group of nations in which every colour, race and creed was represented with equality. Continued membership of the Commonwealth should result in the policy of apartheid being changed: this could be the only peaceful answer. Fraser held out hope that the white people of South Africa would act to remove the government. 'After all, is this not the right answer to this problem? South Africa is a democracy (if we can for a moment forget that Africans have been denied political opportunities). It is a country in which government can be changed peacefully and legally.'[19]

It was not to be. In March 1961, South Africa left the Commonwealth in the face of persistent criticism of its policies. The other Commonwealth prime ministers, including Menzies, had decided not to oppose its application for renewal of membership so long as its leaders were prepared to join in a statement affirming racial equality, but South Africa had refused. Fraser regretted the action: 'Now South Africa stands alone'.[20] But he had begun to move away from Menzies's view that this was a purely internal matter, and that the world had no right to intervene. Two principles were in conflict, he told the people of Wannon in a radio address. One was the policy of non-interference in other nations' affairs, and the other was

> the great principle of human rights, that all men are born equal and have an inalienable right to their place in the sun, no matter what their colour, race or creed ... When one country initiates policies which obviously discriminate against people of one race and when people of that race are free and equal in other Commonwealth countries, it is too much to expect complete indifference by the various Commonwealth countries.

Fraser remained an optimist that change would be achieved from within. 'I cannot see South Africa pursuing her present policies standing alone in the world. She will have no friends, only foes, and critics wherever people or nations may be gathered together.'[21]

A few weeks later, he made an even stronger statement, in parliament and in front of Menzies, who was now the only Commonwealth Prime Minister who had not publicly condemned South Africa. Fraser was strongly arguing the line that he continued with for the rest of his career: that the implications of apartheid were of international significance. And for the first time he made reference to Australian racism, and the White Australia policy. 'The spirit and emotion of our times are represented in the emancipation, freedom and self-government of coloured people. Anything that flies in the face of this spirit cannot stand and will be pushed aside in this present age.' Blacks in South Africa were second-class citizens without rights, while their 'blood brothers or cousins—people who are racially the same'—elsewhere in Africa were completely equal and free.

> To expect Asians and Africans to take a detached legal view of this matter is to expect too much. I do not think that there are many Australians who can take a detached view of the White Australia policy. How much reason, then, have we to expect Asians or Africans to take a detached view of this other problem ... Although we ourselves are not free from some of the prejudices or sins of the past in these matters—I do not think that any Commonwealth country is free from them—we hope and try, or believe we are trying, to rid ourselves of these inherited prejudices.

The only thing that linked the various members of the Commonwealth, all those millions of people from every colour and creed, was an ideology based on human rights and equality.

> I regard the Commonwealth as a bridge between the people of different races and colours, and we must try to

> maintain this bridge. Having regard to the circumstances, I think it was inevitable that South Africa would have to go, however deplorable I may consider the event … I am convinced that we must make the Commonwealth work. If it cannot be made to work, then I believe the world cannot work and that there will be little hope for us.[22]

Fraser was disagreeing with Menzies on other matters as well. In 1961, when Britain was considering joining the common market, the Australian Liberal Party was sharply divided. Jim Killen toured Britain arguing passionately against the move. Menzies, too, was distraught at the idea. Fraser, though, was an internationalist, and took a different view. He spoke on the topic first to the electors of Wannon—many of whom had intense concerns about the effect on markets for their produce—and then in parliament. The common market, he said, was 'an embodiment of the postwar European ideal of unity and cohesion'. It was inevitable that Britain would join eventually. As for Australia, it must face its geographic position: it was part of Asia.[23]

⋆ ⋆ ⋆

Fraser was now approaching his third election campaign. Australia was in recession, thanks to a credit squeeze. Evatt had been replaced as Opposition Leader by Arthur Calwell, who was still enjoying a honeymoon with the press and the electorate. The 1961 federal election was one of the closest in Australian history. There was a massive swing against the Menzies government. Both Labor and the coalition won sixty-two seats, but two of Labor's seats were in the Northern Territory and the Australian Capital Territory, whose representatives at that time had limited voting rights. For the next two years, Fraser's weekly addresses to his electorate were full of accounts of who was ill, and who had been forced to go in to parliament despite illness—rugged up, drugged up and feverish, for fear of the government not having a majority. In all this, Wannon was a bright spot in the dismal result for the government. Fraser increased both his primary vote and his overall lead. Once again, Democratic Labor Party preferences had flowed strongly to Fraser.

Fraser's increasing grip on his electorate was in large part due to his activism on behalf of the Portland harbour. In 1960, Fraser had made a speech to parliament about the harbour being opened. Crucial to its success would be wool sales, he had said. But it quickly became clear that the brokers of the day did not want competition. In 1962, with the first sales about to be held, the brokers' organisations refused to allocate dates and issued threatening letters to their members effectively ordering them, on pain of dismissal from the associations, to boycott Portland. Fraser swung into action. At this time, the Attorney-General Garfield Barwick was preparing legislation that was the cousin to the US competition legislation that Fraser had been quizzed on all those years before at his pre-selection presentation. The new legislation—the Trade Practices Act—would prohibit anti-competitive practices and abuse of market power. Now Fraser grabbed Barwick and urged him to look at what was happening at Portland. Would the new legislation include a provision preventing boycotts of this kind? Barwick assured him that it would, and Fraser passed on the assurance in his weekly radio address to his electors. In parliament, he announced that he had asked the Attorney-General to ascertain whether the brokers had breached any existing laws.[24]

Fraser's actions caused a storm among the settled relationships of privilege that had grown up around wool marketing in Melbourne and Geelong. Dick Hamer, a minister in the Liberal Bolte government in Victoria, rang his old friend Neville Fraser and told him his son should back off—that he was making enemies with his persistence. There was a particular poignancy to the way in which this pressure was applied. A few months before, Neville had been travelling overseas when he had fallen ill. He stayed with the Frasers in Canberra on his return, and they had taken him to a doctor who insisted he see a specialist as soon as possible. An operation followed, but no surgery was carried out: it had become clear that Neville had only months to live. He had cancer of the liver. It was during this last illness that he was 'worried sick' by Hamer's call, and by the possibility that his son was making enemies.[25] Neville died in January 1962. Hamer was an executor of the will. The rapid illness and death had been an enormous shock, but in the months following the family reoriented itself. Una Fraser moved full-time to Melbourne, and, when they were not in Canberra, Fraser, Tamie and their two children—Angela had been born in 1959—moved back into the old Nareen homestead.

Meanwhile, the battle over Portland continued. The first sale was held in the face of the boycott, but failed. In the aftermath, a meeting of 5000 furious growers elected Fraser as their spokesperson. Fraser allied himself with the Labor state member for the area Bob McClure, who was a shearer and, according to Fraser, 'a good bloke from the old-fashioned Labor mould'. Together, they flayed the Bolte government for its inaction. In April, Bolte called a meeting to discuss the matter. Fraser was to attend as a representative of the growers, but the resentment against him by now was intense. Knowing the precarious position of the federal parliament and the fact that every member must be present for the government to maintain its majority, Bolte set the meeting on a parliamentary sitting day. Fraser was convinced that this was designed to make sure he would not be able to attend.

At that time, pairing—the system by which a member who must be absent is 'paired' with one from the opposition—was not operating. Fraser tried, and failed, to get a pair, then went over the head of the party whip Fred Chaney (senior) to Menzies, who agreed to talk to Arthur Calwell. Fraser and McClure cooperated in encouraging every rural organisation in the district and over the border in South Australia to lobby both Menzies and Calwell so that Fraser's pair could be arranged. Fraser got his pair. When he walked into the meeting with Bolte, he was greeted with a double take and the words 'How did you get here?'

In November 1963, just days before the federal election, Fraser was able to announce 'a wonderful day in the history of western Victoria and south-east South Australia'. The first wool sale had gone ahead and had been very successful. Portland would now go on, Fraser said, to be an alternative centre to Geelong and Melbourne—and right in the middle of the electorate. A few days later he announced that in the next parliament, the government would legislate to control restrictive trade practices.[26]

By this time, there were local government politicians in Portland who had become almost volunteer campaign staff for Fraser. When the election votes were counted, Fraser had received more than 50 per cent of the vote and had opened up a 13.8 per cent lead over Labor. Wannon had become a safe seat, and Fraser had established a pattern for his political battles.

He believed in will—in strength of purpose and argument. As Tamie would put it, he had pushed both colleagues and opponents right to the limits of their tolerance, and won through—though not without building up resentment. Remembering Portland today, Fraser looks into the distance and says, 'I was stirring the pot, of course'. A pause, then a grin. 'It was fun.'

* * *

The Frasers had had a house built for them in Canberra—also designed by Guilford Bell—but were travelling back to Nareen whenever parliament wasn't sitting. Another child, Hugh, was born in 1963. Phoebe, perhaps the child closest to her father in temperament and ambition, was born in 1966. Home movies from the time show Tamie in butterfly sunglasses and white flares at a picnic by the lakes around Canberra, Fraser fishing, the toddlers dirty and happy around an impromptu campfire, or splashing in a tiny square paddling pool in the backyard of the Canberra home. At Nareen there were picnics in the paddocks, and hours of film were shot of Fraser and Tamie leading the children on their ponies.

But during those sun-dappled days, as he grew into fatherhood and politics, Fraser's view of the world was darkening. Hopes seemed to flare up only to be dashed.

He was overjoyed by the election of Senator Kennedy as the US President, telling the electors of Wannon that 'The new President ... has given the free world a new hope that a fresh approach to some of the world's outstanding problems may place peace on a firmer basis than it has been in recent times'. Kennedy would not be soft on communism, but he would 'explore every avenue of access to try to clear up some of the outstanding problems that exist between East and West'.[27] Fraser endorsed Kennedy's handling of the Cuban missile crisis, in which, through staunchness mixed with negotiation, Kennedy had extracted the world from the worst crisis of the Cold War, and from the point at which the world had come closest to nuclear conflagration. Fraser told Wannon in November 1962 that the greatest danger to world peace would be if Russian leaders formed the view that the United States would not fight. 'If this happened, the Russians would make one advance after another, taking more territory and enslaving more free people until the United States, Britain, France and Germany would be forced into a position in which they had to fight.' In both Cuba and his support for Berlin Kennedy had shown that the West would stand firm.[28]

Now, though, Fraser perceived a new danger. The battle had shifted, and the West faced a different challenge. Instead of direct confrontation, communist powers—and he blamed China more than Russia—were using subversion. In 1962, Fraser spoke in one radio address about the visit to parliament of the king of Thailand, and used it as a way to talk about the communist threat. Thailand was ringed by Laos, Cambodia and Burma. 'In every country of South-East Asia which is adjacent to a communist country, guerrilla activities have begun, such as in South Vietnam.' Thailand was an outpost of Australia's defence, he said.

> The greater the communist subversion, the more countries that fall under communist domination, the greater our

> own danger ... The main struggle in the next few years is likely to involve South-East Asia rather than Europe. This means that we are no longer on the edge of the world power struggle; we are being drawn towards its centre.[29]

A new catchcry appeared in speech after speech, radio address after radio address: 'Australia is in a dangerous part of the world'.

When Kennedy was assassinated, in 1963, Fraser wrote a short and emotional note to his friends at the US embassy. Kennedy was, he said,

> a President who has earned his place among the great of your nation, who could have been the greatest of them all. He did not shrink from the challenges of our times; he offered the free world life and lent us courage. He let us believe sanity would prevail. This is the loss the world will count and history measure. His memorial must be a building on his achievements so that the work of his leadership can continue. To this perhaps each of us in our own part can contribute.[30]

* * *

Fraser was now in his thirties, a mature man, head of his extended family, a relatively experienced backbencher, Chair of the Parliamentary Committee on Defence, and an accomplished politician. Yet he had been passed over again and again for ministerial office. For the first seven years, this had been easy to take. He knew he wasn't ready. Now, however, he thought he was. The other ambitious young men who had entered parliament in 1955 had streaked ahead of him. Peter Howson was Minister for the Arts; Doug Anthony was Minister for the Interior. Fraser and Tamie had made friends among the Canberra diplomatic community, and several of the most senior members, including the US Ambassador William Battle, made no secret of the fact that they saw Fraser as one of the most able young

Liberals. But he was passed over by his own side. He thought there were several reasons: Menzies's caution, his own independence of mind, and a perception, conquered in Wannon but still dogging him in Canberra, that with a privileged background like his, he must be a conservative. When would his chance come? In 1965, he received a letter from Alexander Downer (senior), now High Commissioner for Australia in London, consoling him on once again being passed over.

> Keep going, as you cannot help but succeed. I know you are highly regarded by senior ministers; when your breakthrough comes you will zoom ahead with a rapidity that will astonish you. You just can't miss, Malcolm, and I never lose an opportunity myself with visiting ministers to London to urge your claims.[31]

In the end, though, Fraser had to wait for Menzies to depart. With Harold Holt as the new Prime Minister from January 1966, Fraser decided he had to push himself forwards. There was nobody to do it for him; he was not aligned to any faction. He had few friends. He went to speak to Ian Potter, the Melbourne businessman and financier who was known to the Frasers, and who was also a close friend of Holt. Fraser told Potter that he did not want to spend any longer as a backbencher; if he was not to be a minister, he thought it best that he leave politics and let somebody else have a go. Potter advised Fraser to talk to Holt directly, and tell him how he felt. 'So I went to Harold and I said, "Do you want me or don't you want me?" It really was without any sour grapes. If he had said no, I would have said "Fine"; I would have let Wannon know that they could get another candidate for the next election. And he actually said, well, he wished other people had the same attitude and would speak so frankly. I know he checked me out with some other senior party members. Then, for better or worse, he put me in as minister.'

Sometimes, history seems like a fast-moving torrent approaching a tunnel. Options and alternative selves peel off one by one as the torrent narrows, and we are carried on the current into the darkness ahead. Back in 1959, as a relatively new backbencher, Fraser had given a radio address on the topic of Anzac Day to his electors. He always felt awkward on Anzac Day: everyone older than him had fought in the war. Returned servicemen were everywhere. 'It seemed everyone had been in it except me, and there I was expected to speak, and it was just embarrassing.' On this occasion he said that the younger generation should ask what the men who went to World War I and World War II had been fighting for. Normally the qualities were described in general terms: freedom, liberty, the right to lead their own lives unhindered, the right to choose their own government and the rule of law. But, most of all, Fraser said, they had fought in the belief and 'supreme hope' that this would be the last of such conflicts. 'If there was a hope in their heart, I think it may have been "I hope my son will not have to go through this in twenty or thirty years' time".' He moved on to talk about the Returned and Services League, and what a fine organisation it was, but said that if politicians were successful in maintaining the peace, then it would eventually cease to exist. 'If this does happen, then we can say we have won the peace and that our debt to those who fought and who died has been fully repaid.'[32]

Fine hopes, but they were not fulfilled. Fraser had been made Minister for Army, and Australia had just introduced conscription. The country was entering a long, dark tunnel. Vietnam.

5

Vietnam, Act I

Malcolm Fraser thinks now that the Vietnam War was a mistake, that it would have been better if young Australians had not been sent away to kill and be killed. Yet at the time of the war he was one of the main government members speaking in favour of the fight and of conscription. If it is possible to be an idealist about war, then Fraser was one, initially at least. When the first national servicemen were called up in mid 1965, he said in one of his radio addresses to the people of Wannon that he hoped service in Vietnam would come to be regarded 'as a point of pride, and that the community will come to recognise that national service can be something to make a person a better citizen'.[1] In a letter to *The Age*, rebutting the anti-war stance of Jim Cairns, he said:

> It is sometimes forgotten that we are fighting for something positive in South Vietnam. It is not mere opposition to communism, however much merit there may be in that. We are fighting for the right of a small country to go its own way unmolested by its neighbours and secure in its own independence. This is the right that the communists would deny.[2]

He says now, 'Those were innocent days, when I believed what the United States said ... It is easy to say, with the beautiful clarity of retrospect, that perhaps Australia should never have gone to Vietnam. It probably was a wrong decision. But at the time that the decisions were made, things looked very different'. He says that, while keeping the United States involved in Asia and the western Pacific was part of the Australian Government's motive, the United States would probably have been involved anyway, given the way the communist threat was perceived. 'Again, with the delicious clarity of hindsight, the great mistake of policy analysts was to grossly underestimate the extent to which genuine nationalist movements took on the communist cloak if communists gave them allies and resources. The distinction between communism and nationalism would have been difficult to make, but at the time it wasn't even on the agenda.'

A key moment in Fraser's reconsideration of his support for the Vietnam War was his reading of the former Secretary of Defense Robert McNamara's memoir *In Retrospect*, published in 1995. McNamara had been one of the architects of the war, and in his memoir he wrote a forensic dissection of the mistakes that had been made and his own part in them. Fraser learned for the first time that the Central Intelligence Agency (CIA) and the US Government had been complicit in and indeed had initiated the deposing and assassination of the South Vietnamese leader Ngo Dinh Diem, in 1963, when Fraser had been an idealistic backbencher. The Americans had concluded that Diem could not effectively unite the South Vietnamese, but they had given no consideration to finding somebody to do a better job, and nobody did. The South Vietnamese Government never worked well and, after if not before Diem's assassination, became a puppet of the United States. McNamara wrote:

> We of the Kennedy and Johnson administrations who participated in the decisions on Vietnam acted according to what we thought were the principles and traditions of this nation. We made our decisions in light of those values.

> Yet we were wrong, terribly wrong. We owe it to future generations to explain why.[3]

While promoting his book, at the age of seventy-nine, McNamara was known for weeping publicly. Says Fraser, 'He became the darling of the campuses and the chat circuit'. When he says this, Fraser raises an eyebrow, works his mouth, and shrugs. It is certainly not envy. Nor is it admiration. Fraser does not weep over Vietnam. His response is similar to that of Dean Rusk, McNamara's colleague as Secretary of State, who told his son, 'I believed in those decisions at the time they were made. There is nothing I can say now that would diminish my share of responsibility. I live with that, and others can make of it what they will'.[4] The comparison is in any case invalid. Fraser was not, like McNamara and Rusk, one of the architects of the war. His involvement was first as a rising backbencher with a passionate interest in foreign policy, then, from January 1966 to February 1968, as Minister for Army, and, most intensely, from November 1969 until March 1971, as Minister for Defence.

When Fraser became Minister for Army, the key decisions about Australia's involvement had already been made. Selective conscription, administered by a lottery system based on birth date, had been introduced. Prime Minister Holt had announced the dispatch of Australian troops to South Vietnam, and the first national service intake had begun recruit training. Although Fraser did not initiate these policies, he supported and advocated them. To begin with, his was a popular stand; the Holt government won the 1966 election in a landslide, based almost entirely on its support for the war.

Almost sixty thousand Australians served in the Vietnam War. Five hundred and twenty-one were killed or presumed dead, and over three thousand were wounded. The psychological cost is harder to count. The journey through the Vietnam years changed Fraser. As a young backbencher, he had said many times that the purpose of life, and the main consideration of governments, was the pursuit of human happiness. Afterwards, in 1971, he spoke differently. While still drawing on the philosophers who had inspired him at Oxford, he coined the phrase for which he is perhaps best remembered: life wasn't meant to be easy.[5] When he gave the speech that made the phrase famous, Fraser had recently resigned from John Gorton's ministry. His resignation had cast him into the political wilderness and plunged him, midlife, into a period of fundamental reconsideration of the roots of liberalism and the nature of political life. The immediate reason for his resignation was a battle that was, fundamentally, about proper process—the line of command and the manner in which the armed forces are governed and accountable within the democratic system. It was also about civic action—the work Australian soldiers were doing to help the Vietnamese.

Civic action had always been part of Australian troops' work in Vietnam, and before Vietnam it had been part of military involvement in Malaya and elsewhere. From early in Australia's days in Vietnam, medical units had offered help to all who came. Fraser remembers them treating people who had had ears and hands cut off. 'That was how you knew the Vietcong had been recruiting. If a man was reluctant to go, they did this to his mother or his sister or whatever.' Schools, windmills and water storage facilities had been built. Fraser was always passionate about this work. In April 1967 he had announced the creation of the Australian Civil Affairs Unit solely to give aid to the South Vietnamese, with welfare and building programs as well as medical assistance. Although army involvement in this type of work was not new, the unit was his idea, and the cause was close to his heart. In one of his radio addresses to his electorate, Fraser spoke about 'the other war … the fight against ignorance, sickness and poverty', which he said was as real as the casualties on the battlefield. The practical assistance being given by troops to enable the Vietnamese people to improve their standard of living 'may ultimately be the measure of the success of the Australian commitment'. Fraser told the people of Wannon about the Returned and Services League's 'Operation New Life', under which almost 50 tons of household items and garden tools had been donated to help refugees. Ordinary Australians had given bicycles, saucepans and school supplies.[6] Now Australian troops were moving into their own area of responsibility, the province of Phuoc Tuy, and Fraser wanted the work expanded. 'I had this naïve hope that the last experience the Vietnamese would have of Australians would be not negative, but positive. That they might be seen as having built something that was helpful in their lives.' But Vietnam became a quagmire from which it was difficult to extract anything positive.

The journey to Fraser's present position on Vietnam—bitter reflection on the gaps between what he was told, what he believed, what he hoped for and what actually happened—has been a slow one. Even now he does not think it was wrong to advocate war, based on what the Australian Government knew at the time. And he believes that the war gave the countries of South-East Asia time to consolidate and ally themselves to confront the communist threat. Nobody really knows what would have happened had the West stayed out of Vietnam, he says. 'I never believed in the domino theory … which as stated represents an inevitability. And nothing is inevitable. But what certainly was true was that if one country fell it would make it more likely that a neighbour would be under threat. That was true at the time. It was true.'

As the years have gone by, it has become clear to Fraser that Australia was told very little about how the United States was conducting the war in Vietnam, or about the role of the CIA in setting up what he suspects was always a puppet regime in South Vietnam. 'At the time of my resignation, I probably still hoped for a good outcome from Vietnam, but I couldn't help but also doubt', he remembers. 'I was seeing what was happening in Vietnam and looking at body counts and claims of success that were totally unreal. And earlier I had seen the political restrictions placed on the war, with President Johnson saying "We are not at war" … despite all the troops and bombs. How can a country pretend it is not at war when it has so many people fighting in a foreign country?' Fraser also disagreed with the tactics that were being employed. Johnson made a great point of saying that the United States offered no threat to North Vietnam. Fraser thought it foolish to say this. 'You don't tell your enemy the limitations you are imposing on your own actions. That is not how you win wars. There was so much foolishness and hypocrisy.'

The lessons that Fraser drew from Vietnam have led him to oppose the war in Iraq. Vietnam taught him that the Americans will always pursue their own interests, that allies can be trusted only so far. He learned the limitations of liberal ideals, the importance of independent foreign policy and the foolishness of assuming that the merit of liberal democracy is clear to all. He says, 'You cannot impose something on another country by force of arms, and I never really believed you could. That's why I so strongly supported civic action. Our ideas of democracy have evolved over centuries. We are foolish and arrogant if we think it is our role to visit that on everyone else. If you have a totally committed enemy, the only way you can win a war is to deny your enemy the capacity to gain recruits. You were never able to do that in Vietnam, and you are never going to be able to do that in Iraq. So much of what the West has done has made it extraordinarily easy for them to gain millions of recruits. The same thing is true in Afghanistan. So I don't know how you win in those circumstances. I don't think you do'.

Fraser recalls that Holt was never at ease with conscription. He remembers Deputy Prime Minister John McEwen making a point of congratulating Holt and praising him for his courage both in the joint party room and in cabinet when the conscription decision was announced. 'He was trying to support him, to make him feel better about it', but 'Harold himself hated the idea of conscription. I've got no doubt: he really hated it. He just believed it was necessary and I think he really worried about sending conscripts into war'. Fraser believes that Holt would have lain awake at night worrying about the conscripts, whereas he, Fraser, never did. 'I thought it was the only solution. The decision had to be made and therefore the decision was made, and there is not a great deal of purpose lying awake about it at night. It wasn't going to help anyone who went to Vietnam ... That might make Harold Holt a better person than me, but it also left him with concerns that he couldn't do anything about, that he should really have tried to put aside.' Fraser remembers a conversation he had with Robert Menzies in later years. 'Menzies wasn't often disparaging about people, but he said something to the effect that Harold was a nicer man than the Prime Minister sometimes needed to be.'

There was a natural tension between Fraser's liberal views, his belief in individual liberty and the idea of conscription. He wrestled with the conflict in his radio addresses to the people of Wannon, but his fullest working-through of the issue was in an article he wrote for Melbourne University's Liberal magazine *Today Ad Lib* in 1967. In a return to the political philosophers he had studied at Oxford, Fraser wrote about Rousseau, who had believed that the state could become the perfect instrument of government, 'with a will and being of its own'. Marx and Hegel had also seen the state as providing a final answer: 'the end of the struggle, the end of the reform, perhaps even the end of conflict between nations'. But all of these solutions raised the state above the individual.

> The error of these philosophers was twofold. They argued from imperfect experience to an absolute ... They were in fact establishing a deductive system in which all rules and laws flowed from the central metaphysical assumption. Thus, they sought to devise a framework for the state which would make it free of the fears, faults and shortcomings of the states they had known ... But in doing so they forgot the material with which they were working. They forgot that man is not perfect and his entire history is one of change and development—that there is no evidence in all of time to show that it will not continue to be so ... Our liberal philosophy works from the other end. Our judgement of human values, and of the political institutions and objectives that enhance them, is made only after

> experience ... Perhaps this only shows that liberals refuse to enter the fruitless debate that seeks to circumscribe man as though he were a number in a system of mathematics.

Fraser went on to recount the history of socialism sympathetically, as a response to the hardship, exploitation and injustice of the nineteenth century, but, he said, it was a philosophy born of the particular needs of a particular time. It was now essentially out of date.

> Liberal philosophy, by its nature and by its definition, can never become dated in this way. We do not believe there are any absolute or easy answers to the problem of social evolution, but that the problems which do and probably always will occur must be judged against human values upon which no price can be set.

How then to justify conscription and national service, if the needs of the individual were more important than those of the state? Fraser said that even in the liberal philosophy it was recognised that the citizen had certain obligations to the state.

> An obligation to the state, in this sense, is an obligation to the collective well-being of the people with whom we live and, in the final analysis, therefore, is an obligation to ourselves. To preserve harmony in our community there are certain things which we just do not do, and others which we must do in order to uphold the law and order in our society upon which every member depends.

He pointed to the 1966 election result as evidence that the policy of national conscription had been accepted by a majority of citizens. 'Its implementation is not so much a denial of individual freedom as the exercise of a concerted judgement that the building of a strong and viable defence force is necessary to the long-term interests of every one of us.' He concluded:

> I believe that our generation will be judged not on whether we were able to reach some perfect state of man,

> but on the way we have acquitted ourselves in the great human adventure, on our response to the continuing demands of participation in that adventure and our success in expanding areas of human freedom and equality.[7]

Popular support for the war didn't last. By the time Fraser became Minister for Defence in 1969, the first enormous moratorium marches were being planned. The war had become a political liability and a mess, and Fraser knew this, even as he argued that it should be fought, if anything, more strongly and with more vigour. But Gorton did not believe in the 'forward defence' policy that was the underpinning of Australia's involvement in Vietnam. The Menzies government's policy of forward defence, which Fraser strongly supported, was about engaging with and being active in the region with a view to keeping conflict as far as possible from Australia's shores. This was why Australian troops had been in Malaysia. This was why Australia had a vital interest in Vietnam. Fraser argued that the South Vietnamese should not be betrayed and deserted; Gorton, on the other hand, toyed with the notion of Fortress Australia: a country self-sufficient in defence, with little regional role.

The month after Fraser became Minister for Defence, the United States began withdrawing troops, and Gorton said that Australia would not increase its commitment. By the time the Americans and Australians had withdrawn and Saigon had fallen to the Vietcong and the North Vietnamese, in early 1975, Fraser was Leader of the Opposition. It was bitter to watch the frantic clamouring of South Vietnamese people, pleading to be allowed to leave on the departing US and Australian helicopters. It was difficult to hear of the desertion of the staff of the Australian embassy, and of others who had helped our people at war. These remained central preoccupations for Fraser, and when he became Prime Minister a sense of moral responsibility for the South Vietnamese was the core motivation for his government's welcoming large numbers of refugees—reversing the Whitlam government's callous approach.

* * *

American involvement in the Vietnam War was the product of the Democratic administration of John F Kennedy, the man whom Fraser, along with many others, saw as such a golden hope. The war was the product not of US conservatives but of US liberals—the postwar generation that had learned that enemies could not be dealt with through appeasement. In his inaugural address, on 20 January 1961, to which Fraser had listened with a glad heart, Kennedy had promised to stand by countries seeking freedom.

> To those peoples in the huts and villages across the globe struggling to break the bonds of mass misery, we pledge our best efforts to help them help themselves, for whatever period is required—not because the communists may be doing it, not because we seek their votes, but because it is right.[8]

Kennedy had been briefed on the domino theory by the outgoing Eisenhower administration. The South-East Asian region seemed turbulent and dangerous in ways that are difficult to imagine today, and Vietnam was at the centre of this. The first Indochinese war had been between the Viet Minh nationalists under Ho Chi Minh and the French. It ended with the Geneva Accords of 1954, under which the country was divided into two—South and North Vietnam. General elections were meant to be held in 1956 prior to the reunification of the country under an elected President, but that deadline came and went. Meanwhile, the more populous North had become a grim Soviet- and Chinese-sponsored communist dictatorship, while the South under Diem was mired in mismanagement, nepotism and corruption.

This was not the only unrest in the region. China under Mao Tse Tung had invaded Tibet, entered North Korea and threatened India and Taiwan. Indonesia was unstable: the Sukarno government depended largely on support from communists and was conducting insurgency against the new nation of Malaysia. Meanwhile, the European powers were leaving South-East Asia. It seemed, as Fraser said in speech after speech, that Australia was an increasingly lonely European outpost in a dangerous part of the world.

South Vietnam's leader Ngo Dinh Diem visited Australia in 1957. Fraser, at the time a lowly backbencher, does not remember meeting him. 'I may perhaps have shaken his hand.' Menzies affirmed his support for the already embattled leader. Australian military advisers were sent to South Vietnam from 1962 onwards, in support of the Americans. Their numbers were increased as the Diem regime faced increasing subversion, but Diem lost the support of his own people. By the mid 1960s, it seemed certain that if nothing was done South Vietnam would fall to the communist North. In 1963, after the assassination of Diem, and faced with an increasingly unstable South Vietnamese Government, Kennedy had to decide whether to scale up US involvement or accept the fall of the South.

McNamara wrote in his memoir that he believed had Kennedy lived he would have disentangled the United States from Vietnam at this stage, recognising that the South Vietnamese were unable or unwilling to defend themselves. But Kennedy was assassinated. The new administration of Lyndon B Johnson was deeply divided. 'We held meeting after meeting and exchanged memo after memo', McNamara wrote. Some wanted the United States to seek a political solution through negotiation; others wanted an aggressive intervention. The United States was at a fork in the road.[9]

At this stage, 1964, Fraser was carried into the heart of US power. Fraser and Gough Whitlam, then Deputy Leader of the Opposition, became the first Australian recipients of grants from the US Government providing foreign parliamentarians with insights into the processes of US policy formation. Fraser was to meet and be briefed at the highest level—involving a top secret security clearance.

Fraser and Tamie arrived in Washington on 13 May 1964. They spent almost a month there. It was an extraordinary, exhilarating experience. Fraser took a tape recorder with him, which he used to record 'Reports from Washington' for his weekly radio spot in

Wannon.[10] He talked to his electorate about the differences between the Australian and US political systems, and the varying ways in which political leadership worked. He spoke about US attitudes to beef and wool, and the hopes for growth in markets for agricultural products. Mostly, however, he talked about Vietnam—in modulated language for the people of Wannon, and in raw, uncensored impressions for his own notes. 'It ... seems to be recognised by everyone that I have spoken to that the present activity in South Vietnam is not sufficient and much more will have to be done. It is better to go in deeper than to resign oneself to defeat', he said into his tape recorder.

The global consequences of allowing guerrilla warfare to be successful were unthinkable, he had been told. He noted that the Americans felt isolated and didn't want to be left alone in the battle, and that they didn't want to be accused of imperialism.

> They don't want to feel lonely, and they do feel lonely, and therefore it is important for Australia of all nations ... to play some part in assisting. This isn't a question of giving a great deal of material aid; it is a question of giving enough token aid to show that you are prepared to stand up and be counted, to show that you are prepared to help ... I think there is a view that the effort that we have in the past put into this is not commensurate with the risks that now face us.

Fraser met Dean Rusk, Marshall Green—the state department's leading expert on East Asia and later Ambassador to Australia—and Ambassador at Large Averell Harriman. He liked Rusk the best: 'Rusk was the most reasonable and rational of them and got handled very hard and roughly after the Vietnam War. He got blamed for a lot of things'. Fraser's tape-recorded notes show that these men claimed that victory or turning the tide in South Vietnam would

> have a multiplier effect throughout the whole area, in Cambodia and also perhaps affecting Indonesia's attitude.

> Of course, any further defeat would have a multiplier effect in the opposite direction, and that is widely recognised. There is a complete determination that nothing will be resigned and what needs to be done will be done.

Fraser was reassured by what he saw as the Americans' widespread determination to 'do the job properly'. The view of the administrators was that 'nuclear blackmail' had been faced and defeated over Cuba, and that the one remaining challenge to the West was 'this business of subversion, which is cheap to the communists and which so far they've been able to get away with ... I would have thought that our backs were against a brick wall and that these matters must be faced now'.

He asked senior official after senior official if there was any discontent with the level of what Australia was doing in South-East Asia, 'defence-wise, development-wise or in any other way'. There was an acceptance, he concluded, that Australia had needed to build up its industrial base, 'so that we could play a more useful part in the area', but it was now necessary for Australia to do more for its own defence.

So far, all this was in tune with Fraser's own opinions, but on 27 May he went to the Pentagon and met senior officials. Here, Fraser received a more confused message. He recorded:

> It seems to be very difficult, and quite understandably very difficult, to get out of anyone the actual policy and the policy changes that may be made so far as South Vietnam is concerned. If they are in the middle of making policy changes, it is only natural that they would not want to speak to strangers about it.

Using nuclear weapons was one of the things being discussed. Fraser was told that

> The tactical nuclear weapons are now so small and so clean from fallout that there doesn't seem to be much moral

> difference between them and between conventional weapons so-called. While people seem to admit this, they say that the degree of escalation possible with nuclear weapons does create a difference, and therefore the difference in people's minds will remain, and this is probably so.

In conversations, he queried why the United States was so quick to rule out a nuclear option. Surely, he argued, if you are going to war, you should not telegraph to the enemy the things that you will not do? Meeting the same people shortly after Fraser, Gough Whitlam got wind of these arguments, and later alleged that Fraser had been advocating the use of nuclear weapons. Fraser claims he was doing no such thing: he was saying that if you are at war you should be serious about it, and determined; you should not declare to the enemy that they have nothing to fear from you.

Fraser also met Vietnam War sceptics. An academic, Professor Charles Lerch, who lectured on foreign affairs in South-East Asia, took a 'non-administration line'. 'He doesn't believe in a domino theory that if South Vietnam falls, other countries will. He thinks that this sort of subversion can only be present if there are the internal conditions that make it possible.' Fraser listened, but did not agree. Nevertheless, even at this stage he was mystified and concerned about the way in which policy was being made—or not being made.

In his tape-recorded notes, Fraser commented on how many different agencies were involved in US foreign policy: the Department of State, the CIA, the Institute of Defence Analysis, and private think tanks like the Rand Corporation. 'All these can do various things and sometimes have a policy that is in conflict. The importance of any one ... depends on personalities. There is no clear chain of command.' Some of this concern found its way into his Wannon radio addresses. 'There seems to be a complete conviction on every side that the United States will do what is necessary to win in South Vietnam.' After all, he noted, three US presidents had laid the prestige of the country on the line. But things were not completely clear cut. 'If I try to find out what means are to be used to achieve victory in South Vietnam for the forces opposing communism, it is much more difficult to get an answer', he reported.

In July, Fraser was in Los Angeles visiting the Rand Corporation, the right-wing US think tank that was both briefing and briefed by the CIA. He met the head of the Asian section Guy Pauker; in the years ahead, they maintained contact and swapped information on South-East Asia.

Fraser returned home via Vietnam. He visited the Australian embassy in Saigon and met Tran Thien Khiem, the South Vietnamese Minister for Defence. His visit was brief, but confirmed him in his opinions.

In his official report on his overseas trip, Fraser said it was obvious that US policy was under reappraisal and it was therefore 'reassuring' to find determination that everything should be done that needed to be done to achieve victory in South Vietnam. However, 'To say that the war in South Vietnam must be won is relatively easy, but to say how it can be won, to analyse and isolate the problem, is not'. He noted the lack of will in South Vietnam to fight the war. It was essential that ground troops be committed, he argued, if subversion was to be overcome.[11]

A few weeks after Fraser's visit to the United States, on 2 August 1964, the destroyer USS *Maddox* engaged three North Vietnamese torpedo boats in the Gulf of Tonkin, off Vietnam. Warnings were sent to Hanoi about the consequences of any further attacks. Two days later, in the middle of a storm, the *Maddox* again believed itself to be under attack. It was later concluded that this was a mistake—there was no attack—but the incident became the impetus for President Johnson's seeking and gaining sweeping powers to bomb North Vietnam and prosecute an undeclared war. The Americans had chosen escalation, and Australia followed. In November 1964, Australia introduced conscription. Fraser supported the decision, as did almost everyone else. 'As I remember, there was no opposition in the party room to speak of at all.'

At the end of that year, Fraser went overseas again, this time to Indonesia, which seemed at the time to be one of the most unstable countries in the region, and the one most likely to 'go communist'. Thanks to the Australian Ambassador Mick Shann, Fraser met everyone, including Dipi Nusantara Aidit, leader of the communist PKI, then the largest non-ruling communist party in the world. Fraser travelled to a dilapidated shanty town to visit Aidit in his home; the two men got on, and Fraser came away thinking that the communists were well organised, and doubted the ability and the will of the Sukarno government to resist them. Fraser sent his report of this Indonesian trip to Guy Pauker at the Rand Corporation, and stressed to Pauker that Australia could and should have a dual role in Indonesia, providing

> complete firmness and resolution in opposition to confrontation on the one hand, coupled with an open door to negotiation and friendship on the other. As matters are going, we may be the last country to be able to put the Western point of view in a manner that will not be too open to suspicion.[12]

Fraser felt pessimistic about Indonesia, but his reservations about the army's ability were proved wrong. In September 1965, there was an attempted coup—blamed on the Communist Party—which was brutally suppressed by the army. A new regime headed by Major-General Suharto emerged. Suharto presided over an anti-communist, strong and centralised government. US Secretary of Defense Robert McNamara later reflected that these developments in Indonesia should have caused the United States to reassess whether the nature of the communist threat in South-East Asia had declined. This is the luxury of hindsight; by that time, Australian troops were already in Vietnam.

There was nothing in Fraser's public statements at the time to suggest he had doubts about the decision to send in Australian troops. Yet the archives show that, even at this early stage, he did not entirely trust what the Americans were telling Australia. On

9 March 1965, just before Menzies announced the dispatch of an infantry battalion, Fraser wrote a letter to Alan Renouf, Australia's chargé d'affaires at the Australian embassy in Washington. Fraser told Renouf that he had been hearing stories from 'mutual friends' that had disturbed him.

> The stories go this way. If conditions get so bad in Vietnam that the Americans can't stay there, if the Vietcong have in fact won, then so that they could withdraw and minimise the danger to the rest of the South-East Asian area the Americans would try to create some chips which they could use at the bargaining table. They might create chips by bombing Vietnam or by putting in a division or two to bargain with. When they have developed a position of apparent strength, negotiations could start. The idea would be to develop a situation in which they could get out with some status left. If they have to get out this is, of course, important to the rest of South-East Asia.

Fraser told Renouf that this had been described as a 'worst possible' scenario, but,

> I fear that the administration might have come to the conclusion that the worst possible circumstances have in fact arrived and that even now they are in the process of putting this kind of plan into effect.
>
> If what is now being done is part of the long-term plan for withdrawal this should give us some cause for thought about any additional strength that we may one day be asked to put into South Vietnam. To do something in Vietnam in support of friends who are determined to stay there is one thing; to do something in Vietnam as part of a concerted plan for withdrawal is quite another thing, and I am not sure that this would serve our interests particularly well.[13]

Fraser doesn't remember writing this letter; nor does he recall who the 'mutual friends' might have been. If there was a reply, it does not seem to have been kept, and he does not remember receiving one. 'Probably events overtook the whole thing', he says. In fact, as McNamara's memoir reveals, Fraser's suspicions were correct. Elements in the administration were indeed trying to arrive at a position from which negotiations could lead to something other than humiliating defeat.

* * *

Fraser had wanted to be in the ministry, but the position Holt gave him at the beginning of 1966—Minister for Army—was not what he had had in mind. It was not a powerful position. At that time, each of the armed forces—navy, army and airforce—had its own minister. None were in cabinet: the service ministries were almost administrative jobs, acting as proving grounds for promising politicians. Fraser had only a tiny personal staff. The Minister for Defence Allen Fairhall was the man in charge of policy. The permanent Secretary for the Department of Army Bruce White and the heads of the armed forces sat on defence committees from which Fraser was excluded. Although Fraser had responsibility for administering aspects of national service and conscription, even here he had limited power, with Leslie Bury, the Minister for Labour and National Service, chiefly responsible. Often Fraser's senior bureaucrats knew more than he did about how decisions were being made. For a man like Fraser, who was always inclined to make the most of any post he held, it could be frustrating. And there was another barrier: he was uneasy with the post. He had not himself served in wartime, and he felt awkward about dealing with older army men; and he was well aware that not all of them welcomed answering to him. 'I didn't even understand the ranks to begin with, or the insignia.'

Army could easily be a 'seen and not heard' post, and it was not in Fraser's make-up to accept this. His concern that Australia didn't know enough about how the United States was thinking continued, and he soon became aware that he wasn't the only one in the dark about the progress of the war and US strategy. Fraser remembers arguing with Fairhall in his office. 'I can remember saying to him, "For heaven's sake, Allen. You say you agree with me with what I'm saying about Vietnam. Why don't you go to Washington and express these concerns in the strongest possible way? Why don't you try to have an Australian input into the policies? We don't really know what we are doing. The overall American strategy we know nothing about, really, and where their plans might lead and what they regard as their options. Now, if we are a fairly full partner in this war, we should be having an input". And Allen would say, "Oh yes, oh yes", but he never wanted to stir himself. It would have been an unpopular thing to do anyway. The Americans wouldn't have appreciated it.'

Fraser set about doing what he could do—which was to look after the men. He found that even this apparently simple job was not easy, particularly in an army that was expanding quickly as the new conscripts flooded in. An enormous amount of his time was taken up in controversies over individual soldiers and individual families. His parliamentary speeches became more confined than they had been when he was a backbencher, focussed on answering questions on logistical and human resources issues.

Meanwhile, behind the scenes he was fighting a characteristic battle. Fraser is a great believer in the Westminster system and the role of the public service. He also recognises the ability of the bureaucracy to treat ordinary citizens with insufferable arrogance. A couple of weeks after he had become minister, Fraser was given some paperwork to sign with the assurance that all the decisions were minor and that he needn't trouble himself with them too much. Fraser found himself confronted with about a hundred letters responding to complaints received from soldiers and their families. Each letter in reply, drafted for his signature, was the same—a paragraph asserting that the complaint had been investigated and had been found to be groundless. Fraser demanded to see the files of the investigations before he would sign a single letter. He recalls, 'They told me, "You can't do that".

'I said, "I can, and I'm not going to sign the letters without seeing the files".

'They said, "Nobody has ever asked to see the files. They are too big. There are too many of them. You can't do it".

'Anyway, they wheeled the files in on two wheelie wagons, and they just about filled the office. So I went through the first half-dozen files and found that in most cases there had been no inquiry at all'. Fraser told the public servants, 'Tell the army officers to go back and do their work and then I will look at the file and then I will see what sort of letter I will write'. The result was that during his period as Minister for Army, when there was a complaint, there was at least an investigation.

At the time Fraser became minister, Australian troops were serving under the operational control of the US 173 Airborne Brigade. Now they were to be given their own command, and their own job—pacifying the province of Phuoc Tuy. This change had been brought about largely at the behest of Australia's senior military officers. The advice they gave Fraser was enough to deepen his reservations about how the Americans were conducting the war. 'I said, "Do we have an integrated operation with the Americans or is it a separate bit of geography?"

'They told me, "Minister, we would strongly recommend against an integrated operation".

'I said, "What is the problem? They are allies, aren't they?"

'"Yes, but if you want to have reports of Americans shooting Australians, and Australians shooting Americans, have an integrated operation."

'"Right. Well, we will put that aside."'

Fraser remembers another discussion over whether the Australians should have their own army jail. 'They told me, "Oh, we can use the American brig, but then you will have to respond to a lot of parents who will write in about the total brutality of American soldiers guarding the brig".

'I said, "You really believe that?"

'And they said, "Yes. We don't believe it. We know it".'

The Australians were set up with their own jail.

In March 1966, Fraser was approached by the Australian Association for Cultural Freedom, the Australian arm of the Congress for Cultural Freedom, which, with its international secretariat in Paris, had been established by the CIA as a key element in the strategy to combat Soviet propaganda. The Australian arm was the brainchild of Richard Krygier. Its public face was the conservative magazine *Quadrant*, set up in 1956 and edited by the poet James McAuley. Now Krygier wrote to Fraser asking to see him, to 'put to you some suggestions' about conducting an 'information campaign' on Vietnam. The two men met, and Krygier sent a follow-up letter in April containing a summary of his suggestions. He and his colleagues had been concerned with the 'irresponsible campaign' against the war.

> It seems to me that the major sources of trouble in the present campaign are to be found at universities and among churchmen, and if this part of the propaganda campaign could be won, the response of the general public should not present major problems. On the other hand I am convinced that if the vicious smear campaign among the 'opinion formers' is not addressed soon it is bound to seep through to the public at large.

The Australian Association for Cultural Freedom had, Krygier told Fraser, recently arranged a trip to Vietnam for three 'distinguished persons': Professor James McAuley, Peter Coleman, who was then editor of *The Bulletin* magazine, and Sibnarayan Ray of the University of Melbourne. They also hoped soon to send Owen Harries of the University of New South Wales (who later became a key foreign policy adviser to the Fraser government). 'The experience', Krygier wrote, 'has convinced the Australian Association for Cultural Freedom that there was a great deal to be gained by increasing the number of such visits'. Krygier proposed that there be more trips to Vietnam for editors of intellectual journals and other members of the press. He suggested that invitations should be limited to supporters of the government's policy. The association could suggest names, and then use them on their return to address public meetings. 'Should you think that there should not be too much overt government sponsorship of these visits, we could assume sponsorship of some of them.'

Fraser passed a copy of Krygier's letter to Allen Fairhall, as Minister for Defence, saying, 'If it is possible for us to help in any way I think we should'. Fairhall was not impressed. He agreed that Krygier's suggestions were meant to be helpful, but pointed out that there were several existing schemes under which the government assisted overseas visits by Australians. No new ones were needed, and, in any case, 'Some of the invitations could prove difficult'.[14]

Today, Fraser's comment on being shown this correspondence is that the idea of sending people to Vietnam was a good one, but the idea of specially selecting them so they would support government policy was foolish and would soon have come unstitched. He did not know Krygier well, but was on good terms with the *Quadrant* editor James McAuley, who was 'a wonderful person: a total idealist, obviously a very devout and strong anti-communist who did a lot in quiet ways to oppose communism or communists'. Did he know of the links between the Congress for Cultural Freedom and the CIA at the time? Fraser says he did not. Would knowing it have altered his view? 'Probably. But the idea of sending people to Vietnam, I think, was a good idea; the problem was that selection process.'

Shortly after the Australians were established at their base in Nui Dat, Phuoc Tuy province, Fraser wrote to Holt seeking permission to visit the battalions regularly, to gain an understanding of the conflict and to 'demonstrate government interest and concern'. Holt agreed, although Fraser's plans to visit heads of government in other countries as well were cut back after Fairhall complained to Holt that Fraser's trip was becoming too 'inflated' for a junior minister.[15]

The Australian troops now had their own discrete task—to 'pacify' the province of Phuoc Tuy. It was not an easy job. Phuoc Tuy covered about 70 square miles of mountains, swamp and jungle bounded by the South China Sea, with a population of about one hundred thousand people in thirty villages and numerous hamlets. It was the perfect terrain for guerrilla warfare, and was also strategically important—controlling the deep-water harbour of Vung Tau at the mouth of the Saigon River. Every night the Vietcong would infiltrate the villages, taxing the people, threatening them, often murdering them. Some of the villages were communist, but more were neutral or terrorised into submission. Most people obeyed the Vietcong, whether willingly or not. The Australian army's job was to make Phuoc Tuy secure, to try to demonstrate that the allies could protect the people from the Vietcong, thereby securing their loyalty for the South Vietnamese Government.

When Fraser arrived at the Australian base at Nui Dat, in the middle of the jungle, he found there were no defence stores, due partly to Australian wharf labourers' refusal to load transport ships. The toilet blocks were roofless shacks situated above huge holes with an extraordinary stench. The heat was overwhelming. There was mud everywhere: every weapons pit, latrine, gun placement and building involved digging out mud. Already the soldiers were suffering from skin conditions. Meanwhile, everyone knew the Vietcong were watching and taking stock of this new enemy.[16]

Some photos of Fraser on that visit show him, sleeves rolled up and arms akimbo, in the middle of the jungle talking to soldiers who are leaning on their shovels, interrupted in the act of digging pits. Just a few weeks before, the Australians had destroyed the village of Long Phuoc, a few miles south-east of the base. It had been a fortified Vietcong-controlled area, standing on a maze of tunnels, one of which ran nearly 2 miles to Long Tan. As the Australian troops had set fire to the houses, the ammunition hidden in the roofs started exploding. Other photos of Fraser's visit show him grim-faced, inspecting Chinese-manufactured rifles and deadly Vietcong booby traps that had been captured in the raid.[17] At this stage, Fraser, in common with many others, thought that China was chiefly responsible for backing the Vietcong. Now, he says, 'About 60 per cent of the equipment was from Russia. China was much less to blame than we thought'.

Fraser wanted to visit the troops every six months, but on this he was partly frustrated. Holt knocked back his request to be allowed to visit again in early 1967. Fraser wrote again—a long letter pleading his case. Small matters, such as the late arrival of mail, were having a bad effect on morale, he said; it was important the government showed that it cared.[18] This time he was given the go-ahead, and made his second trip to Phuoc Tuy in July 1967. By that time the troops were better established.

On his return, Fraser made one of his few long speeches to parliament on Vietnam as Minister for Army. He said that the Australian soldiers could be proud of what they were achieving. Fraser claimed there was now 80 to 90 per cent security in Phuoc Tuy province. He acknowledged the opposition to the war:

> No war has been so publicised as this war and no war has been so much reported. I believe at the same time that public opinion has never been so confused ... It is, I think, the first war when there has been no censorship of any kind, and thus the full horror of the war is reported, very often on a daily basis. This strikes a sensitive chord in all our minds ... Because we are removed from the struggle and because we want nothing but peace we often forget the lessons we have learned in the past, that not all people or all countries share these objectives.

The paramount objective, to allow South Vietnam to work out its own future, had to be kept in sight, he said. He talked for the first time in parliament about the topic dear to his heart—civic action—but also argued that the war could not be fought 'entirely with clean hands'. Fraser said that no war in history had been as circumscribed by social and humanitarian considerations as the Vietnam War.

> When the enemy troops withdraw into Laos, free world forces cannot follow them. When they withdraw north of the demilitarised zone, they cannot be followed. Wherever they withdraw out of Vietnam, they are now safe from pursuing troops and on countless occasions actions have been curtailed or altered because of a wish and a determination to avoid civilian casualties whenever this is possible. But it is idle to suggest that these will not occur. Despite all our best efforts the wrong people will sometimes be hit. This should not be taken to mean, however, as it sometimes is, that the price is too high. I do not know how you measure this kind of cost. Did the Britons say that the price was too high in 1940? Did the Greeks between 1945 and 1949, when struggling against communist insurrection, say that the price was too high? Did the South Koreans, who were blatantly attacked in 1951, suggest the price was too high? If in all the course of history free people had said the price was too high there would be no freedom today.[19]

Fraser was arguing privately that the war should be pursued with more determination, and without broadcasting to the enemy the limits the allies were setting on themselves. But Fraser was not in cabinet, and for that reason was not privy to the one occasion on which Australia managed to have a significant impact on US policy in Vietnam.

In July 1967, two advisers to President Johnson, Clark Clifford and Maxwell Taylor, visited Australia as part of a tour of their allies. They were seeking an extra commitment to Vietnam. In a long meeting with Holt's cabinet, they argued that Australia should concentrate all of its overseas military resources in South Vietnam; after all, Australia would be more at risk than the United States if South-East Asia went communist. Holt was not willing. Clifford later wrote that Holt presented a long list of reasons why Australia was already close to its maximum effort. Despite the catchphrase by which he became known, 'All the way with LBJ', Holt was far from uncritically accepting of the US priorities in the war. In front of Clifford, only Deputy Prime Minister John McEwen argued strongly in favour of a greatly increased Australian commitment. Clifford later wrote:

> I returned home [from Australia] puzzled, troubled, concerned. Was it possible that our assessment of the danger to the stability of South-East Asia and the western Pacific was exaggerated? Was it possible that those nations that were neighbours of Vietnam had a clearer perception of the tide of world events in 1967 than we? Was it possible that we were continuing to be guided by judgements that might once have had validity but were now obsolete?[20]

On 19 May 1967, US Secretary of Defense Robert McNamara had written a long, anguished memorandum to President Johnson arguing that the war could not be won, and that the United States should do all it could to disengage. This marked the beginning of the end for McNamara's position as an adviser to Johnson. A few months after it was written, Clifford, with memories of the Australian cabinet fresh in his mind, succeeded McNamara as Secretary of Defense. Clifford had been a hawk on Vietnam, and in sharp disagreement with McNamara, but Australia changed him from a hawk to a dove.

At the time, Fraser knew none of this; nor did more senior ministers. 'We had no awareness at all of how the Americans were thinking.' In October 1967, the decision was made to increase Australia's commitment to South Vietnam by 1700, including a third infantry battalion and a tank squadron. It was less than the United States and Clifford had wanted, but it was something.

At the beginning of the school holidays in December 1967, Fraser took a call at Nareen from Prime Minister Holt. Could he come to Canberra? There was to be a series of meetings of top ministers to review Australia's defence policy, and Vietnam in particular. Fraser had only just arrived at Nareen and was looking forward to some rare time with the children. Holt sensed the hesitation in his voice. Fraser remembers, 'I said of course I could get to Canberra if it was important, but he said, "No. You don't have enough time with your family. You stay there. This is just the first meeting, and there will be others. I can brief you. You won't miss anything of importance"'.

That was the last conversation Fraser had with Holt. A few days later, on 17 December, the Prime Minister disappeared while swimming at Portsea, Victoria. Fraser has no doubt that Holt's disappearance was pure accident. 'The conversation I had with him was hardly the kind that you would have with a man planning to commit suicide', he says. Fraser liked Holt, and was not among those agitating for his replacement at the time of his death. Nevertheless, their conversation has led Fraser to believe that, had he lived, Holt would have reviewed Australia's role in Vietnam. This would have been done, he believes, 'in an orderly fashion. It wouldn't have been chaotic, which is what we got from Gorton'.

It was true that by that time—the end of 1967—Phuoc Tuy province seemed relatively secure, but we now know that the Vietcong were preparing for the Tet offensive of January 1968, which, although it was a defeat for the North in every real sense, turned into a major propaganda victory. The communist forces launched concentrated attacks against every major city and regional centre. Tet sowed the seeds of doubt. If, after all this time, and after all the bombs that had been dropped, the Vietcong were still able to strike so hard across the country, perhaps the war could not be won. By the time Fraser received his report on Tet, his period of responsibility for the Australian army was in its last days.[21]

Today, looking back, Fraser believes that the Australian role in Phuoc Tuy was a success, as far as it went. The province did become much more secure, and the South Vietnamese regarded the Australians comparatively favourably. But, 'I think the Vietcong knew that we didn't matter and also knew we would have been harder to tackle, probably because as much as anything we treated villagers with respect. Australians wouldn't so readily shoot villagers, calling them Vietcong, as the Americans would have. But, you know, the Vietcong knew that it was the Americans they had to unsettle, not us. They knew that, and the villagers knew that too'.

* * *

Holt's disappearance had many consequences. One was that John Gorton became Prime Minister, with Fraser's support. As a reward, Fraser was promoted out of the army portfolio and became Minister for Education and Science on 28 February 1968. For the next twenty-one months, his involvement with Vietnam was largely as a spectator. When he returned to the field, as Minister for Defence, in November 1969, a great deal had changed.

6

Too Near the Sun

High above Collins Street in Melbourne, in the ordered calm of Malcolm Fraser's current office, there is a filing cabinet that contains notes he has made in recent years about his relationship with John Gorton. They are reflections made in tranquillity, about one of the most distressing periods in Fraser's life. They read:

> One can get too near the sun. See too far into the behaviour and heart of a man. If you lend money to a man, you lose a friend. There are things that a man cannot accept having another know of him. A man who wants to be strong, known to be weak. Who wishes to be secure, but has known only insecurity since birth, who is believed to hold views strongly and firmly but who acts as a straw man when the pressure is really on … [Gorton was] a sad character in many ways, he was certainly his own worst enemy, but I think this was just the way he was made, I don't think it could have been different.

Fraser and Gorton began as friends and ended as enemies. Gorton replaced Harold Holt as Prime Minister with Fraser's support, yet these two men brought each other down. At the time, people thought they had destroyed each other. Gorton's prime ministerial career was indeed over, but Fraser, cast into the wilderness, emerged reinvigorated and ultimately victorious.

John Gorton was born in 1911 in Victoria, the illegitimate son of an English orange orchardist and a railway worker's daughter. His childhood was insecure and disordered. His mother died when he was only nine years old, and he was brought up by his father's estranged wife and his half-sister before being returned to his father a few years later and packed off to boarding school. He was educated at the best schools and, thanks to the intervention of the headmaster at Geelong Grammar, was sent to Oxford. He was essentially a lonely boy, and an anti-establishment adult. He had been a handsome young man, but serving as a fighter pilot in the Royal Australian Air Force during World War II had hit his face during a forced landing while operating out of Malaya, crushing his nose and breaking both cheekbones. His face never recovered from the mutilation, but his charm resurfaced undamaged. Later on, even when he was out of favour with many of his political colleagues, he remained easy to like and popular with the public.

Gorton had been a member of the Country Party before the war, and when he entered the Senate for the Liberal Party in 1949 he was at first considered an extreme right-winger, but by the time of Holt's death he had reinvented himself as a moderate.[1] It was the progressive and the maverick in Gorton that Fraser liked, and that led Fraser to back him for the leadership after Holt's disappearance.

Fraser hadn't been close to Holt, but he had supported him. Holt's tenure as Prime Minister had been remarkable for several actions: the beginning of the end of the White Australia policy through reforms introduced quietly in 1966, the 1967 referendum which resulted in Commonwealth power to legislate for Aboriginal Australians, and the expansion of government support for the arts. Yet Holt's leadership also saw the beginning of the Liberals' internal turmoil in the wake of Menzies's retirement.

Meanwhile, Gough Whitlam had replaced Arthur Calwell as Australian Labor Party leader in early 1967. Today, Whitlam is a hero of the left, but at the time he was seen as a right-winger. He was hissed and booed repeatedly at Labor Party conferences in Victoria because of his determination to counter left-wing inflexibility. He stood up to the unions and the communists with the famous words 'Certainly the impotent are pure'.[2]

Whitlam was winning, at least in parliament, and he had the Liberals more than rattled. Under Whitlam, Labor was declaring its place as a party of vision: a progressive party, but also a party of the centre. Labor was looking electable for the first time since the split of the mid 1950s. Holt had been criticised within government ranks as too weak, and just too 'nice'.

The assumed successor to Holt was the Liberal Deputy Leader Billy McMahon, but the day after Holt disappeared McMahon's chances were wiped out by the Country Party leader and Deputy Prime Minister Jack McEwen, who made a public statement in which he declared that neither he nor his colleagues would serve in a coalition if McMahon was leader. McEwen refused to give his reasons, but he said that McMahon knew what they were. If McMahon wished to publish them, he could, but if he published them wrongly he would be corrected.

As a junior minister, Fraser didn't know what McEwen's reasons might be. He wasn't privy to the disputes the two men had had in cabinet. Nevertheless, it wasn't hard to guess what McEwen disliked: it was widely believed that McMahon was a habitual leaker, to the Packer press in particular. Years later, when Fraser was in the habit of visiting the ailing Menzies in his home, he was told that McMahon had once made a signed confession about leaking to the media, and that Menzies had kept this in his safe. McMahon had known it was there, and that it would be used if Menzies was sufficiently provoked. Fraser asked Menzies why he had never used the letter to get rid of McMahon. Fraser remembers, 'I said, "You could have done something about McMahon and you left him there. He was never going to be helpful to anyone". Menzies said, "Yes,

Malcolm, perhaps I should have done something". McMahon had an insatiable ambition. He had no sense of value. He wasn't immoral; he was totally amoral'.

McEwen's veto on McMahon meant the leadership was an open contest. With the government suffering at the hands of Whitlam in parliament every day, it seemed to Fraser essential that they should choose a good parliamentary performer. McEwen was sworn in as Prime Minister on the understanding that his commission would continue only until such time as the Liberals could elect a new leader. Fraser remembers that the lobbying began even before Holt's memorial service. The contenders, now that McMahon was vetoed, were Paul Hasluck, the Minister for External Affairs, and Gorton, who was then in the Senate.

Shortly after Holt's memorial service, Hasluck approached Fraser on the steps of Parliament House. Gorton, Hasluck said, was a 'lazy, sloppy minister'. Fraser wished Hasluck well in the battle, but he was already leaning towards Gorton. He liked Gorton's knock-about manner, his charm, his lack of pretensions and his energy. Fraser believed that he would be better able to counter Whitlam in parliament, but this was not his only reason for backing him: he also thought that Gorton would be a progressive, whereas Hasluck spoke more to the party's conservative traditions. He lobbied for Gorton, though not, he says, as actively as some believed. Nevertheless, Fraser was crucial to Gorton's support across the party.

McEwen spoke to Fraser the day before the ballot for the leadership, and asked him if he was entirely committed to Gorton. 'He would be a gamble', McEwen said; 'Hasluck would be safe'. Fraser replied that Hasluck wouldn't be able to deal with Whitlam in parliament. 'McEwen didn't deny it. I wish he had.' Today, the notes that sit in Fraser's filing cabinet conclude that Hasluck was beaten for the wrong reasons.

> It was said he could not beat Whitlam in parliament and that his press image was not good. The first was probably false and the latter probably unimportant. He was able,

> dedicated, of intellectual integrity. He was the more able man. He was beaten narrowly, by three votes, because of the intensity of the Gorton campaign. If he had spoken to a few more he may have won.

Gorton was elected Prime Minister on 10 January 1968. The next day, Fraser gave one of his regular radio addresses to the people of Wannon, and told them the new leader would 'bring an excitement to Australian politics; and it is my firm belief that he will capture the enthusiasm and support of Australia'. There were many challenges in front of Australia, Fraser noted. There was the drought, and the war in Vietnam and the proposed British withdrawal from South-East Asia. Every member of the cabinet would be dedicated to overcoming these problems.[3]

But just a few days after he delivered this address, Fraser was having doubts about whether the right choice had been made. Tamie remembers him coming home one day and telling her that he thought Gorton was making mistakes in the appointment of his personal and senior departmental staff. A Prime Minister, Fraser thought, needed people around him who could work closely and cooperatively with the public service but who were also prepared to argue with the boss and offer competing points of view. There needed to be proper process. He wasn't confident that those closest to Gorton satisfied these tests.

Two weeks later, Fraser was promoted in reward for his support for Gorton, and in recognition of his record as Minister for Army. He was made Minister for Education and Science—his first cabinet post. For the next ten months, the portfolio took up most of his energies, but Fraser never took his eye off foreign policy, and this meant he was increasingly disillusioned with his leader. Gorton was clearly not a supporter of forward defence, yet the review of defence policy that Holt had apparently intended to begin never took place. Instead, Gorton's various public statements left the impression of ambivalence. Hasluck, still Minister for External Affairs and a passionate supporter of Australia's role in Vietnam, held the line, but for most of 1968 it was hard to say what Australia's position was on South-East Asia and Vietnam—yet the troops fought on.

Just a few weeks after becoming Minister for Education, in March 1968, Fraser made a speech to the South Australian Jaycees that was a conscious warning to Gorton. There could be no security in Asia for anyone unless all countries were secure, he said. The main objective of security in the region was to establish conditions in which political institutions could develop and the countries of Asia could raise the standard of living of their own people. Australia's foreign policy was not, and could not be, selfish. 'Given that we are a nation of only twelve million people, there is a limit to what we can do, and we cannot be self-sufficient or isolated in our island continent.' He linked defence policy with his new responsibility of education: it was essential that Asian history and languages were taught in schools.

> When we are making judgements about Asia we need to make quite sure that they are not prejudiced by our own background and origins. If more of us had a wider understanding of Asian history and Asian customs we would be in a better position to form opinions that would have some validity.

The school curriculum was in the hands of the states, he said, but as Minister for Education he intended to do all he could to promote and encourage the teaching of Asian languages.[4]

This became a major preoccupation during his time in the portfolio. Within a year he had announced an advisory committee on the teaching of Asian languages, and in a ministerial statement he coined the term 'multi-racial society' to describe what Australia needed to become.[5] This speech was probably the first in which the notion of multiculturalism was referred to in an Australian parliament. Fraser used the word 'multiculturalism' itself later that year, in a speech in which he argued that love of and loyalty to Australia were in no way incompatible with differences in culture and affection for the homeland.[6] Fraser rejected the conventional wisdom of the times that minority groups should assimilate with the European mainstream. People who came to Australia would want to keep some of their own traditions, and have choices over how they ran their own lives, he said. Fraser saw these as basic human rights—needs, even—and the essence of liberalism. Migrants should have the right to find their own expressions of what it meant to be Australian, within the overarching framework of respect for others and the rule of law.

* * *

So much for foreign frontiers and recent arrivals. Just a few weeks after he took up the education job, Fraser was confronted with another kind of frontier, and another kind of challenge to mainstream ideas of what it meant to be Australian. He went on a tour of the Northern Territory, and had his first close-up encounter with Aboriginal Australia. Fraser travelled with Bill Wentworth, who had become the first ever federal Minister for Aboriginal Affairs in the wake of the 1967 referendum that gave the Commonwealth law-making powers for Aboriginal people. Wentworth was a vehement anti-communist—more so even than Fraser. He was 'a controversial figure, always interesting and stimulating and often provocative', Fraser told the electors of Wannon when he reported on the tour in one of his radio addresses.

But Wentworth was far from a single-issue politician, and he was a determined man, able to go up against his own party when he felt the matter was important. Aboriginal welfare had been Wentworth's longstanding preoccupation. He had been one of the main supporters of the referendum, and now he was determined to make the most of his new portfolio. Education was key to Aboriginal futures, he thought, and he wanted the new Education Minister alongside him on this trip. Fraser told the people of Wannon, 'Bill Wentworth's aim is to find out how to help the Aborigines help themselves … This is the only approach that will lead to a long-term solution to the position of the Aborigines'. As for himself, Fraser said he believed education should be available to students no matter where they lived. He wanted to understand one of the puzzling problems in Aboriginal education: 'They seem to do very well until the end of primary school and at the beginning of secondary school, but after that for one reason or another their interest seems to wane and they find it hard to keep up'.[7]

Wentworth and Fraser started in Alice Springs, where Fraser was a guest speaker on the School of the Air, which brought education to children on remote stations and outposts all over the centre of Australia. The two men moved on, touring the 'very fine' missions at Hermannsburg, continuing to Tennant Creek, and by light aircraft to Groote Eylandt and the boom mining areas around Gove, then to Darwin, Katherine and Arnhem Land. Fraser was impressed with the missions he saw, the new housing and the productive gardens, 'although much is still to be done'. Around the Daly River he was shocked to see that leprosy was still rife in the communities. On the other hand, Catholic missions were

> doing a great deal to develop the resources of the area. Cattle, citrus fruit and gardens of different kinds were flourishing ... The mission here is filling a very useful purpose because the Daly River Aborigines had had a very rough contact with white people over a period of fifty to eighty years and the early history of contact with white people is probably one of the saddest of any of the Aboriginal tribes.[8]

Fraser and Wentworth were getting on well in these remote surroundings, surveying the great red and green tropics from the windows of aircraft and other vehicles. Canberra seemed to be a long way away, and yet they carried with them a sense of responsibility: they had power; they represented government. They wanted that to mean something to these people, who were so far out of sight and too often out of mind in the settled south. Fraser remembers Wentworth expressing the opinion that the words 'assimilate' and 'integrate' really meant the same thing. 'They both meant "Live like us". Wentworth's ideas were much more in line with multiculturalism, that Aborigines should be able to preserve their own traditions and culture, and still be part of mainstream Australia.' On this, the two men were in agreement.

Wentworth was particularly determined to visit a group of Aboriginals already in the headlines—the Gurindji stockmen—who, under the leadership of Vincent Lingiari, had walked off the job on the vast Wave Hill Station, leased by the Vestey Group of companies. Wave Hill was to become the seminal dispute that gave birth to the land rights movement. The Gurindji inspired stories and songs that transcended race barriers, among them Paul Kelly's quiet anthem 'From Little Things Big Things Grow'. At the time of the Northern Territory tour, the Gurindji's supporters were mostly left-wing trade unions and communists, such as the author Frank Hardy. What had started as a dispute over pay and conditions had become something much more fundamental: a statement about the rightful ownership of the land. The Aboriginals had set up camp at Wattie Creek, a place of traditional significance. So far as white man's law was concerned, they were trespassing: Wave Hill Station was Commonwealth leasehold. The previous year, the Gurindji had petitioned the Governor-General for the return of their traditional lands, but had been knocked back after a decision of the Holt cabinet. Wentworth hadn't been happy with that decision. Now he wanted to meet the Gurindji and hear from them first-hand. The two men were told in Darwin that they would have to abandon their trip: the road was washed out. They set out nevertheless, prepared to hike if they had to. In fact, they got through, and ended up sitting down with the elders.

Fraser and Wentworth were told that the Gurindji wanted enough land to set up a village and paddocks for a brumby breaking centre. Wentworth could make no promises on the spot, but Fraser commented in his address to the electors of Wannon: 'It seems to me they had been making moves in the direction of looking after themselves and deserved support. They were good types with a native dignity and a good deal of resolution'. In another address, he said, 'The Aborigines must become involved in their own future, a future which contains human dignity and which enables them to be self-supporting'. Wentworth, Fraser told the people of Wannon, believed white Australians had 'given Aborigines the feeling that all people are out to exploit them'. He continued:

> A certain degree of paternalism will probably be inevitable for some time, but Mr Wentworth's view is that the government has overemphasised this approach in the Northern Territory. He strongly believes that the Aborigines should be made less dependent than they now are. He believes that the Aborigines must be placed in a position where by their own efforts they can see they are improving their own position in life.[9]

Wentworth was, in fact, a convert to the cause of land rights, although he might not have used the term. He fought in cabinet against Country Party colleagues for the Gurindji to be given control of Wave Hill Station. He was defeated. Meanwhile, landholding interests accused him, incredibly, of being 'communist-inspired'. It took until 1972, and the Whitlam government, for the Gurindji people to be given their land. Whitlam presided over a moving ceremony in which he poured a handful of soil into Vincent Lingiari's hand with the words 'I put into your hands part of the earth as a sign that this land will be the possession of you and your children forever'.[10] Fraser, who at this stage was Leader of the Opposition and within months of forcing Whitlam out of government, remembered the dignified men he had met on the trip with Wentworth years earlier and reflected that he, too, would have done what Whitlam did. It fell to Fraser, as Prime Minister, to conclude what Whitlam had begun. One of the first actions of his government was the passage of land rights legislation, giving Indigenous Australian people freehold title to traditional lands in the Northern Territory. Fraser fought, and won, the battle that Wentworth had lost. He, his Minister for Aboriginal Affairs Ian Viner and the leader of the National Country Party Doug Anthony persuaded their colleagues to support land rights and, short of overriding states' and territories' rights, did everything they could to encourage the passage of land rights legislation Australia-wide. Today Fraser says, 'On that kind of thing, Whitlam and I never disagreed. He was right. He had a vision. And those on my own side of politics who opposed land rights were wrong'.

* * *

A few months after his trip to the Northern Territory, in August 1968, Fraser's attention was hauled back to foreign affairs when the Soviet Union invaded Czechoslovakia, crushing the first signs of liberal reform under Alexander Dubcek. The invasion was 'a day of infamy', Fraser said in one of his radio addresses. 'The brutal repression of the Czechs served notice on the countries of the non-communist world that a new analysis, a new accounting had to be taken of the apparent harmony that had begun to characterise Soviet–West relations in recent times.'[11]

For a while it had seemed that China was the main threat to freedom, and that the Soviets were prepared to deal honestly with the West over issues such as the non-proliferation of nuclear weapons. Now that hope was dashed. For Fraser, two realisations combined. In the early days of the Vietnam War, he with many others had understood China to be the main country supplying the Vietcong. By now it had become clear that most of the military equipment, and certainly the sophisticated equipment, was coming from Russia, and that the Chinese and Russians were rivals as much as allies. 'Communism was not monolithic', he says today. 'When the war began, I think we thought it was.' The Czech invasion, or, as he described it, 'the swift red thrust into the heart of Czechoslovakian freedom', had killed any notion that the Russians were peaceful and had renounced the use of force. 'For the brave Czechs, the light of freedom has been snuffed out once more', Fraser said in his radio address.[12] He would never again trust talk of thaws in Soviet relations with the West. Through the next ten years, as the world talked about détente, Fraser remained wary, even hostile. This was one of the things that made it easy, later, for his political enemies to characterise him as a right-winger.

At the time, the events in central Europe bolstered him in his conviction that the Vietnam War had to be fought and won. It increased his desperation over the state of Australian foreign policy. So far as he could see, Australia still didn't have a coherent position on the war. Meanwhile, there was a new area of concern and a new frontier: Soviet submarines were active in the Indian Ocean. The Democratic Labor Party wanted the government to take a firm stand and to encourage US bases, yet Gorton seemed ambivalent about everything Australia was doing by way of forward defence.

There were some things on which Gorton and Fraser agreed. One was the need for an independent Australian foreign policy. But whereas Fraser thought this meant greater and more intense alliances within the region, Gorton seemed to want to reduce regional engagement. Gorton was also toying with the idea of Australia acquiring a nuclear weapon; he wanted to avoid signing the Nuclear Non-Proliferation Treaty so as to leave options open, and he explored building a reactor at Jervis Bay to produce weapon-grade plutonium. Fraser had heard talk of Gorton's ideas on this, but, he says, nothing came to cabinet while he was there.[13]

One of Gorton's first actions as Prime Minister had been to freeze the troop numbers in Vietnam. Since then, in May 1968 he had made the obligatory trip to the White House, and had turned in a performance that bemused his US hosts and the Australian press corps. In one media conference he displayed a fundamental ignorance of the ANZUS treaty. *The Australian Financial Review* editorialised:

> It is difficult to decide … whether Gorton is a very raw tourist casually tossing thoughts this way and that from the top of his head, or whether he is the Prime Minister of a troubled nation delineating policies for the future. Either way he comes perilously close to making an ass of himself. If he is to be taken seriously … he is setting in train drastic alterations to the fundamental polices that guide the Australian nation. He has chosen to inform his nation and its friends of these changes from the capital of a friendly but nonetheless foreign power.[14]

In October 1968, the Americans decided to pause the bombing of North Vietnam in an attempt to advance peace negotiations. As usual, they did not bother to tell Australia about this beforehand. Gorton received notification the day after the pause began. Amid all of this, Fraser was painfully aware that there were still soldiers in Vietnam in the muddy, humid hole that was Nui Dat, risking and sometimes losing their lives and health in the struggle to do their duty, while the politicians sent them mixed messages. 'It was hard to bear the thought', he remembers.

* * *

Sometimes the responsibilities of the education portfolio were a welcome distraction. He had a characteristically idealistic view of what his job was about. In a speech in May 1969, he said:

> The ability to pass on knowledge and wisdom is the distinctive characteristic of humanity. If a society fails in that critical function, we speak of its sinking into the Dark Ages. When that function revives, we speak of the Renaissance … To be a good teacher is something more than to have successfully undergone a course in university or a course of training. It is to possess a quality of character and an intellectual skill which are essential for the maintenance and improvement of our civilisation.[15]

But education, he said in other speeches, had to be about more than the needs of industry and society. And, despite the space race and the 1960s' emphasis on technological marvels, it had to be about more than science.

> We have heard a great deal in recent years about the material wealth of our people. But there is more to life than that. However difficult the prospect, we need to bend our efforts to seek peace between nations ... Some may say there will always be wars because of the nature of man. If I ever come to accept that view I would walk right out of politics.

There had been huge advances in science, but they were a mixed blessing. Science had unleashed nuclear power, which could 'be used to the benefit of every person on earth or could destroy the earth'. In the social sciences, in understanding the problems of human relationships, 'We are not much advanced on where we were decades ago'. Once again, Fraser returned to his hero, John Maynard Keynes, whose economic insights he described as

> perhaps the only discovery in the social sciences that ranks with the great discoveries in the physical and biological fields ... The enormously difficult and complex problems of human relationships present the greatest challenge confronting the world. How to solve it has bedevilled well-meaning men throughout the centuries. Is it too much to aspire to end conflict within communities or between them? This is not only a task for politicians; it is a task for communities, for the advanced thinkers in the universities and for the people.[16]

Two issues dominated Fraser's brief first period as Minister for Education and Science: state aid for independent schools and the growth of tertiary education, in particular the proper role for colleges of advanced education as opposed to universities. Both issues are a reminder of how wrong it is to think of political issues as being firmly and forever defined in terms of left-wing and right-wing. Before the Labor Party split, it had been the left of politics, with its strong Catholic base, that had favoured state aid for non-government schools. By the time Fraser took up the portfolio, this had changed. The Democratic Labor Party was backing the Liberals, and so it became the party favouring state aid. Labor had been opposed, but one of the issues on which Whitlam had rebuilt the party was reversing this policy. When Fraser introduced comprehensive state aid, the main difference between the parties, and the main area of controversy, was the way in which the aid was distributed—across the board, or on the basis of need.

In our own time, education is understood to be one of the top three issues in the public's mind when it votes in federal elections, but in Fraser's day education had until recently been seen as exclusively a state responsibility. Fraser took over the education portfolio at a time when the Commonwealth's role was fast expanding. One of the biggest achievements of the Menzies era had been the expansion of universities: in 1958 there had been only 100 tertiary education graduates for every 100000 people in the Australian population; in 1968 the figure was up to 200 graduates, and was still expanding. A succession of government inquiries through the 1950s and 1960s had led first to the creation of the Universities Commission and then to the establishment of colleges of advanced education. Fraser presided over the consolidation and expansion of this system. He supported the idea of distinct difference between universities and colleges of advanced education. Human beings had one of two different kinds of mind, he said: they were either practically minded or analytically minded. Universities should serve the analytical mind; colleges of advanced education should offer instruction to those who were practically minded, as well as offering university graduates training that might better fit them for jobs.[17]

In the schools, there was a drift of students from the independent and church-run institutions into the state system. In the years before Fraser's appointment, the Commonwealth had begun to make grants to allow non-government schools to establish and improve science labs. Fraser promised that he would act on evidence of a 'crisis' in independent education. Public opinion was behind him: Gallup opinion polls found that two-thirds of Australians favoured state aid for church and other independent schools. What Fraser did was nevertheless controversial. In August 1969 he announced that, rather than granting aid to independent schools on the basis of need, he would distribute the money across the board, with the grants being determined purely by the number of students. The wealthiest schools would receive the same amount per student as the poorest. In his public speeches, Fraser justified both state aid in general and his specific approach.

> We believe it is the democratic right of persons to be allowed to establish independent schools such as we have in Australia. We do not believe in government monopoly ... We categorically reject the argument that because a significant number of citizens choose to seek a form of education for their children which they preferred to the state system and are prepared to make financial sacrifices, those citizens cannot expect any help from the state even though they are easing its financial and physical burden.

He argued that distributing the money on the basis of a means test would discourage schools that were trying to help themselves, and provide an incentive to reduce fees in the hope of receiving more grants. As for distributing funds to those schools that were underperforming academically: 'To deny a school assistance on the grounds that it was already producing good academic results would be to penalise excellence'.[18]

Fraser had an even stronger reason for not giving aid on the basis of need, which he kept to himself. It was to do with the sectarianism that had overshadowed his childhood, and a fear that he might be responsible for reigniting it. 'It was still alive. I could see it in cabinet. To be a Catholic and a Liberal in those days was close to unheard of.' He believed that the hatred that Billy Hughes, the World War I Prime Minister, had fanned by allowing the conscription referendum to be about anti-Catholic sectarianism still lay beneath the surface of Australian life. If federal government aid to schools was distributed on the basis of need, Catholic schools would be the overwhelming beneficiaries. Fraser feared this result, and his fears were reinforced by the vehement campaign conducted by those opposed to state aid. In particular there was the group Defence of Government Schools, or DOGS, which went on to run seventeen candidates in the 1969 federal election, and which was still campaigning hard into the early 1970s, when Fraser had his second stint as Education Minister. DOGS campaigns included illegal occupations of Catholic schools by picnickers who were encouraged to swim in the pools and use the facilities 'provided by church money which state aid freed up'.

DOGS campaign material is filed in Fraser's office, and some of it is marked heavily in his characteristic hand, including paragraphs making the point that the constitution prohibited Commonwealth assistance to religion, and saying that, even under the Fraser formula, over 80 per cent of the schools receiving increased aid were 'separatist and sectarian' Catholic schools. 'The bulk of state aid undeniably goes to support the indoctrinating tools of this one church', said one leaflet.[19] Fraser saw this as confirmation of his fears. He had no problem with the principle of state aid: he saw it as a matter of giving parents choice—the essence of liberalism. Simple justice would have suggested a distribution of money on the basis of need, but Fraser thinks that if this had been done, there would have been violence. He says today, 'They weren't dead, those old hatreds. They really weren't. In today's terms people don't understand how powerful it was back then. I wasn't going to do anything that would help that. I remembered Billy Hughes's effect on my father and his generation. I wasn't going to do it. I wasn't going to have that as the legacy of my time in the portfolio. That was that'.

As Minister for Science, Fraser was called upon to support the organisation he had had a hand in founding—the Australian Conservation Foundation—and to increase the Commonwealth's role in environmental management. The foundation was struggling, and close to collapse. In October 1968 its Chairman, former Liberal Attorney-General Garfield Barwick, wrote to Fraser as Minister for Science asking for a federal grant to help it to maintain a secretariat. Why, Fraser asked in reply, had the foundation not made use of its tax deductable status, which Fraser had organised in the first place, to raise more funds? Barwick acknowledged that this had not been done, but told Fraser that without full-time staff the foundation would fold.[20] Simultaneously, Fraser was being pressed by the senior scientists at the CSIRO for the Commonwealth to take a more active part in conservation, and in particular in issues such as species preservation and collaboration over the Great Barrier Reef and the Australian Alps.[21] Fraser organised a grant to the Australian Conservation Foundation, and approached Peter Nixon, then Minister for the Interior, suggesting that officers of their departments meet regularly with CSIRO scientists on conservation issues. He was responsible, during his time in the portfolio, for initiating the establishment of the Australian Institute of Marine Science.

On 3 May 1969, Fraser spoke at a symposium organised by the Australian Conservation Foundation using government money. The topic was the future of the Great Barrier Reef, a sensitive issue at the time, with the Queensland government planning to allow drilling for oil. Fraser waded in to the controversy in uncompromising terms. 'When man settles a new area, when he pushes down timber and destroys the native vegetation, he sometimes does not realise the damage that can be done to fauna and flora that, as a result of his actions, could well disappear.' Because Australia was relatively sparsely populated, the impact of settlement had been largely hidden. But now the Commonwealth felt that a national approach was needed, he said. Consultations had begun between federal and state ministers. 'Conservation of the natural resources of this earth is emerging as one of the basic challenges to mankind', he said. And, on the Great Barrier Reef:

> Let me state the Commonwealth view in what I hope will be regarded as unequivocal terms. We regard the reef as a priceless asset. We believe we have an obligation to preserve it so that it may survive for all time as one of the great wonders of the world. In so far as the Commonwealth has the power, it will use this power to prevent the reef's being despoiled.[22]

As Fraser struggled with the controversy over state aid and pushed the cause of conservation, he feared that the government was in danger of falling apart or taking the country off the rails. In the budget talks of 1969, Hasluck came close to resigning over the way in which his foreign aid budget was treated. 'He walked out of the discussion', Fraser remembers. Then, shortly afterwards, Fraser went into the anteroom of the cabinet room and to his surprise saw Gorton and Hasluck clearly celebrating together. He was puzzled. 'There was a rapport and an understanding between Gorton and Hasluck that had never been there before.' Sometime afterwards, Gorton announced that Hasluck would be appointed as the next Governor-General.

Before this happened, Fraser had hoped that Hasluck would replace Gorton. Now that possibility was gone, and, looking at his cabinet colleagues, Fraser could see nobody, other than himself, with the capacity to stand up to the Prime Minister. Tamie remembers long gloomy talks far into the night, while the children slept. It is a measure of Fraser's experience of the Gorton prime ministership that at this point—just over a year since Gorton had promoted him to cabinet—he made a private resolution. In the notes on Gorton kept in his filing cabinet, Fraser has written:

> I despaired for the good government of Australia. Hasluck was a man of integrity and courage who was prepared to speak his mind, qualities the government would be much in need of. I determined that if for any reason my authority

> were to be reduced or my position challenged in a way that could remove me from cabinet, then I would have to do my utmost to see that the PM accompanied me. The PM's judgement was so faulty, his performance so erratic, that his position as Prime Minister could only be tolerated while there was someone in the cabinet prepared to put his own reputation and career on the line in challenging Gorton if the need arose.

Following Hasluck's departure from cabinet and just two months before the federal election due in October 1969, the Minister for Defence, Allen Fairhall, caused a stir by announcing his own retirement. The reason he gave was ill health, but to Fraser and other cabinet ministers it was clear that his decision was based in part on the frustration of failing to persuade Gorton to commit either to forward defence or to a coherent alternative policy. Fairhall had been another potential candidate for Prime Minister when Holt disappeared, but he had declined to nominate. He might have won. Following Fairhall's departure, *The Sydney Morning Herald* opined that the front bench was now 'bantam weight'.[23] Privately, Fraser agreed. But his own star was rising: in August 1969 the Melbourne *Herald* published an article that began:

> It is an embarrassing thing for Malcolm Fraser when he walks through the lobbies of Parliament House these days. There are whispers and knowing looks as he goes by. What people are saying, or thinking, is: 'There goes a future Prime Minister'. He is only thirty-nine ... but he has achieved more in politics and learned more than many men twenty years older.[24]

Fraser was being tipped as the next Minister for Defence. The same article quotes him as saying that he didn't want the Prime Minister's position, because it was 'one hell of a job'. He was described as 'still very much a Gorton man', and a man with few friends, but no enemies.

* * *

The October 1969 election was a disaster for the Liberals and a personal disaster for Gorton. Although Labor lost, it won the majority of the two party preferred vote. The government majority in the House of Representatives was reduced from forty to seven, and the swing to Labor was 7.1 per cent, which at the time was the highest recorded swing to the party in the postwar period. It was clear that unless something changed the Liberals would lose government when the next election was called; Whitlam would be Prime Minister. It was beginning to feel inevitable, particularly since the divisions within the Liberal Party between those who backed Gorton and those who despaired of him were increasingly bitter.

Gorton was vulnerable. He had made plenty of enemies by now, not only in cabinet but also among Liberal state premiers, who resented his view that Australia should be regarded not so much as a collection of states but as a centrally governed whole. David Fairbairn, the Minister for National Development, publically criticised Gorton's style and cavalier attitude, refused to serve under him and challenged for the leadership. Three days after the election, Fraser issued a statement denying that he was contemplating a challenge. Gorton was re-elected with Fraser's support; Fraser could simply see no alternative. Fraser's reserve becomes evident when we consider that, at this stage, most people still thought of him as a Gorton supporter. Only Tamie knew his true mind. Fraser was a supporter of states' rights and suspicious of centralised power. The issue went to the heart of his political philosophy. He says today, 'How do you protect liberty? How do you stop anyone from having too much power? In America they have the Bill of Rights. Here we have a system that compels consultation, with the state government and the states' representatives in the Senate'.

On 10 November 1969, Fraser made a speech which could have been taken as dissent from Gorton's attitude. The viability of state governments, Fraser said, was

> at the root of the philosophy of the government which I support ... I do not want to see all political and financial power in Canberra. I believe that the best guarantor of the perpetual liberty of the Australian people is maintenance of the sensible division of power between the Commonwealth of Australia and the states. This could sometimes mean that some matters might be pursued a little more slowly, perhaps even less efficiently than would otherwise be the case ... Even if that were so, it would be but a small price to pay for the constitutional arrangements that provide the best future guarantee of Australian liberty. This view goes to the very depths of our liberal philosophy. It is a view that has continuing validity.[25]

Gorton apparently did not have ears attuned to hear the implied criticism. The next day, in reward for his apparent support of Gorton, Fraser was promoted to Minister for Defence. It was 11 November 1969—the second, but not the last, time that Remembrance Day was to be significant in Fraser's political career.

By the end of his time as Minister for Defence it would no longer be true that Fraser had few friends but no enemies. He would still have few friends, but there would be a substantial number of members of his own party determined to bury his political career.

7

Victory and Withdrawal

Malcolm Fraser sees two threads running through his time as Minister for Defence. To him they stand out against the personalities and the politics and the messy, angry crisis at the end. They represent the lessons to be learned. The first thread, of which the Vietnam War was part, was to do with Australia's place in the world, its foreign policy and in particular the US alliance. The bitterness of having to follow in America's wake with no independent power over the course of the conflict convinced Fraser that Australia should never again take part in a war alongside the United States, or any other ally, unless 'we have access to the centre of power, unless we are involved in the inner councils that discuss strategy'. The second thread was what led Fraser to risk his political career in a conflict with his Prime Minister. It was this that caused John Gorton's downfall. To Fraser this thread was about good government, proper process and the use and abuse of power. Fraser thinks his actions in resigning from the Gorton ministry have never been properly understood.

Fraser's view of the two threads is born of contemplation. The themes were not always clear at the time; things were messier. He says, 'People look back at the Vietnam War and think that it looks obvious how things would turn out. But it wasn't obvious. Politics as it is lived is different from history: you have principles; you try to put them into action; you get information; you make decisions. There are always a hundred things happening at once. Time passes, and people look back and say, "This is what it was about. You should have done this". We didn't have the luxury of historians'.

Tamie remembers Fraser's time as Minister for Defence as one of the most difficult of their life together, 'or at least the most tiring'. For much of it, she moved in a fog of fatigue supporting a husband burdened with great responsibility. She was busy too: they now had four children. The eldest two were at boarding school, but Phoebe, at four and a half, was still at home, and Hugh was shuttling between two primary schools—one in Canberra, one in Nareen. The time was approaching when Fraser and Tamie would give up the attempt to move the family life from Canberra to Nareen and back again several times a year: in the future, Fraser would have to 'batch' when parliament was sitting. He became a lonelier man, the times with family rarer and more precious, but when he was Defence Minister they were still trying to make having two homes work. Tamie remembers, 'Things would happen in Vietnam and the generals would come in at two o'clock in the morning, and they'd be there until four'. She would get up and make them coffee. Two hours or less after they left, she would have to get up again because the children were awake. Often, Fraser would have stayed up through the night reading through the boxes and boxes of papers, scoring the margins with his characteristic marks and impatient notes. Always, he wanted more and better information about what was going on in Phuoc Tuy province, where the Australian troops were stationed. In the background was the knowledge that most Australians had turned against the government, and the policy on Vietnam in particular. 'It was a bad time', Tamie says.

* * *

It is hard to believe that Australia in late 1969 and early 1970, when Fraser resumed his involvement with the Vietnam War as Minister for Defence, was the same country which, just three years before, had delivered Prime Minister Harold Holt a landslide victory largely because of the popularity of the war. The students, church leaders and activists who, during Fraser's time as Minister for Army, had been a vocal minority were now leading majority opinion. Until 1968 most Australians supported the fighting in Vietnam, but by November 1969, when Fraser became Minister for Defence, 51 per cent wanted the troops brought home.[1] The first moratorium marches were being planned.

The history that is written not with facts but with feel-good ethos credits the Whitlam government with extracting Australia from the Vietnam War. It is true that Gough Whitlam ended conscription and released the draft dodgers, but the retreat had already happened—led by the United States, with Australia carried along in the slipstream, never consulted but forced to follow. When President Nixon was elected, in January 1969, he had promised to bring 'peace with honour'. By the middle of that year, he had announced that 25000 US troops would be withdrawn immediately, and that there were plans to withdraw another 50000. Australia was not consulted before this decision was made. The withdrawals continued, so that by the beginning of 1972 the ground war was almost exclusively the responsibility of the South Vietnamese. In December 1969, just after Fraser became Minister for Defence, Gorton assured voters that any further reductions in allied forces would include Australian troops. In April the following year, he announced that one of Australia's three battalions would not be replaced when its tour of duty was over. By the end of 1971, a full year before Whitlam came to power, all but a handful of the Australian troops had come home.

Nixon had proclaimed what became known as the Guam doctrine, signalling that much of what Australia had most feared was coming true. The United States was retreating into isolationism; like Europe, it would depart from the region. The United States would now expect its allies to take care of their own military defence: it would help only those prepared to help themselves.[2] Fraser remembers: 'We had no impact at all on American strategy or policy. We had no information. The students who were demonstrating on the campuses of American universities had more influence over the conduct of the war than did the Australian Government'.

The US policy was now 'Vietnamisation' of the war. The emphasis was on training and encouraging the South Vietnamese to defend themselves, so that the United States could extricate itself. Fraser thought it a policy formulated in good faith and a legitimate strategy, but it was soon clear that Vietnamisation was never going to work. The South Vietnamese Government was a puppet regime, hopelessly infiltrated by the Vietcong, corrupt and without popular support. If the Americans left, it would be only a matter of time before North Vietnam was victorious. From Fraser's point of view, the South Vietnamese who had fought communism were being betrayed, but the Australians could hardly stay once the United States had gone. Australia was powerless, and the United States was careless of its allies. 'The preparations for betrayal were all there. The Americans wanted to proclaim victory ... Well, I think it was obvious they would proclaim victory and withdraw. And everyone in America was so utterly fed up with it they were not prepared to question it. If they were going to get out, then they would get out. That was what they wanted. That was what the message. Out.'

Fraser had the task of trying to recalibrate Australia's defence policy to meet both the realities of what the United States was doing and his own understanding of what was needed and what was right. 'Right up until my resignation, I was probably hoping for a good outcome from Vietnam, while realising that it was getting very unlikely.'

When peace talks began between the Americans and the North Vietnamese, Australia was not consulted. When the talks broke down and bombing was resumed against the North Vietnamese, Australia was not consulted. Finally, in January 1973, after the election of the Whitlam government, a ceasefire was signed in Paris and the Governor-General Paul Hasluck announced an end to hostilities in

Vietnam by Australian forces; but the truth was that Whitlam had no more power over the making of peace than Holt, Gorton or McMahon had had over the making of war.

Fraser had always thought himself an activist and a progressive. As Minister for Education he had welcomed the new passion and activism among young people—subject to limits. In his own thoughts, he compared the student activists opposing the war with himself when he began at Oxford, and with his own emergent idealism. He had told a seminar of university governing bodies in 1969 that they should embrace student activism while maintaining discipline:

> Young people of this age are no longer prepared to accept blindly the rules and dogmas of earlier generations. They question and probe; they have an idealism that is to be applauded; they want to know the reason and they want to understand. They are more adult and more mature than were their counterparts a few years ago.[3]

Now, as minister presiding over an unpopular war, he struggled with the implications of young people's activism. The Labor opposition was encouraging young people to break the law and not register for the draft. Notes that Fraser kept on the moratorium marches read: 'Logic of statements by Whitlam, Cairns. That they want enemy to win. That they want aggression to succeed. Logic of moratorium equals communist win'.[4]

As usual it was the electors of Wannon who were given the most intimate glimpse into Fraser's wrestling with his political ideals. He told them in his weekly radio addresses that the comments by Gough Whitlam, Jim Cairns and other Labor members urging young men not to register were tantamount to treason. He noted that moratorium marchers in Adelaide had carried a banner with the words 'Victory to the Vietcong'. Could this really be happening while young Australians were still overseas, engaged in battle with a ruthless enemy? Dissent was not wrong, Fraser said; it was an inherent and necessary part of democracy, but, 'The concern is caused by the nature of dissent, and the methods and techniques that it advocates and uses'. People who wanted change should work through the established political processes. Violence was unacceptable, and there had already been violent demonstrations. And where, he asked, were the demonstrations against Vietnamese aggression in Cambodia? Where were the marchers decrying the North Vietnamese slaughter of children in orphanages? It seemed that the demonstrators believed that everything Australia and the United States did must be wrong, and nothing that the North Vietnamese did could be other than right.[5]

What was the balance, he asked, between rights and responsibilities? Between duty to country and duty to one's own sense of conscience? This was when he first began to use the words 'life wasn't meant to be easy'—not in the speech that later made the phrase famous, but in a newspaper profile of him published just after he became Defence Minister. He was speaking about himself, his sense of duty and his decision to enter politics. 'Growing up and taking over the property, which is what I like doing more than anything else, just seemed to make life too easy—and I don't think life is really meant to be easy.' The article described Fraser as the outstanding ministerial talent in the party. He was 'tall, modest, handsome, with wavy brown hair and a look of natural confidence and authority ... Authority comes naturally to him, and he has the gifts to back it up'. The article noted that Fraser was known to be close to Robert Menzies, calling on the old man in his Melbourne home.[6]

By now it was clear to most that Fraser would one day be a candidate for the leadership. It seemed to outsiders that his progression might be untroubled. To Fraser, though, it was becoming apparent that the price of a smooth accession to power might be too high. Gorton expected more than normal loyalty from his minister; he expected a blank cheque. Fraser was not the man to give it to him.

The issue that first brought them into open conflict was states' rights. As Fraser settled in as Defence Minister, Gorton was pushing through new federal Seas and Submerged Lands legislation. The constitution gave the Commonwealth powers over waters beyond the territorial limit, and states had powers within it. Both Menzies and Holt had presided over a benign federalism. The need to find and drill for oil on the continental shelf and in the Bass Strait oil field had been dealt with by negotiation. Gorton's approach would change that. The new laws would give the Commonwealth power up to the high-water mark. Gorton wanted his way, and his insistence had made him enemies, including premiers Sir Henry Bolte in Victoria and Robert Askin in New South Wales. Fraser had been talking to them, and to other party members. Gorton had heard about it and was seriously displeased. On 19 May 1970 the two men met in Gorton's office. Gorton demanded Fraser's support. The offshore legislation, he said, was a matter of his own power and prerogative. He didn't intend to consult cabinet: ministers should simply back him on the issue, and Fraser should give unquestioning support. If he did, then there would be a reward. Fraser remembers, 'He told me he only wanted three or four years as leader, and if only he and I stuck together, we could do anything, and I would be his successor'.

Fraser went to bed deeply troubled. The next day, he sat down to draft a letter to Gorton. He recounted the conversation and Gorton's demand of unquestioning support, then said:

> That you made such a request indicates a deficiency on your part, not mine … I indicated as I had on an earlier occasion that no man should demand or seek to demand loyalty irrespective of the issue and of his own actions, that loyalty is a quality attracted by example and not by demand, that no man irrespective of time, of issue or of circumstance could affirm absolute loyalty and remain master of himself. Thus I had to answer last night: 'It depends on the issue; it depends on what you do'. You made it clear that this was not good enough. Thus we came to our present relationship. There is an issue that you believe touches in particular on your view of your own prerogative and power. I have sought to sway you from an

> attitude that I believed on judgement would not sustain the unity of the party. You consequently regard my loyalty as deficient.[7]

Now, if not before, the Gorton–Fraser special relationship was over.

In the meantime, Fraser had been getting to grips with defence. Immediately he had been given the job, in November 1969, he had begun preparations for a ministerial statement. He told the head of the department, Henry Bland, that he wanted to deliver this by March. Much of the preparation had already been done. The direction in which the Department of Defence needed to move was clear, determined by inquiries and reviews over the previous few years. Once little more than a coordinator of the service ministries, the department was becoming more powerful and important in its own right, with its own intelligence assessment capability and its own strategic advisers. Successive ministers had initiated reforms, and there was widespread agreement that the constant warring between the services, each keen to protect its own budget and prestige, needed to end. This was a long-term program, continued under successive governments. Eventually—after Fraser's time—the cumbersome arrangement of each service having its own minister ended, but when Fraser took up the post a great deal remained to be done, and there was inevitable resistance and friction as the services were called on to give up their treasured autonomy. Fraser attacked the problems with characteristic determination, making enemies as he went.

Fraser put his own mark on the ministerial statement, and in the process cemented his enmity with Billy McMahon, who was now Minister for External Affairs. Normally, defence statements were full of detail on budgets and the amount of hardware needed, without any insight into where and how that hardware and manpower might be used. Fraser's speech began by canvassing relations with Indonesia, China and Japan and with a discussion of the United States' 're-appraisal' of its role in South-East Asia. McMahon was furious when he read the draft. The first half of the speech was all about foreign affairs! Fraser was trespassing on McMahon's turf. On

6 March 1970 the two men had a fierce confrontation in Fraser's office, which was alarming enough for Fraser to make careful notes about it immediately afterwards. They still sit in his filing cabinet. McMahon insisted that Fraser cut out the first section of his speech. If he refused, then McMahon would let the party and the press know that Fraser was 'overstepping the line'. Fraser told McMahon he would not give in to threats, and that, particularly in the wake of the Guam doctrine, it would be a nonsense to talk about defence without talking about the trends and changes in the world.[8] Having been threatened, Fraser was in no mood to seek compromise. He referred the matter to Gorton, and Gorton backed Fraser. Four days later Fraser rose in parliament and made one of the boldest and longest speeches of his career to that point.

'We are entering a new era', he said. In the newly independent nations to the north, the first post-colonial generation had emerged. Many nations were undergoing transition and reappraisal. The United States had in the past taken up the main burden of defence of the free world, but the Guam doctrine was 'full of meaning' for Australia. US assistance would be more readily forthcoming to those countries that helped themselves, meaning that insurgency situations would have to be contained—or, better still, prevented from developing—without US combat manpower. Fraser spelled out a new threat: Russia had moved into the Indian Ocean. 'Australia cannot confront the Soviet Union, but we must take account of her Indian Ocean activities in our defence policies and planning.' Two approaches were available to Australia: isolationism and engagement. He rejected the first.

> How long could we stand aloof in armed—or unarmed—detachment from our environment? One can only guess—probably a decade, perhaps a generation … For you do not make South-East Asia or the Indian Ocean disappear by turning your back on them … We reject the concept of detachment. We accept the risks and opportunities of involvement.

Fraser argued for a flexible, well-equipped defence force that could be deployed within the region as well as directly in defence of Australia. He went on to outline the detail, which formed the agenda for his remaining time in defence.[9] The language he used in parliament was moderate, but the plans were, in a conservative organisation like the armed forces, destined to annoy vested interests and tread on the toes of the service ministers—Jim Killen for navy, Andrew Peacock for army and Senator Tom Drake-Brockman for the air force.

Fraser had by now developed a style that remains with him to this day and that even strong people can find disconcerting. He had become a bruiser of egos. Fraser had never entirely lost his shyness, though he had found ways of dealing with it. He almost entirely lacked small talk and the ability to jolly people along. He rarely gave praise for good performance, and often people who had worked long and hard had no idea whether he appreciated their efforts or not. His manner when dealing with work-related matters was abrupt: he just wanted to get the job done. His activism meant that he had a questioning style that could feel like interrogation, and he could be extraordinarily impatient at delay or at failures to provide him with complete and accurate information. He could be kind, and generous, but he never pandered to people's vanity. The capacity to bruise people's sense of self is one of the themes of his career. Tamie says that her husband often won't realise that he has been rude and abrupt, so fierce is his focus on the work at hand. If she points it out to him, he will go out of his way to try to fix it—but he isn't necessarily good at doing that.

What many people miss about Fraser is that he likes—even needs—to be argued with. Tamie says, 'Arguing is how he works out his own ideas. If you won't argue with him, then sometimes he won't act, because he's not absolutely sure that he's right'. But in argument he can be aggressive and unfair. He can take people to the limit—or past the limit—of their tolerance. Not many people find it easy to stand up to Fraser when he is seized with the need to act, or with the full passion of an idea. But as Minister for Defence, he found a man prepared to take him on toe to toe: the new Secretary of Defence Arthur Tange. Today, Fraser says of Tange: 'He was one of the best public servants Australia has ever had'.

When the existing Secretary for Defence, Henry Bland, had announced that he wanted to retire, he presented Fraser with a list of possible replacements. Fraser rejected them all, although he knew they were good public servants. He told Bland that he wanted someone who would argue with him. 'I express my point of view, and when I do it strongly, which I am inclined to do, they'll just accept it. I've got to have somebody who will argue; otherwise, we won't get to the right answers.'[10]

Bland replied, 'You didn't seem to enjoy the arguments you had with me'.

'I might not have enjoyed them, but they are necessary.'

Bland went away and returned with a sheet that had only one name on it. Arthur Tange.

In some ways Tange and Fraser were similar: neither believed in holding a position merely for the sake of it; both were activists. Tange was High Commissioner to India, but before that had been Secretary of the Department of External Affairs. As a result he had his own strong ideas about what needed to be done in defence. Tange and Fraser shared a vision of a defence department with real clout, able to get the armed forces working as one with a coordinated administration and joint chiefs of staff.

Tange began work in March 1970. Eleven weeks later—the day before Fraser's fortieth birthday—he wrote Fraser a blistering ten-page minute stamped 'Personal' and headlined 'State of Departmental Organisation. Ministerial Demands on the Department'. It was a royal ticking-off.

> I have observed the frequency with which, in extensive conversations with me and other senior officers, you have expressed a sense of urgency about a large number of matters and that you wish to see them brought to

> fruition. I am convinced that intensive detailed ministerial supervision and requests for explanations and reports, while doubtless seeking to satisfy the requirements that you believe you have, aggravate the delay by distracting senior officers from substantive work. Indeed this is a matter of fact and not of opinion. It is a matter of fact and not a matter of ministerial authority.[11]

This was the first time anyone had taken Fraser on about his style. As Army Minister, he had forced the department to respond properly and promptly to complaints. In education, there had been conflicts as Fraser ordered a blistering pace. The archives are full of correspondence in which Fraser demanded more information and to know why things were taking so long. He had usually got his way. Now Tange wrote: 'I do not need ministerial help to extract hard work from my officers'. Tange went on to tell Fraser a 'plain truth': that the department was not equipped to do all the things that Fraser had promised in his ministerial statement on 10 March. Fraser should have been told this. The department was 'close to collapse under the weight of the demands made upon it'. Some of what Fraser had said would be done would have to be delayed or put on hold.

Fraser went through this memorandum with his characteristic method, underlining Tange's central points and writing questions in the margin. Beside the comment about some demands being put aside, he wrote 'What?' This was the beginning of a number of terse exchanges.

On 10 September 1970, Tange sent Fraser another strongly worded memorandum about Fraser's plans to meet chiefs of staff and other staff rather than going through Tange as head of department. Fraser says today that Tange was used to ministers who were reactive. Fraser believed that while he wanted frank advice, if there were matters he wanted addressed in that advice it was appropriate for him to talk to the public servants concerned to make sure they were canvassed, and all the options and arguments presented. 'Tange was busy. It was silly for everything to go through him. I think in time he understood my approach.' This, too, was about proper process, but, unlike Tange, Fraser did not think proper process demanded ministers who could react only to what the public service dished up. He was stung into the clearest statement he had ever made of how he saw his job, writing to Tange: 'Perhaps I need to explain the approach I adopt to my responsibilities as minister. I think you recognise I am not prepared to wait to see what a particular departmental machine throws on my desk and then react to it'. Fraser left Tange in no doubt that he would continue to delve into the services, without necessarily going through either Tange or the service ministers but, says Fraser, 'The head of department would always know what was going on'.

The defence portfolio, Fraser told Tange, was unlike any other because it was so concerned with personnel. One of the main problems was an inability to attract people to the armed forces. This issue was a pressing concern throughout Fraser's time in the ministry. It was his attempt to address it, and set proper pay and conditions for the armed services, that brought him into contact with the man who would later appoint him Prime Minister—Sir John Kerr.

More stiff correspondence followed between Fraser and Tange, but by the end of the month, the men had come to an understanding. On 21 September, Fraser sent a handwritten note to Tange. 'Dear Sir Arthur, Before writing formal notes I ask you to come over and discuss the matter that apparently disturbs you. It might be best to choose an hour when we can put a whisky in our hands.' They did so, had it out, and for the rest of Fraser's term as minister became one of the most formidable teams the Australian Department of Defence had ever known. They achieved a remarkable amount in a short period of time. Tange continued the work after Fraser's departure, and brought it to fruition under both the Whitlam and the Fraser governments. But Tange and Fraser never stopped arguing. Fraser says, 'He was strong-minded. If he thought I was making a wrong decision then he would say so. So that made him a very comforting person to have around'. Fraser keeps his correspondence with Tange in his personal filing cabinet; he is clearly fond of it.

Tange later credited Fraser with overcoming entrenched resistance to reform in the armed services. Even though the reform agenda took many years longer than Fraser would have liked, Tange rated him as the best Defence Minister he had seen during his career. As for Fraser's personal style, Tange said, 'He had opinions about most things and was sometimes impetuous in forming them. He expected his advisers to disagree with him and some found his personality hard to endure. He was not always considerate enough to recognise the pressures felt by some'.[12] Elsewhere, he commented:

> It took a man with some breadth of vision, and energy, and some other characteristics I've no doubt led to him becoming Prime Minister, to say 'This is not good enough'. He began a process of interrogation of activities by the armed services of the kind to which years of much more lethargic and more timid examination and supervision had left them unaccustomed.[13]

Tange clearly understood Fraser: 'While always determined to get his own way, his insistence on consulting colleagues when Prime Minister later has been commended by some as desirable practice. On my observation of him in defence, I incline to the view that he needed the reassurance of support before acting'.[14] This is almost exactly what Tamie says: Fraser wants ideas to be tested through argument. He *needs* argument, but not many are strong enough to stand up to him.

Fraser and Tange were giving large amounts of time to the Five Power Defence Arrangements between the United Kingdom, Malaysia, Singapore, New Zealand and Australia. The idea was to keep Britain involved in the region, however weakly, as well as strengthening the links between the non-communist South-East Asian nations. Negotiations had begun before Fraser was minister, and he was determined to bring them to a good conclusion—despite Gorton's seeming opposition to overseas entanglements. Fraser remembers, 'Gorton was against the Five Power Arrangements. I wasn't at all sure that he understood what we were trying to achieve'.

In 1970 a final conference was being planned to try to clear away the remaining obstacles to the agreement. Fraser was so worried about what Gorton might say or do that he made use of his personal friendship with the British Secretary of Defence, Peter Carrington, whom he had come to know when he was British High Commissioner in Canberra. 'I said to Peter, "I don't care where you have this conference but I want it as far away from Canberra, Australia, as you can possibly manage". Well, you see, I was frightened that Gorton would wreck it ... He didn't believe in forward defence or forward defence arrangements. It would have been very easy to make a speech that would have had people going away saying, "This is a waste of time". Peter said, "Yes, Malcolm, I quite understand". He was good. You never had to explain the detail to him. He got it.' The conference took place in Singapore, and the Five Power Defence Arrangements were confirmed shortly after Fraser left the ministry.

In the Arrangements, Fraser was dealing with the philosophy and rationale for alliance—the need for a country like Australia to bind itself to bigger nations, to act in concord with its neighbours, yet also to retain an independent foreign policy. Fraser wanted Australia to use its weight strategically, seeking to gain influence where it could. He had long since ceased to be an idealist about US foreign policy. He knew, now, that the United States was, to say the least, 'careless of its allies'. This was the background to one of the toughest tasks he took on during his time as Minister for Defence: the renegotiation of the contract under which Australia was buying F-111 fighter planes from the United States. If the United States was a friend to Australia, what could be expected of that friendship? The answer, it seemed, was very little.

The F-111 purchase had become a running sore for the Australian Government. It had been announced by Menzies in 1963, with delivery expected in 1967. Australia needed a replacement for its obsolete Canberra aircraft. Technical and military advisers had searched the world for a suitable strike reconnaissance aircraft, and hit on the TFX (Tactical Fighter Experimental), later to become the F-111, being developed in the United States. It was a highly experimental aircraft, groundbreaking and unique.

The first plane was ready for delivery to Australia in 1968, but by then a great deal had changed. First, Indonesia was no longer seen as an imminent threat. Second, fatigue tests on the wing box had revealed concerns about the plane's useful life. Finally, the main problem was that there were doubts about whether the plane would meet Australia's needs. Previously, it had been assumed that if an aircraft or other piece of defence hardware was good enough for the US or British armed forces it would be good enough for Australia. But, Fraser says, 'With the F-111 we learned that protection was not adequate'. The Americans were planning to use mid-air refuelling, but Australia needed a long-range aircraft that could reach targets without being refuelled. The Americans were planning for the F-111 to carry nuclear weapons; the Australians had no such intentions, and therefore needed a larger carrying capacity for heavier conventional weapons. Gorton had tabled documents on the purchase in 1968 showing that Australia was committed to an uncomfortably open agreement, obliged to take delivery of the aircraft when they had been inspected and certified by the US airforce—whether or not they met Australia's quite different operational requirements. Yet the Americans would not cut their Australian ally any slack or take into account Australia's needs.

In July 1969, before Fraser became Minister for Defence, the secretary of the department, Henry Bland, had visited the United States to try to win some concessions. He had got nowhere. Bland reported that there was no assurance that the aircraft would meet the promised performance, and no willingness from the United States to allow Australia to cancel the order if the aircraft was not fit for Australian needs. 'We received no satisfaction', Bland reported.

Allen Fairhall, then the Australian Minister for Defence, had written pleading with Nixon's Secretary of Defense Melvin Laird for some concessions, but the Americans wouldn't budge.[15]

Yet in the wake of the Bland mission Gorton had proclaimed himself satisfied and announced that Australia would accept the aircraft, subject to a modified wing box passing tests. It seemed Australia had little choice. The government was stuck: it had already paid millions, and millions more were to be paid. If the order was cancelled, there was no provision for a refund.

In his early weeks as minister Fraser went through the Bland report and resulting correspondence. In the meantime the United States had, without consultation with Australia, announced that the tests on the wing box would be indefinitely delayed, leaving Australia at a loose end. Then, a little over six weeks after Fraser became Minister for Defence, an F-111 crashed during exercises. Investigations showed that the left-hand wing had broken off. All F-111s were grounded. This gave Fraser the excuse he needed to re-open negotiations.

On 27 February 1970 he proposed to cabinet that he should go to the United States to get to the bottom of the problems, 'probe for the latest information' and 'the overall policy intentions' of the United States, 'lay the ground' for the possibility that the project might be cancelled, and 'encourage the Americans to come up with proposals that would be satisfactory to us', including meeting some of the costs of cancellation and helping Australia to purchase an alternative aircraft.[16] Fraser believes today that the mission he led to the United States 'was not meant to succeed'. After all, Bland had failed, and Gorton had staked his personal credibility on taking the F-111 despite the doubts. There is support for Fraser's view in the archives: on 5 March 1970, the Secretary of the Department of Prime Minister and Cabinet Lenox Hewitt wrote a note to Gorton telling him that Fraser's proposed visit to the United States was 'premature'. Hewitt wrote:

> I really do not think that even the minister would get any sense out of the Pentagon, who would simply rest on their oars and say, as indeed Mr Laird has already said, that they will wait until the investigations are completed ... But apart from the real possibility that the minister's visit would be fruitless, I think we could damage our negotiating position. Our main card is the assurance you had in your own discussions with President Nixon.[17]

Fraser says that whatever Gorton's understanding with Nixon was, it was never revealed to cabinet.

Yet Fraser got his way and was off to the United States, with Arthur Tange at his side and Air Vice Marshal Colin Hannah as part of the team. In the United States they were joined by an Australian technical team that had been based at Fort Worth, where the F-111 was built. These men were experts in the highly technical subjects of metal fatigue and service life. It was clear to Fraser that they knew more about the fine detail of what was going on with the aircraft than the senior staff of the US defence forces. He was to depend on them heavily, encouraging them to express their views strongly, 'which they did'.

The Australian press did not give Fraser much chance of success. The pessimism was understandable: on the face of it, the United States had no reason to budge. But the Fraser who went to Washington in 1970 to talk about the F-111 was a harder man than the wide-eyed backbencher who had gone there on a study tour six years before. He no longer took American good will for granted.

Fraser began talks with the Secretary of Defense Melvin Laird on 6 April. Fraser, with hardly a negotiating card in the deck, made a largely political case. He told Laird that Australians had been 'mild' in their public statements about the problems with the F-111 in comparison with the political embarrassment the government felt. Australia did not want to retreat into isolationism, and since the British had retreated there were increasing risks for Australia. 'Uncertainty and turmoil are increasing in the region.' Knowledge of Australian possession of a deterrent could be expected to keep Indonesia on 'its present cooperative path'; in the absence of a deterrent, the situation would inevitably become less stable. All this—Australia's willingness to have a regional role—fitted with Nixon's Guam doctrine. The delays in the F-111's production lent force to the government's critics: the United States, Fraser suggested, might have more difficulty 'doing business' with the Whitlam opposition, should it come to power.[18]

Laird had little to say in reply. As Gorton's staff had anticipated, he merely urged Australia to await the outcome of the tests. Journalists reporting the meeting were given scant news, but wrote that Fraser was 'grim-looking'. Discussions continued with the Deputy Secretary for Defense, David Packard, but went nowhere. The scheduled day of departure arrived, but Fraser made a decision that he would not go home; he would stay for as long as it took. He remembers, 'Laird came and said, "You are off home tomorrow, then", and I said, "No, I am staying".

'"Why?"

'"Well, because I haven't got an agreement I can take back yet."'

Fraser was bitter. 'We had supported America in Vietnam, in Korea, and we had supported them on most Cold War issues, and it meant absolutely nothing. Nothing at all. That was a lesson for Australia: you don't win brownie points with big powers by simply toeing their line. You have to be independent. The truth was all the Americans wanted was to have us take the aircraft so they could get our money.'

A few days later, Fraser again delayed his departure. Laird talked to him on the telephone to bid him farewell, but Fraser told him he would not be going. 'We are otherwise engaged', he told Laird. 'We are going to be up on the hill.' Fraser had arranged for the Australian technical experts to join him in giving evidence before a Senate committee investigating the F-111. The evidence they would give, both Laird and Fraser knew, would be immensely embarrassing for the United States. 'I told him, "I'm going to take them up there and I will be there myself. I'm going to tell them what the Australian attitude is, and I'm going to let them know that I am perfectly happy for all the evidence to be given in public".' Laird was horrified. Fraser remembers, 'He said, "Malcolm, this is serious".

'I said, "I know it is. I've got no option".

'He said, "Isn't it a very unfriendly act to a friend?"

'And I said it was unfriendly to force us to buy an aircraft that might not meet our needs. Laird said that if our technical experts told the Senate what they had said in negotiations, then the Senate would cut off funding immediately and there would be no F-111. I said that might be the best outcome from our point of view, because then we would owe them nothing and we would expect them to pay back the money we had already given them.'

Within ten minutes, Laird had turned up at the Australian embassy to see Fraser. 'He came into the room and he said, "It is about time we kicked the generals out and do a deal".' Fraser had ready in his hand a page from an exercise book on which he and Air Marshal Colin Hannah had worked out the ten points they wanted the United States to agree to. Laird took it, and read it over.

'He said, "This is all eminently reasonable, Malcolm".

'"I know it is."

'"Well, why haven't you told me before?"

'"I have been telling you for two weeks."

'"Yes, but now I'm listening."'

Fraser pauses in the telling, and then says, 'Bastard'.

The two men initialled the page on the spot. Sadly, the one-page typewritten document is not in the archives. Laird said, 'Now will you pull your people out of the Senate?' Fraser said no, not until the initialled page was turned into a binding legal document. The lawyers were set to work over the weekend, and by the end of Sunday, the ten points had been turned into a memorandum of agreement that Laird signed, and Fraser took back to cabinet in Australia. The Australian technical experts never gave evidence before the Senate committee.

The memorandum of agreement, dated 14 April 1970, contained a huge concession. If Australia's operational and technical criteria were not achieved, then Australia could cancel the deal and the Americans would reimburse part of the money already paid—between $130 million and $150 million. The second major concession was that the US Department of Defense would explore the possibility of leasing Phantom aircraft to Australia while it was awaiting the delivery of the F-111.[19] This memorandum was not made public. As a result, the media commentary on Fraser's visit concentrated almost entirely on the possibility of leasing Phantom aircraft. The financial concessions remained a secret. Fraser's deal was greeted with a lukewarm press. *The Age* editorialised: 'Mr Fraser has bought his government and his Prime Minister time by his negotiations. He has achieved little else'.[20] It was partly this experience—the contrast between what had actually happened and what was reported—that helped to convince Fraser that he needed more help in dealing with the media.

In the meantime came another embarrassment for the Australian Government, and the alliance. On 29 April 1970, the United States invaded Cambodia to help establish the US-friendly Lon Nol regime. Once again, Australia had not been consulted. The resulting outrage helped to fuel the Australian moratorium marches.

Fraser was still wrangling with the Americans. He wanted to make a statement to parliament in which he would table the memorandum of understanding, minus the highly confidential technical details. Partly, this was in order to receive credit for what he had achieved, but it was also because he didn't trust the Americans not to try to back out of the deal. In early May, cables travelled back and forth between Fraser and the Australian embassy in Washington, seeking Laird's agreement to the tabling. The Americans baulked. On 6 May, Fraser was told that at a meeting with senior defence officials 'a firm negative' had been given to the suggestion that the memorandum be tabled. The reason, Fraser was told, was that Nixon's enemies in Congress were trying hard to demonstrate the existence of secret

US commitments in relation to Cambodia. A statement by Fraser quoting the memorandum would open up ground for attack along the lines that the government was entering into secret deals with its allies. Fraser cabled the Australian embassy:

> Would you please impress on the US administration that it will be essential for the Minister for Defence to make a full description of the financial arrangements, the options and the consequences of the new technical understanding in his statement to the Australian Parliament. I cannot see how this can be done in such a way that does not make clear there is a new understanding between Secretary Laird and myself ... If the US administration attempts to insist that these matters not be referred to in the Australian Parliament in a definitive way, I would then be compelled to resubmit the basic decision to the Australian Government since the present decision rests on the ability to tell the Australian Parliament what is being negotiated.

The Ambassador tried again, and was greeted with a request for a delay long enough to allow the Senate and House Armed Services Committee to be consulted. Fraser replied that there was already great pressure for a statement of the results of the mission. Further delay would seriously aggravate the position. Even if he could not table the memorandum, could he not refer to it? The reply came back that Laird was willing to agree to the tabling of the memorandum, but now he wanted changes. As Fraser had feared, the Americans were trying to back down on the deal—limiting the circumstances under which the United States would reimburse the Australians.

More cables flew back and forth. Australia would not cancel in a 'frivolous or arbitrary' way, Fraser emphasised, but Australia, and Australia alone, should be able to decide if the F-111 met its requirements. Things seemed to be back where they had been in March. Fraser threatened to go direct to Laird again, over the heads of the Deputy Secretary for Defense David Packard and the US airforce, who after all had not been there when he and Laird initialled the crucial piece of paper. Finally, after a frantic week, there was a result. Packard signed a letter in terms agreeable to Fraser: the right to cancel remained in Australian hands.[21]

As it turned out, Australia did take delivery of the F-111. The aircraft were stored until final acceptance, in 1973. In the meantime, twenty-four F-4E Phantoms were leased to Australia to provide an interim attack capability.

Fraser received little thanks from Gorton or his own side of politics for his negotiations. Something of the flavour of his reception is reflected in a letter that Tony Street wrote to him on his return, apologising for the treatment he had received before the Government Members' Defence Committee. Street wrote: 'I personally thought the committee was at times downright discourteous, and several members afterwards came up to me to say how embarrassed they were at the conduct of the meeting'.[22]

Harmony was in short supply for Fraser in the Gorton cabinet, and within a couple of months of his return from the United States he was involved in another dispute with his Prime Minister. This too, from Fraser's point of view, was about a fundamental principle: good government. Since his earliest days in public life Fraser had been proud of Australia's record in Papua New Guinea. In July 1970, a conflict was developing in Rabaul, on the Gazelle Peninsula of the country. There was a land shortage, and the administration had bought a number of plantations and made them into small-scale settler blocks. The Mataungan Association, a village-based political movement, had encouraged its supporters to squat on the land. Gorton had visited Papua New Guinea and made a speech promising that the illegal occupation would be stopped. Now, on his return, he asked Fraser to agree to a call-out of Australian armed forces—the Pacific Island Regiment—in case the local police weren't able to deal with the situation. Fraser refused. Calling out the military to intervene in domestic upheaval was a serious thing to do. At the very least, cabinet should be consulted. Admittedly, the call-out was only precautionary: it was expected that the police would be able to handle the dispute. But if the situation turned nasty it could have all kinds of unpleasant implications: the troops might have to be reinforced from Australia. Ultimately, Australian soldiers might find themselves firing on the people of Papua New Guinea. So much for Australia's international reputation, and all the idealism and high hopes for Papua New Guinea!

Even if everything turned out well, Fraser thought, there was still an important matter of principle. The armed forces were not the Prime Minister's private concern, available for him to use on a whim. Fraser sought legal advice, and then told Gorton that he would not consent to the call-out without the matter being considered by a meeting of senior ministers—preferably cabinet. Gorton flatly refused. Fraser told Gorton that he would seek the advice of the Defence Committee, which was the primary advisory and coordinating body on matters of defence. It included Tange as Chairman, together with the Chief of the General Staff, Sir Thomas Daly, the armed forces chiefs and the secretaries of the Department of Prime Minister and Cabinet, the Treasury and the Department of External Affairs. As Fraser expected, the committee recommended caution.

Fraser went back to Gorton, again pleading with him to call a cabinet meeting. The two men had another argument. Gorton was adamant: he said that if Fraser continued to frustrate him he would sign the request to the Governor-General himself. He would not call a cabinet meeting. Seriously worried, Fraser returned to his office. Gorton did not seem to understand his objections. Fraser drafted a letter to his Prime Minister. 'I wanted to lay it all out clearly for him, thinking he couldn't help but get the point if I did so.' The letter pleaded with Gorton to reconsider and hold a cabinet meeting, 'which in such emergencies should be routine in our system of cabinet government … Without it, consistently good government is not possible'. Without such a meeting, he, Fraser, could not sign an order for a call-out, and Gorton should not do so. 'I underline the grave responsibility you accept in so moving against the weight of available advice.' The move Gorton was contemplating had 'possibly grave and tragic consequences'.[23]

As he finished this letter, Fraser received word that Gorton and the Minister for External Territories were already on the way to Government House. It was almost too late to prevent the army being used without cabinet consultation. Fraser dropped all convention. He rang the Governor-General, his former cabinet colleague Paul Hasluck, and told him that while the Prime Minister was on his way to ask him to sign a call-out order, the Defence Committee opposed it, he as Minister for Defence opposed it, and cabinet had not been consulted. Fraser's legal advice was that the Prime Minister's imprimatur alone was not sufficient to legally call out the armed forces in a case of domestic upheaval. Hasluck understood the point, even if Gorton did not. He refused to sign the order. Fraser never sent the letter he had been drafting to Gorton; it remains to this day in his filing cabinet.

Fraser thought that he might have to resign at this time. The tensions at the heart of government remained secret. The media knew nothing of the dispute, but Fraser felt he would have few options if Gorton continued to push for the call-out order without consulting cabinet. But Gorton backed down. On 18 July 1970, he invited senior ministers to the Lodge to discuss the call-out. Fraser was there, and still insisting on a full cabinet discussion. It was decided that Tom Hughes, the Attorney-General, would fly to Papua New Guinea to acquire first-hand knowledge of the situation and see whether or not the state of civil disorder was sufficient to justify a call-out order. This was a face-saving move for Gorton. Hughes was in Papua New Guinea for less than twenty-four hours. Predictably, he came back advising that the call-out was justified. Cabinet received his advice and on 19 July, in a long cabinet decision that spelled out all of the history, it was agreed that the administrator could request a requisition for the call-out on the expectation that it would be approved, if the situation threatened to overwhelm the control of the police. An order-in-council would be signed as a precautionary measure, but the power to approve the requisition remained in the hands of the Australian Government.[24] Fraser worked hard to have the safeguards written into the decision, and then concurred with it. He was still uneasy about the call-out, but he had been granted his request: cabinet had met.

There never was a requisition: it wasn't needed. The Mantanguans withdrew their squatters.

Fraser felt that Australia had been to the brink so far as its international reputation was concerned. More worrying, though, was that the Prime Minister had been prepared to use the armed forces without proper process and on his own authority. In this sense the Papua New Guinea affair was a precursor for the end game between Gorton and Fraser. Perhaps it was inevitable that this end game would bring together the two threads of Fraser's time in defence: Australia's role in the world, and proper processes of government in a democracy. Perhaps it was also inevitable that it ultimately concerned Vietnam, and the aspect of Australia's involvement that represented the last shreds of Fraser's idealism about the war.

The events that led to Fraser and Gorton's final falling-out were later described as 'a Greek tragedy' by one of the actors in the drama, Chief of General Staff Lieutenant General Sir Thomas Daly. The drama brought down Gorton and caused Fraser to resign. It was one of the most dramatic events in a dramatic political decade. Yet at the time most of the key players, including Fraser, had only a partial knowledge of what was going on. New details have emerged as a result of the research for this book. Unanswered questions remain, but the man who might provide the answers, John Gorton, is no longer with us. Judging from facts available, it would seem that, wittingly or otherwise, Gorton brought about his own downfall. Why he behaved as he did we may never know.

⋆ ⋆ ⋆

Civic action—the use of Australian troops to give aid to the South Vietnamese—had always been important to Fraser. He had spoken on the subject frequently and passionately. His insistence on giving civic action a high priority had caused tension throughout his involvement in army and defence. Some in the army shared his idealism, but there were others who didn't think it was army work. In Phuoc Tuy province, civic action had undoubtedly improved living conditions: Australian medical teams had virtually wiped out plague and malaria; children were inoculated and educated, markets opened up and roads repaired. Fraser believed that civic action should continue, perhaps even increase, as fighting troops withdrew. This idea had never been contradicted either within cabinet or by Gorton. Continuing civic action was thus government policy.

But Fraser's conviction that civic action should continue or be scaled up as troops withdrew was not shared by some in the senior levels of the army, and in particular by the Chief of General Staff, Sir Thomas Daly. In an unpublished account of what became known as the 'civic action affair', Daly later said that once troops were withdrawn it would have been impossible to protect civic action teams from attacks by the Vietcong. By the end of 1970, he wrote, it was clear that a withdrawal of Australian forces was likely. He had told the commander of the Australian forces in Vietnam, Major General Colin Fraser (no relation), 'that it would be wise to look carefully before committing his civic action teams to complex long-term projects'. Daly regarded the suggestion that civic action should be maintained or increased as the troops withdrew as a 'face-saving exercise' and 'quite unacceptable'.[25] The problem was that Daly had not shared his reservations with Fraser or with the defence department. Today, Fraser insists that he would have been open to discussions along these lines. The idea of maintaining or scaling up civic action depended on 'pacification' being successful. Although Phuoc Tuy province was still more or less under control, it was becoming clear that if civic action teams were left behind when other troops had withdrawn, they would not be safe. 'If Daly had come to me and said he had problems about civic action, if he had said, "Look, we really think the Americans are going to cut and run and we don't want entanglements that might keep us in Vietnam after they have cut and run, because it will become a very dangerous place", you would say, "Oh sure, I can see the merits in that. Well, how do we handle it?" And you would talk it through. But nothing had come from army to defence or to me as Minister for Defence.' Nevertheless, the view that civic action would be wound down rather than maintained clearly framed the army's planning.

Fraser and Daly had first rubbed up against each other when Fraser was Minister for Army. They worked together well enough. Daly was a soldier's soldier, a veteran of Tobruk and Korea. Fraser admired his courage. 'He was without doubt a most honourable and admirable man', he says today. However, he also suspected that Daly's first loyalty would always be to the army, rather than to a minister—perhaps particularly to a minister like Fraser, who had never served in the armed forces. Fraser says, 'He was an army man through and through. The army would have been everything to him'. Daly was, though, close to Gorton, who was an ex-serviceman. Just how close the two men were can be judged from the strange events of February and March 1971.

For the troops in Vietnam, early 1971 was a particularly dispiriting period. It was common knowledge that the allies were withdrawing under the rubric of Vietnamisation. Already Operation Timothy—the withdrawal of between 600 and 650 Australian troops—was underway. Further withdrawals, possibly at short notice, were expected, yet every day men were still risking their lives. The army in Vietnam was engaged in preparing its bid in the 1971–72 budget. There were many civic action projects that were not completed—schools without roofs, bridges without decking and the like. There was concern that if they weren't finished, they would remain as 'monuments to Australian inefficiency'. The budget planning was conducted with a view to completing the outstanding projects, and not taking on any more.[26] Once the plans were complete, they were to be sent to Canberra for decision. Major General Fraser dictated some guidelines for the budgetary planning. The order was signed, at his direction, by Colonel John Salmon, a new Chief of Staff who had been in Saigon for only a few weeks. Salmon, harassed on the day, had recently fielded complaints from the task force that orders from headquarters tended to be too wordy. With this in mind, he cut a lengthy preamble that made it clear that the document was a guideline for budget planning. He has regretted making this cut ever since: the result was that the order was easily misinterpreted. Six paragraphs remained which appeared to give a bald order that civic action be wound up—in contravention of government policy. (See appendix for the text of this document.) Someone committed to civic action must have read it as an intention to end the involvement, and leaked the substance of the order to an ABC correspondent, Andrew Swanton. On 19 February, Malcolm Fraser heard on ABC Radio in Canberra that the army was winding up civic action. He was staggered—and suspicious. Fraser was a man who liked to be kept well informed. The pressure of his demands for complete and full information had been a theme in every ministry he had held. He was already frustrated by the difficulties of extracting information from the army in Vietnam. Headquarters in Saigon did their best to brief Canberra, but saw their role as including shielding the commanders on the frontline from too many demands.

Colonel Salmon was sitting in the Saigon headquarters on 19 February when flash messages began to arrive from Canberra demanding to know what was going on with civic action. Major General Fraser was away and Salmon, still new in the job, was left to cope as best he could. 'The flashes were arriving so fast I could hardly keep up', he remembers. When Major General Fraser was contactable, he tended to dismiss the whole affair as a 'storm in a teacup', and said, 'We are dealing with a 48-hour wonder'. He declined to authorise two signals prepared for him to send to Canberra endorsing the actions taken during his absences.

Meanwhile, in Canberra the temperature was rising. Malcolm Fraser issued a press statement saying that if any instruction to wind up civic action had been issued, then it was 'contrary to government policy ... A reduction in civic action is not in contemplation ... It is government policy that the Australian army would maintain their civic action activities in Vietnam'. Later, having been briefed by Salmon's responses to his cables, he issued another statement saying that while civic action continued, it was being Vietnamised. The 'guidelines' that had been issued by army headquarters had been 'misunderstood'.[27]

Yet the media continued to suggest that civic action was being wound up. Fraser was suspicious that the army was making decisions without keeping him informed, but he had no evidence. Questioned about civic action on the ABC current affairs program *This Day Tonight*, he said, with some emphasis, that he didn't believe the army wanted civic action wound up, but, in any case, 'The policy in this matter is going to be governed by the government's view'.[28] Still the media insisted that Fraser was being ignored by the army. *The Australian* editorialised on 23 February that, despite what Fraser said and wanted, 'thanks to some sort of indiscretion within the Australian army headquarters', it was now clear that 'Australia has abandoned all pretensions of playing a meaningful policeman's role in Phuoc Tuy province', and that in any case the army now lacked the means of running a civic action program.[29]

Fraser was frustrated and embarrassed. With a sense of desperation about his ability to get the correct story out, he decided to brief selected journalists. He chose Alan Ramsey, the respected Canberra correspondent then with Rupert Murdoch's *Australian* newspaper, and Peter Samuel of *The Bulletin*. Fraser talked to them about the importance of being given full briefings from Vietnam, and admitted to some frustration with this. He mentioned that he was receiving reports from the Joint Intelligence Organisation on the progress of pacification and Vietnamisation. He emphasised to the journalists the important principle that the armed forces should be under civilian control, through the Minister for Defence, and governed by policy as determined by cabinet. They should not go about making their own policies. Fraser insists today that while he expressed his concern about acquiring adequate information from Vietnam, he was not critical in these briefings of either the army or Sir Thomas Daly. It was clear to him, though, that 'the journalists had other sources and they believed those sources over me'. He believes today that one of the people stirring the media pot was Billy McMahon, the Minister for External Affairs.

Ramsey's story came out in *The Sunday Australian* on 28 February.[30] It rehashed the allegations about civic action being wound up and accused the army of intransigence. When Sir Thomas Daly picked up his copy of the paper, he was horrified. As he wrote later in his unpublished account, it was an 'outrageous article' and 'too much for the army to stomach'. The Army Minister Andrew Peacock was in hospital, and Fraser was out of contact in Victoria. Unable to appeal to them for a statement rebutting the article, Daly decided for only the second time in his career to brief journalists himself. Before he could do so, he received a strange telephone call from John Gorton. If Daly didn't know what was going on, said Gorton, then he should. He summoned Daly to his Parliament House office. There, Gorton went further: he told Daly that the press gallery was claiming that senior people in defence were briefing journalists with material very critical of the army, and of Daly in particular. Did Daly have any idea who could be behind this? Daly said that Malcolm Fraser had been 'upset' by Andrew Swanton's report on civic action. Gorton responded that civic action should be seen in its proper perspective—'as a minor part of our overall effort in Vietnam'. There must be more behind the briefings, he suggested. Daly had in mind that the motive must be political. He wrote later:

> It would not be the first time one of the services had been attacked through the press as a means of discrediting the government or a minister. I had in mind, although I did not mention this to Gorton, that there had been

> ill feeling between Andrew Peacock and Malcolm Fraser during previous months ... It had occurred to me that [Fraser] might see Andrew Peacock as a rival for the party leadership, and that the attacks on army were designed to undermine his credibility.

On Daly's account, he did not confide these thoughts to Gorton. 'I did not want to say anything which could be seen as critical of a minister who was my superior officer, and in any case I had no real evidence.' Nevertheless, voicing these thoughts to the Prime Minister—accusing Fraser of disloyalty to army and to Peacock—is exactly what Daly was later accused of doing. Was he less than honest when he denied having done so? Perhaps. Or perhaps it is simply that he and Gorton were close enough to know each other's minds without the words needing to be said. Certainly the rest of Daly's account suggests that the two men were thinking along similar lines. Gorton asked Daly how he got on with Fraser; Daly said they disagreed about some things, but got on well enough. As Daly left, Gorton told him that he had complete confidence in the army and its leadership, and he would support them in the event of any attacks on army. Daly remembered, 'He said he would come out fighting and meet them head on'.

Gorton's motivation in holding this meeting with Daly is hard to divine. Whatever his intention, he seems to have encouraged, if not planted, the idea in Daly's mind that Fraser was undermining him. He had also—without any recourse or consultation with Fraser—promised Daly his support. It was, at very least, a strange thing for a Prime Minister to do.

Tony Eggleton, who was Gorton's Press Secretary at the time, remembers a feeling among some of Gorton's closest confidants, including his Principal Private Secretary, Ainslie Gotto, and the head of the Prime Minister's department, Lenox Hewitt, that Fraser needed to be taken down a peg. 'I had picked up some snippets of conversation to that effect that surprised me, because I thought Malcolm was doing well—almost the Defence Minister from central casting.' Whether it was the previous fallings-out between Fraser and Gorton, or a reaction to the strength of Fraser's personality, there was a view that he needed a 'rap over the knuckles', says Eggleton. 'I thought at the time and I have always thought since that when the civic action affair blew up, they saw it as an issue on which they could cut Malcolm down to size.'

Meanwhile, the Canberra hothouse had been at work. Bob Baudino, Canberra bureau chief for Frank Packer's Australian Consolidated Press, had received word that Fraser was briefing journalists, and had acquired a garbled version of what Fraser had said. He drafted an article that made numerous references to things Fraser had allegedly told his cabinet colleagues, including that he didn't think army reports reaching Canberra were adequate. Today, Fraser is convinced that one of Baudino's main sources was Billy McMahon. Most damaging, Baudino's lead stated that Fraser had set the Joint Intelligence Organisation to spy on the army in Vietnam. This was damaging nonsense. The organisation gathered information from all over Vietnam, including from the army; it included army officers, and its work was done with full army knowledge and cooperation. Baudino did not speak to Fraser in compiling his report, but he ran through the main points with Gorton, including an allegation that Fraser had claimed Daly had made a decision to phase out civic action in contradiction to government policy. On request, Baudino sent Gorton proof copies of the story that evening. They were returned without comment.[31] Gorton did not correct the article, but he did ring Daly at home late that night and told him the substance of what Baudino was saying, and again assured him of his support. Gorton did not ring Fraser.

The next day, 1 March, the Baudino article hit the streets. Fraser went to see Gorton with a prepared statement rebutting the story. Fraser was now in a more than awkward position. In briefing the journalists, 'I had tried to explain the facts of what was going on. Obviously I had done it inadequately or badly, because the journalists went to other sources and believed what those sources said about what I thought, not me. And so the message got out that I was being critical of the army, and that I didn't trust them, and that I was organising spying on them, which was wrong and a nonsense'. Meanwhile, journalists had the impression that Gorton was weeping no tears about Fraser's discomfiture.[32]

The crisis continued. The next day, Peter Samuel's *Bulletin* article came out. Headlined 'The Australian Army's "Revolt" in Vietnam', it alleged that the civic action affair was only one example of the army 'going its own way', that the army's acceptance of civic action had always been 'forced and grudging' and that it had decided to cut out civic action in an attempt to present the government with a fait accompli. This went well beyond the briefing that Fraser had given Samuel. Later, *The Bulletin* declared that Fraser's briefing had been supplemented by information 'from other ministers'.[33]

This article was, Daly thought, 'the worst so far'. The next day he insisted on seeing Fraser, who was preparing to leave for Tasmania. Daly told him, 'The army was fed up with continued press attacks and would take no more of it'. In his later account, Daly said, 'Malcolm Fraser gave me one of his well-known down-the-nose looks and asked in a somewhat aggressive tone what I meant when I said the army would "stand no more"'. Daly said he wanted Fraser to issue a statement refuting the unfair allegations. Fraser agreed to do this, and the two men sat down together to prepare a draft, Fraser delaying his departure for Tasmania in order to complete it. It described suggestions of a 'revolt' in the army as nonsense. Daly left Fraser's office satisfied, and believing the controversy would die.

So far, on the journalist Alan Reid's later account, the whole affair, while embarrassing, 'was only a minor one, with Fraser losing some political skin and having some damage inflicted on his public image, but nothing more'.[34] It was about to become fatal. The press gallery's best and brightest had been following the story from all sides, and the focus of curiosity had become an encounter to which there were only two witnesses: Gorton's meeting with Daly on the day that Ramsey's first article had appeared. What had Gorton said to Daly? What had Daly said to Gorton? The journalist who got the breakthrough was Alan Ramsey. He was told by a good, though third-hand, source that at the crucial meeting Daly had accused Fraser of 'extreme disloyalty' to the army and to Peacock as its minister, and that Daly had said Fraser was trying to discredit the army as part of a political campaign against Peacock. This, of course, was on Daly's own account exactly the thought that had been in his mind—but he claimed that he had not voiced it to Gorton. Today, though, Fraser has learned the identity of Ramsey's source, and he believes that the account Ramsey received of what Daly said to Gorton was probably accurate.

Ramsey had his story—but from a third-hand source. He needed confirmation. He drew up a letter for Gorton asking five questions: Had he called Daly to his office? Had he questioned him about 'army versus defence'? Had Daly said that Fraser was being disloyal to the army? Had he, Gorton, called Fraser in to 'sort the matter out'? And had he discussed the matter with Peacock? Ramsey gave this memorandum to Gorton's Press Secretary on 3 March. In response, Gorton called Ramsey in and confirmed four of the five points—but would neither confirm nor deny the allegation that Daly had accused Fraser of disloyalty. In the context of the Canberra hothouse, a politician failing to deny something in a background briefing with a journalist is as good as confirming it. Ramsey went away satisfied that he had enough to publish. The resulting story was on the front page of *The Australian* on 4 March. It began:

> The chief of the army general staff, Lieutenant General Sir Thomas Daly, has accused the Defence Minister, Mr Fraser, of extreme disloyalty to the army and its junior minister, Mr Peacock. He has told the Prime Minister, Mr Gorton, he believes the army, its department and its minister are being discredited by defence sources as part of a political campaign against Mr Peacock.[35]

Fraser rang Daly from Tasmania. Was it true? Of course not, said Daly.

Then, in one of the strangest developments so far, Daly was again invited to visit Gorton, this time at the Lodge. Gorton was in the middle of having his portrait painted. He asked Daly to draft a statement, to be released under Gorton's name, denying that Daly had accused Fraser of disloyalty. As Gorton sat still for the portrait painter, Daly sat and wrote the appropriate words. They were typed up there and then by Ainsley Gotto, and released to the press gallery. The statement was a denial that Daly had ever said the words that, clearly, Gorton had helped to encourage in his mind. Gorton had now denied the conversation—but why hadn't he done it before the story was published, when Ramsey gave him the chance?

Gorton's denial was a direct hit to Ramsey's credibility as a journalist, so in the next day's paper Ramsey revealed that Gorton had had the chance to deny the story before it hit the presses. Fraser now knew, thanks to Ramsey, that Gorton and Daly had been meeting without his knowledge, and that Gorton had promised the army his support. Fraser believed that Daly had accused him of disloyalty. Meanwhile, the army seemed to be going its own way on civic action without any reference to him as minister, or to the Department of Defence, or to cabinet, and Gorton seemed to be supporting them in this. It was intolerable, and deeply worrying. Today Fraser says, 'It is absolutely fundamental in a democracy that the armed forces answer to civilians, through the Minister for Defence and cabinet. If the Prime Minister is going to run them without reference to cabinet, we are on a very dangerous path indeed'.

Fraser also now knew that Gorton had been given the opportunity to rebut the initial story, but had failed to do so. It seemed to Fraser that he had no option but to resign. He talked it over with Tamie. 'She basically agreed that I had no choice, although she was saying all the time, "Is there another way?" Fraser rang Robert Menzies in Melbourne and told him, 'My position is intolerable'. Menzies agreed, but forbore from giving Fraser advice.

By the following morning, Saturday 6 March, Fraser had made up his mind, and began to draft his resignation speech. Tamie remembers the weekend well. Fraser was seeking advice of different kinds, and there were times when she had to show one person into a room and prevent them from seeing that somebody else was also in the house. Fraser called in the Chairman of the Chiefs of Staff Committee, Admiral Victor Smith, and showed him his resignation speech, instructing him to say nothing about the politics but to alert him if there were any factual errors in his account of the correct chain of command in defence matters. 'He said there were no mistakes. He didn't say anything else.'

His best political friends, Doug Anthony and Tony Street, offered him no advice. Anthony told Fraser later that he had deliberately stayed away 'because he knew what I had in mind and did not see what else I could do'. Street told Fraser that it was his decision alone. 'Tony didn't like tough decisions', says Fraser. It was by now clear to Canberra insiders that either Fraser or Gorton would have to go. They could hardly continue to serve together. Yet Gorton was to claim later that he did not realise how dire things had become, and that he had no idea what was on Fraser's mind. The journalist Reid commented later, 'If Gorton did not hear warning bells … he must have been tone deaf'.[36]

On the Sunday night, Tamie settled down in the living room to watch the television program *Meet the Press*. The Fraser–Gorton conflict was the topic, and Baudino, Samuel and Reid were the main commentators. Reid was asked whether the Liberal Party would do anything about Gorton's position, and he replied that it depended on what Fraser did. If Fraser resigned and stated the reasons, there could be a successful revolt against Gorton's leadership. Gorton had already made enemies of the state premiers, and there were plenty of reservations about his leadership, although he remained popular with the public. 'The test here will come with Mr Fraser. If Mr Fraser accepts this, he becomes hence forward a puppet.'[37] Many commentators, including Gorton himself, believed afterwards that this statement by Reid was what decided Fraser to resign. Tamie knew differently: the resignation letter and speech were already drafted and sitting on the dining room table. She says today, 'Reid was the only one who got it, who saw the situation clearly'.

Gorton rang Fraser that night after the *Meet the Press* program to tell him he thought the show was vicious and distorted. Fraser replied, 'Don't worry, boss. Sleep well'. Today Fraser says about this deception, 'You don't give your enemy a chance to get in first. He could have sacked me before I had a chance to resign'.

Eggleton remembers that night as a time of considerable distress among the Prime Minister's confidants—those who had wanted Fraser taken down a peg or two. 'They had had no intention of causing Fraser to resign.' As their strategy came unstitched, Eggleton says, 'They realised they had totally miscalculated'.

On Monday 8 March, Fraser did not attend the scheduled cabinet meeting. Word of this leaked out. It was now clear to everyone that resignation was likely. Anthony called Fraser in the middle of the morning. Fraser recalls, 'He had just come from the Prime Minister. Gorton had started by saying that he would not have me back. Anthony said he must'. Anthony had been sent to parley. Fraser told him that the only conditions under which he could stay would be Gorton's giving his full support and publically admitting that he had acted wrongly. 'I did not tell Anthony that I would stay on these terms, but that they were the only possible terms on which I could consider staying. I did not believe Gorton would accept. I should have remembered he was a straw man.'

Early in the afternoon, Fraser issued a press release saying that he would seek to make a statement in parliament the following day after question time. At the same time, he sent a letter to Gorton announcing his intention to resign. Pointedly, he said that he would be delivering his resignation letter to the Governor-General—not to Gorton himself. Fraser had not intended the letter to Gorton to become public immediately, but within hours its contents had been leaked by Gorton's office and were known all over Canberra. Fraser learned that the news was out when he listened to the four o'clock radio news bulletin. He says today, 'If my resignation had not been confirmed by Gorton, if it had remained secret, it may have been possible to hold events. Gorton's confirmation denied that possibility. It is just as well that it did'. Cabinet was meeting, in crisis mode. Meanwhile, Fraser, having heard the news report, drove to Government House to submit his resignation to the Governor-General.

The next day was one of the most tense in modern parliamentary history. 'Adjectives don't exist that adequately describe the tension that has pervaded this building today. It's been an absolutely incredible day', said the ABC's Richard Carleton on television that night.[38] Gorton, recognising his peril, made an attempt to save the situation. At a meeting with Fraser, also attended by Anthony, who was Minister for Primary Industries, Nigel Bowen, the Minister for Education, and the Postmaster-General Alan Hulme, Gorton tried to broker a deal. He said he was surprised at Fraser's resignation: there had never been any tension, any disagreement between them. Fraser reminded him of their disputes over offshore legislation and the Gazelle Peninsula before saying that there was no point in revisiting the past; it would not lead to a solution. Anthony then read out Fraser's conditions for staying—that Gorton should admit behaving wrongly and give Fraser his full support. It was all far too late, but, to Fraser's amazement, Gorton indicated that he might consider agreeing.

A party meeting was scheduled for 11.30 a.m., but it was delayed as Fraser thought things through. Fraser remembers being in an office with Tony Street and Bert Kelly. 'I told them that I had written a speech, and that if I delivered it I thought it might be the end of Gorton. I asked them, "Do I make this speech, or don't I?" They both said to go ahead.' In the notes he keeps in his filing cabinet about the crisis, Fraser has recorded:

> My mind remained as it was. Not without anguish. No one could tell the outcome of my course, for our party, and for Australia. I kept to the course for two reasons. I believed Gorton was and would be out to destroy me and in my view that would remove the one bar to his complete autocracy. Perhaps I overestimated the power of

> a PM to destroy another but certainly, if I had withdrawn, the influence I may have had in the party would have been weakened ... It was still awful. No one likes that kind of decision or the consequences that will flow. A man I had supported strongly. A man whom I had regarded as a friend.

There was principle at stake. Gorton had shown that he didn't believe in proper process, even when dealing with the armed forces. He had promised Daly his support without any reference to his Minister for Defence.

The proper chain of command would collapse under such conditions. In parliament that afternoon, straight after prayers, Whitlam moved that standing orders be suspended to allow Fraser to make his statement. Fraser rose to his feet—speaking for the first time in many years from the back bench. What followed was the most severe pasting ever delivered to an Australian Prime Minister by one of his own side. Today, Fraser thinks he didn't do himself justice in this speech. He was trying to make a central point about the importance of proper process—that the army must, in a democracy, be answerable to the civilians, through the Minister for Defence. If a head of armed forces, such as Daly, believed he had a direct line of appeal to the Prime Minister, and if the Prime Minister believed that the armed forces were his to direct at will, as the Gazelle Peninsula affair and the civic action affair suggested, then the whole apparatus broke down. 'The problem is', Fraser says today, 'I took too long to get to the point, and that caused some confusion'. But there was no confusion about his condemnation of Gorton. Fraser recounted the recent events over civic action and admitted his own background briefings to the media, before moving on to the suggestion that he had been disloyal to the army.

> My responsibility ... is to this parliament and through it to the people of Australia. My ultimate loyalty must

> be to Australia … If there is anyone in this House who believes that loyalty to a service requires uncritical and universal support of its activities, that is not a concept that I can embrace, for it would be a denial of parliamentary authority. I do not deny that there have been differences of opinion—the press has labelled it 'abrasion'—with some service relationships in Canberra. But I assert that any Minister for Defence who seeks to do his duty will have to seek to move people from old views and from views that may not embrace the total defence concept.

He moved on to talk about how Gorton had behaved in assuring Daly of 'unequivocal and absolute support' before talking to Fraser. This violated the chains of command. Gorton had been 'impetuous' and this was 'characteristic'. Gorton had also failed in preventing Ramsey's damaging article from going to press. 'One sentence would have killed the report. The Prime Minister, by his inaction, made sure it would cover the front page. As I have indicated in my letter of resignation, I found that disloyalty intolerable and not to be endured.' These actions by Gorton were not isolated, Fraser said. There were other occasions on which Gorton had shown 'a dangerous reluctance to consult cabinet, and an obstinate determination to get his own way'. Fraser then made the dispute over the Gazelle Peninsula public for the first time.

> The original plan and the call-out were both matters of the highest importance. The Prime Minister fought to prevent cabinet discussion. If such a discussion had not been held, at my insistence, I would have resigned then. I have now done so as a result of what I have regarded as the Prime Minister's disloyalty to a senior minister. The Prime Minister, because of his unreasoned drive to get his own way, his obstinacy, impetuous and emotional reactions, has imposed strains on the Liberal Party, the government and the public service. I do not believe he is

> fit to hold the great office of Prime Minister, and I cannot serve in his government.[39]

Gorton stood. Richard Carleton reported that night that there were 'audible groans of disbelief at the lack of fire' in his reply.[40] Gorton agreed that he should have denied the Ramsey story and that this had been a mistake. As for the events of the Gazelle Peninsula, he did not have them clearly in mind. When he came to Ramsey's role, Gorton claimed that he had replied to the question about the conversation with Daly by saying it was wrong to discuss or comment on what a third party had said, and Ramsey had replied 'Fair enough'. Ramsey was sitting in the public gallery as Gorton said these words. He yelled out spontaneously, 'You liar!' The Speaker had him removed from the house. Later, Ramsey apologised for his outburst.

Gorton was finished. The next day, he called a Liberal Party meeting and there was a motion of confidence in his leadership. The vote was tied; Gorton resigned. McMahon was made Prime Minister. In a surprise move, Gorton contested and won the position of Deputy Leader, and ironically chose the portfolio of Defence Minister for himself. It was a situation that didn't last for long: McMahon sacked him within months for disloyalty.

On the last Sunday of March 1971, Fraser gave his regular radio address to the people of Wannon. He thanked the many well-wishers who had contacted him. 'In what was a period of great personal stress, the letters and telegrams were a comfort for Mrs Fraser and myself.' He offered to make a copy of Hansard available to anyone who wanted to read his speech. Apart from that, he didn't want to comment on events. He went on to talk about assistance for wool growers.[41]

It was only at this point, after the resignation, that Fraser received from an anonymous source a copy of the army order signed by Salmon that had started the whole controversy. To his eyes, it seemed clear enough. It was an order that civic action be wound up. For many years—until the research for this book—he took it as confirmation that, despite all the denials, the army had indeed been making policy on its own, without reference to him or to cabinet.

Was he right? Had the army decided off its own bat to wind up civic action? The man who signed the original order, John Salmon, insists today that nothing could be further from the truth. In fact, the result of the budget planning process was that the budgetary allocation for civic action was increased. Nevertheless, it seems clear from Daly's own account that the expectation that civic action would be wound up was at the very least framing the army's planning. Daly had told Major General Fraser to think carefully before committing his teams to new and complex projects. Daly did not communicate his thoughts to the Minister for Defence, and no evidence has been found in the archival record to suggest that he communicated his views to the department. Fraser is convinced that if Arthur Tange had heard about it, 'He would have brought it to my attention'.

Within the Liberal Party, there are many that have never forgiven Fraser for what he did to John Gorton. Some believe that had he not brought down Gorton, it might have been possible for the coalition to win the 1972 election: the Whitlam government might never have been. Certainly, Gorton was more popular than McMahon proved to be, but it seems unlikely that he could have won in 1972, given the ground that Whitlam had already gained in 1969. From his resignation onwards, there were always plenty of Liberals who wanted to see Fraser's political career ended. The ill feeling goes on. In May 2002, Malcolm and Tamie Fraser went to Sydney to attend the funeral of John Gorton. The eulogy was delivered by Tom Hughes—Gorton's Attorney-General and friend. Hughes used the occasion to launch a scathing attack on Fraser, not modulating it because of his presence. What Fraser had done in March 1971 was, Hughes said, a political assassination. His resignation had been 'quite unnecessary'; Gorton had intended no disloyalty. 'The judgement of history upon John Gorton will be kinder than it will be upon those who conspired to bring him down', said Hughes. Fraser sat there, listening. According to reporters, after Gorton's funeral, former Labor Prime Minister Bob Hawke skipped away grinning, pronouncing that the Liberals were much better haters than Labor.

Today, Fraser says that Hughes missed the point. He seemed to suggest that Fraser resigned because of the Gazelle Peninsula affair, when in fact that had been resolved; Fraser had raised it in his resignation speech only as evidence of a pattern of behaviour. Hughes missed the point about proper process and, as for saying that Gorton intended no disloyalty, the record speaks for itself. Fraser says that two separate issues brought about his resignation: the failure of Daly to share his concerns about civic action—'That was a major mistake'—and the way in which Gorton dealt with Daly, apparently using the civic action affair for political purposes, to attack Fraser.

* * *

The immediate outcome of his final fight with Gorton—McMahon as Prime Minister—was not to Fraser's liking. The Liberal Party was on the way to defeat, and Whitlam was looking better by the day.

The confrontation with Gorton had shown how far Fraser was prepared to go to defend principle. It had shown what he would do when, in his view, the situation demanded that men such as himself took action in the interests of good government, proper process and the nation. He was an activist.

There was something else as well—another seed sown for the future. Amid the maelstrom of Fraser's final days in defence, he had formed a relationship that became crucial to Australia's political history. He met John Kerr in circumstances that allowed him to make a shrewd judgement of the man.

From his earliest days as Army Minister Fraser had been concerned about the armed forces' pay and conditions. The forces had trouble recruiting—this had been one of the justifications for conscription—and the situation was becoming worse. Fixing the problem was not easy: the system of pay, as Kerr later described it, was 'almost incomprehensible'. There were different pay scales for each of the armed forces, and for sections within them. Compensating adequately for overseas service and for skills and qualifications had defeated the bureaucracy until then. Tange was too busy to handle it, so, in October 1970, Fraser had announced the appointment of an inquiry to fix the problem. The appointment of John Kerr as its head was not Fraser's personal choice—it was departmental recommendation—but from the moment he took the position, Kerr made it his job to get to know the minister. One of the last things Fraser did as Defence Minister—on the very day he resigned—was to extend the terms of reference of the inquiry so that it could consider allowances for rental accommodation and education as well as pay. 'I knew I was probably going, but I knew this was important. I didn't want it mucked up just because I was on the way out.'

Kerr kept in touch with Fraser after his resignation. Kerr initiated the contact. Fraser remembers, 'John used to consult me unofficially, obviously, about different aspects of the tasks that he was doing, that needed resolving, during the course of his inquiry. Gorton was the Defence Minister now and he didn't really know anything about it. And I was glad to be consulted because I thought it was important. So, I got to know John Kerr then'. These conversations were, if not secret, then certainly discreet. Sometimes they talked by phone; sometimes they met face to face. Given the relationship between Fraser and Gorton, it would have caused a scandal if the meetings had become public, but, as Fraser says, 'Nobody was looking at what I was doing. I was on the back bench. And it wasn't the sexiest subject—pay inquiries into the services ...' The meetings allowed Fraser to see Kerr up-close, to watch him as he tried to find the best way of acquitting his responsibilities. 'He had a very good mind. But he was very concerned to be remembered as doing the right thing. And that's what the meetings were, really. Him checking out what he was thinking, to see if it was the right thing and would be well regarded. We met at different places; we might have spoken on the phone a few times ... If he had a problem and he didn't know quite which direction to go, or what sort of recommendation to make, then he would bounce ideas off me and that sort of thing.' In the process, the men developed a habit of speaking to each other frankly in conditions of political tension. It was the knowledge that he had gained of Kerr's personality that allowed Fraser on that other occasion when good government was at stake to make a shrewd assessment of what to say to the man. In the lead-up to the dismissal of the Whitlam government, Fraser chose words that he knew would resonate with Kerr's concern to be judged well by history: 'You are in the unfortunate position of having to make a choice, and, whichever way you go, you will be condemned. But you have a choice of whether to be condemned for doing the right thing, or for doing the wrong thing'.[42]

8

Life Wasn't Meant to Be Easy

Malcolm and Tamie Fraser divide their lives between two homes. The first and most important is their property on the Mornington Peninsula, with its view of Westernport Bay, its lawns and avenues of lemon-scented gums, and its camellias, tended and bred by Malcolm. Here he conducts interviews from the straight-backed chair in the entrance hall that doubles as a library. His old university textbooks and other serious works of non-fiction fill the shelves on one side of the front door. On the other side is popular fiction, including Colleen McCullough's historical novels set at the time of the Roman Republic. He has been reading these at night time, enjoying the political intrigue between the senate, the tribunes of the plebs, the courts and the assemblies, as strong men like Caesar and Octavian transformed the governance of their city-state into that befitting an empire. It makes a good story, and Fraser is told that McCullough does her historical research very thoroughly. The Frasers also have a flat in Toorak. Both homes are calm and elegant, even on those days when the telephone hardly stops ringing and Fraser is once again in the headlines. It is Tamie who maintains stability. This was always her job. In the days when they were dividing their lives between Canberra, Melbourne and Nareen, it was her aim to keep chaos at bay. Amid the whiplash ups and downs of politics, she tried to prevent the children from feeling that they were always in transit, and their lives out of control. So far as she could manage it, for them family life was the main event and politics the sideshow. There were few constants. 'We always took the vitamiser with us', she remembers. 'It was the only one we had.' Everything else changed.

Now Tamie sits in the soft light of the net-curtained window of the Toorak flat and reflects on the events that brought Fraser to the prime ministership. 'His life has always been so *big*. Nothing he has done has been little. If he leads an aid organisation, it will be the world's biggest. If he had headed the Commonwealth, it would have been a rival to the United Nations. There have been no little crises, only big ones. No little victories, only big ones. Big, big, big.' She remembers 21 March 1975—the beginning of the most dramatic year of their lives together. She sat in Kings Hall, Parliament House, biting her nails and watching a crowd of journalists surging back and forth in the corridor to the Liberals' party room. Politics and the way it was reported were more visceral then, the tides of fortune evident from the movements and the gossip across Kings Hall. Then the journalists poured out of the corridor, and she saw her husband's Press Secretary carried forwards on the tide, his hand held aloft in a sign. It was 'V' for victory. Her husband was Leader of the Opposition and in all likelihood the next Prime Minister of Australia. It was just over four years since he had resigned from John Gorton's ministry in what had seemed at the time likely to be the end of his political career.

In Tamie's and Malcolm's memory and in the written record, the four years between Fraser's casting himself into the political wilderness and becoming Leader of the Opposition are a chiaroscuro of depression and hope. There were achievements, certainly. As well, Fraser made speeches and wrote articles that stand out as statements of liberalism and how it ought to be expressed in the 1970s. Today, these speeches seem like peaks, or viewing platforms, in the journey of his life. One can discern the path that leads up to them—the intellectual framework he acquired at Oxford, the impact of the hard lessons of the Vietnam War and the struggles with his own party—and the path leading on, through the Whitlam years and up to the crisis that brought him to power. Yet, at the time he wrote these speeches and articles, Fraser had every reason to despair of his political future. His private correspondence shows that he was frequently depressed about the Liberal Party, the future of the country and the Western world.

Tony Eggleton remembers encountering Fraser sitting morose in a big green chair in a corridor of Parliament House. 'He looked deeply unhappy. A really sad figure. He said he thought he might as well go back to the farm, because his political career was over. And I said that he should cheer up, because I was sure he would be Prime Minister one day. I had thought so ever since he was Minister for Army.' Fraser was not in any case a man to sit idle and despairing. The political wilderness might be uncomfortable but it was a good place from which to reflect. It was clear to Fraser at the time of his resignation that liberalism was in trouble, and that the government of which he was part was on the skids. He wasn't even sure that it deserved re-election. He set about trying to think through what needed to be done, beginning with his former portfolio of defence. Nobody, it seemed to him, had really got to grips with what Australia should be doing in the aftermath of Nixon's Guam doctrine. Within weeks of his resignation he met Australian National University academics with specialities in international relations and told them he wanted to work on a 'philosophy of Australian defence'. They told him that if he succeeded in satisfactorily defining and prioritising Australia's national interests in the new climate, then he would be 'the first to have done so'.[1]

At about the same time, and with the same mission, Fraser sought out Bob Santamaria. The two men had never met, but had been watching each other for a long time. Santamaria's intellect, connections and strategising had been influential in Australian politics for almost all of Fraser's life. Now they shared a concern about the

Soviet move into the Indian Ocean. Santamaria had been intensely worried about this and about the drifting of defence policy under Gorton.[2] Santamaria's pressure, exercised through the Democratic Labor Party, persuaded Gorton to promise a greater defence presence in Western Australia—something Fraser, too, was advocating. Dick Casey, the old Fraser family friend, had passed on suggestions from Santamaria during Fraser's time as Minister for Defence. Fraser had rejected as impractical most of the particulars, including a push by Santamaria for Australia to buy aircraft carriers being sold by the British.[3] Nevertheless, Fraser had admired Santamaria from afar.

They met face to face for the first time in late March or early April 1971. After their meeting, Santamaria wrote on 5 April telling Fraser that it was essential that cabinet 'make the essential naval/ Indian Ocean decision in the 1971–72 budget ... My friends in the Senate could and would play a constructive role', but that they needed to speak 'from knowledge, and not merely in terms of generalities'. Would Fraser be prepared to help them on a confidential basis? In response, Fraser sent Santamaria copies of speeches he had made, including his resignation speech, and other items on the public record that contained the factual information Santamaria was seeking.

It was the beginning of a correspondence that continued, off and on, throughout the rest of Santamaria's life.[4] Santamaria lobbied Fraser before, during and after his prime ministership on foreign and domestic policy. He wanted Fraser to move against reporters at the ABC, and was disappointed when this was not done after Fraser became Prime Minister.[5] He also encouraged Fraser to block supply in the lead-up to the dismissal of the Whitlam government and, unasked, drafted a speech for Fraser justifying the decision. He sent advice and figuring on key government decisions such as tax indexation and Medibank. Even after Fraser had left political life, Santamaria had plans for him, but he often did not get his own way. 'He was someone I admired, but he was only one of the people I spoke to', says Fraser. Later, Santamaria was to say that he had a 'kind of friendship' with Fraser. They shared many things, most obviously anti-communism, but also a deep concern for rural life, a suspicion of centralised power and, in the early 1970s, a passionate concern that state aid to independent schools should be given on a per capita rather than a needs basis, for fear of stirring anti-Catholic sectarianism. Today, Fraser says, 'I think that on social justice issues we would have had a similar attitude. He led me to respect the Catholic Church, and the way it looks after its people, and this was at a time when most of my colleagues were very suspicious of Catholics. He would have believed that the American alliance was very important, but he wouldn't have been like a compliant puppy dog in relation to it. He was too individualistic for that. And I agreed with him'.

Meanwhile, Fraser was bringing the products of his reflection on defence policy to his speeches, both in parliament and elsewhere. Australia, he said, would now no longer have the luxury of waiting for a major power to commit itself to a conflict before acting.

> This does not mean that Australia should be put in a position of accepting unequal responsibilities beyond our physical strength. But it may mean that we will not again be given the luxury of being able to stand in the shadow of decisions previously announced by major powers on matters we regard as important.

After Vietnam, 'however that unhappy conflict ends', there would be pressure on the democracies to avoid new entanglements. There would be people who would argue that wars should not be fought unless Western Europe or the United States were directly threatened. Australia was only a middle-sized power, but Fraser thought it could be influential. It could show by example 'that we take the pursuit of life and liberty and the pursuit of happiness for our citizens and for others seriously'.[6]

One of the most significant outcomes of Fraser's reflections was a shift in his attitude to China. In his early speeches about Vietnam, he had blamed China more than Russia for provoking and funding insurgency and war. He had seen China as a communist threat equivalent to the Soviet Union—and not really distinct from it. Now he had a quite different view. He said that Australians should ask themselves how much of China's policy was motivated by communist ideology 'and how much of it by her own past and often tragic history'. China had no cause to love any of the great powers, he said, 'least of all the Soviet Union, who still occupies the territories that China regards as her own'. The independence of Taiwan should be maintained 'with skill and with tact', but not by a blanket opposition to mainland China. Concern for Taiwan should not stand in the way of 'dialogue and communication with the most populous country on this earth'.[7] In his attitude to China, and some other matters, Fraser was closer to Whitlam and the Labor Party than to his own side of politics, but none of this was picked up by the media. Because he still supported the Vietnam War, he was more likely to be portrayed as a reactionary.

The Liberal Party was trying to be hip. Faced with Whitlam's vision and stirring rhetoric, the Liberals responded by distancing themselves from the Menzies legacy of long, stable government. Fraser, with his shyness and aloof, abrupt manner, was never going to seem fashionable. He welcomed idealism in the young, but, having watched how public opinion had shifted against the Vietnam War, he asked himself whether a conflict in defence of freedom could ever be won if this generation governed it. What would happen to the ideals that had motivated him, Fraser, in his youth? Once again it was the electors of Wannon who might first have detected, in Fraser's weekly radio addresses, a new emphasis in his thinking: what the media later labelled as 'Fraserism'. It was an emphasis on duty, as well as freedom, and on rigour and endurance, as well as happiness. It was unacceptable for Labor to advocate breaking the law: the law had to bind everyone. 'Young people today are perhaps more idealistic than ever before', and this was something to be proud of, but there was 'another stream' which gave no cause for pride: 'an unwillingness to accept the minimum discipline that is necessary for an ordered society, an unwillingness to work within the framework of the law in our efforts to change that law'. The riots at universities and the statements from public figures were encouraging mutiny in the armed forces: 'These things are all part of a discernable trend which can only lead to the breakdown of the law and all respect for the society in which we live'.[8]

As for the new permissiveness, the sexual promiscuity, Fraser instinctively revolted. He had always thought that the law should so far as possible stay out of the bedroom. Sexual behaviour was a private matter, so long as everyone involved was a consenting adult and nobody was hurt. But he was vocal in opposing abortion on demand, and he hated the way in which sex was hawked from every street corner. Newspapers were publishing pages and pages about sex, he said in his radio addresses. There was hardly a theatre in the capital cities where R-rated films did not dominate. Fraser was discovering that, despite seeing himself as a progressive, there were some matters about which he thought a liberal *should* be conservative: the family, and the rule of law.[9]

At that time, the touchstone of controversy over the permissive society was *The Little Red School Book*, a manual of frankly expressed advice on drugs, sex and how to challenge authority, which was distributed at school gates. Fraser described the book to the electors of Wannon as 'an untidy, insidious and dirty little publication'.[10] He wrote about it to the Minister for Customs and Excise Don Chipp, although he stopped short of advocating its banning. Chipp, in any case, had no such intentions. He told Fraser that the book was mostly political, advocating dissent against authority. Only some of it was about sex, and the only way this differed from marriage manuals was that 'Anglo-Saxon words' were used for sex organs. Such words, Chipp told Fraser, were used in every school yard.[11]

Fraser told his electors that he did not want to return to the Victorian era. He welcomed freedom and idealism. But,

> a society cannot survive without some minimum of discipline, without an element of self-restraint, without a

> high regard of one person for another. Unlicensed sexual behaviour, abortion on request, a less rigorous attitude in relation to drugs, legalisation of prostitution, the pandering to the lowest community standards in literature: all these strike at the heart of values which are important to Australia and which every decent Australian and every family will want to protect.[12]

Fraser thus seemed to have set himself against permissive society and the tide of the times, and this was a gift to his political enemies—those who had seen Gorton as a modern man and who lamented his downfall. Fraser says today, 'That is when it began, that whole idea that I was to the right of Genghis Khan. It was put about by friends of Gorton, by my own side of politics. And it was never true'.

Fraser was in a strange position. He had friends, but few allies who were useful to him. He was increasingly close to Menzies, visiting the old man in his home. One of his best friends, Doug Anthony, was now Deputy Prime Minister, having succeeded John McEwen. Peter Nixon, also from the Country Party, was a friend. Yet among the progressives in his own party, including Jim Killen, Don Chipp and Andrew Peacock, he had no allies or friends. Killen and Peacock had been the service ministers when he was Defence Minister, and at the rough end of the tensions created by his push for reforms. Tom Hughes made no secret of his enmity. Fraser was deeply pessimistic about his ability to rise above all this. He despised the playing of the image game. It seemed so hard to get a simple message out. The media often bemused him; it had worked against him during the F-111 negotiations and during his confrontation with Gorton. Fraser was being forced to realise that while he could talk about big ideas, he was not good at communicating about himself—who he was and what he believed in. Meanwhile, men of greater charm and with better media contacts were rubbishing his name.

So it was that, on a chilly July night in 1971, when he arrived at Melbourne University to deliver the Alfred Deakin Lecture,

Fraser was feeling only pessimism about his own career, the Liberal Party and the future of the country. The lecture he gave, though, turned out to be a pivot point in his political career. Delivered just weeks after he had brought Gorton down, it became the speech for which he is perhaps best remembered and most misunderstood. It contained the words 'life wasn't meant to be easy', which were ever after quoted against him, accompanied by the observation that he had never known poverty. Few people looked for the context.

Fraser had asked Menzies, the Chancellor of the university, to chair the meeting at which the speech was to be delivered. The old man gave Fraser a surprise: he introduced him by noting that he was 'languishing on the back bench', and then, turning to Fraser, gave him an effective endorsement, saying, 'But your day will come, Malcolm. Your day will come'.

Fraser began. The speech was titled 'Towards 2000: Challenge to Australia'. Its schema was drawn straight from the Modern Greats that he had studied at Oxford. Once again, he spoke of Keynes. Once again, and even in the title of his speech, he returned to the idea he had gained from Arnold Toynbee of nations surviving or falling on their responses to challenge. Now, though, the idealism was overlaid with the bitter lessons of recent political life, with the experience of Vietnam, with his mixture of hope and despair for the current generation. Fraser started by talking about how Deakin had understood the challenges of his time: to unite the separate and quarrelsome colonies into 'the great free land we now know'. Now Australia stood in the final thirty years of the century, looking towards 2000, and the challenges came from within and without.

> Arnold Toynbee once wrote twelve volumes to demonstrate and analyse the cause of the rise and fall of nations. His thesis can be condensed to a sentence, and is simply stated: that, through history, nations are confronted by a series of challenges and whether they survive or whether they fall to the wayside depends on the manner and character of their response. Simple, and perhaps one of the few

> things that is self-evident. It involves a conclusion about the past that life has not been easy for people or for nations, and an assumption for the future that that condition will not alter. There is within me some part of the metaphysic, and thus I would add that life is not meant to be easy.

He spoke, then, about domestic conditions and laid out for the first time his understanding of what Keynes would have prescribed for the times—not more government spending, but restraint. Since Keynes, strong unions unconstrained by the experience of unemployment had pushed unreasonable wage demands. Governments had allowed people to think that all things could be provided. Sound economic management and the need for restraint had been laid aside.

Today, reading Fraser's speeches of the early 1970s, what sticks out as unconventional is his insistence on a big role for government in regulating markets, the centrality of trade unions to Australian life, and the importance of investing in education and combating disadvantage. At the time, what was remarkable was his call for restraint and self-reliance. Fraser remarks, 'The times have changed more than I have'.

Fraser turned to the external threats, repeating the view that Australia would have to become more self-reliant and would not be able to wait for great nations to act. 'We live at the beginning of a new era which we do not yet fully comprehend. More than ever in our history we need to stand up, to tread our own path, not in isolation, but in partnership with countries great and small.' He rejected isolationism, criticising Labor explicitly, but implicitly including those in his own party who advocated a reduced role for defence.

Finally, he brought his themes of internal and external threat together under the heading 'Understanding and Will'. This section of the speech was about leadership. How was it possible to persuade people of the need for sacrifice and for a united response to challenge? How could liberal values be combined with the need for forthright action and unity of purpose? Fraser was offering more questions than answers.

> Democracy protects independence of mind and action; it encourages debate; but how does a democracy accept discipline unless there is a present need? Democratic leadership must maintain the essential unity of a people not easily marshalled to a common purpose. We criticise our own objectives; we give the benefit of every doubt to our opponent. Do we want to be able to go on our way so much, do we want peace so much that we cannot recognise that others do not all share our objectives? … What is the catalyst that will unite a people—an obvious danger? But that can be too late. Can it be love of country or obligation? Is it liberty, philosophy or material standards? True democracy is so diversified in its constituent parts that it is difficult to find the catalyst that will light the hearts of men, except when that democracy is threatened. Such a catalyst is the 'Holy Grail' of democracy. Its search places particular responsibility and a particular challenge on those who aspire to leadership.
>
> …
>
> We must be particularly aware of the great weakness of man's idealism, which is to forget the frailty of the human race, to believe that man is something that he is not and so construct a view of society that can only exist in the mind. We can only draw reality from our idealism when we can accept that while we strive for perfection, we will not reach it in this world, nor our sons after us. Recognition of this truth should soften the radical, bring tolerance to the fanatic, temper the extremes of love and hate. But it will not make our vigilance or struggle any the less necessary.[13]

Menzies might have thought that Fraser's time would, and should, come, but not everyone agreed. A few weeks after Fraser delivered the Alfred Deakin Lecture, Prime Minister Billy McMahon offered him a ministry, but the offer could be understood only as an insult.

The job was Minister of State for Supply—the most junior non-cabinet portfolio. Fraser wrote declining the post, with the words: 'I do not really believe that a man ought to serve his apprenticeship twice'.[14]

Yet, just a few weeks later, Fraser did indeed return to cabinet and ironically he had John Gorton to thank. The journalist Alan Reid had published a highly critical book about Gorton's rise and fall, and Gorton had responded in the pages of *The Australian* with a series of articles that included unflattering reflections on his cabinet colleagues.[15] McMahon sacked him for disloyalty, making the position of Deputy Leader vacant. Seven people stood, including Fraser. He knew he was unlikely to get the post—he had too many enemies—but he also knew that if he received a respectable number of votes it would be impossible for McMahon to deny him a place in cabinet. He came third—after Billy Snedden and the Minister for National Development Reginald Swartz, but beating Jim Killen, David Fairbairn, Don Chipp and Bill Wentworth. As he had predicted, his strong showing forced McMahon's hand. On 20 August 1971, for the second time in his political career, Fraser was made Minister for Education and Science.

Six weeks later, he made a ministerial statement that foreshadowed big increases in expenditure for education—increases that from the perspective of our own time seem nothing short of astonishing. He was delivering on a view that he had expressed in the Deakin lecture: education was not a cost, but an investment. Commonwealth expenditure on education had now increased by 100 per cent since 1967–68. Once again, Fraser emphasised the social role of education:

> We ought to strive harder than ever before to achieve what no generation has yet achieved: a community composed of men and women for whom human values are more important than material advantage; a community for whom inter-relationship of man with man has become the most important concern; a community in which tolerance

> and understanding reign and prejudice is abandoned ... If anyone suggests such an ideal cannot be achieved, let those who can believe strive the harder [16]

Within months, Fraser had announced the setting-up of a commission to advise on colleges of advanced education. Over the next twelve months, large increases were announced in government assistance for both independent and government schools—still on the per capita system. Meanwhile, Whitlam was campaigning hard for grants to schools to be made on the basis of need, and the Defence of Government Schools' campaign was increasing in vehemence.

Towards the end of 1971, the year in which he had by his own hand seemingly ended his political career, Malcolm Fraser sat down to write a Christmas letter to his sister, Lorri, in Rome. 'We both enjoyed the five months out of the cabinet and often wish it could have gone on longer', he said, without giving any hint of how busy he had been. He told her about the new family dog Droopy, before leaping back to politics. He said that it was going to be hard to tell which way the economy would go. 'For the first time we are faced with the real problem of attempting to curb inflation without causing too much unemployment and general economic difficulty. No country seems to have mastered that very well so far.' He wrote that he had been to see Robert Menzies, who two weeks before had suffered a second stroke. The first, in 1968, had been mild; this one had been more severe, leaving him paralysed on one side. Fraser told Lorri:

> The Old Man is pretty depressed. His voice and mind are still good, but this stroke has attacked the leg and arm which were not affected [by the earlier stroke] in London ... At the moment he has no movement at all in his left leg or arm, so the prospects of remaining immobile are, unfortunately, high.[17]

* * *

The following year, 1972, was a depressing one in which to be a member of the Liberal government. The Prime Minister, Billy McMahon, was increasingly a figure of ridicule, easily bested in parliament by Gough Whitlam. There was nothing to suggest that the government was getting to grips with inflation, or embracing the tough medicine Fraser thought appropriate. Today, Fraser says, 'The foolishness of Whitlam, the belief that government expenditure could keep going up and up, began with our own side of politics. He increased the foolishness, of course, but it wasn't unique to him'. Thanks largely to Fraser's power in cabinet, virtually all the financial recommendations of the Australian Universities Commission and the Australian Commission on Advanced Education were accepted, leading to big increases in Commonwealth spending on tertiary education. This was the period that saw Griffith, Murdoch and Wollongong universities established, together with the Flinders University School of Medicine. In August 1972, Fraser announced that the action he had taken in 1969 to ensure that Asian languages were taught in schools had borne fruit: the Commonwealth and the states would cooperate over a range of measures to stimulate the teaching of Asian languages and culture. Meanwhile, scholarships for students in secondary school and at university were more than doubled.[18]

But, by comparison with what Whitlam was saying, Fraser was easily painted as conservative. Whitlam was promising needs-based funding for schools, and fee-free tertiary education. Fraser thought that abolishing university fees was inequitable. In a radio address in November 1972 he said that Labor's policy of free tertiary education 'would result in the gigantic inequality of a wharf labourer paying taxes to subsidise a lawyer's education'.[19] Today, Fraser still believes the best way to address equality of opportunity in tertiary education is to offer plentiful scholarships to the less well off, rather than to abolish fees or ask young people to go into debt. In his time, the scholarships included a living allowance for families who otherwise could not afford to support a student at university, meaning that people from low-income families could go to university. Abolishing fees did not greatly change the social mix seeking higher education.

But by now, the electorate had stopped listening. McMahon had already begun to acquire the reputation that has stuck to him ever since—one of the worst prime ministers in Australian history. Behind the scenes he was harassing his ministers and public servants for policy and political advice. Ironically, given his own reputation, he was plagued by cabinet leaks. Everyone knew that the Liberals were on the way out. Whitlam was ascendant. With the big swing in 1969, he had reaped the rewards of the hard years of party reform. Since then, he had released policy after policy, convincing the electorate—and some in the Liberal Party—that he had the vision that McMahon and the government lacked. On 2 December 1972, twenty-three years of Liberal–Country Party rule came to an end. The Australian Labor Party did not secure a big swing: the real change in voting figures had taken place in 1969. Whitlam gaining power had an air of inevitability; as the campaign slogan had said, it was time. Today, asked whether the Liberals deserved to lose power in 1972, Fraser hesitates only for a moment, then gives a decisive nod of his head, accompanied by a grimace. 'Oh yes.' A longer pause, then: 'We had lost all sense of vision. And Whitlam had vision. He had seized the imagination of the people. But the problem with Whitlam is he didn't know how to manage anything, including his own party. And he had no idea about economics. He thought economics didn't matter at all'.

Once Whitlam was in power, he moved with astonishing speed. As soon as the result was beyond doubt, he had himself and his deputy, Lance Barnard, sworn in as a two-man government, and immediately began a massive reform program, beginning with formally ending Australia's involvement in Vietnam and releasing the draft dodgers, then moving on to Medibank, free tertiary education and needs-based aid to independent schools. Meanwhile, McMahon stepped down as Liberal Party leader. Fraser stood for the leadership against Nigel Bowen, the former Treasurer and Deputy Leader Billy Snedden, John Gorton and Jim Killen. Fraser was eliminated after the third ballot, and Snedden became the new leader.

In March 1973, Fraser made his first radio address to his electorate as a member of the opposition. He told them:

> Clearly, the role is quite different from that of a private member supporting the government or that of a government minister ... The Liberal Party faces the task of reconstruction, of regaining the confidence of the majority of Australians. We will be working to achieve that. We will try to be a constructive opposition. If the government introduces measures that we believe to be good, we will support them ... There will be other occasions when we will clearly oppose what the government is doing, because we believe the government to be wrong. On these occasions we will use all the strength and vigour that are available to us.[20]

Fraser received reams of private correspondence commiserating with him on the loss. In his standard reply to these letters, he was blunter than he had been on the radio. He made it clear that he thought the Liberal Party had lost its way. It needed 'the closest scrutiny at every level—our polices, our organisation, our attitudes and approaches to government ... The party must start straightaway'.[21]

Fraser told his electors that he was 'pleased' to have been made Shadow Minister for Primary Industries, particularly since it gave him responsibilities that directly affected Wannon. In truth, he was less than delighted: he thought this was another attempt by his own side to bury him. Primary industries could not be further from the areas in which he had had most to say—foreign policy and economics. In a letter to a friend, the former United States Ambassador William Battle, he said: 'It is not and has never been my main area of concern in parliament. It's been difficult to attack the Labor Party on primary industry matters because they have no policy'.[22] So it was that, through 1973, Fraser's few speeches in parliament were not on agriculture, but on immigration, migrant education and defence.

Privately, Fraser and Tamie talked about Snedden. Neither of them thought he was the man to lead a thoroughgoing review. 'He was a nice man,' says Fraser today, 'a fine fellow and a good bloke. But he was not the most inspiring leader'. Fraser says that it was at this time—only after the McMahon defeat—that he began to allow himself to think that he might one day be leader. 'Up until then I had always thought of leaders being men like Menzies, or Hasluck or Barwick. And for most of my career they had been so far above me. I always said that what I wanted in politics was to do the best job I could of whatever was given to me. But then with Snedden and before that McMahon—well, you begin to look around you and think that perhaps you could do a better job.' Yet it seemed impossible that he would ever be given the chance.

True to his word, Fraser was not always critical of Whitlam to start with. He bemoaned many of his foreign policy moves and criticised his budgets, but he also saw things he liked. When Whitlam gave the vote to eighteen year olds, Fraser said in his weekly radio address that he wished the Liberal Party had done it first. Young people 'show a concern for the underprivileged; they show a concern for the general nature and direction of Australian society. In addition there are many who take a keen interest in international affairs and feel strongly about matters they believe to be right'.[23] Fraser also approved of Whitlam's recognition of the People's Republic of China. He spoke in support of the abolition of the last vestiges of the White Australia policy, while noting that the process of ending it had begun under Menzies and Holt. Whitlam had removed the last legal remnants. Fraser was also in favour of Whitlam's attempts to introduce self-determination for Aboriginal Australians, overturning decades of assimilationist policies.

Six months into Whitlam's prime ministership, Fraser wrote to Lorri and told her that politics was in a state of flux. Nobody could say what the future would bring. 'Whitlam is riding high, but he has changed Australian policies more than anyone envisaged, and, if the theory of the mandate means anything, as far as defence and foreign policy are concerned he has gone far beyond his mandate.' But, Fraser noted, there had been good rains and high prices for rural products, which made it easier for Whitlam to pay for his promises. So far, Whitlam's government looked at least viable.[24]

Then, in October 1973, came the defining economic event of the postwar years: the first oil shock. The Organisation of the Petroleum Exporting Countries (OPEC) initially embargoed oil sales to much of the Western world, then cut production of oil and raised the price. The price of oil quadrupled over just a few months. The world financial system was already under pressure: President Nixon had in 1971 unilaterally stopped the direct convertibility of the US dollar to gold, imposing great strains on the world economy, and leading to the collapse of the Bretton Woods agreements that had regulated international monetary management since World War II. Now the oil shock brought to an end the long postwar boom, together with the assumptions about prosperity and easy living that Fraser had in the Deakin lecture bemoaned, because they had made young people unfamiliar with struggle and adversity. Fraser had been warning about high inflation, and suggesting ways in which Keynes, had he been alive, might have modified his advice to fit the times. Keynes would have advocated restraint, said Fraser, but the oil shock had taken the trends that Fraser had identified into a whole new territory: stagflation, or recession combined with inflation. The conventional view was that Keynesian economics had no answers to offer.

It was a bad time to have as Prime Minister a man who was not a good manager and who did not think economics mattered. Whitlam's visionary program was predicated on the assumption that economic growth and low unemployment were the norm, rather than freaks of the postwar 'golden age'. The oil shock made his program appear not only ambitious, but disastrous. This, together with all the rapid change in social policy, meant that many Australians felt, as Fraser put it in an electorate address in late 1973, that Whitlam was turning 'many aspects of life upside down'. Interest rates were now up to 14 per cent, he told his electorate. Government policies on oil and mineral exploration were 'in turmoil'. And all this was taking place in the 'dangerous' international economic situation caused by Arab oil restrictions.[25]

* * *

The move to opposition had spurred the Frasers to make changes to their family life. Moving back and forth to Canberra had become more of a strain than a help. Now Fraser was no longer a minister, they decided that Tamie and the children should be based at Nareen. The older three children were in boarding school. Phoebe had been enrolled in a Montessori primary school in Canberra. Tamie had chosen it, aware that her daughter was unusually 'bright and lively'. Now she moved to the Nareen state school, and to everyone's surprise preferred the more conventional structure and discipline.

This arrangement, though, was short-lived. The following year, Mark began secondary school at Melbourne Grammar. He wanted to be a day boy rather than a boarder, so the family moved again, buying a house at Fairlie Court near the botanical gardens in South Yarra. Tamie calculated that she had now moved home seventeen times in nineteen years. Nareen was still the refuge and the constant; they spent as many weekends and holidays there as possible. Tamie has memories of driving back and forth, begging the children to sing to her or tell her stories to keep her awake. Fairlie Court, though, was the workaday home base for the family until Fraser became Prime Minister.

When in Canberra, Fraser was 'batching' and, as is often the way with Canberra's transient population of politicians, sharing his house with two others: his old friend Tony Street—'one of the nicest men that ever lived'—and a relative newcomer to parliament, Tony Staley, who became one of the most crucial people in Fraser's political career. It was Staley who engineered Fraser's progress to the party leadership, and, through his talent-spotting of key advisers, he had great influence over the intellectual foundations of the Fraser government.

Today Staley is not Fraser's friend. He is one of those who cannot forgive Fraser for what he sees as his disloyalty to the party through the years of the Howard government. 'I, like many others, was dismayed that he made his criticisms so frequently and so publically. We are courteous to each other, but we don't talk much', says Staley. He believes that Fraser has changed, becoming more left-wing. But Staley is proud of his own role in the Fraser government: it was a good government, he says—sound, sensible, consultative, prudent and well managed, not corrupt. Meanwhile, Fraser believes it is Staley who has changed. 'When I first knew him, he was interested in ideas. Perhaps something happened to that. He took a different view, I think, as time went by.'

Staley was born to the Liberal Party. Like Fraser, he believed politics was a matter of passion and conviction, and that ideas mattered. After a Scotch College education, he studied politics at Melbourne University and went on to become a senior lecturer. He knew all the bright young students, and, even before he entered federal parliament in 1970 as member for the eastern suburbs seat of Chisholm, he was talent-spotting. Easy to spot was David Kemp, first as a graduate student and later as lecturer in political science, who himself came from a family steeped in the intellectual basis of liberalism. Kemp's father, Charles, had established the Institute of Public Affairs, a think tank that had provided much of the policy groundwork for Menzies when he founded the Liberal Party. Kemp became one of Fraser's key advisers during his prime ministership. Kemp recalls, 'I really feel we had a relationship like no other. He never yelled at me like he did with some others. Oh, we argued, and he argues very aggressively, but I was brought up in a family where that was common. I understood it'.

Kemp remembers that Staley was trying to involve him in federal politics as early as 1971. Staley arranged for him to meet John

Gorton when he was still Prime Minister. Then, after Whitlam's 1972 victory, he arranged for Kemp to sit in on a shadow cabinet meeting. The idea was that Kemp should write a document to help the party prepare for the next election. This was the first time that Kemp set eyes on Malcolm Fraser. He remembers, 'I saw him interact with the other members of that Snedden shadow cabinet and I was very impressed with the forceful way in which he spoke and the clarity of his views. I thought, "This is a potentially powerful leader"'.

Kemp wrote an article shortly after this encounter. Titled 'A Leader and a Philosophy', it analysed the roots of liberal philosophy and acknowledged that socialism had forced it to change—to acknowledge that while freedom was a necessary condition for human dignity, it was not enough. 'A man could be free but destitute.' Freedom had to be tempered with concern for others, liberty with a consideration of when it was justifiable to curtail liberty. He analysed Liberal Party policies on taxation, education, abortion and Aboriginal welfare in the light of these reflections, and concluded:

> Liberalism has the enormous strength of being both a conservative and a reforming philosophy—conserving the values of human dignity and fulfilment while liberating human energies ... The issues of leadership and philosophy are inseparable, for the effective leadership of an opposition party requires authority, and leadership in the restatement of the basic guiding principles of policy is potentially an important source of that authority. The future of the Liberal movement in Australia will be decided by the response to this challenge.

Only a strong leader who was also in touch with the roots of liberal philosophy could unify the party and make a successful appeal to the electorate, said Kemp.[26] This article was published in 1973, and was, as Kemp had intended it to be, influential. By now, through

Staley, they were part of the same intellectual circle. Unlike Staley, Kemp doesn't think Fraser has changed. Kemp, today the President of the Victorian Liberal Party, says that Fraser, 'unlike a lot of people connected to political parties', is always aware of the big issues—the ideas that go beyond the sound and light show of party politics. 'He thinks we have to see ourselves in the flow of history, and the important principles for which we stand ... are more important to him than current political leaders and political parties and organisations. All of that is subordinate to the bigger picture. That has led him to do things which some people have seen as disloyalty to the Liberal Party. If you think about it, the Gorton episode is an example of that. So he is seen as someone who doesn't have a high level of political loyalty, and yet I think that that doesn't do him justice. I think that if you pressed him on the point, he would probably say that loyalty is a subordinate value, whereas many people who are active in political life put loyalty at the top of their list ... He is an interesting character as well, of course; as a person I think that he has got enormous strengths and he has got some quirks and foibles, if I may put it that way ... that don't always help him.'

Whatever their differences today, in 1973 Staley and Fraser—both determined men of ideas—saw very much eye to eye. They had known each other since the 1960s, but it was only when they shared the Canberra house that they became close. Fraser was not an easy man to get to know. Staley comments that with most people one starts with small talk and gradually moves to more important topics. With Fraser it was the other way around. 'The closer you got to him, the more small talk you got. He couldn't do small talk until you were close.' They sat up late into the night arguing about politics. About Snedden, they were in sad agreement: he had none of the vision, none of the appetite for thoroughgoing reform and reinvigoration that was needed if the Liberals were to deserve a return to power. But Staley had not agreed with what Fraser had done to Gorton. 'I had stood back and watched that with dismay. Yes, there were problems with Gorton. But Billy McMahon was not the answer.' Unlike Fraser's enemies within the party, though, Staley had forgiven him. For the present, there seemed to be nothing that could be done. There was no appetite in the party for Fraser as leader; rather, the reverse. There were sections of the party dedicated to making sure he never again amounted to anything.

* * *

Fraser spent most of 1973 and 1974 trying to revive his political hopes. In mid 1973 the position of Shadow Minister for Foreign Affairs became vacant due to Nigel Bowen's moving to the New South Wales Supreme Court. Fraser and Andrew Peacock were the contenders. Fraser took a private overseas trip to boost his claim, visiting his sister in Rome and doing some trout fishing in Canada, but also seeing the Indonesian Foreign Minister, catching up with Lee Kuan Yew in Singapore and with the British Foreign Secretary and former High Commissioner to Australia Peter Carrington in London. In Canada he visited his old university friend John Turner, who was now Finance Minister, and later to become Prime Minister. Home movies from this trip show Fraser and Tamie in the wilds, wrapped up against the chill and wading deep in icy lakes, rod and tackle in hand. They look young and happy. Yet, before he left Canada, Fraser heard that his hopes had been dashed: the foreign affairs job would go to Peacock. Once again, his party had rejected him. Instead, he was given the job of Shadow Minister for Industrial Relations. Once more, it seemed like an attempt to finish him off. Industrial relations was an issue 'owned' by the Labor Party; it was a long time since a Liberal had had anything much to say about it. Fraser returned to Australia more depressed than ever about his prospects. Something had to be done.

It was at this point, convinced that he was indeed being buried, that Fraser allowed himself to be persuaded to rethink his opposition to the business of political image-making. He knew he was being portrayed as a deep conservative. Earlier that year, his conservative image had been cemented in many people's minds by his being vocal in opposing a private members' Bill decriminalising abortion. Fraser had told his electors in a radio address that abortion struck at the heart of family life. He would never support abortion on demand. Yet his views were not easy to summarise. In the lead-up to the 1972 federal election, the newly founded Women's Electoral Lobby had surveyed members of parliament and scored them on their attitude to women's issues. Fraser had scored seventeen—much better than his Liberal colleagues, who often had minus figures.[27] Fraser had been interviewed by the founder of the lobby, Beatrice Faust. She later remembered Fraser as 'actually quite a decent chap but he wouldn't answer yes or no. We'd developed the survey for tick boxes and I had to write down every word the man said because he wouldn't give me anything for the tick boxes'.[28]

Complexity did not translate easily in tick-box surveys, or in the minds of the electorate, or in the minds of Liberal Party members. So it was that with many reservations and forebodings, Fraser approached a 'low-key' public relations firm, John Royce and Associates, for help with his public image. A young adviser, Alister Drysdale, was assigned to the case. 'I was just a whippersnapper', Drysdale remembers today. 'I was learning on the job.' Drysdale had a taste for a bold approach, but soon realised that there were strict limits to what his new client would and would not do. He would not alter his hair style, or smile more, or change his way of speaking. Drysdale didn't even suggest it. 'He would have just thrown us out of the office. He had absolute contempt for playing those sorts of games.' Fraser was also remorselessly serious-minded.

Drysdale, who went on to be Fraser's Press Secretary when he was Prime Minister, found that his client didn't even read most of the newspapers, regarding their coverage as superficial. 'He would read the editorials, and I said to him, "But Malcolm, nobody else reads those. They aren't want makes the difference". And he would argue with me that in any case they set the tone of the newspaper. I always had trouble getting him to read the rest of the paper. Right through the prime ministership.' Fraser comments, 'It took twelve minutes to go through the papers. For the most part, if you read the headline and saw the byline of the journalist, you could more or less write the rest yourself. It was all so predictable, and you knew what they thought'. He would read an article if it interested him, and his department ran a clippings service designed to bring to his attention anything that really should be read. Other than that, 'All I needed to know was broadly what they were writing about, and the attitude they were taking'.

It was clear to Drysdale that Fraser had natural strengths. He had always been good at dealing with working people face to face, as his success in turning Wannon into a safe seat had shown. 'Far too many beers in far too many front bars', Fraser remembers. His new portfolio gave him a perfect opportunity to show that side of his personality. Drysdale organised magazine articles that focussed on Fraser on the farm and his family life.

All of this left Fraser only partially convinced that it was the sort of thing a man such as himself should do. 'I was never comfortable with it', he remembers. But in late 1973 a series of events convinced him, as Drysdale puts it, that 'Sometimes the media can be on your side'. Fraser's enemies had begun issuing t-shirts designed to send him up and portray him as hopelessly old-fashioned. The mottos read: 'Relieve Mafeking. Vote Fraser', 'Put Value Back in the Pound. Vote Fraser' and 'Support Our Boys in Korea. Support Malcolm Fraser'. It was an act of political bastardry that makes contemporary politics look tame. Fraser was more depressed than ever, but Drysdale sensed an opportunity to have his client talked about and to present him in a new light. A press conference was booked, and Drysdale and *Age* photographer Bruce Postle organised a photo opportunity. Two models were paid to dress in the t-shirts. Meanwhile, Fraser was in the dentist's chair on the other side of the city. Postle, characteristically, was determined to make what could be a boring photograph into a front-page image. He drove to Fraser, got him out of the chair and took his photograph. Then he went to the dark room and enlarged the picture to a life-sized head and shoulders. He returned to the two waiting models and posed them lying down on a black carpet and holding the image of Fraser while kicking their legs. Postle climbed on top of the furniture to take a picture of them from close to the ceiling. The result was a striking and 'mod' image. Later that day at the press conference, Fraser told the media that he thought the t-shirts were wonderful, and a great joke. Tamie owned a 'Put Value Back in the Pound' version, and he thought they would make excellent Christmas presents for members of the Labor front bench. Postle's photograph meant that the press conference was transformed from a dull political story to an image that dominated the front page on 15 December 1973. The spoof was spoofed, and thus ended. Drysdale had also established his credentials with his client. It was a new experience for Fraser: he had never before felt that the media could be on his side. There were to be precious few occasions, over the next ten years, when they would be.

* * *

As Fraser struggled with his own party, the Whitlam government struggled with the Senate. The Upper House of federal parliament had been untouched by the enthusiasm for change that had seen Whitlam elected. From early in the new government's term, it was clear that it was here that Whitlam would face his biggest political battles. The Australian Labor Party had twenty-six senators, the Liberal and Country Party a total of twenty-six. There were also five Democratic Labor Party senators and three independents. The government typically could not muster more than twenty-eight votes, and the Democratic Labor Party normally voted with the opposition. Reg Withers, the Liberal Party's leader in the Senate, believed that—with Whitlam turning so much on its head—now was the time for the Upper House to fulfil the intention of the founding fathers. 'Let us remember', he said in the early days of the Whitlam government, 'that the Senate was deliberately set up by the founding fathers with its enormous powers to act as a check and a balance'.[29]

Withers's opposite number was Lionel Murphy, the Labor Attorney-General. Murphy's image had been dented in the first months of the new government when he led an extraordinary raid on the offices of the Australian Security Intelligence Organisation without consulting cabinet. Whitlam later described it as his government's greatest mistake; it made the new government look amateurish and unstable, but, more importantly for how things played out in the Senate, it tapped into deep anxieties about Labor and whether it was 'loyal' to Australia or to Moscow. The raid cemented the Democratic Labor, Liberal and Country parties' senators in opposition to Murphy. Any hope he might have had of negotiating the passage of legislation was gone.

By the end of 1973 it was clear to all sides of politics that an election was likely early in the new year, through either a double dissolution or the blocking of supply. Among the Bills the opposition had rejected were the legislation setting up Medibank and the Commonwealth Electoral Bill, which would have allowed for more regular redistributions and a lower tolerance for variation in the population of electorates. Also blocked was legislation setting up the needs-based system of school funding. On this issue, Fraser led the opposition, but the popular mood was against him. Preserving grants to the wealthiest schools was hard to sell. Whitlam, already armed with the requirements for a double dissolution, was clearly keen to fight an election on this issue. In December 1973, he went so far as to tell the premiers to make polling preparations. It was the Country Party that cut a deal and defused the crisis.

Whitlam clearly believed he could win an election, but the Liberal Party also had reason to feel encouraged: Liberal governments had been returned in New South Wales and Victoria; the economy was deteriorating; and Whitlam had taken the country to a referendum, seeking the power to set prices and incomes, and had been soundly defeated. Even if he regained government, Whitlam was unlikely to gain control of the Senate. An election would not fix his problem. So it was that, in early 1974, Labor devised an extraordinary ruse. Vince Gair, who had recently been deposed as Democratic Labor Party leader, was offered an effective bribe: a post as Ambassador to Ireland. The idea was that if Gair resigned from the Senate before the forthcoming half-Senate election, there would be six Senate vacancies contested in Queensland instead of five, and this would give Labor a chance of winning the extra position and gaining control. It was an act of extraordinary political cynicism. Gair's new appointment was approved amid tight secrecy on 21 March. On the same day, Whitlam announced that there would be a half-Senate election on 18 May. Then the story of Gair's appointment was broken by the media, and confirmed by a triumphant Whitlam in parliament. But even as Gair was celebrating with his new Labor friends, the plot was foiled. Whitlam had overlooked the detail: Gair had not yet formally resigned from the Senate. Queensland Premier Bjelke-Petersen ordered a special printing of the *Government Gazette*; thus, Gair was still a senator when the writs were issued, so only five vacancies were contested, and Whitlam could not win control.

To Fraser the Gair affair confirmed that the Whitlam government was without principle. In his weekly radio address he told the people of Wannon that it showed how Whitlam was prepared to 'use virtually any means to gain complete control over both Houses of Parliament. The Prime Minister has talked about a mandate, but there is also a mandate for people who have been elected to the Senate'. Whitlam's actions were unprecedented since William Pitt the Younger had 'decided it was time for the Irish Parliament to disappear in 1801'.[30]

The affair marked the beginning of the many breaches of convention in the manipulation of Senate appointments that played such a crucial role through 1974 and 1975. The fact that Whitlam had breached convention made Snedden and the opposition more willing to consider unusual moves. At a lunch meeting on 4 April 1974, the Liberal and Country parties accepted a recommendation from their joint front benches to force an election by blocking supply. This was a precursor to the dramatic election of 1975 that confirmed Fraser as Prime Minister. The difference was that in 1974 Whitlam embraced the push for an election, rather than resisting it. He chose to make it a double dissolution, which gave him a slim chance of winning the Senate and would in any case allow him to secure the passage of the blocked Bills if he was returned.

Fraser was ambivalent about Snedden's tactics. During 1973 he had argued that an early election would let Whitlam off the hook. 'In my view, [Whitlam] will want an election before he is forced to do something about inflation. He'll use the states as a scapegoat.'[31] Privately, he doubted that the Liberals could win: Snedden had moved too fast, and the electorate was not convinced of a need for change. Fraser was aware that many of his colleagues could not quite grasp that Whitlam had won an election. They thought it was an aberration, that the voters, given a chance, would naturally return them to power. Fraser thought differently. In key areas, Liberal Party policies had either not been prepared or were undercooked. The hard work of remaking the party had not been done. Bad though he thought Whitlam was—and Fraser was increasingly alarmed by the direction of the government—he recognised that the Liberals had not yet earned a return to power.

Meanwhile, Fraser had been making ambitious moves in the industrial relations portfolio. His approach was proving a surprise to some unionists. He was touring workplaces, and insisting on talking to the workers—sometimes against the wishes of employers. Jim Begg, then President of the Waterside Workers Federation, remembers being asked by the radical communist State Secretary Ted Bull to show a 'visitor' around the docks. He waited by the wharves in Melbourne, and at about seven-thirty in the morning saw 'this great hulk of a bloke getting out of a car'. It was Malcolm Fraser, and Begg was instantly worried that he was in for trouble. How would he keep his visitor from being abused? Fraser and his party were deeply unpopular with the members. Begg took a route he hoped would avoid running into too many of 'the lads', but instead ran into a crowd of over a hundred. Fraser insisted on talking to them. Begg was called away, and when he returned he found Fraser surrounded by wharfies laughing and joking. 'I realised that about half of the lads were new Australians, and education was important to them. They wanted to put their kids through university, and Fraser had been Education Minister, so he could relate to that.' Fraser was bawled out by only one member, who objected to his even being brought onto the wharf. Fraser took it well.

Begg was beginning to warm to him. The visit became extended. Begg took Fraser to the Station Pier, where working conditions were appalling, and wharfies were forced to labour unsheltered from the bitter winds off Bass Strait. Then they went on to the newly refurbished Swanston Dock, where crane cabins had heating and air conditioning, and workers were provided with subsidised meals, a decent mess and good boots, wet-weather gear and sunglasses. Fraser spent hours talking to the men and ended up being invited to lunch. By the end of the day he had struck up a lasting connection with Begg, had gained a keen appreciation of the difficulties of wharfies' lives and had forced at least some of them to reconsider their attitudes to him and his party.

The industrial relations policy that Fraser released in the lead-up to the 1974 election cut new ground for the Liberal Party: it actively encouraged union membership. 'While membership of organisations should be voluntary, employees and employers should be positively encouraged to take a responsible and active part in their respective union and industry organisations … Unionism is basic to the Australian way of life', it said.[32] Fraser pledged the Liberals' support of trade union training and consultations between employers and employees. Speaking in one of his radio addresses, in the week that the policy was released, he said, 'We want to see employees given a greater sense of involvement and participation. They cannot be regarded as just another input in the production process'. Underlying this policy was support for negotiation, conciliation and arbitration. Once an agreement had been reached, said Fraser, both employees and employers should be obliged to honour it. The policy advocated the setting-up of an industrial relations bureau with the power to ensure that both employers and employees stuck to the letter of awards and industrial agreements. 'The view that, of all legal agreements, industrial agreements should be the only ones that need not be binding on one party is contrary to our liberal philosophy in law and to our democratic system.'[33]

The election on 18 May 1974 was one of the closest in Australian history. Whitlam was re-elected, but his majority was reduced from nine seats to five in the Lower House. He had failed to gain control of the Senate. There were now twenty-nine Australian Labor Party senators, twenty-nine coalition senators and the South Australian Steele Hall representing the Liberal Movement. Hall supported the government on questions of supply. The Democratic Labor Party had been wiped out; after nineteen years, the child of the Australian Labor Party split was destroyed as a force in Australian federal politics.

Fraser and Staley watched Snedden's press conference after the defeat with sinking hearts. 'We were not defeated', Snedden said, 'but we did not win enough seats to form a government'. It was the born-to-rule mentality, naked for all to see. Snedden expressed satisfaction with his own campaign and denied that Whitlam had a mandate 'in any significant form'. Soon afterwards, Snedden bizarrely interrupted one of Whitlam's parliamentary speeches by shouting 'Woof woof'. He was easy meat for Whitlam's ridicule. Later that year, Fraser wrote to Lorri that he had

> never been so depressed in my life about the future of Australia … I can find nothing here or anywhere in the world to relieve the gloom about the future. Unemployment is going to go through the roof; inflation will hit 20, 25 and perhaps even 30 per cent next year; the cost of running farms has doubled in the last two and a half years; and returns will be half what they were last year. Australia is likely to be internationally bankrupt

> in twelve or so months on present policies … There is going to be a very large number of people in very great difficulty. Our last general election was a fiasco, as you would obviously have heard by now. We chose the time, the issue, everything, and still we could not win. Whitlam has lost popularity at the polls but so has Snedden steadily since the election.[34]

Fraser began work on an article in which he tried to articulate the way forwards for the party. It was published in the Melbourne *Herald* in August 1974, and Fraser had offprints made and bound for distribution. Kemp remembers reading it at the time, and being confirmed in his view that Fraser was the man the party needed. The article began by defending the record of the Menzies years and criticising those who had allowed them to be denigrated: they had been years of growth, friendship with Britain and the United States 'when that was what heritage suggested and security demanded', and warm relations with Asian neighbours.

> How often since the retirement of Menzies have the achievements of those years been proclaimed by the Liberals? We have put them too much aside and allowed our virtues to be seen as a liability … We have allowed people to say the policies were right for the '50s and '60s but not for the '70s or '80s. The point being, of course, that the polices were right for those years.

Jim Cairns, then the Deputy Prime Minister, had described the Menzies years as the McCarthy years. 'At that time, no one spoke in defence of our party', said Fraser. The criticism of Snedden was more than implicit: Fraser was not suggesting a return to the past. 'A political party must move forwards or die. I am saying, however, that in those years the party provided good and appropriate government.'

What was needed now? Fraser restated the principles at the heart of his liberalism: the primacy of the individual in society, responsibility of government to the people, the right of men and women to choose their own life, and the rule of law. 'These are high principles. The specific acts needed to protect them, to give effect to them, will change as the years pass.' Liberals, he said, should be 'radical often, revolutionary never'. He moved on to attack the idea of factions within the party, and the claimed differences between small-'l' liberals and large-'l' Liberals: all liberals should resist such categorisation, he said. Then, clearly a statement of how he saw his own position:

> Those who are hard-line on defence are often regarded as conservative; those who believe that the world is a changing, peaceful place where little defence is required, as progressive. Perhaps the latter group are really looking backwards to the tragic, treacherous days of the 1930s when people still thought wars were ended. Their blindness led to the greatest destruction of all. The hard-liners of those days were not only right; they were the most far-sighted and progressive.
>
> Let liberal alone be name enough for every liberal. Let us take our liberal belief from our minds and our hearts. It is not hard to find our principles. They need emphasis, they need expression, they need proclamation so that the Liberal Party may harness the idealism of all Australians in the service of Australia.[35]

The article reads today like a companion piece to the Deakin lecture of three years before. In that lecture, he had expressed doubt, outlined problems and asked more questions than he gave answers. In this article, he demonstrated more confidence and offered answers: it was like a manifesto. Snedden was effectively on notice.

The Frasers' Canberra house had now been sold, and Staley was no longer spending the evenings locked in political debate with Malcolm. Instead, he was staying in the Rex Hotel, but not sleeping well. During the day, he was Parliamentary Secretary to Snedden, which allowed him to see the man close-up. It was a dispiriting experience. He remembers, 'I had come to the awful view that we were led by a man who should not be Prime Minister. The key question was then whether I had the courage to do something about it'. One night in November 1974, Staley did not sleep at all. By the time the sun came up he had decided to act. He knew Fraser was not a natural candidate: there was no groundswell for him. 'It is not as though all I needed was to light a match to make a big fire', Staley says; 'there were still people in the party who thought he was the devil incarnate'. But there was also widespread dismay with Snedden, and few alternatives. The *Herald* article and the Deakin lecture meant that it was difficult to deny Fraser his intellectual claim on the job. Staley decided that he would try to establish a pro-Fraser group, and that if he failed in the attempt—'if all I succeeded in doing was wrecking'—then he would resign from the party that had been his main interest since childhood. 'That decision was crucial', he remembers. 'It freed me to act.' For a week, Staley avoided Snedden—'I couldn't have looked him in the eye'—while sounding out other parliamentarians. A nucleus formed. Nine days after Staley's sleepless night, the group had grown to the point that they decided to confront Snedden and ask him to resign.

Staley confirms what Fraser himself has always claimed: that Fraser did not know that moves were being made on his behalf until the course of action was decided. Staley waited until he had half the party on side before telling Fraser what was afoot. They were walking down Collins Street on their way to lunch. Fraser stopped in mid stride, lifted his hands to his face and said in horror, 'Oh my God, I can't bear to think about it'. Staley told Fraser that their minds were made up: even if Fraser wanted to stop them, he couldn't. Fraser remembers, 'Tony said I didn't have power to stop them: that was the way he put it. Well, I could have if I got out of the parliament or something—I could have publicly condemned it—but I wasn't going to do that. Billy Snedden was a fine bloke, but he wasn't really all that impressive. He was able, but, at the end of the day, he wasn't an adequate leader. I hated it, but I can't say I didn't want it done'. In the months that followed, Staley remembers, there were at least two occasions on which Fraser tried to persuade him to stop the attempt to unseat Snedden. 'He'd say, "You have to stop, Tony". And I'd say, "We aren't stopping. You can't stop us".'

On 26 November 1974, Staley led a group to confront Snedden and asked him to resign in Fraser's favour. Staley tendered his own letter of resignation as Parliamentary Secretary. Snedden began by saying, 'Yes, well, I have made some mistakes'. Staley's heart leaped: perhaps this would be easier than he had feared. What would Snedden say his mistakes had been, Staley asked. 'I made a mistake not having some of you bastards in for more grog.' To Staley, this was typical: cynical, out of ideas, missing the point entirely. He was more than ever convinced that Snedden had to go, but Snedden refused to resign. The battle was on.

In the party room the day after the confrontation in Snedden's office, Staley moved that the leadership be declared vacant. A number of people spoke in favour. Fraser said nothing. There was a secret vote for the leadership, and Fraser lost. Staley and Fraser knew, though, that the vote was closer than the media was led to believe. Both Staley and Fraser made the rote promises of loyalty expected in these circumstances. Fraser told the truth, if only part of the truth, in saying that he had played no part in the moves against Snedden, and had asked nobody for support. Staley, meanwhile, believed Snedden's downfall was only a matter of time.

So began months of instability. In the weeks following, Drysdale arranged for the *National Times* newspaper to visit Nareen. The resulting article ran with what became some of the defining images of Fraser, with Tamie on trail bikes, and a headline: 'Watch Out Bill, Watch Out Gough, Malcolm Still Wants Your Jobs'. A few weeks later, in January 1975, Fraser made another key speech, this time to the Australian and New Zealand Association for the Advancement of Science congress. This was the first speech in which he had the help of David Kemp, but its ideas were consistent with those he had been developing since the Deakin lecture.

Snedden hung on. The destabilisation and media speculation were all-consuming. Snedden's support in the polls had plummeted to 28 per cent. In February 1975, Snedden asked Fraser for a declaration of loyalty, including a guarantee that he would not seek the leadership before the next election. Fraser refused and issued a qualified statement: Snedden had his full support; nobody to his knowledge or with his consent had done anything to re-open the leadership question. But he did not rule out a challenge.

It was Andrew Peacock—a Snedden supporter and a Fraser rival—who brought matters to a head. In a media interview on 14 March 1975, he said that the leadership question should be brought on and resolved. Four days later, Fraser declared that if the office of leader became vacant, he would be a candidate. The crucial party meeting was held on 21 March 1975. Bill Wentworth moved and won a motion that the leadership be vacated. Fraser and Snedden were the only candidates; Fraser won by a convincing thirty-seven votes to twenty-seven.

That night Tamie rang her sister Eda from Canberra and asked what she should do. She was about to be interviewed as the wife of the Leader of the Opposition. How could she make herself interesting? Eda replied, 'Tam, you can't. You'll just have to be yourself and bluff it out'.

9

Extremis

More ink and tears have been spent over the eight months in which Malcolm Fraser was Leader of the Opposition than any other period in Australian political history. Fraser alone of the major players has never given his own account; nor does he want to now. In the interviews for this book he had to be persuaded to talk about the crisis of 1975 and the dismissal. The idea made him more than cross. 'To me, this whole issue has been so chewed over. I'm so totally bored with it. Why do we have to go over this? There's a tenth anniversary, a fifteenth anniversary, a twentieth anniversary, a thirtieth anniversary, and it gets regurgitated every time.' After the dismissal of the Whitlam government, he won an election with a record majority. Didn't that speak for itself?

He was persuaded by the argument that it was not possible to write his story without addressing the crisis of 1975. He rejected the suggestion that it was the most dramatic event in Australian history. That label, he says, belongs to the conscription issue during World War I, and particularly to the anti-Catholic sectarian feeling stirred up by the Prime Minister Billy Hughes. Fraser has described Hughes's turning the conscription referendum into a vote on 'the merits and demerits of the Irish and Irish Catholics' as 'perhaps the worst act of any Prime Minister in Australia's short history'.[1] The results were still being felt when Fraser was a child, overhearing his father's remarks about whether or not Catholics could be regarded as loyal Australians. The wounds, in Fraser's opinion, did not start to heal until the 1950s. The dismissal was divisive, certainly, he says, but nowhere near as profound or long-lasting in its effects. Unlike Hughes's actions, forcing the Whitlam government to an election was necessary, he believes, and the only responsible thing for an opposition to do.

After two interviews spent trawling the events of late 1975, Fraser was worried. 'I might have said a few new things', he said. 'But if when this book comes out the headlines are "New Information about the Dismissal", then in my view we will have failed, and failed utterly.' So far as he is concerned, the story of his political life is, or should be, about enduring liberal values, about government and about the lessons that the past holds for the present and the future. 'Any book I am involved in should not spend too much time talking about issues that are entirely past and done with.' Yet the events leading up to the dismissal of the Whitlam government fit within these themes. They are about process and convention, and conflicting principles. They are about what we should expect from governments and oppositions, and what it is permissible for an opposition to do.

Fraser's reluctance to speak on his own behalf is not new. By the time he became Leader of the Opposition, in March 1974, he had perfected his method of digesting documents. He would mark, delete and query in a heavy black pen. On the speech notes for his first press conference as Leader of the Opposition, there is a significant deletion. He wrote under the headline 'Philosophy' the following words: 'My own position has often been misrepresented by those who like to apply labels and present me as a conservative. My actions and my policies will speak for themselves and I believe the public will soon judge that I have at heart the interest of all Australians'.[2] But before the Australian people heard these words, the black pen came out, ruling through everything in the paragraph except 'My actions and policies will speak for themselves'. It was a typical Fraser act of editorship, showing the reserve, perhaps even the pride, that prevented him from pleading his own case. He would not, then or in the future, ask for personal understanding or even personal relationship with the electorate. By the time he became Leader of the Opposition, Fraser had more than found his voice. He was forty-five years old, far away from his childhood of being seen and not heard. Yet in the years to come he was often heard without being understood or trusted, at least by that section of the population that had hung its hopes and ideals on the peg of the Whitlam government. Tony Staley remembers, 'He understood that you couldn't be both loved and respected by the electorate. He wanted to be respected. He thought in politics that was more important'. Fraser now is the same as Fraser then. Actions should speak for themselves, he says. 'Whitlam was a popular hero to the left. You can't take that away from him. Many people will always love him. But how many really respect his record in government?'

Mike Steketee, now *The Australian*'s national affairs editor and at the time of the dismissal a young Canberra press gallery journalist, has written recently that at no stage has the relationship between the press gallery and a government been as cosy as it was with the Whitlam government. Michael Gawenda, later editor of *The Age* but at the time also a member of the press gallery, has said that most young reporters were 'infatuated with Gough, with his wit and his arrogance and his energy. With his largeness. Why, Gough could match it with any politician in the world. His predecessor, for God's sake, was Billy McMahon'.[3] Alongside this, there was Fraser—with no desire to be loved, bruising egos, appearing aloof and arrogant and, at his very first public outing as Opposition Leader, striking through the words of self-explanation and leaving the bare statement that his actions and policies should speak for themselves.

At the time, other things in his first press conference as Opposition Leader were more significant. Ever since the Snedden opposition had threatened to block supply the year before, it had seemed likely that it might happen again. Now Fraser said he would not be holding the threat of an election over the government. The Senate was 'primarily a house of review—and apart from exceptional circumstances should not frustrate, certainly not on a purely obstructionist basis'. He left open the possibility that if the government became 'reprehensible' the opposition might have to 'use whatever power is available to it'.[4] He told the electors of Wannon in his first radio address after becoming Leader of the Opposition: 'A majority in the Senate does not automatically bring with it a right to obstruct government … This means that an early, or a mid-term, election is unlikely unless Labor attempts to pass legislation of a most reprehensible nature'.[5] The story of 1975 is largely about how Fraser came to believe that the government had indeed become so reprehensible that the opposition had a duty to act.

When he became leader, Fraser's office was deluged with congratulations, urgings and offers of help from some of the most powerful in the land. Fraser began compiling a list of people who had offered assistance. The media mogul Kerry Packer wrote, 'Please feel free to call on me to do whatever you feel I may be able to do at any time'. James Fairfax, proprietor of *The Sydney Morning Herald* and Channel Seven, sent a handwritten note: 'I think it is the best thing that could have happened both to the Liberal Party and to the country'. Other letters offering congratulations and help came from John Valder, at the time Chairman of the Sydney stock exchange, and the Jewish community leader Isi Leibler.

Bob Santamaria wrote a brief note of congratulations and enclosed a copy of his regular weekly newspaper column, published a few days after Fraser's election. It put Fraser's success in an international context. The communist world was ascendant—about to swallow Vietnam and the whole of Indochina, said Santamaria. 'The Soviet is winning in every part of the world. The democratic world, centred on the paralysed United States, is being thrashed.' If Whitlam stayed in office, Santamaria wrote, within three years Australia would not have effective defence. The present Australian Government should be forced to an election and defeated, not prematurely but at the first appropriate moment. Fraser, said Santamaria, would not find it easy to prove himself, but he 'possesses a large intellectual capacity ... [and] a basic political philosophy which his rivals lack'.

A partner of the Ord Minnett stockbroking firm, Gilles T Kryger, wrote with congratulations, and offered Fraser access to any information the company might hold that would help him. Alexander Downer (senior), who was High Commissioner in London, wrote saying he 'hooted for joy and opened champagne' when he heard the news. Alan Jones, later to become the notorious Sydney radio shock jock, but at that time a schoolmaster at the Kings School, Parramatta, telegrammed Fraser with some advice—'Restate why you are standing and what you stand for'—and suggested which members of his front bench should come and go. Later, during Fraser's prime ministership, Jones was one of his speechwriters. 'Only for a little while,' says Fraser, 'but for far too long. He could write a good rah-rah speech for the party faithful, but he couldn't handle ideas'.

Other letters of support came from the former Liberal Party politician and Ambassador to the United States Sir Howard Beale, the Director of the Victorian Employers Federation Ian Spicer, business tycoon Peter Abeles and the public opinion pollster Roy Morgan. Sir Henry Bland, former Secretary of the Department of Defence and at that time a private citizen, wrote with some advice: 'Gough Whitlam's flash point is low. You've got to provoke him to throw a glass of water at you. Getting your suit cleaned will be a small price. So niggle away—the break spot is there'.[6]

There was plenty of material here, had it been made public, that the government's supporters might have taken as evidence to support their view that the establishment was united in its determination that Whitlam should not be allowed to remain in office. Many of Fraser's correspondents claimed that if Whitlam remained in power the free enterprise system would be dead. They clearly believed that the sooner Whitlam could be brought to an election and defeated, the better. Yet while Fraser wrote in his replies about his determination to defeat Whitlam's 'socialist' policies, in other correspondence he showed a different aspect of his convictions. Fraser received a letter from Harry Turner, who had until the previous year been the Liberal Party member for the Sydney seat of Bradfield. Turner wrote with mixed congratulations, summing up the ambivalence of those who had seen Fraser as a wrecker of the party.

> As you know, I have felt for a long time that this would be your destiny, though concerned to the last that your driving ambition (otherwise an admirable trait) might overbear your prudence and create for you too many enemies. It is of course much more important, even than your deserved satisfaction and the natural rejoicing of your friends, that the nation should have the kind of statesmanlike leadership that I believe you are capable of giving.

But Turner told Fraser that there was a 'great need' to make some Labor initiatives 'our own'. Fraser agreed. He wrote back thanking Turner for his 'marvellous letter'. 'I take your point about the particular lack of Liberal policy. Up to date we have basically pedalled furiously to catch up with Gough.'[7]

Fraser was saying similar things to others in the party. Ian Macphee, then a relatively new but influential Liberal backbencher, had been one of the first party members to support Fraser for the leadership. Today Macphee recalls that too many of his Liberal colleagues suffered from a born-to-rule mentality, regarding the Whitlam government as illegitimate and an aberration. Fraser was not one of these, which is why Macphee supported him. Fraser and Macphee agreed that much of Whitlam's vision was correct; it was the implementation—the lack of cogent economic management and discipline—that was flawed, together with the tendency towards socialism.

Not all of Fraser's correspondence on becoming leader was from the great and powerful. He also received a note from Nancy

MacPherson, who had briefly been his governess when he was eight years old. She had followed his career with interest, and told him a story from his childhood. They had been on a picnic at Balpool-Nyang.

> You were getting a little too adventurous for safety, climbing on old tree stumps, and I kept trying to get you to come down. Eventually I said, 'Malcolm, will you please get down immediately and do as I say'.
>
> 'All right', you answered. 'I'll do what you say now and when I grow up and am Prime Minister you'll do what I say.'

Mrs MacPherson said she now wanted this to come true. Fraser replied to her, 'From the present vantage point I am sure that even the authority of the prime ministership would not give me the power which I appear to have longed for over you as an eight year old'.[8]

Tony Staley's wife, Elsa, sent Fraser a letter that reflected her growing hatred of politics. 'Congratulations and good luck. But I have suffered enough on our behalf, so you'll have to be damn good—as I think you will be.' Fraser replied:

> I am sure you and Tamie are soul mates, so I understand you only too well when you say you have suffered enough on my behalf. The suffering of wives of depth and sensitivity is perhaps the ugliest part of political life. And there does seem to be an awful element of unfairness for you in having to suffer on my behalf as well as Tony's.[9]

Then there were the letters from ordinary people. Although many Australians were caught up in the idealism of Whitlam, in the mood for change after years of lacklustre leadership from the Liberals, others were clearly terrified by the speed and direction of the change. Marlene Stephens wrote in April 1975: 'Please act now. Set us a course. Surely this Vietnam issue, the economy, what has to be a disastrous budget, plus socialised medicine must give us grounds for an election'.[10] Alan Lambert, manager of his own small business, wrote that he had been listening to Whitlam on the radio and had had

> a sudden cold feeling that I, and my family, would be marked people if by some remote chance this government were to continue in power and finally gain the ultimate dictatorial power they are so obviously after—reprisals are not out of the question. If this sounds a little dramatic then it is brought about by the terrifying likeness of the Whitlam rise to power as to that of Hitler.

He appealed to Fraser to 'bring down the Whitlam regime'. Fraser responded phlegmatically: 'Thank you for your recent letter. I appreciate your expressions of support'.[11] There was a standard paragraph that Fraser included in most of his letters to ordinary citizens: 'I share your concern about the Labor government's policies which threaten the viability of the free enterprise system. Equally dangerous to the survival of that system is the increasing failure of Labor's economic management'. Another common line was: 'It is the very basis of the Australian way of life that is at stake'.

In June, Fraser was interviewed by *Catholic Weekly* magazine. Asked how he described himself, he said, 'As a Christian'. He cited the family and Oxford University as the main influences on his moral outlook. On laws to make homosexual acts between consenting males legal, he said, 'I think I am against it ... Well, one can't absolutely approve of it, but on second thoughts can one legislate effectively about private morals?'[12] In July, Fraser received protest letters about the ABC's sex-farce program *Alvin Purple*. The replies were classic Fraser: 'I have not seen the programs of which you speak, but from your description of them I am sure that I would not find them entertaining. Nevertheless, I am sure you understand that it is wrong in principle for a government to dictate the viewing decisions of the public'.[13]

Other correspondence came from people concerned about the Whitlam government's Family Law Bill, which introduced no-fault divorce. But here, too, Fraser was not as conservative as some of his correspondents. He opposed allowing divorce after one year of separation; he thought the period should be two years. He also moved amendments to give more protection to women who were not in the workforce, but wanted to continue as full-time mothers. Yet he supported the establishment of the Family Court and the introduction of easier and more private means of ending unhappy marriages.[14] His amendments were about choice. The Fraser government went on to set up the Family Court and administer the legislation.

Fraser agreed with much of Whitlam's agenda, but there were parts to which he was implacably opposed. Whitlam was trying to establish an Australian Government Insurance Office. Fraser was deluged with correspondence from the insurance companies, which saw this as an attempt to nationalise the finance industry. In parliament, Fraser said that the insurance office legislation would mean that 'a minister at the stroke of a pen can take measures that can send any insurance company in Australia out of business'.[15] Most importantly, he opposed the government's economic management. There had been increases in taxation and a salary and wages policy (Whitlam had encouraged excessive wage demands), which, Fraser said, had contributed to what was by early 1975 the highest levels of inflation ever known in Australia. There was runaway government spending, squeezing out private investment. Key to the Liberal idea of individual freedom, said Fraser, was the principle that so far as possible people should have a choice in how to spend their income. Free enterprise was inseparable from other kinds of freedom, and Whitlam threatened free enterprise. Business could not get credit or plan for the future. Keynesian pump priming would not work because the pre-conditions for business recovery did not exist. There was no stability in the economy. The government seemed to understand none of this, and to be completely at sea in understanding basic economics. 'Today, the business objective is simply to survive, and it is very hard for many to achieve even that.'[16] In parliament in June 1975, Fraser noted that:

> The government has established a number of records … In its first year it established record unemployment, record inflation, record interest rates and record industrial unrest. In its second year it broke each of its own records. In its third year it is likely to break its records again. The Prime Minister blames a number of things … but never blames the real causes—the mad expenditure policies of the government, the unreasonable across-the-board tariff cuts which have led to great unemployment … revaluation policies and the complete lack of business confidence that has flowed from government policies.[17]

At the time this speech was made, inflation was at 17 per cent. Fraser said that advisers to the government predicted it could reach as high as 30 per cent. The 1974 budget had been based on a 33 per cent increase in government spending and a 46 per cent increase in income tax collections. In the following year, budget outlays were to soar another 42 per cent.

* * *

There was another matter on which Fraser and Whitlam did not agree, which came to a head within days of Fraser becoming Leader of the Opposition. While he was speaking to farmers in the South Australian town of Murray Bridge, Fraser heard that tanks were rolling in to Saigon. The 'retreat with victory' strategy of the United States was revealed for the sham it had always been. Fraser was dismayed, but hardly surprised. Just the week before he had issued a statement about the forces overrunning Vietnam and Cambodia. 'The world is displaying its inherent instability and its incapacity to protect the weak. Détente has not been achieved in any certain or lasting fashion, and, regrettably, the United Nations is not proving as effective as many of us would have hoped.' Fraser had said that the Whitlam government had appeared preoccupied with making overtures to China and Russia, and indifferent to aggression in Indochina. Diplomats had been advising Canberra of the 'impending disaster', but Whitlam had not spoken out in the relevant capitals or to the United Nations; nor had he begun making plans to help refugees. Dr Jim Cairns was driving Australian foreign policy, Fraser said, and he was 'virtually exultant at the prospect of a North Vietnamese victory ... Dr Cairns portrayed himself as a great humanitarian when he led the moratorium marches. He was concerned for peace and good will. It now appears he is much more concerned for a communist victory'.[18] Now, with harrowing pictures of the invasion of Saigon filling the evening news, Fraser told his electorate that the Whitlam government had to act. Australia should be prepared to take 'some thousands of refugees, adults and children'.[19]

Whitlam assumed responsibility for all issues concerning Vietnamese refugees. He oversaw so-called baby lifts which brought 281 orphans to Australia, and the evacuation of the Australian embassy on 25 April. He announced that Vietnamese and Cambodian students already in Australia would be allowed to stay under temporary residence visas, and would also be permitted to bring in their spouses and children for temporary residence. Meanwhile, the government would consider case by case applications by Vietnamese 'with long and close associations with the Australian presence in Vietnam whose life is considered to be in danger ... The number of such persons is expected to be small'.[20]

Fraser argued that the guidelines about keeping families together were a fraud: they were narrower than normal immigration guidelines. Meanwhile, due to government procrastination, the provisions for other Vietnamese associated with Australia were not implemented in time. By 30 April, only seventy-eight Vietnamese refugees, excluding those who arrived on the two baby lifts, had been brought to Australia. Another 350 people had been approved for entry to the country, but this clearance came so late that they were unable to get out by the time the last Australian officials left Vietnam.[21] Fraser told parliament that the Whitlam government's approach was mean and despicable.[22] 'One can only hope that the North Vietnamese troops who are now overrunning the country show more compassion than the Whitlam government.'[23]

As the year wore on, Fraser wrote repeatedly to Whitlam on the refugee issue in general and on behalf of particular refugees. In July he said:

> Few issues in my memory have stirred the conscience of the Australian community as much as the Indochina refugee situation. I can only ask you once again to reconsider your narrow and inhumane policy which has prevented all but a very few refugees from achieving a permanent home in Australia.

It took a fortnight for Whitlam's secretary to acknowledge the letter, and another two months—until 14 September—for Whitlam to reply. He said that he was investigating the credentials of the individuals concerned, but only spouses and dependent children of people already in Australia would be allowed to settle here.[24]

Whitlam's approach to the refugees brought him under increasing pressure from the media and the opposition, yet Fraser's advocacy did not endear him to all of the electorate. Fraser received letters asking why he didn't support the White Australia policy and instead wanted Australia to take 'reffos' and 'wogs'. Fraser had a standard response:

> The White Australia policy was laid to rest by Mr Harold Holt's Liberal government. I have called for a limited number of Vietnamese orphans and adult refugees to be accepted by Australia in response to the vast human tragedy which has been caused in South Vietnam by the communist aggression. I do not think Australia can do less.[25]

The following year, after Whitlam's defeat, a Senate standing committee concluded that of 5629 nominations for refugee status from South Vietnamese, only 542 had been approved—355 for permanent residence and 187 for temporary residence. 'As unpalatable as it may be, we are forced to conclude that the [Whitlam] government acted reluctantly and, as expressed by one witness, in order to placate an increasingly suspicious Australian public.'[26]

Meanwhile, out of the public gaze, the Whitlam government was preparing to take an even tougher approach to refugees. By May 1975 the government was being warned by foreign affairs officers that hundreds, perhaps thousands, of Vietnamese were about to make the journey to Australia by boat. Interdepartmental meetings were held to consider the response. Australia's obligations under United Nations conventions on the status of refugees and the Universal Declaration of Human Rights were discussed, but apparently did not weigh heavily with Whitlam, who decided that if any Vietnamese refugees reached Australia by sea, they would be put into custody.[27]

The Whitlam government's stance contrasted with that of the United States, which was taking in tens of thousands of refugees from South Vietnam. It was also a break from the ways in which the Menzies and Holt governments had dealt with refugees from Hungary and Czechoslovakia. The Whitlam government had relaxed the normal immigration selection criteria for Chilean refugees escaping the overthrow of the Allende government[28], but through April and May 1975, Australia's refugee policy was being revised, and those involved in formulating the policy had been told to exclude Vietnamese and Cambodians from sympathetic consideration under any revised formula 'where decisions of acceptability have been made by the Prime Minister'.[29] The Whitlam government was planning to discard many of the humanitarian and human rights considerations that had previously informed Australia's refugee policy. None of this was debated in parliament at the time.

By the time the boat people began to arrive, in late April 1976, Whitlam's policy was no longer relevant: the Fraser government was in power. The boat people were allowed to land, were given temporary residence permits a day after their arrival and access to full social security benefits. Soon afterwards they were granted permanent residence. Today, Fraser counts his government's management of the South Vietnamese refugees as one of his proudest achievements.

* * *

Fraser was trying to build the opposition into a credible alternative government. He had appointed key advisers. David Kemp he already knew through Tony Staley, and Kemp had already helped Fraser with speeches and ideas. When they were getting to know each other, they had had lunch together. According to Fraser, Kemp was concerned that Fraser might be too conservative. Fraser laughs about this now. When Kemp was a minister in the Howard government, Fraser used to say to him, 'Which one of us is the most conservative now?' In 1975, though, Kemp and Fraser were of largely similar mind. As time went by, differences emerged. Kemp was a 'dry'—more inclined to faith in the free market than Fraser. But in early 1975 the wet–dry distinction did not exist. Fraser and Kemp were progressive liberals. That was what mattered and what drew them together.

Fraser interviewed candidates for another key adviser position; the successful candidate was Petro Georgiou, a postgraduate student from the University of Melbourne and another example of Staley's talent-spotting. Georgiou, Staley remembers, was 'probably the brightest student I had ever seen'. Staley arranged for him to be interviewed by Fraser in his Melbourne office. Meeting Georgiou afterwards, he asked how it had gone. 'No good', Georgiou replied. 'We argued.' Staley went in to Fraser and asked him what he thought. 'Excellent', said Fraser. 'He argued with me.' Georgiou, Greek-born, had emigrated to Australia at the age of four. He went on to be the driving force behind the multicultural and immigration policies of the Fraser government.

Dale Budd was Fraser's Chief of Staff, and went on to manage his office once he was in government. Budd had been with Fraser before that, in both defence and education. 'He was totally unflappable, and he ran the office with total efficiency', remembers Fraser.

In a radio address to his electorate in July, Fraser was able to report that the opposition had launched 'the framework of philosophy and ideas which is the basis of our developing policies'.[30] The opposition's industrial relations policy—virtually identical to that which Fraser had developed as Shadow Minister for Industrial Relations—had already been announced. Over the next few months policies on federalism, education and foreign affairs were released.

The federalism policy rested on the principle that those levels of government responsible for spending money should also be responsible for raising the taxes. Commonwealth, state and local taxes were to be separately identified on one tax assessment so citizens could see the amount levied for each government, and hold them accountable. *The Australian Financial Review* commented in an editorial on 25 September 1975 that this would be the most significant move in the area of federal–state legislation since taxing powers were taken from the states during World War II and never returned. Fraser saw this as a key way of decentralising power. The Fraser government passed the relevant legislation, but it was stillborn. No state picked up the opportunity—and responsibility—that it offered. Fraser says today, 'I still think it's a good idea'.

Fraser's shadow cabinet also spent time on Medibank. The Liberals had been opposed to the government's universal medical insurance scheme, or 'socialised medicine', as it was described. The Medibank legislation had been among the Bills that had been blocked by the Senate, then passed after the 1974 double dissolution election. Now the Fraser shadow cabinet reviewed its position. Fraser himself was not opposed to Medibank as a universal scheme, but he was suspicious of the way in which it undermined the private insurance industry, forcing people to rely on government. The debate in shadow cabinet was about the extent to which the scheme should be universal, and how it should be funded.[31]

When Bill Hayden delivered his first budget, in August 1975, most commentators in the media were mildly congratulatory. Hayden had acknowledged a need to slow the growth in public expenditure. Fraser was less sanguine: in part, he was influenced by a leak of a Treasury briefing paper that disclosed a blowout in the budget deficit for 1974–75 of almost $2 billion, with the government headed for a $5 billion deficit if nothing changed.[32] Meanwhile, Hayden's starting point was that government spending would go up by $3000 million and the tax take would increase by 43 per cent. Fraser said in his radio address to his electorate, 'That [Hayden] should win praise from commentators merely for identifying the problem while still failing to take steps to remedy it is a paradox easily explained by the low esteem in which this government is now held, and the low expectations people have of it'.[33] Responding to the budget, Fraser announced that the coalition had committed itself to tax indexation—another policy urged upon him by Santamaria, among others.[34] The idea was that tax scales would move with inflation, eliminating the 'creep' that saw ever-increasing amounts of individuals' income go to government. It was, Fraser said, a way of keeping governments honest.[35]

In October came a statement, largely written by Fraser himself but heavily influenced by Owen Harries, then advising the Shadow Foreign Minister Andrew Peacock, on what was described as a 'realistic and enlightened' foreign policy. Labor's foreign policy, Fraser said, was 'based on a naïvely optimistic assessment of the international political scene'. Too much faith was placed on détente, 'and any talk of its possible breakdown was automatically dismissed as a manifestation of outdated Cold War mentality'. Labor had been too critical of old allies, and had discriminated in favour of new communist regimes. It had supported militancy in the Third World without doing anything to address the problems of the Third World. The coalition policy, on the other hand, recognised that 'power is still the main arbiter in international politics, and that nation-states normally give priority to what they conceive as their own interests'. Yet, 'It recognises it is self-defeating for a country to interpret its interests in narrow, short-term and purely materialistic terms'. Countries were interdependent, and must 'contribute energetically to the solution of those global problems which are the source of many conflicts'. Labor saw South-East Asia as a region of flourishing democracies, and the world as a place of spreading stability and security. 'We assert that this is not a recognisable picture of the world we are living in. The international system is faced with serious and multiple crises.' South-East Asia was unstable, the policy asserted. The Whitlam optimism about peace in the region was not justified. Australia should work to maintain a political balance and to strengthen the Association of South-East Asian Nations. A major concern was the Soviet presence in the Indian Ocean. The Whitlam aspiration of a neutral zone was not likely to be achieved, given the way the Soviets were moving. Australia should seek a balance of superpower naval forces and extension of the US naval facilities at Diego Garcia in the Indian Ocean. On China, the attitude should be one of neither opposition nor ideological identification and sympathy, but Australia should 'explore cooperation with an open mind'. On the Middle East, the policy advocated a non-partisan stand, and support for the United Nations resolutions calling on Israel to withdraw from the occupied territories.

Along with all this, the foreign policy also flagged issues that were to be central concerns of the Fraser government. The biggest problems the world faced, it said, were 'the food crisis, the energy crisis, the population explosion, the widening gap between poor and rich countries, inflation, the recession in world trade and the growing danger of nuclear proliferation'. Trade and resources had to be considered not in isolation, but as part of preventing the hardening of relations between industrially developed countries and the Third World.[36]

By now, October 1975, most of the coalition's policies were in place or about to be released. Meanwhile, the shadow cabinet minutes show that Fraser was advising his colleagues to 'look bored' in parliament when Whitlam was 'grandstanding'.[37] While all this policy work was being done by the opposition, the Whitlam government was staggering from crisis to crisis. In October, Fraser and his colleagues decided that the Whitlam government was indeed so reprehensible that it must be forced to an election: they decided that they should block supply. This decision led to a constitutional crisis, and to the sacking of the elected Australian Government by the Governor-General, the Queen's representative, Sir John Kerr.

* * *

The seeds of the Whitlam government's dismissal had been sown in December 1974, before Fraser became Leader of the Opposition, with a series of events that have been described by the political journalist Paul Kelly as 'without parallel in Australia's political history ... so fantastic they defy belief'.[38]

While the Liberal Party had been sweating through the aftermath of Fraser's first challenge to Snedden, the government had been discussing the acquisition of a very large overseas loan. The idea, so far as we know, came from the Minerals and Energy Minister Rex Connor, who dreamed of an enormous resources and infrastructure program with maximum Australian ownership. Thanks to the surge in oil revenues after the oil shock, there were huge amounts of money available in the Middle East, and plenty of middle men who claimed to be able to secure the funds. The Whitlam government decided in December to bypass the normal means by which the government raised loans, and instead seek Middle East petrodollars. The middle man was to be a Pakistani money dealer, Tirath Khemlani. It was later suggested—including by Fraser—that part of the motivation for this extraordinary decision might have been to give the government access to funds outside parliamentary control, to guard against the possibility that the opposition would block supply. If this is correct, it has never been established.

Treasury officials were horrified by the plans. The Secretary of Treasury Fred Wheeler and his deputy John Stone did everything they could to deter the government from its course, but their concerns were ignored. There was a sense of urgency: Khemlani was claiming that the funds were available now, and Connor needed authorisation to cut the deal. On 13 December senior ministers gathered and decided the loan should be pursued. An Executive Council meeting was needed to give Connor the necessary authorisation. Normally, the Governor-General would have convened the meeting and been present, but Sir John Kerr, who had been appointed to the post by Whitlam earlier in the year, was in Sydney, having been led to believe that no Executive Council meeting would be held. Late that night at the Lodge, and without contacting Kerr, Whitlam convened a meeting of the Executive Council. Present were Whitlam, Cairns, Connor and Lionel Murphy, the Attorney-General. The meeting authorised Connor to seek a loan of up to US$4000 million. (For comparison, the total income for the federal government in 1974–75 was US$15643 million.[39]) The next morning, Whitlam told Kerr by telephone that the meeting had had to be called because of exceptional circumstances. According to his memoirs, Kerr came to the conclusion that he had been bypassed, either on purpose or because Whitlam did not take his constitutional role seriously. Kerr's trust in Whitlam was fatally undermined.[40]

One problem with the extraordinary loan that Connor was now authorised to negotiate was that the minute said it was for 'temporary purposes'. This meant that the approval of the Loan Council, a statutory body including the state governments charged with coordinating government borrowings, was not needed. The Khemlani loan would never have been approved by the Loan Council, says Fraser; describing it as 'temporary' circumvented this, yet the purposes of the loan as later described by Connor in parliament were clearly anything but temporary. They included huge infrastructure projects: natural gas pipelines, petrochemical plants, uranium milling plants and natural gas extraction infrastructure, rail freight infrastructure and solar energy research.[41] The minute that Kerr had been presented with recording the decision of the

Executive Council meeting referred to none of this, saying instead that the government needed 'immediate access to substantial sums of non-equity capital from abroad for temporary purposes'. The purposes were 'exigencies arising out of the current world situation and the international energy crisis', and to deal with unemployment. No written legal advice on the description of the loan as temporary was given to the Executive Council or to Kerr. Instead, Whitlam said later, Lionel Murphy had given oral advice that the borrowing could be regarded as being for temporary purposes. This extraordinary opinion went against the advice of Murphy's own staff in the Attorney-General's department, which had joined with Treasury in opposing the government's course.

Khemlani did not come up with the goods. The funds did not emerge, and Connor's authority was revoked by another Executive Council meeting, on 7 January 1975. A few weeks later, on 28 January, he was given a fresh authority at a properly constituted Executive Council meeting, this time to arrange a loan of US$2000 million.

Treasury officials feared the government was on a course for disaster. From the time Fraser became Leader of the Opposition, in March 1975, Treasury leaked consistently and copiously to the Shadow Treasurer Phillip Lynch. Some of the documents remain in the archives.[42] Fraser says, 'They thought that the government was mad, they really did, and I can't blame them. But, you know, when you see a public service leaking and sneaking against a government, it's not something you can condone, although I understood why they thought it was necessary, and it was clearly something that they had agonised over'. Officially, Fraser did not know the identity of the leaker—'Phillip kept it all very close to his chest'—although naturally he had a shrewd idea who was involved. The flow of information was extraordinarily rich: as well as information on the loans affair, the shadow cabinet received copies of Treasury briefing papers in the lead-up to the 1975 budget. As the crisis of 1975 developed, the opposition knew exactly when supply would run out and was privy to the details of the attempts by Whitlam to negotiate with the banks to bankroll the government in the absence of supply.

By May 1975 news of the loan negotiations was becoming public, and the Liberals were making good use of the information they were receiving from Treasury and as a result of their own investigations. The fact that Australia had been about to borrow such huge amounts in such a dubious manner caused first incredulity, then horror. As Fraser was later to say, there seemed to have been no consideration about the impact of the loan on the economy. The proposed loan would have increased the debt for every Australian family by $1000 and quadrupled the country's overseas debt. 'Quite apart from the burden, that must be about the greatest overseas currency gamble in history.'[43] As a result of the controversy, Connor's authority to seek the loan was withdrawn, but the scandal continued with a cast of strange middle men and dubious dealings. It was revealed that the Treasurer Jim Cairns had also been involved in seeking loans through an Australian businessman, George Harris. On 6 July, Cairns was sacked for misleading parliament over his role in the affair. The government, Fraser said, had forfeited its claims to efficiency, propriety and common sense. The loans affair had made Australia a laughing stock in international circles, and the country's credit rating had been impugned.

> It is not just the Americans, the Swiss and the British who have been made to laugh at us. The revelations in the newspapers indicate that even the Saudi Arabians are taken aback by Australia's funny money dealings with brokers and fix-it men in London's Half Moon Street and Hounslow.[44]

A few days later, on 9 July, there was a special sitting of the parliament in which all the loan documents were tabled. Fraser described the Executive Council meeting of the previous December as 'an illegal conspiracy to evade the constitution', and 'clear evidence of … a deliberate conspiracy to deceive and to defraud'. He called for a royal commission.[45]

There was speculation in the media and in parliament: had Kerr been compliant, deceived or overruled? All this had a deep impact on Kerr. He wrote later in his memoirs:

> I learned some lessons from the loan affair ... I did not intend to deal with any crisis which might involve exercise of the reserve powers acting automatically as a rubber stamp for whatever the Prime Minister might advise; and I stiffened myself against the need to be ready to make an informed and neutral assessment should critical discretionary matters arise for my decision.[46]

Kerr did not talk to Whitlam about his concerns. Right up until the day he was dismissed, Whitlam had no idea that he had lost the trust of his Governor-General many months before.

In June 1975, there had been a by-election in the Tasmanian seat of Bass, caused by the resignation of the former Deputy Prime Minister and Minister for Defence Lance Barnard to become Ambassador to Sweden. Barnard, Fraser says today, was 'one of the most sensible people Whitlam had. Whitlam should never have let him go. It was Barnard and Arthur Tange who stopped the American alliance from being permanently damaged'. Fraser said during the campaign for Bass that one of the worst things about the government was that the list of matters to criticise was now too long to be conveniently covered.[47] The by-election resulted in a massive loss for Whitlam and a 17 per cent swing to the Liberals. From that point on, if not before, it was clear that Whitlam had probably won his last election. Whenever the country went to the polls, Fraser would almost certainly become Prime Minister, but another election was not due until 1977. There were many in the opposition and the Liberal Party across the nation who were urging Fraser to do what he could to force Whitlam to go early.

* * *

In early 1975, the opposition's ability to act was limited. In the May 1974 double dissolution election, the Senate result had been Labor twenty-nine, coalition twenty-nine and two independents—Michael Townley from Tasmania, who backed the opposition, and Steele Hall, a former Liberal from South Australia, who backed Whitlam on supply. So on the key question of supply, the numbers were split evenly. This meant the opposition could reject supply, but not delay it. The preferred tactic, worked out by the Liberal Senate leader Reg Withers months before, was to delay rather than to reject supply, thus retaining control, including the ability to pass the Bill the minute an election was called. If the Bill was rejected, on the other hand, it would be up to the government when and how to present it again.

Shortly before Fraser became Leader of the Opposition, Whitlam had appointed his Attorney-General Lionel Murphy to the High Court. Under the constitution, state parliaments appoint to fill casual Senate vacancies. The convention is that they choose a candidate from the same party as the departing senator. In this case, though, the Liberal New South Wales Premier Tom Lewis broke with convention and appointed Cleaver Bunton, a long-serving Albury mayor without party affiliation. It was the first of two appointments by which state premiers deliberately weakened Whitlam in the Senate.

Fraser, who at the time of this appointment was in the final stages of his battle of attrition with Snedden, says today that he had no advance warning of what Lewis was doing. 'If he discussed it with anyone, he didn't discuss it with me.' There was no discussion in shadow cabinet before the appointment was made. If Snedden knew what Lewis was doing, he did not share his knowledge with Fraser. Fraser believes that Lewis was acting off his own bat; he also believes that what Lewis did was wrong. 'I knew Tom Lewis fairly well, and nothing would surprise me very much. Well, you know, people are unpredictable, react emotionally and without due process. And he wanted to get rid of Whitlam. If you make that sort of judgement about a person, then you are never surprised about whatever they do.' The appointment weakened Labor in the Senate, but on the key issue of blocking supply Bunton supported the government, so this left the numbers on the key question unchanged. The real significance of the Bunton appointment was that, on top of the Gair affair, it created a precedent in a period when conventions were stretched past breaking point.

In September 1975, fate delivered a weapon into the hands of Whitlam's greatest political enemy—the Queensland Premier Joh Bjelke-Petersen. A Queensland Labor senator, Bert Milliner, died, and Bjelke-Petersen refused to appoint Labor's nominee, and instead chose Albert Patrick Field, an obscure French polisher who described himself as a 'true' Labor man, but declared that he would never vote for Whitlam and would support any moves to force an early election. Bjelke-Petersen had delivered control of the Senate to the opposition. Today, Fraser acknowledges that he could be accused of hypocrisy over the Field appointment. It was not his doing: Bjelke-Petersen, he says, acted on his own and without consultation. It was Whitlam who had opened the door to manipulating Senate numbers with the Gair affair. Nevertheless, Fraser says today, 'The process of appointing Senator Field was quite inadequate. It was a breach of customary process. It was wrong. And, yes, I would have thought at the time that it was wrong. But I took the advantage'. A pause, then Fraser says with emphasis, 'But we made sure it could never happen again'. One of the early actions of the Fraser government was to hold a referendum on the issue of casual Senate appointments.[48] On Fraser's forty-seventh birthday, 21 May 1977, the Australian people voted by an overwhelming majority to alter the constitution so that state parliaments were obliged to replace senators with members of the same party. Was initiating this referendum an act of expiation? 'We made sure it could never happen again', Fraser repeats. 'Because it was wrong.'

On 12 September, Whitlam made a speech foreshadowing that supply might be blocked and asserting that 'There is no obligation by law, by rule, by precedent or convention for a Prime Minister in those circumstances which are threatened, to advise the Governor General to dissolve the House of Representatives and have an election for it'. Whitlam, the shadow cabinet noted, was preparing to tough it out.[49] Nevertheless, at the time of Field's appointment it was not Fraser's intention to block supply, despite the fact that many people were urging him to do so. He was hearing two kinds of advice—from those who thought the opposition should use its numbers to force an election, and from those who opposed it. In September, after Field's appointment, Santamaria sent Fraser a draft speech, apparently hoping he would deliver it. It argued that the opposition should breach the conventions of the constitution and block supply if not doing so endangered 'the future of Australia':

> The spirit of the constitution—emphatically not the letter—regards a refusal of supply by the Senate as an extraordinary act, to be taken only in the last resort in a position of great emergency. Nevertheless, in such an emergency, the Senate has the legal right and the positive duty to act.[50]

Ian Macphee, on the other hand, was telling Fraser that any move to block supply would alienate too many of the people whose support they would need to govern well. David Kemp had concurred with the initial decision to let the Hayden budget pass, but changed his view as crisis followed crisis through the spring of 1975. By October, he was advising Fraser that no Leader of the Opposition could refuse to act without seeming incurably weak. Senators who were initially against blocking supply also changed their view. Senator Peter Baume remembers being unhappy about the idea, and meeting Fraser, who told him he would not ask him to take any action to which he was opposed. At this stage, Macphee remembers, Fraser was himself inclined against blocking supply, but told Baume and Macphee that he was 'monitoring things closely'.[51]

On 29 September, Fraser's Chief of Staff Tony Eggleton wrote in a note briefing Fraser for shadow cabinet: 'You may find it necessary to say at least something about the election speculation, even if only to repeat your public stance and ask them all, meanwhile, to "cool it"'.[52] Sure enough, the minutes of the next day's meeting show that the shadow cabinet was arguing that the climate would never be better for forcing an election. Fraser put a dampener on the enthusiasm and 'made it clear that the discussion was not intended to lead to a decision at this stage ... MPs/senators should do nothing to encourage media speculation'. On the same day, Fraser advised members at a joint party meeting to 'play it cool': 'Decision will be made at appropriate time. Meanwhile do not fan speculation'.[53] As late as 6 October, Fraser admonished the shadow cabinet that 'No decision had yet been made about forcing an early election. It was extremely misleading for anyone to give briefings along the lines that a decision had been reached'. Shadow ministers were briefing the media anticipating that supply would be blocked, but Fraser had said that the government would be allowed to govern—providing there were no more scandals, no more reprehensible behaviour.[54]

Four days after that shadow cabinet meeting, the rules of the game changed. The High Court declared that legislation allowing the Australian Capital and Northern territories to be represented in the Senate was valid. At the next Senate election, two senators would be elected from each territory. There was a chance that, if Whitlam called an early half-Senate election, he might temporarily gain control of the Senate and be able to pass all his Bills, including supply. There were discussions in the Liberal Party about the possibility of premiers refusing to direct the issuing of the writs if Whitlam chose this option. On 12 October, Fraser addressed the Federal Council of the Liberal Party and asserted that 'The constitution quite deliberately gives the Senate the power to reject appropriation Bills', but then went on to say, 'This tactic should be used with the greatest of reluctance; anyone who seeks to read into these statements a decision on either side would be wrong'.[55] He asked the premiers for their views. All the Liberal premiers were in favour of blocking supply, except for Max Bingham in Tasmania and Dick Hamer in Victoria.

But even as Fraser told the Federal Council that no decision had been made, the Whitlam government's final scandal was about to break. Tirath Khemlani had flown to Australia on 10 October with suitcases full of documents about his dealings with the Australian Government. On the day that Fraser addressed the Federal Council, Khemlani's documents arrived at the Melbourne *Herald*. The next day, 13 October, they were published. They showed that Connor had remained in contact with Khemlani, seeking petro-dollars even after his authority to negotiate the loan had been withdrawn. Whitlam himself was tainted: could it really be believed that he had known nothing? Connor was forced to resign. This resignation of yet another minister was the last straw. If Whitlam could not prevent one of his ministers from acting contrary to his own orders, what else might be going on? The country was at risk. Something had to be done. The senators who had not liked the idea of blocking supply were convinced; Peter Baume recalls, 'When Rex Connor resigned, I was ready to come on board. I was disgusted with the government'.[56]

On 15 October, the shadow cabinet minutes show, Fraser put the motion. The decision to block supply was unanimous. The minutes noted:

> Mr Fraser went around the table and all 'ministers' indicated their support for the move. Mr Fraser said he shared Mr Killen's reluctance about taking this course of action, but, following the sacking of Connor, the opposition would have little respect if it did not try to get rid of the government. Mr Fraser warned the 'ministry' that a tough political fight lay ahead. Emphasis should be placed on the government's dishonesty. We must not get on the defensive.

He warned them to be calm in the House of Representatives, and not to react to provocation.[57] At the party room later that day,

Senator Alan Missen spoke passionately against the move, although he gave Fraser private assurances. 'He came to see me and said that the media would talk about him as one of the senators who would cross the floor, because he had made it clear how he felt. But he gave me his word that he wouldn't cross the floor and he was a man of his word. I never worried about Missen.'

While Reg Withers, the Opposition Leader in the Senate, announced in parliament that the budget would not be proceeded with until Whitlam agreed to an election, Fraser rang the country's media owners. He began with Rupert Murdoch, the proprietor who had supported the election of the Whitlam government. Fraser had known Murdoch from childhood: when the two boys were under ten, Keith Murdoch had taken Rupert and the young Malcolm out fishing on Westernport Bay. Since then, they had remained friendly, but not friends. Now, Fraser asked for his support. Fraser remembers, 'I had only one conversation with Rupert. He asked, "Will your Senate stick?"

'"Yes," I said, "the Senate will stick".

'And he said, "I'll stay with you as long as they do"'. Murdoch was as good as his word. Throughout the crisis and the election that followed, the Murdoch press backed Fraser so completely that reporters at *The Australian* went on strike, accusing their boss of making the paper into a propaganda sheet. The paper lost circulation as a result, but Murdoch never wavered. Fraser regarded his support as locked in: 'If he gave his word I knew it would last'. What difference did it make in the subsequent election? 'I find it hard to judge.'

Then Fraser spoke to Kerry Packer, who also promised support. Packer, though, was not as steadfast as Murdoch. Over the next few weeks, as pressure intensified, 'Kerry would ring up the office and have wobbly knees. He'd say, "You've got to change; you've got to give in". And the way we dealt with that was to get Eggleton to ring up Rupert, and get Rupert to talk to Packer, and tell him to straighten up. And that worked'. Fraser also spoke to James Fairfax, but in the knowledge that the Fairfax newspapers ran differently to

News Ltd—the views of the proprietor were not necessarily reflected in the copy the reporters wrote. As for Packer and Murdoch: 'We did not believe the fiction that media barons do not control the policies of their papers'. It was this reality that later, after his parliamentary career, influenced him in campaigning for the greatest possible diversity of media ownership. A powerful media proprietor can bully a government, he says.

Did Murdoch ever ask anything in return for his support? Fraser says not. 'He never asked for anything from me, except to be treated the same as other people. He didn't want discrimination against him.' Packer was a different matter. Later, when Fraser was in government, he came looking for favours—effective control over regional television stations. 'But he didn't get what he asked for,' says Fraser, 'and once you show you are going to stand up to that kind of bullying, generally the bullying stops'. Packer got what he wanted from the Hawke Labor government.

On 19 October, preparing for a shadow cabinet meeting, Eggleton wrote a list of options for the opposition, including everything from 'sitting tight' to withdrawing 'as gracefully as possible'; but the shadow cabinet minutes state that Fraser's team was 'united and determined'. They would stick to their present course. On 21 October, the shadow cabinet discussed whether now was the time to approach the Governor-General and reject the budget Bills outright. It was decided that there were advantages in further delaying tactics. 'An approach to the Governor-General was not favoured at the moment. There was complete solidarity over the opposition's stand. The view was expressed that, far from weakening in their resolve, they were twice as firm as they were when they made the original decision last week'.[58]

Fraser claims today that he was certain throughout that the senators would stick. Neville Bonner, in later years, claimed that on 11 November he was about to cross the floor and pass supply.[59] If so, Fraser was not aware of it, and he is inclined to think that Bonner was rewriting history. At the time, all the senators were firm, save one. On 20 October, South Australian Senator Don Jessop sent Fraser a copy of a telegram from former South Australian Liberal Premier Thomas Playford, who said, 'Grave consequences must follow present decision which will be disastrous repeat disastrous to country's economy. Strongly suggest defer action until normal Senate election held'. Jessop commented that he had received similar views from many 'Liberals of equal integrity and importance as Sir Thomas Playford'. Jessop, says Fraser, was also 'wobbly at the knees'. Fraser organised for Jessop to receive a rush of telephone calls supporting what the opposition was doing. Jessop, like all the other senators, held to the course.[60]

There were other powerful doubters. Dick Hamer, the Liberal Victorian Premier, wrote Fraser a long letter on 27 October begging him to 'review the position calmly': 'I want you to be Prime Minister of Australia as soon as possible, but in our present national difficulties, I want you to take office with a full head of public confidence and support and without the active resentment or mistrust of a substantial segment of the Australian electorate'. Hamer's wife, April, sent Fraser a personal handwritten note. She said she had always admired him, though she had the impression that he found women 'rather boring and frivolous'. She didn't believe the 'bad publicity' about Fraser being an entrenched right-winger: 'You are too intelligent and clear-thinking'. But now she begged him to withdraw from the impasse. Doing so would show him to be a stronger man than Whitlam. 'If you continue, of course we shall all support you in public to the best of our ability, but with such deep reservations that they will cause long-term disruption in the party.' Fraser replied to April Hamer promising that he did not consider her boring or frivolous. 'I am sometimes shy and have the impression that you might also be, but perhaps that impression of you is as misleading as yours is of me.' He could understand her unhappiness at what was happening.

> Few people anticipated how rough the road would be, or how vigorously an irrational Mr Whitlam would cling

> to office no matter what the cost. So much of what has happened cannot be used publically. The destruction of the High Court, appointments in all sectors of the public service and the very high probability that after two more years of Labor Australia would never again be governable in a reasonable and sensible manner.

He could not in conscience withdraw.[61]

The public opinion polls had begun to turn against the opposition: the public certainly wanted an election. The vast majority had long since sickened of the Whitlam government, but they didn't like Fraser's tactics. How was the crisis to be resolved? Today, Tony Staley and David Kemp remember that Fraser was always confident that it would be through the intervention of the Governor-General. Staley says, 'We spent many hours talking about Kerr, analysing his psychology'. Fraser himself was so confident that Kerr would act that he had no fall-back plan, no Plan B. He says today that while he was sure of Kerr, he was not certain that Whitlam would be dismissed. He thought it equally likely that Kerr would give Whitlam an ultimatum and that Whitlam would then agree to call an election which he would contest as Prime Minister. As the pressure grew, as the media reported that public servants were stocking up on canned food in case the money ran out, Fraser held firm. How did he feel? Asked this question today, he looks blank. 'How did I feel? Well, I suppose I was determined.'

Fraser was not a man to do nothing when he believed the country was in crisis. He was an activist by conviction and temperament. He was convinced, as he wrote to April Hamer, that lasting damage was being done and that the country could not wait for relief. It was not the sort if situation in which people—leaders—should do nothing. Fraser believed in convention. He believed in the principle that a government with the numbers in the House of Representatives should in normal circumstances be allowed to govern. These, though, were exceptional circumstances, and he also believed that oppositions have a duty. He says today,

'So often in politics, principles conflict, and then it is a matter of judgement. No matter what your political system, there is a need for judgement. You can have the best system in the world and bad people will still manage to wreck a country. You can have the worst system in the world and good people will bring about good results. People have to act from principle, but they do have to be prepared to act'. Connor's resignation was not only the straw that broke the camel's back, says Fraser, but the proof that there was no reason to think things would improve. 'You have to understand: the country was in extremis. It was everything. Scandal after scandal. Ministers resigning, the economy, the contempt for the constitution, the loans affair, the speed of change which meant that public servants couldn't deal with it all or give sensible advice.'

In mid October, Fraser had been to see Robert Menzies. The old man was by now a lonely figure, not often visited by his former colleagues. Fraser remembers, 'He probably had no real personal friends. A lot of his relatives had died and a lot of other political colleagues had died or they lived in other places'. Fraser hoped that Menzies would make a statement supporting what was being done or at least not speak in opposition, but he didn't know what his attitude would be. He did his homework, and went prepared to persuade. 'I found a paragraph in *The Argus*, in the late 1940s, and it was the Leader of the Opposition, Robert Gordon Menzies, calling on the Victorian opposition to block supply in the Victorian Legislative Council, so that the people of Victoria could express their total dislike, their anathema, towards the federal Labor government. So, he wanted to force an election in Victoria. I thought, "Fine, I've got him".' They sat down and talked. Menzies began by saying, 'I don't like what you've done much'.

Fraser replied, 'I don't like it either, Sir'.

Menzies went on, 'But you had no option. You had to'. Menzies agreed to write a statement.

After the discussion was over, Fraser asked, 'Sir, do you remember issuing a statement from Victoria as the Leader of the Opposition a long, long while ago, calling for the Victorian Upper House to block the supply Bill to the Victorian parliament?'

Menzies smiled and said, 'If I thought hard, Malcolm, I might'.

Fraser says today, 'But he knew: he knew that I'd done my homework on this'.

Menzies's statement was released to the media. In five elegantly worded pages he said that he had refrained from entering into political controversy, but now felt compelled to break his silence. There was no doubt the Senate had the constitutional power to block money Bills, he said. The constitution had been written deliberately to give these powers to the states' House. 'It would be absurd to suppose that the draftsmen of the constitution conferred these powers on the Senate with a mental reservation that they should never be executed.' Menzies went on to say that the Senate should not exercise its powers in every case.

> Everything depends on the circumstances. For a government fresh from the people, with a victory, to be challenged in the Senate … would be, in my opinion, wrong. Not illegal, no, but politically wrong. But these are not the circumstances today. The government has, in the last twelve months, itself put up a record of unconstitutionality and, if it is not too strong a word, misconduct on a variety of occasions.

He recapped the history—the scandals and the sackings—and said that the Senate could not 'accept them with complacency'. If ever there had been an occasion on which the Senate should act to force an election, then this was it. Finally, Menzies said it would be 'a singular piece of impertinence' for Whitlam to ask the Governor-General, 'whose reputation is high, and who understands these things very well', for a premature half-Senate election in the hope of gaining control for a month or two.[62]

Fraser could hardly have hoped for anything better. Not only did Menzies's statement exactly echo his own views; it was also likely to catch the ear of and flatter the man who was now the pivot of the crisis—Sir John Kerr, the Governor-General. On the same day that Menzies's statement was issued to the media, Fraser had the first of several meetings with Kerr. There was no secret about it: Fraser had sought Whitlam's permission, which had been willingly given. Fraser is sure that very few people, including his own shadow cabinet, believed him when he told them that he knew Kerr better than Whitlam did. Certainly, Whitlam had no knowledge of the intensity of their previous connection. At this meeting the two men sat and talked over a drink for more than an hour. Fraser told Kerr that a firm decision had been made to block supply and this would continue until the Prime Minister faced the country. The Senate and the coalition were 'firm and solid'. Kerr asked why supply had been blocked rather than rejected. Fraser replied that this was so it could be passed immediately in the case of an election being called. Fraser did not try to give Kerr advice, but he did make it clear that he thought they were already in a constitutional crisis and that there was reason enough for the Governor-General to act.

Fraser says that Kerr, both at this meeting and at the two following, was entirely proper: he did not give Fraser any explicit signals about what he intended to do. Nevertheless, Fraser came away with some firm impressions. Knowing Kerr's character, he was sure that he was most concerned for how history would regard him. 'I don't think that is a weakness. A man who cares how history regards him is likely to make noble decisions that will stand the test of time.' Kerr's view was that the worst thing he could do in the eyes of history would be to involve the Queen in a constitutional crisis. He told Fraser at one of these meetings, 'Of course, I am keeping the Palace informed. But I will not ask the Queen's advice'. Fraser understood. Kerr wanted to protect the Palace. Fraser also came away from the meetings with the strong impression that Kerr believed his own position to be at risk. We now know that Kerr believed if Whitlam suspected he was to be sacked, he would try to get Kerr sacked first. Fraser divined this at the time and realised that it would mean Kerr would not give

Whitlam any warning: it was more likely that Whitlam would be dismissed. Today, Fraser says, 'If Whitlam had advised the Queen to sack Kerr, she would have had to do it, and then there she is, bang in the middle of the crisis. Kerr wasn't just concerned for his own tenure; it would be completely misrepresenting him to say that. He was concerned for the position of the Queen'.

Much later, after the events of 1975 were over, Kerr told Fraser that he had believed ever since the notorious Executive Council meeting of December 1974 that if he opposed Whitlam he would be sacked and a 'patsy' put in his place. What would happen then? The Queen would be in the middle of the crisis, and the country would be at Whitlam's mercy. Fraser says today, 'His concern with the Queen's position was very sensible. He was concerned for the whole way Australia and the constitution operate'. Fraser believes that if Whitlam had advised the Queen to sack Kerr, the hopes of the monarchists that the Queen might act independently of the Prime Minister's advice would have been 'proved to be a nonsense'. Kerr would have been sacked, and the Queen would have appointed whomever Whitlam chose to replace him. 'That would place her and the monarchy in the centre of the crisis.'

After the first meeting with Kerr, Fraser issued a deferential statement declaring that the opposition would abide by any decision reached by the Governor-General. 'I have a very high regard for the office ... If he gives advice we would give the greatest possible weight to it because of the respect we have for the office and the man.' This was interpreted by the media as a back-down. There were even suggestions that Fraser had been ticked off by Kerr. Neither was true; Fraser was acting tactically. He was positioning himself as Kerr's friend, as the one who understood his dilemma. Fraser reported to shadow cabinet that the media had 'completely distorted the position'.[63] By late October, Whitlam had reason to think he was averting the crisis. The voters disliked Fraser's tactics and Fraser seemed to have softened. Privately, as we know from Kerr's memoirs, Kerr had long before decided he could not confide in Whitlam.

Meanwhile, the government was running out of money. On about 22 October the shadow cabinet had received another leaked document—a memorandum to the Deputy Commissioner of Taxation from the Commissioner. It stated that the funds available to pay salaries and administrative costs would run out on or around 14 November. The Commissioner urged the utmost economies, but also said that, inevitably, if the taxation department could not spend money, its ability to collect revenues would be affected.[64] Publically, it was thought the government had enough to last until the end of November. Fraser now knew differently.

Kerr and Fraser met again on 30 October. Kerr suggested a compromise: would Fraser agree to pass supply on condition that Whitlam agreed not to call a half-Senate election until May 1976, so ensuring that the government could not acquire temporary control of the Senate? Fraser remembers this as a short conversation. He rejected the compromise. 'I made it clear I thought we were in a constitutional crisis and, while it wasn't explicit, it would have been clear to him that I thought he should act.'

Whitlam, meanwhile, was taking the crisis to a new level, making plans to govern after the money had run out. The shadow cabinet heard about these plans almost immediately they were made, and before the public announcement, through its links into Treasury. Whitlam intended to approach the banks and ask them to pay public servants and government suppliers in return for a certificate of indebtedness from the government. Fraser had thought that by this point he was beyond being shocked by Whitlam, but the plan shook him. The principle that governments hold power only with the support of parliament is fundamental to democracy. If a government intended to hang on despite being refused money by parliament, then it was on 'the first grave step to dictatorship'. Fraser drew on his understanding of history gained at Oxford all those years before. The last time a leader had thought he could govern even when parliament denied him money was when Charles I had dismissed parliament in the 1600s. He had believed in the divine right of kings, and his actions had led to civil war. Did Whitlam realise the implications of what he was doing? '[Mr Whitlam] believes that he alone is the constitution, that he alone is the parliament', Fraser said.[65]

Privately, the banks were already assuring the opposition that they would not cooperate. The Federal Treasurer of the Liberal Party Sir Robert Crichton-Brown was on the board of the Commercial Banking Company of Sydney, and received legal advice that showed that any payment under such a scheme would be illegal—and that the bank directors would be personally liable for prosecution. The plan was simply never going to work. Nevertheless, in Fraser's view Whitlam's intention to use the banks was an abandoning of fundamental democratic principle, perhaps the most damaging and worrying thing that had happened so far.

At just twenty-four hours' notice, Fraser arranged for the Liberal state and federal leaders to gather in Melbourne, on 2 November. They issued a combined communiqué in which they spoke about the risk of dictatorship and the breach of constitutional principle. They instructed Fraser to call on the Governor-General 'to report on the outcome' of their discussions. Surely, now, Kerr would have to act?

That night, Ian Macphee was waiting in hospital with his wife, who was at risk of miscarrying. He saw the evening news, which reported on the communiqué, that the opposition was standing firm and that Fraser was going to see the Governor-General the next day. Macphee was troubled enough to take time away from his wife's bedside to write Fraser a long and anguished letter.

> We must all hope that the Governor-General will give you some reason to hope that he will act if the PM does bypass parliament for supply. I write in ignorance of what the Governor-General has already said to you and in anticipation of his not giving you the above expectation.

Macphee reminded Fraser of the arguments that he, Macphee, had been advancing since August—that Labor would destroy itself and that blocking supply risked losing public good will. 'Election would not be a problem but re-election may be if the public tired of our relative austerity and someone like Hawke, Hayden or Dunstan then led the ALP and plausibly claimed a combination of economic expertise and social reform to contrast with our dull economic management.' Blocking supply, said Macphee, would polarise the community. There was a risk of actual violence.

He begged Fraser to withdraw. 'People do not want Labor but they do not want *us in this way*' (emphasis in original). Macphee was worried about their capacity to govern if almost half the electorate was hostile. 'Whatever damage [the Whitlam government] might do in another eighteen months … may be exceeded many times over by a decade of extremism and instability (a likely consequence if we adhere to our present course for much longer without the Governor-General intervening to dissolve the House)'.

Fraser replied on 7 November with two paragraphs, the first expressing sympathy. Macphee's baby had been lost. As for the rest, he had read the letter carefully and would keep it in mind 'as events progress'.[66]

By the time Fraser wrote that note, the end game had begun. On 3 November, Fraser had met briefly with Kerr to present another compromise. The opposition would be prepared to pass supply immediately if Whitlam would undertake to hold a House of Representatives election at the same time as the next Senate election, which had to be before 30 June 1976. Whitlam rejected the compromise. Fraser's offer was blackmail, he said: the only difference was that the time for the payment of the ransom had been extended. There was now no way out, Fraser believed, other than for Kerr to act. He was sure he would do so and that he would leave it until the last possible moment. Others were not so confident. Sometime in the final days of the crisis, Fraser spoke again to Menzies, who told him, 'I don't think you are going to get an election out of this man. You will have to retreat'.

Fraser replied, 'Sir, on this issue, I don't know how to retreat'.

On 6 November Fraser met with Kerr again. Both men had done their maths. They knew that if an election was to be held before Christmas, the last viable date was 13 December, meaning parliament would have to be dissolved in the week following their meeting. Fraser was sure that Kerr would not allow the nation to remain in crisis over Christmas. Knowing that this was the last meeting they would have before Kerr would need to act, Fraser used every inch of leverage and every insight he had into Kerr's character. He assured him that the senators would hold firm; he told him that if he did not act then the opposition would be forced to criticise him: they would have to say that he had failed in his duty and that he had imperilled the reserve powers of the Crown forever; he said that supply running out and Kerr's failing to act would effectively destroy the reserve powers. Fraser also said that he believed he would win the election. Despite the polls being as they were, once the election was called, the people would move back to the underlying issue: economic management. Kerr had a duty to obtain an election, Fraser said. Australians wanted an election. 'I told him frankly that this was a wretched government. There needed to be an election, and he should do everything he could to achieve it. I said something like: "You know, Sir, I regret that you are in this position. It is a terrible position to be in, but you are in the unfortunate position of having to make a choice, and, whichever way you go, you will be condemned. But you have a choice of whether to be condemned for doing the right thing, or for doing the wrong thing. The people believe that there ought to be an election. They will not forgive you for not calling an election and they'll say that you've betrayed your power, you've betrayed your position, by not using the powers which are very clearly available to you. They believe that the country is in extremis". I asked him whether he wanted to be condemned for not using the powers deliberately placed there by the founding fathers to give the people of Australia relief from the most wretched government in the whole history of federation, or did he want to be condemned for doing what was right?'

What did Kerr say to this? Today, Fraser smiles. 'I don't remember. He probably said something like "Thanks very much, Malcolm". I knew that he wanted to be seen as doing the right thing. It was part of my judgement of him, as a man, that he did not want to be condemned for *not* doing the right thing. I left it to the last minute, you know, to let some pressure build. I never asked for a comment on this. This wasn't a discussion. It would have been improper to have a discussion, and he didn't seek it. I said that I wanted to give him a view, and he listened to me do that.'

Fraser says that while he was putting immense and well-calculated pressure on Kerr, he was still not sure that this would result in Whitlam's dismissal. He thought it possible that Kerr would speak to Whitlam and tell him what was in his mind, and that at the last minute Whitlam would then agree to an election. But he had also divined Kerr's fear that if he warned Whitlam, then Whitlam would sack him first.

Later that day, Kerr saw Whitlam and told him that Fraser had no interest in a compromise. Whitlam told Kerr that he would probably advise a half-Senate election to be held on 13 December. He said nothing about provision for supply, which would have run out before the election could be held. The government was relying on its shaky plans to use the banks. Whitlam was supremely confident that Fraser would have no option but to back down. Kerr's memoirs reveal that it was on this day, after his meetings with Fraser and Whitlam, that he decided to sack the government. Nevertheless, he consulted the Chief Justice Garfield Barwick and High Court judge Sir Anthony Mason. Fraser knew nothing of this until afterwards, but he says today, 'Gar was steel. He would have helped him do what was right'.

The morning of 11 November dawned crisp and blue. At nine o'clock, Fraser, Phillip Lynch and Doug Anthony went to Whitlam's office. Whitlam offered again the option of a late Senate election; Fraser rejected the offer. Fraser again offered his compromise—elections for both houses in May; Whitlam refused. Fraser looked at Whitlam, and sounded the warning that Kerr had not given him.

'You know, Prime Minister, the Governor-General can make up his own mind what to do. You can't necessarily assume he will do just as you advise.'

Whitlam dismissed the suggestion: 'Nonsense', he said.

Fraser left and was preparing for a joint party meeting when the telephone rang. It was 9.55 a.m. On the other end was Sir John Kerr. 'He opened by saying that this would have to remain confidential', recalls Fraser. What followed was one of the most momentous phone calls in the history of Australian politics. Fraser turned over the agenda for the joint party meeting that he had in his hand and took notes on the back. That piece of paper remains in Fraser's possession today. It records, in Fraser's unmistakeable scrawl, the substance of the undertakings that Kerr sought from him. If Whitlam was dismissed and Fraser was made Prime Minister, would he agree to call a double dissolution election? Would he agree to run a caretaker administration, making no policy changes? Would he obtain supply straightaway? Would he advise a dissolution on that very day? There was a further condition—less expected, but highly significant. Kerr asked Fraser to guarantee that no action would be taken against the ministers of the Whitlam government over the loans affair, and that there would be no royal commission. Fraser understood this commitment not to pursue Whitlam and his ministers to be a permanent undertaking, applying not only for the period of the caretaker government, but for good. He was glad to give the commitment. Although only months before he had called for a royal commission into the loans affair, that had been before he knew there was to be an election.

Fraser held firm to this promise, despite the urgings of his colleagues and claims that there was evidence that pointed to more than just incompetence in the loans affair. In the months following, keeping this promise and refusing to even consider investigating allegations against Cairns, Whitlam and Murphy cost Fraser one of his most valuable ministers, and a man he still respects—his first Attorney-General, Robert Ellicott. Of all the ministers he lost, Fraser regrets the loss of Ellicott most of all. Ellicott was responsible for driving law reform, in particular human rights–based legislation. While Kerr extracted the commitment, it accorded with Fraser's convictions. Fraser had accused Whitlam and his ministers of corruption, but he had meant political corruption. If there was to be an election, then Whitlam and his ministers would be judged by the people, and pay a political price. That was appropriate, Fraser believed. There should be no other cost. Here, too, there was a principle at stake. 'Governments pursuing previous governments through the courts is the kind of thing that happens in a dictatorship', he says today.

The phone call with Kerr ended. Fraser wrote the time and date on his note of the conversation, and signed it. He knew now that today was the day that Kerr intended to act. He still wasn't certain that, once faced with an ultimatum, Whitlam would not back down and choose to go to an election as Prime Minister.

There has been some controversy about this telephone conversation. Kerr later denied that it ever took place. There can be little doubt that it did. Fraser's Principal Private Secretary at the time, Dale Budd, remembers seeing the signed note of the conversation on Fraser's desk later on 11 November.[67] National Country Party member of parliament Peter Nixon was in the room at the time of the call and remembers it, although he heard only one side—Fraser's monosyllabic responses. So why did Kerr deny that the call took place? Fraser believes that this was a measure of the pressure Kerr was under in the wake of the dismissal, with conspiracy theories being floated. There was nothing improper in the call, Fraser thought. Kerr was simply doing the sensible thing: making sure that if he sacked Whitlam and called on Fraser, he knew how Fraser would act. Fraser says, 'Look, denying it was a sign of weakness. There are many signs of weakness in his character, and that is probably true of most of us. It was an error of judgement and it was a weakness not to explain it how I've explained it'.

After the telephone call, Fraser walked into the joint party meeting, which started late, at 10.30 a.m. The minutes show that at eleven o'clock, the members stood for two minutes' silence to mark Armistice Day. Lynch briefed the room on the meetings that had been held between banks and senior public servants. Eggleton's briefing notes for the meeting read:

> Pressures on government as banks declined to cooperate. Two major banks have already told Hayden that they cannot be in his scheme ... Believe we are close to crunch point ... With money running out and grave doubts about the legality and practicality of alternative financing schemes, it cannot be long before the Governor-General will feel compelled to intervene. Meanwhile we must remain resolute and united. Federal fundraising ahead of target.

Anthony told the room that 'things are building to a crisis in the next twenty-four hours and to stay firm and resolute'. Fraser asked his colleagues not to press him on current events. Matters would soon be resolved.[68]

The events of the rest of that day have been recounted many times. Parliament sat at 11.45 a.m. and Fraser moved a motion of censure against the government for planning to continue without supply. At 12.34 p.m. Whitlam delivered his last speech as Prime Minister, moving an amendment censuring Fraser. Whitlam had announced his intention to call a half-Senate election, and was planning to call on Kerr to arrange it. Kerr, meanwhile, was preparing for the dismissal and had arranged for Fraser to go to see him immediately after Whitlam. There was a mix-up. Fraser arrived first and was kept waiting.

Kerr and Whitlam have given differing versions of what occurred between them. According to Kerr's version, he warned Whitlam, saying that he would be dismissed if he continued in his determination to govern without supply. In this version, Whitlam had a few moments to reconsider. Although the documents dismissing him were ready and waiting, he was not actually dismissed until they were handed to him. He could, had he been able to think very quickly indeed, have gone to the election as Prime Minister. According to Kerr, Whitlam responded by looking at the telephone and saying, 'I must get in touch with the Palace at once', thus confirming that, if he was given the chance, he would advise the Queen to dismiss Kerr. It was after this that Kerr handed him the documents, and formally dismissed him. According to Whitlam, there was no chance to reconsider, and no mention of telephoning the Palace: Kerr dismissed him without warning.[69] Fraser, who walked into the room minutes later, says today that he believes Kerr's version. 'It was always my understanding that Whitlam had a choice, that he could, at that very last minute, have agreed to call an election, and he would then have contested that election as Prime Minister.'

How would we remember the events of 11 November 1975 if this had happened? Would Whitlam still be a Labor hero? Would Fraser have been a better loved Prime Minister? Would Kerr have been so reviled? Whatever happened in those few moments, Whitlam seems to have been stunned. He did not return to parliament to speak to his advisers; he left and went to the Lodge, and rang his wife, his departmental head and office chief and invited them to join him. When they arrived they found him eating his lunch. It was steak.

Meanwhile, Fraser was shown in to Kerr's office. Kerr again asked him for the commitments agreed to earlier that day by telephone. Fraser gave the same answers and was sworn in as Prime Minister, returning immediately to Parliament House to organise the passing of supply. In an atmosphere of deceptive quiet, the word was passed among the coalition senators: 'Do not allow your expression to change, but Whitlam has been sacked. Malcolm is Prime Minister and we will get the budget as quickly as we can'. Labor's senators were not briefed: they didn't know the government had changed. As planned previously, Labor moved that the budget Bills be declared urgent and put immediately, expecting the opposition to block as usual. Reg Withers, on behalf of the coalition, agreed to what Labor proposed and the budget was quietly passed at 2.24 p.m. Too late, the Labor senators realised what had happened: the opposition was no longer the opposition but a caretaker government, and it had just been given supply.

Crowds were gathering on the lawns in front of Parliament House as Fraser left at 3.15 p.m. to advise Kerr to call a double dissolution election. Protesters gave him fascist salutes and pounded on the roof of his car. Kerr dissolved parliament and David Smith read the proclamation on the steps, followed by Whitlam's famous speech: 'Maintain your rage'. Fraser's office—still that of the Leader of the Opposition—was a flurry of senior bureaucrats, many struggling with the fact that when they were told the Prime Minister wanted to see them it meant Fraser, not Whitlam. In the halls of Parliament House, Labor ministers were evacuating their offices, loading boxes with papers. There was confusion and panic.

How was Fraser feeling? Those who saw him that day recall him as mostly impassive. Kerr wrote in his memoirs that when he told Fraser that Whitlam had been dismissed, his face 'revealed nothing of the impact this news must surely have had upon him'. Normally a new Prime Minister would stop for a glass of champagne with the Governor-General, but because of the stressful circumstances and the need to acquire supply, this was dispensed with: 'I feel sure you would rather get back to your desk—there's a lot to be done', Kerr had said. At this, according to Kerr, Fraser had smiled slightly.[70] David Kemp remembers seeing Fraser return to Parliament House surrounded by security men. 'Nothing symbolised for me quite so dramatically the change which had occurred in his status than that group of strangers invading the territory of our opposition office in Parliament House.' Kemp congratulated Fraser and was given another fleeting smile. Later, there was an 'electric' media conference, at which, according to Kemp, the journalist Mungo MacCallum was giggling with emotion.[71] Fraser remembers his dominant emotion as relief. 'But, really, I don't remember the emotions much at all.'

Fraser tried to ring Tamie, in Melbourne, without success. She first heard the news when she returned home to Fairlie Court from a trip to the hairdresser. Mark was there, studying for Higher School

Certificate exams. He greeted his mother with the words 'What on earth's going on? The radio's saying Dad's the PM'. Fraser was soon on the line. 'Whitlam's been sacked. Can you come?' All the children were day students at Fraser's old school Melbourne Grammar. Tamie waited to talk to them before boarding a plane for Canberra, 'to be', she says, 'what is loosely termed "a support"'.

That night Fraser, Tony Staley and Fraser's personal staff—Dale Budd, David Kemp, Petro Georgiou and David Barnett—dined in the Lobby restaurant. The mood was subdued—relief and weariness in equal measure. Tamie arrived at Canberra airport and was met at the stairs of the plane by the manager of the airport, who steered her away from an angry press pack and into a Commonwealth car.

On the way back to their hotel later that evening, Tamie noticed a flag on the front of their car and realised they were riding in the prime ministerial vehicle. She told Fraser she didn't think it was right; after all, he was only the caretaker Prime Minister. He hadn't been elected. Fraser told her it was necessary: it was the position that was important; the position had to be protected. They arrived at the Rex Hotel, where they were staying, and security people shepherded them through a kitchen door, down a long passageway then into the service lift. When, finally, they closed the door to their room and were left alone, Tamie turned to Fraser and said, 'I can't believe it. It's hideous. Is this the freedom we've been fighting for?' Then she realised. She knew. Their lives were no longer their own.

Part 2

Governing

10

How to Govern

Fraser says today that he has no regrets over his actions in blocking supply and bringing about the crisis that led to the dismissal. In the interviews for this book, he said that blocking supply should be done again if an opposition had the numbers in the Senate and the government was so 'reprehensible' that it should answer to the people. While it is commonly argued that the House of Representatives is the 'people's house', Fraser says this is to misunderstand the Australian system. We are not like the United Kingdom, with an Upper House that is appointed or hereditary: both the Senate and the House of Representatives are the people's houses—differently elected, but both answerable to the people. The Senate is a house of review, and powerful. The founding fathers meant it to be so. 'Certainly, the founding fathers would never have believed that the Senate would be a rubber stamp. That was what it was *not* meant to be', he says. When the opposition has the numbers in the Senate, this brings with it a responsibility.

So what kinds of circumstances justify using the power to block supply to force a government to the polls? 'I don't think that you can define it. It is an accumulation of events, and the final act might not necessarily be the worst of the acts, by any means.' In 1975, says Fraser, the Australian people, and certainly the Canberra press gallery, had become 'almost punch drunk. You know, in the boxing parlance. When you get hit on the head so much that you don't really understand what is happening. If you have so many crises all around you, then crisis becomes normality. But if any one of the events of the Whitlam government and the loans affair had happened by themselves, it would have been blazoned in the headlines'.

The decision that the Whitlam government was so bad and so damaging to the country that the blocking of supply was justified was made because of a combination of many factors, Fraser says today. There were the crises. There was the speed of change, with the public service struggling to provide proper advice or caution. There was the dire state of the economy and, in Fraser's judgement, the lack of a credible plan to put it right. Finally, there were the scandals, the lack of propriety, the resignations of the government's most senior ministers in crisis after crisis, and the evidence that Whitlam could not or would not control his ministers. 'I think, at the end of the day, for me, I just had an instinct: this is wrong, or this has gone too far; you can't go down this track.' Thus, the decision to force a government to an election is one not only of principle, but also of politics, judgement and leadership. In 1975, those three came together. The popular support for an election was there. The opposition had the numbers in the Senate, giving it both power and responsibility. Fraser provided the leadership.

Two fundamental principles conflicted, 'as they often do in politics'. The first principle is that an elected government should be allowed to govern. The second is that the opposition has a duty to protect the country from fundamental damage. 'When principles conflict, you have to exercise judgement. That is what we did. I didn't like the idea of blocking supply, never did, still don't. It is a power that should be used only in a significant emergency.' Could he not have waited for the electoral cycle, given that he almost certainly would have won the next election? No, he says. The damage would have been too deep. The Hayden budget, while a retreat from the worst excesses of Whitlam, was merely 'less bad' and not a recipe for recovery. The economy might never have recovered had Whitlam stayed in power. Just as importantly, the government had proved it could not be trusted. What else might Whitlam's ministers have been getting up to, given that Connor and Cairns had misled both Whitlam and the parliament?

Did the improper appointment of Albert Field and Cleaver Bunton undermine the right to block supply? Fraser points out that it was Whitlam, with the Gair affair, who first broke convention on the question of Senate positions. But in any case, 'I think we would have been held in contempt if we had said, "Oh we really ought to block supply and have an election because the country is going down the gurgler, but we can't act because Bjelke-Petersen and Tom Lewis did the wrong thing". That would have been pathetic. I'm not saying it was justification of what Bjelke-Petersen and Lewis did. It was an improper change to the Senate. But that opened up a possibility of starting to put right a lot of the things that were going wrong in Australia. And it wasn't a coup d'état, as people have said. All we did was force the calling of an election, and a country is never so democratic as when the people get to vote'.

* * *

The 1975 election campaign was one of the most emotional in Australia's history. It was marked by enormous and passionate rallies of Whitlam's supporters. Badges reading 'Shame Fraser Shame' had begun to be distributed during the blocking of supply. Now there was 'Give Fraser the Razor' and 'Kerr's Cur is a Mangy Mongrel'. The Liberal Party campaign slogan was 'Turn on the Lights', which made driving with headlights on a political statement. The Liberal campaign song, belted out by Renee Geyer, was accompanied by a television commercial showing a montage of the Whitlam government's darkest moments—the Murphy raid on the Australian Security Intelligence Organisation, the Gair affair, unemployment, inflation, industrial unrest and the sacking of Jim Cairns.

On the day of the dismissal an estimated twenty thousand people rallied in the capital cities. There were strikes in several states, and calls for a general strike. It could have been worse. Bob Hawke, then President of the Australian Council of Trade Unions, from the first advised the union movement to keep cool heads. He rejected the idea of a general strike, instead advocating that unionists donate a day's pay to the Labor campaign. Hawke has said since that he thought the idea of a strike was 'stupidly counterproductive' and he was not deceived by the euphoria of the pro-Whitlam rallies. 'One didn't have to rely on the polls to know that the government was widely unpopular ... The broader electorate had the baseball bat in hand and it was not Fraser's head they were waiting to smash.'[1]

Amid all of this, Fraser was outwardly unemotional. The Liberal Party tactic, thought out before, was to concentrate on the economy. There had been discussions during the crisis about how to conduct the election. It had been agreed that there was no point in courting the Canberra media: they were hopelessly biased in favour of Whitlam. Rather, the emphasis should be on local media and on members of parliament and ministers attending as many community events as possible. The minutes of the joint party room meeting on 12 November, less than twenty-fours hours after the dismissal, show that Fraser started in phlegmatic fashion, telling everyone that meetings must begin on time and that ministers' attendance was obligatory. Later in the morning, he said, he would form a ministry that would be smaller than normal. Fraser concluded the meeting with the words 'We are going out to win. Work hard'.[2]

Tamie remembers many times in the weeks that followed sitting on a stage behind Fraser, scanning the crowd and wondering if that night would be the one on which she would see a gun or a knife—someone wanting to take her husband's life. Fraser himself says that he was never frightened. 'I guess at heart I never thought an Australian crowd would do it.' There was plenty of anger, but no serious violence directed against them. Once, at a rally at the Northcote town hall in Melbourne, Fraser was hit on the head by beer cans in a potato sack. Another time, Tamie collected an accidental blow to the head from a banner—and received a profuse apology from the protester concerned.

Even before Fraser became caretaker Prime Minister, his family had had to come to terms with the impact of what he had done. Blocking supply infuriated so many people that the security services were convinced the Frasers were at real risk. During the election campaign, Tamie's parents came to stay at Fairlie Court to help when Tamie was away. When the children left for school, they were accompanied by bodyguards. Sometimes the security precautions deteriorated into farce. Tamie recalls one day during the supply crisis when the family were at Nareen, and there had been a threat to maim the Fraser children. The family had planned one of their customary picnics with the children in the paddocks, but as they packed and got ready to leave, Fraser was caught up on the phone. Tamie scribbled a note, left it for him, and departed with the children. She returned later to find Nareen in a state of siege, with security officers on high alert. She was told they had found a threatening note on the table. They showed it to her: it was her own note to Fraser. In big black texta were the words 'I'll fix the kids and be back after lunch for you'.

During the crisis leading to the dismissal, the public opinion polls had shown that most Australians did not support the blocking of supply, but, as Fraser had predicted to his colleagues, once the election campaign was called the figures changed. Polls published in *The National Times* showed that on the weekend of 19 and 20 November—a week after the dismissal—41 per cent of Australians thought the main election issue was the way in which Whitlam had been sacked. Only 21 per cent saw the main issue as being the economy. By the weekend of 3 and 4 December, only 27 per cent saw the manner of Whitlam's departure as the main issue, and the number who thought the economy was what mattered most had risen to 37 per cent.[3] Fraser was campaigning in Tasmania when he received the first information to show that the shift was on from public opinion pollster Gary Morgan. He remembers, 'The whole thing started to move. Gough was talking about the wrong issues. He was talking about the Senate and the use of the Senate. I was trying to talk about the realities of people's lives and how they lived in the economic circumstances of Australia, and I really believe that at the end of the day that is what they focussed on'.

During the campaign, Fraser and Tamie were busier than ever. Tamie remembers 'briefings at 6 a.m. and debriefings at 11.30 p.m. and during the day breakfasts, morning coffees, lunches, street walks, drinks and dinners or rowdy evening meetings. We were new and not awfully clever at pacing ourselves, but we were young and keen and determined to give it our best shot ... Finally, election eve came and we were going to win. I wept a tear silently in the night for the acknowledged permanent loss of a cherished privacy'.

Not surprisingly, given the strain of the previous few weeks, shortly before his formal policy speech Fraser fell ill. Tamie remembers a Liberal Party function on a hot day at a race course in the electorate. Fraser was in a long-sleeved shirt, two jumpers, a sports coat and a heavy overcoat, shivering with fever. He watched Whitlam's policy launch speech on 24 November from his bed. Whitlam concentrated almost entirely on the manner of his dismissal. 'The whole future of democracy is in your hands', he said. Because of Fraser's illness, the Liberal Party launch had to be delayed until 27 November. Fraser's speech had nothing of the elegance, big ideas or flourish of his Deakin lecture; the tone was downbeat, practical, focussed on the economy and the record of Whitlam. Fraser was making the obvious claim: to be a better manager.

> For three dark years our freedom, our prosperity, the self-respect of many Australians have been eroded—eroded by the highest taxes in our history, more and more inflation, more and more unemployment, more and more power to Canberra. More and more dependence on government, more and more regulations, more forms, more controls, more bureaucracy.

Fraser promised tax indexation and home savings grants, together with strategies to promote growth. Kemp remembers struggling with Fraser over the question of industry protection. Whitlam had cut tariffs to manufacturing industries—one reason for his unpopularity. Kemp was even then much more of a free trader than Fraser. He remembers, 'I felt it would be a great mistake to have in that speech a view that we were for high protection or that we weren't prepared to tell Australian industry that the age of high protection was over. So I had quite a discussion with Malcolm about this and we eventually came up with a formulation, which we laughed about at the time. Malcolm said, "Well, look, I'll tell you what we'll do: we'll say that Australian industry will have the protection that it needs", which of course could be interpreted either way'. The phrase survived in the final version of the policy speech. Fraser said: 'We will give Australian industry the protection it needs. We would sooner have jobs than dogma'.[4] Attitudes to protection played an important part in the story of the Fraser government. Today Fraser says he was always a free trader by instinct, but that there was no point in lowering tariffs when other countries would not. 'My view was that you always use these things as bargaining chips. There is no such thing, even today, as perfect free trade.' Yet he pushed hard for developed countries to open their markets to agricultural produce, making common cause with Third World countries.

Fraser received regular advice from Robert Menzies during the campaign. On 2 December, Menzies wrote a letter telling him he hadn't looked good in a broadcast the night before.

> You appeared to be using the 'idiot board' and looking everywhere except at the lens of the camera. You are easily at your best when you are speaking your own words direct to the audience. When, as on the last occasion, you appeared to be reading what someone else had written, you lose the impact of your own personality, and it is your own personality which will win this election ... In all this rubbish they are talking about the Governor-General

> the real issues are the ones you have indicated. Stick to the real issues, those which made them tremendously unpopular two months ago, and we will win ... I cannot contemplate defeat because in reality this is the last chance the Australian voters will have to avoid disaster, so my prayers and hopes are with you.[5]

In the week before election day, Tamie received a note from Menzies, whom they had invited to join them on polling night.

> My very dear Tamie,
>
> May an old campaigner tell you how much he admires what you have been doing in the course of this campaign. You have not only handled your interviews with great charm and skill, but you have been of tremendous assistance to Malcolm. I am now convinced that he will win on Saturday. I would like to convey to him my belief that this will be a great personal triumph, a complete vindication of his character and attainments. I notice that some people have been promoting themselves for future consideration in a rather curious way. Do get Malcolm to believe, as is the truth, that his personal prestige will be so great that he can exercise his choice of ministers without feeling that he must please anybody but himself. It is essential that the new government should be competent and cohesive, for the work they will have to do will be of extreme difficulty. Don't let Malcolm be too modest about it all. In my opinion he will have the same amount of personal authority and prestige as I always hoped for in my own case in my own time ... You will know where my thoughts are because this is, in my opinion, the most vital Australian election in my time.[6]

When the election was held, on 13 December, the result was the worst for Labor in the postwar period. The coalition had a record majority, and became the first government since before the 1961 election to hold a majority in the Senate. On election night, Fraser says, he felt mainly relief, but also a sense of crushing responsibility and 'a recognition that there was an enormous amount of damage to repair'.

In recent years, Fraser's former colleagues have suggested that his government was plagued by a sense of lack of legitimacy, and that this made it more cautious than it would otherwise have been. Fraser denies it. What better kind of legitimacy can there be than a record election majority, he asks. The next election, in 1977, more or less confirmed the result. The Australian Labor Party, still led by Whitlam, failed to recover much ground, winning only an extra two seats. It was not until Bill Hayden replaced Whitlam that Labor began to look competitive again, making up substantial ground in the 1980 election. The Fraser government lost control of the Senate in the same year. Yet Fraser admits that he was keenly aware of the need for healing after the events of 1975, and he was concerned that his actions should demonstrate that he wanted to govern for all Australians. This was one of the factors that determined how he dealt with the aftermath of the dismissal and the persistent allegations against Whitlam, Cairns, Connor and Murphy.

* * *

Tamie arrived at the Lodge to be greeted by a letter from Margaret Whitlam saying she hoped that the Frasers would enjoy their time there. Tamie was touched by the gesture, after so many weeks of acrimony. In 1983, she was to write her own note to greet Hazel Hawke. Tamie was surprised to find that the Lodge was by no means a grand home. There had been no new crockery purchased since Stanley Bruce was Prime Minister in 1929. There weren't enough matching plates to allow a formal dinner to be served to a dozen people without washing up being done in between courses. Menzies, conscious of the bad feeling towards politicians who spent public money on their own comfort, had been frugal and used his own furniture and fittings. There was no official body to take care of the house. Tamie remembers, 'By the time we arrived, there was Zara's carpet, Sonia's curtains and Margaret's chairs. The place, through no one person's fault, looked like a dog's breakfast'. There were no paintings, decorative arts or furniture to give the house a sense of history. The staff quarters were squalid. The Frasers dealt with this by asking the appropriate union to inspect them and insist on an upgrade—not for the comfort of the Frasers but for the union members. On their tours overseas, Tamie was struck by how most of the official residences they visited were living museums of their country. By comparison, Australia's four official establishments—the Lodge, Government House, Kirribilli and Admiralty House in Sydney—were bare. In response, Tamie founded the Australiana Fund to collect money from the private sector to buy major pieces of Australian furniture, paintings and sculpture for the four official establishments. The fund survives to this day.

Fraser and Tamie decided, regretfully, that the children should go to boarding school. It was the only way they would be able to have anything approaching a normal life, without bodyguards accompanying them. Phoebe, the youngest, was only nine. 'It was an incredibly hard decision', Tamie remembers. During 1976 the house at Fairlie Court was sold, and once again Nareen became the family home whenever they were able to get away from Canberra. The security services recommended that a perimeter fence be erected, at enormous cost, to keep them safe. Fraser rejected the idea. Instead, a station hand's cottage was made available for security guards, and a sentry box was erected at the gate.

Tamie's diary was soon almost as full as her husband's. She remembers the years of the prime ministership as 'really hard work. I did a lot of stuff on my own account, and then I attended the things with Malcolm as well. So it was full on'. He would often ask her advice. She is reluctant to admit it: 'I don't want to be seen as like Janette Howard', she says. She was not the power behind the throne, and she knew that she was never the only person he listened to. Nevertheless, they would 'thrash things out', often into the small hours. In particular, her advice was important in those areas where Fraser's party colleagues were inevitably partisan—the occasions on which a minister was in trouble, and Fraser had to consider whether to ask him to resign. 'Mine was a layperson's point of view. I would have to say what message people would take from it if they resigned, or if they didn't.'

It took the Frasers some time to adjust to the protocol and formalities of their new position. In March 1976, King Hussein and Queen Alia of Jordan arrived on a state visit. Tamie and Fraser met the royal couple at the airport. The motorcade on the way back to Canberra was enormous: Hussein had motorcycle outriders; there was an Australian security vehicle, then more outriders, and Fraser and Tamie in the prime ministerial car. A civilian car driving on the same side of the road was forced to pull over in the ditch. Fraser was horrified. Tamie remembers, 'He shouted at the driver, "We can't push people off the road. Stop! Stop!" and he got out and strode over to the people and said, "I'm terribly sorry we pushed you off the road. I do apologise", then got into the car and rushed off again, leaving them gobsmacked, I am sure'. Hussein's contingent believed that the delay must mean there had been an assassination attempt. King and queen ducked down and were driven away at high speed. Fraser says, 'There was no need for all that cavalcade. Driving along like that, pushing people off the road. That's the sort of thing dictators do. We don't do that in Australia. Or we shouldn't. Tamie makes an amusing story out of it, but I was really annoyed'.

* * *

A Prime Minister does not belong to himself, or to his family. He belongs to the process of government. He is somewhere between conductor, composer and lead singer. He leads the orchestra, yet depends on the orchestra. He directs the process of government, yet is owned by it. At the point at which he becomes Prime Minister, the story of Malcolm Fraser ceases to be only his story. The memoir of a Prime Minister is not only about him; it is also about his ministers, his advisers and the nation. It is about the interaction between the man and the people, the politically possible and the nature of the times. Even in Fraser's memory, the organising principle of chronology falls away. Everything happened at once.

The suite of offices that Fraser and his staff occupied in the old Parliament House is tiny by present-day standards. All day long, every day, it would be full of people and events. Typists would be hammering away at drafts of statements and letters. Ministers would come and go. Advisers would push ideas, argue and think. Fraser would leave to attend parliament, or some public event, and return. Fraser's diaries as Prime Minister show him holding his first meetings at 8 a.m. He would have already given a dozen directives to his staff—almost comic in their variety—about questions he wanted answered, matters on which he wished to be briefed. He would issue instructions about whom he wanted to call that day, and the order in which the calls should be placed. His demands for briefings covered everything from the price of steel to aviation charges at country airports to the family members of the Japanese Prime Minister. Appointments with ministers, backbenchers and public servants would be stacked one on the other. In between there would be encounters with the few people—senior ministers, senior advisers—who could walk into his office at any time. There were public events, dinners at the Lodge for visiting dignitaries and others, long meetings of cabinet and its subcommittees. He read his briefs, letters and cabinet submissions on aeroplanes, in cars and in bed, getting through them by the caseful. He didn't write much, but he did annotate—the thick black pen scoring in the margins, and questions in his now barely legible scrawl: 'Find out more'. 'Why?' 'Yes'. 'No'. Or there would be a note to seek the opinion of a minister or senior public servant. Fraser read every letter that went out under his name, and often demanded redrafts. He would initial documents he had seen, so there could be no doubt about what he had read and what he had not. Fraser says he had by that time developed a particular ability—it might be called prime ministerial. It was the capacity to pay intense attention to something for a period of time, then to switch to another topic, and pay it equally intense attention. In between, he issued instructions and asked questions. Fraser's appointment diary would typically list the last event of the day at around 10 p.m., but after that there was the work done at home, the reading and thinking and telephone calls made in the small hours to overseas heads of government. In this maelstrom, on any single day a dozen separate stories were advanced.

Fraser also argued—perhaps most of all with those closest to him. David Kemp remembers, 'He would pull any argument out to win the point. Sometimes he was quite unfair in the way he argued. But in the end, he would think about what you had been saying and he might well modify what he ended up with. I have always found him an extraordinarily rational person. He is one of the most rational people I know'. Not everyone could stand the style: the all-out arguments, the lack of praise, small talk and those small emblems of personal warmth that can make a leader loved. Kemp says, 'You've got to be a certain kind of personality to deal with these things. Some people were vulnerable to the way he argued a point and were crushed by it. They would go along with him, then resent the force of his personality'. Among those were some of Fraser's cabinet ministers. Alistair Drysdale remembers that on Fraser's fiftieth birthday, in May 1980, the staff had an impromptu birthday party, with a cake. Someone made a speech to the effect that Fraser wasn't always easy to work with but they were proud to be doing so. Fraser responded, unsmiling, 'Well, it's all voluntary, you know. None of you have to work here'.

Fraser's speeches were mostly written by others, but he would provide whole paragraphs of text and demand that drafts were sent out to others. The most important speeches were indeed the work of an orchestra, many instruments in the making. Owen Harries, who became one of Fraser's key foreign affairs advisers, remembers, 'He always knew what he wanted to say, where he wanted to end up. But he often had no idea of how to get there'. Finding the way was the job of the advisers and the speechwriters.

In conversations to decide the title for this book, Fraser suggested that the words 'Enduring Liberal' should have a question mark after them. 'I don't think I want to say that I always got it right. I held these principles. I tried to put them into action, but, in all the hundreds of things one deals with, I don't want to claim that I always lived up to my ideals. That is for others to judge.'

How does one judge the Fraser government? It is only by looking back that one can take up the threads of the ideas and principles that Fraser took in to government, attempt to trace them through the tangle of daily events and judge whether they were still intact, and what had been achieved, at the end. We have to abandon chronology, and consider themes.

* * *

Fraser was Prime Minister from November 1975 to March 1983. He won three elections—in 1975, 1977 and 1980. He took office before Margaret Thatcher became Prime Minister of the United Kingdom, and before Ronald Reagan became President of the United States. He spanned the years between unquestioning acceptance of big government and the rise of equally unquestioning faith in free markets as an organising principle in human affairs. He also spanned the years between faith in détente as a means of achieving world peace, the Soviet invasion of Afghanistan and the beginning of the collapse of the Soviet Union. There were immense social changes. Computers went from being tools for scientists to an essential part of government and business. International air travel came within reach of the ordinary person. In 1975, conservation of the environment was not a major issue for the majority; by the time Fraser lost government, it was at the heart of politics. In 1975 the popular press was full of talk of hippies and the permissive society; by 1983 it was power dressing and the beginning of the decade that became known for the phrase 'Greed is good'.

The record of the government that emerges from the archives, and from Fraser's memory, overturns conventional ideas of what his years in government were about. Those outraged by Whitlam's dismissal have seen the Fraser government through the prism of their fury. And this wasn't the only barrier to a clear view. The rubbishing of Fraser's record by his own side of politics began even before he lost government, and quickly accelerated once John Howard led the party. At least since the fall of Gorton, Fraser had had as many enemies in his own party as on the other side of parliament. That, at least, has not changed.

When he became Prime Minister, Fraser had been in politics for twenty years, serving under five different leaders, and had been a minister in three governments. He had also watched the Whitlam implosion. He had spent a long time thinking about how things should run. Now he put those ideas into practice.

He appointed his cabinet. He took Menzies's advice about regarding himself as free to choose, but he also wanted to maintain balance, between the states, between the coalition parties and between different points of view. 'I wanted diversity of life experience but also of politics. I wanted to hear the arguments in cabinet. The worst thing that can happen in government is to make a decision and then suddenly be exposed to a range of arguments that you haven't considered.' There was also the simple matter of competence. 'You don't want to appoint somebody beyond their ability, because it won't do them any good. You can't ignore the states, but keeping the balance there might mean that a person of higher ability has to wait longer than he or she should have to wait, and somebody else might get in quicker than they should. Sometimes you can't get rid of someone because of the state they come from, or there isn't an obvious replacement or they are going to make a great fuss and you don't need a great fuss ... And so a cabinet is always a less than ideal balance. If you've got four or five people in a cabinet who are really good, then you're lucky.'

Fraser regarded himself as lucky in his first ministry and particularly lucky in having Doug Anthony as Deputy Prime Minister and leader of the Liberal's coalition partner, the National Country Party. Anthony was also Minister for National Resources and for overseas trade. Fraser recalls, 'At first there were rumours in the media about tensions between us, but they didn't understand the nature of our experiences together'. Long before Fraser was Prime Minister, he and Anthony had gone on fishing trips in the Snowy Mountains. One day they had had a frustrating time, catching nothing, when they saw a big trout between two rocks. They dangled flies in front of it with no response. They put a net in front of it and prodded it with sticks. Still no success. Finally, they decided to try to tickle it out of the water. It ended with them taking turns to dangle each other by the ankles over the icy torrent. Fraser says, 'What you have to understand is that we were each in a position to let go, and we didn't. Well, once you have been in that sort of position with someone, there is a level of trust and understanding'. (They didn't catch the fish.)

Members of Fraser's own party were liable to see him as too close to the National Country Party. He, on the other hand, thought it important that rural Australia had strong representation in a parliament and in a government otherwise likely to be city-dominated. He took care to include the National Country Party in the greeting of foreign leaders. He made sure its position and role were acknowledged and respected. He was always aware that the leader of the minority party in a coalition has to be prepared to walk away if the party's principles are compromised, but he and Anthony agreed on many things. Anthony later backed Fraser's liberal agenda on key issues, including Aboriginal land rights.

Phillip Lynch, whose office had played the crucial role in handling the Treasury leaks and in the opposition's pursuit of the loans affair, was Treasurer in the first Fraser cabinet. Tony Street was Minister for

Industrial Relations, charged with a difficult role given the anger of the union movement. Ian Sinclair was Minister for Primary Industry, and Peter Nixon was Minister for Transport. Andrew Peacock took foreign affairs. Although Peacock had always been a political rival, Fraser was glad to have him in the portfolio that was perhaps closest to his own interests. 'Andrew and I have always had very similar views on most things to do with foreign affairs. Where we disagreed later was really about emphasis and timing rather than principle.' Jim Killen, also not a Fraser supporter, took defence. In the outer ministry there were positions for two talented men who had come into parliament at the 1974 election: John Howard was Minister for Business and Consumer Affairs, and Ian Macphee was Minister for Productivity. Tony Staley was Minister for the Capital Territory and Minister Assisting for the Arts. The immigration portfolio was held by Michael MacKellar. The Western Australian Ian Viner took Aboriginal affairs. Of the people in his first cabinet, those Fraser regarded as personal friends included Nixon, Anthony, Street, Staley and Macphee, but personal friendship, he says, had to be entirely put aside in making choices. 'It is a funny business, in politics, you know. Because it is not about friendships, but it is about relationships.'

A notable omission from the ministry was Don Chipp, who had held portfolios in both the Gorton and the McMahon governments and who had been Minister for Social Security during the caretaker period. Now Fraser replaced Chipp with the only woman in the team, Senator Margaret Guilfoyle. Chipp was also left out of the Fraser ministry following the 1977 election. He resigned from the Liberal Party shortly afterwards and founded the Australian Democrats. Fraser says today that his omission of Chipp was not an oversight. He will not elaborate.

Another continuing omission was the longstanding Victorian Senator Alan Missen—in many ways a liberal after Fraser's own heart. Missen, too, was vehemently opposed to racism and had criticised apartheid long before the rest of the party took a stand on it. He had also opposed the Menzies government's attempts to ban communism. Missen became the most consistent campaigner for freedom of information legislation, a Fraser government reform. Why did Fraser leave Missen out of his cabinets? Fraser says, 'I suppose that I felt he wouldn't have fitted … I'm not sure that he wanted the discipline of cabinet. I could have discussed it with him and I confess I didn't. Maybe I felt that too many issues were issues of principle for Alan, and that is not being critical of him, but in cabinet you can't make everything an issue of high principle. You've got to be selective'.

Fraser was determined to make cabinet work. He had experienced the bypassing of cabinet processes under Gorton. In Fraser's view, good government demanded that important decisions were taken to cabinet and openly discussed, even if this meant slower decision-making. Fraser felt an argumentative cabinet in which advice was challenged was more likely to arrive at the right decisions than one filled with ministers who simply concurred with the leader. 'Proper processes. It sounds dull, but it is what government is all about. With proper process, you are less likely to get dangerous things happening.' Proper process, Fraser still believes, is not a matter of technocratic nicety; it is intimately related to that fundamental liberal principle the rule of law. 'Due process is the protection against arbitrary, autocratic or dictatorial government. The law might say one thing, but if due process isn't observed you end up with arbitrary government in any case. So if you want to govern well you use the advice that is available and you use the people that are available. You get cabinet decisions. You keep cabinet at the heart of things.'

How is judgement exercised amid the enormous amount of material that a government must deal with, when the luxury of hindsight is not available and every move will have its critics? Fraser says, 'You take advice from as many sources as possible and discuss it, sometimes for too long or what people would say is too long. People say now that my cabinet meetings went on until everyone was exhausted. And sometimes, if I wasn't sure of a cabinet decision, I'd say, "I want to defer this discussion; I'll come back to it at another point". And so it might take longer. But you were more likely to be prudent that way. More likely to avoid being arbitrary, which so often means oppressive'. On the other hand, he tried to chair cabinet meetings firmly, to keep people on topic and make sure that non-contentious material was moved through briskly. 'One of the worst things you can do is continue cabinet meetings after dinner. I tried not to do it, and when we did it never went well.' While ensuring that important matters went to the whole of cabinet, to help with the overwhelming amount of material, Fraser made good use of a cabinet committee system. The important committees included foreign affairs and defence, monetary policy and general administrative. There were also ad hoc committees set up for particular tasks, such as handling the uranium mining issue and the never-ending work of setting budgets, with the constant battle between being across the detail and not allowing that detail to swamp philosophical thrust and coherence.

So far as was possible, cabinet submissions were circulated well in advance, with the idea that ministers would have time to read them and think. Fraser did his best to prevent ministers discussing issues privately and caucusing. 'I wanted them to have the arguments in cabinet. I didn't want deals stitched up outside.' Ministers were also banned from announcing publically what they planned to take to cabinet, which would have had the effect of making it difficult for cabinet to decide differently. Important decisions almost always followed consideration of a comprehensive cabinet submission. Often there were also detailed papers from within the public service, or from the advisers in Fraser's or another minister's private office. Some matters came before cabinet several times, with ministers being sent away with instructions to acquire better information from their departments.

Fraser kept on several of the senior public servants that Whitlam had appointed. John Menadue, a Whitlam appointee, remained as head of the Department of Prime Minister and Cabinet, which in the preceding year he had restructured and turned into a powerhouse of ideas, with the ability to vet cabinet submissions and oversee the rest of the public service, warning Fraser of any areas of weakness. Another key figure in Fraser's department was Brian Johns, also a Whitlam appointment. Fraser remembers, 'I believed, and this is now fantasy in today's world, but I believed in an apolitical public service, and while there were a few Whitlam appointments who I knew probably wouldn't want to tolerate us, and we probably wouldn't want to tolerate them, there were also some seriously talented people. I think John Menadue behaved impeccably at that time, and I thought that having him and the others would demonstrate that we wanted to govern well, and that an apolitical public service was something that was worth preserving'.

Fraser initiated legislation designed to discourage the politicisation of the public service. 'I tried to come up with a device that the Labor Party would accept as well, in the hope that it would survive.' Under this scheme, when a permanent headship fell vacant, a committee of senior public servants chaired by the head of the public service board compiled a list of recommended appointees. If the government appointed someone from the list, they would have permanence. If instead the government chose its own candidate, they would hold office for only five years and could be sacked by an incoming Prime Minister of a different political party. Fraser's hopes that this scheme would survive his government were dashed: the Hawke government repealed the legislation, criticising it for placing too much power in the hands of a few public servants.[7]

Having assembled his ministerial team, Fraser took cool assessment. Not every minister was as good as they should be. Not every public service department was strong. Deliberately, Fraser and Menadue made sure the Department of Prime Minister and Cabinet reflected in its divisions the whole range of the public service. Fraser remembers, 'In any area where you had some doubt, you'd make sure you had excellent people in the relevant division of the Department of Prime Minister and Cabinet to compensate. I tried to be across everything. I would try to know as much as I could, and if I found that when a submission came to cabinet I knew more about it than the minister, well, you knew you had a problem and had to be on the alert'. Ministers who were across their portfolios, though, 'were left alone to get on with it', he says. Others sometimes tried to cover up their shortcomings by protesting they needed more private staff; these tended to be the ones that Fraser and his advisers watched most closely.

Fraser would receive from the Department of Prime Minister and Cabinet a brief on all cabinet submissions, including a summary of the issues, and usually a recommendation—sometimes disagreeing with that of the minister or suggesting some refinement or alteration. Fraser's private office, designed with the help of Kemp, was an extension of him, a source of advice and, perhaps most importantly, argument from the best minds that could be assembled. Fraser showed his respect for academics in the appointment of his private staff. Many of his most trusted advisers came from universities. There were nineteen people on his private staff in 1976, later expanding to twenty-one. About one-third to a half were advisers; the remainder of his staff were in charge of administration and press relations. But in the hectic day to day, anyone could be called on to do anything. Kemp and Georgiou were important from the beginning. Later, Owen Harries of the University of New South Wales briefly became a key adviser on foreign affairs. Professor John Rose—another former colleague of Tony Staley's from the University of Melbourne—joined in 1977, and became a crucial adviser on moves towards economic deregulation. Dale Budd continued as Chief of Staff. Ian Renard, 'kind, thoughtful, very valuable', joined later. Steve Vaughan was 'extraordinarily good on figures. He never gave me a figure that was wrong'.

Fraser consciously tried to diversify his sources of advice as much as possible. Nobody could be sure that they were the only person briefing him on an issue. He was always ringing people up, sometimes at short notice, to seek opinions. He took care to maintain a network in industry and elsewhere. His determination to diversify advice caused tension, and bruised the egos of those who expected to have an uncontested right to prime ministerial attention. Today Fraser says, 'It is all about a government harnessing the best advice and the best expertise and the best minds. You can't be expert on everything; nor can your ministers. You want the public service and your advisers to serve you up a menu of options, and you want to hear all the options, not just the ones they are attached to. Then you want advice, and a diversity of that. Then you exercise judgement. The machinery I set up was to try to achieve those ends, and for the most part it worked well'.

* * *

The national economy and the hunt for savings dominated Fraser's first months of government, yet the early cabinet records show that these were not the only issues he was dealing with. There were also matters of symbolism. Whitlam had dropped the term 'Commonwealth Government', replacing it with the theoretically more democratic-sounding 'Australian Government'. Fraser's cabinet decided to restore the word 'Commonwealth', but, in keeping with the mood of economy, with the proviso that the stock of stationery be used up first.[8] They also discussed the national anthem. After a public opinion poll, the Whitlam government had dropped 'God Save the Queen' and adopted 'Advance Australia Fair' as the anthem to be played on all except royal occasions, when 'God Save the Queen' would also be played. When the Fraser cabinet discussed the issue, Fraser said he preferred 'Waltzing Matilda' to either of the other songs.[9] 'God Save the Queen' was reinstated for royal and vice-regal occasions, and a decision was made to conduct a plebiscite to find a song to use on other occasions when Australia's separate identity was being celebrated. 'Advance Australia Fair' won, but wasn't officially declared as the Australian national anthem until 1984. Fraser still wishes it was 'Waltzing Matilda'. 'It's the tune everyone associates with Australia. People say the words are inappropriate, and I say, "Well, what about the Marseillaise? The words of that are hardly appropriate either". And I thought and still believe that 'Advance Australia Fair' is un-emotive. And the second verse! "Girt by sea." Why should we have language in our national anthem that nobody in their entire lives would ever use?'

Meanwhile, the man who had sacked Whitlam, Sir John Kerr, was lonely and besieged. There were angry demonstrations almost every time he appeared in public. In March 1976, Tony Eggleton, now Federal Director of the Liberal Party, was advising Fraser on the problem of the media looking for 'hostility' angles on the Governor-General. Eggleton advised that the government arrange maximum coverage of those events not marked by demonstrations, so the public could see that Kerr was out and about doing his job. 'Hosts should arrange for "spontaneous" support in strategic locations.' In April, Kerr wrote to Fraser begging him for leave at the end of the year. 'I do urge you to make it possible for me to do what I want to do about this', Kerr said. He wanted to get away overseas. 'You will appreciate, I am sure, that a holiday in Australia is extremely difficult for me.' Fraser replied that he was sympathetic to the idea of leave, but that in the atmosphere of cuts he could hardly pay for it out of the public purse. He would be happy if Kerr covered his own expenses. From the caretaker period onwards Kerr had raised with Fraser several times the possibility that he should resign to relieve 'the national tensions which inevitably resulted from the 1975 crisis'. It was Fraser who urged him to remain in his office, saying that if he resigned it would cast doubt on whether Kerr thought his own actions had been correct. But, by early 1977, Kerr had made it clear to both the Queen and Fraser that he would not want to continue past the end of that year. In June 1977, Kerr wrote a long letter to Fraser saying he had agreed to stay this long because he had not wanted to do anything that would call into question the legitimacy of his decision in sacking Whitlam, or the legitimacy of Fraser's government. Now, though, he foreshadowed that he would resign at the end of the year.[10] Fraser offered Kerr a post as UNESCO

Ambassador, but Kerr resigned from this post under the pressure of public outrage.

Today Fraser agrees that Kerr was a broken man in the wake of the dismissal. He regrets that he was not more attentive to him, and is aware that Kerr felt abandoned. 'Well, I probably didn't discuss with or inform the Governor-General as much as I should have. I can remember someone telling me that Kerr was put out because I wasn't telling him what was going on, and I said, "Well, he is briefed on everything, isn't he?"

'"Yes, he's briefed on everything."

'But I think that he thought that I ought to be briefing him.'

There were some other legacies of the extraordinary events of 1975, concerning the determination of some in politics to punish Whitlam and his ministers for the loans affair—to pursue them through the courts. There were two threads to this: persistent allegations that there was more to the loans affair than incompetence, and the strange court case brought against Whitlam, Cairns, Connor and Murphy by an obscure New South Wales solicitor, Danny Sankey. (Murphy, the Attorney-General who had advised on the key Executive Council decision to seek the loan, was by this time a High Court judge.) The Sankey case has almost disappeared from histories of this era. It was ill founded in law, as events proved. Yet it was significant in several ways. It gave rise to an important High Court precedent on the issue of cabinet privilege, but that is not really part of this story; more important for present purposes is that it sheds light on the 'what might have been' of Australian history: what the remaining term of the Whitlam government might have been like had the coalition not blocked supply and forced the crisis that led to Whitlam's dismissal. Specific to Fraser's story, it demonstrates the strength of his determination that Whitlam and his ministers should not be further investigated or pursued. Fraser, in fact, protected them.

Fraser's determination on this led to the resignation of his first Attorney-General, Robert Ellicott. Today, Fraser says that of all the ministers he lost during his eight years as Prime Minister, he regretted the loss of Ellicott as Attorney-General the most of all. Yet this was the price that had to be paid for Fraser to keep his undertaking to Sir John Kerr, and his personal commitment to the principle that a government should not use the courts to pursue its predecessors. It was the Queensland Premier Joh Bjelke-Petersen and the former Prime Minister Billy McMahon who would not let the matter go. After the blocking of supply and before the dismissal, at the meeting of state and federal Liberal and National Party leaders on 2 November 1975, Bjelke-Petersen had told some of those present about information he had received from one of his friends, Wally Fancher, a US cattleman from northern Queensland. By the end of the meeting, Bjelke-Petersen believed he had been asked by the two coalition parties to ask Fancher to pursue an investigation. Fraser says today he knew nothing about this: the first he heard about Fancher's activities was during the election campaign, at which point he told Bjelke-Petersen to stop the investigation immediately. If it became public it would be seen as a breach of Fraser's undertaking to Sir John Kerr. Bjelke-Petersen did not obey. Meanwhile, Billy McMahon had his own ideas on what should be done. A few days into the period of the caretaker government, McMahon's staff and then McMahon himself contacted David Reid, the Secretary of the Executive Council. Reid was so disturbed by the approaches that he made a note for the file and informed his superiors.[11] He wrote that McMahon had asked to be given a copy of the documents relating to the Executive Council meeting of 13 December 1974.

> I declined to do so on the grounds of propriety. This disturbed him. He said he understood Mr Fraser had given the Governor-General an undertaking that the caretaker government would not initiate a court case against the ministers who participated in the meeting on 13 December 1974, but that he (Mr McMahon) had overcome this problem by arranging for a private person other than a member of the Liberal–Country Party

> government to initiate a court case ... He said that if I would agree to make the documents available he would send Mr Ashley to Canberra the following day to collect them from my home. I again declined and asked him whether, if he were Prime Minister, he would expect an officer of his department to accede to such a request. He laughed. He stated that if the court case proceeded it would probably be necessary for these documents to be obtained by subpoena.

Sure enough, three days later, on 20 November, solicitor Danny Sankey began the bizarre case accusing Murphy, Whitlam, Cairns and Connor of offences under the Crimes Act. Two charges were laid against each defendant: that the loan proposal would have contravened the Commonwealth–State Financial Agreement of 1928, under which Loans Council approval was normally sought, and that the defendants had conspired to deceive the Governor-General in the performance of his duties. It was widely believed at the time that the Liberal Party was in some way behind the Sankey case. Today, Ellicott and Fraser confirm that they believed it was McMahon, 'and not', emphasises Fraser, 'anyone else in my government or the Liberal Party. Just McMahon. I knew McMahon was running around up to his tricks. I couldn't control what he did, but I could make damn sure that the government, my government, did not get involved'.

The Secretary of the Attorney-General's department Clarrie Harders told the caretaker Attorney-General Ivor Greenwood that it would seem McMahon might be guilty of an offence under the Crimes Act for encouraging Reid to leak, and that this was all the more serious because the documents he was trying to acquire were to be used in criminal proceedings: 'committing an offence ... in order to have others charged with an offence'. Greenwood placed the matter before Fraser in a letter dated 16 December 1975—the Tuesday following the election. No action was taken. Fraser says today that he doesn't remember the reasons why not, but his main concern was that there should be no opening-up of the issues surrounding the loans affair before the courts. 'We had had an election. The people had passed their judgement. That was it, so far as I was concerned.'

On 22 December, Fraser made Ellicott Attorney-General. It was now Ellicott's job to handle those aspects of the Sankey case that involved the Commonwealth. Ellicott took very seriously the principle that, as first law officer, an Attorney-General should exercise independent discretion and not be bound by the decisions of cabinet or by political affiliation. Yet he was now in a potentially awkward conflict: in opposition, he had already said in parliament that he thought Whitlam and his ministers were guilty of an 'illegal and unconstitutional act'.

Bjelke-Petersen's man Wally Fancher had by this time returned from his overseas investigations claiming that there were documents available, signed by Cairns and Connor, that established that they would have received big kickback commissions had the loans to the Australian Government ever come to pass. In a memorandum to Fraser, Ellicott recommended that steps be taken to acquire the documents, if they existed, including giving immunities from prosecution to the Swiss bank officials who were said to have them. Once again, no action was taken.[12] Fraser says today, 'You have to understand that I was absolutely determined that I was not going to be involved in this. There were all kinds of people with an axe to grind against Whitlam, and lots of people disliked Murphy. Even if documents did exist, who is to say that they weren't forged? And what would we have done to the country, at that time, by trying to pursue it?' As for Bjelke-Petersen, Fraser regarded the Queensland Premier as 'gullible'. There were good reasons, too, to doubt Fancher's credibility. Ellicott nevertheless aired Fancher's allegations in parliament, on 19 May 1976. Predictably, Whitlam claimed this was evidence that the government had breached its undertakings to Kerr.[13]

Meanwhile, Sankey was trying to subpoena the key Executive Council documents. The Fraser cabinet claimed cabinet privilege, and the Queanbeyan magistrate hearing the case upheld the claim. His decision was appealed, and eventually made its way to the High Court. (Lionel Murphy, then on the court, did not sit on the matter.)

When Whitlam and Connor asked Ellicott to take over the Sankey case on behalf of the Commonwealth, clearly they were hoping that he would do so in order to terminate it. Ellicott, though, was of the view that before he could make such a decision he should have access to all the evidence so he could decide whether or not the allegations had substance and should be heard. He sought access to the Executive Council minutes and cabinet approval to interview the senior public servants who had advised the Whitlam government during the loans affair. The files on the Sankey case from this point on are fat with memorandums from senior public servants, including the Secretary of Treasury Sir Frederick Wheeler, vigorously protesting against the idea that they might be asked to give the Fraser government an account of the doings of the previous administration. There were longstanding conventions, they said, fundamental to the Westminster system, that a government should not look into the affairs of its predecessors. For some of these public servants it was clearly a matter of principle over which they were prepared to resign. Ellicott appreciated the principle, but thought that there was 'no place where the criminal law does not run'. The matter came before cabinet on 26 July 1976. As Ellicott said later, in his resignation speech:

> Cabinet made it clear to me that in its view I should take over the proceedings and terminate them. I took the position that I could not do so unless I first ascertained all the material facts, according to my duty. I also made it clear that only I could exercise the discretion ... I regarded cabinet as preventing me from exercising my duty.[14]

In early August, at a meeting at the Lodge, Ellicott told Fraser that he planned to take over the proceedings so that the public servants could be subpoenaed and all the evidence obtained. Fraser was dismayed. They argued. Both stood firm.

From Fraser's point of view, the risks were enormous. 'You could easily make a country ungovernable by pursuing something like this. Can you imagine how we would have looked, what people would have said, if we were seen to be pursuing Whitlam? And if public servants like the Secretary of Treasury were resigning over it? Apart from anything else, Ellicott's reputation would have been significantly compromised. The public interest, the good of the nation, demanded that government have no part in the case, other than to close it down.' With characteristic thoroughness, Fraser burrowed into the literature on the position of attorneys-general, and their independence or otherwise from the political process. The idea that the Attorney-General was or should be different from other cabinet ministers and 'independently aloof' from the political process dated back to the fifteenth century, but had gained its modern expression from William Shawcross, the Attorney-General in the Atlee government in 1950s Britain. Shawcross had said that an Attorney-General should 'acquaint himself with all the relevant facts' when deciding whether or not to prosecute. This was the principle Ellicott was adhering to. But Shawcross had also said that the Attorney-General should consider the effect of a case on 'public morale and order and … public policy', and that he should consult with his colleagues. In this case, says Fraser, the whole of cabinet was opposed to Ellicott taking on the case.[15] It was yet another case of conflicting principles. On the one hand, there was the independence of the nation's chief law officer; on the other hand, there were the potentially awful consequences of being seen to pursue Whitlam—the real likelihood that the country would become ungovernable.

Fraser sought the opinion of the Solicitor-General Sir Maurice Byers, who wrote that the case was misconceived. Even if the Whitlam ministers had conspired to deceive the Governor-General, it was not a criminal offence. The relevant section of the Crimes Act 'does not, properly construed, apply to the actions of ministers', and the Financial Agreement Act was not a criminal law. There were other strong reasons why the government should not pursue the case: prosecution would have 'a divisive effect for significant sections of the community ... It would run the risk of being identified with party politics, no matter how fairly [the case was] conducted'. Byers quoted the eminent British lawyer and former Attorney-General in the Atlee government Sir John Simon on the issue of an Attorney-General's independence. Simon had said that it was 'nonsense' to suggest that an Attorney-General ought to prosecute merely because there was a case. 'It is not true, and no one who has held the office supposes that it is.' A government might decide that an action should not proceed as a matter of public policy. In that case, it would be quite proper for an Attorney-General to withdraw from the proceedings. For an Attorney-General to

> start of his own motion prosecutions which involve grave matters of public concern—treason, sedition, corruption and the like—I should regard it as a very grave mistake if he did such a thing without knowing that, in the view of his colleagues, public policy was not offended by undertaking such prosecution.[16]

Ellicott had by now offered his resignation, but Fraser had refused to accept it. Then, on 5 August, Ellicott received a letter from Lionel Murphy saying that while he would not object if Ellicott took over the case in order to close it down, he would object if he planned to pursue it. Reluctantly, Ellicott decided that he would have to leave the Sankey case alone to run its course without Commonwealth intervention, but he remained deeply unhappy at what he saw as Fraser and cabinet's interference with his independence.

On 6 September 1977 Ellicott delivered his resignation speech in the federal parliament. He had never wanted to pursue the matter to incriminate Whitlam, Murphy, Cairns and Connor, he said; he had merely wanted to ascertain the facts. Until that was done, 'No public in this country will be satisfied about this case ... The simple fact is that there is a great public interest in having this matter cleared up'. In reply, Fraser paid tribute to Ellicott's achievements as the 'driving force' of reform.[17] For Fraser, the greater public interest lay elsewhere: in good government. He says today, 'Democracy as we know it in Australia simply couldn't survive if incoming governments developed the habit of prosecuting their predecessors through the courts'. Even if there had been incontrovertible evidence of financial corruption, Fraser says, 'I am not sure I would have acted. If there had been evidence, it would have had to be weighed very carefully indeed, and the impact on the body politic weighed in the balance as well'. Fraser rejected all suggestions that such evidence should be sought out.

The Sankey case dragged on. In late 1978, the High Court ordered that the Executive Council documents for which the Fraser government had claimed privilege should be produced: not even cabinet documents should be immune from production before the courts. The High Court also found that one of the charges brought by Sankey was bad in law, and dismissed it. On 16 February 1979, the Queanbeyan magistrate found there was no prima facie case on the remaining charge against Whitlam, Cairns, Connor and Murphy, and dismissed the case. Today Fraser describes the Sankey case as so tenuous that it was 'almost fraudulent'. As for the Fancher allegations, no firm evidence emerged. The allegations were revived later when two *Age* journalists pursued them, but they failed to persuade their newspaper that there was sufficient evidence to publish. They wrote a book, but it made no impact, being largely speculative.[18] Fraser says that he never believed that Whitlam and his ministers were corrupt in the sense of personal gain. 'I had said in parliament that they were politically corrupt, and I meant it. I believe they deliberately deceived the Governor-General. They corrupted the political process, but they paid a political price.'

After the crisis of 1975, it was time for governing. It was a time for healing.

11

Balance

There are ideas in the columns of figures produced by governments, and there are dramas. Line by line, program by program, the action advances. Ideas and ideals meet that other imperative, the politically possible. Those who have the luxury of looking at government budgeting with hindsight can boil it down to a few figures. Surplus or deficit. Government spending as a proportion of gross domestic product. Such numbers are taken to spell success or failure. Off stage, though, there are different measures. Each number is connected with a human story—a cause advanced or thwarted, sometimes tragedy, sometimes hope. Budgeting forces governments to make choices, and so in the columns of figures we see the lineaments of character and priority, and how the nation moves.

In opposition, Malcolm Fraser had made stirring speeches. He spoke of idealism, of the search for the 'grail of democracy' and the need to 'light the hearts of men'. As Prime Minister, he was more likely to say things like 'Our resources are limited', a phrase repeated in speech after speech. Fraser had made good economic management the main theme of his bid for power; it remained a dominant narrative. Good economic management was what the voters wanted, as the 1975 and 1977 elections demonstrated. Nevertheless, economics leads to dry and dreary words. Soon the cartoonists were depicting Fraser as a grim Easter Island statue. Most people forgot, if they ever knew, about the activism and the liberal values expressed in his earlier political speeches. They remembered 'Life wasn't meant to be easy', and heard in that statement only the dismal economic theme. Yet the liberal Fraser was still there, apparent in the decisions recorded in the columns of figures.

On 23 December 1975, the day after his second ministry was sworn in, Fraser wrote to all ministers: 'Our overriding task during the months and indeed years ahead is to rein in the rate of growth in government spending and reduce the relative size of the government sector. This task is central to our whole economic and social strategy'. He went on to warn his ministers that they would have to 'face up to many very hard options and take many very hard decisions' and that just because expenditure had been approved this did not mean money could or should be spent. Straightaway, cabinet began a review of all spending programs with a deadline of 16 January 1976. Ministers, Fraser said, should identify all programs under their control, list them in order of priority from highest to lowest, and detail steps that could be taken to cut the low priorities. Decisions on cuts should be made by 23 January.[1] Behind the scenes, work was being done at a frantic pace, but, so far as the public was concerned, there wasn't very much to be seen. After all the high drama of 1975, things in Canberra had gone quiet.

In January 1976, *The Sydney Morning Herald* observed that Fraser

> seems to be avoiding the grosser errors in the style of the former government simply by doing the opposite. Whereas Mr Whitlam took off in a whirlwind of decision-making after his victory in 1972, Mr Fraser quietly submerged on 14 December ... A lot of people who work in Parliament House have still not sighted Mr Fraser in the flesh since the elections, although apart from spending the Christmas week at his property, Nareen, he has been at his parliamentary desk on most days.

The government was not coasting, the article said. Sir Henry Bland had been appointed to an administrative review committee to find savings in the public service, and ministers had been given a tight deadline to find cuts for the rest of the financial year.[2]

Behind the scenes there was struggle, as the archival record reveals. The information on programs and cuts came to cabinet and its sub-committees—folders and folders of detail, portfolio by portfolio, program by program. At every step, choices had to be made. Everywhere there are Fraser's marks—'Make cut possible this year', 'Must be protected', 'More work' or a simple question mark. Possible cuts were divided with deceptive cleanliness into columns of 'Easy' and 'Hard'. From early on, Treasury tried to assert primacy. Fraser resisted: he, and cabinet, would make the decisions.

Tamie remembers Fraser coming home one evening in this period with 'everything sagging'. He told her he wasn't sure that the economy could be fixed. 'It's just gone too far down.' Fraser remembers, 'Industry were the worst. They'd say, "Oh, yes, we support the government's general thesis. Yes, do cut expenditure, but not in areas that affect our industry"'.

The work went on, the detail always threatening to overwhelm any attempt at philosophical thrust. The planning documents tell the tale:

> Aboriginal Affairs: don't proceed with projects of low priority—savings $3.68 million.
> Don't proceed with Whitlam initiatives on consumer protection—savings $0.84 million.
> Increase house rents in the Australian Capital Territory—savings $1 million.
> Defer new contracts for buildings and works—savings $6 million.
> Increase passport fees—savings $1.4 million.
> Pharmaceutical benefits: review list of drugs—savings $3 million.

In Fraser's handwriting is a note to retain the contraceptive pill on the list. There were savings the ministers favoured and others they opposed. There were pleas for special consideration. Cabinet discussed the reintroduction of tertiary education fees, but the idea was rejected. The National Gallery's overseas purchase requests were reviewed. The National Capital Development Commission received a firm Fraser cut. In a file note, Fraser wrote that $4 million in cuts should be made possible in this year. The commission would have to review its plans in the light of the much slower growth expected in the public service. 'There are no soft options for the building and construction industry in Canberra. Some of them will have to leave.'[3]

The idea of limited resources and a limited government role became commonplace over the next thirty years, part of public understanding of what can and cannot be expected from government. In Fraser's time it was a new theme. Placing economic management at the centre of politics was an important part of Fraser's legacy.

During the long postwar boom, governments had been determined to build a better world. This was the time of Maynard Keynes, and of Fraser's intellectual awakening. In the good years that followed, growth and prosperity had come to seem like natural rights. It had appeared that governments could spend without limit. After the oil shock, the world became a different and more difficult place. Fraser later said:

> I have great respect for Keynes as he wrote for the 1930s, but for those who use Keynes to justify every extravagance and stupidity of government ... I have only contempt, and Keynes must shudder in his grave at those who have falsely claimed his name in support of what they have done.[4]

The Fraser government was the first in the Western world to make the need for government restraint a dominant part of its narrative. Fraser was ahead of Britain's Margaret Thatcher, who was elected in 1979, and of the United States' Ronald Reagan, who became President in 1981. But Fraser was not Thatcher; nor was he Reagan. He was the same liberal who had wrestled with justifying conscription by referring to an individual's duty to society and who had talked about the importance of philosophy over science because it helped to teach individuals to live together. This Fraser was hardly likely to say, as Thatcher did, 'There is no such thing as society'. There was common ground between Thatcher and Fraser, but there were also many points of disagreement. Thatcher's full 'There is no such thing as society' statement read:

> I think we've been through a period where too many people have been given to understand that if they have a problem, it's the government's job to cope with it. 'I have a problem; I'll get a grant.' 'I'm homeless; the government must house me.' They're casting their problem on society. And, you know, there is no such thing as society. There are individual men and women, and there are families. And no government can do anything except through people, and people must look to themselves first. It's our duty to look after ourselves and, then, also to look after our neighbour. People have got the entitlements too much in mind, without the obligations. There's no such thing as entitlement, unless someone has first met an obligation.[5]

In his Deakin lecture, sixteen years before Thatcher said these words, Fraser had said:

> Many forget that the budget is primarily an instrument for sound economic management. It must also achieve a proper and equitable use of national wealth. It can create the climate in which wealth can be generated but it cannot of itself create wealth. As each budget approaches, how many ask 'What will be in it for me?' Many have come to regard budget time as they regard Christmas. It should not be so regarded. No responsible government can behave like Father Christmas and look after the affairs of this nation.[6]

But in the same lecture he had talked about the task of statesmanship and the need to find common cause, to temper zealotry and idealism with an understanding of 'the frailty of the human race'. Fraser was not a zealot. He was, more than anything else, pragmatic. He believed in small government because he believed in freedom. For the same reason—individual freedom—he also believed in the need for government. He believed in society.

Fraser articulated the balancing act in a speech in 1987, after he had left parliament. Echoing Menzies, he said that the bulk of public policy should be directed to forgotten people—those who are not represented by powerful interests and factions. Menzies, Fraser said, had been aware of two conflicting requirements in the tenets of liberalism. One was expressed by John Stuart Mill as the tendency for society to diminish the power of the individual. The other was expressed by Edmund Burke, who said, 'The only liberty I mean is a liberty connected with order, that not only exists along with order and virtue, but which cannot exist at all without them'. Fraser commented, 'The first quotation expresses the dangers of government involvement; the second expresses the necessity of such involvement ... There is a role for government that transcends economics, to maintain equity, to create opportunity, to maintain the balance'.[7]

During Fraser's time in government, the ideas that later became known as neo-liberalism were gaining their advocates. Fraser's adviser David Kemp was making sure the boss was aware of them. He sent him articles by the Australian philosopher Lachlan Chipman and the US economist Milton Friedman, then the leading advocate of small government. Kemp told Fraser that Chipman mounted an 'interesting argument about the relationship between liberty, justice and private enterprise' and that Friedman gave 'an exceptionally clear account of the relationship between excessive government spending, the present economic crisis and the danger to freedom'.[8] Fraser read these writers. He met Friedman and the free market evangelist Friedrich Hayek in the early months of his government. He was aware of them and respectful of them, but he was guided chiefly by his understanding of what Keynes would have done in the environment of the 1970s and 1980s. This was an understanding of economics in which the role of government was seen as important, indeed essential. It was an optimistic view, even at a time of economic gloom. It was a view of the world in which it was possible for governments and leaders to make a difference. Fraser later said:

> There is all the difference in the world ... between those who argue that regulations are bad and must be abolished and those who argue that regulations should be as few as possible. Some regulation is necessary to preserve the interests of the forgotten people. It is the balance between too much and too little regulation and between wise and foolish regulations that appears so elusive in today's debate. Those who argue for deregulation often seem to suggest that there is no role for government. That is not the position of the true liberal.[9]

While he was Prime Minister, Fraser was criticised by the Left for being too harsh, for not having enough heart. He was seen as anti-union and a hard-line right-winger. Since then he has been excoriated by the Right, and by economic rationalists across the board, for not being hard enough—for not cutting more and deregulating more. Both critiques hold him to standards that were not his own. Fraser tried to reconcile Burke and Mill; thus, the Fraser who derided the Whitlam government for bringing the country to its economic knees was also the Fraser who shared and continued with much of Whitlam's social vision. He didn't always succeed. There were failures, and initiatives conceived in hope and idealism that fell by the wayside or were sacrificed to political and economic pragmatics. In judging his record, though, it helps to understand the ideas behind all those columns of figures. Fraser tried, in difficult economic times, for balance.

* * *

The Fraser government's story can be divided into three periods: the early years, when the emphasis was on rebuilding the economy after the first oil shock and the Whitlam government; the middle years, when Fraser could claim success; and the final years, when, beset with crises both political and economic, many of his achievements came undone. At the time, of course, such cool judgements were not possible. Actors on the stage are caught up in the imperatives of the moment, carrying the story forwards. It is the critics who make assessments with the luxury of hindsight.

There were two treasurers during the Fraser years. The first was Phillip Lynch. Fraser and Lynch had their disagreements, but Fraser says of him today, 'Phillip was all right. He was a good deputy; I think that he was basically a good Treasurer. He was strong enough; he fought the main issues in cabinet well; he was loyal to me as Prime Minister. When we disagreed we had open arguments and I knew what he thought and where he was coming from. He would say, "Prime Minister, I'm going to put a note on the file about this discussion". I'd say, "That's all right, Phillip, you put your note for file"'.

When Lynch resigned as Treasurer before the 1977 election, he was replaced by John Howard. For Howard, this was a big promotion. He had entered parliament just three years before. Howard had backed Fraser against Snedden during the 1975 Liberal leadership battle, and had been Minister for Business and Consumer Affairs. Fraser says today that he put Howard in the job because 'He was bright and he got across a brief well, and he was a good manager'. Fraser did not think of Howard as an ideas man. In the years that followed, says Fraser, Howard rarely argued or fought his corner either with Fraser personally or in cabinet. 'I couldn't understand it. There would be some small issues that he would push quite hard, and then quite big things that affected his area would go through without him saying much at all.' At first, Howard was a young and relatively inexperienced Treasurer. Not surprisingly, he was not dominant in debates, including with his own department. Later, as he grew in confidence, he allied himself with the emerging 'dry' faction of free market adherents, which was usually seen as in opposition to Fraser. Today, Fraser says that very few disagreements were had openly. Often, he was not even aware that Howard disagreed with something he was doing until he heard it from others. Later, there was political manoeuvring. 'Again, I heard about what he was doing from others, and at first and for a long time I didn't believe it. I didn't want to believe he was playing those political games.'

Lynch was not an independent economic thinker. Nor was Howard, for the first years of his time as Treasurer. For that reason, the main battles over economic policy were not between Fraser and his treasurers, but between Fraser and the bureaucracy, in particular one of the most aggressive intellects in Canberra, John Stone. When Fraser came to power, Stone was deputy to Treasury Secretary Sir Frederick Wheeler. From 1979 he was Secretary, but at all times he was the dominant personality in the department.

Treasury had lost its supremacy over economic policy during the Whitlam years; now it hoped to regain it. Yet on this most vital part of governance, Fraser was determined to diversify his sources of advice. So from the very earliest days, Fraser and his advisers were engaged in a struggle. Every time they went against Treasury advice, they were accused of being, as Fraser remembers it, 'not only wrong but positively sinful. And they would brief the media, so you'd get hammered, seeing the Treasury line coming at you from all sides. Treasury wanted to be the boss. They tried to totally dominate the treasurers'. Stone, says Fraser, had a good mind, but also a tendency to present only one option in his advice to government. 'I always wanted more than one option, and he resented that. I think he always wanted to be a politician, really, and later events proved that.' (Stone left the Treasury in 1984, in the first term of Bob Hawke's Labor government. He went on to become an adviser to the abortive 'Joh for Canberra' push in 1987, in which the Queensland Premier Joh Bjelke-Petersen toyed with the idea of becoming Prime Minister. Stone was elected as a National Party senator for Queensland in

1987 and resigned in 1990 in an unsuccessful attempt to enter the House of Representatives as member for the seat of Fairfax. Since the mid 1980s, he has emerged as a leading critic of the Fraser government's record.)

Fraser came to see that too many of the views he was hearing—whether they came from the Reserve Bank or from Treasury or even from the media—were really Treasury views. He remembers talking to Harry Knight, the Chairman of the Reserve Bank. 'I would say, "Harry, I can't believe that you always totally agree with Treasury. You're the Governor of the Reserve Bank. It's an important position, probably a more important position than the head of Treasury. Now, I am entitled to know what your view is". Well, it took about six months before I asked "Harry, what's your view?" and he gave a view that was different from Treasury's. I remember quite distinctly he opened it by saying, "Now, there's a different way of approaching this problem". Fred Wheeler and John Stone almost fell off their chairs. They had lost one major battle.'

In Fraser's view these conflicts were not chiefly a matter of personality. He had no personal animosity with Stone, and valued him highly. He appointed him head of Treasury in 1979. Rather, the struggle was about the important principle of a government receiving sound information, diverse advice and a menu of options from which to choose, having heard all the arguments. Instead, Treasury advocated for one position only, and any other position was, as Fraser remembers it, 'not only wrong, not merely less than the best outcome, not merely against their advice, but disastrous and apocryphal. Really, Treasury could be bullies'.

For others, Stone's personality did appear to be key. John Rose, Fraser's principal economic adviser in his private office after early 1977, remembers an occasion on which one officer of the Department of Prime Minister and Cabinet was too frightened of Stone's aggressive style to engage him in argument. David Kemp, a key adviser, says, 'Stone didn't help his cause by the way in which he pursued it. John Stone and Malcolm Fraser are two extraordinary characters in Australian history. They don't share many things, but one of the things they do share in their characters is that they are both incredibly strong personalities and very determined and they believe in will with a capital "W". They believe that if you will something strongly enough and you are in a leadership position, you can make it happen; and in many cases they are correct. They didn't agree on economic policy, and Stone set out to basically use the force of his personality to stop the Treasurer and the Reserve Bank from doing anything inappropriate. He had magnificent skill with language. Now Stone would say, "Oh, look, you can't criticise people if they are just swayed by rational argument", and in a way that is true, but you have to understand the personality involved to really understand the full politics of it'.

The battle began in the early months of Fraser's government, as ministers brought forward their lists of cuts, and Lynch and Fraser worked towards a May economic statement. Fraser had promised to retain Medibank. Work had already been done, in opposition, to find ways to protect the private health insurance industry while retaining universal taxpayer-funded health insurance. Now it was discovered that Medibank was costing a massive 6.4 per cent of total budget outlays, and the amount was increasing quickly. This was simply unaffordable, cabinet was told. Not only was there no incentive for those who could afford it to insure privately; there was no reason for either doctors or patients to be economical. It was decided to impose a levy of 2.5 per cent of taxable income to fund Medibank. Those on high incomes could either pay a premium, or, if they chose to insure privately, gain exemption from the levy.[10] Fraser had also promised to deliver tax indexation. To him, this was an important principle. Tax indexation meant that as inflation caused wages to rise, taxpayers would not automatically see higher and higher proportions of their income disappear. It was a means of keeping government honest and preserving maximum individual freedom. The dispute was over how soon tax indexation should be introduced and how much government expenditure should be cut in order to be able to introduce it responsibly. This was the main battleground for Lynch and Treasury.

Fraser remembers that in January 1976, after cabinet had spent weeks poring over programs and making cuts, the Secretary of Treasury Fred Wheeler told him that, in his view, the government had now identified enough cuts. Any more might be counterproductive. Fraser says, 'I wanted to press on further with expenditure cutting, and Wheeler, not in Stone's presence, said that he wouldn't do more: the country had had enough shocks. He said, "The budget will be coming around and you will have plenty of time to have another go later". Unfortunately, he persuaded me'. Treasury officers later said that they did not remember giving this advice.[11] There is some documentary support for the Reserve Bank being worried about cutting too deep, but the bulk of the archival record shows that in its usual 'our way or disaster' tone, Treasury was advising that either more cuts be made or tax indexation be delayed. Meanwhile, Fraser was telling his ministers that, although fighting inflation was the first priority, they had also to introduce reforms outside the economic area 'consistent with our political traditions of progressive and enlightened reforms'.[12]

One of Fraser's principal advisers at this time was Ian Castles, a senior policy adviser in the Department of Prime Minister and Cabinet and a refugee from Treasury. He confided in Fraser that he had left because he couldn't stand the intellectual aridity of pretending there was only one answer, and one way forwards. 'He knew there are always multiple options', remembers Fraser. As cabinet wrestled with cuts, Castles suggested what Fraser now describes as 'one of the best reforms we made for social equity'. The idea was that the government would abolish tax rebates for dependent children and instead introduce generous family allowances. Even more radical, the proposal was to pay the new allowance not to the family breadwinner but to the mother. It was a fundamentally progressive idea. The tax rebates had benefitted the rich more than the poor. Family allowances would redistribute wealth to the poorest families. At the same time they would alter the balance of economic power, giving tens of thousands of housewives income under their own control for the first time. When family allowances were announced in the May 1976 economic statement, *The Age* described them as 'one of the most important advances in social welfare since federation'.[13] They were revenue neutral—the increased revenue from the abolition of the tax rebate was simply paid out again in the form of the allowance—but nevertheless they were opposed by both Treasury and Lynch. It was Fraser's determination, together with that of the Minister for Social Welfare Margaret Guilfoyle, that saw the idea pushed through cabinet. Fraser says, 'It made me happy. I liked that we were doing something so innovative even at such a hard time. We never took the view that just because we had to cut expenditure that that was all we had to do. If there was an area of extreme need, a really important need, then it didn't preclude progressive reform. Now that might not please an economic rationalist, but it is looking at how government can help, how it can be a force for good and a force for change'. Why give the money to the woman? Fraser says, 'Because that was the right person to give it to'. Was he a feminist? Fraser baulks at the word, but says he had been 'well educated' both by Tamie and by the formidable women who had been influential in liberal politics since before Menzies founded the Liberal Party.

The increasingly vehement battle of words over tax indexation and the size of the deficit continued. Finally, cabinet decided that enough cutting had been done, and that full tax indexation would be delivered from July. Lynch and senior Treasury officials made a last-ditch attempt to alter the decision. On 14 May, Lynch sent a thirteen-page letter to Fraser at Nareen. Fraser was well aware, as he read it, of the Treasury style in the drafting—'the usual "our way or damnation" stuff'. The letter argued that introducing full tax indexation would destroy the credibility of the government:

> I firmly believe that the decisions that we are on the point of finally taking and announcing will have major consequences for our future as a government and it is because,

> despite my utmost efforts, I cannot believe that those effects will be to our overall advantage that I presume to burden you with what is, I suppose, one last appeal.[14]

Fraser was irritated that the letter attempted to overturn a cabinet decision made after full debate, but nevertheless went though it, showing it to Kemp and Castles, who visited him at Nareen, and asking Castles to provide comments. Fraser decided the arguments did not stand up to scrutiny, and held firm.[15] The dispute had been heard in cabinet, and cabinet had made its decision.

A week later, on 20 May 1976, Lynch delivered an economic statement telling parliament that the government was taking early action to 'regain control of the national budget'. Difficult decisions had been made. Medibank would be retained. Tax indexation, which would 'by itself produce a desirable discipline upon future government spending decisions', would be introduced from July that year. Lynch said that budget outlays for the rest of that financial year had now been cut by $360 million. The number of public servants had declined by 2.5 per cent, or 8250 people. Treasury forecasts before the cuts had implied that there would be a budget deficit of $4800 million in 1976–77 and a $4700 million increase in budget outlays. Now this had been reduced by almost $2600 million, as a result of which the task of formulating the next budget had been 'reduced to manageable proportions'.[16] Today, this economic statement is among Fraser's regrets. 'I think that we should have gone further then. It would have made it easier afterwards. The reason is simply that once your ministers have settled in, they become attached to all the programs of their area, and they don't want to put a hot knife through them, so it gets harder to cut. I gave Maggie Thatcher that advice when she was elected. I told her to take an axe to things early, because it was harder later, but she didn't really do it either.' At the time, though, most commentators were bemoaning cuts and worrying that too many shocks might push the economy into recession.

There was no let-up after the May statement. Cabinet straightaway began to prepare for the 1976 budget. In July, Lynch was warning

Fraser that there were 'pressure points' on the budget, in particular from Aboriginal affairs, which was pushing, partly successfully, for a more liberal approach. Papers to cabinet from Lynch warned repeatedly that Keynesian economics offered no solutions to their present problems. 'Inflation is now recognised as the fundamental economic problem. No sustainable recovery in activity can be counted upon so long as inflation and inflationary expectations go unchecked.' The language was pure Treasury—cogent and forceful—but this was not the only opinion that Fraser and his ministers were hearing. Increasingly concerned about the dominance of Treasury, Fraser had taken care that his own department was in a position to give strong and independent advice. While endorsing Treasury's overall approach, Fraser's other advisers constantly questioned its assumptions and insisted that there were unacknowledged margins of error in the figuring.[17]

In government as elsewhere, information is power, and this is never more true than in the difficult and expert business of economic reporting and modelling. The archives reveal that through much of 1976, Fraser, his department and his staff had to struggle to acquire the data—both raw figures and modelling—on which Treasury and the Reserve Bank were basing their advice. In February 1976, the Economic Committee of Cabinet asked for regular detailed reports on the state of the economy from Treasury. It didn't happen. On 12 June 1976, Fraser wrote to Lynch saying he was aware that quarterly forecasts on the economy were prepared in the Treasurer's department. As Prime Minister he should be advised in detail about those forecasts. He asked Lynch to arrange for this to be done. In a handwritten note on the bottom, he said, 'It is essential that this information and bank reports be available to my department'. Four weeks later, the Department of Prime Minister and Cabinet complained that it still wasn't receiving the information from Treasury needed to brief Fraser. More demands flowed back and forth until in mid July Fraser demanded that Lynch fix the problem.

> It is not possible to have a situation in which any department of state is prepared to deny the Prime Minister or his department information for advice to the Prime Minister. I know the position the Treasury is adopting is not a new position. It has, as I understand it, been traditional but it is not one that I believe you and I can accept in the interests of good government.

It is a measure of the stubbornness of Treasury that even the full force of Fraser determination did not succeed. In August, cabinet was still not receiving the quarterly forecasts they had requested six months before. The last straw came in October, when Fraser discovered that there had been a decline in Australian financial reserves, but neither he nor Lynch had been informed. In a letter to Lynch, he said:

> I regard that omission as most serious. You and I both agree that a full and free flow of information is absolutely critical if we are to make appropriate decisions. I find the omission incomprehensible because I cannot believe that the Secretary of the Treasury and the Governor were not aware of the figures.[18]

Only in November—a year after Fraser had come to power—did the monthly economic papers begin to flow. They showed, in that month and through the first months of 1977, the beginnings of patchy but vulnerable economic recovery that gained in strength through the following years.

Fraser says today, 'The truth is they didn't trust any politicians. They thought politicians weren't capable of making hard decisions. They thought they should be making the decisions, not us. I guess given what they had been through during the Whitlam years it was understandable, but it was quite undemocratic in attitude'. Fraser believes that the struggle over information was 'a power play, pure and simple. Phillip Lynch might have disagreed sometimes with the advice I was getting from Prime Minister and Cabinet and others, but he always agreed absolutely that we should get the basic information, and in the end it was him who sorted it out. So far as I am aware, no government since has had to fight that battle. It would be extraordinary in today's terms'.

This struggle over basic information formed the background to an historic decision made against the advice of Treasury and the Reserve Bank—the devaluation of the Australian dollar and the move from a fixed exchange rate to a flexibly managed system—the so-called 'dirty float'. Fraser and Treasury were agreed that fighting inflation was the first priority, but for Fraser it was not the only priority. He feared industry collapse and resulting increased unemployment. Inflation had to be combated, he thought, but not at any cost. Once again, it was a matter of balance, of pragmatics over zealotry. Treasury agreed that the dollar was overvalued—deliberately so to keep inflation in check. Fraser was worried about the impact on the international competitiveness of agriculture and manufacturing. From October 1977 onwards he received briefings from his own department canvassing the options, including the possibility of floating the dollar. Fraser thought industry activity was flatter than Treasury believed, and his private conversations with industry leaders had made him sceptical about the Treasury belief that devaluation would be inflationary. In October, Fraser received a visit from the Managing Director of the International Monetary Fund Johannes Witteveen. As soon as Witteveen left, Fraser dictated a note of the conversation.

> He said, do not be dogmatic about the exchange rate. The fund would not look askance at a devaluation. He recognised the damage done by wage increases. He said it was not only a question of balance of payments. It was also a question of relative costs. He recognised the problems posed by imbalance. He also recognised that because Australia had started late, the inflation rates in many European countries, Japan and the USA would be lower than ours for another year. Therefore our position would get worse for another year. He was clearly giving

> me a warning not to be too dogmatic, and for Australia not to be too dogmatic.[19]

On the same day, Fraser received a briefing from his department that the market was clearly expecting devaluation. Other briefings followed over the next few days, canvassing devaluation rates of around 15 per cent. Treasury was vehemently and vocally opposed. Lynch argued the Treasury line hard in cabinet through October and November; Fraser remained unconvinced. It was at this point, Fraser remembers, that he pushed the Reserve Bank Governor hard for an independent point of view from that of Treasury.

At a cabinet meeting on 28 November 1976, Fraser broke off the discussion and asked the Reserve Bank Governor Harold Knight and Lynch to talk privately in his office. There were no Treasury officials present. Cabinet had agreed to devalue; the question on which Fraser wanted advice was the amount. Fraser knew that Treasury might agree to a small devaluation—between 7 and 8 per cent—but he had seen other countries take that course only to have to devalue again and again, prompting speculation on the currency and undermining confidence in their governments' economic management. He was determined not to get caught in the same trap. If there was to be a devaluation—and he was convinced of the need—he wanted there to be only one. Fraser remembers, 'I got them in my office, and I asked, "Harry, what is the smallest level of devaluation which will guarantee that the next move is an appreciation?"

'And Harry said, "Fifteen per cent".

'And I said, "Well, you're not going to murder me, are you, if I add 2.5 per cent for safety?"

'And he laughed and said would I settle for 15.5 per cent, and I said I would prefer to have the insurance, and he said no, he wouldn't murder me. So he had given an independent view from Treasury, which was a great relief to me. Treasury weren't in that conversation because I knew I couldn't get sense out of them. Harry Knight would talk sense. All I would have got from Treasury was a lecture about how perfidious it was, and that governments that don't accept their advice are never any good. Harry Knight, once he stopped blindly going along and once he accepted that you needed to give the government independent advice and a range of options, was generally pretty balanced'.

The cabinet meeting reconvened, and made the decision to devalue the currency by 17.5 per cent. The focus of media commentary at the time was the devaluation, but of even more long-term significance was the second part of the decision: to introduce a flexibly administered exchange rate, or, as the cabinet decision described it, 'a managed float'. This was a landmark in the history of the Australian economy: the first significant move to a more flexible financial system. The people urging more flexibility were the public servants in Fraser's department, not Lynch and not Treasury. The decision stated that a group comprising the Governor of the Reserve Bank, the Secretary to the Treasury and the Secretary of the Department of Prime Minister and Cabinet was to keep the level of the exchange rate under review. This key decision was made without submission, but had been preceded by weeks of discussion, debate and briefings on both devaluation generally and the possibility of floating the dollar.[20]

Two days later, Fraser told parliament that the only alternative to devaluation offered by government advisers had been 'going into hock' to the International Monetary Fund. Devaluation was 'a warning of a weakness in our national economy which will take a total national effort to correct'. Again, he was arguing for balance. 'Throughout this year we have acted to maintain a balance between the four arms of national economic policy—budgetary, monetary, external and wages policy.'[21] As Fraser had hoped, the next move was upwards. On 7 December, Knight announced an adjustment upwards by 2 per cent. 'The change is the first of more frequent and smaller shifts in the relationship of the Australia dollar to the "basket" of currencies', said Knight's statement.[22] The devaluation and managed float had worked. A few days later, Fraser spelled out the philosophy of balance in economic management more explicitly:

> In balancing the arms of economic policy, the government considered inflation as the number one priority, but we have never contended that it was the only priority ... If inflation had been the only priority there would have been no family allowances, no indexation and no increases in money for social programs. There would have been no budget deficit, and there would have been more extensive cut-backs in government programs. If inflation were our sole objective we should have had a balanced budget. I do not recall the government being urged to bring down a balanced budget on this last occasion. The reason is obvious. The hardship in other areas would have been vast and much too great. In other words, there must be a balance in objectives, although there is one major objective.[23]

No commentators had argued for bigger cuts; rather, there were fears that the cuts had gone too deep. The advocates of small government were smiling on Fraser. Milton Friedman wrote an article in *The Australian* supporting the devaluation, but saying the government should go further and float the dollar. Australia, Friedman said, was 'very well regarded internationally because now—and this is comparatively rare among Western nations at the moment—it appears to be pursuing a mature and steady course'.[24] Fraser was proved right: the devaluation decision did not lead to inflation. Meanwhile, although Fraser remained opposed to a full float of the dollar, early the following year the flexibly managed exchange rate was fine-tuned for further flexibility, with a threesome of government officials from the Reserve Bank, the Department of Prime Minister and Cabinet and Treasury meeting regularly to decide on small adjustments. The group became known in government as 'the troika', and the Monetary Policy Committee of Cabinet considered its recommendations frequently. Never again would an Australian government be caught having to make such a massive one-off devaluation.

★ ★ ★

Meanwhile, Fraser had become so frustrated with the dogmatism of Treasury and the struggle to acquire a range of policy advice that he had decided to split the department into two, establishing the Department of Finance alongside Treasury. The decision is bitterly remembered by Stone to the present day. In an article in *Quadrant* in 2007, he described it as being a fit of pique and vengeance by Fraser, sparked by his fury at being initially bested in cabinet debates by Lynch on the devaluation question.[25] Fraser denies this. The cabinet debates had been fiery, certainly, but that was appropriate in the lead-up to a big decision. The splitting of Treasury happened because of a year's experience of the downside of having one department regarding financial advice and management as its preserve, and frustrating the government by its attempt to hang on to control. Lynch supported the decision. 'As to whether it was the correct decision or not, I think the verdict of history is on my side', Fraser says. No government since has seen fit to reunite the two departments.

Wages were the fourth arm of economic policy, but in this the government had to seek balance without having control, its only real influence moral suasion and negotiation. Both were constant themes of Fraser's time in power. In his first year as Prime Minister, the Arbitration Commission went against the government by passing on the full consumer price index increase instead of half, as requested. After that, cabinet considered many measures to gain more control over wages policy—including asset freezing, constitutional referendums to give the government the power to set wages, and deregistration of unions—but most of them were rejected in favour of yet more negotiation and persuasion. Hours were spent with employers and unions, talking and talking, sometimes pushing hard, yet never able to govern the final outcome. At the time, the Fraser government was seen as anti-union, and even anti-worker. Fraser thought it was the unions, not him, who lacked concern for those who were most disadvantaged: the unemployed. He said in a speech in 1979: 'In most markets when a product is in surplus supply and people want to sell more of it, they seek to reduce their price. In the labour market, however, people forget that economic truism. Even though labour is in over-supply, union leaders still seek excessive wage increases'.[26] Fraser made the same point in speech after speech on the economy during his time in government. He was heard but rarely heeded.

To begin with, negotiations with the President of the Australian Council of Trade Unions (ACTU) Bob Hawke were courteous. Hawke had not been afraid to criticise Labor leader Gough Whitlam, and Fraser found he was intelligent and 'could be talked to'. Hawke was appointed by the Fraser government to key bodies, such as the Australian Population and Immigration Council. One result of negotiations with Hawke was that the Prices Justification Tribunal, a Whitlam invention which Fraser had promised to scrap, was instead retained. As Hawke's own political ambitions developed, towards the middle of the Fraser government's years, the relationship began to deteriorate. Today Fraser says, 'I always thought that if you could get good union leaders to be responsible, it should be possible to achieve things. And I never thought that unions weren't needed. Business might say to you, "Oh, of course we will treat our workers well". But I would have accepted then and accept now that somebody without skills that are in scarce supply would find it very difficult to negotiate with major corporations. There needs to be somebody to help represent people. Who can do it apart from a union?' Fraser's guiding principle, he says today, was the rule of law. He believed that it should apply as much to the industrial field—to the agreements between employers and employees—as to any other area of life. He found precious few allies.

With Fraser's support, John Howard as Minister for Business and Consumer Affairs pushed through a reluctant cabinet moves to make parts of the Trade Practices Act an effective weapon against unions. The so-called 'secondary boycott provisions' made it illegal for a union to use industrial action to prevent businesses from supplying or trading with those involved in a dispute. These changes later became an important weapon for employers trying to combat union power, but during Fraser's time he found that employers lacked the will for the fight. They preferred cosy and not-so-cosy deals to the application of the law. Fraser remembers, 'There was no real pressure for a deregulated labour market of the kind that exists now. Employer groups would ask us to pass laws to help them with unions, and I would say, "We just passed [the changes to the Trade Practices Act]; why don't you use them?" And they would say they didn't want to. They wanted the government to rescue them. And these were the same people who in other contexts would argue for small government and rolling back government regulation'.

Fraser's other attempt to bring the rule of law to unions was the Industrial Relations Bureau—first proposed in the policy he had written as shadow minister. It was an idea taken from the United States. Conceived as an 'ombudsman' in industrial disputes, the bureau had the power to initiate proceedings against either unions or employers to ensure compliance with industrial agreements. It was controversial. Unions saw it as an example of union bashing. Fraser had quite different aspirations for it. A respected unionist, Des Linehan, was appointed as its first Director. Today Fraser says, 'I thought it should start off by pursuing a couple of big employers who were most blatantly in breach of awards, and then once it had built its credibility, look at unions who were in breach'. In practice it was ineffectual: 'Neither the unions nor the employers were really interested in the rule of law', Fraser says. 'It was too uncomfortable a concept for them.' By the end of the Fraser government, the Industrial Relations Bureau was described by both the Labor Party and employer representatives as 'almost an irrelevancy'.[27] It was abolished by the Hawke government.

By 1979, it seemed that the hard slog of cutting and restraint had worked. Apparently Treasury thought so too, despite its apocalyptic predictions in 1976. Fraser was invited to give a speech at the Economic Club of New York. As Fraser remembers it, the invitation had been organised by John Stone, who also had a hand in drafting the speech. Fraser recalls, 'He told me we had a wonderful story to tell, and he would be glad to help tell it'. Fraser was speaking to a pre-Reaganomics United States, but already the calls for lower taxation had begun. Fraser opened the speech by saying that in 1977 he had made a bet with the Chairman of the board of governors of the US Federal Reserve System, Arthur Burns, that he could get the Australian rate of inflation below the United States' before the June quarter of 1978. Now he was here to collect. Doing it had not been easy, he told the Economic Club; 'It never is'. Australia, Fraser said, had lessons for the United States. The spirit of restraint in government spending had been in place in Australia for three years. Growth in Australian federal government spending had been cut from 46 per cent in 1974–75 to less than 8 per cent. 'We still think that's a bit too high.' Taxes had been reduced and indexation introduced 'to keep government honest'. The budget deficit—over 5 per cent of gross domestic product when he came to government—was now at about 2.8 per cent, and inflation was down from 17 per cent in 1975 to about 7.5 per cent, lower than for the OECD as a whole. Business investment was rising.

Not all the problems were over. Unemployment was better than it had been, but was still high. 'When an economy has been so fractured as the Australian economy was a few years ago, it takes time for the steady application of policies to put things right', Fraser said. Inflation was still the main enemy: it distorted everything. Already in Australia people were calling for more government spending to create new jobs, but, 'In the end, new jobs will only be created if our economies grow faster than they have been'. For that to happen, inflation had to be kept down. The Fraser government, he said, would be holding to its course.

> It is sometimes said that in democracies, where there are elections every few years, it is difficult to persevere with firm, anti-inflationary policies. Implicitly—or even explicitly in some cases—this view is based upon a low opinion of our democratic electorates. This is an opinion that I do

> not share. What our democratic electorates do require is leadership and constant explanation of policies.[28]

In 1979, Fraser had every reason to feel proud of his government's economic achievements, despite there being shadows on the record—hard lessons learned and initiatives failed. Tax indexation, which Fraser had seen as part of the philosophical bedrock of keeping governments honest and individuals with maximum freedom over their resources, had fallen by the wayside—first being limited to half of the consumer price index increase and later abandoned. In 1977, the government had gone to the election with an unsubtle 'fistful of dollars' election campaign in which advertisements showed money from promised tax cuts being thrust at the voter. The tax cuts, too, had proved unsustainable, and were partly taken back by the introduction of a 1.5 per cent levy in the 1978 budget.

Fraser says today that he never liked the fistful of dollars campaign. 'Eggleton produced this as the idea from the advertising people and I think that it was going to air almost when I first knew about it. It was effective, but it held long-term damage.' The partial cancelling of the tax cuts, the detail of which was agreed between Howard and Fraser, cost the government heavily in terms of credibility. It was, pure and simple, a broken promise and not something that Fraser is proud of in retrospect. The introduction of the levy clawed back $560 million. With other measures, it reduced the projected deficit in the 1978 budget from $3046 million to $2486 million. Today Fraser says that the difference was not enough to justify the breaking of a core election promise. 'In political terms it was clearly a mistake. It shouldn't have been done. You would have gotten away with getting rid of tax indexation, I think, but it would have been better if the deficit was out another $560 million and we had kept the commitment. The Treasury arguments about budget deficits, budget surpluses and so on could have been put aside. That is one of the occasions when we let the weight of the Treasury argument dominate commonsense, which I hope that we didn't do too often.'[29]

As for tax indexation, it was unsustainable. Fraser points out that no other comparable country has introduced and retained it. The Howard government was later to fight to the High Court to prevent information being released on the amount of revenue raised by 'bracket creep'. Fraser thinks the information should be made public: 'It is one of the main ways in which government revenue increases year to year, and if you believe that people are capable of making choices in a democracy, then those choices have to be informed'.

Despite all this, the years from 1979 to 1981 were the high point of the Fraser government's economic record. In 1980–81, the budget was in surplus. Industry profitability was recovering. Unemployment dropped to below 6 per cent—the lowest level since the first oil shock. It wouldn't be so low again until the late 1980s. Yet 1979 was also the year in which three events, all of them out of the government's control, had their beginnings. In time, they were to undo the Fraser government's success.

The first was the Iranian revolution in late 1978, followed by the Iran–Iraq war in 1980. These events caused a second oil shock. The two oil shocks of the 1970s were at the time the worst blows to the world economic system since the Great Depression. The first hit Whitlam, the second Fraser. In 1979, it seemed that Australia might get off lightly, thanks to investment in resources, but, as the decade turned, the briefings cabinet received on economic prospects became gloomier and gloomier. By early 1982, the government knew the economy was in serious trouble. Fraser says that from early 1980 he tried to talk to the President of the ACTU Bob Hawke about the implications, but Hawke was now a different man with different priorities—preparing for his own entry to parliament in October 1980.

In 1979 the ACTU had adopted a policy of campaigning for a 35-hour week with no loss of pay, and seeking pay rises outside indexation guidelines. The government and employers were victims of the recovery. Profitability was returning, and the unions wanted their cut. By May 1980 there was strike action in a number of industries. With the world economy in shock, Fraser saw the ACTU campaign as a disaster for Australia, but employers were tempted to concede union claims on the basis that they would make up the cost through increased profits later on. Faced with lengthy industrial disputes or giving a wage rise, many thought the best commercial decision was to give the rise. The government used everything short of legislation to try to stop employers from giving in.

Today, Fraser is cynical about Hawke's motivation in leading the union push. 'He was intelligent enough to know that it would do the economy harm', he says. 'He kept saying, "Have a national council", but, you know, I couldn't really see what good would have come out of that.' Hawke as Prime Minister was later to call a national summit including unions and employers, resulting in the Accord under which the unions agreed to wage restraint in return for more government spending on education and welfare. Fraser says, 'He was able to get the unions on board, but I would have never believed that he wanted to get the unions on board for me'. Once Hawke entered parliament, Fraser found the new ACTU President, Cliff Dolan, 'much more responsible', and the government was able to negotiate more reasonable pay rises within the indexation system.

Fraser was everywhere at this time, personally involved in negotiations. 'It was talk, talk, talk', he says. Yet his fiercest words and actions were aimed at employers, not unions. In March 1981, spurred by reports that the management of the chemical company ICI was planning to negotiate a reduction in working hours, Fraser made a speech threatening a reduction in tariff protection for any company that granted the 35-hour week. The ICI management was summoned for a series of acrimonious meetings in which Fraser was at his most forceful. He threatened the company with reductions in tariff protection and punitive tax. ICI responded by saying it would suspend investment in Australia. Days of heated argument followed. Finally, ICI backed down and issued a statement refusing to negotiate on working hours. Fraser remembers this period as one of 'constant jawboning, constant negotiation and, yes, force or the threat of it'. But the push for bigger wage increases outside the system continued. The Arbitration Commission effectively abandoned indexation in favour of collective bargaining. More and more employers gave in and the wages breakout cascaded from industry to industry. It seemed that all of industry was in ferment. This was the environment in which Bob Hawke acquired his reputation as a peacemaker, appearing as though from nowhere to settle disputes—although, as Fraser observes, there were those in the union movement who were prepared to say that by the time Hawke appeared the hard work of negotiation had often been done. The impact of the union push was, as Howard reported in his 1982 budget speech, that wages increased by nearly 4 per cent more than the rate of inflation at the same time as the international downturn came home to Australia.[30]

The third disaster for the Fraser government's economic record was the 1981 drought—the most severe of the century. By the end of August 1982, the wheat crop in eastern Australia was on the verge of failure, and sheep prices plummeted as graziers reduced flocks. Things were breaking down. The country was in trouble, and so was the Prime Minister. Fraser says now, 'I allowed myself to get tired. It is a very difficult thing, for prime ministers, to prevent that from happening. You don't realise. I had good stamina. I could beat most of my staff in that respect. But only looking back you realise that you were weary, and perhaps it was affecting your judgement'.

In June 1982, just before the budget, John Howard told cabinet that while there was 'significant variation in the tone of the economy' and while he rejected the 'extremes of gloom', there was no doubt that the economy had slipped into a period of little or no growth, with the causes being world recession and increased labour costs. Treasury recommended firm action to contain the deficit. The advice to Fraser from the Department of Prime Minister and Cabinet, though, was that Howard's assessment was 'excessively pessimistic and the prescription excessively harsh particularly in view of the worsening in domestic economic conditions'.[31] This budget was the one in which Fraser was accused, both at the time and afterwards, of abandoning his principles of government restraint. It was a spending budget; it was also an election budget. Fraser was considering going to the polls early throughout 1982. This budget was the only one in which the government planned for an increase in the deficit—to $1.7 billion—still one of the smallest for many years.

It is true, Fraser says, that the 1982 budget was a Keynesian response to a downturn. It was, in a modest way, pump priming—but not to the extent that has been portrayed in retrospect. The planned-for deficit would be less than 1 per cent of gross domestic product, and in the previous year the budget had been in surplus. As well, there was to be a domestic surplus, meaning that the overall deficit would not be inflationary. 'It was hardly a spendthrift budget', says Fraser. 'I think Keynes would have regarded it as very modest, and very affordable and appropriate for a country in the middle of a downturn.' The problem, he says, was that the Treasury forecasts on which the budget was based were dramatically wrong. Within weeks of the budget being delivered, they had begun to come unstuck. Treasury, Fraser says, had assumed an end to the drought and had grossly underestimated the impact of the drought and the world downturn. In fact, a more recent analysis shows that the Treasury estimates of growth in the 1982 budget were the biggest forecast error of the twenty years at the end of the last century. The budget prediction was for growth of 3 per cent; the reality was negative growth of 2.5 per cent.[32] The planned-for deficit of $1.7 billion blew out to $4.5 billion. In the budget papers for the following year—1983–84, when Labor was in office—Treasury gave its explanation for the blow-out: 'A major part of the deficit overrun was attributable to the automatic response of receipts and outlays to the sharp decline in the economy'.[33] In other words, the blow-out was because of a recession not foreseen by Treasury.

* * *

The year 1982 was one of continual crisis for the Fraser government. Not only were the wheels falling off the budget figuring, but Fraser was coming under attack from within his government. He had been weakened in 1981 by a challenge to his leadership from Andrew Peacock. The 'dry' faction contained increasingly vocal critics.

Fraser's back had been troubling him for years, ever since the damage he had done to it by driving all over Wannon on the bench seats of his old ute, and lifting big bags of superphosphate on the farm. In October the constant niggling pain began to worsen. A doctor had to be called to Nareen in the middle of the night to give him a shot of morphine. 'You wouldn't wish the pain on your worst enemy', Fraser remembers. He battled on. He attended a public function designed to raise money for the Royal Melbourne Botanic Gardens to dig out its lake, and found he had to use a shovel to symbolically begin the process. 'I had to bring up a bit of mud to show how much muck had collected over the years. So I picked up the shovel and did it, and the mud was very sticky and heavy. Anyway, I dug up a couple of shovels, but it was agony. I walked away from it, but afterwards all they could do was give me another good shot of morphine.' On 31 October he was admitted to hospital for surgery: he had a trapped nerve. He had been thinking seriously about an early election, but now, for the moment at least, that option was wiped out.

Recovering and forced to stay in bed, Fraser realised how tired he was. The enforced rest yielded some benefits. Fraser told Tamie's mother, who visited him one day, that every Prime Minister should undergo surgery at least once a year, to force them to step back from the day-to-day demands of office, the detail and the overwhelming pressure. Tamie walked into his hospital room one evening to find him watching the BBC comedy *Yes, Minister* with his head of department Geoffrey Yeend, and Doug Anthony, 'and all of them laughing in different places'.[34]

It was this rest that gave Fraser his big idea—the negotiation of a wage freeze. Before he was on his feet again, he issued a press statement that had some of the ring of his old speeches.

> The nation is now divided—between the great majority who have jobs and the growing minority who do not ... We must shake off the attitudes, the prejudices that have led to too much division in the past. We must reunite this nation in one cause based on the dignity and on the rights of all Australians, based on our feelings and duties to each other as Australians.[35]

The core of Fraser's plan was a freeze of wages in the public sector. Government wages would be pegged and the savings used to create jobs, with some of the money going to the states as bait to lock in the premiers, including those from Labor states. The public sector would then set the pace for private industry. The ACTU indicated acceptance of a six-month wage freeze, so long as the savings went to a 'national employment fund'. A special premiers' conference was called in December. Fraser reported that in the September quarter real wages had risen by about 5 per cent, while productivity was virtually unchanged. Profits had fallen by about 13 per cent. 'Drastic action is needed to meet the situation. A twelve-month pause in wages throughout the entire economy would materially help to reverse recent trends.' He offered the states the savings—about $300 million—from a wage freeze to be spent on employment-generating activities. 'The Commonwealth would like a very frank discussion to take place. It has to be clearly understood, however, that the Commonwealth sees a twelve-month wage pause as crucial.' If agreement could not be reached, the Commonwealth still intended to do all in its power to achieve a wage freeze.[36] The result was an agreement from the Liberal premiers for a twelve-month freeze, and six months from the Labor premiers. It was an enormous achievement.

Meanwhile, however, Bob Hawke, who was now Shadow Minister for Industrial Relations, had got the ACTU to agree in principle to a prices and income policy for Australia. Hawke was capitalising on his image as a peacemaker—the man who could bring tranquillity and unity to a troubled nation. Today Fraser sees what Hawke later achieved with the Accord as an 'evolution' of the wage freeze. It was a difference he tried to sum up in his policy speech for the 1983 election, when he said that his government would work *with* the trade union movement, but not *for* the trade union movement 'as Labor does'.[37]

By now, though, the government was embattled and beset by crises both economic and political. Encouraged by an unexpected win in a by-election in December 1982 in the seat of Flinders, Fraser called an early election. He was hoping to contest against Hayden. 'I suppose I thought I could beat Hayden. It was an awful decision, to call that election when I did.' On the day of the election announcement, Labor replaced Hayden with Bob Hawke. It was the most dramatic day in politics since the dismissal. Tamie says she knew straightaway that they were beaten.

* * *

In early 1983, as Fraser campaigned, the nation halted to mourn the victims of the Ash Wednesday bushfires in Victoria. The country was once again in economic trouble. Unemployment climbed to 9 per cent that year, and the economy went into reverse. It was, as Fraser says, 'a gloomy time to be in Australia'. On 5 March 1983, he was defeated. His economic record has been debated ever since. What did he achieve? What is his economic record?

The Fraser government had to struggle with an international economic environment that was not helpful at any stage. Nevertheless, Fraser dramatically slowed the growth in government spending. It was years before his record in this was matched. Between 1976 and 1982, federal budget spending grew by an average of 2.7 per cent each year in real terms, compared with an average of 11.9 per cent under the Whitlam government, and in the region of 4 per cent under Holt, Gorton and McMahon. If the last year of the Fraser government is excluded—a time when the government faced international downturn and the worst drought in the country's history—the average growth in government spending during Fraser's prime ministership would have been just 2.1 per cent each year.[38]

Changes in the composition of government figures, with alterations on both sides of the ledger, strain the ability to make comparisons over the decades. Nevertheless, in judging how well Fraser did it is worth considering the growth in spending of the governments that came after him. In the first three years of the Hawke government, spending increased at an average of 6.8 per cent per year in real terms. The Hawke–Keating government then reversed the growth in spending for three years, delivering an average annual growth over its term of 2.8 per cent in real terms. During the Howard government, from 1996 to 2007, the average growth in government spending was 3.3 per cent in real terms—above that of the Fraser and Hawke–Keating governments.

The economic debates of 2009 shed some light on how Fraser's record might be regarded. After the 2009 budget, the opposition Treasury spokesman Joe Hockey described plans by the Rudd government to hold spending growth to 2 per cent as 'heroic, ridiculous assumptions'. If that definition is accepted, then it is the Fraser government that over the last fifty years has come closest to heroism over the whole of its term—although its record is bested by the last ten years of the Hawke–Keating government. The present Secretary of Treasury, Ken Henry, has rejected the 'heroic' tag, but has made it clear that keeping growth in government spending to around 2 per cent will require firm discipline and 'no reform fatigue'. He has said that the aspiration is only 'heroic' in the context of the last seven years of the Howard government, in which budget outlays rose by a total of 25.7 per cent.[39]

What about the size of government? Spending by the government as a percentage of gross domestic product was 24.6 per cent in the first year of the Fraser government. It hit a low of 23.9 per cent in 1981–82, before climbing to 26.3 per cent in the context of the drought and the recession of 1982–83. During the Howard years, government spending hit a high of 25.7 per cent of gross domestic product in 2000–01. Howard's lowest figure was 23.7 per cent, in 1999–2000. When Howard left government, in 2007, and the economy was booming, government spending was at 24.2 per cent of gross domestic product. It is predicted to go to 28.6 per cent under Rudd in 2009–10. Given the differences in the economic times, the Fraser government delivered on its promise to restrain the size of government in proportion to the rest of the economy.

Under Fraser, until the second oil shock, the drought and the wages push, unemployment was declining, inflation had been brought under control and corporate profitability was recovering. There were failures. Tax indexation fell by the wayside. Wages policy did not succeed. Plans to introduce the rule of law to the industrial realm failed, largely because neither employers nor employees wanted law, rather than negotiation and power politics, to govern industrial relations. In this field, Fraser was alone in his belief in the rule of law. He remained committed to wage indexation, arbitration and negotiations with the union movement. Nobody at the time was pushing for a deregulated labour market. To sum up, in the context of the economic climate and compared with the records of governments before and since, the figures make Fraser look not so much a soft-hearted liberal as a comparatively hard-line and tough-minded manager.

Yet a government's economic record cannot be judged solely on its success in reducing expenditure. Fraser wanted balance. He had always argued for government activism in pursuing social reform. He retained Medibank as a universal taxpayer-funded means of health insurance. Other vital social welfare programs were retained. Family benefits delivered significant new power to women and poor families. In other areas, as the following chapters in this book show, the vision for Australia was carried forward. The Fraser government reformed immigration policy. It achieved real advances in foreign affairs and domestic social policy. Columns of figures do not tell the whole story.

So how well does Fraser feel he achieved the balance—the reconciliation of Burke and Mill; the need for small government and individual freedom on the one hand, and social order and obligation on the other? Fraser sits in his high-backed chair by the fire in his Mornington Peninsula home. The dogs are at his feet; the table in the dining room is laid for a dinner with friends. The garden outside is cloaked in a light mist, and water drips from the leaves. It is a scene of ease and conviviality, of the obligations and pleasures of connectedness. The telephone keeps ringing. Fraser is engaged in drafting a press statement in conjunction with Aboriginal leader Lowitja O'Donoghue opposing the Howard government's intervention in Aboriginal communities. Howard, says Fraser, is taking away all human respect, all freedom of action. In a different way, Fraser is still wrestling with that balance—order on the one hand, freedom on the other. With the wisdom of hindsight, what would he do differently in economic management?

He would have cut more deeply in those precious first few months when he had a recent mandate behind him and ministers who had yet to become attached to their programs. 'People say, "You could have handled the unions better", but I am not sure how realistic that is, given that Hawke was going to enter politics and obviously had his own agenda.' As for the rest, he is not sure what he could have done differently. In the climate of the times the economic record was a cause of pride—and a mark in John Howard's favour. Why his own party chose to tear down the pride in the Fraser government's record 'is a matter for comment by others'. How well did he do in striking the balance? Fraser shifts a dog from one foot to the other. He says, 'That is for others to judge'.

12

The Difficulties of Freedom

Aboriginal Australia and Human Rights

In the autumn of 1978, Malcolm and Tamie Fraser flew from Alice Springs to Katherine and on to the Top End. They toured the Aboriginal communities of Arnhem Land, and the fringe camps around Alice Springs. Photographs show Fraser in a tweedy suit, sitting in the dust of the Todd River talking to an Aboriginal man. He had a go at riding a camel. He helped to brand cattle on the Aboriginal-owned Haasts Bluff cattle station. In safari suit and slouch hat, he went fishing with the Chair of the recently formed Northern Land Council, Galarrwuy Yunupingu. A photograph shows Fraser and Yunupingu grinning in a tin boat, holding up fish as long as their arms. He visited Papunya, three hours' drive west of Alice Springs, and was photographed in a crisp white shirt and mustard-coloured tie against the improbably red sand and blue sky. His hands are on his hips. With a barefoot Aboriginal man on one side, he is surveying the sheets of corrugated iron the Aboriginals called home. A photograph was taken on the plane on the way back to Canberra. Fraser sat erect, smiling tightly. Tamie, in slacks and shirt, was cross-legged on the floor, laughing at the camera. Staff and media sat around, beers in hand. The Frasers looked happy, as though returning from a joyful adventure. It had indeed been a happy trip, in parts, but the experience was bitter-sweet, and the photograph is deceptive. Fraser was dismayed, and angry.[1]

The camera did not capture everything that Fraser had seen. In Papunya, a community of nomadic people brought in from the centre only about twenty years before, he had visited the new medical centre and saw a filthy labour ward with afterbirth still sitting on the floor. The school had been vandalised, with broken windows and fittings torn out. The Minister for Aboriginal Affairs at the time, Ian Viner, says today, 'I remember the visit vividly. None of us who were there could avoid the memory'. Viner and his staff believed what Fraser saw in Papunya was partly a put-up job. The white advisers did not like what they thought Fraser represented. Most of them, and most of the Aboriginal population, had left town without any attempt at a clean-up or putting on a good face.

There was another side to Papunya. The Papunya Tula art school—working out of that same vandalised school building—had begun to produce its unmistakeable and powerful work, which later transfixed the international art world, yet Fraser was shown none of this. Those behind the art movement did not see anything to gain in introducing this tall and phlegmatic Liberal to their depictions of country.

Papunya was in any case a place of dislocated hope, a small part of the dilemma and ambiguity of government action in Aboriginal affairs. Alongside the beauty of the art, there were Third World rates of infant death, trachoma and heart disease. There were men and women dying in middle age, children malnourished, lives blighted by alcohol and hopelessness: children were being brought up without prospects. And, Fraser remembers, there were 'the most awful white do-gooders. I said to them, "Why don't you clean the hospital?" And they said it wasn't their job, and I said, "Well, if you set an example maybe other people would help". But with people like that you could see it wasn't going to work. They might have been very sympathetic to Aboriginal people, but you could see that they thought of themselves as superior, and an Aboriginal person will sense that several miles off, and then you can do nothing'.

Viner remembers, 'Malcolm on that trip was grappling with the problems face to face'. For Fraser, Aboriginal affairs was about human rights, and about freedom. It was of a piece with other reforms conceived to give individuals the right to determine their own lives. Fred Chaney remembers that he and the backbencher Alan Missen wrote to Fraser in 1976 with a list of human rights reforms that would establish the government as reformist. Even in a time of budget cuts, they argued, there were things that could and should be done. On that list were freedom of information legislation and a human rights commission. These reforms were linked by common principles: the belief in the rights of the individual over government.

The red sands and blue skies of Central Australia may seem a long way from courtrooms and administrative law, but for Fraser they were connected. He says, 'All of it was about the ability of people to have recourse against oppressive administrations, to scrutinise and to question. If Aborigines had had the rights and the ability to query administrative decisions, if they had had a human rights commission, then their children could not have been taken away'. Yet freedom is never easy to achieve, and is in any case not a simple concept. In 1978, as in our own time, remote Aboriginal Australia was the saddest and cruellest testing ground for the most fundamental tenets of liberal philosophy: that all individuals should have the right to choose how they live, subject to the law and the rights of others. Then, as now, not all of those involved believed that freedom should be part of the answer. Governments over many generations since white settlement had denied Aboriginals both freedom and responsibility. In 1978, there was bipartisan commitment to self-determination, but freedom was young. Freedom was hope, but freedom was also dilemma.

In Alice Springs, Fraser saw the alcoholism and the despair. Brian Johns, then a senior public servant in the Department of Prime

Minister and Cabinet, remembers Fraser wandering into the dry bed of the Todd River. 'He was wearing some kind of worsted suit, and he sat down, this great tall man, in the dust and asked this Aboriginal man what he wanted from government, and the man told a long story about wanting a bore so they could get water, and how they had asked for it and it was never done. Malcolm listened, and said to me, "Fix it". And as he moved off, this old man asked us, "Who was that?"'

Johns found himself following around an increasingly terse Fraser and being told to 'fix it' many times, until he had a long list of problems. On his return to Canberra, Fraser called together Viner and the ministers for health and education, Ralph Hunt and John Carrick, and, as Viner remembers, 'bawled us out'. He wanted action. He responded with what in retrospect seems almost naïve determination. To Viner, he wrote that the specific issues—vandalism, the dirty hospital at Papunya and the broken school windows—should be addressed 'as a matter of urgency ... I would expect the problems to be resolved within a period of four weeks'.

It was clear that despite many efforts and best intentions, something in Aboriginal policy was not working, and Fraser wanted it put right. His trip to the Northern Territory resulted in the first attempt to have an all-of-government approach to Aboriginal affairs. Previously, the Department of Aboriginal Affairs had been isolated, and not well regarded. It was seen as having splashed money around with insufficient accountability during the Whitlam years. Now Fraser set up an interdepartmental committee to try to get to the bottom of the problems. He demanded papers be prepared on:

> Self-management: a summary of the current situation, new initiatives pending and an analysis of the problems. Cattle stations: a review ... e.g. over-stocking, late branding etc. raises the suspicion that Aboriginals see cattle stations only as a means of acquiring land and are not so concerned about keeping them viable. Outstation movement: a paper outlining the ramifications of the movement and the

> Commonwealth strategy for dealing with it. Staffing and training: what people are being recruited—and should be—to work with Aboriginals?

Fraser believed many problems were the product of a lack of coordination between departments and between state and federal governments. Perhaps, he suggested in his letter to Viner, there needed to be a 'Peace Corps–type operation' or use of experts from the overseas aid bureau. 'These are just ideas, but I see the papers as a useful means of focussing ministerial attention and encouraging a process of continual review of policies.'[2]

Hunt responded to Fraser by questioning the fundamentals of policy. He doubted that Aboriginal people should have self-determination. He told Fraser: 'We have inherited this idea from a previous government but that should give greater impetus to examination of the concept'. Asking Aboriginals to run their own health services when they lacked expertise was a 'dangerous concept'. The outstation movement, in which Aboriginals chose to move back to their traditional lands to escape the dysfunction and violence of the fringe camps and other settlements, had been embraced by the Fraser government as evidence that Aboriginal people were making freely exercised choices about their own lives, but Hunt said the infant mortality rate in the Northern Territory had risen in the last year and that this was due to the outstation movement. 'If the outstation movement increases then the problems will increase.'[3]

Hunt's view was not one to gain traction in the Fraser government. The problems were immense, but Fraser and his ministers held firm to the view that there could be no solution that did not respect the right to self-determination. Aboriginals, like all other Australians, should be free.

The interdepartmental working committee set up as a result of the trip got underway. Brian Johns remembers the problems of trying to wrestle, in a time of razor gangs and cutbacks, with the stubborn, multifaceted nature of disadvantage and the limitations of what government could do. Having the bore drilled, for example, was not simple. It was the responsibility of the Alice Springs council and needed funding from the territory government. An endless network of bureaucracy was involved, all of it reluctant to move or to accept responsibility. Today, Johns still doesn't know whether it was drilled.

The reports from the committee came back to cabinet. Self-management was welcomed by Aboriginals, they said, but, 'The immensity of the task of implementing government policy should not be underestimated'. The main problems were an historical lack of recognition of the importance of land to Aboriginals, and the speed with which government management and control had been withdrawn, allowing insufficient time for training, adjustment and self-reliance.

> The economic potential of most communities is low, poverty is chronic and dependence is thereby being promoted. Outstations are recognised as genuine Aboriginal initiatives in a choice of lifestyle based on self-management, but also exemplify the difficulties of achieving key policy objectives. Their remoteness poses serious administrative and logistic problems in support supply and provision of services.

There were differences of opinion and approach between federal government departments and between the states. 'In some communities immense social problems persist—alcoholism, juvenile delinquency, truancy, vandalism, poverty and unemployment. The standard of management is poor and white staff employed by communities are often incompetent or worse.' Yet the report urged continued commitment to self-management—'the principle that all Aborigines and Torres Strait Islanders should be as free as other Australians to determine their own varied futures'. The report urged cabinet to recognise that self-management

> must mean that certain projects will fail, and money will not be spent as wisely as could have been expected had other policies been adopted. The only way these aspects

> could be entirely overcome would be through a policy of direct control, although even then there would be no guarantees against failure and fiasco.

There were recommendations for resolving the differences within governments, and a standing committee was set up to stay on the problem. Fraser's own department commented that the existing policy set long-term targets that were difficult to attain. 'Any failures and setbacks should be seen in that context.' The work went on. Evidence of progress was hard to find.[4]

Fraser had wanted at least the obvious problems solved in four weeks. Today, reminded of this, his face grows long. 'I expect it is exactly the same now as it was then. Or worse. I don't suppose anything has changed.' The failure to make greater improvements in the lives and prospects of many Aboriginal people is one of his biggest regrets. Indeed, today, the problems in much of remote Aboriginal Australia are no better and are possibly worse than they were in Fraser's time. In Papunya and other communities, petrol-sniffing has ravaged the bodies and brains of a generation.

During Fraser's time, Aboriginal policy was more or less bipartisan, the differences between Whitlam and Fraser matters of detail and implementation. Whitlam's and Fraser's policies overturned decades of assimilationist ideas in which the assumption had been that Aboriginals could and should become just like white Australians—that being an Aboriginal was in itself a problem to be solved. In our own time, self-determination has been abandoned as federal government policy. It has been suggested that the whole idea of self-determination was somehow misconceived and that the policies of Whitlam and Fraser did no good, and may have done harm. In June 2007, the Howard government announced a 'national emergency' in Aboriginal Australia, signalling a return to paternalism and government control, at least in the Northern Territory. The army was sent into Aboriginal communities. There was the threat of compulsory health checks. Welfare payments were partially withheld. The talk was not of freedom but of 'mutual obligation', 'normalisation' and 'mainstreaming'. Fraser says, 'Really, it all means assimilation. It means governments forcing people'. It is still an approach he rejects.

There are more sophisticated, less ideologically loaded critiques of self-determination. The anthropologist Peter Sutton has suggested that Western liberal notions of freedom cannot be simply applied to cultures that were, pre-contact, scattered, stratified and nomadic, and in which the dominant obligation was to family rather than broader notions of social well-being. There are many regional differences, Sutton says, and continent-wide generalisations are difficult, but in some places lives were safer, more ordered, in the paternalistic missions of the past. Sutton suggests that cultural change cannot be simply imposed, but perhaps the agenda today should be not assimilation but self-modernisation.[5] Fraser knows that freedom is complicated. It is not, to him, a lofty ideal or abstract notion to be asserted without recognition of context and practicalities. Freedom for Aboriginal people means, simply, the same sort of control over their lives that is enjoyed by most Australians. Such freedom is meaningless without health care, housing, education and opportunity. Freedom therefore implies order, and order implies government. Once again, it is a matter of the balance between John Stuart Mill and Edmund Burke—on the one hand the tendency of government to diminish the power of the individual, and on the other the need for social order if any meaningful kind of liberty is to prevail. In the chaos and anarchy of the worst Aboriginal settlements there is no order, little safety and therefore no liberty. To echo another of the philosophers Fraser studied at university, Thomas Hobbes, life is brutish and short. Fraser suspects, as he has always suspected, that government action cannot be the whole of the solution. Government must help people to help themselves. Precisely what that means is what Fraser's government and every government since has wrestled with.

Yet basic human rights are just that. The principle of 'self-determination of peoples' is contained in United Nations charter. It forms part of Australia's international obligations. It may require different things in different situations, but it cannot be regarded as less important or as not applying merely because of culture or the colour of skin. Australia, Fraser fears, is entering a new era of racism. We have regressed. And in Papunya and many other places, he suspects, the windows are still broken, the hospital is still dirty, men, women and children are still suffering and hope is still in short supply. 'It's shameful. It's something every Australian should be ashamed of and aware of', he says. Yet what is to be done, and how much of what he and his ministers did was right? At the time, the policies Fraser adopted and pursued in Aboriginal affairs were radical, particularly for the Liberal and National Country parties. Today, though, Fraser says, 'I think we were timid. I think we didn't go nearly far enough'. He has come to this conclusion since he left power. Partly it is from the evidence that the problems remain; partly it is that he has acquired an increased understanding of history, and what it requires of the present.

* * *

Fraser was always interested in Aboriginal affairs, but his understanding altered over time. In 1961, when he was a backbencher, he took part in a debate on 'native welfare' and supported the assimilationist policies of government. He described them as the opposite of racism, and contrasted them favourably to apartheid in South Africa. He said:

> Unfortunately some doubt has been cast upon the meaning of the term 'assimilation'. Surely it means that ultimately the Aborigines will have the same privileges, responsibilities and rights that other Australians now have. In other words Aborigines will live in the same street as other Australians and will be treated as their equal, as indeed they are in certain areas already … The marriage of two persons of different colour would be part of their assimilation. It may well be that by that means the

> Aboriginal race will be absorbed over a period of time. As far as I can see, assimilation and absorption are part of one and the same thing.[6]

Four years later, during the move to equal pay for Aboriginal stockmen, Fraser wrote to the Minister for Territories CE Barnes, expressing concern that it would place many Aboriginals out of work, but that 'Frankly my own view is that Australia can no longer afford, in the international scene, to have two standards'. Fraser argued that equal pay should be introduced, but that the government should avoid placing the whole of this burden on the pastoral industry in one go. Government should subsidise the wages over an adjustment period. Barnes wrote back acknowledging the problem and saying it was under 'active consideration'.[7]

Yet Barnes did nothing, and Fraser was prescient. Before equal pay, pastoralists had allowed Aboriginals to live on the land; they had provided shelter and food for the extended families in the camps. Conditions varied. There was racism and little freedom: the pastoralists were still benefitting from the history of dispossession. Yet Aboriginal people had some security. When equal pay came in, pastoralists saw no reason why they should continue to support Aboriginal encampments. At about the same time, Aboriginals became entitled to social security. As a consequence of this combination of policies they moved to the fringe camps and the settlements with some money but no role and little opportunity. This formed part of the background to the despair that Fraser saw on his 1978 trip to the Northern Territory, and to the outstation movement, which was largely a response to Aboriginal people's desire to escape from the alcoholism and violence into which many fringe camps had descended. Who could deny the justice of the principle of equal pay? Who could deny that Aboriginal people should have access to the same social security benefits as other Australians? And yet the consequences had been disastrous. It was a failure of governance and a failure of planning—not the first, and certainly not the last. Justice, like freedom, is rarely simple.

By the time he was Prime Minister, Fraser was horrified by the assimilationist policies of the past. His ideas had changed, not least through his experiences as Education Minister, in particular his tour of Aboriginal settlements in the company of his activist colleague Bill Wentworth. As Prime Minister, he said that trying to enforce conformity 'denies people their identity and self-esteem. It drives a wedge between children and their parents. We cannot demand of people that they renounce the heritage that they value, and yet expect them to feel welcome as full members of our society'. Diversity was 'a quality to be actively embraced, a source of social wealth and dynamism'.[8] These ideas drove his policies on immigration and refugees. They also drove Aboriginal policy.

* * *

Just five days after he became Leader of the Opposition in 1975, Fraser called for a report on Aboriginal affairs. He was told that there had been big increases in spending under Whitlam: from $62 million in 1972 to $164 million in 1975. There had been a royal commission, presided over by Justice Ted Woodward, which had recommended the granting of land rights in the Northern Territory. The Whitlam government had introduced, but not yet passed, the necessary legislation. There was a newly created Department of Aboriginal Affairs and an elected advisory body, the National Aboriginal Consultative Committee. 'Broad initiatives have been undertaken but many have experienced implementation problems', the report said. At this stage, the opposition's policy was not complete. In particular, shadow cabinet had not come to a view on land rights.[9]

Fraser appointed Robert Ellicott, an eminent lawyer who had been Solicitor-General under both McMahon and Whitlam, as his Shadow Minister for Aboriginal Affairs. As the various crises of 1975 were brewing, Ellicott drafted a policy that broke with decades of Liberal Party support for assimilation. It recommended that the 'useful and beneficial' policies of Labor should be continued. The policy was grounded in the fundamental tenets of liberalism. 'Individuals should be able to develop their own personality in their own way, always subject to the rights of others', it said. 'Traditional groups and communities within our society should have a like capacity.' Aboriginal programs should be generously funded:

> We regard these expenditures as nothing more than just to people whose freedom and self-expression have been inhibited by past policies and community attitudes ... A Liberal–National Country Party government will therefore seize every opportunity and support any innovation likely to ensure a higher level of mutual tolerance, trust and enterprise than has so far marked our history.

Crucially, the policy embraced land rights—an unprecedented move for parties whose support base included the mining and pastoral industries.[10]

Where Whitlam had spoken of self-determination, the Liberal and National Country parties chose a different word: self-management. In Ellicott's mind this was more than just rebranding: self-management implied responsibility as well as freedom. This accorded with the liberal philosophy that not all problems could be solved by government. But for most observers over the next decade, the terms 'self-management' and 'self-determination' became interchangeable.

Once Fraser was in government, the new policy was put into action. Ian Viner had a miserable first few months as Minister for Aboriginal Affairs. He faced the full force of Treasury determination to slash expenditure in the lead-up to the 1976 budget. 'It was indeed a drama', he remembers. 'There I was, a junior minister, with John Stone leading the gang and my budget disappearing from under me.' His budget was cut by $26 million on the previous year's expenditure. He did not give up: he spoke to Fraser and Lynch, and was allowed to make a special cabinet submission arguing for clawing back the funding. He succeeded, with Fraser's support, in restoring almost all of what had been cut, despite tartly worded warnings from Treasury that 'If the government is to adhere to its policy of expenditure restraint it will be important that *all* attempts to reopen earlier decisions be resisted' (emphasis in original).[11] Fraser says today, 'Yes, we had to cut, but I never took the view that meant higher priority areas wouldn't have extra funds if necessary'. For the rest of Fraser's term, the budget allocation for Aboriginal affairs was progressively increased.

Meanwhile, the Department of Aboriginal Affairs' delivery of services had been subjected to a review, which had found some successes and many problems. Under Whitlam, there had been 'massive ministerial initiatives' in housing, legal aid and local governance. The planning had been inadequate and the speed of change had meant that many programs had not been properly managed. Not enough attention had been given to training. There had been a lack of consultation, and too many programs were still delivered to Aboriginal people rather than by Aboriginal people, the review said. There had been significant achievements, but also waste and stupidity. Some Aboriginal communities had wanted to buy prefabricated houses to solve their housing shortages, but had been told by bureaucrats that this did not fit in with ideas of self-determination. They should build their own houses. Other housing associations were in bad shape: 'In one case after financial support over a period of three years there was one completed house of which the occupant was the white project manager. In another, no houses had been built, the association had collapsed and building materials left on the site were rotting on the ground'. Gradually, more accountability and better systems were developed.[12] The man who conducted this review, David Hay, was later appointed to head the department.

Viner was faced with the seemingly enormous task of negotiating land rights legislation in the Northern Territory against the bitter opposition of the Country Liberal Party territory government, the Minister for the Northern Territory Evan Adermann and the federal Department of the Northern Territory. Viner found that both his main antagonists and his main supporters came from within his own party. His allies included the first Aboriginal federal parliamentarian, Neville Bonner, Fred Chaney (junior), later to take over as Minister for Aboriginal Affairs, and Philip Ruddock. He remembers today, 'Fraser gave me unhesitating, unequivocal support'. Ellicott, the man who had drafted the government's Aboriginal policy, says, 'If there was one thing that got Malcolm Fraser emotional, it was land rights'. Why was Fraser so committed to the issue? Brian Johns, working in the Department of Prime Minister and Cabinet, gained the impression that Fraser had an emotional connection to the cause: that it was to do with his own deep connections to land, his childhood memories of Balpool-Nyang, and what its loss had meant to him. Fraser says today, 'That's too long a bow. That wasn't it. I thought it was just. It was as simple as that'.

The party had committed to land rights, but what exactly did that mean? The mining lobby and pastoralists were arguing for a token form of land rights, under which Aboriginals would not be able to veto or earn royalties from mining development. The territory government wanted the Commonwealth to pass only 'framework' legislation, leaving the detail to them, to minimise 'discrimination as between Aboriginals and other citizens'.[13] Viner remembers 'very strong debates, both in committee and in the party room, with some very antagonistic debaters'. He had adopted and modified the legislation that the Whitlam government had drafted, which carried with it the ability for Aboriginal people to veto and receive royalties from mining. Fraser was key. Viner says, 'If you've got the Prime Minister on side, well, you've got a much better chance of getting contentious matters through the system'. When pressure from the mining lobby was at its height, Viner arranged for Fraser to meet Silas Roberts, Roy Marika and Wenten Rubuntja, three Aboriginal leaders from the Northern Territory. Roberts and Marika, used to white man's politics, arrived for their meeting dressed in suits. Rubuntja was also a leader of his people, and Chairman of the Central Land Council, but he was less used to environments such as Parliament House. He arrived in Fraser's office in a white shirt dusted with the red soil of the centre, and carrying what appeared to be a bundle of newspapers. 'Fraser was obviously impressed, if not moved', Viner remembers. As the meeting drew to an end, Rubuntja unwrapped the newspapers and pulled out a wooden churinga—the sacred object that acts as a traditional title deed to land. He showed it to Fraser, and quietly pointed out the marks that represented his people's claims to land. Fraser bent over and considered it, then thanked Rubuntja for coming all the way to Canberra to show the sacred board.

The Aboriginal Land Rights (Northern Territory) Act became law in December 1976. It was a high point of political achievement, and for many Aboriginal people was evidence that the Fraser government was on their side. Viner remembers a lift in 'hope, in aspiration, in determination and participation'. The main difference from the legislation introduced but not passed by the Whitlam government was that urban Aboriginals could not make claims on the basis of need. Traditional associations had to be proved.

In the years that followed, the Fraser government used all its powers of influence, example and persuasion to get state governments to follow suit with land rights. New South Wales and South Australia did so; Queensland and Western Australia were intransigent. But Fraser stopped short of imposing land rights on the states by law. The Fraser who had fallen out with Gorton over the seabed legislation was still a federalist, yet there were times when he was prepared to go further. When principles conflicted—Aboriginal self-management versus states' rights—he sometimes came down on the side of the Aboriginals. In the weeks before the 1978 trip to the Northern Territory, Fraser had been confronting the Queensland Premier Joh Bjelke-Petersen over the Queensland government's intention to revoke Aboriginal reserve lands at Aurukun, on Cape York, and Mornington Island. The Queensland government wanted to remove the influence of the Uniting Church, which had been a strong advocate for Aboriginal people, and put the communities under the management of the unpopular Queensland Department of Aboriginal and Islander Affairs and its head Pat Killoran.[14] The issue had been brewing since the days of Fraser's caretaker government. Within weeks of the 1975 election, Fraser had dispatched Viner to consult the Aboriginal people. Reporting back, Viner said the community was unanimously against being administered by the Queensland government, and against mining. The people had vivid memories of what had happened further north, at Mapoon, when the miners had arrived. Communities had been forcibly moved on by police, their homes burned to the ground. 'One speaker summed up their feeling of identity with the land and their fears by explaining that their names were taken from trees, animals and other totems associated with their land, and that if these were "swept away" they would become "people with no name, no land"', Viner told Fraser.[15] Neither the Queensland government nor the miners had consulted Aboriginal people. Over months of negotiation, Viner and Fraser used everything at the federal government's disposal, including threats to use foreign investment review guidelines and the federal power over export licences, to persuade the Queensland government and the miners to negotiate with the Aboriginals.

A turning point in dealing with Bjelke-Petersen came early in the piece. Viner believed he had reached a compromise agreement to preserve the reserves, but, as he flew out of Brisbane, Bjelke-Petersen was already on radio news gloating that he had stood up to the Commonwealth. Viner remembers, 'When I landed in Sydney, Fraser was on the phone travelling from Melbourne on his way to Nareen. He told me to go to Aurukun and Mornington Island the next day to find out what the people wanted and to report to cabinet. He said: "I'm going to authorise you to break the cabinet rule not to say publicly what you will be taking to cabinet. You can say there has been no agreement with Bjelke-Petersen and you are going to Aurukun and Mornington Island to consult the people"'. After Bjelke-Petersen's antics, Viner found that he had the support not only of Fraser but also of Doug Anthony, despite the discomfort the confrontation caused in the National Country Party. Viner took Aboriginal people from Aurukun and Mornington Island into the cabinet room—the first time this had been done. 'They had a profound effect', he remembers. There were all-day meetings with Bjelke-Petersen and Queensland government minister Russ Hinze. In letters to Bjelke-Petersen, Fraser continually asserted the right of the federal government to be involved. 'As a result of the 1967 referendum, the Commonwealth Government regards itself as having paramount responsibility for Aboriginal affairs', he said.[16]

The Queensland government was not to be swayed. The federal parliament passed legislation granting the reserves self-management, but on the same day Bjelke-Petersen revoked the reserves, which made the federal law irrelevant. More negotiations followed. Viner remembers that in the days before Fraser's Northern Territory trip, Bjelke-Petersen was in Fraser's office complaining about the churches' advocacy for the Aurukun Aboriginals. Bjelke-Petersen told Fraser that the bishops wanted him to meet the Aboriginal people. He said to Fraser, 'I'm not going to go and meet with them. You wouldn't sit down and have breakfast at the same table with them, Malcolm'.

Fraser replied frostily, 'Well, as a matter of fact, Joh, I'm going to go and have lunch today with all the members of the National Aboriginal Conference'.

Bjelke-Petersen groaned and threw up his hands in exasperation.

Fraser did have lunch with the National Aboriginal Conference. It was its first meeting. The conference was the consultative body set up by the Fraser government to replace the Whitlam-initiated National Aboriginal Consultative Council, which was in conflict with both its own people and the new Department of Aboriginal Affairs. The main difference between the two bodies was the electoral base, which was altered to be more regionally focussed after a government-commissioned report by the anthropologist Les Hiatt. Fraser gave a speech at the lunch, saying that it would take persistence and determination to overcome Aboriginal disadvantage, but that 'Throughout all our work together we must never forget that any policy based on the superiority of one race over another is policy doomed to failure'. He pointed out the link with South Africa and apartheid: 'Just as the government's policies towards Southern Africa are founded on this fundamental principle, so in Australia we must achieve nothing less than real equality of all Australians—equality of rights, equality of opportunities, equality of protection under the law'.[17]

What did not become public at the time was that cabinet had decided that as a last resort it would use its power to compulsorily acquire the reserves from the Queensland government—an extraordinary move that would almost certainly have resulted in a states' rights test case. It would also have cost hundreds of millions of dollars in compensation.[18] Ultimately, though, negotiation succeeded. The reserves became unique self-governing areas with the land leased to the new Aboriginal local government authorities.

There were other times when negotiation with state governments failed. In 1980, the Western Australian government wanted to force drilling for oil at Noonkanbah, a pastoral lease bought by the Fraser government for the Aboriginal community in the face of the state government's opposition. Fraser engaged in vigorous correspondence with the Premier Charles Court, urging negotiation with the Aboriginal people, who claimed the drilling site was sacred. Court was scathing in reply: sacred sites were being 'manufactured', he claimed, as part of 'a well-orchestrated attempt to frustrate mineral and petroleum exploration and development on pastoral leases'. Court told Fraser that Aboriginals were being 'expertly manipulated' and used to foment 'insurrection' aimed at undermining elected government. Fraser's sympathetic ear merely encouraged the 'stirrers'. Today Fraser says, 'There were all the usual claims that Aborigines were being used, that they manufactured sacred sites. I thought that by and large they were very genuine, and they deserved to be treated with respect. Charlie made it very difficult'. Fraser agreed that mining could not be prevented on pastoral leases, but again urged

Court to negotiate. He failed to persuade him. A convoy of forty-five non-union drilling rigs and trucks left Perth, protected by hundreds of police, on 7 August 1980. Federal parliament was sitting. Late at night Fraser called in Viner and Fred Chaney, who had replaced Viner as Minister for Aboriginal Affairs. Fraser was aghast at the overriding of Aboriginal interests and fearful for Australia's international reputation. He rang Ray O'Connor, who was Acting Premier while Court was overseas. It was a long conversation, in which Fraser used all his powers of persuasion, telling O'Connor he was putting Australia's international reputation at risk. Finally, O'Connor said he would stop the convoy, but within forty-eight hours Court vetoed that decision. The convoy went ahead. There were violent confrontations between police and Noonkanbah protesters as the drilling rigs forced their way through community picket lines.

Chaney continued to intervene, with Fraser's help. They were talking to the oil drillers, Amax Exploration, and the Australian Mining Industry Council, urging negotiation. Court was furious, writing to Fraser:

> There is nothing I can do to stop you talking to the mining and petroleum exploration companies, or to the Aborigines, but based on past experience this will finish up as yet another intrusion into the erosion of a true federal system ... I have to repeat what I said previously, namely, that we would not be in the present situation of Noonkanbah had it not been for Commonwealth interference.

As for negotiations with the Aboriginals:

> My considered view is that there comes a time when we have to call a halt to appeasement ... It is no time for bleeding hearts. If we are going to get a degree of sanity into this question then the federal and state governments have to be seen by the public to be fulfilling the responsibility of government.[19]

Fraser had used everything short of overriding the state government, which he would not do. Federation won the day. The drilling went on, to the distress of the Aboriginals. No oil was found, and Australia was embarrassed when the National Aboriginal Conference took the matter to the United Nations in Geneva, making international headlines.

* * *

In 1980, the Fraser government set up the Aboriginal Development Commission, with Charlie Perkins as its first Director. The commission served as a 'bank', helping Aboriginals to buy land on the open market, set up businesses and acquire finance for housing, as well as advising the minister. In 1998, near the end of his life, Perkins described it as 'the high point in Aboriginal affairs in an economic sense' and the first time that Aboriginal people had been given control over significant assets.[20] The government had also begun a national campaign designed to overcome the crushing levels of unemployment suffered by Indigenous Australians. The national employment initiative was to have two strands—one aimed at Aboriginals in remote areas, the other to address unemployment among those in the mainstream labour market. The main scheme for remote areas was the Community Development Employment Project, under which the unemployed were paid to work in their communities. It had significant success, building participation and responsibility in local communities. For the mainstream labour market there were publicity campaigns aimed at promoting Aboriginal people to private employers. Private companies working for the federal government had clauses inserted into contracts obliging them to seek opportunities to employ Aboriginal people. State governments were encouraged to do the same.

When the statistics came to cabinet showing that, despite these efforts, there was little impact on Aboriginal unemployment, Fraser considered going even further and introducing legislation enforcing positive discrimination in the Commonwealth public service. Despite reluctance in the public service, he pushed for a cabinet submission on the topic. It took eighteen months, with the bureaucrats in the Department of Employment and Industrial Relations being constantly prompted by Fraser's departmental staff. The issue, the bureaucrats protested, was 'particularly complex'. When the submission finally emerged, in August 1978, both Ian Viner as Minister for Aboriginal Affairs and Tony Street as Minister for Employment opposed the idea, and so did the Public Service Board, arguing that selection for public service positions should be on merit alone, and that quota systems were divisive and inefficient.[21] Positive discrimination was too radical for the times, but today Fraser says, 'How else are you going to get change? We should probably have gone ahead and done it, and today there might be real differences as a result'.

* * *

The idea of a treaty with Aboriginals was raised by the National Aboriginal Conference in the middle of Fraser's time as Prime Minister. His cabinet rejected the word 'treaty' because of its suggestion that Aboriginal Australia formed a separate nation, but in 1980 cabinet embraced the idea of a makarrata. The word meant, cabinet was told, 'the end of the dispute and resumption of normal relations'. This, it was agreed, might be consistent with the government's policy of recognising the impact of dispossession and dispersal. The National Aboriginal Conference wanted the agreement to include land rights in those states yet to grant them, and compensation through a fixed proportion of gross domestic product. Cabinet rejected these demands, but funded the conference to further develop the idea. Chaney remembers that both he and Fraser were active in encouraging the conference to bring forward proposals that the government had some chance of negotiating past vehement opposition, including that of Bjelke-Petersen in Queensland and Court in Western Australia. Negotiations did not succeed: the conference would not give up its claims to big compensation and land rights. In the dying days of the Fraser government, the Department of Prime Minister and Cabinet was telling Fraser that there seemed to be little likelihood of a realistic agreement.[22]

Today, this is one of the areas in which Fraser thinks his government was too timid. At the time, he thought Australia was leading the way in the treatment of Indigenous people. Since then, he thinks, we have gone backwards. Other countries, including the United States, Canada and New Zealand, are doing better in combating Indigenous disadvantage—and all of them have some kind of treaty as the foundation for their approach. In Australia, the word 'treaty' has been taken to mean an agreement between nations, but in other countries it has been understood differently and has led to more national unity. 'The idea that it means separate sovereignty is a nonsense', Fraser says today. As for compensation: 'It is necessary. It is just. All the countries that have succeeded in this area have paid real compensation'. But could such ideas have been pushed through in the 1980s, with premiers like Bjelke-Petersen and Court in opposition and much of cabinet opposed? Chaney doubts it. 'We did the best we could to come up with a proposal that was practical.'

The Hawke government that replaced Fraser's also failed to sign a treaty or other agreement, but did set up the Aboriginal and Torres Strait Islander Commission, an elected body with real powers over money and the administration of Aboriginal programs. Fraser, by that time out of politics, supported the idea, but was bitterly disappointed by its 'ghastly failure' after Lowitja O'Donoghue, its first Chairperson, departed. Meanwhile, the poverty, the health problems, the alcoholism and the dysfunction became worse under Hawke and Keating, as they had under Whitlam and Fraser.

* * *

Much was done in Aboriginal affairs under Fraser. There was enormous energy and good will. Fred Chaney says today, 'Fraser was a valiant fighter for change'. Ian Viner remembers a fresh spirit that blew through Aboriginal Australia once it was accepted that this was a government in favour of change. New leaders, particularly women, began to emerge within Aboriginal communities. Today, both Viner and Chaney maintain close friendships with the Aboriginal community. They are remembered well, as two of the best ministers.

Charlie Perkins, the radical Aboriginal activist who was made a senior bureaucrat by Whitlam, told an interviewer in 1998 that after the dismissal he hadn't known what to expect from Fraser.

> I didn't know how to take him ... I thought what a dour, sullen person he looks, but then I found out that on Aboriginal affairs he was absolutely A-1. He was tops. He was the best of them all on Aboriginal affairs. And Gough is good, but you know the problem with Gough ... sometimes he thinks he started everything and you know ... he didn't. Fraser was very good on Aboriginal affairs and he produced the goods.[23]

Under Fraser, Perkins became Deputy Secretary of the Department of Aboriginal Affairs—the first Aboriginal to rise so high within the federal public service.

But did it work? Did Fraser deliver the goods? Today, Fraser reflects on these questions with some bitterness. Despite the intentions and the achievements, it is hard to point to measurable outcomes to show that the Whitlam and Fraser governments' policies succeeded in combating what is euphemistically called 'Aboriginal disadvantage'. As Peter Sutton has said, 'A murdered mother is not "disadvantaged"—she has lost her life'.[24] Chaney says that Fraser's strength was holding to the liberal principles on many occasions when it would have been easier to let things be. Chaney has remained closely involved in Aboriginal affairs since his time in government. Today, he says, governments continue to wrestle with the problems and with the limits of what government can do. He said recently in a speech that 'The fundamental challenge for governments today is no different from the fundamental challenge we have faced over the last thirty years: how do we deliver on our good intentions? ... The past is a land full of good intentions'.[25] Some lessons have been learned, Chaney says. Centrally administered programs fail. Engaging Aboriginal people is essential, and programs that fail to do that will also fail. Localism and flexibility are essential. And, Chaney says, it is a fiction that before self-management was a 'golden age', as is today suggested by critics of the Whitlam and Fraser eras. 'I visited some of those camps and missions in the old days, and they were bloody awful. There never was a golden era.' Chaney says the Fraser government brought a new level of respect to dealing with Aboriginal people. 'Like all successive governments, it struggled to achieve changes as rapidly as it wished, but the directions it set were correct.'

Fraser was against big government: he believed in individual responsibility. The key difference between liberalism and socialism, he had said in a speech before he became Leader of the Opposition, was that socialists turned to government for solutions, while liberals asked, 'Can individuals solve it for themselves? Can the government create the climate in which that can happen?'[26] Yet he did believe in a role for government in overcoming the prejudice, oppression and dispossession of previous generations. Governments, after all, had created many of the problems. This was the way in which the Fraser government's policies in Aboriginal affairs were linked to its wider human rights agenda. Fraser knew, as Prime Minister, that the policies of prejudice were not a matter of far-off history; they had continued into his own time as a parliamentarian. People had doubtless meant well—he had meant well when he had spoken in favour of assimilation back in 1961—yet, for Aboriginal people, governments had been part of the problem, not the solution.

* * *

It is no accident that the man who drafted the Aboriginal affairs policy that Fraser took to the 1975 election was Robert Ellicott, who went on to be Attorney-General in the first Fraser government. Ellicott was responsible for the legislation setting up the Human Rights Commission and what was at the time the most far-reaching system of judicial review of administrative decisions then operating in a Westminster system. Nor is it any accident that Fred Chaney and Peter Baume, who succeeded Ian Viner as ministers for Aboriginal affairs, were also both leading members of the liberal-minded ginger group that helped to keep the human rights agenda alive after Ellicott's resignation over the Sankey affair. Fraser does not claim the main credit for the freedom of information and administrative law reforms: 'I was advised by others'. But it was due to his support and intervention that they succeeded, despite the bitter opposition of the public service and the reservations of many in cabinet.

The reforms that the Fraser government brought to fruition had been brewing for a decade. In 1968, the Gorton government had established a committee under Sir John Kerr to review administrative law. This was the same era of Kerr's life in which he chaired the inquiry into armed forces pay that first brought him into contact with Fraser. In this inquiry, Kerr recommended the establishment of a 'general counsel for grievances', or an ombudsman, to act as an advocate for citizens, together with a comprehensive system by which citizens could have the courts review public service decisions. This agenda had been adopted by the Whitlam government but not brought to completion. It fell to the Fraser government to appoint the first ombudsman in March 1977 and to set up the Administrative Appeals Tribunal, which had the power to conduct merit-based reviews of a range of specified government decisions. Whitlam had also introduced a human rights commission Bill, but it never became law. Ellicott introduced a modified proposal. Instead of a 'Bill of Rights' approach, the Fraser government's Human Rights Commission was conceived as a body that could handle complaints, investigate breaches and make reports and recommendations.

When Ellicott resigned as Attorney-General, legislation establishing a comprehensive system of judicial review of administrative decisions under which the federal court could review the legal validity of government actions had been passed but not proclaimed. Legislation to set up a Human Rights Commission had been introduced, but was left lying on the table. For a long time nothing seemed to be happening. In late 1979, the backbenchers and ministers most concerned with the human rights law reform agenda—Ellicott, Chaney, Missen, Baume and Philip Ruddock—formed a delegation to see Fraser and insist that the agenda be advanced. Ellicott remembers, 'A lot of people would think that Fraser would be light years behind people like Chaney and Missen on this, but that's a superficial impression. We said to him, "These are major reforms of our government; they are really important. What's happening? We should be doing something about it". And he sat up and took notice, and once his attention was drawn to it he made sure that things moved quickly'.

The Administrative Decisions (Judicial Review) Act came into force in October 1980. It was not the kind of reform that made headlines, but its impact on the Australian system of government is still being felt today. The Human Rights Commission was established in 1981, and in time it brought Fraser back into active involvement in Aboriginal affairs, long after he had left government.

Freedom of information legislation took longer, resisted at every step by the most powerful figures in the public service. The idea of legislation giving the public the right to access government documents had been part of the Whitlam government's election campaign in 1972, but as with much of his law reform program had not been pursued once his activist Attorney-General Lionel Murphy left for the High Court. The idea was kept alive chiefly by Alan Missen, who made freedom of information his personal mission.

Cabinet decided in principle to introduce freedom of information legislation in December 1976.[27] Ellicott brought draft legislation to cabinet in May 1977, and ran straight into public service resistance. The head of the Department of Prime Minister and Cabinet Geoffrey Yeend warned that the legislation would result in 'administrative chaos ... departments keeping dual filing cabinets'. In a handwritten note dated 20 May 1977 and marked 'not for file'—which nevertheless did end up on the cabinet file—Yeend wrote to Fraser: 'Were I not under the threat of my advice being made public I would be questioning with you the wisdom of this whole legislation. It is a can of worms, political commitment notwithstanding'.[28] Other senior public servants, including Arthur Tange in the Department of Defence and Frederick Wheeler in Treasury, also opposed the legislation. Fraser and his cabinet persisted; Yeend continued to advise Fraser against proceeding. In October 1977, Yeend succeeded in having the draft Bill put aside for further examination.[29] There were more delays, more reconsideration, more public service advice. Legislation was finally introduced—considerably weakened from Ellicott's first draft—in June 1978 and was referred to a Senate committee, while the public service continued its campaign, with departments demanding broader and in some cases blanket exemptions. Yeend wrote in 1980, after the report of the Senate committee had been received, that the proposed law would go further than any other country with a similar system of government, and was an 'experimental step of major dimensions ... Whatever the politics of the decision it is certainly a gamble in the administrative sense'.[30] Yeend asked for the legislation not to come into effect until mid 1983, which, as it happened, would have put it off until after the Fraser government lost power. Nevertheless, against all opposition, the cabinet persisted, though not without delays and misgivings. On 1 December 1982, Australia became the first Westminster system to introduce national freedom of information laws. Over the next two decades, every state in Australia followed course. Today in most states all three levels of government—local, state and federal—are covered by freedom of information.

Fraser is disappointed in the legacy. The legislation his government introduced has been progressively weakened and grudgingly implemented. He believes it has fallen victim to the very public service opposition that his cabinet attempted to overcome. As this book was being written, freedom of information laws were under review in several states. Federally, the then Special Minister for State John Faulkner had released legislation designed to greatly improve public access to documents, including the creation of an information commissioner to conduct merit-based reviews of agency decisions and to promote a culture of disclosure in government. Faulkner called for heads of federal government departments to 'loosen up' their approach.[31] Fraser commented that the main opposition to reform was still coming from within the public service, and the fact that heads of department are now not permanent but political appointments 'doesn't seem to have changed things one iota. We need a fresh spirit in these things. We need to understand that it will always be opposed, particularly by a politicised public service, but the ability to find out what government is doing and to challenge it—that is fundamental to freedom'.

As for the Human Rights Commission, today Fraser would go much further. At the time he agreed with Ellicott's approach: relying on the common law and the power of report and recommendation to protect human rights. There are now, he says, abundant examples to show that the common law is 'grossly inadequate'. An Act of parliament can override the common law, and Australian governments have been increasingly willing to pass and use such laws. For example, the High Court has found that the federal government has the right under the Migration Act to indefinitely detain failed asylum seekers.[32] In recent years, asylum seekers, including children, have been locked up even though they have committed no crime. Australian citizens have been deported and falsely imprisoned. David Hicks, an Australian citizen, has been imprisoned without charge overseas, without the Australian Government having any legal obligation to intervene. As for Aboriginal Australians, Fraser says, 'Our system has patently failed to protect Aboriginal people's rights. The circumstances of Aborigines is one of the strongest arguments I know for a Bill of Rights'.

The Fraser government had conceived the Human Rights Commission as a body that could bring human rights abuses to public prominence. In 1997, the organisation that had replaced it, the Human Rights and Equal Opportunity Commission, did exactly that when it issued the *Bringing Them Home* report, an investigation into the practice of taking Aboriginal children from their families. This was the issue that brought Fraser back into active involvement with Aboriginal Australia. The report had been commissioned by the Keating government, but by the time it was finished Howard was in power. Witnesses to the commission had told stories of trauma, shedding light on some of the reasons for persistent dysfunction in Aboriginal communities. Very few Aboriginal families were untouched by the policies of child removal. The commission recommended that state and federal governments make apologies and restitution to the stolen generation. In the months that followed, all states issued apologies. Thousands of people signed 'sorry books', but the Howard government refused both an apology and compensation, suggesting instead that the commission had exaggerated the evidence—that there was no such thing as a stolen generation.

In May 1997, at the National Aboriginal Reconciliation Convention, at least one hundred Aboriginal delegates turned their backs on Howard as he thumped the lectern in angry response to talk of apologies and compensation. It was a low point in the relationship of government and Indigenous people. At about this time, Fraser and Ian Viner were talking. Fraser asked if it was true that children had been taken away from their parents as late as the 1950s, when Paul Hasluck—a man he had admired—was Minister for Territories. Viner replied that it was true. He remembers, 'Malcolm looked astonished. He said, "Well, the policy was never reported to the party room. I must look into it"'.

Some years later, researching a speech, Fraser burrowed into the documents and discovered ordinances from 1911 giving police wide powers to take Aboriginal 'half-caste' children into custody, and not only when they were being neglected or mistreated. Fraser read reports from the 1928 Queensland Protector of Aborigines

JW Bleakley, who asserted that it wasn't true, as generally thought, that 'half castes' were treated harshly in Aboriginal camps. On the contrary: they were happier if raised with other Aboriginals. Yet the removals continued. Fraser found documents from 1950 on the removal of 'half-caste' children from Wave Hill. Patrol Officer Evans reported to the Administrator that there had been 'distressing scenes the like of which I wish never to experience again'. Evans recommended that children should be left with their mothers at least until they were six. These documents proved that there was an awareness that the practice of removing children might be in breach of the Universal Declaration of Human Rights, which had by this time been adopted. There was pressure for a policy review, and there were recommendations that the practice of taking 'half-caste' children be abandoned. The matter went to the Minister for the Territories in February 1952. That minister was Paul Hasluck.

Here, Fraser found confirmation of what he had been told. The Administrator said that removal of 'partly coloured' children was in accord with assimilation and in the children's best interests. He recommended a policy which stipulated that any 'partly coloured' children could be removed if the Director of Native Affairs thought it in their best interests, but not unless the child was neglected, the mother willingly gave up the child or 'a painstaking attempt has been made to explain to the mother the advantages to be gained by the removal of the child'. The Administrator also recommended that no child under the age of four should be removed, except when it was neglected or in need of medical care. On this document Fraser found, in Hasluck's own writing, the unmistakeable evidence that he had endorsed the policy. 'Approved' was written under each clause, and in a handwritten amendment Hasluck had overriden the recommendation that only children over four years be taken: 'No age limit need be stated. The younger the child is at the time of removal the better for the child'. The fundamentals of the removal policy did not change, and it lingered on into the 1960s.[33] Fraser comments today, 'It would be interesting to know what Hasluck thought of that when he was Governor-General, in the 1970s'.

This led Fraser to his current position: the view that the moves his government took, while radical at the time, were not enough. He believes that the inhibition to real change, both at the time of his government and today, is a failure to come to terms with history. 'Some people accept that the history of settlement in Australia was brutal and bloody. Some people accept that there was dispossession, and that generations of children were taken from their families. Others either deny the history, or refuse to consider it. Non-Indigenous Australians need to do much more to come to grips with what happened and to understand that it creates obligations. It demands action in the present day to deal with the legacy.'

When the National Sorry Day committee was formed in 1998 Fraser became its co-patron, first with Lowitja O'Donoghue and then with the Aboriginal author and member of the stolen generation Doris Pilkington. He left that post in 2006 and became instead a co-patron of the national representative and advocacy organisation the Stolen Generations Alliance, again with O'Donoghue. In 2000, when hundreds of thousands of Australians streamed across the Sydney Harbour Bridge in a symbolic walk for reconciliation, Fraser was among them. He called on Howard to make the apology to the stolen generation. In the Olympic year, he said, 'Australia must not become an international pariah because of one person's blinkered vision'.[34]

Later that year, Fraser delivered the Vincent Lingiari Memorial Lecture, held to remember the Wave Hill activist that Fraser had met decades before when as Minister for Education he had travelled to the interior with Bill Wentworth. Fraser brought to his speech his historical research—the indisputable record of government decisions from the beginning of white settlement until his own time as a parliamentarian, all of it predicated on the belief that dying out or becoming 'like us' was the only future for Aboriginal Australians. At the time Fraser gave this speech, members of the stolen generation were fighting through the courts for compensation. The first test case, of Lorna Cubillo and Peter Gunner, had just been decided, with the government victorious. It was not disputed that the children had been subjected to cruel treatment, but child removal had been legal at the time, the judgement claimed. Fraser said that the law had been unjust, and that if the government had to fight its case on current laws it would lose every case. Therefore, what was needed was political and moral leadership: 'The injustice done to individuals was substantial. So many were tragically and traumatically affected. Surely it is reason enough to shut the doors of the courts and solve the issues politically'.

Now Fraser was not as worried by words like 'treaty' as his cabinet had been in the early 1980s. He noted that the Canadians were not frightened of such language. Terms like 'sovereignty', 'self-government' and 'self-determination' did not mean separateness; they meant giving Indigenous people the same control over their lives already enjoyed by other Australians.

> We have supported the Universal Declaration of Human Rights. We have ratified the International Covenant of Civil and Political Rights, the International Covenant on Economic, Social and Cultural Rights, the Convention on the Elimination of All Forms of Racial Discrimination and the Convention on the Rights of the Child. Did we mean it when we took these steps? Or were we trying to say: 'We ratified these instruments so that we can apply them to the rest of the world but they do not apply to Australia'?[35]

In another speech, Fraser examined the evidence. Was it inevitable that the situation would simply become worse in Indigenous Australia? Were the problems really intractable? Overseas experience said not. In Canada, land claims had been granted with cash settlements and administrative autonomy. In New Zealand, a reinvigorated Treaty of Waitangi had led to settlements of cash, land and autonomy. In Australia, the gap between Indigenous and non-Indigenous life expectancy was widening. In Canada and New Zealand, it was narrowing.

> Forty years ago in New Zealand, Canada and the USA, the gap was about fifteen years, while in Australia it was twenty years. Today in New Zealand it is five years; in Canada it is seven years, in the USA it is three and a half years. But in Australia the gap is still twenty years or more ... Australia has the competence, resources and goodwill to make the health improvements seen elsewhere. But we have become the home of unfunded policies, which are worse than useless because they give the illusion of action without the substance.

He quoted health experts who said that an extra $300 million per year in Aboriginal health would increase life expectancy by 30 per cent within a decade. But neither Labor nor the Coalition was prepared to commit these resources. The notion that more was spent on Aboriginal health than on the health of other Australians was a complete fiction, said Fraser. The idea that there is something uniquely intractable about despair and dysfunction in Aboriginal Australia was wrong, and implicitly racist. And, he said, the overseas experience suggested that any solution had to be grounded in freedom and self-management if it was to work.[36]

Fraser was dismayed when in 2005 the Howard government abolished the Aboriginal and Torres Strait Islander Commission without replacing it with anything else. Australia now lacked an elected national representative Aboriginal body, and remains today the only Western government with an Indigenous minority that does not have elected representation. Fraser says, 'How can you consult, how can you deliver policy and services, how can you advance self-determination when there isn't a mechanism for consultation, when there isn't anyone who can claim to be representative?' But self-determination was no longer part of government rhetoric; instead, there were the new terms 'mutual obligation', 'shared responsibility', 'mainstreaming' and 'normalisation'.

Then came the intervention.

In June 2007, as the interviews for this book were underway, the Howard government used the latest report cataloguing child abuse in Aboriginal communities to announce a national emergency. In truth, there had been an emergency for many years—at least since Fraser's own trip to the interior in 1978—but now the Howard government had decided to do away with consultation. The army was mobilised. Unprecedented powers were given to civilians and police. Welfare payments were to be garnisheed. To allow all this to be done, the Racial Discrimination Act, passed by the Whitlam government with bipartisan support, was suspended. The authors of the report that had prompted the intervention had recommended urgent action, with Northern Territory and federal governments collaborating in 'genuine consultation' with Aboriginal people. This recommendation was ignored. Quoting Fred Chaney, the report had recommended that action be locally based, not run by a centralised bureaucracy. This too was ignored.[37]

Fraser was one of the intervention's most vocal opponents. He did not deny—had never denied—the need for urgent action. He regretted his own government's failures in the area. Nor did he deny that when a community turns violent, the human rights of the victims—women and children chief among them—are invaded. But why, he asked, had so little planning been done? It was like a re-run of the equal pay decision, only without the justification of principle. 'Why are survey teams visiting Aboriginal communities only after the announcement of the plan? Normally assessments are made before policy is announced. Then there is a clear idea of how many doctors and nurses are required, and how much money will be needed.' Most Aboriginal communities still lacked adequate schools and teachers. What was the sense, then, of saying that all children should be in school?

By early 2008, it was clear that one of the consequences of the intervention was that Aboriginals dependent on alcohol were moving to the towns, and there were no resources to deal with them. The town camps were sinking further into despair. 'That was entirely predictable', said Fraser in one of the interviews for this book. 'Why didn't they plan for it?' More fundamentally, urgent though the problems were, any solution that did not respect human rights was bound to fail. Today, Fraser reaffirms his foundation belief. Human beings, including Aboriginal Australians, must be free to determine their own lives. Freedom may be complex. Liberal ideas may need to be applied differently in different cultures. Close attention needs to be paid to how money is distributed, and how government intervention affects the authority of local leaders, but, 'I refuse to believe that there aren't local leaders there who if they were listened to would step up'.

So what would Fraser do if he had his time in government again? Partly, he says, it is about money. Self-management or self-determination was not meant to signify simply a withdrawal of government; the intention was to encourage and help Aboriginal leaders to manage their own communities' affairs. When self-determination and self-management became government policy in the 1970s, there needed to be many, many more dollars spent on training and supporting Aboriginal people to manage their own affairs—and this needed to be done for decades, not years. Would this have been possible in a time of razor gangs and cut-backs? 'It would have been difficult. It was difficult to do what we did do. But we should have done it.' If Fraser had his time again, he would make sure the issue of a treaty remained on the agenda, and he would further consider moves for positive discrimination in employment. Mostly, he would persist, plan, listen to Aboriginal people, review policy regularly and persist some more.

Would more radical changes have been possible? Fraser believes probably not at the time. Particularly in Queensland and Western Australia, federal government moves were always likely to be challenged in the courts. Any moves to change the Constitution would certainly have been resisted. The state departments of Aboriginal affairs in any case had more people on the ground and could have effectively undermined any action with which Charles Court and Joh Bjelke-Petersen disagreed. Moves for a treaty, for more land rights and for compensation were probably not politically possible at the time.

* * *

In 2007, the Howard government was defeated. As the research for this book continued, Kevin Rudd was preparing to make an apology to the stolen generation. Fraser spoke about this to both his own side of politics and the new Minister for Aboriginal Affairs, Jenny Macklin. He was trying to convince the Leader of the Opposition Brendan Nelson to be part of the apology, to endorse it. He was trying to convince Macklin that compensation should form part of the apology. Did he really think this would happen, that it was politically possible? 'It has to be', he said. 'Without compensation there will just be more anger, and no healing.' But the word came back quickly enough: compensation was not being considered.

Fraser also tried to convince Macklin to delay the apology, so as to make time to organise it as a major national event supported by a public education campaign. He wanted ethnic groups, schools and the Returned Services League all to have their own apology ceremonies. He wanted Australians to better understand their own history and what it required of them. He wanted the entire nation to focus on what was being said and why. He wanted to see real political leadership. In the end, the government opted for speed over inclusiveness. Nevertheless, the apology was a significant and moving national event.

Fraser was invited with other former prime ministers to go to Canberra to witness the apology. It was a fine day, and a fine speech by Rudd, Fraser thought. He was disappointed with Nelson's speech, but relieved that part of what he had wanted had occurred: the apology was bipartisan. Afterwards, the press photographers captured an extraordinary moment. Gough Whitlam and Malcolm

Fraser—two tall men—were standing together, and Whitlam was leaning on Fraser's shoulder. The photograph was prominent in the next day's newspapers. Away from the main stage, here was another small moment of reconciliation.

A few days later, Fraser participated in one of the interviews for this book. How had that moment with Whitlam come about? 'Well, he needed someone to lean on', said Fraser, slightly impatient at the question. 'He is an old man, you know.' Fraser was seventy-seven. Whitlam was ninety. It was many years since they had been enemies. They agreed on many things; Aboriginal Australia had always been one of those things. So too their mutual passion for human beings, whatever their race, to be able to live in dignity and freedom.

Freedom is not just a word. It is a complicated, living principle. Human rights are not an add-on, able to be ignored in an emergency. For Fraser they are the solution, the touchstone of human advancement. They may require different things in different circumstances, but they remain the foundation for action.

13

Leadership

Immigration and Refugees

On 28 April 1976 a single vessel slipped unnoticed into Darwin harbour, carrying five unexpected travellers. The arrivals barely made the news, although they were refugees from the aftermath of one of the most divisive wars in Australia's history. They were processed quickly, given social security benefits, and allowed to stay. Soon there was a trickle of desperate souls making their way to Australia's shores, and then the trickle turned into waves. For periods towards the end of 1977, Indochinese boat people were arriving in Australia almost daily—sometimes in several boats a day. There was no reason to think they would stop coming.

'I am not able to predict the limits of the flow. It could amount to hundreds of thousands of people', the Minister for Immigration Michael MacKellar told cabinet in November 1978.[1] Enormous numbers of Vietnamese had fled their homes since the defeat of South Vietnam. They were crowding refugee camps in South-East Asia. First the boat people came to Australia in tiny fishing boats. By the middle of 1978, they were arriving in record numbers; Australia had never seen anything like it before. By 1979, Vietnam seemed to be deliberately exporting its unwanted citizens—particularly ethnic Chinese and small businesspeople who were out of sympathy with the communist regime.

Headlines appeared in Australian newspapers suggesting that the refugees would bring problems and political strife. The Chief Secretary of the Northern Territory, Paul Everingham, accused the federal government of 'irresponsibility' for allowing Australia to be exposed to the risk of disease.[2] It was said that the Fraser government was losing control. Questions were asked. Were these people really refugees? Many of them had no papers. Could they be trusted? Did they deserve Australia's compassion?

Papers and submissions came to cabinet suggesting urgent action. Perhaps Australia was too 'hospitable', it was suggested. Perhaps the boat people should be denied social security benefits. Perhaps boats should be turned back—although this would be abhorrent. Perhaps 'discreet inquiries' should be made of the Northern Territory government about suitable locations for a refugee 'reception centre' or 'holding centre' in an area remote from capital cities, to which the boat people could be sent.

In May 1978, the Secretary of the Department of Immigration and Ethnic Affairs LWB Engeldow told MacKellar that the boat people threatened the orderly refugee program. There were only two options: stopping the boat movements in transit or sending arrivals to

> a reception centre to be established somewhere in Australia where they can be held pending further decisions ... In the present circumstances ... it is doubtful if we can much longer afford to adopt a more in sorrow than in anger approach to boat arrivals in Darwin ... Indeed many would judge that the situation is already out of control ... These people are 'queue jumpers' who are virtually self-selecting themselves for migration to Australia. For the most part they have rightly judged that once here they have little or no prospect of being turned away.[3]

Engeldow saw the reception centre as a last resort, but likely to be necessary. MacKellar asked for urgent in-principle approval to establish the reception centre. In a joint cabinet submission with Peacock, he said the intake of Indochinese refugees was 'significantly altering the ethnic composition of Australia's migration intake'. A fifth of that year's intake would be from Asia. Only a small minority of the refugees being settled in Australia had arrived by boat: most were coming through proper processes, selected in the refugee camps of Thailand and Malaysia. Yet the boats were the focus of publicity and fear.[4] By June 1978, 1037 boat people had arrived in Australia. None had been sent back or refused entry. Labor's spokesman on immigration Dr Moss Cass wrote an article for *The Australian* describing the boat people as 'queue jumpers' and saying their arrival should not be tolerated.[5]

By the middle of 1979, the documents coming to cabinet were apocalyptic in their predictions. One memorandum, apparently from within the Department of Immigration and Ethnic Affairs, said:

> If the refugee problem were to get out of control it would impose very serious strains on the unity and character of Australian society ... This new situation has all the ingredients for one of the most controversial and divisive issues in Australia's history. A hostile public reaction, stimulated by traditional fears of the 'yellow peril' and by concern about present high levels of unemployment, could not only jeopardise government attempts to resolve the refugee problem but could also cause a head-on collision between domestic public opinion and Australia's foreign policy interests. If that were to happen Australian governments would face impossible choices in sustaining an effective foreign policy in the region.[6]

All the rhetoric and the harsh solutions that have been used in our own time to deal with refugees were available to, and being urged upon, the Fraser government. There was the term 'queue jumpers'. There was the option of compulsory detention. There was the suggestion that the military be used to intercept the boats and turn them back. Yet the Fraser government chose differently. Fraser remembers the idea of the reception centre coming before cabinet. He says that MacKellar did not push it. It originated within the Department of Immigration and Ethnic Affairs. 'We disposed of it in about thirty seconds. I thought it was a piece of racist barbarism.' He goes on, 'There was a hard core within the immigration department that opposed a genuine compassionate and humanitarian response. It was ultra-conservative and reactionary with a strong racist streak'. Fraser suspects that the advice his government received from the department was much the same as that received by the Hawke, Keating and Howard governments. The difference was not in the advice, in the gravity of the crisis or in public attitudes, but in the choices his government made.

The archival record confirms that, in paragraphs marked by Fraser, his own department consistently advised against the ideas of a reception centre and of refusing refugees social security. Desperate people would not be deterred by being refused benefits, Fraser's advisers said. As for the reception centre: there were 'grave reservations'. It was not a viable option. It would damage Australia's international reputation. Most important, it was not humane or in accord with Australia's international obligations to refugees. On a Department of Immigration paper asserting that it was not possible to tell whether people without papers were genuine refugees, one of Fraser's advisers wrote that nor was it possible to prove that they *weren't* refugees.[7] Fraser says today, 'Of course people arriving in those circumstances weren't going to have proper papers, and the department would know that perfectly well'. The United Nations Refugee Convention, signed by the Menzies government in 1954, specifically prohibited the imposition of penalties on those seeking asylum for arriving without permission or papers. The Fraser government observed its international obligations.[8]

Yet the idea of compulsory detention did not die easily. In September 1978, as the boats continued to arrive, a committee of cabinet agreed to contingency planning for 'possible sites and operational modalities' for a centre.[9] Fraser says he made sure no such planning was done. 'If you do the planning, then you have opened the door to the idea.' In 1979 and early 1980 the whole of cabinet considered suggestions that the Darwin quarantine station should be used as a 'refugee holding centre', and that 'discreet inquiries' be made about other possible sites. But each time the idea raised its head, it was rejected.[10] 'It was kicking around for a while', Fraser remembers, 'but I wouldn't have a bar of it'.

In opposition, Fraser had argued that Australia had a moral obligation to take 'many thousands of refugees' from Vietnam. In government, the solution chosen for the problem of 'queue jumpers' was to attempt to make sure there was indeed a queue, and that it was working properly and fairly. The solution to people coming in the back door was to open the front door wider.

MacKellar argued in his submissions to cabinet that if refugees in the camps believed they had a chance of getting into Australia through proper processes, they would not risk their lives at sea. As the number of boat people arriving increased, so too did the Australian government's willingness to accept more people. In decision after decision, cabinet gradually increased the quota of refugees Australia would take. More Department of Immigration personnel were sent to the refugee camps to process applicants. There were good reasons for this other than the purely humanitarian. Australia was able to select refugees, and gained credit with the other countries of South-East Asia. But Australia's approach went well beyond the token. Fraser says, 'I can remember talking to Michael MacKellar about it and saying, "We've just got an ethical obligation. We were fighting alongside these people in Vietnam"'.

In 1979, Asia was the largest regional source of immigrants to Australia, at 29 per cent of the intake. Most immigrants were refugees or entering under the family reunion program to join relatives who had arrived as refugees.[11] By the end of the Fraser government, almost seventy thousand Indochinese refugees had settled in the country, only 2059 of whom were boat people. Per head of population, Australia had taken the largest number of Indochinese refugees of any country in the world. In absolute terms, Australia was fourth in the world, behind the United States (468 463), Canada (79 908) and France (79 684).[12]

The Whitlam government had swept away the last vestiges of the White Australia policy, but had at the same time greatly reduced immigration. In 1975, Australia's total immigration was only 52 748—the lowest since World War II. More people emigrated from Australia than arrived to settle, meaning there was a net migration loss. The Fraser government continued an immigration policy that did not discriminate on the grounds of race, and at the same time increased immigration to an average of ninety thousand a year over its term. This, together with its compassionate approach to refugees, meant that it was Fraser's government that gave substance to the ending of the White Australia policy. Entry of refugees together with family reunion programs meant that by 1995 there were 238 000 first- and second-generation Indochinese living in Australia—more than 1 per cent of the population.[13] The Fraser government changed the ethnic mix of the Australian population forever, and its reform of policy concerning both refugees and immigration more generally remains one of its most important legacies.

* * *

The advice and the fear that surrounded the arrival of boat people did not dissipate with time. Nine years after Fraser lost power, the Labor government, faced with more desperate people arriving on Australia's shores, accepted the view that reception centres were needed for refugees, although now they were more frankly termed 'detention centres'. Those entering the country without a valid visa were compulsorily detained, usually in places remote from legal and compassionate aid. The Howard government continued and refined the policy. Under Howard, the term 'queue jumpers' formed part of the election rhetoric of government ministers. Australians were encouraged to feel affronted and threatened by the refugees. Between 1999 and 2001, over two thousand children were locked up inside immigration detention centres. The centres became desperate places. There were demonstrations, suicide attempts, hunger strikes and the sewing together of lips. Detention, the government said, was necessary.

On 24 August 2001, at dawn, 433 Afghan refugees were rescued from a sinking fishing boat in international waters by the Norwegian container ship MV *Tampa*. The Howard government refused the vessel entry to Australia, denying our country's obligations under international law. When the captain of the *Tampa* nevertheless entered Australian waters, his passengers suffering from dehydration and dysentery, Australia sent troops to board the vessel and threatened the captain with prosecution as a people smuggler. The *Tampa* affair led to the so-called 'Pacific solution', in which refugees were sent to detention camps constructed in Nauru and Papua New Guinea. The constitutions of those countries, which had been drawn up with the help of Australian lawyers, contained guarantees of human rights, including that people should not be indefinitely detained without charge and should have the full protection of the law.[14] Now Australia was collaborating in the breach of those provisions. Yet in time nearly all of those dealt with under the Pacific solution were found to be genuine refugees. Unauthorised arrivals who were eventually accepted into Australia were issued with temporary protection visas, denying them certainty and social security benefits.

The Human Rights and Equal Opportunity Commission—successor to the Human Rights Commission set up by the Fraser government—held an inquiry into the mandatory detention of children and found that the government's actions amounted to 'cruel, inhumane and degrading treatment'. Australia was in breach

[top left] Malcolm Fraser's paternal grandmother Anna Fraser with his father, Neville. *[top right]* Malcolm Fraser's paternal grandfather, Sir Simon Fraser (1832–1919). 'Immigrant from Nova Scotia', contractor, pastoralist and politician. *[bottom left]* Malcolm Fraser's maternal grandmother, Amy Woolf, with his mother, Una. *[bottom right]* Malcolm Fraser's maternal grandfather, Louis Woolf.

[top left] Malcolm Fraser's parents, Neville and Una, on their wedding day in 1927. The reception was held in the home of Una's Hordern relations. *[top right]* Malcolm aged about five, with a toy kangaroo. *[bottom]* Una with Lorri and baby Malcolm.

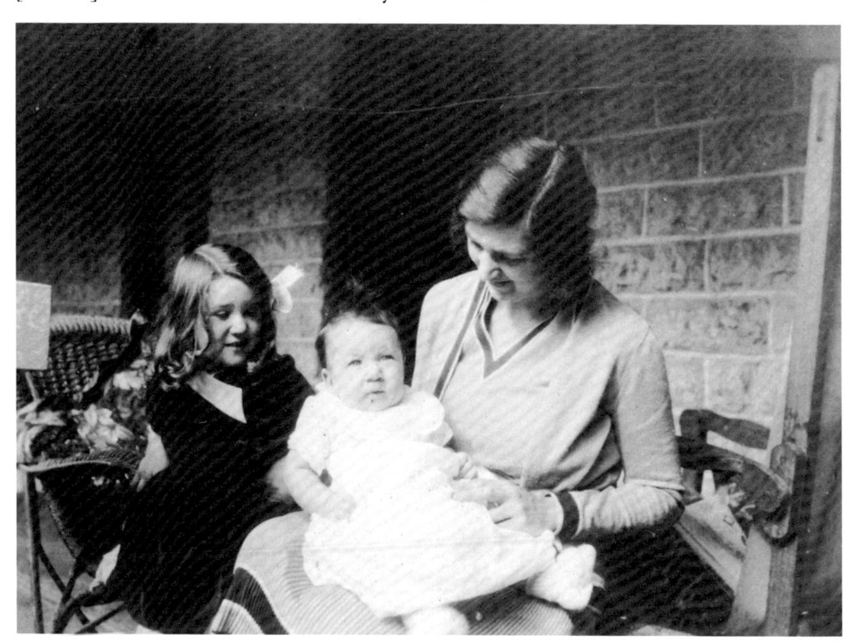

[top] Ten years old, and free. Malcolm at Balpool Nyang with his pet bird, Chakra. *[bottom]* Picnic at Balpool-Nyang. Malcolm, Neville, Una and Lorri.

[top] The Oxford undergraduate with his first car, a Jowett Javelin, c. 1950. *[bottom]* The candidate for Wannon. Fraser on Nareen in 1954.

[top] Tamie and Malcolm. Their wedding was held the day after the closing ceremony for the Melbourne Olympics—9 December 1956. *[bottom]* Tamie and Malcolm with the children. Left to right: Angela, Mark, Phoebe and Hugh.

[top] Mud everywhere
Fraser as Minister for Army visits the troops at Nui Dat, Vietnam, in June 1966, shortly after the base was established. *[bottom]* Guest speaker on School of the Air. Fraser as Minister for Education in Alice Springs, April 1968.

[top] Coalition partners Doug Anthony and Malcolm Fraser at Casino. Anthony said to Fraser, 'Here, Malcolm, you'd better take the reins'.
[bottom] Spoofing the spoof: Bruce Postle's front-page picture sending up the nasty campaign by Fraser's enemies.

[top left] The Leader of the Opposition and his wife. Taken at Nareen on 22 March 1975—the day after Fraser defeated Snedden to become leader of the Liberal Party. *[top right]* The notes Fraser took of the telephone call he had from John Kerr on the morning of 11 November 1975. They read 1) Double Dissolution Bills 2) Caretaker 3) No policy changes 4) No Royal Commission 5) + supply 5) Dissolution today. Fraser signed the notes and gave the time of the call. They are on the back of the agenda for the joint party meeting, which was about to begin when Fraser took the call. *[bottom]* The first Fraser government. Ministers after swearing in. Left to right: Malcolm Fraser, Governor-General Sir John Kerr and Deputy Prime Minister Doug Anthony. 13 November 1975.

[top] Malcolm and Tamie on the night of the December 1975 election victory, at the Southern Cross Hotel in Melbourne. *[bottom]* Malcolm and Tamie read the morning newspapers following the Liberal victory in December 1975, Windsor Hotel, Melbourne.

[top] Fishing with Galarrwuy Yunupingu in April 1978. This fishing trip resulted in Fraser facing criminal charges. *[bottom]* In the Todd River with Charlie Perkins and local Aboriginals, April 1978.

[top] Attending a state funeral for a true liberal: Robert Menzies died in May 1978. *[bottom]* With US President Jimmy Carter at the White House in 1980.

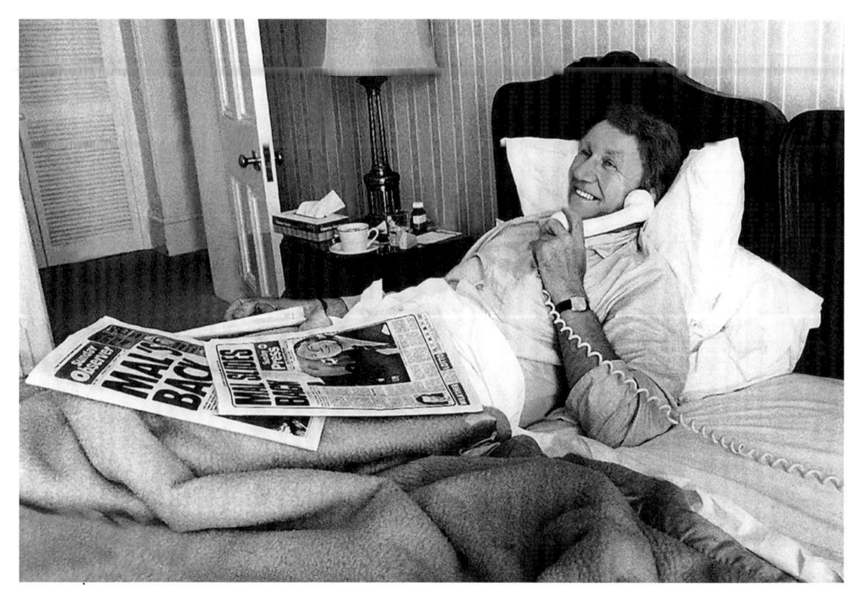

[top] Fraser on the morning after his third election victory in October 1980. *[bottom left]* Engaging the mind, not the heart. With British Prime Minister Margaret Thatcher at Yarralumla at the time of the Melbourne CHOGM in 1981. *[bottom right]* Fraser with the President of the United States Ronald Reagan, in May 1982.

[top] The 1981 Commonwealth Heads of Government Meeting in the Melbourne Town Hall. *[bottom]* Bringing the region together. Indian Prime Minister Indira Gandhi at the 1981 Commonwealth Heads of Government Regional Meeting, which was a Fraser initiative.

[top] Fraser leaves the Southern Cross Hotel in Melbourne after losing the federal election on 11 March 1983. *[bottom left]* Olusegun Obasanjo on the whites-only beach at Port Elizabeth in South Africa, February 1986. *[bottom right]* Oliver Tambo and Fraser at Nareen, 5 April 1987.

[top] Malcolm and Phoebe at the launch of the CARE Emergency Response Unit in Sydney, 20 May 1993. *[bottom left]* CARE Australia became known for emergency relief. It was one of the first agencies to respond to the Bangladesh floods in 1989 and to the famine in Somalia in 1992. *[bottom right]* Steve Pratt, the freed CARE worker, with Fraser and UN Secretary-General Kofi Annan in February 2000 at the Canberra Hyatt.

[top] Sharing a platform with Whitlam in 1991 during the 'Maintain Your Age' campaign. *[bottom]* Reconciliation. Former prime ministers Bob Hawke, Gough Whitlam, Malcolm Fraser, Paul Keating and Prime Minister Kevin Rudd on the day of the national apology to the stolen generations, 13 February 2008.

of its international obligations. Petro Georgiou, once Fraser's chief adviser on immigration and ethnic affairs, led a back-bench revolt that succeeded in softening some of the compulsory detention measures. His political career never recovered.

The Howard government claimed that there was no alternative to mandatory detention for boat people, yet, at the same time as these things were happening, most asylum seekers were at liberty in the Australian community. These were people who were 'authorised arrivals'. Most arrived by air on tourist or student visas. Once in Australia, they claimed to be refugees. They were not detained. Most received a bridging visa and some were allowed to work. In 2001—the time of the *Tampa* crisis—only 19 per cent of these 'authorised arrivals' were found to be genuine refugees, but, of those who arrived 'unauthorised' by boat, 95 per cent were found to be genuine. Numbers varied year by year, but the pattern remained the same. Australia was running one humane system for those who arrived by air and who were least likely to be genuine refugees, and another inhumane one that applied to the most desperate and the most likely to be genuine.[15] 'We will decide who comes to this country and the circumstances in which they come', said Prime Minister John Howard in the lead-up to the 2001 election, making the boat people an election issue. Through all this, the government's popularity rose.

What happened to Australia between the years 1978 and 2001? The difference, Fraser believes, was political leadership. The scale of the challenge that Australia faced from refugees during the Howard years was less than it had been when Fraser was in government. During the term of the Howard government, the number of refugees settling in Australia peaked at 13 235 a year, or about 10.5 per cent of our total migrant intake. In 2001, the year of the *Tampa* crisis and the beginning of the Pacific solution, we took in just 7640, or about 7 per cent of our total migrant intake. Yet during the last three years of the Fraser government, Australia provided a home for about twenty thousand refugees a year, the great bulk of them Indochinese.

Refugees were close to 20 per cent of all migrants.[16] Our population in 1981 was just 14.6 million; at the height of the *Tampa* crisis, it was 19 million.

Did the refugees taken in during Fraser's time damage Australia? Most people would say not. Racism is always with us. Like most new arrivals, the Indochinese faced problems and prejudice, and some remain disadvantaged, but there was no endemic racial violence or discord, no economic chaos or social collapse. Today, Indochinese refugees and their descendants top our university courses and are among our leading professionals and businesspeople. Fraser says, 'People are never going to say yes to a significant change in migration which is likely to result in people they do not know, whose background they do not understand, coming to this country in significant numbers. Governments are always going to have to set the example if you want an enlightened policy to be pursued'. Immigration policy, and refugee policy in particular, says Fraser, is always going to require political leadership, as well as optimism, reassurance and encouragement from leaders. 'I knew if I asked the people whether we should take in the Vietnamese, they would say no. I also thought that if we did it and explained how and why, then it would be accepted.' He sees the record of his government as part of a history of nation-building through immigration.

Australia had first settled large numbers of refugees after World War II. At that stage the only way it could be done, Fraser says, was by assuring the union movement that the White Australia policy would not be changed. There was controversy, prejudice and opposition, yet the migration program succeeded. The postwar refugees and displaced people were not demonised; the government adopted instead the optimistic term 'new Australians'. The migrants changed the public perception of Australia's future. 'I don't suppose before the event in the late 1940s the people of Melbourne would ever have voted in favour of becoming one of the largest Greek cities in the world, but now most people are proud of the fact.' In Fraser's own time as Prime Minister, 'We had a deliberate approach in what we said in public. We never spoke about fear. We always spoke of tolerance, of diversity, and we planned carefully'.

Fears about settling Asian refugees were not confined to the general public; there were people inside the government who were worried as well. Fraser remembers that at one of the first cabinet meetings at which the commitment to take large numbers of Indochinese refugees was discussed, John Howard sat silently through the debate, but 'sidled up to me afterwards in a corridor and said, "We're not going to take too many of these people, are we?"

'And I just looked at him and said, "John, we have just had a debate in cabinet".

'And he said, "Yes, but we're not going to take too many of them, are we? It is just for show, isn't it?"

'I said, "Look, what you say to me in the corridor is meaningless. If you want to say something, you can say it in cabinet. If you want to re-open the debate, you can say it in cabinet". But he never did'.

Fraser's recollection of this encounter was first aired in January 2008, when the 1977 cabinet records were released to the public under the thirty-year rule. Howard denied that he had ever said these words, protesting that at the time of the key decisions on refugees he hadn't even been in cabinet. This is true. He was Minister for Consumer and Business Affairs, and in the outer ministry. However, junior ministers often sat in on cabinet meetings. The attendance register for the main cabinet meeting at which refugee policy was discussed, on 3 May 1977, shows that Howard was there.[17] In any case, it is not news that Howard did not share Fraser's conviction that Australia could draw strength from diversity. In 1988, as Leader of the Opposition, Howard said publicly that he wanted to see the rate of Asian immigration 'slowed down a little' in the interests of social cohesion. (Howard later said that he had been wrong, and that he had changed his mind.)[18]

* * *

Fraser had since his first days in politics advocated immigration as a means of boosting Australia's population. In his earliest speeches and radio addresses he said that he hoped to see Australia reach a population of twenty-five million in his lifetime—an ambition he is likely to fulfil. As a minister in the Gorton government he had become the first federal politician to use the word 'multiculturalism'.[19] In this he was breaking with the Anglocentric and assimilationist traditions of his party. He was closer to Whitlam than to many on his own side of politics. The Whitlam government had developed the concept of multiculturalism, with the Minister for Immigration Al Grassby its passionate advocate; yet, at the same time, Whitlam cut immigration and all but dismantled the Department of Immigration. It was therefore the Fraser government that gave multiculturalism form and definition. A report by the Australian Ethnic Affairs Council, which had been set up by the Fraser government, defined multiculturalism as 'cultural pluralism'. Australia, the council said, should work towards 'not a oneness, but a unity, not a similarity, but a composite, not a melting pot, but a voluntary bond of dissimilar people sharing a common political and institutional structure'.[20] It was this definition and aspiration that guided government policies from both sides of politics for the next twenty years—until repudiated by the Howard government. During Fraser's time, most advocates of multiculturalism were Labor supporters dismayed by the events of 1975. They were often reluctant to recognise what was achieved in the Fraser years. It is only through the prism of the Howard years, and because of Fraser's vocal opposition to Australia's more recent treatment of refugees, that some have been prepared to reassess.

Fraser says today that he was well aware that the decision to take in large numbers of Asian refugees and their families was a fundamental one, changing the face of Australia and with the potential for vicious electoral backlash. 'Every word I said on the issue in public was to try to say that we could do it, that we were strong enough, that we should be proud of our record as a migrant nation, and that we would be made stronger by diversity.' He believed that sectarianism was an ever-present threat. He remembered the way his own father had believed the things that Prime Minister Billy Hughes had said about Catholics during World War I. Politicians, he believes, have a superior duty to speak with 'discretion and respect' on issues of race and religion.

In speeches during his prime ministership, Fraser asserted that Australia had 'an enormous capacity for social change' and had 'developed a maturity and tolerance that few would have dared predict in 1945'. Migrants had strengthened the country with

> their energies, their commitment and their children ... In multiculturalism we have forged a radically innovative basis upon which we can respond as a nation to Australia's diversity, to its challenges and opportunities. It is a basis which offers at once both an understanding of the present and vision of the future built upon that understanding.[21]

Diversity, Fraser said, in speech after speech, was to be embraced; and he used every opportunity to encourage the nation to have confidence and pride in its ability to do so.

One of the first things the Fraser government did after its election victory in 1975 was to declare that the Department of Immigration, dismantled under Whitlam, was to be reassembled. It was also given a new name—the Department of Immigration and Ethnic Affairs—with the last two words reflecting that the department was now responsible not only for letting people in, but also for helping them after they had arrived. Fraser set up an ethnic affairs unit within the Department of Prime Minister and Cabinet, which worked closely with his adviser, Petro Georgiou, to keep an eye on the department and organise policy priorities. By the end of the Fraser government's term, immigration policy and the relevant machinery of government had been completely recast.

The government also set up a Population and Immigration Council with a broad membership, including Bob Hawke, as

President of the Australian Council of Trade Unions, and George Polites, the Executive Director of the Australian Council of Employers Federation. The council's first task was to write a green paper, which was tabled on 17 March 1977. It estimated that Australia had the capacity to absorb an annual intake of migrants of about one hundred thousand, and up to two hundred thousand in the future, with the aim of bringing the population to 19.3 million by 2001. (The report's calculations proved accurate: at the 2001 census, Australia's population was nineteen million.) 'The major constraint on the acceptance of such a population increase would be community attitudes rather than the availability of resources', the council said.[22] The government set about making sure that community attitudes were as favourable as possible. The green paper was used to encourage Australians to think and talk about immigration. Seminars were held around the nation. By the time the new immigration policy was announced in mid 1978, it had already been the subject of a government-sponsored national conversation. The policy anticipated an annual intake of at least seventy thousand, and laid out nine principles governing who would be allowed into the country. Migrants had to provide some benefit to Australia, 'although this will not always be a major consideration in the case of refugees and family members'; they should not jeopardise social cohesiveness and harmony; and, while they were expected to integrate, they would be 'given the opportunity to preserve and disseminate their ethnic heritage'. From now on immigration would be planned on a triennial basis with annual reviews and adjustments, and with targets linked to government programs for training and assistance. There would also be an appeals process for immigration decisions—part of the new machinery of administrative law and another means to check the integrity of departmental processes.[23]

In the first year of the Fraser government, Vietnamese refugees were not much in the public mind, although they were flooding the refugee camps of South-East Asia and Malaysia, and Australia was under increasing pressure to take in more. The Department of

Foreign Affairs briefed cabinet on the impact that Whitlam's grudging approach was having on Australia's international reputation.[24] In January 1976, just weeks after the election that brought Fraser to power, Michael MacKellar announced that Australia would take an extra 800 refugees from camps in Thailand. He also reversed an obnoxious provision of the Whitlam government under which nine South Vietnamese refugees settled in Australia had been required to sign an undertaking not to engage in political activity as a condition of entry.[25] The government declared an amnesty to illegal immigrants. A total of 8614 people applied for amnesty and nearly all were accepted.

The government adopted a compassionate approach to refugees fleeing East Timor and the war in Lebanon. For the Lebanese, normal entry criteria applying to migrants were relaxed, and 4000 people were allowed in. Nine out of ten were Muslims, whereas previous migrants from Lebanon had been mainly Christians. This was done despite the recognition that many of the migrants would face extra problems. In September 1976, MacKellar told cabinet that large numbers were unskilled or semi-skilled, and as a result unemployment was likely to rise. For every one person admitted as a refugee, three came in under family reunion programs. Cabinet agreed that a requirement be introduced that Lebanese refugees live in Australia for at least twelve months before bringing in family members, and Fraser's department agreed that this was 'a good compromise between compassionate considerations and the potential dangers involved in poor health standards and false claims of … relationship and possible entry of terrorists'.[26] Within months, MacKellar recommended that, due to the 'declining quality' of applicants for refugee status in Lebanon, the normal entry requirements be reimposed. Cabinet agreed. Already, the Department of Immigration said, there were problems emerging in Sydney including overcrowding and unemployment.[27]

In recent times, some in the media have blamed the Fraser government's intake of Lebanese Muslim refugees for continuing problems in the Lebanese community.[28] There is evidence that

Lebanese Muslims have had trouble finding work and establishing themselves on an equal footing with other Australians—although the second generation is doing better.[29] But those who focus on the Lebanese forget the context. The unemployment figures for the Lebanese are only slightly worse than for Vietnamese migrants, who do not attract as much negative media attention. The Vietnamese and Lebanese are two of the most recently arrived migrant groups in Australia. They were settled just before the economy was restructured, with many unskilled jobs disappearing as tariffs were dismantled. This is one of the reasons for the focus of later governments on skilled migration. The Lebanese Muslims don't threaten our way of life. The absolute numbers of unemployed are small. At the 2001 census, there were only about 6500 unemployed Lebanese-born Australians. The problems of the Lebanese are not to do with their culture or their religion; they are a small part of bigger national issues to do with unskilled employment. There is no reason to think that their children and children's children will not overcome disadvantage, unless we allow prejudice to get in the way.[30]

The Lebanese and Vietnamese were refugees from particularly bloody conflicts. By letting them in, Australia probably saved their lives. So was it wrong to do so? Fraser says that if there was a failure of government in those early months it was in resettlement programs and planning. The proper approach to problems of integration, he says, is to find out what the problems are and what can be done about them, rather than to conclude that 'bad' people have been allowed in, or that it was wrong to show compassion.

The month after the Lebanese problems were aired in Fraser's cabinet, a Senate standing committee report examining refugee policy was released. It was scathing of the Whitlam government's approach to Vietnamese refugees, but also criticised the lack of refugee policy more generally. There was 'irrefutable evidence of [a] complete lack of policy for the acceptance of people into Australia as refugees rather than as normal migrants', the report said. The Department of Immigration had failed to provide any extra help to newly arrived refugees. The recommendation was for urgent action.[31] Fraser needed no persuading.

Before the Senate committee report was tabled, and in the same month that the problems of Lebanese refugees had been brought to cabinet, Fraser wrote to MacKellar instructing him to bring to cabinet a 'comprehensive and consistent' policy to allow for a continued intake of refugees. The resulting document was adopted in May 1977. For the first time, the policy made it clear that Australia intended to be in the front line of international responses to refugee situations, and that it would take in large numbers.[32] The taking in and settling of refugees would be a continuous process, with 'quick and decisive' responses to international crises and special administrative arrangements within the Department of Immigration, including in resettlement programs. The Fraser government's adoption of the refugee policy marked the beginning of a dedicated humanitarian program backed by a system of settlement support. Previously, there had been ad hoc decision-making, crisis by crisis.

Within months of the policy being adopted, the trickle of boat people from Indochina had turned into continuous waves, and MacKellar was telling cabinet that it was urgently necessary to increase the numbers that Australia was accepting and send more immigration officers to the refugee camps of Asia. Over the months that followed, the quota for numbers of refugees to be accepted was lifted many times. An important part of the policy was to 'internationalise' the response, encouraging other nations to lift their intakes. Australia became the fourth-largest contributor of funds to the United Nations High Commissioner for Refugees, the United Nations' refugee agency.

* * *

The Department of Immigration and Ethnic Affairs grew in strength and importance. Fraser, though, was not impressed by its culture. He feared that too many of the department's officers held attitudes that dated from the days of the White Australia policy. He abhorred the submissions arguing for harsh treatment of Indochinese boat people. He was suspicious of the department's attitudes to the Lebanese 'Too many of the department were assimilationists.'

Taking in migrants challenges a society on many levels. Fraser believed that if Australia was to absorb more migrants harmoniously, it was essential that they had real equality of opportunity: this was not just idealism but hard-nosed realism. 'If particular groups feel that they and their children are condemned, whether through legal or other arrangements, to occupy the worst jobs and housing, to suffer the poorest health and education, then the societies in which they live are embarking on a path that will cost them dearly', he said in 1981. Attitudes would harden. Strife would result. Multiculturalism *required* equality of opportunity, and ensuring this was the job of government. The problems of the Lebanese refugees had been the government's responsibility as well as that of the individuals concerned, Fraser believed.

> The less constructively a society responds to its own diversity, the less capable it becomes of doing so. Its reluctance to respond, fuelled by the fear of encouraging division, becomes a self-fulfilling prophecy—the erosion of national cohesion is a result not of the fact of diversity but of its denial and suppression.[33]

Fraser had had his first lesson in the problems faced by migrants when he was Shadow Minister for Industrial Relations, during the Snedden years. He had received his education at the hands of two leading lights in the Australian Greek Welfare Association: Spiro Moraitis and George Papadopoulos. Moraitis remembers, 'We had been told he was very open-minded about new Australians'. They approached Fraser in his office, and later took him on a tour of the programs they were running—all without government assistance. There were English-language classes and basic training on how to live in Australian society. Fraser heard about the particular problems of women at home, who often didn't have the same opportunities to learn English as their husbands and children. In time, they would be shut out of family conversations as the others began to speak English at home. He heard about the isolation and loneliness of many migrants. Ever since, Fraser had thought that this was an area in which government should act. He had made it a personal mission.

At about the same time as he met Moraitis and Papadopoulos, Fraser encountered another man who became crucial to his record in government. Frank Galbally was one of Australia's leading criminal lawyers, a Catholic former seminarian, 'silver-haired, silver-tongued, with a soft heart and the ability to mesmerise a jury with his oratory and his flair for the theatrical'.[34] Galbally had a reputation for defending the underdog. He had been an active supporter of Labor for many years, but had become disillusioned with the Whitlam government. He later wrote in his autobiography that he became 'non-political' for a time, but 'was brought back to political consciousness by the plight of migrants'. He was 'not overly enamoured' by the Liberal Party's leadership or policies during the Snedden era. 'However, after a great deal of discussion, certain gentlemen and myself approached Malcolm Fraser—a rising figure within the Liberal Party—and urged him to challenge the then leadership of the federal opposition. He did this and became leader of both the opposition and the Liberal Party.' Fraser invited Galbally to his flat in South Yarra, and asked him if he would join the Liberal Party. Galbally recalled:

> I raised with him the question of policy towards migrants, a central concern of mine. I was particularly concerned about policy relating to the arrival of migrants here and their continued presence in Australia. He himself was clearly interested in improving government assistance to migrants; and so we reached an agreement that, if he were to become Prime Minister, he would look very carefully at the deficiencies that I described. The question of my joining the party again arose and I responded, 'Well, not at

> the moment, but give me some time'. He agreed to do so. I then considered the position very carefully and upon the understanding that my action would not be made public until I was satisfied that Malcolm's intentions would be endorsed by his parliamentary colleagues—I became a member of the Liberal Party. I told Malcolm that, having joined the party, I was happy to use my influence—such as it might be—to back him on any future occasion. The occasion was not long coming.

During the personal attacks on Sir John Kerr, Galbally issued a statement supporting the Governor-General's actions in dismissing Whitlam and announcing his membership of the Liberal Party. By that time, Galbally and Fraser had developed a relationship of mutual trust.[35]

* * *

In May 1977 Fraser took to cabinet a submission recommending a review of post-arrival programs and services to migrants. The inquiry was to report to him personally. He wanted his own department, rather than the Department of Immigration and Ethnic Affairs, to steer it to completion. 'I wanted to keep an eye on it. I didn't want it to disappear.' Fraser chose Galbally to head the review. Fraser remembers having to argue for the appointment: some in the party room didn't like Galbally's record of successfully defending alleged murderers. Fraser says, 'I thought people are entitled to a defence; he's doing his job and if he's too smart for the government prosecutors, well, too bad'. Fraser says today, 'He was a most impressive and able man, and a very humanitarian man, without being at all soft-headed about it'. In the following months, as Galbally toured the nation, he and Fraser kept up a correspondence. Fraser quietly consulted Galbally on his struggles with the Department of Immigration, and Galbally made recommendations for changes, while counselling Fraser not to let it be known that the recommendations came from him, for fear of jeopardising the department's willingness to cooperate with his work.[36]

The Galbally inquiry was Fraser's personal project, something he was determined to see through. He says today, 'I wanted to achieve a total sense of belonging for people, no matter what their origin and background. I wanted us to be able to say that once they're Australian, they're accepted as Australian. That's it. They don't have to look over their shoulder to wonder what somebody is going to shout at them. They don't have to feel apart and different and separate because they speak with a different accent or because their physical appearance isn't a typically Anglo-Saxon physical appearance. And I think that in a large measure this has been achieved in Australia. There are always going to be areas for improvement'. Between them, Galbally and Fraser translated the government's commitment to diversity into practical measures. Fraser presented Galbally's report to cabinet in May 1978. With Fraser's backing, the government adopted all of its recommendations, even though, in a time of cutbacks, they meant extra spending of $50 million over three years. Fraser remembers, 'Quite a number of ministers would have been reluctant, but they didn't argue all that strongly. Probably some of them resented the extra money when their own areas were being cut. But, even if some of them instinctively didn't like the idea of Asian faces in Australian streets, they recognised that on a straight, logical, rational argument, it was very hard to come down against the policies. The policies were appropriate. They were just'.

Fraser told cabinet that he wanted to be the one to table the report in parliament, and he arranged for it to be provided in multiple languages, the first time this had been done with a major government report. He told parliament that Australia was 'at a critical stage in developing a cohesive, united multicultural nation. The government accepts that it is now essential to give significant further encouragement to develop a multicultural attitude in Australian society. It will foster the retention of the cultural heritage of different ethnic groups and promote intercultural understanding'. The extra spending was necessary, he said, because the Galbally report addressed an injustice: migrants were at a disadvantage. 'It always has been in our philosophy to seek out areas of need and disadvantage and to act upon them. It is only in such circumstances that the government is prepared to make exceptions to our general rule [of expenditure restraint].'[37]

Galbally had adopted the liberal principle of self-help—that ethnic communities, rather than centralised government departments, were the best placed to help their own. Settlement services were to be delivered largely through government-funded Migrant Resource Centres representing the different ethnic communities. Money was to be spent on English-language classes, translation services and improved government communication. The report also recommended the establishment of the Australian Institute for Multicultural Affairs, an independent statutory body to promote tolerance, understanding and awareness of the diversity of Australian culture. Galbally became the institute's first Chairman. Fraser's chief adviser on multiculturalism, Petro Georgiou, left his staff to become its first Director. As a result, the institute remained close to Fraser—a government-funded, independent research and advocacy body with a brief to both assert pluralism and ensure that it was a source of strength rather than a threat.

With Fraser's backing, the Galbally agenda proceeded with astonishing speed. The report had taken less than a year to compile, and the new Immigration Minister, Ian Macphee, made sure the implementation was equally quick. A task force was set up, including senior officials from all the Commonwealth departments involved. By 1980–81, nearly all of the recommendations were reported to have been implemented or near implementation.[38]

The month in which the Galbally report was tabled was the worst so far for unauthorised arrivals by boat people. The media didn't help with the Fraser government's promotion of the benefits of multiculturalism. *The Sun Herald* published reports suggesting that Vietnamese settled in Sydney carried serious diseases. A public opinion poll showed that 57 per cent of Australians were against allowing boat people to stay.[39] Meanwhile, the United Nations High Commissioner for Refugees estimated that the global refugee population was at 3.1 million. Australia not playing its part was never an option. Fraser says, 'If we hadn't done what we did, our international reputation would have been mud, and rightly so'.

During the final days of compiling his report—and after writing the recommendations for English-language lessons, Migrant Resource Centres and the rest—Galbally had been haunted by a feeling that it still wasn't enough. He knew, from his tours of the nation, how isolated migrants could be, how cut off from the rest of Australian culture. Often they were too shy to go out much. They couldn't read the newspapers or understand much of what was on the radio. Later he remembered:

> I went out to a park one lunchtime and I just thought, 'Now what would be the best thing really to help this matter, this whole problem, accelerate and be solved?' … And I thought, 'Television! … Open up the world. Open up Australia through television! Well, how in the name of goodness can that be done?' And I thought about it and thought about it. And nearly everyone said, 'Oh no, there's no way known you could get a multicultural television station'. And I said, 'Well I don't see why not'.[40]

The idea of ethnic broadcasting wasn't new. Experimental ethnic radio stations had been set up in 1975, during the Whitlam years. The Fraser government had wanted the ABC to establish ethnic broadcasting permanently. Negotiations went on for almost a year. The ABC resisted too many 'strings' being attached to the extra funding proposed, and Fraser became convinced that the organisation's heart wasn't in it. 'The ABC was very grudging, and I lost interest in them. I thought with that attitude they wouldn't do it properly in any case.' The government withdrew its offer to the ABC and in January 1978 set up the Special Broadcasting Service (SBS) as a separate body.

The Galbally report envisaged something much more ambitious than ethnic stations. It recommended a broadcasting service that would help put multiculturalism into effect. The aim was not 'ethnic television' but use of broadcasting technology to reach both old and new Australians. The programs would increase awareness and appreciation of the diversity of the country. The service would break down prejudice and help new arrivals to adjust to life in Australia. Fraser wanted it to be a means of opening minds and hearts. 'Galbally and I wanted to break down that narrow, introspective attitude that leads to fear and racism. We wanted to use the technology to bring people together.' The plan was to establish a new body, the Independent and Multicultural Broadcasting Corporation, to take over from SBS and provide both television and radio, but the legislation to set it up was frustrated by Labor in the Senate. Senator John Button described the idea as part of Fraser's 'desperate obsession' with providing 'tempting bait electorally' to ethnic communities, and argued that the money would be better spent on the ABC.[41] As a result, the multicultural television service was instead begun by a reformed SBS with a new board and an advisory council headed by Frank Galbally. Fraser says, 'What we couldn't do with legislation we did administratively'. Multicultural television began in October 1980. By the time Fraser gave his speech to the inaugural meeting of the Australian Institute of Multicultural Affairs, in November 1981, he was able to praise Channel 0/28, as it was then known, as 'a service unique in the world' that was already gaining praise and awards for its news services and high-quality content.[42]

By this time, in 1982, the boat people had stopped arriving. Vietnam had been persuaded by the United Nations to agree to an orderly departure program, in which it allowed those wanting to leave to apply for acceptance by other countries. Australia continued to accept large numbers. Meanwhile, Macphee had introduced a new system, the Numerical Migrant Assessment System, selecting potential migrants on a range of factors, including personal suitability and ability to settle. The method was not trouble-free; it was changed several times and the name was abandoned in 1981, but nevertheless it was the precursor to systems still in use today.

* * *

By the time Fraser lost power, in 1983, multiculturalism was widely accepted as a success, and was bipartisan policy. Hawke made some changes—among other things dismantling the Australian Institute for Multicultural Affairs and transferring its functions to a branch of his own department—but there was no suggestion from the new government of a return to discrimination on the basis of race, or an alteration to multiculturalism as official government policy.

Immigration reform is one of the most important legacies of the Fraser government; so too the largely successful settlement of the Indochinese. When he left power, Fraser regarded these changes as 'my proudest achievements ... we had laid down the principles of high migration, of non-discrimination. But we had also put the machinery in place to make sure that it worked, that the non-discrimination was real in terms of how people could live in Australia and the opportunities open to them. It was good planning and good implementation. It was what government ought to do'.

Fraser thought the changes were so entrenched, so well accepted by Australians, that they could not be undone. But he had misgivings, on this count at least, when John Howard became leader of the Liberal Party, and then Prime Minister. His misgivings were confirmed on 10 September 1996, when the independent member for Ipswich Pauline Hanson rose in parliament and gave her maiden speech. Hanson asserted that 'mainstream Australians' were subject to 'a type of reverse racism ... by those who promote political correctness and those who control the various taxpayer-funded "industries" that flourish in our society servicing Aboriginals, multiculturalists and a host of other minority groups'. She said that governments were encouraging 'separatism' by providing opportunities, land, moneys and facilities available only to Aboriginals. But the main thrust of her speech was an attack on multiculturalism, and Asian immigration in particular.

> Immigration and multiculturalism are issues that this government is trying to address, but for far too long ordinary Australians have been kept out of any debate by the major parties. I and most Australians want our immigration policy radically reviewed and that of multiculturalism abolished. I believe we are in danger of being swamped by Asians ... They have their own culture and religion, form ghettos and do not assimilate. Of course, I will be called racist but, if I can invite whom I want into my home, then I should have the right to have a say in who comes into my country. A truly multicultural country can never be strong or united.[43]

Hanson's views didn't surprise Fraser: such opinions had always been present in Australian society. Most people were threatened by change. What dismayed him was that the Prime Minister, John Howard, did not condemn Hanson's views. 'He said they were an example of freedom of speech. Well, I suppose they were, but he could have said more. He could have said things that would encourage Australians to have an optimistic view of themselves and their ability to change. But then, given what he had said about the refugees after that cabinet meeting in 1977, I never expected that kind of thing from John Howard.'

The government insisted during this time that the Pauline Hanson issue and its handling of refugees were not damaging Australia's reputation in the region. Fraser gained a different impression. On a visit to China in 1998, he had a conversation with the Premier Zhu Rongji. 'He said, "Malcolm, as an old friend of China, I can ask you this. Tell me about Pauline Hanson. Why doesn't Howard condemn her?" That was a difficult question to answer.'

Fraser fell out with Howard over many things during the next few years. Those who wonder at the reasons for the gulf between the two Liberal prime ministers could do well to start by looking at immigration, refugee policy and multiculturalism. These were among the most important reforms that Fraser introduced. They had been his personal mission, and they were close to his heart and central to his understanding of true liberalism. He was deeply disturbed at seeing the Howard government take so many backward steps. The treatment of refugees, the Pacific solution, the children behind barbed wire—all that lay ahead.

Fraser watched while his friend and former staff member Petro Georgiou, now a backbencher, paid the price for crossing the floor to vote against a Bill that would have forced the processing of all asylum seekers to be done off shore. In 2006 Georgiou faced a pre-selection challenge backed by key senior Liberals. Fraser says, 'He spoke out. I have nothing but contempt for those Liberals who come to me and say, "Oh Malcolm, I am speaking out, but behind closed doors; I am more effective that way". Well, Petro worked behind the scenes and in front of the scenes and however he thought it would work. Petro and the others paid the price'.

During the *Tampa* crisis, Tamie and Malcolm Fraser seriously considered giving up their membership of the Liberal Party. Tamie remembers long and anguished discussions. How could they remain in a party so patently in breach of the principles they believed lay at its core? She says, 'I felt so strongly and still do about how Howard changed the face of Australia, and how our country is viewed in the world and by itself. Once people think it's okay to behave and have attitudes like Howard had, then it's very hard to reverse. It takes generational change again to get over it'. In the end, by the skin of their teeth, they decided to stay, largely because of Georgiou and the other backbenchers. Tamie says, 'We thought we would be letting them down if we left. And we wanted to say "It's our party too"'. Fraser took to insisting, at public events when he was asked to speak, that there were still some liberals in the Liberal Party. He would decline to name them, because he said doing so would only make their positions more difficult. Within Liberal Party circles the

Frasers' position was sometimes uncomfortable. Tamie remembers choosing carefully which topics to raise, and in what company. 'Sometimes you're surprised by people you know. Mostly you can pick who really you don't talk to about these things and those you do. Just every now and again you get caught and there might be a couple at dinner who don't think as you think. And you've fallen in before you realise and it can all get very sticky.'

Fraser refuses to say how he voted in the 2001, 2004 and 2007 federal elections, but during the interviews for this book he said many times that the Howard government did not deserve to be re-elected. Tamie is more forthcoming. Did she vote for the Howard government? 'No way.'

In October 2007, the Minister for Immigration in the Howard government, Kevin Andrews, told the media that he had cut the number of African refugees accepted into Australia because they had trouble integrating into society. He said this had been done on the basis of advice contained in submissions from an interdepartmental committee to cabinet.[44] Fraser was at the time doing the interviews for this book. One spring afternoon he sat in his office far above Melbourne's Collins Street. He had trouble turning his mind to anything other than Andrews's comments. He recalled the advice that had come to his cabinet from the bureaucrats and the Department of Immigration recommending the 'reception centres' and canvassing the turning-back of boats, predicting the breakdown of Australian society if the refugees continued to come. He remembered the advice his own government had received about Lebanese migrants. The response of his government had been to try to help new people to settle. Why was it that the Howard government didn't ask what it could do to help, rather than encouraging the blaming of the migrants themselves? Didn't the government realise how dangerous that could be? Now was the time, Fraser said, for a new Galbally-style inquiry, to find out what the problems were and what was needed. Where, today, were the mechanisms of government committed to promoting tolerance, support and diversity? Where was the vision?

As for SBS, Fraser believes that the national broadcaster that his government created has lost its way. Mainstream has replaced multicultural. Big money is going into ordinary programming, while the reporting of community events and customs has declined. SBS should be at the forefront of encouraging engagement between African migrants and the rest of the community. Its voice is never heard. 'Australia has veered, in its thinking, back to uniformity, to assimilation, to seeing diversity as a threat rather than a strength', Fraser said. He had heard the things people said about Muslims—how they might be terrorists, how they couldn't be trusted—and thought them similar to the things his father had once said about Catholics. He thought about that compassionate, brilliant Catholic Frank Galbally, and said, 'Surely we have learned something since then?'

Fraser paused. Outside his office window the city lay in spring haze, the loop of the Yarra embracing the city, people of every colour and descent walking its banks, in the streets and working in the offices. Fraser said, 'You know, those who are against multiculturalism have already lost. Taking the word out of government policy won't change the result. We are already a multicultural nation. Anyone who looks at the faces in the street knows that, if they think about it'. The new arrivals, including those who arrived without permission and papers, have done us no harm and a lot of good. He looked out of the window and sighed. 'Who would have thought that we would have grown so afraid?'

14

The World

It is autumn. The sun is up. The newspapers are spread out on the table. There is coffee and porridge. Another peaceful morning in Australia. Almost before the headline on the newspaper has been absorbed, the telephone rings. It is Malcolm Fraser. 'Listen', he says. 'I'm worried about what they are doing with China.' The headline is about the Rudd government's defence white paper which depicts China as a long-term threat.[1] Fraser is worried that the United States is alienating China, and Australia is following too easily in its path. 'There are so many things in the world that one could get depressed about', Fraser says. One of them, 'something that I could lie awake worrying about if I wanted', is the possibility that the United States will be involved in a conflict with China over Taiwan. Our Collins class submarines have been equipped with American command and control systems to maximise cooperation with the United States. They can operate in the Taiwan Strait, which US nuclear submarines cannot do. 'If there is a conflict, America will want those submarines', says Fraser, and yet in such a conflict the United States would have no friends in our region. Conflict with China would be directly contrary to our interests. So would Australia stand up for itself, or would it simply follow the United States?

Australia, Fraser believes, is 'remiss' in not telling the United States that talk of containing China should be put aside. It is all very well to speak of increased defence cooperation with Japan and the United States, but what about defence cooperation with China as well? 'The United States finds it very difficult to deal with other countries on an equal footing', he says. 'She is so all-consumingly powerful that she is unable to resist the strength of her own ideas.' Yet, says Fraser, the best elements of the US character value allies who are open and forthright and don't merely follow unquestioningly. Australia should be a critical friend, and make sure its voice is heard.

The breakfast conversation is over. The message is clear. Peaceful mornings in Australia cannot be taken for granted. Security requires thought, and choices. A middle power like Australia should never coast in the wake of powerful friends. Fraser is now seventy-nine years old. 'Sometimes, these days', he said at one point during the research for this book, 'I have a day on which I have nothing in particular to do'. This, he emphasises, is not to say that he is at a loose end. Rather, it means he can turn his mind to all the things that never get scheduled because he is too busy. In any case, it doesn't happen often. As his former adviser David Kemp says, 'I don't suppose there is a single day in Malcolm Fraser's life when he hasn't been thinking about policy, about how to take things forward'.

Today, the Australia, New Zealand and United States Security (ANZUS) treaty has become a magic talisman of Australian foreign policy. Any political leader who offends, or who is believed to have offended, the United States is unelectable. Keeping the US alliance in good health is taken to be the first and most important aim of foreign policy. Because of the United States, we have gone to war in Iraq and Afghanistan. But what does ANZUS mean? What did it ever mean?

The ANZUS treaty has always been a very limited document, Fraser says. It is not like the North Atlantic Treaty Organisation (NATO), binding allies to respond if any are attacked. Instead, ANZUS commits the parties only to 'consult' if their 'territorial integrity, political independence or security' is threatened in the

Pacific. If there is an armed attack on Australia, then the treaty binds the United States to 'act to meet the common danger in accordance with … constitutional processes'. In practice, any support for Australia would be dependent on the attitude of the US Congress.[2]

As Prime Minister, Fraser was a supporter of the US alliance. In the Cold War world, there were good reasons to be so. The Soviet Union was still an outward-looking and predatory power. Some of Fraser's main foreign policy achievements—not revealed at the time—were directed to keeping the Western alliance strong and unified. Yet, as a result of his experience as Minister for Defence, he was always clear-eyed about the contingent nature of the United States' friendship. During the Cold War, the United States would have responded to any threat to Australia. It would not have wanted to cede the territory to the Soviet bloc. But in today's world, Fraser asks, 'Does it really matter to the USA who governs Australia?' The times demand the striking of a different balance.

Even during the Cold War the ANZUS treaty was recognised by both sides as a limited commitment. Fraser recalls that in the mid 1950s, when the treaty was still young, President Eisenhower moved the US Pacific Fleet into the Taiwan Strait. Menzies told Eisenhower that if there were a conflict with China over Taiwan, Australia would not be part of it and ANZUS would not apply. 'Is there any politician with the strength to do that now?' Fraser says. The United States has also made the limitations of its commitment clear. In the 1960s, when Australia was involved in the Indonesian-sponsored confrontation in Malaysia, the Australian Minister for External Affairs, Garfield Barwick, said publically that Australian troops in Borneo were covered under the ANZUS treaty. This greatly displeased the Americans. The administration of President Lyndon Johnson quickly made it plain to the Australian Government that such presumption was not appreciated.[3]

Even when Fraser was Prime Minister, there were doubts about the US alliance. 'A relationship founded on common interests is ultimately the only relationship that can be depended upon', Fraser said in his first big statement on foreign affairs as Prime Minister. 'The interests of the United States and the interests of Australia are not necessarily identical. In our relations with the United States, as in our relations with other great powers, our first responsibility is independently to assess our own interests. The United States will unquestionably do the same.'[4] Behind the scenes, the language was less diplomatic. Documents that went to cabinet clearly anticipated that Australia could not rely on support in matters where the United States' interests were not directly involved. Cabinet was told that Australian governments had for many years deliberately avoided attempts to define exactly what the ANZUS treaty meant and the circumstances that would result in the United States coming to Australia's aid. Any attempts to reach such definitions would not be welcomed by the United States, and might result in a more limited commitment than was in Australia's interests. Australia should be able to independently handle any situation in which US support was uncertain.

Asked today if he trusts the United States, or trusts China, Fraser says, 'I will trust any country as long as I have a clear understanding of how it sees its own self-interest. Because that is what will count'.

* * *

Fraser could see the National War Memorial from the steps of old Parliament House. The two buildings faced each other at opposite ends of an axis. It was, he thought, an appropriate juxtaposition. The two buildings implicated each other. Democratic freedoms depended on the ability to defend the nation. The chief responsibility of any government was to keep the nation secure. In Parliament House, over the decades, decisions had been made to send young people to war. The memorial stood as a reminder. Perhaps sometimes it was a reproach. 'Too many Australians have died in places remote from their home—in Europe, in the Middle East, in Korea, in South-East Asia—for us to be unconcerned about the preservation of world peace', Fraser said in 1981, when he was being called on to justify his meddling in the affairs of superpowers. 'Their sacrifice not only confers a right but imposes a duty on Australia to speak on these issues.' In an echo of the injunction that had haunted his childhood, he went on, 'It would not only be foolish, but a political and moral failing to assume that nations such as Australia should be seen but not heard on the great issues'.[5]

During Fraser's time in politics, the affairs of the world were dominated by the clash of ideologies and ambitions represented by the Soviet Union and the United States. This was known as the conflict between East and West. What could Australia do, other than shelter behind our great and powerful friends? As Prime Minister, Fraser rejected the idea that Australia should be compliant, or silent. There were few debates in which he didn't insert our point of view, and few world leaders that he didn't argue with. Margaret Thatcher felt the force of his will; Henry Kissinger disagreed with him about China. Fraser thought President Carter naïve and President Ford insufficiently determined and, in the nicest and most diplomatic fashion, he told them so. He also told US and European leaders that they were hypocrites in their relations with the Third World. On the one hand, they preached the benefits of a free-market system; on the other hand, they closed their markets to agricultural products, denying developing countries their best chance of an escape from poverty. In 1980, Fraser said:

> It is one thing to recognise one's limitations; it is another to exaggerate them and make them the excuse for passivity. Australia is not a great power, but neither is it a negligible factor in international politics. It is a significant middle power which will be listened to—is listened to—when it advances informed and reasonable views.[6]

To the extent that Fraser was effective in foreign affairs—and he changed the course of a number of world events—it was not because he saw Australia as subservient or a 'deputy' to any superior power.

It is because he was seen *and* heard. David Kemp remarks, 'It was very rare for Malcolm to conclude that the correct thing to do was nothing'. In foreign affairs, as in other matters, Fraser was an activist.

* * *

One of the defining issues in international affairs during the years of the Fraser government was the conflict between the interests of the developed countries and those of the Third World. This was known as the North–South dialogue. The term recognised that most of the developed nations were in the Northern Hemisphere, and the poorest nations were in the South. Fraser made common cause between Australia and the Third World. He argued for justice in trade, and became one of the leading activists against racism and apartheid. This offended many conservatives, including in his own party. At the time, the media were liable to see a contradiction between his position in the East–West conflict and his activism in North–South dialogue. Fraser saw no contradiction: they were related. If the developed nations did not deal justly with the Third World, then poor countries would be pushed into the arms of the Soviets.

Fraser's particular contribution was to take the dominant narratives of his time—East–West and North–South—and frame Australia's self-interest within them. Australia's position was unique—a developed nation, but in the Southern Hemisphere. We were a member of the Western alliance, yet positioned in the East—geographically a part of Asia. Like the Third World nations, our most significant exports were commodities and agricultural products. Fraser conceived Australia's self-interest in the broadest, most outward-looking terms—as encompassing action for a better, more principled world. Today Fraser says, 'If you are interested in a better world then you have to be interested in foreign policy'. Yet he also said, in 1976, that ideology, while not irrelevant, could not guide foreign policy. In speech after speech, the idea recurred. All countries would look after their self-interest, and Australia should too. We should expect this of our allies as well as our enemies. An optimistic conclusion followed from this: dialogue was always possible. Even when we most disagreed, there would always be room to search for areas of common interest. As Prime Minister, Fraser tried to marry idealism and pragmatism.

It didn't always work. Before it had even been elected the Fraser government was faced with a bitter example of hard, unjust international real politics. On 16 October 1975, the day after the Fraser shadow cabinet made its decision to block supply to the Whitlam government, the Indonesian army began a covert invasion of the former Portuguese colony of East Timor. Five Australian journalists were killed in the town of Balibo. It is now a matter of historical record that the Whitlam government knew of the invasion before it happened. Whitlam had, in 1974 and early 1975, made it clear to Indonesian President Suharto that he believed East Timor should become part of Indonesia. Suharto, who might have been dissuaded from the invasion if Australia had strongly opposed it, had instead taken comfort. While Whitlam said he thought that the East Timorese people should be able to determine their own futures, it was clear from his conversations with his staff that he regarded this as mere formality.[7] As Australia went through the agonies of late 1975, the Indonesians tightened their grip. On 7 December, when the Fraser government was still in caretaker mode, there was a full invasion and the East Timorese capital of Dili was captured. The caretaker Foreign Affairs Minister, Andrew Peacock, issued a statement saying that the events in East Timor were 'deeply regretted'.

Behind the scenes, Fraser was troubled and conflicted. A fortnight before the full invasion, the Department of Foreign Affairs and Trade had told him that it was vital to Australia's long-term relationship with Indonesia that he send Suharto a message to indicate that a Fraser government would not change the Whitlam government's policy on Indonesia.

Fraser shared Whitlam's concern that East Timor should not become a communist enclave in the underbelly of Indonesia. On the other hand, no principled government could endorse the use of force. Fraser remembers, 'It really was put to me with the utmost urgency that it was most vital that I communicate to Suharto. On the one hand, I abhorred the incorporation. It was contrary to everything we believed about self-determination of peoples. On the other hand, I couldn't change policy anyway in caretaker mode and Indonesia was our most important neighbour, and I was being told it was vital that I do this thing'. Thus began the tightrope walk of every Australian government since over East Timor—principle on the one hand and pragmatism on the other.

Fraser was very reluctant to do what the Department of Foreign Affairs was recommending. After a phone call to the Australian Ambassador in Jakarta, Richard Woolcott, Fraser ultimately refused to send a letter but instead authorised the sending of a top-secret cablegram to Woolcott worded in the third person and authorising him to pass a message to Suharto. Fraser chose his words carefully. 'I was trying to say as little as possible. The draft came to me, and I remember altering the words to try to weaken them.' Woolcott was to tell Suharto that Fraser recognised 'the need for Indonesia to have an appropriate solution for the problem of Portuguese Timor', and regretted 'irritants' to the relationship such as protests over the invasion by Australian trade unions. Woolcott was to say that Fraser would not receive representatives of the independence movement Fretilin should they visit Australia. Fraser ensured that this commitment was given only 'pending the elections'. Finally, he made it clear that he wanted the message he had sent to remain secret. Five days later, Woolcott reported back that Suharto 'greatly appreciated' the message, and had asked for 'amplification' on Fraser's recognition of the need for an 'appropriate solution'. Woolcott had used diplomatic niceties, telling Suharto that he assumed Fraser meant 'a solution which accommodated Indonesia's policy interests'.[8] The invasion proceeded.

Once elected to government, the Fraser cabinet had time and power to reconsider, but by this stage there was little that could be done. In February 1976, Peacock told cabinet that Indonesian forces were 'well on the way' to integrating East Timor into Indonesia. 'The tragedy is that integration might have been achieved in more peaceful ways, but that is now history.' Peacock said that Australia had no tangible national interests involved. If anything, it would favour integration, but, 'It must be of concern … that the largest country of South-East Asia, one contiguous to Australia and one firmly controlled by generals, has used force'. Australia now had 'very limited' ability to alter the course of events, but should not 'connive' in the takeover. He recommended that Australia continue to call for the withdrawal of Indonesian forces and an act of self-determination, but he recognised the likelihood that none of this would have any effect.[9]

East Timor was formally incorporated as a province of Indonesia on 18 July 1976. Fraser still hadn't been to Indonesia for a formal visit—something which, he was advised, was causing some tension. By the time he did visit, in October that year, the Indonesians were making it clear that the Australian policy of calling for withdrawal and self-determination would no longer be accepted. Fraser was asked by journalists to restate the policy. He wouldn't do so, saying merely that it had been spelled out many times. He took action to suppress two-way radio links between East Timor and Fretilin supporters in Darwin. At the United Nations, Australia abstained from voting for resolutions condemning Indonesian military intervention. In January 1978, the government surrendered to realities: East Timor was part of Indonesia, and would be 'recognised de facto' even though Australia remained 'critical of the means by which integration was brought about'.[10]

Today, having had the benefit of looking at the documents released as part of a Senate committee inquiry, including records of Whitlam's discussions with Suharto, Fraser believes that Australia was cleverly manipulated by the Indonesians.[11] 'There is more than a suggestion in the documents that Suharto was very much concerned at what Australia thought', says Fraser. 'He did not want to incorporate East Timor into Indonesia if Australia were to be outspoken and active in opposition.' Fraser says that diplomats at the time thought they had high-level access to classified information from the Indonesians, but it is more than likely that they knew only what the Indonesians wanted them to know—so they would be locked in once the invasion took place.

The option of a United Nations intervention to oversee a vote by the East Timorese on its future was never seriously pursued. The Whitlam government could have advocated for it from as early as 1974. Fraser believes it would probably have made no difference, but there was a small chance. The last opportunity for Australia to influence the course of events was mid 1975, Fraser believes. That opportunity was not taken. After that, 'The overriding concern with domestic politics at the end of 1975 made it difficult to focus adequately on what was happening in Timor. That's not an excuse; it is the reality. Real politic, in the harshest sense of the term, governed the day'.

East Timor was an horrendously difficult foreign policy problem. Strong advocacy for East Timor after the invasion would have meant unmanageable tensions with Indonesia for years. Australia would have had no support from the United Kingdom or other European powers; nor would the United States have come to our aid. 'Imagine if we had asked the USA for support over East Timor. It would have been refused. They saw Fretilin as communists. And if an Australian government allowed it to be exposed that the USA had preferred Indonesia to Australia, then the whole fabric of foreign policy would come unravelled.'

At a time of superpower politics, with Soviet submarines in the Indian Ocean, armed build-ups by the Warsaw pact countries in Europe, and the still real possibility of nuclear war, the future of East Timor was a comparatively small matter. Nevertheless, for the rest of Fraser's term, as resistance to Indonesian rule continued and news of human rights abuses increased, East Timor stood as an example of the choices governments make to maintain security. Perhaps most of all it was a reminder of the consequences of Australia's having failed to use its influence when, just maybe, it might have made a difference. Under his government, Fraser resolved, Australia would be seen and heard.

* * *

Everything happens at once in government. In early 1976, at the same time as Fraser was dealing with the push to cut government expenditure, the negotiation of land rights legislation, the beginnings of immigration policy review and the May economic statement, he was also preparing one of the most important parliamentary speeches of his prime ministership. It worked its way through successive drafts throughout April and May, being sent out for comment to the Secretary of Foreign Affairs Alan Renouf, to Arthur Tange in defence and to the Minister for Foreign Affairs Andrew Peacock. It became known to Fraser's staff as the 'State of the World' speech. David Kemp worked on it, but one of the moving forces behind the ideas was Owen Harries, the small Welsh academic who later became an adviser on Australia's foreign policy and, after the Fraser government, influential in Washington. As an academic, Harries had been in the forefront of support for Australia's involvement in the Vietnam War. He was seen as a hard-line Cold Warrior and was involved with the anti-communist Congress for Cultural Freedom that had courted Fraser during his days as Army Minister. Harries had gone on to draft the Liberal Party's 'enlightened realism' foreign affairs policy in opposition.

When Fraser was in government, Harries became the head of policy planning in the Department of Foreign Affairs and then an adviser to Peacock before Fraser poached him for his own staff. Later, in 1982, he became Australia's Ambassador to the United Nations Educational, Scientific and Cultural Organization, and after that he moved to Washington, where he edited the influential journal *The National Interest*, which was a key forum for neo-conservative ideas during the years of the Bush government in the 1990s. More recently, Harries broke with many of his neo-conservative friends over his opposition to the Iraq War. Fraser says today, 'I didn't agree with everything Owen did in Washington, but he was never in favour of American unilateralism. He had a lot more sense than that'. In the mid 1970s, Harries's approach to Australia's foreign policy was strong anti-communism and a suspicion of the Soviets together with a concern for justice and humanitarianism. In these ideals he and Fraser were as one.

The State of the World was a big speech for a small country.[12] Fraser stuck his neck out. Whitlam, standing in parliament immediately after it was delivered, described it as

> one of the most regrettable and reactionary speeches we have heard in this House. It was depressing … it will do nothing but provoke alarm, needlessly offend one of the world's superpowers and set back the cause of détente and international conciliation. What was the need for such a speech? … [What] was its mixture of Cold War rhetoric and apocalyptic doom saying, all this rattling of antique sabres and blowing of rusty bugles?[13]

Whitlam should have seen the drafts. He was not the only one to question the need for a country like Australia to speak so loudly. The notes for the speech, the drafts and the comments on those drafts fill six fat folders in the archives, testament to the way in which Fraser threw out and tested his ideas in the crucible of argument.[14] Amid all the other issues that the new government was dealing with, the preparation of this speech took an enormous amount of intellectual energy. Due to the State of the World address, another planned major speech on the government's human rights agenda—freedom of information, the human rights commission, Aboriginal land rights and judicial review—was postponed and then abandoned. As

Fred Chaney, one of the prime movers, put it, that speech would have articulated 'the consistent philosophy behind all we have done and all we aspire to do'. Perhaps Fraser's record would be better understood if that speech had been made.[15]

Part of the background to the State of the World speech, Fraser says today, was the Department of Foreign Affairs's opposition to the new government's attitude to the Baltic States. Whitlam had recognised their incorporation by the Soviet Union; the Fraser government had, as one of its first deeds and in fulfilment of a policy commitment, withdrawn this recognition. Fraser was lobbied on the issue by the Australian Ambassador to the Soviet Union Sir James Plimsoll, who had been brought back by the department for consultations. Fraser says, 'I am sure Jim had been organised by the Department of Foreign Affairs. He warned me there would be terrible consequences to annoying the Soviets; it would be dreadful: we would lose trade, we would never recover, the Soviets would do this, the Soviets would do that and so on. And I said, "Look, Jim, I just don't believe you. There won't be any alteration to Soviet behaviour. They will try to behave as though it hasn't happened". And he persisted and went on and on until I almost had to ask him to go'. Fraser was right. There was no Soviet reaction, but the Department of Foreign Affairs was, according to Fraser, 'very annoyed' that its advice had not been followed.

This annoyance flowed over into the disputes about the State of the World speech. The arguments were about how scathing Fraser should be about détente and how far he should go in risking the alienation of the Soviet Union, criticising the Western alliance and leaning towards China. In early drafts, the speech described détente as a 'failure'. Peacock recommended toning the speech down. Alan Renouf said that the tone of the comments was likely to 'mark Australia out for USSR hostility … Is it for Australia to launch another anti-Russian campaign? … Is this not really a matter for others more directly threatened?' Fraser should not say that détente had failed, argued Renouf. Rather, he should say that it had had 'limited success'. It was 'not necessary to be so blunt'. The speech 'leans towards China too much' and 'would make Australia an ally of China second only to Albania. There is no need to go so far'. References to the lack of resolve of the Western alliance would not be appreciated in Bonn and Paris, Renouf said. Tange agreed that Fraser was too harsh on détente: 'While scepticism is justified, it is a bit early to give a final verdict of failure'. It was Tange's advice that weighed with Fraser. He underlined Tange's comments, and the next draft adopted his suggested wording.

By May both Renouf and Peacock thought the draft State of the World speech much improved and 'more measured'. Peacock commented: 'Such a speech needs to be made because if the analysis it gives is right, and I think it is basically right, then there is an urgent need to dispel illusion and complacency at home [and] to articulate the government's thinking and intentions'. He thought the speech would have adverse effects on Australia's relationship with the Soviet Union, but, in the longer term, 'The USSR respects a clear understanding of power realities'.

The speech that Fraser delivered, on 1 June 1976, was still strongly worded, and opened a new and original era in Australian foreign affairs. It was controversial domestically, and noticed internationally—an announcement of Fraser's arrival on the world stage. Far from annoying Bonn and Paris, Fraser says, it was greatly appreciated by the German Chancellor Helmut Schmidt, at least. In its scepticism of détente and its calls for clarity and determination in US foreign policy, the speech was more hard-line than either the US President at the time, Gerald Ford, or his successor, Jimmy Carter; Fraser anticipated the approach that was later taken by Ronald Reagan. The speech called on the developed nations to cease their hypocrisy over Third World trade, and it went much further than any previous Australian government in sympathy for China. Today Fraser makes the point that this speech, and his approach to foreign policy generally, did not strain the US alliance or adversely affect Australia's standing in world affairs. 'On the contrary, it was respected', he says. 'They knew we weren't a pushover.'

Fraser began by urging a

> realistic assessment of the state of the world ... free of self-deception, self-delusion. We must be prepared to face the world as it is, and not as we would like it to be. Only in that way can we avoid becoming involved in the pursuit of policies whose assumptions are so remote from reality that their failure is inevitable. Only in that way can we effectively advance our objectives of peace and security.

Australia should seek to further its 'deeply held values of democracy, freedom and respect for the individual', but ideology could not be the guiding principle in foreign affairs. Under Whitlam, the economic chaos at home had been echoed by a neglect of power realities abroad and unrealistic notions that an 'age of peace and stability had arrived'. The truth was that countries were still prepared to use force. The Soviet Union still sought to extend its influence. In many countries, minorities were oppressed. 'We have come far beyond the point where anyone can pretend that the denial of rights to minorities, or of basic rights to majorities, is not a matter of international concern.' The 'appalling widespread problems of poverty, hunger and disease are not only an affront to human dignity, but constantly threaten discord and conflict between nations'.

A successful Australian foreign policy, said Fraser, had to be 'flexible, alert and undogmatic', recognising that the superpowers were dominant but also that other major powers—China, Japan, Europe and groups such as the Association of South-East Asian Nations—could influence events. 'Although our capacities to advance our interests are limited, we should be active and constructive in pursuit of a peaceful and favourable international environment.'

His wording on détente, much softened from the original draft, was still strong, likely to affront both the superpowers. 'Despite the hopes placed in détente, it has not stabilised relations between the great powers. Indeed a renewed arms race now looms as a real prospect.' What was needed was a true, tangible sign from the Soviets that they were serious about peace. They needed to reduce their armaments. The United States came in for criticism as well. It remained the power with which Australia had most in common, said Fraser. It was important to keep ANZUS 'in good repair'. Australia could ill afford any reduction in US credibility, yet the Vietnam War and the Watergate scandal that had led to Nixon's resignation had undermined the United States' self-confidence and sense of purpose.

> Let me not be misunderstood. This is no plea for any power to be a policeman for the world, nor to do what small powers should do for themselves. A country without the fortitude to defend itself does not deserve help. But … there are many things that only the world's greatest free power can do. If she leaves them undone, they remain undone.

Privately, Fraser had already sent a version of these sentiments to President Ford in the United States. It was a very deliberate letter, written in the earliest months of his prime ministership, which had also been through several drafts, with Peacock rejecting earlier bland versions from the department, telling them that what Fraser wanted was a letter that 'advises the President of Australia's grave concern at the continuing uncertainty of US policy throughout the world'.[16]

In his State of the World speech, Fraser said it had been hoped that détente would lead to a relaxation of tensions. 'Unfortunately, the reality has not matched these aspirations.' The Soviets had assisted the North Vietnamese to take over South Vietnam, had intervened in Angola and had expanded their armed forces. While talks had proceeded on nuclear arms limitation, the Warsaw pact countries now had a major advantage in conventional forces. 'Reasonable people can … reasonably conclude that the Soviet Union still seeks to expand its influence throughout the world in order to achieve Soviet primacy.' Negotiation was not a substitute for military balance; indeed, negotiations could not take place unless there was a military balance. It would be foolish to think that 'unsupported goodwill' was enough.

China, Fraser said, was a 'great unknown', but that was all the more reason to seek good relationships with it. China had everything to fear from the Soviets on her frontier. Australia and China shared an interest in seeking a balance of power in the region. 'We can therefore expect Chinese support for our own views on the need for an effective American presence in the Pacific and Indian oceans. Such support has, in fact, been given.' At the time, this suggestion—that China could be more ally than enemy—was largely overlooked domestically. Fraser was challenging the tendency of the West to lump the communist countries together. 'They were not monolithic', he says today. 'There were differences, and I thought we should be very interested in what those differences were.' Commentators at the time saw only the 'sabre rattling' about the Soviet Union. But Fraser's message was heard loud and clear in China, the United States and Russia.

The picture Fraser had painted of the world was one of multiple threats: from inequality, injustice and unfairness, Soviet aggression and lack of will among the democracies. He wanted Australia to be

> an example of the vital strength of the values of freedom and democracy ... In finding our way in such a world, the democracies must not lose their sense of purpose. There must be no failure of will or resolution ... Let history not record that this was the time when the democracies abandoned their faith.

⋆ ⋆ ⋆

Three weeks later, Malcolm and Tamie Fraser found out just how well the speech had been heard in China. Stepping off a plane in Peking, they were met by the kind of greeting only the Chinese can give. Massed columns of soldiers marched up and down. Thousands of school children cried out 'Welcome, warmly welcome' while dancing in formations of breathtaking precision. Tamie remembers,

'It was such a barrage of colour and sounds and movement you felt quite battered by it'.[17]

In a deliberate token of his intentions, Fraser had chosen to make his first overseas visit as Prime Minister not to the United States or Europe, but to Japan and China. In Japan, he had been greeted with a rendition of 'Waltzing Matilda' that had confirmed him in his belief that this should be Australia's national song. 'It was played by a Japanese military band. They made it exciting, uplifting, with verve and spirit.' Tamie remembers them both 'getting teary' at the sound. Fraser had signed a treaty of friendship and cooperation with Japan that set the framework for the relationship between the two countries for the rest of the century. The treaty was a Whitlam initiative, but Fraser had indicated from the beginning of his leadership that support for it was bipartisan, and as Prime Minister he had demanded that the relevant bureaucrats negotiate face to face and stop 'legalistic nit-picking' so that agreement could be reached.[18]

In China, the Frasers were most honoured guests. They were being wooed. The Peking newspaper *People's Daily* published material congratulating the Fraser government for its scepticism on détente and its stand on the Soviet Union's 'social imperialism'.[19] The Frasers were given gala banquets. They visited the Great Wall of China—Fraser had to remove his leather-soled shoes and walk in his socks to avoid slipping on the steep parts. After three days in Peking, they travelled by train to the far-north-western city of Urumqi. From there they travelled into the remote mountains. It was rare for Western leaders to visit the province, and the Frasers and their party—the first Westerners that many of the locals had seen—were stared at everywhere they went. They dined in a Mongolian farmer's yurt on cheese made from mare's milk. They were asked to join in traditional dances. Fraser—who hates dancing—kept his seat, but the next day the Australian press corps reported that amid the snow-capped mountains on the Russian border, Tamie Fraser had 'revived the spirits of the tiring Australian party' by kicking off her shoes and learning 'lively' traditional Mongolian steps.[20]

Most importantly of all, in diplomatic discussions Fraser was given new insights into China's thinking. Chairman Mao Tse Tung was ill—he died three months later—so Fraser's discussions were with the Premier Hua Kuo-Feng. They were very frank with each other. Fraser confided his worries on the Warsaw pact and the lack of US will. They talked about how the relationship between Japan, China, the United States and Australia might be developed. The discussions of the first day were leaked to the media by someone in Fraser's party, as were details of a late-night discussion he had with accompanying advisers and staff in which he speculated that one day China, Japan, the United States and Australia might have a defence arrangement. The story was written up in the Australian press as though he was trying to negotiate a four-power pact there and then. The culprit, Fraser believes—a senior official in foreign affairs—was motivated by antagonism to his strong anti-Soviet line. No pact was being discussed, but Hua and Fraser went on to agree that they had a common interest in opposing Soviet expansion in the region. By their fourth discussion, relations were good enough for Fraser to ask Hua about China's history of support for insurgency. Would China automatically support communist movements in the region? What was going to be most important for China, Fraser asked: relations between governments or relations between parties? Hua gave Fraser an unequivocal answer: from that time on, relations between governments would be the most important thing; the history of Chinese support for insurgency in South-East Asia was over. Fraser was the first overseas leader to have heard about the shift in policy. He was quick to communicate it to other leaders in the Association of South-East Asian Nations and to the US Secretary of State Henry Kissinger.

Four weeks later, Fraser was in the United States with Peacock, meeting Ford and Kissinger face to face. Fraser told them they weren't consulting China enough—that they should be trying to draw China into the international community. Kissinger was not impressed. He responded by saying that the Chinese were 'the most cold-blooded balance of power specialists in the world' and were using Australia to bring pressure on the United States. The record of this discussion shows Kissinger as saying that America briefed the Chinese more than any other country, except its closest allies such as Australia. Given Fraser's personal experience of how little the US told its allies, it is perhaps understandable that he didn't draw much comfort from this.[21] Fraser also met the future Secretary of Defense Donald Rumsfeld. From him and Kissinger, he heard what he already knew to be true: in the United States' view, the ANZUS treaty led to only a marginal increase in Australia's security. Australia was expected to handle regional problems, such as those concerning Indonesia and Papua New Guinea, by herself.[22] Today, Fraser says that Kissinger was a 'juggler': 'If he didn't see a solution to a problem he was brilliant at keeping all the balls in the air, so a solution might emerge in the future'.

By the time of Fraser's visit to the United States in 1976—an election year for the Americans—it was already clear that a Washington outsider, the former Governor of Georgia Jimmy Carter, had captured the imagination of a country wearied by Watergate and too many cynical administrations. Owen Harries visited the country in November 1976, and after discussions with Carter's advisers reported to Fraser that the President Elect had yet to work out his foreign policy, but that he took advice from many sharply opposed camps. 'He is much too strong and clever to be captured and used merely as a conduit for the views of others. He is in command of the situation and using others, rather than being used. The degree of respect shown for him by his advisers is striking.'[23] A briefing note from the Department of Prime Minister and Cabinet agreed that Carter's foreign policy was 'largely unformed' and suggested 'an intensive study of the psychology of Carter's handling of power'. The resulting document was brought to cabinet by Peacock in November. Carter, said Peacock, would differ from Ford in substance. He was using the word 'architectural' to describe his foreign policy approach. This contrasted with Kissinger's 'acrobatic' approach, or 'brilliant improvisation to maintain the status quo'. Carter wanted a 'less inflated and more pragmatic approach' to the Soviet Union. He was particularly concerned about nuclear proliferation, and wanted to 'restore a moral basis for American policy'. Carter was concerned about human rights, and this might cause Australia difficulties because of 'the vulnerability of some countries that are important to Australia, and the possibility that Australia itself could come under criticism if a polemical atmosphere develops'. The risk, Peacock said in his summary, was that Carter would downgrade issues of interest to Australia, such as the Indian Ocean, and focus on relationships with Europe and Japan, at Australia's expense.[24]

Early in 1977, with Carter in power, some of Australia's fears were being borne out. In a media conference in March, Carter stated that he would be trying to move towards a demilitarisation of the Indian Ocean, 'consulting closely with our allies and friends'.[25] In fact, Australia had not been consulted. Fraser feared that Carter might make an agreement with the Soviets in the Indian Ocean that would take precedence over ANZUS, and limit the United States' ability to respond to Australia.

Peacock went to Washington in May 1977 and reported back that he had 'received all the right assurances' but that he was sceptical about the follow-through. Vice President Walter Mondale and the Secretary of State, Cyrus Vance, had told him that the administration had not meant to 'shock' Australia with the Indian Ocean announcement. Peacock was only partly reassured. He told cabinet that the policy-making process in the United States was fragmented and prone to domestic pressure, and that Carter often tended to think aloud—which was probably what he had been doing with the Indian Ocean announcement—but, 'It was clear that Australia's priorities and interests will not automatically be taken into account'.[26] Fraser rapidly began to plan his own trip, wanting to talk to Carter before the Indian Ocean policy became 'locked in concrete'.

Fraser found in Carter a man he instinctively liked. He was full of good intentions, but as a leader of the free world he was astonishingly green. Fraser remembers, 'He had a naïve view that if you were nice to the Soviet Union, they would behave nicely back. He was an idealist. He was a relatively fast learner but totally ignorant about foreign affairs when he took the office. He made terrible mistakes in his first eighteen months'. Arthur Tange, who was with Fraser, later observed that the idea of a demilitarised Indian Ocean was 'one of Carter's woollier foreign policy forays'. Both Tange and cabinet were wondering what the political consequences might be if, in a Senate election, the voters of Western Australia were told that there was an agreement that forbade the Americans from defending Western Australia, but that the eastern coast states were not affected.[27]

Carter did not remain a foreign policy naïf. Fraser remembers a telephone conversation with him later in the negotiations over the Indian Ocean in which Carter confided in shocked tones that the Russian leader Leonid Brezhnev had lied to him in a conversation on the presidential 'red phone'. 'I said, "Well, what did you expect?" That changed his view. He learned quickly.'

By the time Carter left office, in 1981, Australia was more worried about military build-up in the Indian Ocean than demilitarisation. By that time, everything had changed. Fraser was able to claim that his State of the World speech five years before had been right. Détente was over.

* * *

When Fraser was an idealistic young undergraduate, he had come to understand the hope for a better world represented by the new Keynesian machinery of international cooperation growing up in the postwar years. In the aftermath of the oil shock in the early 1970s, that machinery had largely collapsed. Now there were some new attempts for a better world—one in which poverty and injustice would be eased. The developing countries in the United Nations had proposed a New International Economic Order. Unlike the Bretton Woods system, which had benefitted the developed countries, the new order would improve the terms of trade and reduce the tariff barriers that prevented the Third World from fair access to the markets of Europe and the United States. This push, and the rounds of trade talks that took place throughout the 1970s, gave rise to the North–South dialogue in which Fraser's was an important voice.

If Fraser was seen as a conservative on East–West issues, he was a radical liberal on North–South matters. In his State of the World speech he had said: 'The appalling widespread problems of poverty, hunger and disease are not only an affront to human dignity, but constantly threaten discord and conflict between nations'. The developed countries had given tied aid and tied loans but had completely failed to open their markets. 'They can take no pride in their actions in this area.' He had warned that the European Economic Community, a body he had welcomed since his earliest days as a backbencher, risked becoming inward-looking and selfish.

Fraser pursued these ideas in every international forum at which he had a voice, and at almost every meeting he had with world leaders during his term of office. It took up an enormous amount of time. The North–South issue connected Fraser the Prime Minister to Fraser the idealistic young man. His original contribution was to frame Australia's interests as being the same as those of the Third World. Like the developing countries, Australia was an exporter mainly of commodities rather than manufactured goods. Like them, Australia was locked out of world markets. The developed nations were pushing hard for financial institutions to have open access to worldwide markets; the developing nations wanted the right to form trade associations and to regulate the activities of multinational corporations. Not surprisingly, the North–South dialogue was full of tension, resentment, distrust and difficulties.

Australia consistently sided with the South while trying to use its unique position to engage the North. Fraser's pursuit of these ideas was largely frustrated. Again and again, he came up against the self-satisfied apathy of Europe and the United States. Fraser was in favour of globalisation; what he thought was lacking was a recognition of the need for justice, for the benefits of globalisation to be felt by all.

In May 1977, Fraser went to Europe to advocate for Australia. He hoped that Australian uranium, which his government was planning to exploit, would give him a bargaining chip. Europe needed an assured supply of uranium; Australia was interested in access to markets and stability of trade. Perhaps a treaty embracing all trade was necessary, he suggested. It cut no ice. Arthur Tange, who travelled as part of the Australian team, later remembered the trip to Europe as

> frantic activity, serving the Prime Minister's demands for up-to-date briefings ... In each capital we saw little beyond the walls of hotel rooms where the team wrote papers at night, not on the country outside but on the one about to be visited next morning. In Brussels I was given a seat at the table of a European Economic Commission meeting headed by the President Roy Jenkins and listened to our Prime Minister wade into the commission ... There was much agitation on the part of several commissioners ... I came away with the distinct impression that Fraser's brusque diplomatic methods in a formal European environment might have been more likely to shock than to persuade.[28]

Jenkins clearly didn't want to negotiate with the Australian Prime Minister. Fraser had just one relatively modest aim: to gain a commitment that once a year the Europeans would agree to negotiate with Australia over trade. 'I wanted a meeting where we could put our grievances on the table and they could put theirs and we could talk in a genuine way. I didn't think that would fix the problems, but it would create a forum in which you might over time get some movement.' He recalls that while the senior officials from each side talked, he went into Jenkins's office and found him mixing martinis. 'Jenkins said, "We don't have to take this afternoon too seriously, do we? We can leave it all to the chaps, can't we?"

'And I said, "Sure, provided you will agree to meeting once a year for negotiations".

'And he said, "Oh, I don't think we can do that, old chap"

'So I put down my martini and said, "Well in that case we are going to have to take it seriously. Perhaps we should go and join the others".'

They talked until three, with Jenkins 'turning and weaving all the time, refusing to be tied down'. Finally, Jenkins made a verbal agreement to negotiate regularly with Australia about trade grievances. Fraser asked for it in writing. 'Jenkins said, "Well, we can leave that to the chaps, can't we?", and that's when I made my first mistake for the day, because I agreed.' That evening Fraser was at a reception. While he socialised, he was waiting for the Secretary of the Department of Foreign Affairs Nick Parkinson to bring him the written agreement. 'Nick came in with a very long face, looking quite pale and distressed. I asked him if he had the document, and he said, "You don't want to see it".

'I said, "That makes me want to see it even more".'

The agreement Parkinson had in his hand said that if Australia had problems or complaints, it could put them in writing, and, if the European Community deemed it necessary, a discussion might follow.

'That's not what Jenkins agreed to', Fraser said.

'I know it isn't', said Parkinson.

Fraser told him to go back and try again. Parkinson said the European negotiators had 'flown to the four corners of Europe'. There could be no going back.

'Someone will be around, and I want you to find them', said Fraser.

Fraser and his party were due to leave the next morning, but that night Fraser told Parkinson to let it be known that he was prepared to leave the senior public servants in Europe indefinitely to continue negotiations until the agreement he had reached verbally with Jenkins was confirmed in writing. 'I also let it be known that before I left the following morning I was prepared to call a press conference and make it clear that Roy Jenkins couldn't keep his word. He had agreed to something in front of sixteen people at three-thirty in the afternoon and by the evening he had gone back on it. I was prepared to say that Roy Jenkins's word didn't last more than three or four hours.' At close to midnight the Australian team finally emerged with a piece of paper that reflected what Fraser and Jenkins had agreed.

In the long run, it did little good. John Howard was appointed Minister for Special Trade Negotiations, but despite his best efforts he got little more from the Europeans than sympathetic noises. The Europeans, then as now, remained impervious to any but their own interests. Today Fraser says, 'Nothing has changed. They talk free trade, but there is no free trade. The Europeans were never going to shift'.

According to Howard's recent biography, his frustration at the hands of the Europeans was one of the things that made him an advocate of lowering Australia's tariffs, on the grounds that Australia could expect no special favours.[29] Fraser says that if the European negotiations, or any other serious world trade negotiations, had come to anything, Australia's tariffs on manufactured goods would have been a bargaining chip. 'I was trying to make the point that if we could get better access for the things we could do best, we would find it much easier to reduce protection on other things where Australia was a high-cost producer. That argument never got taken up. Australia's officials knew full well that was my attitude, and it would have been translated into policy if we had been given any indication that agriculture protection would come down substantially.'

In the mid to late 1970s there was a series of international meetings of heads of governments on trade issues. Fraser tried to turn the emphasis from manufactured goods—which were the main concern of the developed countries—to agricultural products. He was one of the advocates of the idea of a Common Fund to be established within the United Nations to stabilise price fluctuations for commodities and to support developing countries in improving and diversifying their products and trade. Fraser pursued this idea in all his talks with world leaders in the early years of his government, and through both the United Nations and the Commonwealth. He wanted the developing countries to see contributing to a Common Fund as a matter of interdependence rather than aid. As always with the topics closest to his heart, Fraser made the Common Fund the subject of one of his addresses to his electorate. He told the people of Wannon that the failure of the major trading blocs to deal with agricultural protectionism posed one of the most testing challenges for world leaders. 'Australia, while recognising the limits of our influence on world economic affairs, will continue to press our case with vigour and reason.'[30] Australia was one of the first nations to offer to put money into a Common Fund, and one of the first to ratify the United Nations' instrument under which it was established, in 1980. Once again, though, Fraser was unsuccessful. Not enough countries ratified the agreement, and the Common Fund did not come into force until 1989—long after Fraser had left the scene.

* * *

Fraser and Peacock wanted an intellectual framework for their insight that Australia had interests in common with the Third World. Fraser had always valued academics. As Minister for Educaion he had insisted on their role in teaching human beings how to live together in peace. As Prime Minister he had sought out scholars such as David Kemp, Petro Georgiou and John Rose for his personal staff. Now, Owen Harries was appointed to head a task force to consider Australia's relationship to the Third World. The result was a 450-page volume released in September 1979.[31] It was an extraordinary document, described by one foreign policy expert as 'one of the best and most unusual state papers I have seen produced by Australian government sources ... One cannot imagine its being produced at earlier stages of our national history. It is a true sign of growing maturity'.[32] The Harries report included a mix of hard-nosed foreign policy advice with appendices on moral philosophy in which concepts such as equity, justice and responsibility were discussed in the context of the developed world's duties. The report was digested, commented upon and criticised all over the world. Harries laid out ninety-two recommendations and thirteen general conclusions. He argued that a distinction needed to be made between radical and moderate forces in the Third World. The first wanted fundamental change; the latter wanted improved conditions and opportunities within the existing system. 'Policies which simply resist all change are likely to strengthen the radicals; those which are responsible to limited and practicable proposals ... are likely to strengthen the moderates.' Australia, Harries said, was a 'Western country with a difference', being isolated from the centres of power in Europe and the United States. It should not necessarily follow the prevailing Western line towards the Third World, but should be 'moderate, sympathetic and cooperative' in reacting to Third World proposals. He also recommended that Australia detach itself from the western European group at the United Nations, and instead attach itself to the Asian group. Europe's increasing cohesiveness made Australia's membership of the group 'anomalous'.

Not all of the recommendations accorded with government policy. Harries said that Australia shouldn't try to act as a bridge between the Third World and the West, or seek a prominent role in African affairs; yet Fraser was doing exactly these things (see chapter 15). The report also advocated Australia's reducing tariffs as quickly as possible, particularly for products from the Third World, to 'facilitate the transition to a more outward-looking Australian industrial structure'. Cabinet welcomed the report, and Fraser adopted it as a guide for policy formation, but he retained his own view on tariffs. He says today, 'We certainly needed to drop them, but not without some indication that there would be movement internationally'. It fell to Hawke and Keating, in the years after Fraser, to lower Australia's manufacturing tariff walls, but little was received in return. 'They talked about a level playing field, while America and Europe still subsidised their farmers', says Fraser. Today, Third World countries are still prevented from accessing the most lucrative markets. 'In the essentials', says Fraser, 'absolutely nothing has changed'.

* * *

The Fraser family spent the summer of 1979 at Nareen. It was the mid point of Fraser's time as Prime Minister. There were many reasons for satisfaction. Domestically, the economy was recovering. It still seemed as though the Common Fund might succeed. Immigration policy was being reformed. Then, as the year drew to a close, Fraser received a visitor with unwelcome news. It was the Soviet Ambassador, and the reason for his call was the Soviet invasion of Afghanistan. The Ambassador tried to tell Fraser that the Afghan Government had requested Soviet assistance. Fraser was having none of it. Shortly afterwards he described the invasion as the greatest threat to world peace since World War II.[33] Here was proof that the Soviet Union was still an aggressive, imperial power. The United States would have to wake up.

President Carter was already in the middle of a foreign policy crisis. Just weeks before, in November 1979, a group of Islamist students had invaded the US embassy in Iran and taken sixty-six Americans hostage. Carter was trying to negotiate their release. Just before Christmas, the Australian Minister for Defence Jim Killen had told cabinet that the Iran crisis meant that the United States was likely to want an increase in its naval presence in the Indian Ocean. While that was welcome, it was likely to be matched by increased Soviet forces, which would not be welcome. Cabinet had considered whether Australia might be involved in any direct military action in Iran, although it was not at that time proposed.[34]

Now there was an even more serious crisis. For the first time in many years, the Soviets had invaded a non-aligned country. Why had they done it, and would they stop there? All that was needed, Fraser told the media, was for a pro-Marxist minority in Iran to claim they were being persecuted and that they wanted help: that would give the Soviets the excuse to move further into the Middle East. They would have direct access to the Indian Ocean, the Arabian Sea and the Persian Gulf, and could come to control much of the world's oil supply. They could bring the West to its knees.

When parliament sat in February 1980, Fraser quoted slabs of his State of the World speech. 'When that speech was given in 1976 there were many commentators throughout this nation who regarded it as a hard-line, Cold War statement. As events have sadly proved, it was all too accurate.' The Soviets were now on the move in Africa, South-West Asia and South-East Asia. Tensions in the Indian Ocean were heightened. World affairs had entered a new and uncomfortable era.[35]

The Soviet action, Peacock told cabinet in its first meeting of 1980, had 'changed the unwritten rules' of US–Soviet relations. Carter had declared months before that any attempt by an outside force to gain control of the Persian Gulf region would be regarded as an assault on the interests of the United States. Now that seemed likely to happen. The outlook for the decade ahead was 'truncated, suspicious and competitive East–West relations'. Peacock told cabinet that the Soviets might have many objectives, including a future assault on the Middle East oil fields, but they must also have thought that now was a good time to move. They were betting on the Americans' preoccupation with the hostage crisis in Iran. They saw the risk of retaliation as low.[36]

Fraser knew only too well the weaknesses and hypocrisies of the Western alliance, but in this situation he thought it essential that the West present a united face: Carter had to be supported. There was no chance of persuading the Soviets to withdraw, but, as Fraser told parliament, they must be convinced that the cost of what they had done was so high that they would reconsider any further moves. Over the next few months, all of Fraser's foreign policy efforts were towards this. He was to pay a significant political price.

The United States had already announced trade sanctions, and asked its allies for support. The Australian cabinet considered a long list of sanctions. It agreed not to sign any new wheat contracts, effectively saying that it would not replace the shortages that would be caused by the US trade boycott. Academic, scientific and cultural exchanges were halted.

That year's Olympics were due to be held in Moscow. At first, Peacock told cabinet that an Olympic boycott was unlikely. If there was to be one, then Australia should 'await the lead of the United States … and move only in good company'.[37] Privately, Fraser was against a boycott. The focus of cabinet discussions had been to try to find action that would be sustainable without being divisive. Throughout January, memorandums flew back and forth as cabinet revised the details of the sanctions.

Then, in late January, Carter unilaterally announced a boycott of the Olympics. Once again, he had not consulted the United States' allies, but he did ask them to follow his lead. Fraser was dismayed: he thought the move a mistake. It would be a cruel blow to sportspeople and their supporters, but, even more serious, the boycott was unlikely to succeed. It would become a sign of division in the alliance rather than unity. Nevertheless, in the months ahead, he and his ministers did everything they could to persuade Australian sportspeople to boycott the games, including putting heavy pressure on the Australian Olympic Federation. Today, athletes still remember the pain. Some wanted to compete; some felt that by doing so they would be traitors. The division and the pain took decades to heal. There was only one step that Fraser would not take: he would not refuse the athletes permission to travel, as Carter had in the United States. Despite what was at stake, 'In a democracy, preventing private citizens from travelling is something a government should not do'.

Meanwhile, Fraser had begun an extraordinary, and largely secret, exercise in shuttle diplomacy. He started in late January 1980 in Washington, where he found the Carter administration transformed, with a new willingness to spend on defence and a new concern about the Western alliance. To his shock, Carter had found that in this crucial moment in world affairs the Western alliance was in ill repair. Just weeks before, Carter had written to Fraser congratulating him on his role in persuading Britain's Margaret Thatcher to support black rule in Rhodesia (see chapter 15).[38] Fraser had played a key role in bringing the stubborn Thatcher and the leaders of the angry frontline African states together to negotiate a compromise. Clearly, Carter said, Fraser was talented in negotiation. Now he appealed to him for help in reaching out to Europe.

Fraser flew to Germany to see Chancellor Helmut Schmidt. He found confirmation for Carter's fears: the Europeans were fed up with not being consulted. Schmidt in particular was furious with Carter, and told Fraser that the US President had assured him that there would not be a boycott of the Olympics. (It was not an issue Schmidt wanted to fight in Germany, given that it was an election year.) Yet just hours later Schmidt had seen Carter on the television news announcing just such a boycott. Schmidt was prepared to defend the alliance, even at the risk of his position. He backed the boycott once it was announced, but he remained angry with Carter.

Schmidt made an unusual request of Fraser. Would he change his plans and return to Washington, to take Carter a message from Europe? Fraser remembers, 'I said, "Why don't you ring him up or go and see him yourself?" But he said no. He wanted Australia to be an intermediary. He said they were too angry with each other to be able to talk'. Fraser was reluctant. 'I didn't think this was really something I necessarily should be doing.' He wanted to find out whether d'Estaing and Thatcher agreed. Telephone calls were made. Schmidt said D'Estaing thought it was a good idea and that the British Foreign Secretary Peter Carrington was less enthusiastic but had no objection. As a result, Fraser found himself flying back to Washington. The reasons for his return were not made public at the time. Carter told the media that Fraser had decided to 'stop by to see me again to give me a report on the consultations in Europe', since the meetings had been so 'fruitful'. Fraser, in turn, made a few remarks about how Australia did not overestimate its influence but wanted to play what role it could.[39] In fact, Fraser told Carter in blunt terms that his failure to consult was putting the Western alliance at risk when it was most needed. The result was that Carter called a meeting of foreign ministers for the last week of February. The cracks were papered over.

Back in Australia, and in the midst of his own attempt to make the Olympic boycott stick, Fraser kept up the diplomacy. Carter, meanwhile, plunged deeper into crisis. His negotiations to liberate the hostages in Iran were achieving nothing and, on 24 April, the United States launched a military operation aimed at freeing them. The result was a disaster: two aircraft crashed and eight US servicemen died. The operation had been a gamble, and in international terms its timing could not have been worse. Fraser was advised that its failure would reinforce the image of the President as a bungler. Increased strains had been placed on the Western alliance. Cool heads were needed, and effective communication.

Fraser did his best to be one of those cool heads. In a letter to Carter after the failed operation, he wrote that an overriding imperative was to establish a totally unified approach with Europe. 'There can be no uncertainty about the results of divisions between Europe and the United States; there can only be a cold certainty of a disaster that could lead to a Third World War.' He suggested that Carter should invite the European leaders to Washington for consultations—not just one meeting but a regular process, so that the Soviet Union would know that when policies were announced, they were shared policies. Fraser was using the crisis to try to convince Carter that US unilateralism had to end. There were some things that the free world could not do without the United States, but there were also many things that the United States could not, or should not, do on its own.

More letters were sent—to Robert Muldoon in New Zealand, to Pierre Trudeau in Canada and to Margaret Thatcher in Britain.

Fraser told Thatcher that he wouldn't criticise Carter for attempting the release of the hostages.

> What the Iranians have done is unforgivable and outside the law. The frustration of a great nation such as the United States is something which even those of us who are not American can well understand ... The whole Western world is crying out for a common strategy and a common approach which I believe only you and [Carter, d'Estaing and Schmidt] can achieve ... Let me say that my government is grievously concerned at any sign of lack of unity or approach amongst the four major nations upon whom our freedom and way of life so greatly depends. Unity with the United States is of the highest importance.

He urged Helmut Schmidt to do whatever he could to achieve unity and shared strategy.

> There is one point in the discussions I have had with you on which we have never agreed, and I think you know what it is. You have always expressed a diffidence about the role you as Chancellor of Germany can or should take. I understand the reasons for that diffidence but I do not agree with it, because of the position you have established yourself and a deep respect with which you and your country are held.[40]

Meanwhile, despite pressure of the kind that only Fraser could exert, including personal phone calls to Olympic officials and offering cash compensation to athletes to attend other competitions, the Olympic boycott in Australia had failed. The Australian Olympic Federation was deeply divided, and left the decision to the last possible moment. In May it voted six to five to send a team. Fraser was bitterly disappointed. After all the work he had done in promoting Western unity, he had to admit that his own country would not help Carter to deliver a boycott. The attempt to do so had torn apart the careers of dozens of athletes, and the nation was treated to the depressing spectacle of a much depleted Australian team abandoning their flag to march behind the Olympic banner in the opening ceremony in Moscow. Of the 218 athletes selected, only 125 went. The Australian Government had tested to the limit the loyalty of a small number of its most prominent citizens. The pressure was all the greater because at the previous Olympics, in Montreal, Australia had put in a poor showing, failing to earn a single gold medal. Moscow was meant to have been vindication. Fraser was accused of hypocrisy because some trade with the Soviets continued. He had received advice that a complete trade boycott would be ineffective, but that didn't stop the ill feeling. The swimmer Dawn Fraser condemned Malcolm Fraser for the apparent hypocrisy; 'Fraser versus Fraser' were the newspaper headlines.[41]

One good thing came out of the sporting setbacks of Montreal and Moscow. Robert Ellicott, by this time Minister for Home Affairs, had already been advancing the idea of an Australian Institute for Sport. The distress over Montreal had led to more funding for training athletes before the Olympics, and the Moscow boycott gave impetus to the campaign for more federal involvement in developing elite athletes. Fraser opened the institute in 1981.

Sixty-one countries boycotted the Moscow Olympics, including West Germany, China and Japan. The United Kingdom and France supported the boycott but allowed their athletes to participate if they wished. But it was not the boycott that defeated the Soviets; it was Afghanistan itself. The Soviet troops were worn down by the determined resistance of the guerrilla mujahidin equipped with US arms. The invasion of Afghanistan did not cause World War III; instead, it became one of the first steps towards the weakening of the Soviet Union, leading to its eventual collapse. Fraser's fears about a continuing Soviet advance into the Middle East were not realised.

Carter had received his baptism of fire; he began to re-arm the United States. Fraser says, 'He never gets credit for the things he did in his last eighteen months. People forget that it was him and not Reagan who began to re-arm. Carter is a good man and he has done a lot of good things since he left the presidency, but his learning curve was a very painful one'.

* * *

At the same time, Fraser was facing more problems at home. He had worked well with his Minister for Foreign Affairs, Andrew Peacock. Back in the Gorton and Snedden days, they had been rivals for the leadership but in government they had found only common ground. Fraser remembers today that Peacock 'had been very good, right with me: we agreed on almost everything'. But in 1980 they fell out. For Peacock, it was an issue of principle; for Fraser, it was a question of timing and emphasis. The issue that tore them apart was the Vietnamese invasion of Kampuchea in 1978, and the resulting question of whether Australia should continue to recognise the murderous regime of Pol Pot. Peacock thought the Pol Pot regime so abhorrent that Australia should withdraw its recognition. Fraser and the rest of cabinet agreed with him about the abhorrence of Pol Pot, but gave priority to supporting the countries of the Association of South-East Asian Nations, which did not want Australia to give de facto encouragement to the Vietnamese aggression. As Fraser put it in parliament:

> It is not possible to move away from Pol Pot without moving a distance towards that Vietnamese-supported regime ... The whole world would know that, once derecognised, Pol Pot would never again be recognised. Therefore, if this country were to re-establish any kind of diplomatic relations, it would be with that Vietnamese-supported regime. There is no way of avoiding the fact that a move away from Pol Pot is in part an encouragement to the Vietnamese-supported aggression.[42]

Fraser had previously written to world leaders arguing that Vietnam's invasion of Kampuchea had 'important strategic implications' as part of the Soviet Union's attempts to exert influence in the developing world. This was being done through a 'carefully calculated series of steps' which, taken in isolation, would not provoke a response, but which together threatened to upset the global balance of power.[43]

This was the context in which cabinet decided that solidarity with the Association of South-East Asian Nations in condemning Vietnamese aggression was more important than expressing abhorrence for Pol Pot. In July 1980, Peacock told the media that he thought Pol Pot should be derecognised, but he was then rebuffed in cabinet, meaning a public humiliation. He offered his resignation, but a compromise was worked out in which cabinet agreed to keep the matter under continuing review, with Peacock able to raise it again if circumstances altered.[44] The issue came up again at the Commonwealth Heads of Regional Government Meeting in New Delhi later in the year. The Singapore Prime Minister Lee Kuan Yew spoke in strong opposition to a derecognition of Pol Pot. Fraser remembers that Lee Kuan Yew had spoken to him privately about the importance of the issue. 'Wisely or not, I said, "It might be a good thing for you to press your views on Andrew".' The result was that Lee Kuan Yew and Peacock had a fierce row on the plane back to Singapore.

In Canberra on 10 September, Fraser released a media statement from Lee Kuan Yew on the issue just as Peacock was preparing to raise the matter again in cabinet. Peacock was furious. He accused Fraser of disloyalty.

On the very day on which Fraser called the election, 12 September 1980, Peacock was again threatening to resign. He offered Fraser three options: his immediate resignation, a change of cabinet policy on Kampuchea, or an undertaking from Peacock to remain silent through the campaign and then decline to serve as Foreign Minister after the election. He and Fraser talked long and hard. On

23 September, cabinet reached a decision noting the discussions between Fraser and Peacock and agreeing to an uneasy truce. Australia's recognition of Pol Pot would not continue beyond the short term.[45]

The issue was hosed down during the election campaign, but when the new ministry was sworn in, Peacock was by his own choice not Minister for Foreign Affairs. He took the industrial relations portfolio, and was replaced as Foreign Minister by Tony Street. Within months of the election, however, Peacock resigned from the industrial relations portfolio, again accusing Fraser of disloyalty. Later, he challenged for the leadership. The government never fully recovered its stability.

* * *

In late 1980, the Australian Government was keeping a close eye on the contenders in the US presidential election. Peacock had briefed cabinet in August that a Reagan victory would mean 'an immediate increase in defence expenditure to address the existing military imbalance of the Soviet Union'. A Carter victory would see 'a more consistent and cohesive policy than we have seen during his first term. Carter would also seek to strengthen the United States' defence posture to consult with allies and to improve unity within NATO'. Either stance would be welcomed by Australia, but there were concerns about both candidates. Reagan would be more cautious than Carter in developing relationships with China. Reagan did not have a great knowledge of Australia, whereas, 'in the light of our recent record', Carter was warmly disposed. And on human rights, Regan would be less of an activist than Carter.[46]

Fraser welcomed Reagan's election; the new President's views on the Soviet threat were close to Fraser's own. The United States was now showing the resolve that Fraser had hoped for from both Ford and Carter. But Reagan soon disappointed Fraser in other ways. He had no interest in the idea of a Common Fund or in the continuing moves to begin serious world trade negotiations. World justice was not on the Reagan agenda.

On 2 April 1982, Argentina invaded the Falkland Islands, a British territory 480 kilometres off the coast of Argentina. Britain was outraged. Prime Minister Margaret Thatcher, in full jingoistic mode, made defending the Falklands a matter of national pride. The United States, though, was reluctant and initially remained neutral. The US Ambassador to the United Nations Jeanne Kirkpatrick was arguing fiercely for the USA to support Argentina. The Vice President George Bush (senior) was visiting Australia at the end of April and dined with Fraser at the Lodge. Fraser remembers, 'Inevitably, the topic of Argentina came up, and I asked him if Jeanne Kirkpatrick was going to win the argument, and had he thought of the consequences.

'"What do you mean?"

'"Well, Margaret Thatcher is your most important ally in Europe. If you as the senior NATO partner support Argentina against her, she will see it as an act of total betrayal. If that is what you do, she'll condemn you from one end of Europe to the next. She'll condemn you around the world. If you ever ask her to America, she'll condemn you in the United States. You might end up without NATO. You know, a woman scorned!"

'Bush looked at his watch. He said, "Malcolm, I think that I am going to have to disrupt your dinner party. The National Security Council is sitting down to examine this matter in three minutes' time; I think that I had better key myself in to the discussion. Have you got a telephone?"'

Fraser showed him to the office. Bush made his phone call and emerged about an hour and a half later, giving Fraser the thumbs up. Fraser asked him what would have happened if he hadn't made the call. 'Kirkpatrick would have won the argument in ten minutes', he said.

On 1 May it was reported that the previous day there had been an emergency meeting of the National Security Council at the

White House, and President Reagan had declared support for Britain, and military and economic sanctions against Argentina. NATO survived.[47]

In December 1982, the Fraser cabinet received a mid-term review of the Reagan administration. It said Reagan now had a 'well-established national security apparatus' and that Australia had 'regular correspondence at the highest level with the American administration'. But there was criticism of the 'unsophisticated way in which foreign policy is being articulated'.[48] The assessments reflected Fraser's own views. He was glad that Reagan had taken the hard line against the Soviets; but it was clear that the unsubtle way in which the United States was pursuing foreign policy had alienated the Chinese. Fraser felt an opportunity had been lost. Meanwhile, he had even less joy from Reagan on the issues of free trade and the Third World than he had had from Ford and Carter.

* * *

When Helmut Schmidt left office, in October 1982, he wrote to Fraser to thank him for what he had done on the world stage. Schmidt credited Fraser with helping to create a new form of North–South exchange. 'You have … warned with increasing concern of the dangers of protectionism and I have agreed with you. The hard times facing the world economy will tempt many governments to turn to protectionism. You and I know that this would be the wrong way.'[49] Soon after he received Schmidt's letter, Fraser was voted out of office, but his activism on North–South issues did not stop when he left power; nor did his blunt speaking to US allies. In 1984, Fraser gave a speech in Hong Kong in which he said there were 'fundamental problems' in the international economy that were largely the fault of the United States. If there were no US deficit, interest rates and therefore Third World repayments would be reduced by billions of dollars each year, but

> the US deficit has risen the most under the President most committed to abolishing it … Within three or four years at most, on the basis of current policies, the United States will be a net debtor nation. What kind of world is it when the world's wealthiest country owes more interest abroad than interest due?

The US deficit affected everyone, Fraser said. It sucked in funds from abroad, raised international interest rates and made it harder for poor nations to borrow. 'The single most important factor in world economies in 1984 is the United States' deficit. The second most important factor is the lack of agreement and understanding of the damage that maintenance of that deficit will do to the whole world.' The result, Fraser said, was the risk of 'massive political instability' and the alienation of developing nations from the West. Fraser returned to the idealism of his youth. What had happened to the determination to build a better world that had inspired leaders after World War II, he asked. 'Let me only say that if the men of 1945 were alive today, they would act and not wait until disaster fell.'

Fraser proposed a solution. He had been working on it in government right up to his last days in power, writing letters to Lee Kuan Yew and other leaders in the Association of South-East Asian Nations. What he suggested was a new voluntary code in which signatories would agree not to raise protection in any form against any other signatory. Fraser hoped such an idea might revive the battered hopes for free trade. If just one major trading group signed up, then the negotiations could no longer be inhibited by the developed countries. 'They would not have to sign—but the incentives to do so would be great once a major economic group endorsed [the agreement]', he said. Fraser had instructed the Department of Trade and the Treasury to examine the idea. They had concluded that it would be in the interests of Australia and of the Third World. Australia's levels of protection were there to be dismantled—in return for commitment from others to do the same.[50] Perhaps it would never have worked. Regardless, these hopes died with the Fraser government.

In his 1976 State of the World speech, Fraser had said that Australia's relationship to the Western alliance was not a matter of 'historical ties or ideology or cultural compatibility, important as those things are'; it was based 'four square on an appreciation of what Australia's interests require'.[51] Today, Fraser wonders if governments are still prepared to act on that 'four-square appreciation'. Instead of presenting a unique Australian point of view, we have been too subservient, too reactive. We have been dragged into conflict because of the false importance given to the ANZUS treaty. He fears that our intimacy with the United States during the regime of George W Bush and the Howard government's rhetoric on asylum seekers have alienated us from the countries in our region. Now Fraser reads the newspaper headlines and their talk of containing China, and he worries. It seems to be a backward-looking policy and potentially dangerous. The first objective of foreign policy, Fraser says, should be peace and stability in East Asia and the western Pacific. All our efforts should be directed to that result. It depends on developing relationships of trust between the countries of the region.

There are plenty of problems. There is the behaviour of North Korea and the bad feeling between Japan and China, which is not helped by Japan's refusal to acknowledge or apologise for the atrocities committed by its troops in World War II. As for Taiwan and China, Fraser believes this once seemingly insurmountable problem might now be relatively easily overcome by granting Taiwan a special status similar to or better than that enjoyed by Hong Kong within a unified China.

How helpful is our relationship with the United States in solving these problems? Sometimes it helps, and sometimes it doesn't, Fraser says. When the United States advances good relations between the countries of the region, it is obviously welcome. Sometimes its goodwill is essential. Yet to say, as the 2009 Rudd government white paper implies, that peace and stability in the western Pacific primarily depends on the United States is 'misleading and wrong'. Not all the US actions in the region have helped. In Fraser's opinion, the United States has not learned the lessons about the dangers of unilateralism. In recent years, Fraser has been reinforced in his view that independence in Australia's foreign policy is essential.

Fraser reflects on the history. The United States made it clear that it would not back Australian troops in Malaysia in the days of Garfield Barwick. In Fraser's own time, the United States stated that Australia was expected to handle regional conflicts on her own. The ANZUS treaty has always been a heavily qualified commitment by the United States. 'The USA will always follow its own interests. Everything in our history tells us that this is so', Fraser says. 'ANZUS should never again be used to draw Australia into conflict if our own interests lie elsewhere.' The best guarantee of security for Australia, he believes, lies in developing good relationships within our region—not in sheltering behind the United States.

15

Commonwealth

On 2 June 1977, the British opposition frontbencher Sir Geoffrey Howe sat down to write to his leader, Margaret Thatcher. He wrote a report and a warning: watch out for Malcolm Fraser. Howe had dined two nights before with Fraser and Peter Carrington, the Conservative Party's leader in the House of Lords, at the Australian High Commissioner's house. If the British Conservatives had expected a relaxed occasion, they had had a surprise. After dinner, Howe told Thatcher, Fraser had 'launched into quite a formidable (but not unreasonable) critique' of the European Economic Community's systems of subsidies, tariffs and quotas, and their impact on Australia and the Third World. Howe and Carrington had tried to defend Europe, but, 'I fear that we did not come at all close to winning the argument'. Howe said that Fraser was likely to raise the same point with Thatcher, and Howe had asked that her briefings be updated so that she would be better prepared than he had been.[1]

Thatcher already knew Fraser. They had met years before, when they were both ministers for education. When Fraser was elected in 1975, Thatcher had sent him a telegram:

> My colleagues and I rejoice to see Australia rejecting socialism in favour of personal freedom, wider opportunities

> for private enterprise and stronger ties with Britain. Your success and that of our mutual friends in New Zealand is a shot in the arm for the Conservative Party. We in Britain confidently intend to follow your good example.[2]

Now they met again. Thatcher was still in opposition, but had become the dominant figure in British politics. Fraser made his customary assessment of character. As Education Minister Thatcher had struck him as hard-working but inexperienced. As leader of the Conservative Party, he took her measure. 'You could get Maggie within reach of reasonable results if you could get her to turn her intellect to a question. She had a good mind, but if you engaged the emotions rather than the intellect, you just got this awful jingoism, and then she could be so very stubborn.'

Fraser and Thatcher dealt with each other, on and off, for the next thirteen years. When Fraser was Prime Minister, they went head to head over the future of Rhodesia (now Zimbabwe). After he had left office, Fraser lobbied her over sanctions against South Africa. Throughout these years his constant aim was to engage her head, and avoid her heart. 'If ever she thought her prestige or Britain's prestige was at stake, well, then you just couldn't move her.' Yet he did move her. In Fraser, Thatcher encountered a leader whose determination matched her own.

Fraser was in London in 1977 to attend his first Commonwealth Heads of Government Meeting (CHOGM). He had said in his State of the World speech that ideology 'while not irrelevant' could not be the guiding principle for foreign policy. But he had also said that Australia should 'seek to further our own deeply held values of democracy, freedom and respect for the individual'.[3] If there was a forum through which Fraser was able to bring into alignment his hopes for a better world and his pragmatism, it was the Commonwealth.

* * *

Fraser's roots went deep in the Commonwealth. His grandfather Sir Simon Fraser had been a representative at one of the Imperial Conferences between the United Kingdom and its self-governing dominions in 1894. These meetings led to the creation of what in the post–World War I years became known as the British Commonwealth. Fraser's grandmother Anna Fraser was a member of organisations established to encourage friendship between Commonwealth nations. In those days the Commonwealth represented British heritage. In 1946 it had only five members: Britain, Australia, New Zealand, Canada and South Africa. The Commonwealth was a hangover from the days of empire, dominated by white faces and with Britain indisputably at its head. With the granting of independence to India, Pakistan and Burma (now Myanmar) in 1947, the composition of the Commonwealth began to change. A crucial test was when India became a republic. Could it still be part of the Commonwealth when the monarch of Britain had no role in its internal affairs? The Commonwealth survived. In 1950, India accepted the Queen as head of the Commonwealth and as a symbol of free association. Other Commonwealth countries became republics or constitutional monarchies with their own rulers. The modern Commonwealth had arrived. It grew quickly as newly independent countries entered the post-colonial age. The word 'British' was dropped from its title, and the organisation became instead simply the Commonwealth of Nations—an association of independent countries meeting, in theory at least, as equals. No country has ever left the Commonwealth entirely of its own volition.

Fraser welcomed the modern Commonwealth in one of his first speeches in parliament, in March 1956. 'Although our fathers may not like it, the fact is that the British Empire is passing out of existence and in its place is coming something which will be far more enduring and beneficial to world peace.'[4] In 1961, the member states put pressure on South Africa to end apartheid, and as a result South Africa withdrew. The young Fraser told parliament at the time that this was inevitable: the Commonwealth could not embrace or tolerate racism.

> I regard the Commonwealth as a bridge between the people of different races and colours, and we must try to maintain this bridge ... I am convinced that we must make the Commonwealth work. If it cannot be made to work, then I believe the world cannot work and that there will be little hope for us.[5]

As the new nations bordering Rhodesia and South Africa gained independence and joined the Commonwealth, opposition to apartheid and racism became a central issue. In 1965, largely as a result of pressure from the new African nations, the Commonwealth set up its own secretariat—a dedicated public service. This became the conduit for advocacy from groups opposing apartheid, including the African National Congress (ANC) in South Africa.

The Commonwealth had become a unique international organisation. Unlike the United Nations, it did not include either of the superpowers. Some thought this condemned it to irrelevance. Others—including Fraser—thought of it as a source of strength. In 1971 in Singapore the Commonwealth leaders declared that membership was compatible with being part of any other international organisation—or with non-alignment. The Commonwealth was declaring itself outside the Cold War. In the same declaration, the heads of government committed themselves to opposing racism.

> We believe that our multinational association can expand human understanding and understanding among nations, assist in the elimination of discrimination based on differences of race, colour or creed, maintain and strengthen personal liberty, contribute to the enrichment of life for all, and provide a powerful influence for peace among nations.[6]

Another strength was that Commonwealth heads of government actually got to know each other. At the summits, every two years, the main business was conducted at retreats. The heads of government left behind their staff, their public relations operators and their advisers, and met face to face for long discussions. Fraser says today, 'That doesn't happen in any other international forum. You meet people and come to understand them and to trust them, and things become possible in international affairs that previously were not possible'. In the Commonwealth of Nations, Fraser found an organisation that resonated with his highest ideals. Over the period of his prime ministership he became one of its leading figures.

* * *

The Commonwealth of Nations had by the mid 1970s become a mix of poor and wealthy nations spread across the globe, with little in common other than an historical association with the United Kingdom. It was so unusual, and the agendas of its member states were so often at variance, that many people thought that it would soon break apart, or else become an irrelevant talking shop. The Commonwealth was having to adjust, rapidly, to the post-colonial age. Britain had dealt well with the transition over many years, but in the 1970s there was the potential for schism between the 'old Commonwealth' of white, wealthy nations and the new African nations shrugging off the colonial past. By the time Fraser was preparing for his first CHOGM, to be held in London in 1977, the future of the Commonwealth seemed dim. The issue over which it seemed likely to break up was opposition to apartheid. In 1976, the South African military had fired on black youths demonstrating in the Soweto riots. Officers had shot indiscriminately. Hundreds of people, many of them children, had died. More were injured. South Africa's neighbours, the newly independent majority-ruled nations, were the so-called frontline states. Of these, Botswana, Lesotho, Tanzania and Zambia were members of the Commonwealth. There were other sympathetic Commonwealth nations further afield, including Jamaica. For them, action against apartheid was an issue on which there could be no compromise. The ANC had taken up arms in South Africa, supported by the frontline states. But the old, white Commonwealth nations, with their deep bonds of money and friendship with business and political leaders in Rhodesia and South Africa, saw the ANC and other black movements as Marxists. At a time when South Africa was being internationally condemned, New Zealand had hosted a tour of the country's rugby union team. As a result, African nations had boycotted the 1976 Montreal Olympics and were threatening to boycott the 1978 Commonwealth Games in Edmonton.

In all this, Australia's position had been ambiguous. Only a few years before, in 1971, Australia too had hosted a tour of the South African Springboks. In the minds of many southern African leaders, Australia and New Zealand were lumped together—rich white nations out of touch with the new multiracial Commonwealth and unconcerned about the battle for justice. Fraser was determined to end that impression. In the lead-up to the 1977 London meeting, Fraser told cabinet that Australia had 'a somewhat unfavourable reputation of being indifferent to the Commonwealth, unduly suspicious of any innovative proposals, and niggardly in response to requests for financial contributions'. He and Andrew Peacock made public statements about the importance of the Commonwealth, but said, 'In many ways, our actions have yet to match our words'. Fraser told cabinet that it was on North–South issues—the preparedness of the wealthy white nations to engage economically with the Third World—that the 'real mettle' of the Commonwealth would be tested. To help with this, Australia had to break with its reputation as a white and latently racist nation. In particular, it had to distinguish itself from New Zealand. Australia, Fraser said, should lend support to Western efforts to negotiate an end to apartheid. Australia should 'continue to make clear to the Africans that, while calling for patience, we agree that there is injustice to be remedied as quickly as possible'. Australia should support bans on sporting contacts with South Africa and 'make clear that our own policy is a genuine and practical effort to exert influence on South Africa to modify apartheid'.[7]

The future of Rhodesia was another key Commonwealth issue. The self-governing British colony, bordered by Zambia, Mozambique, South Africa and Botswana, had sought independence from Britain in 1962. Britain had insisted that independence be accompanied by a move to majority rule, but Prime Minister Ian Smith had refused. Instead, he had unilaterally declared independence in 1965. In Rhodesia, blacks outnumbered whites by twenty-two to one, yet they were shut out of all positions of power and condemned to lives of servitude and poverty. The United Nations authorised sanctions against the Smith regime, but Rhodesia still had friends—chief among them South Africa. Meanwhile, the nationalist Patriotic Front, led by Robert Mugabe and Joshua Nkomo, was waging a guerilla war against the Smith regime from bases inside the frontline states. British-sponsored attempts to negotiate a political compromise had repeatedly failed.

There was no obvious reason for Fraser and Australia to become particularly involved in these issues. Senior officials advised that they could see 'no valid ground' for Australia to be one of apartheid's most vociferous critics. The issues of apartheid and Rhodesia were of 'little consequence for Australia's national interests'.[8] Yet, during and after his prime ministership, Fraser became an important figure in the struggle that eventually carried Rhodesia and South Africa to majority rule. In the process, he helped to prevent bloodshed in southern Africa, and a fracturing of the Commonwealth. Instead, during the period of Fraser's government, the Commonwealth became an extraordinary forum concerned, perhaps more than anything else, with international social justice. Fraser says today, 'I thought the Commonwealth was an organisation well worth preserving. Apart from the intrinsic justice of majority rule, that's why I did what I could to make sure it survived. Australia was in a unique position. I thought we should use it'.

Fraser's commitment to the Commonwealth was bolstered by Tony Eggleton. Formerly Press Secretary to Menzies, Holt and Gorton, Eggleton had spent three years in the early 1970s as part of the Commonwealth secretariat in London before returning to Australia for the 1974 election. When Fraser became Leader of the Opposition, Eggleton had been made Fraser's Chief of Staff, and subsequently Secretary to the Shadow Cabinet and Federal Director of the Liberal Party. It was Eggleton who suggested to a willing Fraser that a renewed commitment to the Commonwealth should be part of the opposition's foreign policy. The Commonwealth's ideals were fitting for a progressive Liberal government, and the organisation was, as Eggleton puts it today, 'a ready-made vehicle to raise Malcolm Fraser and Australia's standing in the world'.

* * *

Fraser arrived in London a few days before the 1977 CHOGM was due to begin. Eggleton had used his contacts to arrange for Fraser to give a speech at the Royal Commonwealth Society. There, Fraser called for a fast move to majority rule in Rhodesia. On apartheid, he said, 'Policies based on the false and pernicious premise of one race's superiority over another are the most flagrant violation of fundamental human decency. They offend the moral sense of every person, every nation, concerned about the dignity and equality of man'.[9] As a result, when the black African leaders landed at Heathrow they were greeted by newspaper reports that the Australian Prime Minister, who had been expected to be an arch conservative, had instead announced himself as a champion of black rights. He was a member of the old Commonwealth siding with the new. Eggleton says, 'Really, Malcolm was the surprise of the conference'.

The CHOGM was held in Lancaster House, a Georgian mansion in the West End. In this aristocratic setting the leaders of the former colonies of Britain gathered as equals and advanced their agendas, not all of them pleasing to the mother country. Eggleton remembers standing at the foot of the grand staircase on the first morning of the meeting and seeing Fraser come down with Michael Manley, the Prime Minister of Jamaica. Manley was regarded as a socialist, a friend to Cuba; Fraser as a vehement Cold Warrior. Now Manley had his arm thrown around Fraser's shoulders. The two men became allies and friends.

The CHOGM retreat was held at the Gleneagles Hotel in Scotland. There, the leaders were forced to face each other and to talk, without the insulation of staff and advisers. Together at Gleneagles were Prime Minister Robert Muldoon of New Zealand and the leaders of the frontline states. They could hardly be further apart on the key issue to be debated: sporting contacts with South Africa. The new Commonwealth countries wanted an agreement that all nations would prevent their citizens from going to South Africa for sport. Fraser knew that for countries like Canada, New Zealand and Australia, the idea of preventing private citizens from travelling was politically and perhaps legally impossible. He took the lead in negotiations. He says today, 'I remember taking the words that Muldoon wanted and taking the words that the frontline states wanted and going away and drafting something that had a little bit of each in it, and Sonny Ramphal [Secretary-General of the Commonwealth] was able to get it through'. The final agreement was nutted out in a session from which Fraser was excluded. He remembers, 'Muldoon made it plain that he wouldn't negotiate if I was in the room, and he obviously had to be there, so that meant I couldn't be'.

Muldoon and Fraser never got on. The political journalist Michelle Grattan once wrote that they 'harboured a healthy mutual dislike'.[10] From Fraser's point of view, 'Muldoon thought that everyone, certainly everyone in New Zealand, should agree with him, and he would have expected me to agree with him too, on sporting contacts. Well, I didn't, so that was that'. Fraser also had experience from trade negotiations of the way Muldoon treated his ministers. During one set of talks, Fraser asked Brian Talboys, 'an awfully nice man' and the New Zealand Deputy Prime Minister and Minister for Foreign Affairs, why he wasn't sitting in on the meeting alongside Muldoon. 'He said, "Oh, Rob wouldn't like that"', remembers Fraser. 'For Muldoon, ministers were there to do what he told them to do and I wasn't of that mould and probably made that clear to him in a way he didn't appreciate.' From the London CHOGM onwards, Muldoon and Fraser sparred at every Commonwealth event, with Muldoon doing his best to mock and frustrate Fraser's initiatives.

The Gleneagles agreement was a triumph of negotiation. The opening wording could not have been stronger. Racial prejudice and discrimination were described as 'a dangerous sickness and an unmitigated evil'. Apartheid in sport was 'an abomination'. The agreement accepted that it was the 'urgent duty' of Commonwealth nations to discourage any kind of sporting contacts with South Africa or any other country where sports were organised on the basis of race, colour or ethnic origin.

The paragraphs that made the agreement possible—and that brought Muldoon to the table—were those that Fraser had drafted. They gave enough away for everyone to feel able to sign up. They acknowledged that it was for each government to determine how it might discharge its commitment under the agreement, while recognising 'that the effective fulfilment of [the agreement] was essential to the harmonious development of Commonwealth sport hereafter'.[11]

This gave Muldoon wriggle room. When he returned home he made it clear that no matter what he had agreed to in Scotland, he would not act to prevent South African sporting tours. Taking the hint, the New Zealand rugby association invited a tour from the South African Springboks. The result, in 1981, was unprecedented civil strife. The issue tore the nation apart. Protesters occupied the pitch in Hamilton, chanting, 'The whole world is watching'. Muldoon was recovering from this when, in October 1981, he came to Melbourne for the first CHOGM to be held in Australia.

All this lay ahead, but in 1977 at Gleneagles the anti-racism principles of the Commonwealth had been re-endorsed in the strongest possible terms. The boycott of the games at Edmonton was averted, and the unity of the Commonwealth, for the moment, was preserved.

* * *

Just past midnight on the morning of 13 February 1978, eight months after the CHOGM in London, Malcolm and Tamie Fraser were fast asleep in their bed at Sydney's Hilton Hotel when they were woken by an explosion. Tamie remembers it not so much as a bang, but as a reverberation, felt more in the stomach than the ears. There was a second of silence, then Fraser said, 'My God. I think that was a bomb'. Moments later Andrew Peacock arrived and told them that it had indeed been a bomb. It had been planted in a rubbish bin outside the hotel and had exploded when it was collected by a garbage compactor. Two garbage men had been killed outright. A policeman was critically injured, and later died, and many people were hurt. Outside the hotel there was blood and flesh and glass all over the pavement. Terrorism had arrived in Australia.[12]

The Frasers were at the Hilton to host the Commonwealth Heads of Government Regional Meeting (CHOGRM) for Asia and the Pacific. This was a Fraser initiative. He had raised the idea of such a meeting with Commonwealth Secretary-General Sonny Ramphal during his first weeks as Prime Minister. Ramphal had not been enthusiastic. He feared regional meetings would result in power blocs, detracting from Commonwealth unity. Fraser, on the other hand, thought that in the big meetings small and emerging nations tended to be overlooked. 'The head of government in Tonga might well feel inhibited in arguing with the British Prime Minister', says Fraser today. 'There was a tendency to overlook their concerns.' Fraser was worried that there were no international forums in which the small island nations of the Pacific could be properly heard. They couldn't even afford an office at the United Nations until the Commonwealth funded one for them, and yet all the time issues that affected them were being debated—trade, and the law of the sea among them. With a CHOGRM, the leaders of the tiny island nations could meet the leaders of Singapore, Malaysia and India. They could be heard, share their concerns and gain support. Despite Ramphal's reservations, Fraser had gained agreement for a regional meeting. Now, as a result, the heads of twelve Asian and Pacific countries were in Sydney for the very first CHOGRM.

The day before the explosion, Fraser had been preparing to greet the heads of government at the hotel. When he had seen a crowd of demonstrators waiting for Muldoon, he had ordered that the location for the greetings be switched from the front entrance to one on the other side of the building. Muldoon had arrived, followed shortly afterwards by the Indian Prime Minister Morarji Desai. Later, the consensus among the security forces was that the bomb left at the front entrance had almost certainly been intended for Desai. The change of entrance foiled the terrorists' plans. Fraser says, 'If it was remote-controlled and had exploded when I was greeting him, I would have been killed and so would many others'. Dead-pan, he adds, 'Piggy Muldoon may have accidentally saved my life'.

After the bomb went off, Fraser was told to stay in his hotel room—an instruction he ignored. He threw on his dressing gown. Together with Andrew Peacock, he convened a meeting of the security personnel. Quick decisions had to be made. Should the hotel be cleared? Should the CHOGRM go ahead? Bomb crews were soon swarming all over the building, combing it for more explosives. There was a scare when a hessian parcel was found on a fire escape. It turned out to be a brick. After the Frasers had gone back to bed they were woken again, at about four o'clock in the morning, because there had been another bomb scare, and the floor had to be cleared.

The heads of government decided that they wanted the conference to go ahead. They would not be deterred by terrorism. At ten o'clock, having had next to no sleep, Fraser welcomed his guests. As well as Desai of India and Muldoon of New Zealand, sitting in front of him were the heads of government for the Pacific island nations of Fiji, Tonga, Nauru and Western Samoa, the presidents of Bangladesh and Sri Lanka, and the prime ministers of Malaysia, Papua New Guinea and Singapore. Their nations were scattered across half of the globe, and contained a fifth of the world's population, including most of its poorest people.

In his opening address, Fraser made a brief introductory statement about the bomb, then moved briskly on to the real business. He told the leaders:

> We know that there is hardly anything that one of us can do for our own economy or security that will not concern another. We recognise that none can diminish the dignity of one man without diminishing the dignity of all others. None of us can be visited by calamity, whether due to nature or the misjudgement of men, without affecting the welfare of others. Nor can any nation improve its position without it holding out hope for other nations.[13]

Tamie, who was hosting the wives of the government heads, remembers that some of the women were so alarmed by the bombing that they stayed in their rooms for a day or two, but most

> just shrugged it off. I mean we discussed the bomb and said 'Isn't it frightful', and then we didn't discuss it any more. It was obviously at the back of our minds, but we didn't let it hang like a thunder cloud above our heads. We went ahead with our program.[14]

Meanwhile, Fraser had to deal with the bomb's implications for the rest of the meeting. The heads of government were meant to be travelling to a retreat at Bowral for the last days of the summit. Clearly, the route had to be secured. Fraser talked to the New South Wales Premier Neville Wran. A huge effort was needed. Every crossing, every culvert and every bridge would have to be patrolled. The police simply did not have the numbers. Wran and Fraser agreed that the armed forces would have to be used. Fraser remembered his struggle with Gorton over the Gazelle Peninsula affair. He intended no repeat and took care to follow correct procedure. He asked Wran to make a formal request for the use of the armed forces so the appropriate process could be followed. A cabinet meeting was called, followed by an Executive Council meeting. The use of the armed forces was authorised 'to protect the interests of the Commonwealth'. For the next three days, nearly two thousand army and air force personnel were on the streets of Sydney and the route to Bowral. There were armoured personnel carriers and mine detectors. As a last resort, they were authorised to use lethal force. It was the most dramatic domestic military call-out in Australia's history.[15]

Within days, the security forces were convinced that the perpetrators of the bombing had been the Indian religious sect Ananda Marga. The spiritual leader of the sect had been jailed by Desai's government, and there had been terrorist attacks in India. The Australian security forces had been aware of Ananda Marga being active in Australia and were monitoring the sect. In the months after the CHOGRM, cabinet was told that there had been more acts of violence and harassment by Ananda Marga in South-East Asia and Australia than anywhere else in the world other than India. There had been an attack on the Indian attaché and his wife in Canberra, and the stabbing of an Air India employee in Melbourne.[16] In the years that followed, various conspiracy theories circulated about the bomb, including allegations that the security forces themselves were behind it. Two members of the sect were convicted of the bombing but later cleared on appeal. Fraser says he has never seen any reason to depart from the initial conclusion: Ananda Marga was to blame.

The final communiqué of this first CHOGRM bristled with the frustrations of countries locked out of the means of escaping from poverty. Picking up on some of the themes in Fraser's opening address, the communiqué called for structural changes in the international economic system to enable the poorest nations to earn a more equitable share of the world's wealth. There needed to be urgent action to 'ensure that, in a world which has the means and the resources to do it, the basic needs of all mankind [will] be satisfied within an acceptable period of time'. The meeting called on industrialised countries to take the lead. It reserved particular criticism for the European Economic Community, which, as it expanded in membership, shut out developing nations from an increasing number of markets. Yet the CHOGRM communiqué was also an optimistic document. It committed the leaders to using the structure of the Commonwealth to help each other. Predictably, one of the outcomes of the meeting was an agreement to set up a Commonwealth working group on terrorism.[17] Regional working groups were established on trade, energy—with a particular emphasis on alternative energy sources such as solar, windpower and biomass—and the illicit drug trade. Arrangements were made for the countries of the region to share their technological knowledge. Fraser later told parliament that it was astonishing how much the very different countries had in common. The problems of a small town or village in India were often similar to those of an island nation in the Pacific.[18]

It was generally agreed that the CHOGRM had been a success. The leaders were due to meet again in New Delhi in 1980. Australia wanted to set up a secretariat for the region in Sydney, but the idea was opposed by Ramphal.

Without Australian sponsorship, the regional meetings of Commonwealth leaders did not survive after Fraser left the prime ministership. Fraser thinks this is a shame. Would the Solomon Islands still have been a failed state, he wonders, if that country had had access to a regional Commonwealth secretariat and working groups in which problems could be shared? Would Fiji be so unstable if it had been involved in regular meetings with democracies such as India? Fraser says, 'Today, the problems of the small island states hardly ever get noticed until they become critical'. As the small countries of our region fell into disarray over the last decade, the Australian Government lacked understanding and relationships of trust. Perhaps, if there had been a regional Commonwealth secretariat, more could have been done before it was too late.

* * *

In early 1979, Tony Eggleton was in Britain helping the Conservative Party with the election campaign. The day after Margaret Thatcher's victory was declared, he took a call from Malcolm Fraser. 'Look', Fraser said. 'I am very worried about Margaret's attitude on Africa.'

That year's CHOGM was due to be held in August in Lusaka, capital of the frontline state of Zambia. Formerly known as Northern Rhodesia, Zambia had gained its independence just fifteen years previously. The founding President, Kenneth Kaunda, was a fighter for majority rule who under the old regime had been jailed and persecuted for his political activism. With the other frontline states, he was a key supporter of the Patriotic Front, the political and military alliance between Joshua Nkomo and Robert Mugabe fighting to overthrow the white minority regime in Rhodesia.

The situation in Rhodesia had changed since the previous CHOGM, in 1977. Ian Smith, who as Prime Minister had unilaterally declared independence from Britain to avoid ceding to majority rule, had been forced by the continuing guerilla war to compromise. Elections were held in April 1979—just weeks before Thatcher came to power in the United Kingdom. The Patriotic Front had refused to take part, which was hardly surprising given that the constitution still assured whites twenty-eight of the 100 seats in parliament, and guaranteed that control of the police, the civil service and the judiciary would remain in the hands of whites. Most of the country was under martial law when the election was held. A moderate black leader, Bishop Abel Muzorewa, was elected Prime Minister, and was regarded by Mugabe, Nkomo and the frontline states as little better than a traitor to the cause. Ian Smith, still in government, told a media conference on the day that 'black rule' theoretically began that little would change, and said, 'The less change the better'.[19] The Patriotic Front and its supporters refused to accept the Muzorewa–Smith settlement, and the guerrilla war was continuing, with Nkomo based largely in Zambia, and Mugabe in Mozambique. Both countries had suffered incursions by South African and Rhodesian military.

The future of Zimbabwe Rhodesia, as it was called from May 1979 to 1980, was one of the most pressing moral issues in world affairs. During the British election campaign, Thatcher had seemed to commit her party to accepting the Muzorewa government as a basis for bringing the country to legality. Thatcher saw the Patriotic Front and the frontline states as communists. Fraser, tempered by his reflections on the Vietnam War, thought the African activists were chiefly concerned with nationalism and justice. They would take support where they found it. If the West failed them, they would naturally turn to the East.

In his telephone call to Eggleton on the morning after the Conservative Party's victory, Fraser was searching for ways to prevent Thatcher from locking herself into a position before the CHOGM. Peter Carrington, who became the British foreign secretary, was already trying to persuade his leader to change her view that the elections in Zimbabwe Rhodesia were a legitimate solution to the troubles. Carrington, a charming and shrewd diplomat, was well known to Fraser. He had been British High Commissioner to Australia when Fraser was a raw backbencher in the late 1950s, and later, when Fraser was Minister for Defence, they had collaborated over the Five Power Defence Arrangements. What Fraser wanted to know from Eggleton was whether a delegation of Australian foreign affairs officials might help Carrington to press his case. Within days, public servants from Fraser's own department and the Department of Foreign Affairs were in London conveying Australia's position to Thatcher's most senior advisers.

Meanwhile, Zambian President Kenneth Kaunda wrote Fraser a passionate nine-page letter. On his side, at least, there could be no compromise. The Muzorewa–Smith arrangement was a strategy for more war in Zimbabwe Rhodesia. 'No one can keep the people of Zimbabwe from true independence. No genuine independence, peace and stability will be brought to Rhodesia by tricks no matter how cleverly ... conceived and carried out.'[20] Kaunda wanted Australia and the key countries of Europe to prevail upon the

Thatcher government to reject the Muzorewa–Smith solution, and press for real constitutional change.

Fraser had met and got to know Kaunda in London two years before, and understood his point of view. Kaunda had told Fraser that when he had been negotiating the independence of Zambia, talks had stalled for a long while. One day Kaunda had burst out in indignation, 'Why aren't we getting anywhere?' and a foolish British diplomat had responded, 'Why should we? You're not hurting us'. Kaunda had broken off negotiations, returned home and sent twenty people to China to be trained as terrorists. They came back and oversaw the bombing of bridges and police stations. Fraser recalls, 'Kaunda said, and I believed him, that he told them to make sure there was no one on the bridges or in the police stations before they blew them up'. The British got the message, and the negotiations started again. Zambia achieved independence.

This time, Fraser thought, the Commonwealth might well rupture. Much worse, it seemed possible that the whole of southern Africa might descend into war, with the West effectively defending unjust white minority rule. Thatcher was not known for compromise, and the leaders of the frontline states simply could not compromise if they were to keep faith with their principles and their electorates. Nigeria—not a frontline state but the most populous country in Africa—was already threatening to pull out of the Commonwealth over Zimbabwe Rhodesia. The President, General Olusegun Obasanjo, was, Fraser was advised in the weeks before the Lusaka CHOGM, 'seriously disenchanted with Britain'.[21]

What, if anything, were the white nations of the world, and Britain in particular, prepared to do? With Thatcher in power, Muldoon hostile to majority rule and Pierre Trudeau recently defeated in Canada, Fraser was the only old Commonwealth leader trying to bridge the gap between the African states and Britain. Fraser's stand was not popular in Australia. His electoral correspondence contained plenty of letters querying why he was supporting the blacks against our 'white Rhodesian brothers'.[22] The Western Australian Premier

Charles Court told Fraser that he should support 'responsible black leaders', by which he meant Muzorewa. Many federal Liberal members of parliament felt the same way. Fraser remembers a party room meeting in which three of his colleagues queried why he was supporting 'communist, terrorist people in the ANC against our blood brothers, the Afrikaners. I said, "Well, if you want a government that is going to allow a very small white minority to keep a great black majority in a state of subjection for the term of their natural lives, you're going to have to get another government". Then I said, "That is the end of the meeting now". The issue was never raised again, by anyone. I think that is one of very few meetings where I refused to allow more debate'. Ian Macphee remembers Fraser saying at about this time that in politics a leader could not afford too many points of principle, but that 'Opposition to racism is mine'.

Fraser was talking to Carrington in Britain. They were of similar views: Thatcher had to be persuaded to shift her position. 'He said that he could organise Thatcher to come and talk to me. They were going to Tokyo for an OECD [Organisation for Economic Cooperation and Development] meeting, and he could persuade her to come on to Canberra afterwards.' Carrington gave him some advice: 'She will never change her mind if there are three people in the room. You will have to get her to send out her staff, and not have a note-taker present and just speak one on one'. Carrington himself managed to organise an excuse not to be present.

Fraser and Thatcher met over about three hours. She was, as he had expected, instinctively inclined to accept the internal settlement, and deeply suspicious of Mugabe. Fraser made a rational case, concentrating on engaging her intellect. There were two options, he said. Either a solution had to be imposed on the people of Zimbabwe Rhodesia, or a solution had to be found which the people would accept—and they would never accept Muzorewa. If Britain wanted to impose a solution, then she would have to commit troops. Mugabe and Nkomo would not stop fighting. Nor would the frontline states cease their support. Was Thatcher prepared to pull troops out of Northern Ireland to go to Africa? And for how long? Months, years or decades? Fraser remembers, 'I was trying to get her to think, which she could do very well. She had a good brain'. After about two hours, Thatcher had agreed, almost against her will, that the Zimbabwean constitution would have to change. Fraser called in the officials. 'Then I made my first big mistake. I suggested she tell them what we had agreed, and she reverted right back to where we had been two hours before. It took another hour of talks get her back to what she had said at the end of the first two hours. And it was all gentle stuff, you know, no whips or threats. Just saying, "But Margaret, don't we agree this? And don't we agree that?"'

Sonny Ramphal and the leaders of the frontline states and their supporters knew that Fraser was talking to Thatcher. Later that day they were dismayed to hear that she had made an inflammatory speech to the Canberra Press Club, describing the Patriotic Front as terrorists and saying her purpose in talking to Fraser had been to seek his support to shift opinion towards Muzorewa.[23] Fraser, though, was encouraged. The speech Thatcher gave had been written before their conversation in the morning.

Fraser and Peacock organised a quick ring-around, telling Ramphal not to give up hope. Fraser called Michael Manley, waking him in the middle of the Jamaican night. He told Manley that Thatcher was a proud woman. She had conservative members of her own party who did not want her to back down, and it would be hard for her to be seen to do so. Now, however, there seemed a real prospect that she would shift, if she was given a little space in which to do so. Would Manley help to persuade Kaunda and Tanzanian President and head of the frontline states Julius Nyerere not to humiliate her, not to make violent speeches or allow demonstrators to get her back up? Manley did as he was asked.[24] Fraser recalls, 'At every stage I was just trying to stop attitudes from hardening. Trying to leave open some room for negotiation'. It had seemed that there might be open disputes on the floor of the CHOGM. Now, the frontline states agreed to bite their tongues in the hope that Thatcher would shift ground. 'They were all extremely polite to her', Fraser says.

As the date for the Lusaka CHOGM approached, Fraser's staff put the tactics he was to adopt in writing. Australia, 'having set the game in play' through Fraser's meeting with Thatcher, should adopt a 'monitoring/good offices' position, resorting to pressure only if Britain appeared to be moving off course. Australia should try to 'jolly along Mrs Thatcher' while being sensitive to her concerns that she didn't want to be seen to react to pressure. The potential pitfalls were 'too much rhetoric on either side'. Thatcher had a short fuse, and if she believed her own or Britain's prestige was at stake then there would be a backlash against Australia. On the other hand, if the frontline states were too emotional, it would have the reverse effect of making her feel she was responding to pressure.[25] Yet the frontline states were essential if the Patriotic Front, presently committed to achieving its aims through armed struggle, was to be brought to the negotiating table.

Tamie and Malcolm Fraser flew to Africa in July 1979, a few days before the start of the CHOGM. Fraser wanted to visit the President of Nigeria Olusegun Obasanjo, who had decided not to attend the meeting. It was a frightening time to be in Africa. Tamie later recalled that the whole continent seemed to be 'trembling'. There had been violence all along the boundaries of Zimbabwe Rhodesia and South Africa. Their plane flew hundreds of kilometres out of its way to stay in safe air corridors. Before leaving Australia, Tamie had written letters to each of the children. She hid them in her jumper drawer—there to be found if she and Malcolm never came home. 'When we got back from Africa I didn't read them again. I just tore them up and put them in the wastepaper basket and thought what a stupid woman.'[26]

The Frasers were greeted at Lagos airport by tight security, a brass band and Nigerian officials in flowing national dress. Fraser and Obasanjo got on well. They became close colleagues in the years ahead, during the struggle against apartheid. Obasanjo had taken over government in a coup, but was in the process of setting up a democracy. Fraser came to think of him as 'a very great man'.

* * *

As July came to a close, the Commonwealth leaders gathered in the mountain air of Lusaka, on the central plateau of Zambia. The Frasers were housed in the Mulungushi Village, a cluster of villas within a compound wall. The conference itself was held at Mulungushi Hall—a big, bland building in the middle of paddocks, looking, Tamie thought, like a technical school in rural Victoria. Inside, there were dark-brown woodgrain walls and bright-gold carpet, and the heads of government sat around an oval table in their various traditional costumes, their national flags behind them. Fraser delivered the reply to Kaunda's welcoming speech and announced his position. 'All oppression is repugnant, but there is an obscenity about oppression based on no more than the colour of a person's skin', he said. A solution had to be found to the problems of southern Africa. No matter how difficult, it was vital to discover areas of agreement and build on them. Nobody wanted slaughter and bloodshed. 'As to what happens next, that is not in the lap of the gods; it is to a very large extent in our laps. Time is running out and we may not have such an opportunity again.'[27]

When the discussion on Zimbabwe Rhodesia began, two days later, Thatcher's opening speech was not particularly encouraging. She acknowledged again that the country's constitution was defective.

> I refer of course to the provisions which make it possible for the white minority to block, in the parliament, constitutional changes that would be unwelcome to them. This is a valid criticism—such a blocking mechanism has not appeared in any other independence constitution agreed to by the British parliament.

But on the other hand, she seemed to be saying that the issue wasn't worth fighting over.

> What began as a struggle between the white minority and the black majority has more recently taken on a very different dimension ... There is now an African President,

> an African Prime Minister and an African majority in parliament. There have been elections in which for the first time the African majority have been able to elect the leaders of the government. There are those who seem to believe that the world should simply go on treating Bishop Muzorewa as if he were Mr Smith. But the change that has taken place in Rhodesia cannot be dismissed as of no consequence.[28]

At least she had not locked herself into position. There was room to move.

The next day, Fraser and Peacock acted as brokers in discussions between Thatcher, Carrington and Nyerere. Nyerere wanted the final communiqué of the CHOGM to commit Britain to fresh elections. Thatcher, on the other hand, insisted that Fraser and Peacock not ask too much of her. She was under pressure from conservatives in her own party. She could not appear to be returning to London having come under direction at the meeting. Carrington argued that Thatcher would be letting down Muzorewa and his white supporters if she moved further than the position she had outlined in her speech. Nyerere, on behalf of the frontline states, was prepared to consider an interim British-appointed government while fresh elections were prepared, but Thatcher would not talk about transitional arrangements at all. She rummaged in her handbag—referring to it as her 'armoury' and the most secure place in Whitehall—for notes on the lack of elections in Nyerere's Tanzania. The final communiqué, Thatcher said, must not embarrass Britain or cause problems within the Conservative Party. Fraser pointed out that Nyerere and the frontline states' leaders also had their constituencies to worry about. They needed arguments they could take home—something that they could offer to the Patriotic Front to encourage it towards moderation and negotiation.[29] The key issue now was what the communiqué would say. How far would it commit Britain? How far would Thatcher move from her opening statement?

Two days later, Fraser, Thatcher and Carrington once again met the frontline leaders Kaunda and Nyerere, and Michael Manley of Jamaica. Over a long morning, a nine-point draft communiqué was negotiated. It was an agonising process, each side of the negotiation moving to middle ground reluctantly. Fraser worked hard at helping to find wording everyone could agree to. He wrote in the margins of his copy, offering different forms of words that were incorporated in the final version. The next day, the result was circulated to all the heads of government, with a letter from Kaunda. The suggestion was that it be discussed the following day, and kept confidential until then.

The negotiations had achieved what many had thought impossible—common ground. The draft declaration contained not only the recognition that the constitution of Zimbabwe Rhodesia was 'deficient in certain important respects' but also an acknowledgement that the 'search for a lasting settlement must involve all parties to the conflict'. The draft said there should be a conference, to which all sides would be invited. Thatcher had shifted ground. She had agreed that Britain would negotiate with the Patriotic Front. Even more, the draft said that there must be new 'free and fair elections properly supervised under British government authority and with Commonwealth observers'.[30]

Fraser was not the only one who could take credit. Carrington had worked hard to move Thatcher, and the frontline leaders had played their part as well. Nevertheless, the Australian intervention had helped to achieve what many had thought impossible—an agreed way forward. Fraser and Eggleton were aware that they had a good news story but that the Australian journalists who were with them would be scooped the next day because of the time differences between Australia and Africa. They therefore called the Australian press corps together for a briefing. Eggleton remembers, 'Whether it was a good thing or a bad thing, a couple of British journalists snuck in at the back'. The result was that the British press were soon approaching Thatcher for confirmation of an agreement that was not yet meant to be public. She was furious. She thought Fraser was trying to lock her in before she had made any formal concessions. She was also worried about being humiliated. There was no certainty that the frontline states would stick to the agreement, either. They, too, had compromised, allowing a clause that guaranteed that white minority interests would be protected. What if Britain was seen to have compromised, yet still failed to achieve agreement?

That night the Australian delegation was to host a barbecue at the temporary Australian high commission. Australian wines and food had been flown over in the hold of the Prime Minister's plane. Tables were spread with white linen under the trees. Tamie was rushing around trying to make sure that the evening was running smoothly. The drinks seemed to go on and on until it became a little awkward. Margaret Thatcher was late. The food could not be served until she was there. There were fears that she would not come at all. Muldoon was wandering around, unhelpfully asking in terms of mock wonderment who could possibly have been responsible for the leak of the agreement. Everyone already knew that it was Fraser and Eggleton.

Finally, there was 'a great whisper' and Thatcher was there. She demanded that the draft agreement be approved immediately, or she would withdraw her support. There and then, Ramphal called the lead players together and convened a session of the meeting. The agreement was endorsed, and formally announced almost straightaway. Thatcher did not linger at the barbecue; she had arrived late and left early. The press described her as being 'exhausted but euphoric' about the agreement. She was already facing allegations from journalists that she had sold out the Zimbabweans to appease the Commonwealth, but she denied changing her mind under pressure. 'I believe passionately in the ballot box over the bullet', she said.[31]

Fraser's relationship with Thatcher never fully recovered. They continued to deal with each other, but, as Eggleton remembers, Thatcher and Carrington were convinced that he and Fraser had deliberately leaked the agreement to the media. 'I always felt there was a reserve that hadn't been there before.'

But Fraser had cemented his reputation elsewhere. The next morning, as he walked into the conference room, the African and Asian delegates stood and applauded him. He also had a triumphant return to Australia. He told parliament that Lusaka had been critical in the history of the Commonwealth. 'Had the conference gone badly the institution would have been seriously maimed and could have been destroyed. As it happened the conference did not go badly; it went extremely well, and far from breaking up the Commonwealth has emerged a stronger, more vital and more cohesive body'. Those who thought that the Commonwealth was irrelevant and 'merely the ghost of a vanished empire, a talking shop, a dealer in myths and illusions' had now been proved wrong.

> I believe it is now clear that it is those who hold this view who are the real romantics—pessimistic romantics who refuse to come to terms with a changing world and the changing forms of influence and power … The time when discussion of the Commonwealth tended to be clouded by rather dubious metaphysics and the search for the definition of an essence is long since past. The contemporary Commonwealth is confident enough to take itself for granted, to define itself in terms of what it does. Its form is flexible and accommodating; its bent is pragmatic and problem-solving; its atmosphere is informal and unpolemical.[32]

* * *

Behind the scenes the diplomacy went on. The challenge was to persuade the Patriotic Front, which had hopes of achieving its aims through force of arms, to instead attend a conference with the enemy, trusting Britain to be an honest broker. Fraser stayed on the case, writing to the frontline leaders and urging the view that the Lancaster House conference was the only forum in which warfare could be avoided. The conference began in October, and continued for twelve weeks. It was far from smooth sailing, with the Patriotic Front walking out, but being pressured by the frontline states to return. In December, an agreement was reached under which Muzorewa agreed to step down for supervised elections. A ceasefire was declared; Australia sent peacekeeping troops. Mugabe won the election easily. Australia was the first country to appoint a High Commissioner to the new Zimbabwe, and also committed to a generous aid program. In April 1980, Fraser attended Zimbabwe's independence celebrations.

Mugabe said later that he was 'enchanted by [Fraser] really, and we became friends, personal friends'.[33] Fraser, in turn, was impressed by Mugabe, and moved by his personal story. In the mid 1960s the young activist had been imprisoned by Smith's government for 'subversive speech' and incarcerated in Salisbury prison. While he was in jail his only son had fallen ill. The British Anglican bishop and anti-apartheid campaigner Trevor Huddleston offered to be a hostage: he would go to Salisbury to be jailed if Mugabe could be allowed out to see his son. Smith refused, dismissing the offer as 'a communist trick'. The boy died, and Huddleston repeated the offer—would Smith allow Mugabe to attend the funeral if Huddleston agreed to be jailed in his place? Smith refused again. The fact that the boy had died didn't alter the fact that this was a 'communist trick'.

Later, Sally Mugabe, herself an activist, fled to England when she was threatened with arrest. When her immigration status came into doubt, Mugabe wrote long pleading letters to Harold Wilson. They went unanswered and the British gave no help. At the same time, the Home Office granted a work visa to Ian Smith's stepson Robert. Only after a high-profile media campaign and a petition signed by more than four hundred parliamentarians did Edward Heath's Conservative government finally agree to grant sanctuary to Sally Mugabe.

Fraser understood why Mugabe had resorted to armed struggle, and why he distrusted the British. What he found surprising was that after his election win Mugabe was prepared to sit down with Smith and talk about reconciliation between black and white. Fraser says, 'I was not sure that I would have been able to do that, if I had been treated as he had'.

Fraser also got to know Sally Mugabe. He was even more impressed by her. She was from Ghana, a teacher, an independent thinker and 'a lovely, brave, very human and very intelligent woman'. Mugabe, Fraser soon realised, could be a 'stubborn and an inflexible person', but Sally clearly worked on his better side. To begin with Fraser kept in touch with the Mugabes and watched Zimbabwe's progress.

* * *

Today it is impossible to think of Zimbabwe or its leader without an awareness of its present disasters—an economy in ruins, and Mugabe a murderous dictator. Yet for the first ten years it looked very different. The economy improved. In 1995, the World Bank reported that child malnutrition in Zimbabwe had fallen from 22 per cent to 12 per cent in the ten years after independence. Life expectancy rose from 56 to 64 years. By 1990, Zimbabwe had lower infant mortality and higher adult literacy rates than the average for developing countries.[34] Mugabe managed an uneasy truce with rivals and factional enemies. Zimbabwe played a leading role in the politics of southern Africa. All these were significant achievements.

But Fraser, still in touch with Mugabe until the early 1990s, detected signs of trouble. The civil service was woefully inefficient and in need of reform. He told Mugabe what he thought, but, 'He never did do what was needed, and that was the beginning of some of the problems'. He also thought Mugabe needed to make changes to encourage international investment. Fraser says, 'Perhaps I should have done more to persuade him to that when he would still talk to me. He made all the right noises, but it never really happened'.

In the late 1980s, Mugabe took his secretary Grace Marufu as his mistress. Sally was ill with kidney disease. Fraser heard from 'someone I trust' that when Sally was dying, she insisted that whatever happened Robert should not be allowed to marry 'that woman'. She said, 'It will be the end of Zimbabwe if he does'. Fraser says today, 'What was her motivation for saying that? You might think it was just the normal thing of a woman who had already been deserted by her husband. But, knowing Sally, I think she knew that it would be bad for him. I think she knew what was in him, and that he needed different people around him. I think it was prescience'.

Sally Mugabe died in 1992. As she had feared, Mugabe married Marufu. Fraser was by that time less in touch with Mugabe. 'He was moving beyond reach, less and less willing to talk to anyone with a white face.' When Fraser spoke to the other African leaders he knew, particularly Obasanjo, he heard that they, too, were finding that Mugabe was moving beyond them. He had begun his disastrous land 'reforms', and in 1995 there were reports of the assassination of his political rivals. It is now many years since Mugabe spoke to Malcolm Fraser.

Fraser considered, in the late 1990s, speaking out against human rights abuses in Zimbabwe. He was aware that his words would carry particular weight. He probably would have done so, had he not taken a call from the Director of the Harare-based office of the international aid organisation CARE. At the time, Fraser was the organisation's President. The Director pleaded with him not to make any statements: 'We have staff in remote areas. You will be putting them at risk'. Fraser held his tongue, then and for some years afterwards. Did he consider trying to use his old relationship to talk to Mugabe? He thought by then that it was too late. 'The only people who could have influenced him were other black African leaders. He won't listen to any white man. Only black faces can fix this problem.'

In recent years, since he left the leadership of CARE, Fraser has added his voice to calls for international pressure on Zimbabwe, particularly from the other African nations. Change, Fraser has said, cannot come from the ballot box, because the Mugabe government controls too many of the processes. He has suggested cutting off electricity supplies to force Mugabe to go.[35] The African nations should have done more, he believes. Some leaders, such as Obasanjo, were prepared to be 'very tough', but President Thabo Mbeki of South Africa stood in the way. South Africa and Nigeria are the leading powers in southern Africa. If they had combined to pressure Mugabe, then the other, smaller states would have joined them. Fraser says, 'I think that could have been effective'. He knows that in the 1990s, Obasanjo organised a meeting between Mbeki, Mugabe and himself, 'But whenever there was a difference of opinion, Mbeki sided with Mugabe'. Mbeki endorsed Mugabe's 'wins' in a string of dubious elections, opposed the imposition of sanctions, allowed shipments of weapons across South African territory and into Zimbabwe and sided with Zimbabwe at the United Nations. The reason normally given for Mbeki's actions is filial obligation: he and Mugabe were freedom fighters together. Fraser doesn't buy it. Mugabe did the hard yards—years of guerrilla warfare; Mbeki was never in the front line. 'He was the money collector and the diplomat, operating out of London, Lusaka and Lagos. You can't draw a comparison between what Mugabe did and what Mbeki did.' Meanwhile, the chaos in Zimbabwe damaged South Africa. Thousand of refugees flooded across the border. Fraser knows that Nelson Mandela would have supported action against Mugabe. So why did Mbeki remain the dictator's ally? It is a question that for Fraser remains unanswered.

Fraser feels that with the election of South Africa's new President Jacob Zuma, in 2009, there is more hope. When Fraser last spoke to Obasanjo, in around 2006, the Nigerian leader said that nobody could talk to Mugabe. 'He said he was beyond redemption', says Fraser.

So how does he feel now about Mugabe, whose rise to power he helped to achieve? 'How could anyone be anything but deeply,

deeply disappointed?' The conservative historian Hal Colebatch has suggested that Fraser was wrong in pressuring Thatcher over Zimbabwe. Colebatch says Muzorewa should have been left in power, and that with British support the internal settlement 'could have had a good chance of success'.[36] Fraser thinks that Colebatch has a selective memory. The Muzorewa government could not have been propped up except with the use of armed force, which would have meant a major military commitment by Britain for many years—something Thatcher was not prepared to contemplate. If the settlement that Fraser helped to broker had not been achieved, bloody civil war in southern Africa would have been the almost certain result.

* * *

Two years after Lusaka, in October 1981, it was Australia's turn to host the CHOGM. Forty-one leaders gathered at Melbourne town hall for the opening of the meeting. One of Tamie's sisters, Christine Hindhaugh, was there, and later described the scene.

> Pierre Trudeau was chatting to Lee Kuan Yew, his hand in his pocket, super cool. Margaret Thatcher, impeccable all in black, seemed pensive and detached. Mrs Ghandi was much smaller than I had imagined, a diminutive figure as she stood there in her sari, only her face revealing the steel needed to hold on to power in the world's largest democracy. Prince Mabandla, Prime Minister of Swaziland, looked a splendid figure in gown and feathers, and among the others there was a colourful sprinkling of turbans, kaftans, saris and gold-braided military uniforms. Mr Muldoon of New Zealand, I noted with a smile, wore a suit, tie and expression of dark grey.[37]

Fraser gave the opening address.

> I am convinced that our generation of leaders will ultimately be judged largely in terms of their success or

> failure in reconciling the interests of the rich and poor countries of the earth. For if they are not reconciled, the world in which we shall live out our lives and which our children shall inherit will be an unhappy one, condemned to turmoil and bitterness. Those who fail to recognise the gravity and drama of the issues disguised by the rather bland term 'North–South dialogue' are guilty of a serious failure of historical imagination.[38]

Among the leaders gathered at the CHOGM was Robert Mugabe, attending for the first time, with his wife Sally, the two of them transformed from outlaws to leaders of their country. Other new countries—Vanuatu, Belize and St Vincent and the Grenadines—were represented. Melbourne's Exhibition Building was used for the meeting, with the decorations and furnishings chosen by Tamie. The Queen was in town and gave a reception on the royal yacht *Britannia*. There were helicopter escorts, security men prowling the roofs, closed-circuit television cameras—the most elaborate security arrangements in the country's history.

Fraser wanted to make the Melbourne CHOGM an advance in the North–South dialogue. He had used the Commonwealth at every opportunity to push the Third World's cause. His close relationship with Jamaican President Michael Manley had resulted in him being invited to attend a 'mini-summit' on North–South issues in Runaway Bay, Jamaica, at the end of 1978. As international meetings go, this had been small beer. Only seven nations were invited—but they were very different. Fraser joined Manley, Obasanjo of Nigeria and the leaders of Canada, Norway and Venezuela. The guest of honour was Helmut Schmidt, Chancellor of West Germany. Fraser had suggested to Manley that Schmidt was the European leader most likely to listen. He was right. Schmidt went home from the meeting, Fraser says, 'convinced of the need for a Common Fund, and that it was very important that the Third World nations got a better deal. He was the first European leader to really be persuaded'. From then on, Schmidt supported the anti-protection agenda. It seemed that more progress might be possible, and the Melbourne CHOGM was well timed to play its role. A major international meeting on cooperation and development, or, as it became known, a North–South Summit, was due to be held in Cancun, Mexico, almost immediately after the Melbourne CHOGM. The instigators hoped that this summit would draw up a blueprint for the new world economic order. Fraser hoped that if he could persuade Thatcher to commit herself to action in Melbourne, it would help to make Cancun a success.

In July, he had sent her a draft of the declaration he hoped the meeting would endorse. Thatcher wrote back to him in chilly terms. She didn't want to raise 'unreal expectations' by exaggerating what governments could do through international action.

> It would ... be wrong to suggest that the chronic problems of poverty, over population and underdevelopment can be resolved by a series of international negotiations. It would be a disservice to leave any country with the impression that the main responsibility for its development lies not with itself but with the international community.

She also rebutted Fraser's argument that the inequality of wealth among states was a danger to the peace of the world. She didn't think it was true. She wanted to avoid the implication in Fraser's draft that major institutional changes were necessary to prevent conflict. Thatcher, true to her conservatism, thought that the existing institutions had worked quite well.[39]

Fraser was by this time battling troubles at home. Andrew Peacock was on the back bench, having resigned as Industrial Relations Minister in April of that year. There was constant speculation that he would challenge for the leadership. The economy was beginning to fail under the weight of the wage breakout, the drought and the second oil shock. Labor had recovered from thc ignominy of the Whitlam years under the leadership of Bill Hayden. As a result, during the CHOGM the media spent little time on what Fraser was trying to achieve, and instead ran front-page stories on a possible leadership challenge by Peacock—which in fact did not emerge until the following year.

Bizarrely, there was also a rumour that Fraser had cancer. He had supposedly been seen visiting the Peter MacCallum Cancer Centre. Phoebe Fraser rang Tamie in tears from boarding school. Was it true? Meanwhile, President Kaunda told Fraser that if it *was* true, he would arrange for his personal medicine man to be flown over from Zambia. A frustrated Fraser instructed his staff to find out where the Peter MacCallum clinic was, so that he could be sure to avoid it, for fear of sparking more rumours. Tamie agreed to go on *Nationwide* to rebut the story. She insisted to Richard Carleton that her husband was well, and then stormed off in what the *Sun* called 'a grand exit in heroic mode' and *The Sydney Morning Herald* described as 'undoubtedly the most marvellous piece of theatre on television last week'.[40]

So the CHOGM proceeded largely untroubled by serious media attention. The main achievement was the Melbourne Declaration—sixteen points of agreement on how rich and poor countries could unite to combat world poverty, close in wording to the document Fraser had shown Thatcher months before. The declaration began with a reaffirmation that all men and women had the right to live with dignity, and went on to assert that this imposed obligations on all states 'not only in respect to their own people but in their dealings with all other nations'. It asserted that the 'gross inequality of wealth and opportunity ... and the unbroken circle of poverty' of developing countries were 'fundamental sources of tension and instability in the world'. The Commonwealth countries committed themselves to do what they could to 'infuse an increased sense of urgency and direction into the resolution of these common problems of mankind', and called for a revitalisation of dialogue between developed and developing countries. 'This will require a political commitment, clear vision and intellectual realism which have thus far escaped mankind and to all of which the Commonwealth can greatly contribute.' The need for change was urgent, and the choice was not between change and no change, but between 'timely, adequate managed change and disruptive, involuntary change imposed by breakdown and conflict'. Fraser's theme of enlightened self-interest in foreign affairs was present in the tenth point, which stated that while fairness for developing countries was a humanitarian issue it was also true that 'Self-interest itself warrants a constructive and positive approach'.[41]

The Melbourne Declaration was endorsed by the meeting. There was enthusiasm from India, the African states and Pacific island countries. As for the old Commonwealth, Muldoon dismissed the declaration as pious platitudes, and Thatcher told the media that there had been a great deal of talk about the morality of securing trade for developing countries, but that, 'We were also some of us able to say, "Look, we too have problems, we too have problems with unemployment and we too have problems". Much as we hate protectionism, we do sometimes have problems with things like textiles and footwear which can cause problems of unemployment at home'. The meeting reaffirmed the Commonwealth's abhorrence of apartheid and its commitment to the Gleneagles agreement, but even here Thatcher was less than enthusiastic, saying there might be 'slightly different interpretations' of the agreement, but that it had been 'reaffirmed in a general way'.[42]

* * *

At Cancun a few weeks later, the United States and the European powers killed hopes for real change. Instead, the 1980s were a decade of trade wars and increasing poverty in the Third World.

On Thatcher's return to England from Mexico, the Leader of the Opposition Michael Foot used the Melbourne Declaration to ridicule her claim that Cancun had been a success. The summit, he said, had been 'a cruel and mocking anticlimax to millions of people all over the world'. All that had resulted was 'a promise to have talks about talks. Not an extra penny appears to have been promised—or, in the right honourable lady's words, "committed"—to the poorest people in the world'. Foot went on:

> Does the right honourable lady think that this Mexico summit meeting has lived up to the Melbourne Declaration which she signed? Where is the 'determined and dedicated action' that was promised then? Where is the 'revitalisation of the dialogue between developed and developing countries'? Where is the 'political commitment to a clear vision?'[43]

Cancun marked the beginning of the end of hopes for a new international economic order. The cause to which Fraser had devoted so much energy and time was not to be fulfilled. By the time he lost power, in 1983, few people remembered the Melbourne Declaration.

The battle within the Commonwealth over southern Africa continued. Thatcher continued to oppose sanctions against South Africa, and by 1985 it again seemed that the Commonwealth would fracture over the issue. Thatcher had by that time made it clear that she was reorienting Britain away from its former colonies and towards Europe. In 1985, Sonny Ramphal told Thatcher that to resist sanctions, as she was doing, when everyone else wanted to impose them, came close to being an accomplice in apartheid.

It was another Australian Prime Minister, Bob Hawke, who helped to resolve this impasse. At the Nassau CHOGM, in October 1985, Hawke, together with prime ministers Rajiv Gandhi of India and Brian Mulroney of Canada, negotiated a compromise. The Commonwealth countries would appoint a group of eminent persons, respected internationally, that would try to broker talks aimed at ending apartheid. If there was no progress after six months, then the Commonwealth leaders would meet again and consider tougher action. Hawke had someone in mind for the Eminent Persons Group—the man who only two years before had been his political opponent. Malcolm Fraser.

16

Foundations

Fraser and Financial Deregulation

One of the important ways in which the Fraser government's record has been misunderstood is in alleging that he resisted the reform and deregulation of the financial system. People have assessed Fraser through the prism of the Hawke–Keating era that followed his years in government. They have pointed to what Hawke and Keating did in floating the dollar and ushering in a new financial era, and have accused Fraser of resisting moves along this road. But the main people rubbishing Fraser's record have not been Labor Party politicians; they have been from his own side of politics.

In the last year of the Fraser government the Treasurer John Howard aligned himself with the 'dry' faction. Since then, Howard has allowed a version of history to emerge, and at times has even promoted a version, in which he is remembered as the brave man pushing for deregulation against a controlling and rigid Fraser.[1] In this narrative, Fraser is characterised as a conservative farmer at heart, enmeshed with his Country Party friends and colleagues, suspicious of banks and big business and determined to resist financial deregulation at all costs. This version of history was being developed within the 'dry' faction of the party during the last months of the Fraser government, gained power in the period following his defeat and was reinforced during the Howard prime ministership and since. Elements in the Liberal Party had a vested interest in promoting the narrative, and it has proved astonishingly persistent, despite being contradicted both by the documentary record and the memories of those who were involved in decisions.

The allegation that Fraser resisted financial deregulation has been regurgitated by journalist after journalist as though it were unquestioned truth. In May 2009, as this book was in the final stages of preparation, *The Weekend Australian* editorialised that Fraser had 'declined to deregulate the country's financial system'. The respected political journalist Michelle Grattan wrote that Howard 'initiated the landmark Campbell inquiry'. Even the National Museum of Australia claims on a website used as part of its educational program that 'Fraser proved a true conservative on economic issues, for example resisting economic deregulation'.[2] Such claims have become commonplace in reflections on Fraser's record.

Yet this version of history is the reverse of the truth. It is time to set the record straight.

There were four main reforms in the late 1970s and early 1980s that together formed what has been described as the 'revolution' of financial deregulation.[3] They were the surrendering of controls over the exchange rate, deregulation of interest rates, foreign bank entry and abolishing exchange control over movements of capital inside and outside Australia. All of these advanced under Fraser. Key moves were made because of his initiative and support. During the Fraser years, deregulation was resisted by both Treasury and the Reserve Bank of Australia; the initiatives came from Fraser's department and his personal staff.

This book is the first time that Fraser has defended his government's record on financial deregulation, but it is not the first time that doubt has been cast on the received version of history. All of the writers who have made a study of the archival record and the memories of those who were present during the Fraser years have cast doubt on the view that Howard was trying to push deregulation against resistance from Fraser.[4] Journalist Christine Wallace wrote in her 1993 biography of John Hewson:

> If Howard was such a passionate but vanquished promoter of financial deregulation, where is the pile of cabinet submissions he lost on to prove it? The truth is they do not exist … There *is* no stack of unsatisfied, unresolved, rejected and defeated cabinet submissions on financial deregulation from John Howard.[5]

It has been suggested that Howard was convinced through informal talks with Fraser that making cabinet submissions pushing for more deregulation would be a waste of time, because of Fraser's obstinate resistance.[6] Fraser remembers no such conversations. In any case, the documentary record shows that cabinet was wrestling with the possibility of floating the dollar as early as 1976, before Howard was Treasurer, and the issue remained 'alive' before cabinet for the remainder of the Fraser government, with the Prime Minister leading initiatives to introduce more flexibility in how the exchange rate was set—although it is true that he remained opposed to a full float. Treasury opposed the key moves to greater flexibility, and Howard did not advocate for them.

Yet the myth of Howard the reformer and Fraser the rigid conservative persists, altering only slightly when challenged with the facts. It has been suggested that Howard achieved deregulation by stealth—the stealth being necessary because of Fraser's opposition. In this version, Howard was responsible for key decisions such as deregulating bank interest rates. These undermined the rationale of the old system, making the rest of deregulation inevitable. This narrative was given another run in the recently published Howard biography, although in that case the authors noted that the slow pace of reform did not suggest a Treasurer in a hurry.[7]

It is true that Howard made many important and successful cabinet submissions on deregulating bank interest rates, but most of these moves came after other steps—most importantly the adoption of a market-based system for selling government securities—had been made through the initiative of Fraser, his department and his staff against the resistance of Treasury and the Reserve Bank. The market-oriented system for selling government securities made bank interest rate deregulation inevitable—not the other way around. It is also true that a key advocate for financial deregulation was Dr John Hewson, later Liberal Party leader but at the time an adviser working in Howard's office. It was Fraser who arranged for Hewson to work closely with his departmental and personal staff—which, as has been documented elsewhere, caused considerable tension in Hewson's relationship with Treasury.[8]

Because history has been so distorted, and because memory is unreliable and open to challenge, the account that follows relies mostly on the documents held in the National Archives of Australia. It has been augmented by the memories and contemporaneous diary notes of Fraser himself and of the man who was one of his most crucial advisers on financial deregulation, Dr John Rose.[9]

* * *

The story of the Fraser government's role in financial deregulation is one of ideas, change and the politically possible. It is not, or should not be, primarily about personalities, although inevitably the strengths, weaknesses and dispositions of the people involved in the process are part of the narrative.

From January 1979, the Secretary of Treasury was John Stone. Before that, Stone was deputy to the secretary Sir Frederick Wheeler. At all times, though, Stone was the dominant personality in Treasury. As detailed in chapter 11, he resisted Fraser on many issues, including the devaluation of the dollar in late 1976. He continued to resist deregulation on almost every front. Until the final months of the Fraser government, the Governor of the Reserve Bank was Sir Harold Knight, who also opposed many deregulatory initiatives. He was succeeded in August 1982 by Robert Johnston. Meanwhile,

John Howard was sworn in as Treasurer on 19 November 1977, replacing Phillip Lynch.

Fraser was determined to diversify his sources of advice on the economy. He was frustrated by the fact that at the beginning of his term, Treasury and the Reserve Bank always seemed to agree, with the dominant view—no matter who was voicing it—being that of John Stone. As a result of this, and given that the economy was the most vital issue facing his government, Fraser took care in selecting the economic advisers in his own office and within the Department of Prime Minister and Cabinet. In 1977 Fraser recruited John Rose to his private office staff. This was another piece of 'talent-spotting' by Tony Staley from the University of Melbourne, where Rose was a research fellow at the Institute of Applied Economic and Social Research. Staley regarded Rose as not only the leading expert on securities and finance regulation but also 'a very wise man, which is a good thing in a political adviser'. Rose, though, had already made an impact in his own right in Canberra as an adviser on securities, first to a Senate select committee and then to the Attorney-General. Fraser also made sure that the economic policy division of the Department of Prime Minister and Cabinet was strong and independent. The key senior figures included Ian Castles, one of the most respected policy advisers in the public service, and senior adviser Ed Visbord. These men worked closely with Rose and Hewson, and they were often called in to brief the Monetary Policy Committee of Cabinet.

Fraser was aware that the tensions generated by his trying to diversify his sources of advice might lead to a political divide between his office and that of the Treasurer, and he was keen to avoid this. For this reason, Rose, acting under Fraser's instructions, sought out John Hewson, a bright young economist from the Reserve Bank who had at the end of 1976 been recruited to Treasurer Lynch's staff. When Lynch was replaced by Howard, it was Rose who urged Fraser to make sure that Hewson was transferred to Howard's office. Rose and Hewson were close intellectually and personally. As the story of deregulation advanced, they authored numerous briefing notes and cabinet papers together. To the chagrin of Treasury, they became key advisers to the Prime Minister and the Monetary Policy Committee of Cabinet. Their advice was often preferred to that of Treasury. It was Rose and Hewson's advice, together with that of the Department of Prime Minister and Cabinet, that was key in the decision to switch to a flexibly managed exchange rate after the devaluation of the dollar.

These people—Rose, Castles, Visbord, Hewson and other officers of the Department of Prime Minister and Cabinet—initiated and pushed for the major moves towards financial deregulation during the Fraser government. To the extent that they were successful, it was because they gained Fraser's personal backing. He took their recommendations to cabinet. Fraser was the activist on the issue. The result of Fraser's activism was that his government built the foundations of financial deregulation. The Hawke–Keating government built on those foundations.

Rose says today that he was well aware during his time on Fraser's staff that it was a time of transition—trying to move from a highly regulated economy to one with more market orientation. There were limits to what was politically possible, given that both Treasury and the Reserve Bank opposed key moves in financial markets. Fraser agrees: 'It was a time of transition, but it was also a time of education. There was little electoral support for these moves, and there was a lot of concern. Treasury, in particular, if they thought we were doing the wrong thing, would go direct to financial markets and the media. They could crucify you'. Fraser also agrees that he often had to be convinced of the wisdom of deregulation. 'I relied heavily on Rose and Visbord and Castles.' He was not in favour, at any time, of a complete float of the dollar. Yet it was he who had pushed through the idea of a move from a fixed to a flexible exchange rate. When his advisers made a convincing case, he supported it. There were times, though, when the resistance of the key financial institutions of government delayed reform or made it impossible.

★ ★ ★

The financial system is a tightly woven braid. Pull on one thread, and all the others must move. In the early 1970s, the braid was kept rigid by a range of government controls so tight that there could be little movement without government's say so. Looking at the past from the knowledge of the present is always deceptive. It seems from today's perspective that those advocating deregulation were necessarily on the right side of history, and those resisting it were wrong. At the time it was not so clear. The advantage of regulation was that it gave the government more control. With that power came grave responsibility.

The government regulated the interest rates that banks could charge on loans and pay on deposits, meaning that banks had limited control over their own balance sheets. Banks were also subject to directives on the quantity and types of loans. They were liable to pressure to make loans to particular areas, such as housing. Financial institutions were specialised, with clear demarcations between trading banks, savings banks and finance companies. All transactions in foreign exchange were tightly controlled. Australians, by and large, were not allowed to make portfolio investments offshore. Government securities—the means by which the government borrows money—had a partially captive market, making it easy for the government to fund itself. Banks were limited in the risks they could take. Lastly, the fact that the exchange rate was fixed meant the government could prevent the flow of domestic savings offshore and, in theory, provide a degree of stability.

This system of tight control was under pressure by the time Fraser came to power. A number of developed countries had moved towards a floating exchange rate following the breakdown of the Bretton Woods agreements that had been part of the postwar international machinery influenced by the man who had so inspired Fraser, John Maynard Keynes. Under Bretton Woods, countries agreed to maintain the exchange rate of their currencies within fixed values, with the International Monetary Fund bridging temporary imbalances of payments. That system had collapsed after 1971 in the wake of President Nixon's ending of the United States' participation. As well, globalisation and advances in technology meant that there were increasingly intimate links between Australian domestic finances and the international system. There were also domestic reasons for the system of control being under strain, including the strong growth of non-bank financial institutions, such as building societies and credit unions, that were not subject to the same controls as banks.

By the mid 1970s it was clear to many economists that the system would have to change. But how fast, and by how much? What were the risks of giving up control? John Rose says that he understands why key bureaucrats—such as John Stone—resisted reform. 'People in John Stone's position wanted a well-managed economy, and understood that to be their responsibility. I don't think that was just about their personal power. They knew how vital a well-managed economy is to civilised living and human dignity and people's ability to have a decent life. And you can stuff it up in all sorts of ways.' Rose believes that there are not many countries that have consistently got it right. 'There you are with that responsibility, and the people who make the key decisions are not you, but people who have been elected, politicians, and for the most part you don't think they can be trusted. There are only a few levers you can pull. Wages are controlled by others. So that leaves you with monetary policy and fiscal policy. Why would you weaken control of those, when there is so much at stake? And when tax rates are a plaything of politics? I am sure that John Stone thought he had very good reasons indeed for fighting every step of the way.' Fraser, meanwhile, has sympathy for Howard. Although he grew in confidence as the years went by, Howard was at first a relatively inexperienced minister and Treasurer, squeezed between Treasury and the Prime Minister. One of the leading advocates of deregulation was Hewson, who was in Howard's own office, and the leading resister was Stone, Howard's head of department. 'It would not have been easy for him to take a position', says Fraser.

Fraser's role in the history of financial deregulation in Australia started with his policy speech in 1975, in which he promised 'a comprehensive examination of the ways in which the efficiency of the Australian capital market can be improved with special reference to the availability of finance for the expansion of small business'.[10] Fraser repeated the commitment during the 1977 election campaign. At the time, his driving motivation was his concern over the ability of small business to borrow. In early 1977 he asked the Reserve Bank for briefings on the availability of finance, and was told that government caps on interest rates for small loans might be counterproductive: instead of making it easier for small business and homeowners to borrow, caps gave banks a disincentive to make small loans available.[11]

Fraser's commitment to the capital market inquiry led in time to one of the most significant steps his government took in laying the foundations for financial deregulation: the Committee of Inquiry into the Australian Financial System, which became known as the Campbell Inquiry, after its Chairman, Keith Campbell. The inquiry's recommendations for comprehensive deregulation were picked up by the Hawke–Keating government and had an enormous impact on the economic development of the nation. But long before the Campbell Inquiry got underway, in November 1976, a key decision had been made: to devalue the dollar and move to a flexibly managed exchange rate. Under this new system, a threesome of government officials from Treasury, the Reserve Bank and the Department of Prime Minister and Cabinet met regularly and made small adjustments to the exchange rate. The system, refined in early 1977, became known as the 'dirty float'. It was by itself a big change, but the documentary record shows that in the lead-up to it, more radical steps, including a full float, had been considered by the Fraser cabinet. In October 1976 a briefing to Fraser had stated:

> If the government were to take the *radical* step [emphasis in the original], which is consistent with views expressed in opposition by Mr Lynch as Shadow Treasurer, of floating the dollar and adopted as a starting point a rate devalued by 10 or 15 per cent, it would have most if not all of the advantages of devaluation yet avoid most economic and political criticism. It would be an enlightened step consistent with advanced economic thinking and bring us into line with procedures employed in most developed countries.

A few weeks later, in a paper on the balance of payments and falls in international reserves, Castles told Fraser that floating the dollar was greatly preferable to a fixed rate.[12]

After the move to the flexibly managed system, the Monetary Policy Committee of Cabinet wrestled with the issue of how much and how often the exchange rate should move. The question of whether a full float was justified was often explored, with the impetus coming from Fraser's office and the Department of Prime Minister and Cabinet. Treasury and the Reserve Bank continued to oppose any moves to a more flexible system. Fraser says, 'With both those institutions against you, it was hard to move'.

In early 1978, the Monetary Policy Committee of Cabinet repeatedly called on Treasurer John Howard for reports on the possibility of moving to a market-oriented foreign exchange system.[13] Alan Carmody, the head of the Department of Prime Minister and Cabinet, complained in mid March that action on various issues to do with the money system, including the exchange rate, was being delayed 'because of [claims that] the time is not yet right or pending the preparation of papers which have either been inadequate or themselves further deferred'. Carmody recommended that any changes affecting the exchange rate be considered early enough to be implemented in the next financial year.[14] Finally, on 31 March, almost four months after he had been asked for it, Howard presented a paper from Treasury and the Reserve Bank that concluded that the implications of a move to a market-oriented system were 'important and complex', and that 'Comparison of Australia's recent experience with that of other countries where exchange rates are determined more directly by market forces does not present a convincing case for a basic change from our present foreign exchange arrangements'.[15] An update of this paper was presented by Howard in May. Howard canvassed the views of the Reserve Bank and Treasury, including some differences between them, but did not offer any comment of his own or any recommendation for action.[16]

The Department of Prime Minister and Cabinet was sharply critical of the Treasury and Reserve Bank's line, and advised Fraser to 'support the continuation of the present management policy pending the introduction of a more market-oriented foreign exchange system'. In another paper, the department said:

> We doubt the argument that speculation is destabilising. Some personal prejudices seem to creep into the Treasury/Reserve Bank paper on this issue … In a market system the rate moves. In a fixed system reserves move … We therefore regard the argument as sufficiently strong to move to a market-determined spot and forward exchange rate system, with intervention to be determined from time to time by the government.

Rose and Castles were recommending a review of the whole exchange control question, including removal of controls on overseas borrowings and foreign exchange transactions.[17]

At the end of May 1978, the Monetary Policy Committee of Cabinet decided to make no change for the present, but instructed Treasury and the Reserve Bank to set out 'in clear terms, step by step, the way in which a more market-oriented foreign exchange system could be implemented'.[18] This was Fraser's initiative, acting on the advice of Castles and Rose. But still Treasury and the Reserve Bank resisted. When the paper that the committee had called for was presented, in August 1978, it recapped their previous conclusions almost word for word, saying there was not a convincing case, before outlining possible steps in disapproving tones. Once again, in the absence of any recommendation from the Treasurer, the Monetary Policy Committee decided to make no changes.[19]

Meanwhile, at the same meetings and following a paper from Visbord and Rose, cabinet had been going about the process of setting up what became the Campbell Inquiry. The issue of exchange rate management was to be included in its work, and awareness of this meant that cabinet did not closely consider the exchange rate issue again until after Campbell had reported, in 1981. In June 1980, the Monetary Policy Committee of Cabinet 'reaffirmed its disposition to change the present policy on exchange rates', but agreed that this should be considered in the light of Campbell's recommendations.[20] Had Howard been pressing for the floating of the dollar at this time, he would have been sailing with the wind. The Monetary Policy Committee had indicated its disposition towards exactly that move. Even if Fraser had been opposed, Howard would hardly have been raising a novel issue.

Campbell's interim report was lodged in August 1980. Howard reported to cabinet that most submissions to Campbell had viewed the present levels of government intervention as excessive and the major cause of inefficiency. Howard thought Campbell was doing a good job, but in some areas might have gone further than required by his terms of reference. The Monetary Policy Committee of Cabinet, however, decided it did not want to discourage the broad approach that Campbell had chosen to adopt.[21] From then on, the issue of the management of the exchange rate was subsumed in the broader agenda of the Campbell Inquiry, the final report of which was not received until late 1981.

Fraser acknowledges that at this time and for some years afterwards he was against a complete float of the Australian dollar. He felt it 'let governments off the hook' of having to defend their exchange rate with good economic management. He was open, though, to debate. He was interested in ways of making the financial system work better. 'I wanted to hear the arguments', he says. If Howard had raised the matter with him at this stage, 'I would have said to him that he would have to argue the case in cabinet. He never did so'.

* * *

Over the same period as these decisions were being made, Fraser and his advisers were pushing an issue, which has since been described by the former Reserve Bank Governor Ian Macfarlane, in his 2006 Boyer lectures, as 'second only in importance to the float of the Australian dollar in 1983'. This was the way in which government securities were sold. The issue was whether government or the market should set the interest rates at which the government borrowed money. If the interest rates on government securities were set by the market, deregulation of other interest rates followed naturally. Once again, the movement was coming from Fraser's staff, John Hewson and the Department of Prime Minister and Cabinet, with Treasury and the Reserve Bank resisting and Howard playing no apparent role.

There were two kinds of government securities to which Fraser's advisers turned their attention. First, there were Treasury notes, which were aimed at the professional short-term money market investors. Second, there were Commonwealth bonds, longer term and aimed at a broader range of investors. At the beginning of Fraser's government both were sold at designated times with the terms and rates of return being set by the government in advance. Rose, in Fraser's office, thought both should be sold by tender, with the market setting the rates.

The first trace of this issue in the cabinet papers appears in January 1978. Visbord, Rose and Hewson advised Fraser that the use of formal public loans, with interest rates set by government, was an 'anachronism'. Rose and Hewson wanted government securities to be sold under a tender system. Visbord agreed about Treasury notes, but for Commonwealth bonds he advocated a 'tap and tender' system, meaning that the government would sell parcels by tender every now and again to assist in the setting of a market-based rate. After that, the securities would remain available, or 'on tap', with the government adjusting the rate as it thought necessary. 'This would be in accordance with the practice in most other developed countries', Visbord told Fraser. The issue went to the Monetary Policy Committee of Cabinet, which called for a paper from Treasury and the Reserve Bank.[22]

This decision, and the accepting of advice from Rose and Castles, apparently caused a flurry in Treasury and in relations between the very new Treasurer and his senior staff. On 19 January 1978, a file note by Geoffrey Yeend of the Department of Prime Minister and Cabinet shows that John Stone had rung protesting that Treasury would find it impossible to produce the paper on time. The Treasurer had not understood that it had to be done so quickly, and had failed to mention that Commonwealth bonds, as well as Treasury notes, were involved. Yeend wrote: 'I commented in discussion incidentally that we would after the monetary policy meeting try to talk to Treasury officers about the debriefing they got from the Treasurer so that we could minimise misunderstandings of this nature'.[23] A week later, another note for file showed that the Secretary of Treasury Fred Wheeler was saying that he was not aware of some of the issues that the Treasurer was meant to be briefing him on.[24]

Nevertheless, Treasury and the Reserve Bank met their deadline with a paper that recommended against change in the selling of government securities, because it might contribute to increased instability. The present arrangements had 'developed in an evolutionary way in consonance with the Australian institutional framework', and it was not clear that there would be any net advantage in changing the system. The paper pointed out that Loan Council approval would be needed for any changes—meaning that state premiers would have to be convinced.[25] The Department of Prime Minister and Cabinet disagreed, advising Fraser to support a decision in principle to institute a tender system for the sale of

Treasury notes starting in 1978–79. Howard should be told to report in detail on the necessary institutional steps.[26] Once again, the Monetary Policy Committee of Cabinet preferred this advice to that of Treasury. On 24 February 1978, the committee gave Treasury and the Reserve Bank three months to prepare the necessary in-depth papers, with the idea that the Loan Council would consider them before its June meeting.[27]

By 17 May the requested papers still hadn't come forward, and the committee called for them 'as a matter of urgency'.[28] They were lodged later that day. The paper on Commonwealth bonds was a bucket of cold water. It repeated the arguments for no change: the present system had 'evolved within the Australian institutional framework to meet the needs of monetary policy and government financing'. Any changes would require Loan Council agreement, and this was not likely to be forthcoming. The paper on Treasury notes did not express a strong opinion, but said, 'The balance of advantage and disadvantage does not seem to lie clearly in one direction or the other'.[29]

Once again, the Department of Prime Minister and Cabinet disagreed with the Treasury and Reserve Bank's line. The frustration and determination of Fraser's advisers are clear from a departmental briefing note to Fraser that suggested he should support an approach to the Loan Council to secure the '*early* introduction of a tender system … for selling Treasury notes' [emphasis in original].[30] Sure enough, in July, after the Loan Council meeting, the Monetary Policy Committee of Cabinet instructed Treasury and the Reserve Bank to lay out the steps to implement a tap system for Commonwealth bonds, on the basis that it was to be introduced by September 1978.[31]

When these papers were presented, Rose wrote another strong paper advocating a tender system. Nobody, said Rose, had raised any significant arguments against such a system for Treasury notes. It should be introduced 'as soon as the Reserve Bank can organise it, within say three months'. Visbord agreed. At Fraser's behest Rose's paper was circulated to the Monetary Policy Committee of Cabinet, and the committee decided that it had 'a disposition' to introduce a tender system.[32]

The issue got bogged down. In December, the Department of Prime Minister and Cabinet reminded Fraser that the issue of tenders for Treasury notes and a tap and tender system for Commonwealth securities had still not been decided.[33] Christmas and New Year came and went. In mid January 1979, the department told Fraser that Treasury and the Reserve Bank were still opposing significant change, principally because of the risk that it would upset the market for very little return. The department again strongly advocated a move to tenders for Treasury notes.[34] A few days later, Rose and Hewson prepared yet another paper for the Monetary Policy Committee of Cabinet, again strongly arguing for tenders. This time, they were successful. Two key decisions were made: to move to the sale of Treasury notes by tender and of Commonwealth bonds by a tap and tender system.[35]

Once again, the decisions caused a flurry. A file note shows that there were a number of calls to the department from 'Treasury' and 'Stone' complaining that they had not been adequately briefed on the decisions. It was agreed that the arrangements for informal briefings would be reinstated.[36] Later in February, a senior adviser in the department wrote a three-page file note recording what were apparently heated discussions with Treasury officials at a meeting attended by Visbord, Rose and other departmental officials. Treasury officials felt they now had the job of designing a scheme 'which would not leave ministers with "egg on their faces"'. Treasury was still predicting that the Loan Council would not agree to the new system.[37]

But after negotiations, the Loan Council did agree, and the tender system for Treasury notes was finally introduced in December 1979. A few months later, in April 1980, John Howard announced the new tap and tender system for marketing of Commonwealth bonds.

* * *

It was shortly after this that Howard made a series of important cabinet submissions on the deregulation of banks and interest rates. Howard had made earlier moves in this direction. In January 1979 he had written a cabinet paper signalling deregulation of banks, but had said it was 'neither necessary nor desirable' to make sudden moves. In advice to Fraser, Ed Visbord strongly supported Howard. Now, Howard made a more concerted effort for change.[38] The Department of Prime Minister and Cabinet urged Fraser to support Howard on these deregulatory moves, and by and large Fraser and cabinet followed this advice: for the most part, Howard obtained the decisions he wanted. Some matters were deferred pending the report of the Campbell Inquiry, now in full swing. Sometimes Howard agreed with this. At least once he even suggested delay, but later changed his mind and pushed for early change, at which point cabinet supported him.[39]

Rose still thought that Commonwealth bonds, as well as Treasury notes, should be sold entirely by tender. The tap system was an advance, but not enough, and there were still problems in the government's trying to make adjustments in the yield in the periods between the 'testing of the market' by tenders. In early 1981, urged by Rose, Fraser wrote to Howard inviting his views on moving to a tender system for Commonwealth bonds. Howard responded that 'Such a course is not without its dangers', and said that it would be 'unsettling', although it might be a good idea in the future.[40]

Visbord pushed the matter again in a memorandum to Fraser on 7 July 1981. At this stage, Visbord was not in favour of a full tender system, but believed the tap system wasn't working because adjustments to the yield were too infrequent and large. 'What is required is essentially a commercial approach to the sale of Commonwealth paper. As with other commodities, the price should be adjusted as necessary to achieve the desired sales, and the strategy should be to aim to increase the attractiveness of this paper.'[41] Fraser took the matter to the Monetary Policy Committee of Cabinet. On 15 July, the committee agreed that it was 'disposed' towards introducing a tender system, and called on Howard to bring forward a paper on the matter.[42] Howard's paper, received a week later, said that a tender system would be a 'major departure from existing arrangements' and that the Loan Council was unlikely to approve it. Fraser continued to work on the matter, briefed by papers from Rose arguing strongly in favour. Once more the Monetary Policy Committee of Cabinet decided that it was 'disposed' towards a tender system. The matter was to be considered again after the budget.[43]

In August there was a showdown. Rose's diary notes record that he decided to make another attempt to persuade Visbord of the benefits of a tender system. They talked into the night. To make a point, Rose rang Charles Goode, the Chairman of the finance company Potter Partners, and asked him to find out from his colleagues what they would bid for Commonwealth bonds if they were sold by tender. The results came back and were remarkable for their variety. Rose said to Visbord, 'We've been doing this for so many years and it never works. If these people can't decide the clearing rate, why should the government be able to set a rate that settles the issue? Let the market sort it out'. The next morning, Visbord sent Rose a note: he was convinced. Rose went to see Fraser, who was about to go in to a meeting of the Monetary Policy Committee of Cabinet. When Fraser heard about Visbord's change of heart, he delayed the meeting until a paper advocating the change could be typed up. Then the committee met. Word drifted out that Howard was 'very upset' because he had not been informed about the new developments. Treasury officials were being called over. Everyone was to be asked in to the cabinet room to debate the issue.

The discussion was bruising, with John Stone vigorously arguing the case against change. The debate went on, round and round. Stone said that the premiers wouldn't like such a system and that it would cause instability. Finally, Fraser called a halt. Rose remembers, 'Fraser said he was convinced of the need for change, but without the support of the Reserve Bank and Treasury it was not going to be possible to move'.

After the meeting, Fraser decided to find out the attitudes of the states. Through Rose, he made quiet inquiries, and found that they were open to persuasion and some of them were in favour. So Fraser kept pushing. By now Howard also supported a change. Fraser wrote to Howard on 25 August: 'I believe we are agreed on the desirability of moving as soon as possible to a tender/auction system for selling Commonwealth bonds'. Fraser went on to say that he had been of the view for some time that they made a misjudgement in not adopting a tender system for Commonwealth bonds at the same time as they had for Treasury notes. His recent experience, including a meeting with the premiers the previous week, had strengthened his view. 'As long as we have to set yields on tap securities, it will be difficult to avoid being seen to be responsible for every upward shift in interest rates; we have to get away from this situation.' He asked Howard to request that Treasury and the Reserve Bank outline the form that a tender system might take, with the aim of putting it in place 'as soon as possible'.[44]

By now—late 1981—the final report of the Campbell Inquiry was expected within weeks. Treasury and the Reserve Bank lodged their memorandums, but cabinet decided to defer the matter until after the inquiry had reported.[45] The Campbell Inquiry did indeed recommend, among many other things, a tender system for government securities. The task force set up to consider the report endorsed this approach, but Treasury had serious doubts.[46] Fraser continued to push the issue. He suggested to Howard in February that a special management group be set up to determine the setting of targets and reserve prices if a tender system was adopted. Howard resisted this idea:

> To be quite frank, I do not see the need to the establishment of such a group. It would, in my view, represent an unnecessary derogation from my own responsibilities to advise the government on interest rate matters ... I envisage that I would as appropriate bring recommendations to the

> Monetary Policy Committee of Cabinet in respect of such things as quantities to be auctioned.[47]

Finally, after negotiations with the states, the first tender for the sale of Commonwealth bonds was announced in July 1982—four and a half years after it had first been suggested. The hold-up, at every stage, had been opposition from Treasury and the Reserve Bank. Howard had played no significant role in achieving the change. The time taken is a measure of how hard it is to institute important financial reform—and this was one of the most important of the decade, with far-reaching implications. Against the resistance of the key financial institutions of government, it was almost impossible, and certainly slow.

It has been suggested that Fraser resisted the move to a market-based system for selling government securities. In fact, the record shows that it was Fraser, his department and his staff who were responsible for a change which, in the history of Australia's financial deregulation is second in significance only to the Hawke–Keating government's decision to float the dollar, and inseparable from the related issue of deregulation of interest rates more generally.

* * *

The other important financial initiative of the Fraser government was the establishment of the Campbell Inquiry, which laid the foundations for what the Hawke–Keating government was later to do. The setting-up of this inquiry was also the initiative of Fraser, advised by his department and personal staff.

Ed Visbord and John Rose discussed the matter with Fraser on a flight to Canberra early in 1978—at the same time as cabinet was wrestling with both the government securities issue and the possibility of floating the dollar. Fraser had made a commitment to a capital market inquiry in the 1975 and 1977 election campaigns. Why not make this a comprehensive inquiry into all the issues of government regulation of the financial system? Fraser instructed Rose and

Visbord to do an immediate paper suggesting an inquiry to look at all the issues—government securities, foreign exchange, controls on overseas borrowings and banking regulation. Fraser took the matter to the Monetary Policy Committee of Cabinet without submission on 9 February 1978. He says today, 'I wanted some action. It had taken far too long to move on this, and I was frustrated'. The result was a decision to set up the inquiry. Later that month, Howard was instructed to bring forward detailed terms of reference by 7 March.[48] But a few days later Howard begged an extension of time: 'I expect to have proposals ready in approximately two or three weeks'.[49]

It took much longer. Fraser remembers experiencing increasing frustration at how slowly things were moving. There were good excuses: Howard was at the time a relatively new and inexperienced Treasurer; the issues concerning the marketing of Commonwealth securities were running simultaneously; there was a budget to prepare; and Howard was carrying the finance portfolio as well as Treasury. Nevertheless, any idea that Howard was forcing the pace of change against reluctance from Fraser and cabinet is obviously false.

In May, cabinet gave Howard an apparent hurry-up, noting that he would bring forward a submission on the terms of reference for the inquiry in the week beginning 8 May.[50] Howard missed that deadline as well. Finally, in late July, he presented the Monetary Policy Committee of Cabinet with four alternative draft terms of reference without making any recommendation on which one should be adopted. Those favoured by the Department of Prime Minister and Cabinet—for a broad-ranging inquiry—were adopted with minor changes. Howard was instructed to create a list of suitable committee members.[51] That took almost another three months. The Department of Prime Minister and Cabinet supported the choice of Keith Campbell as Chairman of the inquiry. Other minor changes to its membership were made over the following weeks.[52] The inquiry was finally established in January 1979—more than three years after Fraser had promised it in his 1975 policy speech, and almost a year after cabinet had decided to set it up.

The Campbell Inquiry took nearly two years, with an interim report made in August 1980.[53] By the time the final report was delivered, in late 1981, the Fraser government was struggling with an economy battered by the impact of the second oil shock. Fractures were appearing in the government. Fraser had been damaged by the resignation of Andrew Peacock as Minister for Industrial Relations. Peacock was emerging as a rival to Fraser, and Howard had aligned himself with the 'dry' faction of backbenchers. Howard was also seen as a leadership aspirant. Already, the view had emerged that it was Howard driving the push for deregulation, and Fraser resisting it. The truth was that, by now, the Campbell Inquiry agenda had become an important platform for Howard, who had been convinced of the merits of wholesale deregulation. However, his advocacy in cabinet was still muted.

The recent biography of John Howard asserts that at this time the 'dry' faction of the Liberal Party, including John Hyde, Ross McLean, David Jull and Murray Sainsbury, would 'have a drink in Howard's office on Thursday nights at ten or eleven o'clock when the parliament rose. Jim Carlton would occasionally join them. Howard would sit back with his favourite beer, Foster's, and empathise with the group's complaints that Fraser wasn't supporting deregulation'.[54] If this is an accurate account of what Howard was doing at the time, then his allies were gaining a false impression. Howard had not personally pushed for deregulation of government securities; he had not pushed for the floating of the dollar. He had dragged his feet on the Campbell Inquiry. He had pushed for deregulation of bank interest rates, but only after the previous moves were in place and with support from the Prime Minister's department. Where there had been delay pending the Campbell Inquiry, he had concurred with this and, in at least one case, suggested it.

Nor was Howard to be a strong advocate for Campbell's recommendations for comprehensive deregulation. In June 1981, anticipating the conclusion of the Campbell Inquiry, Howard wrote to Fraser suggesting that a task force group of officials be set up to examine the report, since it was likely to be voluminous and detailed. Fraser agreed: 'I assume that you have in mind that the Monetary Policy Committee of Cabinet should consider the report with the assistance of the task force'.[55] In October, Visbord wrote a note for the file anticipating that the copies of the report would be delivered the following week.

Then there occurred a strange sequence of events. Fraser became aware in the first week of November that Howard had already received the Campbell Inquiry report, and was apparently 'sitting on it'. A copy had been given to senior Treasury officials with instructions that it be tightly held and not given to the task force that had been established to consider it. Fraser rang Howard immediately, with Rose in the room, and asked for a copy of the report. Rose's diary note records Fraser as saying that he was 'very concerned about the politics of deregulation of interest rates'.[56] The result was that Fraser received copies of the report.

Some of these events are reflected in the archival record. On 5 November—the day after Fraser had demanded a copy of the report—Howard wrote to Fraser and referred to 'our telephone conversation yesterday regarding the final report. I understand that you have now received two copies of the report'. Howard said that arrangements were being made for the report to be tabled in the Senate on 12 November 1981 and made available to the news media on embargoed basis the day before.[57] As the letter makes clear, Howard had not circulated copies of the report to any cabinet ministers, or to Fraser himself until asked to do so, yet he was planning to make it available to the media in just six days' time.

It is true that Fraser was seriously troubled by the report—not because he was against deregulation on principle, but because the political implications were enormous and difficult at what was already a politically difficult time. Rose recorded Fraser as saying that 'He didn't mind the economics of it, but in the political situation at the present time, setting so many hares running at one time would not be terribly helpful'. The report offered a package of measures amounting to almost complete deregulation of the financial system, including the floating of the dollar, yet offered little by way of advice on implementation, and nothing on the social effects. When the Campbell Inquiry had begun, home loan interest rates had been at 9.5 per cent and the country was doing well, having recovered from the Whitlam years. Now, home buyers were paying 12.5 per cent, and the economic achievements of the previous six years were being destroyed by the international downturn, the Australian Council of Trade Unions wages policy and the drought. Fraser was considering an early election—the election that he was to lose. He remembers today, 'It's true I was worried about the politics of interest rates. Anyone would be. I wanted us to think very carefully about how to handle it'.

A few days later, on 9 November, there was a heated session in cabinet. The result was a cabinet decision that could have left Howard in no doubt about what his colleagues thought of his actions in sitting on the report.

> [Cabinet] noted that the Treasurer had indicated publicly that the report of the inquiry into the Australian financial system would be tabled in the Senate on 11 November 1981; noted that ministers had not yet had an opportunity to study the report and its recommendations in detail; noted that the report canvassed policy issues which impinge upon the portfolio responsibilities of a number of ministers; noted that in order to give cabinet an opportunity to determine the initial approach to be adopted by the government in relation to the report, the Treasurer would issue a further statement indicating that the report would now be tabled in the House of Representatives in the week commencing 16 November 1981; and agreed to consider the matter further on 13 November when the Treasurer would have available: a draft tabling statement; and advice on aspects of the recommendations of the report which could give rise to presentational difficulties at the time of tabling.[58]

Howard had been rapped over the knuckles, but someone briefed the media with a different slant on events. The delay in Howard's tabling was written up in at least one news article as Howard's having been 'rolled' by a 'panicked' cabinet determined to 'take the scalpel [to the] most sensitive recommendations'.[59]

The reality was that the task force Howard had himself recommended—including representatives from the Reserve Bank and Treasury, as well as Rose and Hewson—had begun work. In mid December, Howard wrote to Fraser saying that it would produce a number of papers on the important and sensitive issues, with the first being available in January. Fraser and Howard had agreed that, rather than taking an 'all or nothing' approach to Campbell, there should be a phased response. If Howard opposed this idea or wanted a faster pace, he didn't say so to Fraser. Instead, Howard wrote:

> Quite clearly it is possible for the government to respond to some of the recommendations reasonably early. Equally, there are others, particularly in the taxation area, which the government may at an early stage simply wish to note and put off for consideration in the budgetary context. There are others which will involve consultation with the states and there are others still which will require further study. This is of course a very preliminary assessment on my part of how we might schedule our response to the report. It is important I think to avoid the expectation of one single all-embracing response by the government. Equally again it is highly desirable in my judgement that the government be seen to be responding in an orderly and methodical manner to what has been recommended.[60]

In January 1982, Howard wrote again saying that because of its 'importance and sensitivity', the issue of housing rates was being considered first, and that there should be papers for cabinet by 26 January. It could not be done more quickly, he said. Since he, Howard, was going on leave, cabinet would not be able to consider the matter until 15 February.[61]

In fact, it was the task force papers on public sector financing, recommending a market-oriented approach to the sale of Commonwealth bonds, that came first, on 26 January. This led, eventually, to the introduction of a tender system for Commonwealth bonds, as described earlier. The task force papers on housing were lodged with the cabinet office on 8 February. Howard's accompanying submission was not a call to action. He wrote:

> While there are many interdependencies in the Campbell report (which require some areas of it to be dealt with ahead of others) it would be going too far to say that the response to it must be an 'all or nothing' one. On the contrary it seems to me that there are a significant number of recommendations where the appropriate government response may be to decide to phase in desirable changes over a period of time; there may be some recommendations where our attitude may be to indicate that the government is unlikely to take them up; and there may be some others to which we can indicate an early favourable response ... It is vital, in due course, that the government is seen to be making a serious and thoughtful response to the report recommendations.[62]

Task force work trickled on throughout 1982. There is little doubt that the process became bogged down. Key papers were considered and more information and papers were called for, but there were few decisions for action—and few recommendations for action from the Treasurer.

Howard lodged the reports on monetary policy and interest rate controls on 18 June 1982. In his accompanying submission, he said there was substantial agreement on the task force that Campbell's recommendations should be implemented, but on the issue of interest rate controls he said: 'While I would not want to exclude the possibility that some of these recommendations might be taken up in coming months ... I reiterate that I'm not putting any specific recommendations for further changes at this time'.[63]

Visbord, meanwhile, was trying to find a date on which cabinet could give the Campbell recommendations comprehensive consideration. Fraser had suggested that at least a day was needed. Visbord was also alerting Fraser to divisions of opinion within the task force on entry of foreign banks and foreign exchange. The Department of Prime Minister and Cabinet together with Rose and Hewson favoured foreign bank entry soon, in conjunction with changes to prudential regulation and interest rate controls. Treasury and the Reserve Bank, on the other hand, wanted to set aside the issue of foreign bank entry until those issues had been settled. On exchange rates, Treasury and the Reserve bank favoured only gradual evolution to a market-based system; the Department of Prime Minister and Cabinet favoured the early dismantling of exchange rate controls. 'Hewson and Rose desire more movement towards Campbell than the Treasury and the Reserve Bank position implies.'[64]

Howard did not adjudicate on this difference of opinion. On 2 July, he said in a submission to cabinet that 'Any changes need to be made carefully and explained well'. They should be seen as 'an orderly continuation of what has been an evolutionary process to a more market-based foreign exchange arrangement'. He endorsed a task force conclusion that some government intervention in foreign exchange was warranted, and suggested that Treasury and the Reserve Bank prepare a detailed report on possible changes. There were no firm recommendations for change, no push towards deregulation. Once again, the more radical deregulatory push was coming from the Department of Prime Minister and Cabinet, which wrote to Fraser suggesting that the government move towards dismantling almost all controls. To be fair, this paper noted the differences of opinion on the task force, and stated: 'The Treasurer's position corresponds to that of Hewson and Rose', but, if so, this position was not reflected in Howard's cabinet submissions.[65]

John Rose remembers this period as one of constant argument and tangling with Treasury and the Reserve Bank—but something significant did emerge. The Reserve Bank representative on the task force was Bob Johnston. 'I was walking back from a meeting at Treasury with Bob Johnston after another round of argument, and I said, "Bob, why are you so opposed to this exchange rate stuff?" and he said, "Well, John, I'm not opposed. I'm in favour of it, but what I am having to argue is the Reserve Bank formal position".' At the time, a replacement was being sought for the Reserve Bank Governor Harry Knight, who had retired. Media reports had floated both Johnston's name and that of former Treasurer Phillip Lynch. Howard favoured Johnston. Rose remembers getting back to the office after his talk with Johnston and going straight in to Fraser. 'I said, "Look, I'll let you know my view. I think that you should make Bob Johnston Governor", and Malcolm said, "Why do you think that?" and I told him this remark Bob Johnston had made. He picked up the phone on his desk, which was the one that connected direct to Howard, and he said to Howard, "Look, the guy for the job is Bob Johnston".' Fraser remembers that Howard was very happy with this, and Johnston was duly appointed on the Treasurer's recommendation. As a result, the Reserve Bank's attitude to floating the dollar and deregulation more generally changed—but not in time to affect the Fraser government. Today Fraser remembers, 'I knew that Johnston was in favour of these changes, and that is why I supported appointing him. I would hardly have done that if I was against deregulation'.

Meanwhile, Fraser had asked for, and received, advice on a package of measures involving reductions in levels of industry protection on the one hand and a devaluation of the dollar on the other. 'Because these two changes have opposite effects on competitiveness, one can be a "trade-off" to some extent against the other.'[66] On 5 July, cabinet wrestled with the issue of reducing levels of industry protection at a time of economic downturn, and decided that more thinking was needed before it could make a decision.[67] Also in July, the Monetary Policy Committee of Cabinet made a series of decisions on Campbell, all of which called for more work rather than for action. Moves towards making the financial system more flexible should 'continue in an evolutionary manner'.[68] In October, Visbord was noting that the question of entry of foreign banks was 'the most urgent issue outstanding'. In December, Howard lodged the task force papers on participation in the banking system. He recommended that up to eight foreign banks be allowed entry. This issue dragged on, with a group of officials asked to examine the matter and the relationship between bank entry and prudential supervision. The Department of Prime Minister and Cabinet supported Howard's approach, but suggested that twelve rather than eight banks be allowed in.[69]

Fraser was becoming impatient. There are letters on the file from November and December 1982 in which he urged Howard to bring forward remaining task force papers as a matter of urgency so they could be dealt with early in the new year. There are other memorandums in which the Department of Prime Minister and Cabinet promises to 'jog' the Treasurer's memory.[70] Finally, on 13 January 1983, cabinet considered a Howard submission on foreign banks and decided in principle to allow for the initial entry of up to ten. It was a decision never implemented: just a few weeks afterwards, Fraser called the election at which his government was defeated.[71]

What about foreign exchange? Cabinet considered another submission from Howard on 13 January, weeks before the calling of the election. There was a decision requesting more information 'revised and updated in the light of recent developments'. This submission was never lodged.[72]

* * *

It was now almost four years since cabinet had decided to establish the Campbell Inquiry. Decisions had been made to move government securities to a market-based system. Some of the controls on interest rates had been removed. It had been decided to allow in foreign banks. There had been a staggering amount of paper, consideration and reconsideration, followed by calls for yet more reports and information. At no stage does the documentary record suggest that Howard attempted to force the pace. Looking back now, Fraser admits that at this stage of the government's life, 'I had allowed myself to get tired'. If he had his time again, he would set up a dedicated body within his own department to drive the Campbell agenda. 'More vigorous action would have helped an economic recovery', he says. 'I was always in favour of freeing up capital markets, but the Reserve Bank and Treasury simply weren't willing to move for most of the time I was in government.'

What would have happened if Fraser had won the March 1983 election? It seems certain that foreign banks would have been allowed in at about the same time as Hawke and Keating made the same move. Bank and interest rate regulation would almost certainly have been further relaxed, if not in the difficult circumstances of 1982 then at least after the breaking of the drought and the 1983 recovery.

Within two months of taking office, Hawke and Keating held their own inquiry—the Martin Review Group—which rapidly endorsed the recommendations of Campbell. That led to the deregulation of the stock exchange, the entry of foreign banks, the removal of remaining ceilings on bank loan interest rates and, most important of all, the floating of the dollar.

In 1983, and for some years afterwards, Fraser was opposed to this last move. The strength of his opposition to floating the currency can be seen in a speech he gave in 1984, in which he called on the big economies of Europe, North America and Japan to provide stability in exchange rates. If they failed to do so, he said, then smaller countries would have no option but to float their currencies, and this was of 'no more advantage to private enterprise than giving every trader on the street corner a right to print currency'.[73] It was just such financial pressures and the crisis they caused for Australia that led to Hawke and Keating floating the dollar. Would Fraser have done the same if he had been Prime Minister? Fraser thinks it more likely that he would have continued to move the 'dirty float' to become ever more flexible, while maintaining an element of government control, but, 'I would have taken advice, and made a pragmatic decision on the evidence and the arguments, and certainly people around me were arguing for a float'.

Rose believes, and the documentary record would seem to suggest, that had Fraser held power, all or most of the financial deregulation achieved by Hawke and Keating would still have occurred. When it comes to the other arms of deregulation—tariffs and the labour market—the Fraser government has less to show. On wages, Fraser was a supporter of arbitration. Deregulation of the labour market was never part of his agenda. As for tariffs, Fraser says it is too simplistic to depict him as opposed to reform. 'I was always a free trader by instinct', he says, but he believed that if Australia were to go further in dropping tariffs on manufactured goods, 'which we certainly needed to do', it should be in return for better access to markets for agricultural produce in Europe, the United States and Japan, all of which remained highly protectionist of their farmers. Tariffs on manufactured goods were 'bargaining chips' in international negotiations. They were elements of foreign policy, as described in chapters 14 and 15. When Hawke and Keating reduced protection of manufacturing, Fraser says, it was without acquiring any significant concessions in return.

So what were the differences between the Fraser government and that of Hawke and Keating on deregulation? One of the key differences was surely the presence of an activist Treasurer, prepared to take strong positions and argue for them. Another key difference was that by the time Keating was pushing the agenda, the economy was recovering and the drought had broken. Finally, there had been a change to the governorship of the Reserve Bank, thanks to Bob Johnston's appointment. The Hawke–Keating government still had to push against the resistance of Treasury, but the Reserve Bank was onside.

Fraser continues to have deep reservations about the more zealous proponents of deregulation, and to believe in a strong role for government. 'The people who are at the extreme on free markets don't really believe in social policy. They wouldn't have views on how to treat refugees or Aboriginals. They wouldn't have views about how Australia might be a force for good in the world, apart from economics. I have always believed those things were part of what governments should do.'

By the mid 1980s, Australia had moved from a system of rigid control further and faster towards a deregulated economy than many comparable countries. In this story, the role of the Fraser government was one of transition and education at a time when the key financial institutions of government had not been convinced of the need for change. The laying of the foundations for the new financial era was the achievement of Fraser and his advisers.

17

Land and Sea

When the Minister for Aboriginal Affairs Ian Viner brought the Aboriginal Land Rights legislation to parliament, he included in his second reading speech some words by the anthropologist William Stanner to describe what land meant to Aboriginal people. 'No English words are good enough to give a sense of the links between an Aboriginal group and its homeland ... Our word "land" is too spare and meagre. We can now scarcely use it except with economic overtones unless we happen to be poets.' Stanner said he had seen Aboriginal people embrace the earth they walked on. To be deprived of homeland, he said, was to be bereft of that which made living intelligible. It was to be faced with 'a kind of vertigo in living'.[1]

Fraser is no poet. As a farmer, he thinks of land 'with economic overtones'. Yet he understood the emotional impact of those words. He is not only pragmatic. We all hold within us the lessons learned in childhood, before the rational mind comes to dominate, and there will always be some part of Fraser that is the solitary, self-sufficient boy, in his boat on the Edward River and wandering free in the red-gum forest of Balpool-Nyang—the childhood home that was taken from him. In his feeling for land there is the 'something of the metaphysic' that also formed the basis of his motivation for being a politician. Yet metaphysics has no place in public policy. Political action, he believes, must be based on reason. As well, politics is the art of the possible.

This chapter describes Fraser's record on environmental issues. The politics of land and sea was never simple. Fraser had to balance progress with preservation. There were also the interests of Aboriginals and Torres Strait Islanders. Most difficult of all, he tried to stay true to his understanding of the role of state governments in the Australian federation. States' rights, he believed, are among the main checks on the abuse of power by the federal government. If Fraser had not believed this, he could hardly have advocated the right of the Senate to block supply and bring down Whitlam. Yet in the battles over the environment he had to deal with some of the most stubborn politicians in the land—state premiers. He used everything he could in negotiation. He both offered big carrots and brandished strong sticks. Only very rarely was he prepared to overrule the states. 'Sometimes,' Fraser says, 'you simply can't resolve the conflict between principles'. The results were mixed. The Fraser government created Kakadu National Park and banned whaling. Fraser's actions saved the Great Barrier Reef from oil drilling and Fraser Island from sand mining. He oversaw the mining and export of Australian uranium, establishing the strictest of safeguards. Yet it is also likely that if Fraser had remained in power the great wild rivers of south-western Tasmania would have been dammed.

Is it necessary for politicians to be optimists? A good politician must surely believe that it is possible to make things better. In our own time, the balance of scientific evidence tells us that human activity is bringing the planet into peril. This challenge cannot be met without good government. Perhaps, then, it is enough for the politicians of the present to believe only that their actions may stop things from getting worse. Malcolm Fraser, though, is an optimist. Liberalism is a hopeful philosophy. It is predicated on a belief in human reason, in the capacity of the individual to grow in understanding, and in the ability of good government to both preserve freedom and bring the order on which freedom depends. The liberal in Fraser believes in progress.

He was not, and is not, a 'deep green' believing in preservation at all costs. He believes, as he put it in 1981, that 'Man surely has the right to utilise the resources of this planet', but also that 'It is certainly not acceptable for this generation to rob the next, or for us to pass on to our children a less healthy, a less beautiful or a less enriching heritage than we enjoy ourselves'.[2] He has always believed that Australia can, and should, support bigger populations. Doing this, he believes, is a matter of management, and of vision.

Those who had been following Fraser during his political career would have known, when he came to the prime ministership, that he was what the Tasmanian Premier Doug Lowe later described as a 'closet greenie'.[3] Claude Austin, the man who had backed Fraser's pre-selection all those years ago, had been a strong conservationist. Through him, and long before the environment was politically fashionable, Fraser became involved in the issues. As a backbencher he pushed through a ban on the export of Australian native birds. He was a founding member of the Australian Conservation Foundation. It was his efforts as a backbencher that gained the foundation tax-deductable status in the mid 1960s. Later, as Minister for Education and Science, he secured its future with federal grants.

The 1970s was a time of awakening for what became the modern environmental movement. Its coming of age was the fight to prevent the damming of the wild rivers of Tasmania. Before that, there was the battle against the flooding of Lake Pedder, the jewel of the Tasmanian wilderness, by the state's Hydro-Electric Commission in 1972. Like every other federal politician, Fraser was lobbied over the lake. In September 1973, he replied to a letter from the Secretary of the Lake Pedder Action Committee, saying:

> As a foundation member of the Australian Conservation Foundation, I have a great concern for matters such as the preservation of Lake Pedder. I have presented a number of petitions from my own constituents on this subject to

> parliament and sincerely trust that no more damage will be done to this beautiful area of Tasmania.[4]

But Fraser was in opposition, and there was little he could do. The campaign to save Lake Pedder was unsuccessful. In the wake of that failure, the Tasmanian Wilderness Society was founded by Dr Bob Brown. The new society's aims were, Brown said, to protect wilderness and to encourage 'a new humility by humankind towards this little planet which nurtures us and from which we've emerged, a relationship with the wild planet to be who we are'.[5]

In the December 1975 election that brought him to power, Fraser made a commitment to help the Tasmanian government establish a national park of world significance in the south-west of the state, as well as promising to jointly fund a survey of the region's resources. Throughout his time in government, the fight over the Tasmanian wilderness continued. Fraser watched and waited. In the last days of his government, this battle involved him in one of the most difficult conflicts he faced between his fundamental beliefs—states' rights on the one hand, and conservation on the other.

* * *

The first test of the Fraser government's environmental credentials, in 1976, was sand mining on Fraser Island. Located off the Queensland coast east of Maryborough, Fraser Island is unique—the largest sand island in the world, and a fragile combination of steep dunes, perched lakes and, thanks to the absence of foxes, goats and mice, a huge diversity of native animals and plants. Its sand had been mined since 1971. The Queensland government, under the leadership of the National Party Premier Joh Bjelke-Petersen, had set aside a small area of the island as a national park, but had failed to protect the rainforest, the lakes, the surfing beaches or the famous coloured sands. Sand-mining leases were held by the Hawaiian-based Dillingham Corporation and Queensland Titanium Mines.

The Whitlam government was ambivalent. The Minister for Mines and Energy Rex Connor was pro-development, wanting Australian ownership of mining companies and increased government control. In 1974, Connor had contravened earlier cabinet directives and approved export contracts for Fraser Island sand, then threatened to resign if Whitlam didn't back him. Yet many in Whitlam's cabinet, including Moss Cass, the Environment Minister, were horrified by the damage being done. Whitlam resolved the tensions by setting up an environmental inquiry in April 1975. The Queensland government boycotted it, saying Whitlam was infringing on states' rights. Dillingham's unsuccessfully challenged it in the High Court, and mining continued apace while the inquiry did its work. By the time it reported, Fraser was in government. The inquiry recommended that all export of Fraser Island minerals be absolutely prohibited.

Bjelke-Petersen, who had played such a crucial role in Whitlam's downfall, had confidently told his cabinet that once Fraser was appointed Queensland development could 'push ahead'.[6] He didn't know his man.

Fraser was initially suspicious of the Whitlam-appointed inquiry, but he investigated and was assured that the report was independent and had unimpeachable scientific credibility. The decision seemed clear. Sand mining and preservation of the environment were incompatible. One or the other had to give way, and the economic benefits of the mine did not outweigh the uniqueness of the island.

Not everyone in government agreed. Fraser remembers, 'Plenty of people in cabinet thought stopping mining would be a disastrous decision. It was a leftie decision, they said. It would make international investors think we were like Whitlam'. Senior Treasury officials were among the most vocal opponents. Fraser was at this time—late 1976—locked in his battles with Treasury over the need for more information and the devaluation of the dollar. He was about to announce the split of the department into two. Here was one more cause of distrust and bad feeling. Fraser says today, 'Treasury were very outspoken, as though they were speaking about something in their domain'.

The issue went to cabinet in November 1976. Fraser carried the day: the export of sand from Fraser Island was banned from 31 December 1976.[7] Later, Fraser was visiting New York and spoke at a lunch for twenty-five senior corporate leaders with interests in Australia. They questioned him about Fraser Island in such detail that he was convinced that they had been briefed by Treasury. Fraser told them that 'Australia's national interests wouldn't always coincide with their financial interests'. One businessman threatened him. Life would become 'very uncomfortable' for the Australian Government if it persisted with a sand-mining ban, Fraser was told. The threat made him more determined. 'I didn't worry about the pressure. If you know in your heart that you've taken the right decision, it makes life much easier to cope with. It makes you happier.'

Fraser thought the decision on sand mining was relatively easy. The scientific case was clear. It was an 'either or' option. Mining and the preservation of the island were incompatible, and could not be reconciled. It wasn't often that decisions between right and wrong were so clear-cut.

⋆ ⋆ ⋆

In the 1970s, only a very few scientists had heard of what was then largely a theory—that the burning of fossil fuels was warming the atmosphere and causing climate change. Instead, one of the most pressing crises facing the world was a lack of fossil fuels. The first oil shock, in the early 1970s, had brought home how dependent the Western world was on a resource that was believed to be running out fast. Credible scientists said that by 2010 the world's known supplies of oil would be exhausted. There were apocalyptic predictions about the impact on civilisation.[8]

Fraser believed that Australia had both special responsibilities and special opportunities in the energy debate. Australia was rich in resources: it was a major coal exporter and had oil and gas. Perhaps most important of all, at a time when Japan and countries in Asia and Europe were building nuclear power reactors, Australia had an estimated 20 per cent of the world's reserves of uranium. The bulk was in a small area about 150 kilometres wide at the northern tip of the Northern Territory, 200 kilometres east of Darwin and on the edge of the Arnhem Land Aboriginal Reserve. The land under which the uranium lay was some of the most remarkable in the continent. It included spectacular tropical wetlands, the Arnhem Land escarpment and some of the best surviving examples of Aboriginal rock art in the country. There was evidence that there had been human occupation for at least 50 000 years.

A national park had been proposed since the mid 1960s, but the discovery of uranium in the early 1970s and the issue of mining leases had complicated and delayed decisions, with the boundaries of the area gradually contracting as the miners brought pressure to bear. Three-quarters of this uranium lay in the Ranger and Jabiluka deposits, with the latter thought to be the largest deposit in the world. Jabiluka was controlled by Pancontinental Mining Limited and Getty Oil. Ranger was controlled by a partnership between the Electrolytic Zinc Company of Australasia, Peko-Wallsend and the Australian Atomic Energy Corporation.

In a radio talk in 1977, Fraser told the electors of Wannon that because of its rich resources, Australia had special obligations to strike a balance between its own needs and those of other countries, and between present needs and future needs.[9] When it came to uranium, he thought there was an additional responsibility. Uranium offered both the promise of human progress and the threat of annihilation. The world was locked in a Cold War. Fraser didn't believe détente was working. Nuclear war seemed possible, even likely, and the only hope lay in non-proliferation treaties—the attempt to reach agreements to limit the number of nuclear weapons. If uranium was exported, could Australia be sure that it would not end up in weapons? As well, there were fears that nuclear power reactors themselves were unacceptably dangerous. Fraser believed that Australia was in a unique position to influence the way the nuclear power industry developed. If Australia was an exporter of uranium, it could insist on only exporting to countries that had signed the nuclear non-proliferation treaty and agreed to strict safeguards. If Australia left its uranium in the ground, then the unscrupulous would find what they needed somewhere else and the opportunity to set standards and safeguards would be lost. Fraser was never in any doubt that Australia's uranium should be mined and exported, but he knew it was a momentous and difficult political decision, and there were many things to be weighed in the balance—the economy, the international obligations, the beauty of the Alligator Rivers region, and the rights of the traditional owners.

The Whitlam government had once again been ambivalent about uranium mining. When Whitlam came to government there were already contracts for the export of 9000 tonnes of uranium. Whitlam was committed to land rights, and it was clear that the Aboriginals of the Alligator Rivers region would have strong claims to the land covered by the mining leases. By the time Whitlam set up the Woodward Royal Commission into land rights, the government had decided at least to delay allowing uranium exporting. The industry was held in suspension. Meanwhile, Whitlam's cabinet was split. Rex Connor wanted the uranium mined, with maximum Australian ownership and government control of the marketing. He also wanted an enrichment plant established on Australian soil to maximise the earnings. Moss Cass, and many Labor supporters, believed uranium should stay in the ground. Once again, Whitlam's solution to the tensions was to appoint a public inquiry, under the leadership of Justice Russell Walter Fox, a senior judge of the Australian Capital Territory Supreme Court. By the time that Fox's first report was released, in October 1976, Fraser was in government.

Doug Anthony, as Minister for National Resources, was keen for uranium mining to proceed as quickly as possible. In early January 1976, he was pressing cabinet to authorise statements expressing support for uranium mining at Ranger, as well as making it clear that overseas ownership would be welcome. Fraser knew it would be necessary to move more slowly.[10] 'I was certainly in favour. I agreed with Doug. But I knew, and I think he knew after a very little discussion, that this was something where we could not move quickly. It was a very sensitive issue indeed, both politically and in terms of how we wanted to do it, but there were plenty in government who were saying, "Let's just get on with it".' Instead, there were seventeen months between the coalition coming to government and the crucial decisions being made. Fraser wanted to get it right—to do the best he could to balance the competing considerations, and handle the politics.

The Fox Inquiry's first report dealt with the international issues—the question of whether it was right for Australia to mine uranium at all. The newspaper headlines were saying: '"Green Light" for Uranium Mining'. Fox had found that the hazards were, if properly controlled, not so great as to justify a ban on uranium export. Yet he also sounded a grave warning: the nuclear power industry, he said, was unintentionally contributing to an increased risk of nuclear war. This was the most serious hazard, and the parliament needed to think carefully about the responsibility it imposed, and what kinds of safeguards were needed. Uranium should be sold only to countries that had signed the Nuclear Non-Proliferation Treaty. It was clear by now that both sides of politics thought uranium mining would go ahead. Bob Hawke, then President of the Australian Council of Trade Unions, told the government that the unions would agree to uranium export, providing it was used only for power generation and mined and sold with appropriate safeguards.[11]

Meanwhile, the Aboriginal Land Rights Act had been passed. Fraser had given Fox the power to consider the Aboriginal claims to the uranium-rich lands. The Aboriginals had a clear case under the new legislation; but what powers would their 'ownership' allow? Thanks to Viner's and Fraser's battles, land rights usually gave Aboriginal people the ability to veto mining, but the Ranger uranium project had been specifically excluded. The traditional owners would not be able to prevent mining. They could only negotiate terms.

Fox's second report, delivered in May 1977, dealt in anguished fashion with the Aboriginal claims. It was clear that most Aboriginals opposed the mining. It was also clear that they knew their views would not prevail. Fox said:

> They feel that having got so far, the white man is not likely to stop. They have a justifiable complaint that plans for mining have been allowed to develop as far as they have without Aboriginal people having an adequate opportunity to be heard ... There can be no compromise with the Aboriginal position: either it is treated as conclusive, or it is set aside. We are a tribunal of white men and any attempt on our part to state what is a reasonable accommodation of the various claims and interests can be regarded as white man's arrogance or paternalism. Nevertheless this is the task we have been set ... That our values are different is not to be denied, but we have nevertheless striven to understand ... their values and their viewpoint. We have given careful attention to all that has been put before us by them or on their behalf. In the end, we form the conclusion that their opposition should not be allowed to prevail.[12]

Fox recommended that mining should go ahead. He also recommended an arrangement that had been anticipated in the Woodward Royal Commission's report: the Aboriginals should be given title to their land, but at the same time the Kakadu National Park should be established. The land would be both Aboriginal-owned and jointly managed as a national park. Meanwhile, Fox laid down the strictest safeguards for mining and recommended the appointment of a statutory official, the supervising scientist, to make sure they were adhered to.

In the wake of the Fox Inquiry, Fraser gave a ministerial statement on the safeguards that the government would adopt if it decided to allow the mining of uranium. Australia had to support moves for non-proliferation. Uranium was a 'special commodity', and mining it meant that Australia would have to be selective about the customer countries. 'It is not the government's view that safeguards should be regarded as something to be balanced against commercial considerations. We view adequate safeguards as a fundamental prerequisite of any uranium export which we would also expect responsible customer countries for Australian uranium readily to accept.'[13]

In the months after Fox's report, cabinet considered more than a dozen submissions on safeguards, national parks, environmental protection and royalties. Finally, in August 1977, Fraser told parliament what everyone had expected: that mining would proceed at Ranger subject to the strictest safeguards. The government had adopted almost in their entirety Fox's recommendations, including the establishment of Kakadu National Park, and the granting of land rights to the Aboriginals.

The decision to develop uranium, Fraser told parliament, was 'motivated by a high sense of moral responsibility to all Australians and to the community of nations'. It flowed from four fundamental considerations: the need to reduce the risk of nuclear proliferation, the need to supply energy to an energy-deficient world, the need to protect the environment in which the mining took place and the need to make proper provision for the interests of the Aboriginals of the Alligator Rivers region. Renewable energy, such as solar, wind and tidal, was being explored but would not be able to provide all of mankind's needs in the century ahead. As for the cause of nuclear proliferation, Fraser said, this was best served by Australia agreeing to export its uranium. Australia possessed 20 per cent of world's reserves.

> In this situation we are in a special position of influence and have a corresponding moral responsibility to maximise protection against nuclear weapons proliferation by

> responding to the needs of many countries for adequate assurances of uranium supplies. If Australia fails in either of these courses, Australia will fail in her duty to the world.[14]

Australia would sell only to countries that had signed the Nuclear Non-Proliferation Treaty. There were to be bilateral arrangements to make sure uranium could be used only for power generation.

The Australian Labor Party had now adopted an anti-mining stance. This was late in the day. In 1975, the party's national conference had supported the mining and enrichment of uranium for sale abroad, under government control. It had been clear that Whitlam, too, planned to allow export once Fox had reported. In 1976, the Labor Party had described its policy on uranium as still being in 'formative stages'.[15] But once the Fraser government's intentions became clear, Labor adopted a policy of complete opposition. There were protest marches throughout Australia. The issue had become a rallying point for the conservation movement.

Fraser knew that this was a government decision that required explanation, and reassurance. The result was a government-run information campaign. This was perhaps the first time that almost as much effort was put into selling and explaining a government decision as into the decision itself. Brian Johns in the Department of Prime Minister and Cabinet was put in charge. Ian Viner, as Minister for Aboriginal Affairs, remembers Fraser ringing him up and saying he hoped he wasn't going home for the weekend, because he had plans for him. Viner ended up spending the weekend with key public servants sitting in an office and in a great 'burst of intellectual energy' writing a series of leaflets explaining every aspect of the uranium package—from safeguards, to the international energy crisis, to Aboriginal rights and the national park.

Fraser and Viner knew that the way in which Aboriginal interests were dealt with would be the first real test of their land rights principles. Two days after Fraser's announcement, Viner travelled to the Alligator Rivers region to explain the government's decision.

He was quoted in *The Sydney Morning Herald* on 29 August 1977 as saying that he knew Aboriginals would prefer it wasn't happening.

> I suppose it's like you and me ... You would not like a big pit dug in your own backyard, and to them that is what an open pit uranium mine will be ... I think like you and me they would probably prefer it didn't happen, but knowing it will happen they want to be satisfied that proper controls are imposed on mining so it doesn't harm the physical environment and that the social impact is controlled as much as possible.

There had been a change in the Aboriginal politics. The Chairman of the Northern Land Council who had given evidence to Fox was Silas Roberts, who was opposed to uranium mining. Now a new leader had emerged—Galarrwuy Yunupingu, who had acted as an interpreter during the Woodward Royal Commission, and came to prominence during the negotiations over the Land Rights Act that resulted. He was, Viner remembers, 'a very, very able man'. Fraser had met Yunupingu during his visit to the Northern Territory in April 1978. The Aboriginal leader had taken Fraser fishing in the Woolonga Wildlife Sanctuary, and they had returned with a boatload of fish. But the trip resulted in an embarrassing legacy. Roy James Wright of Darwin was sitting in the city's jail serving a sentence for taking fish with a gill net. He realised that, technically, the Prime Minister had been poaching by fishing in the national park, and he launched a private prosecution, with the encouragement of the Australian Labor Party. Fraser remembers, 'I had just assumed that if the traditional owner invited you to fish, you could fish'. The case dragged on, to the delight of the media and the opposition. In August, the Darwin magistrate found that the facts were not disputed, but dismissed the charge. Because Fraser had been invited to fish at the invitation of Yunupingu, the magistrate said, he had been placed in a situation where he was obliged to accept the hospitality of the traditional owners of the area.[16] This decision came almost exactly a year after

Fraser had announced that uranium mining would go ahead. It was a nice example of the complications of the politics of land. The Prime Minister was cleared of poaching because of the power of Yunupingu, but Yunupingu had been forced into negotiations over mining because of the decisions of the Prime Minister. The case led to the law being changed, so that traditional owners had the power to invite guests onto their land to hunt and fish.

Yunupingu understood the real politic. The decision to mine uranium had been made; his people could not veto it, but they could try to extract the best possible deal. In the following months Yunupingu drove the process among his people, and argued hard with the miners and the government. Fraser remembers, 'He was very impressive, and not at all backward in coming forward. He argued his corner very well. Played the politics tough and fair'.

There was pressure within the industry to force the pace of negotiations, but Fraser and Viner agreed that the Aboriginal people should be 'given all the room possible' to develop their approach. The issue was as difficult among the Aboriginals as it was among whites. Decisions were never unanimous, but nor were they pushed through—although the government clearly had the power to impose its will if it wished. The negotiations took more than a year and involved hundreds of meetings across remote Arnhem Land. In August 1978, an agreement was reached, but other Aboriginals took out an injunction to prevent the signing. Finally, in November 1978, the agreements were signed. The Northern Land Council had come of age, and Yunupingu was recognised by being made Australian of the Year.

There was another round of negotiations over mining at Jabiluka. Here, too there were strong differences of opinion among Aboriginal people, which remain to this day. An agreement was signed in 1982 to allow mining to go ahead. The Chairman of the Northern Land Council at the time, Gerry Blitner, said:

> We believe it is a fair agreement for both parties … Because of the fairness of the negotiations and the careful

> and delicate way in which they have been handled, and the long-lasting benefit to Aboriginal people, the Northern Land Council is proud to have been part of them.[17]

As in white society, the Jabiluka matter was never settled. When the Hawke government came to power, in 1983, it forbade export licences for Jabiluka uranium under its three mines policy. Some Aboriginals welcomed the policy; others objected that by undermining an agreement made in good faith, the new federal government was breaching the principle of Aboriginal self-determination.[18] The Howard government abandoned the three mines policy, and it seemed that Jabiluka would go ahead after all. Traditional owners claimed to UNESCO that the World Heritage area was under threat as a result, but the World Heritage committee, having considered the evidence, declined to find that Kakadu was at risk. The present owners of the Jabiluka lease, Rio Tinto, have since acquired a reputation for good dealings with the Aboriginal community. Fred Chaney, who succeeded Viner as Minister for Aboriginal Affairs, has in recent times suggested that governments could learn from Rio Tinto in their dealings with Aboriginal people.[19]

Today, Kakadu National Park covers nearly 20 000 square kilometres from the northern coast to the southern planes, including wooded savannahs and rivers. Most of the land is owned by Aboriginals, and Aboriginals have a majority on the joint management board. The mining leases are surrounded by the national park, but are not part of it. Millions of dollars of royalties have been paid to Aboriginal interests. The communities of the region have many of the same problems as other Aboriginal groups: there are low standards of living and poor opportunities. Until recently, the local Aboriginals were not employed by the mines in large numbers. Yet the royalties have also led to the establishment of successful Aboriginal-owned businesses. Some see the mining royalties as giving them 'real self-determination'. Others think that dependence on mining has merely been substituted for dependence on government.[20]

The final agreements that allowed uranium mining to go ahead during the term of the Fraser government were a bringing-together of multiple interests: the energy crisis, the economics, the national park and Aboriginals. Today Fraser sees the making of these agreements as examples of the importance of negotiation, and of patience. It was not easy. The controversy never entirely died. Negotiation was often a thankless task. It was a classic example of the political process. 'But it was worth the time we took. It was worth the patience. We got the national park. Aborigines got land rights. We got the uranium out of the ground. We got the strictest possible safeguards, and Aborigines were involved in that process.'

* * *

There were other environmental issues during Fraser's time in government that were simpler to resolve. In the lead-up to the 1977 election, Fraser received a visit from the people leading Project Jonah, the main Australian group opposing whaling. They presented him with a petition signed by 100 000 people, but Fraser needed no persuading. He was aware of the campaign, and in sympathy with it. Phoebe, his daughter, then eleven, had come home from boarding school and asked him about why whales were still being shot, and didn't he think it should be stopped? He told the people from Project Jonah this, which led to an idea that she was responsible for his view. In fact, he was already dismayed by the hunting. Fraser recalls today, 'It was another fairly clear case where you had two things that could not co-exist. You might be able to have Kakadu and uranium mining, subject to the strictest safeguards, but you couldn't have a sustainable population of whales and harpooning'. Fraser says he would have moved to end whaling immediately but for the attitude of the Western Australian Premier Charles Court. The sole remaining whaling station was in his state, and 'He was really getting ready to create a fuss'. To defuse that fuss, Fraser appointed an inquiry which took submissions from hundreds of individuals and organisations before recommending that whaling be stopped. In April 1979, Fraser announced that the government would not only ban whaling in Australian waters, but also campaign for a worldwide ban.[21]

At that time, Fraser had become disillusioned with the organisation he had helped to found—the Australian Conservation Foundation. He felt it had been taken over by radicals, and he wanted a 'sober, responsible' voice on environmental issues. Fraser arranged for Peter Scott, the co-founder of the Swiss-based international environmental organisation the World Wildlife Fund, to be invited to Australia. 'I organised for him to talk to people about setting up the organisation here', remembers Fraser. He ensured that the organisation gained tax-deductable status for donations, and a small government grant. The World Wildlife Fund grew to be the largest conservation organisation in the country.

* * *

The Queensland government had been wanting to allow drilling for oil on the Great Barrier Reef since at least the mid 1960s. Federal governments of both complexions had opposed it. When Fraser had been Minister for Education and Science in the Gorton government, a royal commission had been set up to investigate the issue. It had reported to the Whitlam government with recommendations that oil drilling not be allowed. As a result, Whitlam had established the Great Barrier Reef Marine Park Authority to recommend areas of the reef for protection. The Queensland government had fought every step of the way.

Fraser was utterly clear that the destruction of the reef could not be allowed. His commitment to preserving it was close to absolute. He could not abide the thought of it being despoiled. It was internationally famous, one of the wonders of the natural world—the largest coral reef on the planet and the largest structure constructed by living organisms, including man. Quite apart from its importance in its own right, it would be a matter of great national shame if it was damaged. Fraser had given the Australian Conservation Foundation firm statements of his views at the time when he was Minister for Education and Science. Research by the Australian Institute of Marine Science, which Fraser had established during his last days in the portfolio, had been vital to the royal commission and continued to inform the management of the reef. There was no doubt about his longstanding commitment to the reef. Yet there was a conflict between principles.

Fraser had fallen out with Gorton over his attempts to push through legislation giving the Commonwealth control over the continental shelf. The issue was whether the states or the Commonwealth controlled the land between the low-water mark and the 3-mile limit of the territorial seas. Fraser abhorred Gorton's use of federal power to overrule the interests of the states. The Whitlam government, immune to such sensitivities, had continued in Gorton's line, and passed legislation. Within days of Fraser being elected Prime Minister, the High Court had confirmed the law's validity. The Commonwealth's power to protect most of the reef from the intentions of the Queensland government was now beyond doubt.

Yet Fraser didn't want to use that power. He had come to government promising a return to cooperative federalism. This was one of the main points of difference between him and Whitlam, and it was fundamental to his liberal beliefs. He says today, 'You've got a total conflict of principles: when does the Commonwealth use its heavy hand over the states and when does it not?' Fraser says that if Bjelke-Petersen had not been amenable to negotiation, then ultimately he would have overruled him. 'We would have used the power if we had had to, but we put a lot of effort into making sure it didn't come to that.'

Bjelke-Petersen wrote to Fraser within days of the High Court decision, saying that while he was prepared to cooperate with the federal government over the reef, he would not tolerate any national park nominations in the areas where Queensland still had sovereignty. Queensland would not 'acknowledge ... the legitimacy of any possible future attempt to encroach on Queensland's rights or territory'. Fraser wrote back saying that the policies of the government on the Great Barrier Reef had not yet been considered in detail, but pointing out that the Great Barrier Reef Marine Park Act 'specifically prohibited' any kind of mining activity.[22]

So began a process of negotiation that became a test of Fraser's commitment to the new federalism on the one side and the environment on the other. Despite his sometimes bizarre and extreme public statements, Bjelke-Petersen was in the end easier to negotiate with than some other state premiers, such as Charles Court in Western Australia and Robin Gray in Tasmania. There were several ways in which Fraser approached him. The Queensland minister Russ Hinze, 'for all his faults', was a good negotiator, with influence over Bjelke-Petersen. Alan Griffiths of the Prime Minister's department had useful relations with senior public servants in Queensland who had the ear of the Premier, and Peter Nixon, the National Party minister, would sometimes be dispatched. Nixon recalls the time he spent negotiating with Queensland as 'mind-boggling'. He, too, worked though Hinze and the National Party President Bob Sparkes. None of it was quick. It all took immense political and personal energy. Sometimes, what Bjelke-Petersen said in public was out of kilter with what he had agreed to in private. Sometimes it was hard to tell what he thought he was doing.[23] Once again, Fraser chose moving slowly—slower than many would have liked—rather than riding roughshod.

The issue of the submerged lands legislation dominated the premiers' conferences in 1978 and 1979, but as he negotiated Fraser also made it clear that the Great Barrier Reef had to be protected. He told parliament in February 1979 that while discussions were taking place with the Queensland government, 'The Commonwealth's position is unequivocal; there will not be drilling on the reef ... Let me give a complete and unequivocal guarantee that this government would not allow any drilling or any mining that would do anything to damage the reef'.[24]

Meanwhile, the Great Barrier Reef Marine Park Authority had recommended that the first stage of the marine park—the so-called 'Capricornia' section—be declared, and Fraser was under pressure from the opposition. Why didn't the federal government simply act? Public opinion was clearly in favour. A poll published at the time showed that 66 per cent of Australians—and 90 per cent of Queenslanders—wanted a complete ban on oil drilling and exploration on the reef.[25] Yet Fraser delayed, and the negotiations went on.

In June 1979, amid catcalls and interjections from the opposition, Fraser told parliament that the federal government believed that the states should have authority within the 3-mile limit. The Great Barrier Reef came close to the shore at a number of points, so this had 'implications' for the Great Barrier Reef Marine Park. But he repeated his commitment that the reef would not be damaged.[26]

Yet still the declaration of the park was delayed. Bill Hayden castigated Fraser: there was no excuse for the delay, he said. But Fraser held firm.

Finally, in the premiers' conference of 1979, the premiers and Fraser cut a deal in which, perhaps for the last time, the federal government voluntarily gave up power. Under a constitutional settlement, the Commonwealth granted the states administrative power over the seabed. However, the deal made it clear that the reef would be governed by the Great Barrier Reef Marine Park Authority—a federal government body. As a result of this agreement, the Capricornia section of the Great Barrier Reef Marine Park was declared in October 1979.

At that time, the Marine Park Authority had recommended that the Cairns section of the reef—an area three times larger than the Capricornia section—be declared. Bjelke-Petersen fought it all the way. Fraser appealed to him from a number of different angles. In March 1980, he wrote saying that he intended to apply for the reef to be included on the World Heritage list—meaning the federal government would have international obligations to protect it. In a separate, confidential letter, he pointed out to Bjelke-Petersen that government members of parliament with marginal seats on the Queensland coast wanted to see the park declared before the next election. Bjelke-Petersen and Fraser were both to be at a meeting of the World Wilderness Congress in Cairns that June. That would be the perfect venue to announce the World Heritage listing, Fraser suggested. Bjelke-Petersen tried to have a bet both ways. He had no objection to announcing an intention to declare the park, he said, but, 'The actual declaration should not be rushed'. The announcement of the intention should be sufficient.[27]

The line Bjelke-Petersen was taking in public gave Fraser good reason to doubt his sincerity about the park. In a press interview in May 1980, in his typically mangled English, Bjelke-Petersen said that drilling the reef for oil was only a matter of time. 'I think before long you and you and every one of us will be saying, "Please get on with the job because I'm sick and tired of walking and things are coming to a halt".' Nevertheless, Fraser went ahead with an announcement at the World Wilderness Congress that the reef would be listed on the World Heritage register. Confusingly, Bjelke-Petersen then assured the congress that the reef would not be 'mined, drilled or blackened by oil'.[28]

The negotiations continued. Hours of public service and ministerial time were expended. The key issue was whether the boundary of the park should be the low-water mark, or a point off the coast, as the Queenslanders wanted. Finally, in November 1981, the federal government lost patience and overrode the Queensland objections. The boundary was drawn by the Commonwealth to take in the seagrass beds north of Cape Flattery, a habitat for dugong, and the high-quality reefs fringing the mainland and the island. Bjelke-Petersen was publically intransigent, claiming that 'Mr Fraser can say what he likes, he can do what he likes; we are not going to recognise it'.[29] Meanwhile, Fraser said in one of his radio addresses to his electorate that the decision had been made after two years of discussion and negotiation. 'We felt it was time for decisions to be made, and I had indicated earlier in the year that the Commonwealth patience was not inexhaustible.'[30]

By 1982, Bjelke-Petersen was declaring that the whole of the reef should become a marine park area. The Great Barrier Reef Marine Park now covers 95 per cent of the World Heritage property. In today's world it is hard to conceive that oil drilling was ever contemplated.

⋆ ⋆ ⋆

Ever since the flooding of Lake Pedder, the conservation movement in Tasmania had suspected that there were plans to dam the wild rivers of the south-west. Suspicions were confirmed in 1980. The Hydro-Electric Commission said the dams were necessary if Tasmania was to have enough electricity for the future. The plan was to dam the Gordon River below its intersection with the Franklin, flooding a vast area of unique temperate rainforest.

In a state with high unemployment, isolated from and often overlooked by the mainland, the Hydro-Electric Commission had a special place. There was an almost religious faith in its promises of a bright industrialised future. Fraser remembers, 'The HEC virtually ran the state. Nobody would question them'. In particular, nobody in the state's government was prepared to subject the wildly optimistic projections of electricity needs to critical examination.

Fraser did not want the dam built. As the dispute began to engulf Tasmanian politics in 1980, he wrote to Labor Premier Doug Lowe, saying he found it 'somewhat surprising' that he had not suggested that the south-west Tasmanian wilderness be listed on the World Heritage register, and asking for his views.[31] This was a significant suggestion: such a listing would mean that the federal government had made international commitments to protect the area from damage. Lowe agreed to apply for listing. Meanwhile, he suggested a compromise designed to save at least one river: instead of damming the Gordon below its intersection with the Franklin, he proposed that the dam be built upstream, above the Olga River. He was successful in getting this plan through the Tasmanian House of Assembly, but the Upper House blocked the legislation. Lowe had to call a referendum to resolve the issue. Voters would be asked to choose between the two schemes. He told the media he planned to include a 'no dams' option on the ballot paper, but his colleagues forced a backdown. About a month before the referendum was held, in December 1981, Lowe lost a no-confidence motion, stood down as Premier and resigned from the Labor Party. Within months, the Labor government was forced to an election after a no-confidence motion, and was defeated by the Liberals, led by Robin Gray. When the Tasmanian dams referendum was held, 47 per cent voted for the Hydro-Electric Commission's preferred Gordon below the Franklin scheme. Lowe's compromise option of Gordon above the Olga received 8 per cent of the vote, but an astonishing 45 per cent of votes were informal. Almost a third of voters had scrawled on their ballot paper 'NO DAMS'.

Through all this Fraser stood back, watching and waiting. The federal Minister for Home Affairs Ian Wilson had suggested that the Commonwealth should declare a national park, because it was clear that with Lowe's position so precarious, any Tasmanian action to do so might well collapse. Cabinet decided not to intervene, but when Lowe, in one of his last acts as Premier, forwarded the application for World Heritage listing, Fraser saw that it was dispatched to UNESCO in Paris as quickly as possible.

Within weeks, the new Premier, Robin Gray, made his attitude abundantly clear. The Franklin, he said in 1982, wasn't anything special. It was 'nothing but a brown ditch, leech-ridden, unattractive to the majority of people'.[32] He asked the Fraser government to withdraw the nomination for World Heritage listing. It was an extraordinary request—quite without precedent. Fraser was dismayed. After consulting the Ambassador to UNESCO, cabinet refused to withdraw the nomination.

In late 1982, the Tasmanian government revoked parts of the Wild Rivers National Park to allow work on the dam site to begin. While Fraser was recovering in hospital from back surgery, work camps were being erected on the banks of the Franklin. The Fraser government was entering its last months, beset by numerous crises. The economy had gone sour. The drought was biting. Fraser had been weakened by Andrew Peacock's leadership challenge. The headlines were full of news about tax avoidance schemes and organised crime. Meanwhile, the Tasmanian conservationists, led by Bob Brown, called on people from around the nation to join them in blockading the river. It was clear to Brown and his supporters that their only hope of stopping the dam was to persuade the federal government to act. Fraser was lobbied to use Loan Council powers to prevent the Hydro-Electric Commission from borrowing the money necessary to build the dam. He refused.

Gray was intransigent. He sent the Deputy Premier, Max Bingham, to Paris to argue against the World Heritage listing. Nevertheless, on 14 December 1982, the World Heritage Committee accepted the south-west of Tasmania onto the World Heritage list, with the rider that it was 'seriously concerned' at the likely effect of the dam, and urging the federal government to 'take all possible measures to protect the integrity of the property'.[33] 'It was a straight-out conflict', Fraser recalls today. 'We had signed the convention and forwarded the nomination. I had made sure it was forwarded, despite Gray not wanting me to do it. We had international duties. But I have always been against the use of the external affairs power to override the states.'

The issue of how much power the federal government has over the states was not as settled in Fraser's time as it is in our own. Under the constitution, the federal government has power to legislate for external affairs. The issue in the case of the Tasmanian south-west was whether the federal government had the power to enforce international treaties, such as those involving the United Nations, including World Heritage conventions. The cabinet was told, both by its own advisers and by legal experts commissioned by the conservationists, that it had the power to stop the dams. Fraser did not want the question tested. Committed as he was to the machinery of international law, he felt that it had never been the intention of the founding fathers that the constitution, with its careful balance of power between the states and the Commonwealth, should be so easily overridden. The World Heritage Committee had accepted the area onto its list despite knowing that the dam would probably be built. 'They knew that, and if the dam had been built it wouldn't have meant the area would be de-listed. People forget that when they say we should have used our power to block the dam.'

Fraser wanted the Franklin to be saved. He was prepared to use both carrot and stick in his negotiations with the state government. But in the last resort, he was not prepared to overrule them.

What was the difference between the Great Barrier Reef and Fraser Island, where Fraser had been prepared to overrule the state government, and the Franklin? The difference, Fraser says, was the source of the law on which the federal government's power rested. In the case of the Great Barrier Reef, the power came from the Seas and Submerged Lands Act—which had been passed by an Australian parliament, and upheld by the High Court. Whatever Fraser thought of the law, the powers it gave originated entirely from within Australia. In the case of Fraser Island, the power came from the federal government's ability to grant export licences—again, a locally based law consistent with the constitution. The case of south-west Tasmania, on the other hand, relied on the external affairs power in the constitution, which was meant to be used to safeguard Australia's relationships with other countries, yet, says Fraser, 'It simply couldn't be said that any nation in the world would not deal with us or threaten us because a dam was built in Tasmania. Even the World Heritage Committee would not have acted. Nobody can say that building that dam was going to alter our relations with any other country or state, and yet that is the sole justification for using the external affairs power'.

On the same day that World Heritage listing was confirmed, the blockade of the Franklin River by conservationists began. More than two thousand people registered at the Wilderness Society headquarters in the tiny town of Strahan at the river's mouth. So began one of the biggest campaigns of non-violent civil disobedience in Australia's history. There was saturation media coverage. Bob Brown, with dozens of others, was arrested. He refused to sign bail conditions prohibiting return to the site, so was jailed. Brown became a national figure. Meanwhile, the Wilderness Society continued to target federal politicians. By the end of the year, Fraser had personally received over twenty thousand letters on the affair, the vast majority begging him to stop the dam from being built.

Fraser wanted to prevent the dam if he could. 'We tried to get Gray off track', he says. On 19 January 1983, he made an extraordinary offer. If the Tasmanian government would forgo the right to dam the Franklin, the federal government would pay the full cost—estimated at $500 million—of building a modern, environmentally clean coal-fired power station to generate an amount of electricity equivalent to that that would be generated by damming the rivers. The offer, he said, was made to give 'breathing space' so that the viability of the dam could be 'assessed in a calmer atmosphere' and so that a management plan could be devised for the south-west in cooperation with the federal government.

> The extent of this offer expresses the magnitude of our concern for the protection of the Australian environment. It also expresses the magnitude of our concern to provide opportunities for industry in Tasmania and jobs in that state. Protection of the environment does not come free. It demands some sacrifice. My government believes that the Tasmanian people alone should not bear the cost of protection of the environment in south-west Tasmania. That cost should fall on the whole Australian community.

Yet Fraser also made it clear that he was not planning to overrule the state government. 'There will be no compulsion or coercion. The offer is on the table; it is for the Tasmanian government to take it up or decline it as it sees fit', he said.[34] Gray gave no sign of backing down. He immediately rejected the offer, saying that it couldn't be serious. Fraser insisted that it was.

Today Fraser believes that, given time, this offer might have carried the day. He had already seen analysis that suggested the Hydro-Electric Commission's figures didn't add up. If both sides had stepped back and taken a breath, reason might have prevented the dam being built. But there was no time for stepping back. The Franklin became part of the battle for the Fraser government's survival.

Fraser called the federal election on 3 February. During the campaign, the Wilderness Society targeted marginal seats. Coalition members of parliament were followed everywhere they went by greenies dressed in platypus suits. The Australian Conservation Foundation—the organisation Fraser had helped to found—was at the centre of the campaign, but nearly every environmental group in Australia had signed up to the cause. Milo Dunphy, the Vice President of the Australian Conservation Foundation, organised rallies in Canberra to mark the opening of parliament in mid February, and accused Fraser of weakness for refusing to use federal power. On election day, 13 000 volunteers from the campaign to save the Franklin staffed polling booths. There were full-page colour advertisements in *The Sydney Morning Herald* and *The Age* featuring beautiful pictures of the Franklin with the caption 'Could you vote for a party that will destroy this?' The text urged a vote for the Labor Party in the House of Representatives and for the Australian Democrats in the Senate.

The campaign against the damming of the Franklin did not decide the 1983 election. Other issues—the state of the economy and Bob Hawke's great popularity—carried the day. Even Hawke has said that he doubts that the campaign won him a single seat.[35]

Nevertheless, for the first time, conservationists had exercised political muscle. As the green vote grew in subsequent years, it became an important factor in the Hawke government's longevity.

One of Hawke's first actions as Prime Minister was to pass legislation to prevent the dam. Inevitably, there was a High Court challenge by the Tasmanian government. On 1 July 1983, the court ruled by a majority of four to three that the Gordon below the Franklin dam could not go ahead. The case, a landmark in Australia's environmental and constitutional history, confirmed the federal government's power to override the states in cases where it had signed international conventions and agreements.

* * *

The Franklin dam campaign was the political coming of age of the Australian conservation movement. Bob Brown entered first the Tasmanian parliament, and then the federal parliament as a senator for Tasmania. The Greens became a force in Australian politics. The Hawke–Keating federal government went on to nominate the North Queensland rainforest, and later the Southern and Lemonthyme forests of Tasmania, for World Heritage status—although the listings were opposed by the states concerned.

Fraser abhors the principle that was set by the crucial High Court decision. The external affairs power of the constitution was meant to be about matters that affected relations with other countries. In the case of the Franklin, he says, 'That simply isn't true … There are many international conventions and agreements to which Australia is a signatory. They affect health, education, industrial relations, all sorts of activities which go very much to the heart of government in this country. On the precedent set by the High Court in the Franklin dam case there is hardly an aspect of the Australian constitution which could not be upset by the Commonwealth appealing to the appropriate convention and taking the case to the High Court … There is little legal doctrine in these conventions. It was never the intention of those who approved the Australian constitution that it could be overturned in this way'.

Shortly after the High Court decision, Fraser was talking to Lord Hailsham, a life peer, and at the time the British Lord Chancellor, one of the great legal and political figures of the twentieth century. They discussed the Franklin dam case. They agreed that its effect was to undermine sovereignty and the rule of law. At the end of their discussion, Hailsham said, 'Pity. In the days of Owen Dixon we used to examine the judgements of your High Court closely. We don't read them now'.[36]

Fraser says, 'He meant that it was unreasonable to use the external affairs power in this way to gain more power for the Commonwealth'.

How does Fraser feel now about the battle for the Franklin? If he had won the election in 1983, what would have happened? Would the dam have been built? Fraser says that once the election was over, he might have tried a number of things. He might have called a full public inquiry into Tasmania's energy needs, and exposed the Hydro-Electric Commission's figures. He would have kept open the offer of funding alternative means of generating electricity. There would have been bigger carrots, bigger sticks.

And if that hadn't worked? Would the Franklin have been dammed? Probably.

Fraser thinks that in principle he was right. Nevertheless, he also says that if he had his time again, he might act differently. He might put politics ahead of principle. 'From today's perspective,' he says, 'it is probably as a matter of raw politics a mistake to argue points of constitutional law when the majority of the population clearly wants the federal government to act, and I accept that that was the case with the Franklin. I think if I had my time again, I would use the federal power, just accepting the politics of it, the will of the majority'.

Fraser visits Tasmania two or three times a year for the trout fishing. He and Tamie own a shack on the Great Lake on the central plateau. He is one of the state's best known anglers. 'Trout fishing gives you an excuse to visit all kinds of exciting places', he says today. Tasmania is one of them.

He is glad that Bob Brown is in federal politics. He says that Brown 'often talks a great deal of sense', although he disagrees with some of the Green Party's 'more way-out' policies. He is also glad that the Franklin runs free.

18

Loyalty and Loss

Australia lost some innocence in the 1970s and 1980s. There was the Hilton Hotel bombing, which proved that terrorism could reach the country. A string of royal commissions and government inquiries forced the realisation that organised crime, with its accompaniment of official corruption, had established itself firmly and that none of the existing law enforcement agencies had the scope, the resources or the power effectively to attack it. The stripping away of innocence began before Fraser came to government and continued after he left. No part of Australia was left unaffected, and by the early 1990s, two state governments—Western Australia and Queensland—had fallen largely as a result of royal commissions. High Court judge and Gough Whitlam's former Attorney-General Lionel Murphy had faced corruption charges, of which he was acquitted on appeal. Senior police and state government ministers were in jail.

It is therefore no trivial thing to say that the Fraser government was honest. The lesson of the 1970s and 1980s was, or should have been, that honesty in government is something that should never be taken for granted. Sometimes there was a heavy cost—both personal and political—to maintaining both the appearance and the reality of high standards.

Today, Fraser reflects on the nature of loyalty. There are three kinds of loyalty: to people, to values and to organisations. A political leader is expected to be loyal to his team and to his party. A human being is expected to be loyal to his friends. 'Most people who aren't political leaders would put loyalty to friends first', says Fraser. He felt that as Prime Minister his first loyalty had to be to values, and to the integrity of government. The result cost him both friends and support.

It fell to Fraser's government to set the direction of responses to terrorism and organised crime. Partly as a result of the Hilton Hotel bombing, the Australia Federal Police was established. During the Fraser government there were three royal commissions into drugs and drug trafficking, all of them revealing complex webs of criminality. A common theme was the lack of information-sharing between law enforcement agencies. In response, the Fraser government, in cooperation with the states, established the Australian Bureau of Criminal Intelligence to collect and share information.

The biggest inquiry of them all was established in 1980 to investigate allegations of criminal activity by the Federated Ship Painters and Dockers Union. The inquiry was a joint venture between the federal and Victorian governments, but it was the Fraser government's initiative.[1] Fraser says today that the Victorian Premier Dick Hamer was at first against setting it up. He had received a police report asserting that there were no problems big enough to justify such an inquiry. 'We had had a report that suggested differently', Fraser remembers. He persuaded Hamer that a royal commission with broad terms of reference was needed. In August 1980, Attorney-General Peter Durack told Fraser that it had not been possible to secure the services of a judge or former judge to conduct the royal commission. Instead, he recommended Francis Xavier Costigan, QC, a barrister with 'a broad general practice which gives him useful background to conduct inquires'.[2] The appointment changed Australia.

Costigan began to pick at the evidence, and found long threads running into the fabric of the country. Using new computer technology, he followed webs of connections and, most important of all, the money trail. By the time he had finished his work there was hardly a section of Australian society left untouched. He had reached everywhere, including into the heartland of Liberal Party support. In September 1982, a report from Costigan found that the Painters and Dockers was not a true trade union, but 'rather a criminal enterprise which deliberately recruits hardened criminals as members'.[3] Such corruption could not exist in one part of society without implicating other parts. In late 1982, as Fraser recovered from back surgery, weekly reports were being tabled in cabinet, each one a small book, detailing the action that was being taken as a result of Costigan's reports.[4] One of the last acts of the Fraser government was to introduce legislation to set up a crimes commission to take over from Costigan, which was to be a permanent national body entrusted with royal commission–like powers and charged with fighting corruption. The legislation was not proclaimed before Fraser lost government, but after Hawke came to power, the crimes commission was recast and established as the National Crime Authority.

Some of the loneliest and most difficult decisions of Fraser's prime ministership were to do with honesty. By 1982, Costigan was investigating tax avoidance. He had uncovered what became known as 'bottom of the harbour' schemes. These involved highly artificial arrangements in which companies were stripped of assets and passed through a number of hands to avoid tax liabilities. Such schemes had been popular since the 1970s and were actively promoted by some lawyers and accountants. It was always doubtful if they were legal, but, as Costigan found, the authorities' failure to act had meant that operators had grown confident that tax could be avoided with impunity. There was a particular history of bungling, negligence and misconduct within the Western Australian Deputy Crown Solicitor's office, and as a result a large number of dubious tax schemes involved businesses and individuals in that state. Many people, including some in the Liberal Party's heartland, felt that avoiding the tax man was in any case hardly a criminal act.

Before Costigan got underway, John Howard as Treasurer had introduced legislation closing off loopholes and making various tax avoidance schemes clearly illegal. In 1980, he had introduced strong penalties, including jail, for deliberately stripping a company so it could not pay its debts. The idea of retrospective legislation—allowing the government to force the repayment of tax that had been avoided before legislation made the schemes illegal—was first raised in Howard's budgetary submissions. Fraser recalls, 'John Howard didn't particularly push the idea, but he didn't oppose it either'. It was a difficult decision. The idea that an action can be made illegal in retrospect was inherently obnoxious and dangerous, but, in this case, Fraser thought retrospectivity was justified. He argued that the schemes were so patently artificial, so corrupt, that the people who engaged in them must have known they were wrong. 'So far as I recall, all of cabinet supported the legislation.' Once the decision was announced, Fraser became the main person arguing the case. He was disgusted at the greed and lack of ethics involved in the tax evasion industry. Tax evasion was a 'cancer on the body politic', he said.[5] He told his staff that he would if necessary stake his leadership on the issue: he was determined to wipe out the tax evasion industry. When the legislation was introduced, political journalist Michelle Grattan quoted Fraser as saying that those Liberals involved in avoiding tax should get out of the party.[6] In one of his radio addresses to the people of Wannon, he said:

> The principle of fairness is absolutely fundamental for liberals; it is more fundamental than any other principle, certainly more fundamental than any element of retrospectivity in the proposed legislation. The Liberal Party was founded to govern fairly in the interests of all Australians … I would not want to lead or be part of any party which failed to stand by that principle.[7]

There are sections of the Liberal Party that have never forgiven Fraser for retrospective tax legislation. Thankfully, perhaps, he was protected from knowing the impact of his decisions on the financial support for the party. Since Robert Menzies there had been strict rules that ministers were not to be involved in fundraising for the party; nor were they allowed to know the identity of donors. Correspondence between Fraser and the Federal Treasurer of the party Bob Crichton-Brown shows them adhering to this 'inflexible rule' even when discussing the overall state of campaign funding. Throughout 1982, Crichton-Brown was telling Fraser that the party's finances were 'anything but good' and counselling him against an early election as a result—but Fraser and Crichton-Brown observed the rule that prevented them from discussing one reason why donations were drying up.[8] Today, things have changed. There is no doubt that the division has broken down, and that ministers and members of parliament on both sides of politics are directly involved in fundraising at every level. Fraser says, 'It has to be corrupting, if not in the strict legal sense then in the sense of improper influencing of decisions'.

One of the main ways in which Fraser had justified blocking supply and forcing the crisis of 1975 had been the need, after the scandals of the loans affair, for the highest standards of ministerial propriety. In opposition, Fraser had insisted that ministers drop private businesses that could be seen to conflict with their shadow portfolios. At the very first cabinet meeting of the Fraser caretaker government, on 12 November 1975, Fraser had demanded that his ministers resign their directorships of public companies and provide him with a list of their pecuniary interests. He had suggested at this meeting that because the government planned to reintroduce the superphosphate bounty, perhaps he and other ministers with farms should consider declining the benefit. He was dissuaded by the head of the Department of Prime Minister and Cabinet John Menadue, who said that it would be 'absurd' if ministers tried to quarantine themselves from all the benefits of government budgetary decisions.[9]

* * *

Like prime ministers before and since, Fraser soon discovered the painful cost of keeping to high standards. Unlike some other prime ministers, he did not compromise. The result was that he lost a number of ministers through forced resignations. These, he says today, were among the most painful and difficult decisions he made as Prime Minister, but, 'If you don't set a certain standard at the top and keep to it even when it hurts, then you are undermining anything you might want to do. You are giving the worst possible leadership message to the community at large'.

Each minister had supporters in the party room and cabinet. Each sacking or forced resignation stoked the view of Fraser as a cold, ungrateful leader. Today the memories of damage inflicted on colleagues still cause him pain, but, he says, 'It is not that I didn't feel the tug of loyalty. But as leader, loyalty to values has to come first. But it is difficult. These were good ministers, most of them. They were people I had worked with, eaten with, drunk with, over many years. You owe them things. And then ... ' He grimaces. Tamie remembers that it was at times like this that she and Malcolm would 'thrash around the issues until late at night', with her role being to offer a point of view from outside the political process and the loyalties of the party room. 'Often he couldn't really discuss it with his colleagues, because they were all friends or rivals or whatever. So it came to me.'

The first painful decision concerned the Treasurer Phillip Lynch. In October 1977, Fraser, Doug Anthony and Lynch were sharing a flight back to Canberra after attending the funeral of the Roman Catholic cardinal Norman Gilroy. Lynch knew that later that day Fraser was planning to see the Governor-General to request an early election. Fraser remembers, 'Phillip was totally preoccupied. He couldn't talk about anything. He was obviously worried about something. I didn't know what'. He found out soon enough. Evidence at a judicial inquiry had linked Lynch to dubious land speculation in Victoria. 'If he had told me what was going on, then I might not have called the election', says Fraser today. As it was, when the allegations broke, Fraser was in the middle of an election campaign. 'Every media conference, the first ten questions were about Lynch', Fraser says. To make matters worse, by that time Lynch was ill and in hospital with a kidney complaint.

The transactions at the heart of the inquiry were complicated. There was no way, in an election campaign, that they could or would be examined dispassionately. It seemed clear to Fraser that Lynch would have to stand aside, at least until the election was over and the allegations could be examined in cooler fashion. To Fraser's distress, Lynch did not at first go willingly. 'There were people advising him not to resign, that he hadn't done anything wrong. And of course he was ill, and that ruins your judgement.' Fraser did not have the heart to confront Lynch personally; instead, he sent Peter Nixon, the Minister for Primary Industries, to visit Lynch in hospital. Fraser dealt with his Treasurer through intermediaries.

Faced with having to force Lynch to resign, Fraser went to see the former Country Party leader Jack McEwen—a man he had respected greatly since his earliest days as a backbencher. 'I trusted Jack's judgement. I knew what I had to do, but because it was so difficult I just needed some support or confirmation. Anyway, we had a drink, and he said to me, "I know what you want to speak to me about. There is only one thing to do: get rid of him now. Fair or not, you just have to cut him off".' Steeled, Fraser forced Lynch's resignation, promising a full investigation after the election.

Two days after Fraser was re-elected, Lynch sent him a four-page letter full of pain. He did not dispute that Fraser had been correct to ask him to stand aside, but he was hurt that Fraser had not dealt with him face to face.

> At no stage did you offer to have a personal discussion with me; nor did you telephone me. You gave me no indication as to your thinking. During the whole of the period that the allegations were being made against me you never at any time expressed your confidence in me in a way that, under the Westminster system, prime ministers have traditionally done.

Lynch had provided Fraser with statements by his lawyers and accountants as evidence that he had done nothing wrong. He wanted Fraser to state publicly that he had confidence in him. To Fraser, it seemed clear that the only way in which the public could be brought to an acceptance that Lynch had done nothing wrong was for the allegations to be examined by an independent Queen's Counsel. Lynch was deeply hurt.

> I ask you, how much more can any man be expected to take? You have not accepted your responsibilities to me and have taken every possible step to place yourself at arm's length from me ... The buck stops at your desk and you cannot stand aside from it. You cannot wash your hands of your responsibilities by seeking to have me investigated by Queen's Counsel. It is for you to take a judgement.[10]

Today, Fraser winces when shown this letter. He has some regrets about the way he handled Lynch. He still believes he had no option but to force him to stand aside, and he has no doubts that the decision to arrange an independent inquiry was also correct, but, 'I should have just got in the car and gone down to see him in hospital. I have always regretted that I didn't do that'. When the Queen's Counsel reported, they found that Lynch had done nothing wrong, either legally or ethically. Fraser announced himself satisfied with their findings and made a statement that showed some signs of the impact the affair had had on him.

> This situation has shown that the Prime Minister is placed in a very difficult position when he is called upon to make judgements on colleagues with whom he has worked closely ... A better means has to be found to make decisions which can have such an impact on an individual's career and on the life of his family.[11]

The result was a committee of inquiry into public duty and private interest, set up in February 1978 and headed by Nigel

Bowen, the Chief Justice of the Federal Court. This resulted in a code of conduct for parliamentarians and public servants, including confidential registers of pecuniary interest for ministers. Later, during the Hawke government, public registers of pecuniary interest were introduced for all federal parliamentarians.

Lynch decided not to return as Treasurer. It was this decision that led to John Howard's promotion to that position, while Lynch took up the portfolio for industry and commerce. He remained Fraser's deputy until the Peacock leadership challenge of early 1982. Fraser and Lynch mended their relationship. Today Fraser says, 'Phillip was all right. I always knew when he was angry, when he disagreed. It was all open and on the surface. And, in the end, he was very loyal to me'.

Hot on the heels of the Lynch affair came the painful forced resignation of Reg Withers. The offence, on any understanding, was trivial. After the 1977 election there were allegations that senior ministers had interfered to influence the names given to electorates. The significance of this lay in whether or not a seat was counted as 'new', and in the resulting impact on pre-selections. In Fraser's view, any suggestion of interference with the electoral system had to be taken seriously, and he established a royal commission to investigate. It emerged that Withers, who was Minister for Administrative Services with responsibility for the Electoral Commission, had telephoned the Chief Electoral Officer to discuss the naming of two Gold Coast electorates. The Royal Commissioner had described what Withers had done as 'impropriety'.[12] Withers refused to resign, and Fraser sacked him.

Fraser says today, 'Look, it was a trivial matter and I thought it was a bit strong to call it impropriety, but if the government rode roughshod over a royal commission on a matter affecting the electoral system it would be very difficult to be regarded as a government of principle'. The bad feeling never entirely dissipated. Withers did not return to the ministry. Immediately after the 1983 election defeat, Fraser wrote to him:

> I want to say something that may or may not have been passed on to you. I think that in the last few years you have paid a very high price for what was not such a very large matter. I wish that I had found some way of redressing the balance. I regret very much that I did not.

Withers wrote back that it was all in the past. 'I have always tried to live for today and tomorrow.'[13]

Another temporary loss was the resignation of National Party colleague and Minister for Primary Industry Ian Sinclair, following the tabling in the New South Wales parliament of a report on the investigation into his business affairs. Sinclair was accused of forgery in a dispute over his father's will. He was acquitted in August 1980 and returned to the ministry. Sinclair, Fraser says today, dealt with the matter in an entirely appropriate way—resigning without having to be asked until the matter could be cleared up.

The ministerial losses that Fraser regards as most 'stupid and pointless' were those of John Moore and Michael MacKellar in the colour-television affair—a confused and messy sequence of events involving the import by MacKellar of a colour-television set without paying duty. There was confusion over whether the set was black-and-white, in which case no duty was payable, or colour, in which case duty should have been paid. Moore was the minister responsible for customs and got caught up in the affair. Fraser says, 'It was so utterly trivial. The television set was worth something like a hundred dollars, and suddenly you are faced with losing two ministers over it'.

Tamie and Fraser discussed the affair into the night. What message did it give? Jack McEwen had once said to Fraser that every citizen, approaching the customs barrier, had an illogical urge to cheat. 'Even if it is stupid, if it makes no difference to how you live your life.' Fraser thought that if the ministers kept their portfolios, the message that ordinary Australians would take was that it was no big deal to cheat customs, or, by extension, to avoid taxes. 'That was not a message I was prepared to send.' The ministers resigned.

On the evening of Friday 17 September 1982, Fraser was relaxing at Nareen, looking forward to a rare weekend with 'nothing in particular planned other than doing some thinking'. He rarely had a weekend off, or an evening, for that matter. He used to read cabinet submissions in bed. 'I think I had good stamina. Certainly I could outlast most of my staff.' On this occasion, his weekend was wrecked by a telephone call from the Minister for Primary Industries Peter Nixon. 'He said, "Malcolm, I am going to have to resign, because I have been criticised in the report of a royal commission".

'I said, "Hang on. I am not going to accept your resignation at least until I have read the report".

'And he said, "Well, it is going to have to be tabled next week".

'And I said, "All right, well, just let me have a look at it".'

The next day, Fraser returned to Canberra. 'I have never worked so hard as I worked in the next forty-eight hours.' He read not only the report of the royal commission, but also the transcripts of evidence and the report of another inquiry that preceded it. It was an immense burst of intellectual energy.

The royal commission, presided over by Justice Edward Woodward, could hardly have been more important to Australia's interests. It had resulted from discoveries in mid 1981 that horse and kangaroo meat had been substituted for exports of beef. There was an outcry on both sides of the Pacific. Australia's reputation as an exporter was at risk and there were soon widespread allegations of malpractice and corruption within the meat industry. Meat made up more than a quarter of the gross value of rural production and was an important export earner. It was, as Fraser later told parliament, 'imperative that Australia's reputation was cleared'.[14]

For years there had been problems with wasteful and inefficient dual meat inspection services. Nixon had established a committee of inquiry under a former Liberal minister, Bert Kelly, which had recommended the establishment of a single federal meat inspection service. The substance of Woodward's criticism of Nixon was that the head of this earlier inquiry had told him about the 'sordid' nature of the industry and referred in general terms to allegations of graft and misuse of meat inspectors' power. Woodward said that Nixon should have been 'jolted out of complacency' by what Kelly had said, but in fact had done little to pursue the allegations. Woodward wrote:

> I have carefully considered the minister's role in this matter, having due regard to the responsibility attributable to senior departmental officers, the heavy workload which ministers accept and the potential unfairness of looking at one issue in isolation. In spite of these considerations, I am bound to record my view that the minister did not deal with these allegations adequately and effectively.[15]

Fraser called into his office all the information that Woodward had had in front of him: the Kelly report, the transcript of the evidence to Woodward and the departmental notes of discussions Nixon had had with Kelly.[16] By the end of the weekend, Fraser was sure that Nixon had not been at fault.

The following week, Fraser tabled Woodward's report in parliament along with a ream of background documentation, and began a forensic defence of his minister. The allegations of malpractice raised by the earlier inquiry had been general, and Nixon had been offered no 'positive or specific evidence or names of people engaged in serious malpractice', said Fraser. Crucially, there had been no mention at all of meat substitution. Instead, the focus of the earlier inquiry and the discussions concerning it had been about the establishment of an Australian meat inspection service. Woodward had acknowledged that Nixon had acted rapidly and effectively once the meat substitution was discovered. It was thanks to Nixon's prompt action that exports to the United States had been quickly resumed. 'Now I ask: How could the minister, given no specific information, have taken any further action to deal with these allegations? I submit that on the basis of all the available evidence he could not have. Where is the substance on which the minister could be blamed or condemned?'[17]

Why did Fraser save Nixon, 'riding roughshod' over a Royal Commissioner, when he had not been prepared to do the same for Withers? Withers's supporters were quick to see it as hypocrisy, and Fraser's defence of Nixon as loyalty for a man who was both a key minister and a personal friend. But Fraser says that loyalty to values was still the guiding rule. Woodward had simply got it wrong. As Nixon was later to point out to parliament, Kelly had told Woodward that he had heard no reports of meat substitution. The issue simply hadn't been raised during Kelly's inquiry. Woodward had chosen to ignore this.[18] Fraser had examined the evidence, and was convinced that there was no case against Nixon, and indeed that he had handled the meat substitution crisis extraordinarily well. Neither Woodward nor the opposition was able to unpick the case he had made in parliament defending Nixon, 'And they would have been quick to do so if they could. I had done the work. It was a question of evidence'. Fraser was also influenced by the fact that, unlike Withers, Nixon had offered his resignation without having to be asked. Nixon had recognised the principle of adhering to high standards. Fraser says today, 'If Reg had come to me and said that he was offering his resignation, I would never have accepted it. It was probably the most trivial of all mistakes over which I lost ministers. But instead he was trying to pretend that nothing had happened'.

A government, Fraser says, sets the standard for the community as a whole. If a government is corrupt, the rest of society will be corrupt. If a government fails to set and enforce high standards, the rest of the community will allow its standards to drop. 'In the end, I still think what I did was basically right. But I wish it could have been different. I just wish I had had the ability to handle these sorts of issues more skilfully. I was dealing with people I had worked closely with. Some of them were friends. Everyone is working under pressure, and when something happens that the press call a scandal, you don't always have the luxury of being able to reflect on it at leisure. It is one of the dilemmas of a Prime Minister to get these things right.'

* * *

On 15 April 1981, Fraser was reading the papers over breakfast and saw a biting cartoon about his relationship with Andrew Peacock. It showed Fraser towering over a blustering, red-faced Peacock, who was saying, 'Now listen here, ya rogue. I've had it with your bullying tactics and dictatorial attitude. My principles are at stake and I'll go to any length to uphold them. I'll … I'll … I'll … I'll have my secretary resign immediately'.[19] Fraser looked up from the paper and said to Tamie, 'That's it. Andrew will resign today'. He was right.

The relationship between Fraser and Peacock had never been easy, although they had worked well together over foreign policy. Since they had fallen out over Kampuchea in 1980, things had been icy. Peacock had chosen not to return as Minister for Foreign Affairs and had instead taken the portfolio of industrial relations. He had also unsuccessfully challenged Lynch for the deputy leadership. From his new position, Peacock had watched while Fraser used his personal muscle to try to persuade employers to resist the wages breakout. On 10 April 1981, Peacock's Principal Private Secretary Barry Simon had given a speech to businessmen in Canberra attacking the way Fraser had used threats to strong-arm the chemical company ICI Australia Limited to hold firm against the unions' campaign.[20] This was not the kind of statement that the government could tolerate coming from ministerial staff. Cabinet insisted that Peacock demand Simon's resignation, but Peacock refused, instead issuing a statement saying that ministerial staff had a right to personal views. Fraser had kept up the pressure. The day before the cartoon appeared, Peacock had backed down and Simon had resigned.

In the meantime, the details of Peacock's threats to resign over Kampuchea on the eve of the 1980 election had become public, and Peacock—wrongly—blamed Fraser for the leak. Peacock drafted a resignation letter in the most vitriolic terms, and he gave a series of interviews that deliberately echoed the speech Fraser had made on resigning from the Gorton ministry.

> The Prime Minister has consistently allowed damaging reports to be published about my capacity as a senior

> minister. He has bypassed the system of governance by acting in a manic determination to get his own way, and I find the constant disloyalty and erratic acts of behaviour intolerable and not to be endured.[21]

Peacock repeated these claims in a parliamentary address at the end of the month. He said he had resigned because of 'irreconcilable differences' with Fraser, who had used the cabinet committee system to 'centralise power around himself'.[22]

By the time this speech was given, Fraser had assembled his defence. Already, senior cabinet ministers had declared their support for him. Anthony and Lynch had issued a press statement that said that, in the Barry Simon affair, Peacock's fight was not just with Fraser but with the whole of cabinet. Every minister had thought Simon had to go. Statistics had been prepared on Peacock's success in cabinet. When he was Foreign Minister, only six out of 272 of his submissions had been rejected or significantly altered. As Minister for Industrial Relations, only four out of seventeen had been altered.[23]

In his speech in reply to Peacock, Fraser defended his use of cabinet committees. As for the charges that he always got his own way:

> I reject those charges totally and I reject them also on behalf of my colleagues on whom they reflect. What does it say of my colleagues that I as Prime Minister can persuade them all to caucus to one particular view? That charge is offensive to them, as it is offensive to me. The principles of cabinet discussion, decision and responsibility have been reasserted and strengthened since the government came to office in 1975, by contrast with the way in which they had been downgraded in the previous three years.

If Peacock had had a complaint about how cabinet was run, he should have raised it with Fraser, or within cabinet. Fraser catalogued their achievements together in foreign policy. He told parliament:

> It seems to me that in the perspective of the issues of great and enduring importance to Australia on which we have

> worked together, personal feelings and difficulties should be treated as of little consequence. This government has achieved great and significant objectives; the honourable member has been a part of that. How can it be that he has now turned aside? How can it be that the concerns he has enumerated today were not raised with me or with cabinet? How can it be that he chooses this place to damage a great political party, even if that is not his intention, and good government? The hopes and opportunities of millions of Australians depend to a very significant degree on what we all do in this place. They expect better from us than we sometimes provide.[24]

Peacock failed to substantiate the charges of lack of loyalty on Fraser's part. As a result the debate following his resignation deteriorated into a more general discussion of Fraser's style. Nevertheless, his resignation damaged the government. For the next year, Peacock and his supporters agitated from the back bench while the appearance of disunity eroded electoral support. Meanwhile, the 'dry' faction, led by John Hyde, had emerged as critical of Fraser. Both Peacock and Howard were courting its support.

In April 1982, Fraser brought things to a head by calling a special party meeting. Hyde was encouraging Howard to contest the leadership, but Howard had refused, believing that Fraser had the numbers to retain his post.[25] Howard's supporters then pressured Fraser to make Howard his deputy, and drop Lynch. Fraser remembers, 'Phillip was getting tired in any case. I would have had to persuade him to stand, and if it was going to be anyone else it was going to be Howard. There was no other contender'. Lynch agreed to step down, but, 'He said to me that he thought he would make me a better and more loyal deputy than Howard would. And he was right about that'. Today, Fraser regrets not persuading Lynch to stay. 'I could have won the day for him as well as for myself. I don't think there is any doubt about that.' Fraser, with Howard standing as his deputy, won the leadership ballot easily, defeating Peacock by fifty-four votes to twenty-seven.

Meanwhile, Lynch's health was failing. In October 1982, he announced his resignation from parliament, forcing a by-election in his seat of Flinders. Fraser had done his best during Lynch's illness to make up for earlier neglect. In his letter of resignation, Lynch said:

> I have appreciated the regular personal contact you have maintained with me during this period ... I would like to record my admiration for the leadership you have provided to the government since 1975. As must be expected in politics we have had our differences. We have nevertheless worked well together and you will continue to have my unqualified support as leader of the party.[26]

The by-election came at a difficult time for the government. To everyone's surprise, the Liberals won the seat. This set off a chain of events that ended in Fraser losing government.

* * *

The disadvantage of writing a thematic account of a government, as this has been, is that the reader loses a sense of the crushing work of prime ministerial office. Everything happens at once, rather than in neat thematic packages. In 1982, as his government entered its last months, Fraser was dealing not only with the troubles caused by Peacock, but also with the Franklin dam controversy, the Costigan report and retrospective tax laws, the attempt to contain the wages breakout, the framing of the controversial budget of 1982–83, struggles with the bureaucracy over freedom of information legislation, attempts to help maintain the unity of the Western alliance over the Falkland Islands, the continuing reform of immigration procedures, the reform proposals arising out of the Campbell Inquiry on financial deregulation, and recovery from back surgery, not to mention a thousand day-to-day matters that were important at the time but have no claim on history's attention. Fraser admits that he was tired. 'You don't notice it when the adrenalin is there and you are involved in doing things. I needed to get away and think more. It is a major challenge for prime ministers, to stop from getting so tired that judgement is affected. It creeps up on you. I am not sure I realised how weary I was until after I had lost the election.'

The other thing that tends to be overlooked in thematic accounts is the role of the ministers who did not oversee nation-changing policies, who never resigned, or challenged, or even complained, but who were nevertheless crucial to government. Several of the important ministers who served under Fraser have been mentioned in other chapters of this book. They were not the only ones who mattered. There was Peter Nixon, the Minister for Transport and later for Primary Industries: 'always straightforward, a good administrator, good in cabinet and a tremendous help in resolving issues and disputes'; Tony Street, the Minister for Employment and Industrial Relations, then, after Peacock's departure, for Foreign Affairs: 'Street was thoughtful, conscientious, never pushed himself forwards, but could do any job you asked'; and the Attorney-General Peter Durack: 'quiet, reserved, but totally committed to the good of the government'. Margaret Guilfoyle, the Minister for Social Security, 'contributed significantly to cabinet debates. She could be totally relied on and she could think for herself. She wasn't a captive to the bureaucracy'. The ministers he most valued, Fraser says today, were not those who always agreed with him, but those who had their arguments openly in cabinet, and who, once a decision had been made, held loyal to the government policy. 'Such people are the backbone of government.'

Then there were the personal staff, with perhaps the main member overlooked so far being Dale Budd. 'The whole world could be falling apart, and he would be totally unfazed and just get on with the job. He was a rock.' Fraser considers himself extraordinarily fortunate in the people who worked in his office. 'They served the government well. They understood the different roles of the private office and the public service, and that sometimes that would cause tension and resentment. They understood that it was therefore vital for those tensions to remain unimportant. In key areas concerning Treasury, important reforms would not have been achieved unless it was for my private staff and the Department of Prime Minister and Cabinet.'

Finally, there was Tamie. What to say about her? 'She doesn't like all those conventional things that people say, like, "I couldn't have done it without her".' So what does she like? 'Probably to stay entirely out of the limelight and pretend she isn't part of this story.' Fraser's chin drops. He thinks long and hard, then says, 'She would never have sought a public role unless it were for me. I suppose it all started that time we came back from our honeymoon and she had to give that speech for me at Edenhope'. Another pause. 'She had a strong sense of duty. Once I was Prime Minister she had a clear idea of what she should do, and she accepted masses of appointments and established the Australiana Fund and did all sorts of things on her own behalf. And she probably would have been happier on the golf course.' The chin grows longer, and trembles. 'If she had been Prime Minister in 1983', he finishes, 'we would have won'.

* * *

Fraser had been considering an early election ever since he had seen off the Peacock leadership challenge. The party organisation was against the idea. The party's Federal Director Tony Eggleton later wrote that he had sensed 'the sourness in the electorate' and advised running for a full term. The option of a late-1982 election was in any case ruled out when Fraser had to go into hospital for back surgery. Eggleton wrote later in his report reflecting on the reasons for the loss: 'The Prime Minister returned from sick leave in mid January 1983 with no preconceived ideas about election timing. However, a number of factors soon began to generate the early election option'. These included the need to gain a mandate for the wages pause, the need for strong and stable government to deal with the economic difficulties and a desire to avoid political instability from ongoing election speculation. There were also fears that interest rates would have to rise in late 1983.[27]

Bob Hawke was the other factor. It was clear that he might soon replace Bill Hayden as Labor leader. Fraser thought he could beat Hayden, but he knew that Hawke was a different matter. Hawke had what Fraser had never received, or sought: the affection of the electorate.

In February, Fraser rang around his ministers. 'You know your ministers. Someone's judgement is always right. Someone else's is always wrong. Doug Anthony was in favour of it, and I obviously paid a lot of attention to him. I rang someone else nearly last, because he had opposed every other election timing, in my view wrongly. And he was agreeing with me and saying "Go now". That gave me a jolt. I wish I had rung him first instead of nearly last.' But the decision was made.

Fraser contacted the office of Governor-General Sir Ninian Stephen to seek a double dissolution election, shortly after midday on 3 February 1983, but Stephen was not available to see him. Meanwhile, Fraser's press secretaries brought news that Hayden was in trouble, and there was speculation that Hawke would replace him. Fraser thought this was good. Labor was in disarray. His calling an election would lock them into Hayden as leader.

Things moved both faster and slower than Fraser had anticipated. While he waited for an opportunity to see the Governor-General, Hayden announced his resignation. The day was shaping as the most dramatic in politics since the dismissal. Hawke held his first press conference as leader, announcing a theme of 'national reconciliation'. Meanwhile, Stephen asked Fraser for more information on the basis for the double dissolution. When Fraser was finally able to announce the election, after 5 p.m., the media asked him if the switch to Hawke had caught him with his pants down. He said, 'No, it makes no difference who the leader may be. The policies of the Labor Party are the same ... The policies of the Labor Party are not altered by altering the shopfront window'.[28]

Others were less sanguine. David Kemp was not on Fraser's staff at that time, but he was in close touch. He remembers, 'I was at a meeting with the advertising agency, talking about the election, and the phone rang and it was Fraser. He said, "They have just appointed Hawke as leader" ... And I thought, "My God". I thought, "What am I going to say to him?" And I said something like, "I think that we can still win", but I wasn't confident of that. I didn't want to discourage him, but I thought that it was a tremendous blow'. Tamie thought the election was lost the moment she heard that Hawke was leader. 'I knew Labor would win, hands down, from way out. I'm sure Malcolm would have been able to beat Hayden, but he would never have beaten Hawke straightaway. If he had waited and run at the end of the year, then he'd have had a chance against Hawke because he would have been able to handle him much better than anyone else in the parliament. He would have been able to wear down his folklore image a bit.'

As it was, the campaign began with Fraser 11 per cent behind in the polls, and he was never ahead. The final week of the campaign offered cruel hope: the Liberals made up some ground. But on election day, the polls showed that Fraser was still 3 per cent short of winning.

Very little went well with the campaign. Just when Fraser most needed to be heard, immediately after his campaign policy speech on 15 February, the Ash Wednesday bushfires forced a halt to campaigning and deepened the gloom of the electorate. Much of southern Australia had been ablaze, from the Adelaide Hills to the Macedon Ranges. Seventy-five people lost their lives. Over two thousand homes were lost. Total property damage was over $400 million. The fires were at that time the worst in the nation's history.[29] The bushfires broke the theme of the government's election campaign, and took the nation's mind off the issues and the arguments. Fraser as Prime Minister naturally had to deal with the issues raised by the fires, while the Labor Party was left free to continue its campaign.

The Liberal Party campaign slogan was 'We're not waiting for the world'. The idea behind it was that the world was in recession, but the Australian Government had taken action to lessen its effect and would introduce more measures aimed at speedy recovery. In his policy speech, Fraser put the best face possible on the dire economic climate. The government had introduced 'a wage pause with a difference. It expresses the Australian ideal of mateship … [It] gives people with jobs a chance to help other Australians without jobs'. He announced new national projects: a bicentennial water resources program, a Darwin to Alice Springs railway and an Advanced Technology Corporation to help small and medium firms innovate. Mostly, he ran on the government's record, but there was no hiding the trouble the nation was in. 'When the world recession finally did hit Australia its effect was greatly worsened by two things', he told the electorate: the drought and the wages 'explosion'. It was true, but hardly the most upbeat message at the beginning of a policy speech. The opposition, Fraser said, was 'the riskiest and most divisible Labor Party in our history'. Hawke, on the other hand, promised national unity and hope. 'The new path … will be national reconciliation, national recovery, national reconstruction.'[30]

Tony Eggleton, the Federal Director of the Liberal Party, later listed the reasons why Fraser had lost, in his report on the election. He said that after seven years the electorate had become 'disillusioned and impatient' with the government. The recession, aggravated by the drought and the wages explosion, was biting deeply into many sections of the community, and unemployment was 'becoming more than a remote escalating statistic; it was looming as a real threat to middle Australia'. Traditional Liberal supporters including the business community had lost faith in the government. The party disunity in 1982 had damaged the government's credibility, and single-issue groups, including those against the Franklin dam, had concentrated their fire in marginal seats. Hawke had captured an electorate hungry for freshness and hope.[31]

David Kemp was with Fraser on election night, 5 March. As the numbers went up, and they knew he was beaten, Kemp realised that Fraser had decided to resign as leader. He tried to persuade him out of it. 'I said, "Look, if you resign now, you will be giving the message that you are not really interested in the future of the country. That you just wanted to be Prime Minister. That is not a good message to give to the country, and I think that you are the best person who can beat Hawke. You are the most powerful debater the party has got, and you will be the one to expose the weakness of the new government". And he listened to that and obviously dismissed it in the end.'

Fraser said to Kemp that he was going to ring John Howard. Kemp remembers, 'So he picked up the phone to Howard, and he said, "John, I am going to resign", and it was just such an emotional phone call. He wasn't crying. It was just an incredible, emotional moment for him. And then they talked for a little bit and then he put down the phone and he turned to me and he said, "I don't think that he was sorry"'.

Fraser's concession speech, at the Southern Cross Hotel in Melbourne, stands as a landmark in Australian history. Most Australians born before 1965 will never forget it. He had kept the media waiting. He had arrived at the hotel at about midnight, but it was almost one o'clock by the time he walked into what one reporter later described as a 'hyperactive knot of humanity, bristling with boom mikes and ballpoints'.[32] He tried to start his speech three times, but the noise prevented him. Most of those watching had thought of him as austere, aloof and cold. Now, as he waited for quiet, it became clear that he was vulnerable. The shock of this, more than anything else, quietened the room. He began:

> Ladies and gentlemen, I have a short statement that I would like to make. Firstly, I would like to congratulate

> Mr Hawke and the Australian Labor Party on winning this election. I hope they can achieve what they intend for the people of Australia. They have set a high ambition and I hope they can achieve it because if they can it will advantage this country.
>
> I want to say that from this moment I resign the leadership of the Liberal Party. I will not contest the leadership of the Liberal Party.

At that point, the cameras caught Fraser's emotion. He fought for control, and went on, his voice slightly raised.

> I would also like to say that I think Australia is handed over to Mr Hawke and the Labor Party in as good a condition or better condition than any other Western country in the world.
>
> I want to make it quite plain that I take total responsibility for the timing of the federal election. I take total responsibility for the conduct of that election. I therefore take total responsibility for the defeat of the government and I would like to thank all my colleagues and the Liberal Party right around Australia for the support they have given me, not just over recent weeks, but over the past seven years.[33]

He was asked whether he would resign from parliament as well, and replied, 'I think that can wait a day or two'. His jaw was trembling. Tamie reached out, took his hand and squeezed. He gained strength. 'There really has been magnificent support in very difficult times. There are many wonderful people who believed in what the government was doing and I thank them for that.'

Malcolm and Tamie stood and left the stage. At the end of the month, Malcolm Fraser resigned from parliament.

Part 3

Changing the World

19

Change

There is a photograph that Malcolm Fraser refuses to have in this book. He tosses it across the desk with a 'No!' before muttering something about 'Awful stuffed shirt'. It is a studio portrait taken at his mother's request in the early 1950s when he was at Oxford. In truth, it is a moving picture, in its way. It shows Fraser somewhere between boy and man, a hint of Adam's apple above the collar and tie. His hair is impossibly neat. In three-quarter profile, he gazes into the distance as though destiny is visible on the horizon. In the style of those times, the picture is suggestive of the idealism of youth.

It is often said these days that Fraser has changed—that he has reversed the usual journey from radical youth to conservative old age. During the research for this book, one senior Liberal Party figure said, 'If Malcolm Fraser had held the views he has now thirty years ago, he could never have been leader of the Liberal Party'. They were referring to his attitude to the US alliance, and his support for compensation to Aboriginals.

Fraser thinks the remark says more about how the Liberal Party has changed than about him. He doesn't think he has changed very much. Certainly, his views became more sophisticated with time and experience. Liberalism, being a flexible and pragmatic philosophy, demands different things at different times. Sometimes, though, the world changes so fundamentally that all those with a sense of politics are forced to reassess which parts of their beliefs remain relevant. The 1980s was such a time.

Fraser had lost power in his prime. He says today, 'I was only fifty-two. I certainly wasn't ready to retire'. He soon discovered that Australia doesn't know what to do with former prime ministers who still have energy and talent to offer. Corporations didn't want him. He made a few abortive ventures in consultancy, only to pull back when it became clear that companies wanted not his advice but for him to use his contacts and connections on their behalf. Fraser felt this was an improper use of his former position. Other corporations feared alienating the incoming government by associating with a defeated leader. Increasingly, Fraser's own party didn't want him either. As a result, Fraser's most important contributions were made overseas. He co-chaired United Nations and Commonwealth bodies charged with attempting to advance the end of apartheid in South Africa. He helped to found CARE Australia, part of CARE International, the international federation of aid agencies. He became one of the most significant Australians in international affairs, and in this he was helped and encouraged by the Hawke government, which shared his determination that Australia should make the most of its influence and position.

How would Australia in the 1980s have been different if Fraser had still been Prime Minister? He doesn't like to think about what might have been. He prefers to think about the present and the future. 'I really don't see the point of a lot of "what ifs". What happened happened. I was defeated. We didn't win. That is all there is to it.' So did the people of Australia get it right in 1983? He bristles a little. 'We live in a democracy, so I suppose the people always get it right.'

Yet a number of alternative histories branch out from his last election. What if he had followed his first instinct, and called the election early in 1982 after seeing off the Peacock leadership challenge? Fraser thinks he might have won. He would have been opposing Bill Hayden instead of Bob Hawke, and he always thought he could beat Hayden. What if he had delayed the election and run his full term, going to the people in late 1983? Fraser is convinced that he could have worn some of the gloss off Hawke. 'The thing to do would have been to demonstrate that he wasn't a very effective parliamentarian, which he never became. It wouldn't have been difficult to do that.' The drought would have broken. Economic recovery would have begun. A late-1983 election would still have been very difficult, but perhaps winnable. What if the Labor Party had not changed leaders on the day Fraser called the election? Was Hayden right when he said a drover's dog could have won? Fraser says, 'Obviously I thought I could beat Hayden, or I wouldn't have called the election, but it was always going to be very difficult'.

What would another term of the Fraser government have looked like? The policies Fraser took to the 1983 election included a bicentennial water resources program, a new dam on the Upper Murray and a promise to explore 'the age-old dream of turning the coastal rivers of New South Wales and Queensland inland'.[1] He promised to complete a Darwin to Alice Springs railway. Today, he says he likes to think that the drought would have spurred him into developing a comprehensive national water policy, embracing both the cities and the country. This is a policy that Australia still lacks. In foreign policy, the Commonwealth Heads of Government Regional Meetings for Asia and the Pacific would have continued. Fraser would have pursued the idea of a Pacific community, the members of which would have pledged not to raise protectionist measures against each other's exports. This might have helped to make a difference in the North–South trade debate. The Campbell financial reform agenda would have been pursued.

The final 'what if' concerns what would have happened if Fraser had not resigned from parliament at the end of March 1983, but had left open the possibility of returning as leader. The Liberal Party would surely have taken a very different course. 'Instead', he says today, 'we have had this awful conservatism. This awful regression'.

* * *

In the three weeks between the election defeat and his resignation from parliament, plenty of people wrote to Fraser trying to persuade him to stay. Garfield Barwick, former Attorney-General in the Menzies government and recently retired Chief Justice of the High Court, wrote a two-page letter commiserating on the defeat. The people of Australia had, according to Barwick, chosen 'a highly speculative venture' in electing Hawke. Barwick attributed Fraser's defeat to three factors: a desire for change, high prices and high unemployment, and 'hysteria' surrounding Hawke himself. 'These three factors would have produced the same result whenever the election was held in 1983', Barwick opined. But if Fraser stayed on, there was no reason to think that he could not win again for the Liberal Party. Fraser wrote in reply:

> My dear Gar,
> The Liberal Party is a slightly different one from your day. There is no option but for me to stand down. If I did not, I have little doubt the party would have torn itself apart gnawing over my bones, and I was not inclined to allow that to happen … Ex–prime ministers, in my view, should get out of the way and make room for their successors.[2]

The people Fraser found it hardest to explain his decision to were those who had, over many years, listened to him each week on the radio and given time and energy to helping get him elected and re-elected. To Dot Grimshaw, Secretary of the Wannon Electorate Committee, he wrote:

> I really hope members of the party understand the reason … because I could also understand if they felt let down over the fact that I have resigned. If I sat in the parliament, whether I spoke or whether I did not, it might be made very difficult for the present opposition leadership, and both Andrew Peacock and John Howard should be given all the support that is possible. Even an ex-PM who does not speak at all would find himself being

> reported approving or disapproving things that were being done, and I could so easily become a source of difficulty and division.[3]

Doug Anthony advised Fraser to take a year's sabbatical and travel overseas before deciding whether or not to quit politics. Today Fraser says, 'That was probably good advice. If I had taken it I might have made a different decision'. Yet at the time it seemed to Fraser that resigning was the only way to give the party a chance to move to fresh leadership and recover from losing government.

Fraser also received many expressions of regret and sympathy after his defeat. The recently retired General Manager of the ABC, Talbot Duckmanton, wrote that he was 'depressed' by the election result. John B Fairfax, proprietor of the Fairfax newspaper group, wrote that Fraser had contributed greatly to the advancement of Australia. Sir Keith Macpherson, Chairman of the Herald and Weekly Times group, wrote:

> I know you don't care for the media much. And at this stage I am inclined to agree with you. Sometimes journalists are even more difficult to control than politicians. Despite this I hope you will accept that you have always had my personal support and admiration … I regard you as one of the great prime ministers of Australia.

Sir Paul Hasluck, former colleague and Governor-General, wrote to congratulate Fraser on his 'correctness of behaviour' on election night. The famous research biologist Sir Gustav Nossal wrote that Fraser's 'great concern for excellence in Australian life has been a shining example to us', and that his support for science was a 'critical factor' in the well-being of the nation. Kerry Stokes, then at the beginning of his career as a media proprietor, wrote that he was disappointed that Fraser would no longer lead the country. Fraser, he said, had 'set a high standard that most Australians looked up to and respected'. Ron Walker, then a businessman, and former lord mayor of Melbourne, wrote: 'It is clear to me that the Whitlam years are about to be re-visited under the Hawke regime'. Clyde Packer, estranged son of Sir Frank and brother to Kerry, wrote: 'Now that it is over I hope that you realise what a good Prime Minister you have been ... I think the scholars will be particularly kind to you'. Fraser also received a letter from a political opponent who had nevertheless become a friend—the Whitlam government minister Clyde Cameron, who wrote: 'I admired you in your moment of defeat. Although you lost the election, you did nothing to lose the respect of those who admire a tough and courageous political fighter'. Richard Krygier, the founder of *Quadrant* magazine, wrote that Fraser 'would always be welcome among the *Quadrant* group'.[4] This last statement proved not to be true. Fraser's allegiances changed as the world changed. *Quadrant,* which had been created to oppose communism, travelled in a different direction. By the turn of the century, 'the *Quadrant* group' was nothing if not hostile to Fraser and what he represented.

Just three days after he had given his concession speech at the Southern Cross Hotel, Fraser wrote careful letters to the two men responsible for leading the Liberal Party into the future. Fraser had not lobbied actively, but had let it be known that he thought Andrew Peacock would make a better leader than John Howard. This came as a surprise to many, and as a disappointment to Howard. It was Peacock who had had the most open falling-out with Fraser, and who had destabilised the government in its last term. Howard, on the other hand, had been deputy and had held the tough Treasury portfolio. He thought himself the natural successor.[5] The truth was that Fraser thought the Liberal Party needed both Howard and Peacock. 'They had complementary talents, and they had the ability to compensate for each other's weaknesses.' Peacock had 'presence and flair'; Howard had the capacity for hard work, and the intellectual ability to master the detail of policy across the spectrum of government. Fraser hoped they would form an effective leadership team. He preferred Peacock for the top job because, 'On issues I thought were important, on the core liberal values, I had learned to have confidence in Andrew's attitude. I had come to be not so confident of John's'.

Fraser thanked Howard for his support as Treasurer and Deputy Leader, and warned him that 'For the future, total unity of purpose throughout the party … is obviously going to be needed'. Later, he sent Howard a telegram congratulating him on being elected as Deputy Leader, and made the point again. 'I have no doubt that you and Andrew in combination will make a powerful team … Total unity and dedication is needed.' To Peacock, Fraser wrote simply that under his leadership 'I have no fears for the success of our cause or the maintenance of liberal values in this country'.[6]

Fraser knew that both men were ambitious, but he hoped they would be able to put that aside for the good of the party. He says today that if he had known they were going to fight each other for the next ten years, he might have decided to stay in parliament himself, sought the leadership and contested the next election against Hawke.

* * *

The first election after Fraser's defeat was called eighteen months early, in December 1984. Peacock did much better than expected. Despite Hawke's personal popularity, there was a 2 per cent swing against Labor, and the government's majority was cut from twenty-five to sixteen. Fraser thought it clear that Peacock had done well enough to deserve continuing support. He soon found out that Howard wasn't giving it to him.

In February 1985, Fraser was in New York visiting Fred Whittemore, a senior executive of Morgan Stanley. Fraser and Howard had dealt with Whittemore during their years in government; they both knew him well. Fraser remembers, 'We were having a tomato juice and talking, because in those offices they never serve grog at lunchtime, and Whittemore said to me, "Oh, you Australians are a rum lot".

'I said, "Why?"

'And he said, "Young Howard was in here last week".

'I said, "Well, what's strange about that? He was my Treasurer. You got to know him then".

'Whittemore replied, "Yes, I know, but it was what he said. Isn't he deputy to Peacock?"

'"Yes."

'"Aren't deputies meant to support their leader?"

'"Of course."'

Whittemore told Fraser that Howard had said almost as soon as he entered the room, 'Fred, you won't have to worry about Peacock. My people will get rid of him before the end of the year'.[7]

Fraser was shocked by this naked evidence of disloyalty. He feared for the party. If Howard was prepared to undermine Peacock within weeks of a creditable election result, there was no chance of the Liberals returning to government at any time in the foreseeable future. He resolved to confront Howard. He had intended to go to Sydney to see him, but as it happened the crucial conversation took place by telephone. 'I told him I thought Peacock had done well enough against Hawke to deserve loyalty and another go. I said, "If you really try to unseat Peacock the party will be torn apart internally and both of you will be in opposition forever. You both need each other. Together you could be a very effective team. Fighting each other you won't be anything and the people of Australia will see that".' The conversation went back and forth. Fraser felt he was getting nowhere. 'John is an extraordinarily stubborn person. There is only one person whom he will consult in a crisis involving his own political fortunes and that is his wife, Janette. Nobody else's advice is worth a crumpet.'

Finally, Fraser laid it on the line, and said, 'If you want to preserve your title "Honest John", more honest than others of your kind, and you want to take on Peacock, then you need to resign as Deputy Leader and do it from the back bench'. Howard made no response, but Fraser knew that a gulf had opened between them. 'You know that if you are going to have that sort of conversation your relationship will never be the same again. That is what happens when you know too much about a person. Once you know too much about someone, it is always very difficult.'

Fraser took every opportunity to make the same points—though with more subtlety—at Liberal Party forums. In a speech at a party function in early 1985 he noted again that Peacock had done 'much better than anyone expected' in the election and that he had 'clearly earned the right to lead the party into the next election, which I believe the Liberal Party should be odds on to win'. For this to happen, he said, 'There must be total loyalty to the parliamentary leader of the party … Any aspirant to the throne must put his ambitions aside until after the next election'.[8] The message was clear enough, but it was not heeded.

Howard continued to undermine Peacock. His criticisms of his leader became notorious in the party and the media as 1985 continued. In September, Peacock brought the matter to a head, organising a challenge to Howard's position as deputy. Howard won the vote, and Peacock resigned. Just as Howard had promised Whittemore, Peacock was gone before the end of the year. By that time, Howard had publically distanced himself from the Fraser legacy. He had said that the Fraser government's lack of 'philosophical clarity' was part of the reason for its defeat.[9] The 'dries' were saying that the Fraser years had been years of lost opportunity. The myth that Fraser had opposed financial deregulation began to gain ground. The Liberal Party was trashing its own record and in the process granting Labor dominance in the debate over the economy. Fraser had a record on economic reform, but nobody in the Liberal Party acknowledged let alone defended it.

Fraser had seen the pattern before when John Gorton, Billy McMahon and Billy Snedden had all felt they had to distance themselves from Robert Menzies in order to appear 'modern' in the late 1960s and early 1970s. How did he feel about the rubbishing of his record? He says today, 'Well, obviously one would prefer it wasn't happening. But they felt they had to destroy what I had been in order to create themselves. Howard was starting to reveal the sort of party he wanted to lead, and it didn't have much relationship to the sort of party I had wanted to lead, or to the sort of party that Menzies founded'. The Liberal Party, he says, is not good at honouring its history. 'Labor has all sorts of myths, and sometimes they manage to make heroes out of their biggest failures. Liberals don't do that, and when they do create a myth it is often a destructive one.'

* * *

Fraser, meanwhile, was having a hard time just being him. 'I think with all the adrenalin running, I hadn't realised how tired I was. I probably should have taken a year off and done nothing. Tamie would have liked that. But I was not used to doing nothing. I still wanted to contribute.'

Tamie describes the period from 1983 to 1985 as a time in which her husband was really 'more lost than I think I realised at the time'. Even simple matters presented a challenge. In the years since he had become a minister, the Nareen telephone exchange had gone from being manual, with a friendly operator who would connect your call, to automatic. Tamie says, 'He actually didn't know how to dial out a number from home. Anyway, we got over that one. Then he didn't know how to go and book a plane. I had still been travelling with the children so I was still a part of the normal world, but he actually wasn't. It was very difficult for him'.

Just six weeks after his defeat, Fraser delivered a speech at a Liberal Party dinner in his honour and described himself as 'mouldering on the farm'. He urged the party not to abandon its core values while doing the soul-searching that inevitably followed defeat. He talked about the recently concluded economic summit that Hawke had held in Canberra. Leaders of big business and big unions had sat in the parliamentary chamber. It was unfortunate symbolism, Fraser thought. To assume that these people knew what ordinary Australians wanted was 'presumptuous in the extreme'. Labor might not be socialist any more, but it was corporatist.[10] This, it emerged, was to be one of the themes of the decade.

Fraser was determined not to get in the way of Peacock and Howard while there was still some chance of them working together. Therefore, he concentrated his energies on international affairs. Former US President Gerald Ford invited him to join the American Enterprise Institute think tank, which, Fraser says, 'was probably liberal republican in those days but was captured later by the neo-conservatives'. Fraser became a distinguished international fellow of the institute. He renewed his connection with Owen Harries, who was by that time a leading member of the Washington intellectual community. Within months of his election defeat, Fraser was at a conference in Vail, Colorado, attended by fifty chief executives of major US corporations as well as former heads of government including Helmut Schmidt, James Callaghan and Giscard d'Estaing. Later that year, Fraser was appointed a senior adjunct fellow of another important think tank, the Center for Strategic and International Studies. Later still, he became Menzies scholar at and a fellow of the Center for International Affairs at Harvard University.

Fraser also joined a new organisation designed to make use of the experience and insights of former government leaders. The Interaction Council was the initiative of former Japanese Prime Minister Takeo Fukuda. At its first meeting, in 1983, the council identified three priorities: peace and security, world economic revitalisation and the attempt to define universal ethical standards. Membership of the Interaction Council was selective, with an emphasis on progressively minded, forward-thinking former leaders; but otherwise the membership was broad, including communist states and spreading across Asia. Fraser says, 'I never had any overweening expectations of what the Interaction Council would be able to achieve. So often things you do internationally are incremental. But I did believe that it could lay down some principles and talk about long-term issues that tend to get pushed aside when you are in active politics'.

All these commitments meant that, while Fraser might have felt underused, he was really quite busy by most people's standards. He was often overseas and never silent, although for a while he exercised a 'self-denying ban' on speaking about domestic politics. Between the years of 1983 and 1989, he gave an average of six major speeches a year in international venues, repackaging the material into many smaller addresses and articles. He criticised the Reagan government's economic record, and the impact of the US deficit on the Third World. He continued to push the idea of a Pacific community.

Fraser supported Reagan's strong stance against the Soviet Union, but by 1984 he was criticising the 'unsubtle' language in which US foreign policy was being conducted. Reagan had referred to the Soviet Union as an 'evil empire'. Fraser thought such language unhelpful, even dangerous. He said:

> If an American President is not respected, if the United States is perceived to be weak and lacking in resolution, it probably does not matter much what that President says. But when a President is perceived to be strong and very determined, when the country is re-arming, it matters very much indeed.

As the Soviet Union faltered, a new idea was beginning to emerge in Washington: the notion that the United States had a unique and sacred duty to bring democracy to the rest of the world. Fraser says today, 'I don't think Reagan was really all that bright. He relied heavily on his advisers'. Among those advisers were the people who later became known as the neo-conservatives. Fraser sensed the trend and didn't like it. In 1984 he told the American Enterprise Institute that Reagan had made the United States strong again. He had rekindled its self-belief, but,

> The management of strength requires a sophistication and a delicacy in touch ... The kinds of words to which I object are the ones which can be construed as implying a sacred duty to the United States to ensure that each person has the right to live in liberty and democracy, with a government of his or her own choice ... Because

> ideologies are so different, relationships must be conducted on a pragmatic basis if there is to be any hope of agreement, any recognition of live and let live, which alone could lead to a reduction in world tension.[11]

* * *

Meanwhile, at home the retrospective critique of the Fraser government was gathering force. Bob Hawke and his Treasurer, Paul Keating, had floated the dollar despite the opposition of John Stone, the Treasury Secretary, who had resigned soon afterwards. Stone, freed from the constraints of his position, began to write and say in public what he had been saying in private for years, and he was as disparaging of Fraser as he was of Hawke. Some strange claims were about. *Business Review Weekly* published an article claiming that Fraser had allowed government spending to 'rise along Whitlam lines'. Fraser provided the figures from budget papers to demonstrate that this was 'a myth'.[12]

Fraser's overseas commitments meant that he often found out about an attack on his record weeks after it had been made. At other times, 'I just didn't see the point in responding. I always hoped that the record would eventually speak for itself'. Sometimes, though, he was provoked. In 1985, Neil Brown, by this time shadow Attorney-General, made a speech criticising the Fraser government for being too 'weak and compromising … In government between 1975 and 1983, we never seemed to be short of time to devote to sand mining on Fraser Island, the preservation of Abbott's booby bird or Aboriginal land rights'. Brown said Fraser should have been more like Thatcher or Reagan—ignoring the fact that Fraser's talk of small government had preceded and anticipated theirs. Liberal frontbencher John Hodges wrote to Brown and sent Fraser a copy:

> I don't recall your protestations either in the party room or around the cabinet table … In spite of Malcolm Fraser's shortcomings, imperfections and deficiencies, of

> which I remind you we all have many, I still believe he will go down in history as one of Australia's great prime ministers.

Fraser wrote back to Hodges thanking him for his letter.

> I spoke with Neil Brown after I saw the reports on his speech and told him that if he ever did that again I would publicly pull him to bits. I am a little tired of Liberals who were part of my government trying to make themselves popular by criticising that government ... Diminishing the Liberal Party's history diminishes the Liberal Party in the present, and I think it is pathetic when current shadow ministers go around saying that they would have been good ministers if only the government of the day had allowed them to be.[13]

⋆ ⋆ ⋆

When Fraser did enter the domestic debate, regarding the new orthodoxy of economic rationalism and free markets, he was arguing a nuanced line.[14] He continued to oppose the floating of the dollar, but on the other Hawke government measures—such as the dismantling of tariffs and the freeing-up of capital markets—he debated the method, not the principle. He pointed out that the 'inevitable' integration of the Australian economy with that of its trading partners meant the government was less able to pursue independent economic policies. The implications needed to be understood and thought through. In particular, if capital was deregulated, 'It is absolutely essential that the labour markets also be deregulated'. He said that Australians needed to work harder, and be more productive. He argued for the industrial relations system to be more flexible, with wages and conditions set at the level of individual enterprises.

Fraser was drawing attention to the conundrum of Hawke's policies. The price of the currency was set by a floating exchange rate, yet domestic prices and incomes were set under the accord between business, government and the unions. One was an economic policy; the other was a policy designed to manage domestic political pressures. Nobody was prepared to resolve the tensions between the two. As for tariffs, Fraser argued that Australia did not have sufficient weight to be able to 'bludgeon our way into markets if the trading world becomes an unregulated jungle'. What was needed were real international agreements to make the 'level playing field' a reality rather than mere aspiration.

'If a policy is dictated by special interest groups … if policy is determined merely by single ideas or ideology, the result is almost certain to be bad', he said in June 1986. 'There are many issues involved in good policy', he went on. Competition should be 'forced' on producers, but it should also be recognised that markets could be used unscrupulously.

> Free markets are important—but not everything that is important to the community will be provided by a free market … Government regulations can be overbearing and stifling, but to suggest that deregulation alone is an adequate objective is a policy that leads only to nineteenth-century laissez-faire … Capital markets should be free, but should they be so free that every speculative movement is encouraged?

The exchange rate should be market-dominated, he agreed, but he asked, should it be influenced most by the underlying realities of the economy, or merely by perception and the speculation that flowed from it?

Fraser was still pursuing the theme that had guided his own economic management—the idea of balance. He said, 'In all of these areas, balance represented by judgement involving a number of values will lead to the best policy. So often, in public policy or debate, that balance is lacking'. In another speech, he said that the lifting of remaining capital controls and inviting more foreign capital into the country was of 'dubious value. I have no philosophical problem with removal of such controls but it should be done when our dollar is strong. Current decisions smack too much of selling off the farm at giveaway prices to sustain current living standards'. He warned that deregulatory ideology would fade in time—as unbalanced approaches always will. Australia needed to be ready for such a shift in the world intellectual climate.

Read in 2009, Fraser's observations seem unremarkable, even prescient. But in the late 1980s, he was seen as old-fashioned. Later, he compared the more extreme versions of belief in free markets to a religion—a matter of faith and 'metaphysics' rather than reason and judgement. Fraser was an unbeliever. When he was listened to at all, he was dismissed as a resister of virtuous reform.

* * *

In March 1984, the leading historian Geoffrey Blainey made a speech in which he criticised the level of Asian immigration to Australia. 'In the past thirty years the government of Australia has moved from the extreme of wanting a white Australia to the extreme of saying that we will have an Asian Australia and that the quicker we move towards it the better.'[15] This was the first time in decades that views like these had been advanced in public by a reputable person. Later, Blainey criticised what became known as the 'black armband' view of history, in which non-Aboriginal Australians were encouraged to feel ashamed of the way in which Aboriginals had been treated. Blainey's academic colleagues denounced him. His entire career, all his previous books and comments, was unpicked in retrospect in the light of his remarks. There were angry demonstrations whenever he appeared in public. Yet significant numbers of people welcomed his views. The Blainey debate, as it became known, was about more than Blainey; it was about what was sayable, and who was allowed to speak. The more the left condemned Blainey, the more he became a martyr to the conservative cause. Views such as his should be expressed, it was argued: to suppress them was political correctness—the action of an elite out of touch with how most Australians felt. Blainey was loyal to an idea of Australia that was still at the heart of many people's sense of identity and patriotism. There was extraordinary passion on both sides of the debate—a feeling of banked-up tension being released. The culture wars had begun.

The Blainey debate lasted for at least two years. Fraser did not take part. He was overseas for much of the time, working against apartheid in South Africa. He was aware that politics in Australia was veering to the right, but it wasn't until 1987 that he was again free to give attention to the fortunes of the political party he had once led. The Hawke government had continued the policy of multiculturalism. The Liberal Party was about to abandon it.

* * *

The second election after the defeat of the Fraser government was held on 11 July 1987. Howard should have had a good chance of winning, but this was destroyed by two matters before the campaign had even began. First, there was his continuing war with Peacock. Second, there was the Queensland Premier Joh Bjelke-Petersen, who launched a bizarre and abortive campaign in which he toyed with the idea of entering federal politics and becoming Prime Minister. Bjelke-Petersen was advised by John Stone, among others, who went on to be elected as a National Party senator for Queensland. Bjelke-Petersen's venture split the coalition. Hawke was only too glad to take advantage of the situation by calling the election early.

The month after the heavy defeat, Fraser wrote some notes intended for the senior figures in the Liberal Party. He reminded them that he had resigned from parliament to give the party a sense of unity and purpose. 'That hope was seriously disappointed … It was only in these circumstances that the Bjelke-Petersen phenomenon was able for a while to get off the ground … The party will deceive itself if it believes the loss of the election was solely due to Bjelke-Petersen.' The election should have been winnable, he said. It had been lost by the opposition, not won by the government. Part of the problem was that the party was becoming increasingly narrow. People who did not agree with the leader were being sidelined. The Liberal Party, Fraser said, had to be capable of accommodating people with significantly differing ideas and of recognising the contribution they could make to policy. 'The party must not be doctrinaire.'

Fraser sent these notes to his former staffers David Kemp and Denis White, for comment. They agreed that Fraser had offered 'an excellent analysis of the problem the party faces ... We both support an active role for you in the process of rebuilding the party'. Fraser had briefly considered trying to become President of the party. But Kemp and White warned that 'The presidency is likely to be a feasible option only if your candidacy is supported by the party leader and carefully engineered'. In the meantime, they noted, parliamentarians had said they did not want Fraser because they thought he would not be 'hands off'.[16] For the moment, Fraser put the idea aside.

After his defeat, Howard released a new immigration policy under the title 'One Australia'. He rejected multiculturalism. It was at this time that Howard suggested Asian immigration should be slowed down. He also spoke out against the idea of a treaty with Aboriginal Australia, saying it was repugnant to the ideals of 'One Australia'. Hawke once again saw an opportunity to exploit the divisions within the Liberal Party, and forced a vote in parliament to affirm that race should not be used as an immigration selection criterion. Three Liberals—Philip Ruddock, Ian Macphee and Steele Hall—crossed the floor to vote with Labor. The Liberal Party was engaged in a battle for its soul.

Ian Macphee had been sent to the back bench by Howard, and had taken on the role of internal party critic. He had become a symbol for the Fraser government's priorities and record. In the process, he lost the support of many Liberal Party members in his seat of Goldstein. In 1989, some of these approached Fraser's friend and former adviser David Kemp, and asked him to contest Macphee's pre-selection. The contest tore Fraser's loyalties. Macphee and Kemp were both friends. As Immigration Minister in the post-Galbally period, Macphee had implemented some of the reforms closest to Fraser's heart, while Kemp had been one of his most important advisers. Kemp remembers taking a call from Fraser, who was travelling in the United States. 'He said, "David, I think that you should step aside. This is very divisive for the party, and people would think better of you if you were to step aside from this pre-selection".

'And I said to him, "Malcolm, you know and I know that that is not right. If I step aside my reputation will be ruined, and I am surprised that you would give me that advice".'

Kemp and Fraser remain friends, but they have never discussed this matter since. To the media, Fraser said that Kemp was a first-class candidate, but should run in a different seat. If Macphee did not gain pre-selection, there would be a perception that the party had rejected the values that he represented. 'That in my view will be very damaging in electoral terms.' Howard dismissed what Fraser had said as 'pure drivel'.[17]

Kemp won pre-selection in Goldstein, but the Macphee battle had weakened the party and eroded Howard's support. Peacock successfully contested the leadership, and had his second chance to defeat Hawke in 1990. He lost. This ended his hopes of becoming Prime Minister. Hawke had now won four elections—the same number as Fraser. As Fraser had predicted, the divisions in the Liberal Party had made it unelectable.

Would Peacock have made a good Prime Minister? Today, Fraser thinks hard before answering the question. He thought the party needed both Howard and Peacock, but on his own Peacock could have been good, 'depending on how hard he wanted to work'. As it was, the Liberal Party of the 1980s 'really didn't deserve to win government'.

* * *

In 1991, a profile of Malcolm Fraser appeared in *Good Weekend* magazine.[18] The magazine's reporter had visited him at Nareen and described him as 'clomping about in his farm clothes and work boots'. The article noted that Fraser was still only sixty-one—six months younger than the Prime Minister, Bob Hawke. Peter Nixon and Doug Anthony were quoted as saying that Fraser's talents were going to waste. Anthony described him as a workaholic. 'I would say work is his number one love, and if he's been unhappy it's because he hasn't had enough to do.'

Fraser told the *Good Weekend* reporter: 'Anything useful that I've done, really, has been outside Australia. I suppose if there's a regret, it's that I haven't been able to do more here'. He was quoted as saying he regretted leaving parliament when he did. Was there a chance of a return to politics? 'I said I'd only consider it if the country was in an absolute mess … My thinking just doesn't coincide with that of the times.' The article commented that both major parties had moved so far to the right that Fraser looked like a bleeding heart in comparison. The new leader of the Liberal Party, John Hewson, had attacked Fraser, saying he 'didn't have the courage to take the decisions that were necessary to change the country'.

The reason Fraser was once again in the news was that he had taken a stand against the Hawke government's changes to media ownership regulation. Rupert Murdoch, who already dominated newspaper publishing, had been allowed to buy the Herald and Weekly Times group. At the same time, a disastrous attempt by Fairfax newspaper heir 'young Warwick' Fairfax to privatise the company had left it in financial trouble and vulnerable to takeover. Kerry Packer was circling. *The Age* newspaper journalists had run a campaign under the cheeky title 'Maintain Your Age' in support of a charter of editorial independence, which they planned to ask any new owner to sign.

For Fraser, the debate over media ownership regulation was part of the wider discussion about the merits of free markets and government regulation. Media was a special industry, he said. It needed government regulation to protect diversity. He argued that if media ownership became too concentrated in a few hands,

> the power is sufficient, I think, to rival the power of the parliament itself... One of the problems in the deregulation debate is that there is often an attempt to draw general rules about regulation or deregulation, when really every different set of circumstances needs looking at on its own merits to come to sensible, pragmatic judgements about what is best.[19]

The campaign on media ownership led to an extraordinary event. Journalists from *The Age* organised a rally in Melbourne's Treasury Gardens, and invited Fraser and Gough Whitlam to share the stage. The pair shook hands, and were greeted with enthusiastic applause. On this issue, and in their mutual scepticism about free market dogma, they had more in common with each other than with their respective parties. Both Fraser and Whitlam believed in the role and responsibility of government.

* * *

Fraser did not foresee the end of the Soviet Union, but he spoke often in the late 1980s about the new spirit of freedom sweeping through Eastern Europe. Changes had taken place that just five years before would have been impossible. 'The entire international climate has changed dramatically.' Market economies and new democracies were emerging. In Hungary, the communist party had disbanded. In Poland, Solidarity was in government. The Soviet Union had withdrawn from Afghanistan, and Vietnam had withdrawn from Kampuchea. 'The politics of fear and ideology are being replaced by a much more hopeful world', Fraser said. Nevertheless, he was sceptical about Mikhail Gorbachev's chances of reforming the 'stultifying' bureaucracy of the Politburo. Meanwhile, in China, protesters had been shot dead by their government in Tiananmen

Square. China, said Fraser, had yet to learn 'that economic freedom without political freedom probably cannot survive'. Fraser thought the changes elsewhere were reason for hope. 'We look on Mr Gorbachev with admiration.'[20]

But Fraser was also aware of new threats as old certainties died. In 1989, his former adviser Owen Harries, at this point editor of the influential US foreign policy journal *The National Interest*, published an article by a state department official, Francis Fukuyama. The article was titled 'The End of History'. It became a manifesto for the neo-conservatives in the Republican Party. Fukuyama argued that the decay in the Soviet Union and the freedom movements in Eastern Europe heralded the ultimate victory for liberal democracy.

> What we may be witnessing is not just the end of the Cold War, or the passing of a particular period of postwar history, but the end of history as such: that is, the end point of mankind's ideological evolution and the universalisation of Western liberal democracy as the final form of human government.[21]

Fraser was not impressed. He said in a speech that two things were surprising about this article.

> First, that a relatively senior officer of the United States state department could write something so utterly foolish, and second, that a normally sensible and rational journal should bother to publish it. In human affairs there is no ultimate, no finite anything. So often our century repeats the mistakes of earlier times ... To suggest that the end of one tyranny and the apparent movements towards capitalism and liberal democracy involve the end of all tyranny is an absurdity. Tyranny can take many forms; it does not have to be called communist, it doesn't have to be called Nazism or fascism.[22]

Fukuyama's article went on to become one of the most discussed and cited of the twentieth century. It had struck a chord. It articulated the mood of the times, and again Fraser was out of step.

One week after Fraser gave the speech criticising Fukuyama, the world watched on television while the people of Berlin pulled down the wall that had divided them for so long. The wall had been erected when Fraser was a young man. For most of his life, opposition to communism and fear of the Soviet threat had been defining motivations. When communism died, so did those parts of Fraser's politics that were most easy to characterise as conservative and right-wing.

The end of communism should have been a time of new hope and possibility, but by the end of the 1980s Fraser was old enough to be cautious and sceptical. There was the opportunity to rethink everything, including Australia's place in the world, without the overshadowing Soviet threat. Yet there were also dangers as old stabilities collapsed. There were dangerous new orthodoxies, including the faith in untrammelled capitalism as an organising principle in human affairs, and the notion that the world's remaining superpower, the United States, had some special mission in the world.

The frame shifted in the 1980s. It was possible to see Fraser in a fresh light. In one way, though, he had not changed at all: he was still an activist. There was never any chance that he would be seen and not heard.

20

Mission to South Africa

Two men stood looking over the Indian Ocean. One was in a suit, the other in white robes. Both were former leaders of their countries. Both had been saddled with the title 'eminent person', but on this day, 23 February 1986, Malcolm Fraser and former Nigerian President Olusegun Obasanjo were simply angry men. The signs along the beach at Port Elizabeth, South Africa, said 'Whites Only'.

Fraser and Obasanjo had first met in 1979, during the lead-up to the Lusaka Commonwealth Heads of Government Meeting (CHOGM), at which the breakthrough on Zimbabwe had been negotiated. A career soldier, Obasanjo had come to power following a military coup but had then devoted himself to establishing democracy. Shortly after Fraser first met him, Obasanjo had become the first military ruler to transfer power peacefully to a civilian-elected government. Fraser regarded him as a great man. The challenges of governing Nigeria, he reflected, made being Prime Minister of Australia look easy. Yet according to the law of this place, Obasanjo could not step onto the sand, and Fraser could not walk on the beach without leaving his companion behind.

Fraser and Obasanjo were in South Africa as co-chairmen of the so-called Eminent Persons Group, appointed by the Commonwealth of Nations to attempt to negotiate the beginning of the end of apartheid in South Africa. They had promised to do their work quietly, without breaking the law and without drawing attention to themselves. They had been, to this point, very restrained. They had sat courteously through meetings with South African Government ministers and resisted provocation. Fraser remembers telling Obasanjo that they might need superglue, to keep their bottoms on their seats, because, 'No matter how we are provoked, we will stay in our seats and keep talking'. The stakes, after all, were very high indeed.

That morning they had planned to meet black African leaders, but, despite government instructions to the contrary, the South African security forces had staked out their hotel. The people Fraser and Obasanjo were meant to meet had 'melted away'. Fraser remembers, 'We had nothing to do. And we were angry. So we thought we might as well take a walk on the beach'. They paused while Fraser took a photo of the 'Whites Only' signs. Then they strode out onto the beach with a commanding air, Fraser with his hand in his pocket and his jacket swinging from the vigour of his pace, Obasanjo with hands clasped behind his back and his chin up. A journalist took a photograph and it travelled around the world, a small talisman of the fight against apartheid.[1]

Fraser had been at Harvard when, in October 1985, he had taken a call from Bob Hawke, the man who had replaced him as Australian Prime Minister. Hawke was attending the CHOGM in Nassau, the Bahamas. Once again, justice in South Africa was the defining issue on the agenda, and once again there was the risk of a schism. Most Commonwealth countries wanted to impose tough sanctions on the racist regime. British Prime Minister Margaret Thatcher was alone in arguing for a policy of 'constructive engagement' with the South African Government. Hawke had brokered a compromise. Under what became known as the Nassau Accord, the South African Government was given six months' notice in which to begin 'a process of dialogue across lines of colour, politics and religion with a view to establishing a non-racial and representative government'. The

Commonwealth leaders called on the South African Government to release black leader Nelson Mandela and all other political prisoners, to legalise banned political parties, including the African National Congress, and to end the state of emergency under which the country had become a police state. If these things were not done, in six months' time the Commonwealth countries would again consider imposing tough sanctions. In the meantime, the heads of government of Zambia, Australia, the Bahamas, Canada, India, the United Kingdom and Zimbabwe were each to appoint an 'eminent person' to a group that would

> seek to facilitate the processes of dialogue ... We are not unmindful of the difficulties such an effort will encounter, including the possibility of initial rejection by the South African authorities, but we believe it to be our duty to leave nothing undone that might contribute to peaceful change in South Africa and avoid the dreadful prospect of violent conflict that looms over South Africa, threatening people of all races in the country, and the peace and stability of the entire southern African region.[2]

Despite their political differences, Hawke had no doubt that Fraser was the right man to be Australia's nominee. As Hawke said to Fraser in a letter confirming the appointment, there was no other Australian who commanded such respect in black Africa and the Commonwealth. 'I am confident that you will be able to make a valuable contribution.'[3] Fraser was happy to accept. He had recent experience of the horrors of apartheid. The opportunity to help end it could not be lightly turned aside.

At the time he took Hawke's call, Fraser was completing work as Chair of a United Nations committee charged with examining the role of transnational corporations in South Africa, and in particular whether their presence was helping to perpetuate apartheid. He had toured the country and heard from business leaders, government ministers and black African leaders. He had tried to get permission to see Nelson Mandela in jail and had been refused, but he had met his wife, Winnie Mandela, and had been, as he wrote in a press statement, 'impressed by her grace, her calm, the authority with which she sees the present position and looks to the future'.[4] Fraser had visited the hostels where black mine workers were forced to live and, with their permission, had taken photos of the living conditions. He reported to the United Nations: 'The hostel was in my view a disgrace to humanity'.[5] The workers slept in bunks constructed in tiers. 'You had to go in feet first or head first. There was no room for anything else', Fraser remembers. 'It was constructed on the same principle as storage for bodies in a morgue.'

Fraser's views about apartheid had been intensified and strengthened.

> As we all know, it denies any semblance of human dignity ... The theory has always been repugnant but before I came here I had not realised that the administration of the policy was as brutal and inhumane as it very plainly is. It's institutionalised. It's all pervasive, affecting pretty well every aspect of an African's life.

Violence in South Africa was intensifying. The government-imposed state of emergency had magnified the police's already substantial powers. Fraser had encountered evidence of police brutality that, he said, he would have found difficult to believe had he not seen it himself. 'Individuals are molested and harassed by the police, sometimes at three or four o'clock in the morning, taken away to detention, where they can be held without trial for six months. They have no recourse to law; they are not allowed to ring anyone up. They just disappear.'[6]

Fraser reported to the General Assembly of the United Nations in November 1985, saying that time was running out for a peaceful solution, and that it was the duty of the international community to act more decisively to accelerate the pace of change. Yet he did not recommend that transnationals should simply leave South Africa;

instead, he recommended that they stay, but only on the condition that they refuse to be part of apartheid. As well as refusing to supply the military, the police and the security forces, transnationals should desegregate their workforces, introduce equal pay for blacks and whites and allow their workers to live with their families in desegregated housing. This was to be understood as a refusal to comply with one of the pillars of apartheid, the Group Areas Act, which designated where people were allowed to live on the basis of their race. Normally, Fraser said, corporations should abide by the laws of the countries in which they operated, but apartheid created an exception. It had been designated a 'crime against humanity', and, 'Exceptional circumstances of this kind require an exceptional response—and to call on transnational corporations to challenge South African apartheid laws and regulations is such an exceptional response'.

Now, thanks to Hawke's telephone call, Fraser had another chance to do something to address this 'crime against humanity', but the Commonwealth mission was much more delicate. The Eminent Persons Group was charged with attempting to persuade apparently irreconcilable groups to talk. Thatcher's nominee to the Group was Lord Tony Barber of Wentbridge. A former Chancellor of the Exchequer, he was seen as a hard-nosed conservative unlikely to be swayed by bleeding hearts. The other eminent persons were Dame Nita Barrow, President of the World Council of Churches, nominated by the Bahamas; the former Tanzanian Foreign Minister John Malecela, who, with Obasanjo, had been nominated jointly by Zimbabwe and Zambia; the former Indian Government minister Sardar Swaran Singh; and the Reverend Edward Walter Scott, a Primate of the Anglican Church in Canada. This group of seven, as Commonwealth Secretary-General Sonny Ramphal later wrote, came from five continents. They were black, white and brown. They were to give everything they had to offer—'integrity, humanity, compassion, understanding and a wide experience—to holding back a darkening storm'.[7]

There were multiple challenges. Black African leaders had hoped for stronger action at Nassau. They wanted sanctions, not more attempts at negotiations. They were enormously sceptical about the Commonwealth mission, and it was not certain they would even see the Eminent Persons Group. The South African Government had already proved itself resistant to international pressure. Mindful of this, the Commonwealth leaders at Nassau had been determined that the Eminent Persons Group should not become an endless talking shop. It was to have a short life—no more than six months—in which to attempt to broker negotiations.

The Group met for the first time in London in December 1985. Fraser remembers that he and Ramphal had a 'stand-up row that went over about two days' over whether or not to insist on guarantees from the South African Government. 'Sonny wanted us to look strong. He wanted us to ask for guarantees that we would be allowed to see Mandela, that we would be guaranteed to do this, guaranteed to do that. You know, it would have been a humiliating set of demands. Well, we might have looked strong, but it would also have been foolish. I said, "You do this, and we'll never go to South Africa. You will abort the mission".' If there was any hope at all, Fraser thought, it was to win the confidence of both sides before seeking concessions. 'In the end, most of the things that were on Sonny's list of demands we did in fact do, but it was a matter of how you went about it.'

The mission to South Africa was another example of Fraser's attitude to negotiation. He believes that it is possible, indeed essential, to talk to people even when you disagree with them on issues of the highest principle. One example is the way that Nelson Mandela was able, in the years ahead, to talk to the South African Government. Thus, in the present day, Israel should talk to Hamas and the United States to North Korea. 'If you start talking and keep talking, little by little you may agree on something, no matter how small, and you can move forwards from that. I mean, what other hope is there in the world than people talking and trying to find areas of agreement?'

Fraser won the dispute with Ramphal. When the meeting ended, Fraser and Obasanjo wrote to the President of South Africa Pieter Botha, saying they were 'anxious to get down to business as quickly as possible in a spirit of helpfulness and with the cooperation of all the parties concerned, working quietly and essentially in non-public ways'. They asked to visit South Africa for consultations with the government and with 'the true representatives of the black population as well as others whose views would be relevant to such a process'. Botha replied on Christmas Eve, saying he was 'prepared to approach this initiative constructively', but warning that 'The Commonwealth group can do incalculable harm if it sees itself as a pressure group charged with the task of extracting concessions from the government and generally engaged in prescribing solutions to problems which are the sole concern of South Africans'. The government, Botha said, was determined to continue its own reform program, 'which has already reached an advanced stage'.[8]

The reform process Botha referred to in his letter was part of the rhetoric of the South African Government at the time. Apartheid was variously said to be 'outmoded' or even 'dead'. Mixed marriages had recently been legalised. Hotels and cinemas were being desegregated, and the pass laws, under which black South Africans were required to carry identity documents and could be imprisoned for failing to do so, were being altered. Yet the main pillars of the system remained in place. Every South African citizen was categorised as belonging to a racial group: white, coloured, Indian or black. The blacks were then further divided into ten 'national units', each of which had its own 'reserve', or homeland. This system meant that the South African Government was able to claim that the country was not one of a white minority and a black majority, but a 'nation of minorities'. It was so only by government fiat.

At the time of the Nassau Accord, the South African Government was claiming to be committed to dismantling apartheid and moving to power sharing. Yet at the same time the government spoke of 'a right of self-determination of minorities', which was clearly understood as embracing segregation of residential areas, schools and health services. It was a system of group rights, as opposed to individual rights. South Africa had a tricameral parliament, with three Houses, covering whites, Indians and coloureds, each of which had some control over its own affairs. Blacks, though, had not even this token control. Responsibility for their affairs was vested in the President. The government specifically rejected the idea of 'one person, one vote' in a unified political system. Instead, each group was to have a right of veto over legislation, meaning that whites could always prevent the economic and social restructuring necessary if apartheid was to be truly ended. Meanwhile, blacks were effectively stripped of their citizenship, because they were said to be citizens not of South Africa but of their homelands.

The history of the homelands was rooted in violence and coercion. During the late 1940s and into the 1950s, people living outside their designated areas had been forcibly relocated. Millions of blacks had been uprooted and dumped in distant arid lands. The homelands were rural slums in which poverty was institutionalised. They were supposedly being brought to 'independence'. This was a fiction: they were dependent in every way on the surrounding white South Africa, and served as sources of cheap labour for white-owned industry. Those who wished to work in white South Africa were forced to leave their families behind. Nor were the homelands large blocks or unitary states; rather, they were jumbles of jigsaw pieces within white South Africa. KwaZulu had as many as twenty-nine separate island blocks. More than 86 per cent of the land in South Africa was in the possession of the white minority.

Almost all genuine black leaders had been 'banned' or jailed. Banning meant they could not meet groups of people or travel, and the media were prohibited from publishing their words or even acknowledging their existence. Meanwhile, the government had taught the white people to fear the blacks. The African National Congress was said to be a communist organisation, which in a way was true: the South African Government had defined 'communist' to mean any group or person causing disturbance aimed at bringing about political, industrial or social change. As the Group of Eminent Persons later reported:

> In its unambiguous insistence on a political structure based on communities the government is in reality seeking to preserve and entrench a society based on racial groups. While in any ordinary circumstances a requirement that 'there is no domination of one population group over another' might seem reasonable, in the circumstances of South Africa these words have quite a different meaning.[9]

This was the South Africa in which Fraser and his fellow Group members had to attempt to bring about dialogue. Most commentators dismissed the effort as an impossible mission. Yet, against the odds, the Group showed that a peaceful change for South Africa was within the people's grasp. As Ramphal later put it: 'For a brief moment, the world—and, pre-eminently, South Africans of all races—glimpsed a path of negotiation to a more worthy future'.[10]

* * *

Fraser, Obasanjo and Barrow made a preliminary visit to South Africa in February 1986. They met both white and black leaders, including the Anglican Bishop of Johannesburg Desmond Tutu, and Winnie Mandela. In their meetings with South African Government ministers, they were conciliatory and refused to be provoked. They told Botha that they would not issue any press statements, they would work quietly and without stirring up trouble, and that nothing they did would be in secret. They would keep the government informed of who they were meeting, and the nature of the discussions. It was during this trip that Fraser and Obasanjo had their planned meetings with black African leaders aborted by the security presence. Shortly before, Barrow and Fraser had been taken to a police station for questioning after they entered the troubled township of Alexandra without a permit, but these were the exceptions—examples of local commanders exceeding their authority. Generally speaking, Fraser's softly-softly approach to the government had proved effective. The Group was allowed to travel as it pleased and meet those whom it wished to meet.

Fraser also saw Frederik Willem de Klerk, who was then Minister for Internal Affairs. Fraser had met him previously on his visit to South Africa while working for the United Nations. De Klerk was the only South African Fraser encountered who attempted to mount a philosophical defence of apartheid. Fraser remembers, 'He went into the history of it. How the Afrikaners had been persecuted for their religion in Europe; how the Germans didn't invent concentration camps, because that was the British during the Boer War. He told me these were the reasons why the Afrikaners would never accept domination by another race'. De Klerk changed his mind over the next ten years. He became President in 1989, and his term was dominated by negotiations that eventually ended the apartheid era. Fraser says, 'Whether he moved because of pragmatism, or because he was convinced of the justice, he was the one who was capable of negotiation, and of bringing white South Africa with him. President Botha would not have done it and could not have done it. While Mandela deserves enormous credit for achieving peaceful change in South Africa, it could not have been done without De Klerk. He deserves great credit as well'.

After their preliminary visit, Fraser and Obasanjo moved on to visit leaders of the frontline states, including Robert Mugabe in Zimbabwe and Kenneth Kaunda in Zambia. Thanks in part to their intervention, Oliver Tambo, the Lusaka-based leader of the African National Congress, was persuaded to see them. Here, too, Fraser and Obasanjo were successful in overcoming initial scepticism. By the time the full Group of Eminent Persons visited South Africa in March, the Commonwealth initiative had gained the cautious support of all sides.

In March and April, the Group travelled throughout the country talking to business leaders, church leaders, the leaders of the homelands and representatives of government. They met Chief Buthelezi,

Chief Minister of KwaZulu and President of Inkatha, the million-strong Zulu political movement. Buthelezi was no friend to the African National Congress. He was seen as a collaborator with the government, and he opposed international sanctions. Yet he told the Group that if Nelson Mandela was released, he would be able to work with him. This was significant: the South African Government portrayed the black Africans as warring tribes, but here was a sign that unity was possible. In general, the Group was 'forcibly struck by the overwhelming desire in the country for a non-violent negotiated settlement'. Nobody wanted violence. Everyone feared it. Yet it was clear that the issue of violence was central to South African politics. The government was refusing to negotiate with black African leaders unless they renounced violence, yet the whole of South African society was based on state-sanctioned violence. Apartheid had been established through force, and force maintained the system. Tambo had told Fraser and Obasanjo that the African National Congress had resorted to violence only late in its life and as a last resort. Now, though, it was black Africans' only weapon; to ask them to give up violence was to ask them to surrender and accept defeat in the battle for justice. This they could not do.

Violence was apparent everywhere the Group went. Deliberately, they went to places where there had been recent trouble. They visited Alexandra the day after twenty-two people had been shot. Fraser met a doctor whose son had been killed by security forces the day before. The boy's body had been found in a morgue with twenty-two bullet holes in his back, yet it was claimed that he had been killed because he was threatening security forces. Later that day, Fraser became aware that the Group—at the time standing at a crossroads talking to more than a dozen people—was being watched. A Casspir—one of the armoured vehicles that patrolled the township—came over the hill towards them, with soldiers peering over the top, guns at the ready. Fraser recalls, 'It had stopped and then I saw another Casspir coming up'. Fraser was not worried for his own or the Group's safety, but he feared that the blacks they were talking to might panic and run, and that if this happened the soldiers would open fire. 'I said to the others, "We had better get out of here and break this up and go in different directions. Now nobody run. We walk to our cars and we just get in totally normally". And we got into our cars and I saw other Casspirs approaching, moving to block off the crossroads. So we would have had four of them with us in the middle. They were obviously called up to see what these whites were doing talking to people, and I'm not sure what would have happened if we had have stayed another five minutes. I was, I must admit, slightly concerned.'

On another occasion, Fraser was warned by an armed Lance Corporal not to take photos of the Casspirs patrolling the townships. Fraser advanced the shutter on his camera, and found that he had a submachine gun pointed at his stomach. Fraser reached out and grabbed the barrel of the gun and moved it aside. 'I told him not to point the bloody thing at me.'[11]

Fraser was accompanied on some of these trips by his first biographer, Philip Ayres. In Soweto, Ayres later recounted, Fraser's camera took in 'acres of huts and shanties which to a casual observer from the First World might have doubled for a vast rubbish dump. A more grossly poor standard of housing could not be imagined'. There were bucket toilets, no drainage, and liquid waste trickling across dirt paths. A mere thirty communal taps serviced 150 000 people. The Group was shown around by representatives of the anti-apartheid United Democratic Front. Five of the guides had spent a total of sixty-seven years in prison. They told Fraser that they could not hold back the people's anger for much longer while maintaining their credibility.

On 8 March, the Group visited the Moutse area in the north-east Transvaal, which had just been incorporated against its will into the KwaNdebele 'self-governing homeland'. They drove along a road fringed with burned-out vehicles. Houses had been abandoned, and some gutted. While Fraser was talking to the local chief, two teenagers were brought in to see him. They had been to a funeral of a young boy who had died in the police station at Mototama, 50 kilometres to the north, after gunfire. The buses taking mourners to the funeral had been stopped at a road block. Shooting had started and a number of people had been killed. Both of the teenagers had been beaten with the hard black rhinoceros-hide whips, or *sjamboks*, that were carried by police. Both were drenched in blood. Fraser examined their wounds then turned to the rest of the Group and said that they should see if they could do something about the people who had been arrested. Within minutes, they were speeding up the highway.

When they arrived at the Mototama police station, Ayres recorded, Fraser

> walked straight up the steps and inside. Behind the counter were two black policemen, seated. Three others were wandering about, shelving weapons or cleaning them. Fraser towered over the counter, leaning on it with his hands, obviously impatient and glaring down imperiously at the policemen below him. 'Who is your commanding officer?' This was clearly not the sort of question, or the sort of tone, these policemen were used to. After some confusion there was a faltering reply to the effect that the commanding officer had gone home. 'I see. Then I suggest you telephone him and ask him to come here. I understand you are holding people in the cells, arrested today at a funeral near here. How many people are you holding?' This produced more confusion. There seemed to be a dispute behind the counter over whether there were any prisoners here at all. One of the police said there were prisoners but he could not say how many. Only the commanding officer could give that information. Another insisted there were none. At some early stage, Fraser told them who he was and what the group were doing in South Africa.

The police were becoming edgy. A riot gun was unshelved. Other policemen were trailing *sjamboks* behind them. Eventually Fraser was told that the prisoners were being held at a white-staffed police station in Krugersdorp, further up the road. It was now about six o'clock. Most of the Group headed back to Johannesburg, but Fraser went on to Krugersdorp. Ayres reported:

> The white police were not pleased to see him and perhaps assumed he would soon go away, but he was sufficiently persistent and authoritative to get something for all his afternoon's efforts. Yes, it was admitted, there had been many arrests at the funeral and people had been injured, though it was denied that anybody had been killed. And yes, in response to repeated requests from Fraser, they finally would allow a lawyer into the cells. They also admitted that the cells in the Motatama station were full of people arrested that day. The police there had simply lied.

The South African police, the Eminent Persons Group later acknowledged, were confronted with enormous difficulty 'in having to try to maintain law and order in an atmosphere seething with discontent, distrust and hostility. But equally clearly they chose in the main to adopt an aggressive and ruthless approach'. Police frequently fired lethal buckshot into unarmed crowds of blacks. Funerals of people killed by security forces often became illegal gatherings. Everywhere, the Group heard stories of gratuitous beatings and point-blank shootings that had 'the unmistakable ring of truth'. On the Group's first visit to Soweto, they had seen a policeman chase and shoot at an unarmed person not 15 metres away from them.

During the time the Group was visiting South Africa, the state of emergency was lifted. This had been one of the things the Nassau Accord had called for, but it had little effect. As the group later reported, 'In reality … South Africa is sliding even further into a permanent state of emergency in terms of the ordinary laws of the land'. Meanwhile, most of white South Africa remained oblivious to what was being done in its name. Away from the townships and the homelands, whites lived in wealth amid rolling green lawns.

Having seen these things, Fraser found it easy to accept the African National Congress's point—that violence was perpetrated on all sides. It was unreasonable to ask the party to abandon violence unless the state agreed to do the same. Fraser believed that the heart of negotiation was to understand what the other side could concede. Clearly, it was not possible for the African National Congress to renounce violence. At the very most, it could be asked to suspend violence in order to allow negotiations to begin. The South African Government would also have to suspend violence.

By this time, the experience of apartheid had worked a change on the members of the Group. All of them, even Fraser, who had previous experience of South Africa, were shaken by what they had seen. The media later reported that Lord Barber had been expected to take Thatcher's side on South African issues, but he had been 'profoundly shocked' by his visits to the country.[12] Instead, together with the other members of the Group, Barber put his name to a report that endorsed the African National Congress's position as entirely understandable.

So far, the Group's visit to South Africa was going better than anyone had expected. The Group had gained the confidence of all sides, and had found that 'No serious person we met was interested in a fight to the finish; all favoured negotiations and peaceful solutions'. Even the government was dismayed that its 'reforms' had not resulted in a reduction of violence. Yet nobody seemed to know how negotiations might begin. The Group saw its role as delineating the necessary steps.

By mid March, the Group had compiled what it dubbed the 'Possible Negotiating Concept'. It was single-page document suggesting a break in the cycle of violence as a condition for the beginning of negotiations. The African National Congress would have to agree to suspend violence, but the document made it clear that the government had to make the most moves. For negotiations to begin, it would have to remove the military from the townships, legalise the African National Congress and other political parties, allow freedom of assembly and discussion, suspend detention without trial and release Nelson Mandela and all other political prisoners.

At the end of its March visit, the Group showed the document to the South African Government and asked for an immediate response. In fact, it was over a month before Botha sent a long letter which the South African Ambassador in London assured the Group 'should be regarded as positive'. Had it not been for that assurance, it would have been difficult to divine the government's attitude. On the one hand, Botha clearly suggested that the existing reforms to apartheid should be enough for negotiations to begin. He failed to deal with the suggestions of further political freedoms. However, he also appeared to make a significant concession: he spoke in terms of a 'suspension' of violence by the African National Congress, rather than demanding renunciation of violence. He also said that he thought the Group was proving useful, and could continue to play a constructive role.

The result was another visit to South Africa in May. On this trip, the Group was allowed what had been refused to all other international figures: a visit to Pollsmoor Prison to meet Nelson Mandela. At this time, Mandela had been in prison for twenty-four years. Under the law, newspapers were forbidden from printing his image or his words, but nevertheless he had become a living legend and an inspiration to the liberation struggle. Much of the world accepted the South African Government's claim that Mandela was a dangerous communist, but Fraser already believed that this wasn't so. He had seen a CIA report which 'in very factual and unemotional language' had said that the African National Congress was a nationalist, not a communist, organisation.

The early days of Mandela's imprisonment had been harsh. He had been forced to do hard labour, but recently the South African Government had begun to treat him more carefully. He was now kept in splendid isolation in a three-room cell on the ground floor of the prison.

In preparation for the Group's visit, the prison authorities called in a tailor and fitted Mandela out in a proper suit—which was taken away from him the moment the visit was over.[13] The meeting took place in a guesthouse in the jail grounds, and came at a crucial time. Mandela was hoping to use the Group to send a message to both the South African Government and his colleagues in the African National Congress: he wanted to tell them that the time was right for negotiations to begin.

Fraser remembers Mandela walking into the room 'with a natural authority and presence'. The first thing he asked Fraser was if the cricketer Donald Bradman was still alive. Fraser said that he was, 'which seemed to please him greatly'. Then Mandela turned to Tony Barber and said, 'I am told Mrs Thatcher says President Gorbachev is a man with whom she can do business. Will you please tell her that it would be far, far easier and very much safer to do business with Nelson Mandela'.

Fraser was instantly impressed with Mandela's authority and intellect, but also with his lack of bitterness. He remembers, 'His language was at first slightly old-fashioned—the product of his decades in prison. But he was very well informed and immensely intelligent'. Mandela told the Group that he was committed to working for a multiracial society in which all people would have a secure place. Fraser says, 'The desire for good will was palpable. After decades in jail, being kept away from his family and his friends, after all he had been through, he wanted to talk reconciliation. He was even on friendly terms with his jailers'. Mandela made it clear that he could not speak for the African National Congress. He had been isolated from his colleagues for years. He told the Group that it would have to deal with Tambo in Lusaka. 'You can tell him what my views are, but they are my personal views alone ... All that being said, I favour the ANC beginning discussions with the government.' The Group showed him the Possible Negotiating Concept, and he assured them that it would have his personal support.

The Group questioned Mandela closely about his political beliefs. Was he a communist? Fraser recalls, 'He told us he was a South African nationalist, not a communist, and that nationalists came in every colour. He said that the ANC shared some aims with communists, mainly those for a non–racially segregated South Africa, but that most of the ANC were not communists, and it was not a communist organisation'. Mandela told them that while he would not renounce violence, he 'affirmed in the strongest possible terms that violence could never be the ultimate solution'.

In its report, the Eminent Persons Group wrote that Mandela was not the violent terrorist of South African propaganda, but

> a man who had been driven to armed struggle only with the greatest reluctance solely in the absence of any other alternative to the violence of the apartheid system, and never as an end in itself … He is an isolated and lonely figure, bearing his incarceration with courage and fortitude, anxious to be reunited with his wife and family but determined that this can only be in circumstances which allow for his unconditional release, along with colleagues and fellow political prisoners, and permit them all to take part in normal political activity … His suffering is seen as the suffering of all who are the victims of apartheid. The campaign for his release has been the galvanising spur for rising black political consciousness across South Africa. His name is emblazoned across the length and breadth of black South Africa … Nelson Mandela has indeed become a living legend. Just as the jailing of nationalist leaders like Mahatma Gandhi and Jomo Kenyatta invested them with a unique aura and helped galvanise resistance to the colonial power, so, we believe, the imprisonment of Nelson Mandela is a self-defeating course for the South African Government to takc.

Mandela, the Group said, was the natural leader of a non-racial South Africa. 'To disregard Nelson Mandela, by continuing his imprisonment, would be to discard an essential and heroic figure in any political settlement in South Africa. His freedom is a key component in any hope of a peaceful resolution of a conflict which otherwise will prove all-consuming.'

Mandela, Tambo and most other black African leaders had now endorsed the Possible Negotiating Concept, but the government had neither accepted nor rejected it. The Group was due to meet the Cabinet Constitutional Committee in Cape Town on 19 May. There seemed every reason to hope. Fraser recalls, 'I actually thought at this stage that we might pull it off, or get some kind of agreement. Nobody had expected us to achieve anything at all, but everyone was saying they wanted negotiations'.

On the very morning of the scheduled meeting, his hopes were dashed. He woke in his hotel room to hear on the radio that the South African Defence Forces had raided African National Congress bases in Harare, Gaborone and Lusaka. This was extraordinary—a violation of international law, and an action against the capitals of the very Commonwealth governments that had helped to set up the Eminent Persons Group. Over breakfast, most of his fellow Group members were convinced that the action was aimed at them. It seemed that the South African Government had deliberately sabotaged the mission. Several of the members wanted to leave the country immediately. Fraser was heavy-hearted, but argued that the 'superglue' rule should still apply. While there was any hope at all, they should keep talking. 'My view was that it was just the government being the government, and you can't see everything that the government does as being aimed at us.'

Soon, though, it was clear that there was no hope. The ministers at the meeting were intransigent. The government had returned to its previous stance: that it was for the African National Congress to make concessions. Once again, they insisted that the party renounce, rather than merely suspend, violence as a condition of talks. This, the Group knew, was neither possible nor a reasonable thing to demand. Later that day, the Group left South Africa. To stay, to attempt further talks, would have been to allow itself to become an impediment to the fight for justice, rather than an aid.

On 6 June, Fraser and Obasanjo wrote to all Commonwealth heads of government reporting their 'reluctant but unequivocal judgement that further talks would not lead anywhere in the circumstances'. The mission to South Africa was at an end. Yet, in another way, it was only just beginning.

* * *

The report of the Commonwealth Eminent Persons Group was released in mid 1986. Within weeks, it had been published as a small book under the title *Mission to South Africa*. It had an enormous impact. From the perspective of the present day it is hard to remember how radical and shocking the book seemed at the time. Many people had believed the South African Government's claims to be reforming apartheid. The Cold War, and the fear that Africa would 'go communist', dominated the thinking of many commentators. Thatcher was still saying that Mandela was a communist, and that sanctions were 'immoral' because they would hurt the very people they were meant to help. Others argued that sanctions would merely 'drive the Afrikaners into their laager'. The 'constructive engagement' policy pursued by Thatcher and Reagan was seen by many as the sensible middle path. Readers of *Mission to South Africa* would have been hard put to adhere to these views. Lucidly written, it was a description and denunciation of apartheid in passionate yet crystal-clear prose, bearing witness to what the Group had seen and illustrated with photos, including some taken by Fraser in the townships and one of Obasanjo standing, hands on hips, on the beach at Port Elizabeth. The report began with bell-like clarity:

> None of us was prepared for the full reality of apartheid. As a contrivance of social engineering, it is awesome in its cruelty. It is achieved and sustained only through force, creating human misery and deprivation and blighting

> the lives of millions. The degree to which apartheid has divided and compartmentalised South African society is nothing short of astounding.

The report went on, with a mixture of forensic analysis and simple yet powerful language, to unpick the South African Government's claim to have reformed apartheid. A chapter was devoted to the central issue of violence, teasing out the impact of state-sanctioned force, and the way in which violence was at the very foundation of the apartheid system. The report described the living conditions in the townships, and gave eye-witness accounts of the behaviour of the South African police and security forces. In these circumstances, it said, it was neither possible nor reasonable for the African National Congress to renounce violence until apartheid had been dismantled. For the first time, a group of people whose judgement and eminence were beyond question pronounced that the South African reforms were hollow, that the African National Congress and Mandela were not communists, and that majority control in South Africa would not lead to a Marxist state. London's *Financial Times* commented that the report was a 'watershed' in the debate on sanctions and apartheid. It was 'extraordinary' that Barber, in particular, had put his name to a document so sympathetic to the African National Congress's world view. *Mission to South Africa*, said the newspaper, had established Fraser and Obasanjo as key figures in the battle to end apartheid. The report had also made it clear that it was the South African Government, not black African leaders, that stood in the way of negotiation. If Thatcher had wanted the Eminent Persons Group to be a device to 'get her off the sanctions hook', then it had 'backfired with a vengeance'.[14]

Fraser, meanwhile, had been reflecting on why, after such a promising start, the South African Government had sabotaged the negotiations. He concluded that the Eminent Persons Group had been a victim of its own success. Everywhere it had travelled, people had expressed their support for Nelson Mandela. All the various black groups had said they would work with him. Before his imprisonment, Mandela had authored the 'Freedom Charter', which had been a rallying document for the anti-apartheid fight. The document was now well out of date. When the Group had asked people why it was not revised and updated, they had been asked in response, 'How can we revise it without Mandela?' The Group had passed all these impressions on to the South African Government. Fraser concluded that while the government had wanted negotiations and an end to violence, this had been because it thought it could control the process. The government had believed its own propaganda: that South Africa was a country of minorities, and, in the case of the black Africans, warring tribes. So long as that was the case, the government had hopes of playing them off against each other; the homeland leaders might be persuaded to embrace the government's proposals for supposed 'power sharing'. But the message of the Eminent Persons Group was that black Africa would unite behind Mandela—a highly intelligent and effective leader. 'I think we were the first ones to bring that message home.' It meant that the government could not control the outcome. 'At that time, they weren't ready to accept that.' As Fraser wrote in the wake of the publication of *Mission to South Africa*, the work of the Group and the potential for a united black population meant that 'A negotiation ceased to be of any use to the government of South Africa'.[15]

* * *

Fraser and Obasanjo began a worldwide lobbying effort in favour of sanctions. Together they wrote an essay, 'What to Do about South Africa', arguing that unless there was real change soon, the country would descend into full-scale guerrilla warfare.[16] If this happened, more violent elements would gain sway and the kind of government that would emerge from violence would inevitably be more radical. The only thing that might—just might—prevent this was for the West to bring real pressure to bear through sanctions. 'Without such actions, the view of black leaders that they are without fundamental support from the West will again be confirmed.' Fraser and Obasanjo argued against the claim that sanctions would hurt black South Africans most of all. First, they said, this was patronising: black South Africans were calling for sanctions, despite the fact that they would suffer. Second, it would be possible to devise some sanctions that would hurt white people almost exclusively. A ban on air links with South Africa would mean that people wishing to travel there would have to do so through Harare or Lusaka. 'At one stroke the dependency of the frontline states on South Africa would be reversed.' Removing consular facilities would mean that travellers would have to go to the frontline states to arrange visas. Freezing of South African bank accounts held overseas would also hit whites more than blacks. These sanctions, they argued, should be added to bans on trade and investment.

> We reject completely the argument that international pressure will force the South African Government to withdraw into itself. That commonly held view is masterly disinformation. It has hitherto been successful in persuading major states not to take substantive measures or impose sanctions against South Africa. The Afrikaners have in fact only changed course when under extreme pressure. Any minimal change which has been achieved in South Africa recently has been as a result of substantial pressure mostly from within South Africa, not as a result of quiet persuasion. Over the last five or six years the two most powerful leaders in the free world, President Reagan and Prime Minister Thatcher, have attempted, by diplomacy, by constructive engagement, to achieve change. At this time the condition of the blacks is worse than it was at the beginning because of the successive emergencies and the use of punitive powers. Why would anyone expect words alone to be successful tomorrow or next year?

Sections of their essay were reproduced in newspapers all over the world. At the same time, Fraser wrote dozens of articles for publication in the Western world's leading newspapers. In the latter half of 1986, these appeared in *The Observer*, *The Times*, the *International Herald Tribune*, *The Washington Post*, the *Los Angeles Times*, *The Age* and *The Australian*. Sanctions might not work, Fraser said, but they might 'offer the last opportunity to avert what could be the worst bloodbath since the Second World War'.[17]

Fraser and Obasanjo wrote to Ronald Reagan, appealing to him to change his hard line against sanctions.

> Mr President, if it had been possible for you to see for one day a small part of what we saw and experienced, we believe that you would want to strain every nerve to redress the situation in South Africa. Words cannot describe the condition of black lives in that country and the thoroughness of the system of racial and economic exploitation which the Afrikaner has instituted.[18]

Shortly after the Eminent Persons Group had reported, the European Economic Community met to consider sanctions against South Africa, but its moves were frustrated once again by Thatcher, who successfully forestalled action by sending her Foreign Minister Geoffrey Howe to visit South Africa in a further attempt at negotiation.

Meanwhile, Fraser was in the United States, lobbying Congress and the Reagan administration. The problem, as Fraser saw it, was not Reagan himself, but the advice he was getting, in particular from Secretary of State George Schultz. Fraser says today, 'Reagan was a very simple man in many ways. It depended on who he had as his advisers. I was never an overweening fan of George Schultz. I'm not sure that he deserved the reputation that he had. In any case, I think that Reagan was badly advised on the issue of South Africa'. Schultz's view of South Africa was dominated by the Cold War and the fear of communism, and this was overriding the simple claim of justice. In the lexicon of the times, the East–West issue of the Cold War was overwhelming the North–South issue of the need for international justice.

Reagan's policy had strong opponents, including within the Republican Party. In June 1985, the House of Representatives had passed tough sanctions legislation with a big majority, but Reagan had headed off Senate action by issuing an executive order imposing much milder sanctions. By 1986, though, a far stronger piece of legislation was before the Congress. In June, Fraser and Obasanjo appeared before the US Senate to argue the case. The US media described Fraser as a 'conservative sheep rancher', and quoted him as saying, 'Some people seem to believe that the yearning for freedom burns less fiercely in the breast of black South Africans than in others. But that is not true. It burns fiercely and it is not going to be put off by gestures'. Fraser admitted that sanctions had no better than a fifty-fifty chance of persuading the South African Government to shift, but if the United States didn't impose them, the world would 'forget that the USA has been the great liberating force in the world. As an Australian I think that would be tragic'.[19] Fraser and Obasanjo were treated to a lecture from George Schultz. 'We went to see him, and he lectured us both about how we shouldn't be running all over town talking to Congressmen and speaking contrary to what Reagan was saying. I think he was more annoyed with me than with Obasanjo. As an ally of the USA, he expected an Australian to support the President. He didn't expect that of Obasanjo.'

Reagan was building up to a major speech on the issue. He was being lobbied by all sides, and particularly by two Republican senators, Nancy Kassebaum and Richard Lugar, who were in close contact with Fraser. The speech had been through numerous drafts. As *Time* magazine later said: 'Republican senators trooped into the Oval Office to argue that it should be toughened; others telephoned White House aides to have it weakened. A committee of competing factions swapped sentences and traded adjectives'.[20] On the eve of the speech, Fraser was expecting to see Kassebaum and Lugar at a reception. They were late. Kassebaum apologised with the words: 'Malcolm, it has been in a good cause. We have been over at the White House and we have redrafted the President's speech and it is one that you will like: it will be a good speech tomorrow morning'. Fraser recalls, 'And so I listened to the speech on the radio the next day, and it was a terrible bloody speech. Richard Lugar rang me back as soon as the speech stopped and said, "Malcolm, I'm sorry, I'm sorry. This is not the speech that Nancy and I left the President with. Somebody got at it after us. We should have stayed there all night"'.

It was indeed a terrible speech.[21] It had been billed as the culmination of a two-month reassessment, but in fact it merely reasserted the policy of constructive engagement. Reagan condemned apartheid as 'morally wrong and politically unacceptable' but praised the South African Government for bringing about 'dramatic change'. He referred to the 'Soviet-armed guerrillas of the African National Congress' and argued against 'the emotional clamour for punitive sanctions', which would be, he said, 'a historic act of folly' that would wreck the economy of southern African nations. He said, 'We need not a Western withdrawal but deeper involvement by the Western business community as agents of change and progress and growth ... We must stay and work, not cut and run'. Archbishop Tutu called the speech 'nauseating'. *The New York Times* columnist James Reston commented: 'Reagan tried unsuccessfully to persuade the extremists on both sides and lost the moderates in the process'.[22]

Thatcher was grateful for Reagan's support, and quoted his speech in arguing her own case. Howe's mission had been an embarrassing failure: Botha had told him firmly that outsiders' views were not welcome. Mandela had refused to see him, as had Tambo. Zambian President Kaunda had agreed to meet him but then delivered a public dressing-down, in which he accused Reagan and Thatcher of being in a 'conspiracy' to preserve apartheid. 'Sir Geoffrey, you people will not be forgiven by history, because South Africa is about to explode. And that you should encourage it to me is incomprehensible', he had said.[23] Nevertheless, Thatcher remained intransigent.

In August, the seven Commonwealth heads of government who had commissioned the Eminent Persons Group met to consider their report and decide on further action. Fraser and Obasanjo were there. They did their best to lobby, but, says Fraser, 'I think Margaret had experienced being persuaded by me once before, and she resented that. So I couldn't get very far, and she was very determined in any case'. The result was what Fraser had spent much of his prime ministerial career trying to avoid: a breach in the Commonwealth. Of the seven countries that had commissioned the Group, six agreed to adopt broad sanctions against South Africa as a 'moral and political imperative … A positive response can no longer be deferred'. As well as trade sanctions, there were to be bans on air links with South Africa, on new investment and on new bank loans. The United Kingdom, on the other hand, agreed only to maintain existing bans, on new investment and tourism promotions. The meeting broke up a day early. In its communiqué, the leaders expressed regret at the 'lack of unanimity, and the heightened strains in our association'.[24] Britain, once again, had turned away from her former colonies.

* * *

In the following month, September 1986, Reagan used his presidential veto to prevent the passage of the US sanctions legislation. Fraser, meanwhile, began a speaking tour of the United States, addressing audiences the length and breadth of the nation on the issue of justice in South Africa.

In the small hours of 14 October 1986, Malcolm Fraser's personal assistant Heather Barwick was awoken in Melbourne by a telephone call from the boss, who was in Memphis to address the local Economic Club. She was still half asleep as he told her that he had been robbed, and that she should urgently cancel all his credit cards and cheque books. It was only later, once she was fully awake and driving to the office to get the details, that she thought over their conversation. Fraser had sounded very strange. She remembers, 'His voice sounded nothing like it normally does. He sounded really awful, as though he had been drugged'. At about the same time as he rang Barwick, Fraser also telephoned Tamie. She remembers, 'He said, "I've been robbed and I've got no clothes and they've taken my wallet", and he sounded really traumatised'.

Barwick cancelled Fraser's cards and cheques, and organised replacements, then set out trying to find him. It was difficult. By the time she eventually got in touch, he was in Los Angeles on the next leg of his speaking tour. He still sounded very strange indeed. Having satisfied herself that he was safe, however, she thought nothing more about the incident until, about three weeks later, the story of what had happened to Fraser in Memphis broke in the Australian media.

So what happened in Memphis? Fraser gave some brief comments to the media at the time, but has never expanded on them. He does not intend to do so now. According to what he said then, on the evening of 13 October, he gave a speech at the Memphis Country Club, where he was meant to be staying. Once the event was over, he set off into the town hoping to find some of the famous live blues venues. The last thing he remembered was having a drink at the Peabody Hotel—the classiest establishment in the city. He woke in a very different place: the Admiral Benbow Hotel, a notoriously seedy dive. He felt dreadful—dizzy and with no sense of balance. He found that his trousers were missing, together with his wallet. His memory of the hours that followed, during which he rang both Tamie and Heather Barwick, is vague, but, as was later revealed, he emerged in the foyer of the hotel wrapped in a towel, borrowed a pair of too-small trousers from the bell hop and got a taxi back to the country club. About two weeks after the incident, an article about it appeared in the Memphis local newspaper, and was picked up by *The Sydney Morning Herald*. Fraser has not been allowed to forget it since.

Today, both Tamie and Heather Barwick are convinced that Fraser was telling the truth, and that he had been drugged. Why and by whom remains a mystery. Probably, he was simply the victim of crime. Businessmen who had travelled overseas contacted him in the wake of the affair to recount similar experiences. On the other hand, by that time Fraser had made plenty of enemies. However, he prefers not to entertain conspiracy theories.

The bitter irony is that October 1986 should have been a month of triumph for Fraser. Just two weeks before he came to grief in Memphis, the US Congress had voted to overturn Reagan's veto on sanctions. The Comprehensive Anti-Apartheid Act became law. This was the first time in the twentieth century that a President's veto had been overturned on a foreign policy matter. It was the biggest foreign policy defeat of Reagan's administration, and the result had been achieved at least partly because of Fraser's work. Memphis overshadowed what was truly a great victory. Once the United States had moved, the European Economic Community, Japan and other countries followed suit.

There was no clear point during Fraser's active involvement in the campaign against apartheid when it was possible to announce victory, yet we now know that the sanctions were indeed crucial to change. We also know, thanks to Mandela's autobiography, that it was after the sanctions started to bite that the South African Government began secret and serious negotiations with Mandela. The financial sanctions were the most effective: the prohibition on lending to the country meant the flow of capital almost dried up. The Reserve Bank advised the government that South Africa was going backwards. The result would be more poverty, more unrest. There was no future in that course. Pragmatism eventually forced the South African Government to the negotiating table. The negotiations were predicated on an identical set of steps to those laid out in the Eminent Persons Group's negotiating concept from years before.

The African National Congress suspended violence. The government released Mandela and other political prisoners from jail, removed troops from the townships, legalised the banned political parties and, over time, ceased much of the state-sanctioned violence.

In 1994, Mandela was elected President by an overwhelming majority in South Africa's first multiracial elections. Fraser says today, 'What our group had done was provide the framework for what had to happen, when the government was ready. They were not ready in 1986. After a few years of real sanctions, they were ready'.

It is surely a cruel irony that what most Australians know and remember about their former Prime Minister in 1986 is not that he played an important role in the end of apartheid in South Africa, and in particular that he helped to persuade Congress to overrule the presidential veto on sanctions against South Africa, but that he lost his trousers in Memphis.

* * *

In 1988, Sonny Ramphal, the Secretary-General of the Commonwealth for the previous fourteen years, announced his intention to retire. He had been an activist, keeping social justice in southern Africa on the agenda for most of the previous decade. The Gleneagles agreement and the move to black majority rule in Zimbabwe were highlights of his term.

Fraser was drawn to the idea of replacing Ramphal. To do so, he would need the support of the Australian Government. He first raised the idea with Bob Hawke in mid 1988, and was delighted to find that he had his unqualified support. The crucial vote was to be taken in October 1989. For eighteen months, Fraser and the entire machinery of Australian diplomacy were involved in an extraordinarily persistent lobbying effort. Fraser had considerable support, but his battle was complicated by a widespread view that it was Africa's 'turn' to head the Commonwealth. The candidate running against Fraser was Ramphal's deputy, the Nigerian Emeka Anyaoku.

Tamie was against Fraser running for the post. She remembers, 'I thought it was too bizarre, frankly'. She knew that her husband was desperate to contribute more to world affairs, but she doubted that the Secretary-General's post would satisfy him. It was by nature a bureaucratic position, acting at the behest of heads of government. 'He's a different sort of person. Mind you,' she says with a laugh, 'if he'd got it he would have tried to make the Commonwealth a rival to the United Nations. He wouldn't have been happy to moulder along with everyone having happy little meetings every couple of years'.

Bob Hawke and the Minister for Foreign Affairs Gareth Evans put themselves on the line supporting Fraser's candidature. Just two months ahead of the crucial vote, the Department of Foreign Affairs and Trade's internal briefing notes were reporting that Fraser was just ahead of Anyaoku.[25] Despite Fraser's strong personal following, most of the African nations—including Mugabe's Zimbabwe—were supporting Anyaoku. Fraser remembers Obasanjo (who was not in office at the time) saying that if the Commonwealth leaders wanted an activist, they would choose Fraser; if they wanted a quiet life, they would choose Anyaoku.

Fraser's main support came from the Asian–Pacific region. His bid was, perhaps predictably, opposed by Margaret Thatcher. New Zealand was also understood to be opposed. By the eve of the vote, at the Kuala Lumpur CHOGM, in October 1989, everyone knew that the result would be close, although convention dictated that, once elected, the successful candidate would be declared unanimously. Hawke pushed for the election to be conducted early in the meeting, and for a secret ballot, thinking that this would minimise the chances of pressure from the big African nations on the smaller countries. None of it worked. Fraser was defeated. Afterwards, Fraser wrote to Hawke thanking him for his support. 'I am particularly appreciative of your own personal involvement. I have some modest understanding of the pressures that can fall on your office and am all the more grateful for the time which you personally devoted to this matter.'[26] Nobody, he acknowledged, could have done more.

Today, Fraser thinks it is probably a good thing that he did not become Commonwealth Secretary-General; Tamie is right. He would have wanted to be an activist—continuing and expanding on Ramphal's legacy. By their vote for Anyaoku, the majority of Commonwealth countries showed that activism was not what they wanted. 'If I had got the job it would have been a constant hassle, because I really wasn't the sort of person they wanted. The Commonwealth has wanted a quiet life ever since.' Anyaoku presided over a period in which the Commonwealth became less active and less influential in world affairs. Fraser would have chosen a different path.

In media interviews at the time of his defeat, Fraser pronounced himself disappointed but not devastated. He said he was finished with politics. He planned to go back to the farm and do some fishing.[27] Yet, even as he licked the wounds of his defeat, he was already enmeshed in another international organisation.

21

CARE

In late August 1992, Malcolm Fraser took a telephone call from Phoebe, his youngest daughter. The child born when he had been serving his first year as a minister in the Holt government had grown into a 25-year-old woman. Now she was ringing from Somalia, where she was working for CARE Australia. She needed Fraser's help to make sense of what had happened. Each time she drove past the city park in Mogadishu, there were more newly dug unmarked graves. Every rural road had its population of walking skeletons. At breakfast time, the smell of the night's corpses wafted over the back wall of the house where she was staying. Each day was an emotional and physical marathon in which an hour's indecision or delay in supplying water, food or shelter could be measured in lives lost. This was the legacy of civil war and famine, and Phoebe was dealing with it. That day, though, had brought her undone.

She had been handing out blankets at one of the CARE feeding centres when armed men had broken through the fence and stolen them. How could they do it, she asked her father. How could anyone take a blanket from a half-starved, half-naked child? Phoebe had already told him about the traditional Somali saying she had heard on her first day in the country: 'My clan against the enemy;

my family against the clan; my brother and I against the family. Me against my brother'. How could she cope with the selfishness, the brutality?

Fraser knew better than to speak anodyne words of comfort to this daughter, his match for idealism and strength of will. Instead, he tried to make sense of what she was seeing. This was what happened, he said, when a country had no laws and no order, no jobs and no government, no welfare, no health system, no dole and no support. This was anarchy—not some abstract concept, but the visceral reality. In such a situation, he said, the strong will always conquer the weak.

Phoebe wrote later that her father's words made dealing with the 'mad environment' a little easier.

> We ask ourselves would the same thing happen in Australia or Britain, and when we look at the newspapers and see the violence within their pages, we know that if there were no checks, no laws, no police, no punishment, that we would have our own people stealing blankets from children too.

After that day, the aid workers learned to rip the blankets in two before handing them out. This made them less valuable on the black market, and they were still big enough to keep little children warm.[1]

Fraser was not only Phoebe's father; he was also, in a way, her boss. Since 1987 he had been the founding Chairman of CARE Australia. Perhaps CARE came along at the right time for Fraser. Certainly, he came along at the right time for it. In late 1986, his work concerning South Africa had been coming to an end. He had once again been confronting the question of what to do with his abundant energy and sense of purpose. Then he received a letter from a man called Ian Harris, who had been commissioned by CARE International to establish an Australian arm of the international aid organisation. Would Fraser consider being its founding

Chairman? Fraser remembered that during his prime ministership, his government had used CARE International to deliver aid to Idi Amin's Uganda. He had been assured that it was a good organisation, and the job had been done well. 'I asked Ian how much time it would take. He said it would be just two or three board meetings a year. I thought that might be a bit of an underestimate.' Fraser was right. CARE, he later said, 'got in my blood'. He was Chairman of CARE Australia from 1987 to 2002—almost twice as long as he had been Prime Minister. For five of those years, between 1990 and 1995, he was also the President of CARE International. CARE gave him 'another life's work'.[2]

It was an easy organisation to be proud of. But helping one's fellow man is a difficult business. Crises bring out the very best and very worst in human beings. Over the years of his involvement in CARE, Fraser was confronted with all the ambiguities, complications and gritty politics of trying to do good.

* * *

CARE began as a collection of US organisations combining to rush emergency food rations to Europe after World War II. The name originally stood for 'Cooperative for American Remittances to Europe'. As the economies of the war-torn continent recovered, CARE's work shifted to the developing world. By the 1970s, CARE International had become a confederation of a dozen national members. The Americans still dominated the organisation, and only CARE USA and CARE Canada were 'operational', meaning that they established and ran their own projects. The other national CAREs were little more than fundraising arms, accessing money available through their governments' overseas aid programs and raising funds from the public.

CARE International had conceived of CARE Australia as just another fundraising organisation. Ian Harris had been given US$250 000 to establish the agency and become its first Chief

Executive. Fraser had a quite different vision: he told Harris that if he was to be involved, he would want CARE Australia to be independent. 'I said to Ian, "All right, if it is an Australian organisation, then it is going to do its own work; it is going to have its own programs, its own representation with governments". Well, that view would have come from both of us, because we had a common mind on those things. I wanted it to be the Australian face of international aid. I wanted young, idealistic Australians to be working around the world, and for our own people to see that money raised in Australia was being spent on Australian projects. I would never have wanted to become involved unless CARE Australia was going to be an active and fully fledged organisation—not just raising money to be spent by the Americans.'

Fraser brought in influential board members from both sides of politics. Ian Macphee joined, as did former Whitlam minister Clyde Cameron. Within a year, CARE Australia had repaid its establishment loan to the international body. Fraser remembers, 'Then CARE International began to ask when they would be getting more money from CARE Australia, and Ian told them there wouldn't be any more money, because we were going operational. We were going to run our own programs'. Harris and Fraser had announced their presence on the international aid scene. CARE Australia was soon able to boast that it was Australia's only fully operational international aid agency.

At the same time as Fraser was getting involved, Phoebe was making her own path. It would be a mistake and a serious misunderstanding of the personalities of father and daughter to think that she merely followed his lead or, for that matter, that he followed hers. The child who had grown up on the edge of the spotlight, seeing her family in the headlines every day, had developed into a tall young woman with a strong resemblance to her father and good doses of his energy and determination. After graduating with an arts degree from the University of Melbourne, she had a brief flirtation with the fashion industry before deciding she wanted to work in international aid. Originally, she had no intention of working overseas. she thought she was better fitted for public relations or fundraising. In typical Fraser style, rather than applying for jobs she wrote to every aid agency in Australia. She remembers, 'I was saying, effectively, that if I liked their replies I might be interested in working for them. Extraordinary front, when you think about it'. The best reply she received was from Harris. After fifteen months of working for CARE in Australia, Phoebe began to travel and 'caught the bug'. Between 1990 and 1996, she worked in the front-line of international aid in twenty-three countries, including South Africa, Kenya, Zimbabwe, Iraq, Bosnia, Serbia and Vietnam. She was in Bangladesh for the floods, Somalia for the famine, Bosnia and Herzegovina during the civil war and Rwanda immediately after the massacres.

Predictably, Malcolm Fraser was a hands-on Chairman. Tony Eggleton, who had worked with Fraser as his Chief of Staff and later as Director of the Liberal Party, was persuaded to take on the position of Secretary-General of CARE International, based in Brussels. Eggleton watched as the former Prime Minister rejected any notion of retirement or personal profit, and instead 'indirectly saved many thousands of lives around the world'. Fraser was able to bring to CARE unprecedented access and power. He toured the projects and the emergency centres.

One 1992 visit to Somalia, made with Eggleton and Harris, coincided with an invasion of nearby Bardere, where a CARE operation was based. It was a tense day. Phoebe advised her father that the situation was too dangerous for the visit to proceed. There was a risk that Baidoa, where Fraser was to visit, would soon be overrun. Phoebe wrote later that her father replied: 'Absolutely not … If it was okay for the team to stay in Baidoa overnight, then it was okay for him to visit'.[3] Fraser toured the feeding centres and the hospital, then went on to Mogadishu and involved himself directly in negotiations with the heads of two of the warring factions, Ali Mahdi and his rival General Mohamed Farah Aideed, in back-to-back meetings. He was asking them both to ensure the safety of the CARE workers in Bardere. Eggleton remembers the meeting with Aideed. 'We walked into this place, and there were half-a-dozen chaps with rifles on their legs, and I thought they could easily shoot us. I was very glad when they stood up and said, "Prime Minister! Welcome!"' Fraser recalls, 'Tony might have thought they could shoot us, but really there was no threat. You can tell when a gun is threatening or not. And both sides said they would do everything they could to help'. The CARE team leader Bob Allen was allowed to leave Bardere in safety later that day, thanks to the intervention of the head of the United Nations peacekeeping force General Imtiaz Shaheen.

On this same visit to Somalia, says Eggleton, 'We were both shocked by the problems of delivering food aid. Malcolm said, "We have to talk to the United Nations about this. I'm going to make a phone call". A few days later we were sitting in an office in New York reviewing the Somalian humanitarian challenge with the United Nations Secretary-General. Life with Malcolm was never dull'.

The growth of CARE Australia was a phenomenon in international aid the like of which had never been seen before, and has not been seen since. It was an extraordinarily energetic organisation, reflecting the personalities of the two men at its head. Fraser liked and admired Harris. 'I don't think there is anyone else who could have got CARE off the ground and made it grow so quickly', he says. But Harris could also be an abrasive man: 'Ian wasn't the easiest person to get on with. He couldn't stomach fools. He was entrepreneurial, sometimes maybe too entrepreneurial. If something needed doing, he would do it, without having to sit around and have a meeting about it. And I suppose he was especially that way because he had a Chairman who would encourage him to do it, or sometimes say, "Why haven't you done it before?" We worked well together'.

They also trod on toes. In the early 1990s CARE Australia was invited to sign an agreement with the European Union to become a provider of emergency aid. None of the European CAREs were operational; CARE Australia had the reputation and the capacity. In 1990, it was CARE Australia that worked with the United Nations to help 370 000 Cambodian refugees return to their homes—an operation that involved considerable logistics, including the building of bridges and roads. By 1995, having started from nothing in 1987, CARE Australia had become one of Australia's largest non-government aid providers. The year 1995 is significant, because it was then that the organisation went through a crisis that nearly brought it undone.

* * *

There are two kinds of aid, and two kinds of aid worker. Different skills and different personalities are needed. Developmental work is long-term and conducted in comparatively stable countries. Programs are implemented that make sustainable differences to people's lives. Phoebe Fraser has commented: 'Development workers are generally more patient and in many ways much stronger people than emergency workers. Their work helps to prevent the types of emergencies more commonly associated with aid work—war, refugees, natural disasters and famine'.[4] Emergency aid workers, on the other hand, must move fast. They run on adrenalin. A day can make a difference to hundreds of lives. The pattern, whether the crisis is war or natural disaster, tends to be similar. First, there must be water. Then there must be shelter and food and medical supplies. Emergencies are about survival, and nothing more. Education and agriculture can wait. Emergency workers have to be resourceful and have initiative. Often, despite the best efforts of their organisation, they are in danger.

One of the main reasons that CARE Australia grew so fast was that from the earliest days it focussed on emergencies. The late 1980s and early 1990s were a tragic period. At the same time as CARE Australia found its feet, there was a string of humanitarian crises: floods in Bangladesh, famine in Sudan, war in Somalia, Rwanda and Bosnia. Harris had a genius for moving quickly. Fraser recalls, 'He knew what was needed in emergencies, and he understood that whoever was there first would get publicity and funds. He wouldn't apologise for making sure that a cameraman went along with the high-protein biscuits and the water sterilising gear, and Australians would see their own people doing vital work, and the funding flowed in'. Within a very short period, CARE Australia had won a high profile and a reputation for doing extraordinary things in trouble spots around the world.

CARE International, though, was at that time chiefly oriented towards developmental work. The practices were correspondingly bureaucratic and rules-bound. Fraser remembers, 'In emergencies, you usually know what you need. You need to work out where people will go to, and where you can set up and help them. And Ian would be in there almost before the emergency had happened working all those things out. CARE International would have a meeting, and then they would want a study done, and then they would have another meeting. Well, you need to do all that for developmental work. In emergencies it is hopeless'.

The focus on fast, effective emergency work suited both Fraser's and Harris's personality. Fraser says, 'I would have been impatient with an aid agency that just wanted to dribble along'. The organisation grew in their image. To suit its emergency work, CARE Australia explored new methods of keeping its workers safe. Private security guards were hired; all projects were equipped with satellite phones. CARE became known for employing a particular kind of aid worker: some had army backgrounds; they were first-class logisticians with a talent for getting things done quickly in awful circumstances. One of these, working in Iraq and later as Country Director in Yugoslavia, was former army Major Steve Pratt, who became the central figure in one of the most dramatic international incidents of the 1990s.

Brian Doolan was another key employee. He was a leftie. He had worked on the staff of a Labor Party federal politician, and for

Aboriginal community–controlled organisations. On the famous night in 1983 when Fraser gave his election concession speech, Doolan had been at a party in an inner-suburban backyard in Sydney. When he saw Fraser weep, he had laughed. Years later, Doolan applied for a job with CARE as a Country Director. He worked in the CARE Middle East Operations office in Jordan, and soon became responsible for CARE's Iraq operation. Phoebe Fraser was based in the same office, working in a unit designed to respond to emergencies in Africa and the Middle East. They became good friends. One day, Malcolm Fraser walked in to Doolan's office. Doolan remembers, 'He just walked through the door and said, "Who are you?"

'And I said, "I'm Brian Doolan".

'And he said, "What did you do before you came to work for CARE, Brian?"

'And I said, "I was an adviser in the Labor Party, Malcolm".

'And he said, "I knew that; I just wanted to see whether you would tell me"'.

Both men laughed. In what lay ahead, Doolan became Fraser's collaborator, adviser and right-hand man. Years later, in Belgrade with bombs dropping around them, he told Fraser that he had laughed on the night of the 1983 election defeat. Fraser took it quite well. 'He said he understood that I had felt that way', Doolan remembers. 'He didn't seem to take offence.'

Doolan recalls, 'CARE Australia in those days had a reputation as the organisation that really got in and did things, and we were caught up in that image. You know, "We are not just an aid organisation; we are a very good aid organisation that can do things others can't do". It became an organisation with a bit of a swagger'. Fraser was not impressed with his first CARE International meetings. Fraser remembers, 'I was waiting for board papers, and I was told they would come in the mail; then I was told they would be given to me the day before the meeting started; then that they would be waiting for me at the meeting. Well, they never turned up. It was just hopeless, and everyone realised that it was hopeless'. When the time came to elect a new international President, Harris encouraged Fraser to run. Fraser recalls, 'I was saying it was too early. I had only been with CARE Australia for a couple of years, but the other person in the race was a Canadian, and he was nearly ninety and wouldn't have done anything or changed anything. Anyway, there was a nominations committee and a slate went up, but the slate got chucked out and I got made President of CARE International. The first thing I had to discuss was the way that business was conducted by the Secretary-General'.

The job of Secretary-General was thrown open. Fraser rang Tony Eggleton, and asked him to apply. Eggleton's qualifications were clearly superior to those of the US candidate, and he easily won the job. Suddenly, the Americans, who had dominated CARE International, were confronted with a fully operational and high-profile CARE Australia, and an Australian President and Secretary-General of the international organisation. Feelings were mollified by the US candidate for Secretary-General being made deputy. He proved very effective. As a long-term worker for CARE, he brought with him the corporate memory of the organisation.

Nevertheless, sadly, international aid is not free of politics and personal tensions. The attitude of CARE USA towards the international organisation began to change. CARE USA suggested a new method of organising CARE International, which was somewhat euphemistically tagged the 'big tent' model. The idea was confused. Fraser says, 'I didn't understand it then and I'm not sure that I understand it now'. It seems that the plan was for the other national CAREs to become little more than franchise operations of CARE USA. As a paper that went to the CARE Australia board put it: 'CARE USA is undoubtedly calling the shots and ... does not see itself as just another equal partner in the confederation'.[5] This was completely at odds with the vision that Fraser had for CARE International. He thought the European CAREs should become self-sufficient and break their dependence on the US arm. He wanted the organisation to be a true federation of equals. As President of CARE International, Fraser was streamlining the administration and improving the links between the different national members. He was moving CARE from being primarily a development agency to an organisation that could also respond quickly to emergencies around the globe and that had a role in advocacy, speaking up for the victims of humanitarian crises. Today, Eggleton says that Fraser, with his international connections and personal energy, 'gave CARE International an influence and clout it had never had before'. But, Eggleton says, 'Malcolm's robust style did not always sit comfortably with other international board members, or the staffs of some member countries'. Chief among these was CARE USA.

Under the rules of CARE International, in each country in which the organisation operated one of the operational national CAREs was designated 'Lead Member'. The Lead Member appointed the Country Director, who was, as Fraser puts it, 'like a little tin god'. Nothing was meant to happen without the approval of the Country Director. All of the administration and the relationships with governments and funding organisations were meant to be organised through the Lead Member. If other national CAREs had projects in the country, they were expected to operate under the Lead Member's umbrella. This worked well enough for developmental projects, but Harris and Fraser thought it broke down in emergencies. As a result, CARE Australia began to push for more independence in the field.

The tensions came to a head after Fraser had visited Sudan in 1994, where CARE Australia was operating a discrete program providing health care to a camp of about seven thousand refugees. CARE USA was the Lead Member, and Fraser as President of the international organisation was treated to what was close to a banquet in the CARE USA compound. He remembers, 'They had lots of deep freezers and lots of refrigerators and all sorts of Western food and, while it wasn't luxury in most circumstances, in the context of where they were, it was certainly very comfortable'. Fraser met two CARE Australia employees—nurses who were working on the Australian project. One of them, Mary-Jane Hammond, spoke to Fraser. 'I said to her, "Where are you staying? Are you part of this establishment?"

'And she laughed and said, "No, not quite".

'And so I said, "Well, where are you?"

'"Oh, we're two or three blocks away."

'She invited me to see it. So when the banquet was over she took me down to see the quarters that she and the other woman were in, and it was a derelict house. The flywire doors were off their hinges; the windowpanes weren't there. There was one tap, cold water only; the only cooking mechanism was a very ancient, worn-out kerosene pressure pump thing; and the loo was a hole in the ground.'

Fraser turned to Harris. 'I said, "Why the bloody hell do you let Mary-Jane and the others live in those conditions? It is an absolute bloody disgrace".

'And he said, "It is up to the Country Director to provide conditions for employees".

'And I said, "I couldn't care less. They are our employees; we're paying them; they're Australians".' The Americans, he told Harris, were to be given one last chance to give the Australians electricity, refrigeration and hot water, or Australia would provide them. 'Ian was delighted to issue ultimatums like that. We were of very similar mind. But he said to me, "You know it will lead to a row with the Americans".

'And I said, "If that's what will happen, let it happen. It is our job to look after our own, and we've got to do it. And if the Americans can't understand that, that's too bad".'

Harris brought the battle on; the US organisation defended its Country Director to the hilt; there were stand-up rows; the bad feeling intensified. But the Australian staff got refrigeration, electricity and hot running water. Fraser comments, 'Ian Harris had a lot of charisma. The staff in the field respected and loved him, because they knew he understood what they were doing and would look after them'.

In late 1994, there was to be a CARE International meeting in Harare. Beforehand, CARE Australia presented a paper suggesting an alternative to the 'big tent' model. Instead, Australia suggested, each country's CARE should be treated as equal, able to operate autonomously within a loose cooperative federation. Australia also proposed changes to the lead member system. Emergency work, the paper said, 'Should be divorced from the more formalised and structured lead membership system. Independent, discrete, loosely coordinated CARE member operations are potentially far more effective in an emergency environment'.[6] The Australian proposal was welcomed by a number of the European CAREs, but meanwhile an ambush was being prepared. Shortly before the Harare meeting, CARE USA, CARE Canada and CARE UK collaborated to lodge an official complaint against CARE Australia, alleging that it had 'violated the established CARE International code' during recent work in Rwanda and Kenya.

There could hardly have been a bigger disjunct between the work being done on the ground and the international politics. Australia had done well in Rwanda. With his usual talent for anticipating trouble, Harris had sent in a team to run a start-up program within days of the massacres. Although CARE USA was the Lead Member, CARE Australia had expanded its operation from neighbouring Zaire, and had insisted on running it independently. Phoebe Fraser was there. At the peak of the crisis there were seven thousand people dying each day. 'At some stage, we all wept', she wrote later. Phoebe was getting up at dawn to do media interviews for prime-time Australian television, then working all day at the frontline, rarely seeing bed before midnight. The Australian public responded, and the operation was able to expand. CARE Australia was asked by UNICEF to run the unaccompanied children's centre, which was taking in up to two hundred lost and orphaned children a day. John Herron, a federal parliamentarian, surgeon and later minister in the Howard government, visited as a volunteer.

All this was fine work, but at the Harare meeting, what mattered was that Australia had broken the rules. The other part of the complaint related to CARE Australia setting up its own office in Kenya, where CARE Canada was the Lead Member. Meanwhile, CARE UK was annoyed because CARE Australia had had meetings with the arm of the British Government responsible for overseas aid. Brian Doolan remembers, 'What particularly annoyed the international CAREs was that Australia was quite unapologetic for what it had done. There was no contrition, no "Oops". That was all part of the swagger of CARE Australia back in those days'.

At Harare, CARE Australia was confronted with a motion—brought forward without notice—under which it would be forced to 'return to compliance' by wrapping up its independent presence in Rwanda and Kenya. The penalties for failing to toe the line would have been other CAREs refusing funding for Australian-run programs, and loss of its Lead Member status in other countries.[7] Fraser was in an awful position, since he had dual roles: President of CARE International and Chairman of CARE Australia. The motion had not been circulated beforehand. Fraser told the meeting that if he was not Chairman of CARE Australia, he would rule it out of order. As it was, he felt his hands were tied. He could not be seen to favour his own organisation. The motion was carried.

In the weeks that followed, CARE Australia received legal advice suggesting that the decision was illegal. The Australian board considered leaving CARE International, but decided in the end to comply, while continuing to push for changes in the lead member system.

Meanwhile, Ian Harris took a call from the Department of Foreign Affairs in Canberra. The substance of the Harare motion had been leaked. 'There is a deliberate campaign to discredit CARE Australia', said Harris in a memorandum to Eggleton.[8] The truth was that CARE Australia was vulnerable. Harris had earned the devotion of many of the CARE Australia staff, but he had also made a few powerful enemies. Among them was a senior bureaucrat within AusAID. Today, Fraser describes this person as 'my least favourite public servant in Australia'.

Trust is crucial for an aid agency. Even in an emergency in which lives are being lost by the minute, all government funding has to be properly acquitted, the accounts audited and reports meticulously prepared. CARE Australia had moved so far and so fast that, in its early years, some of the accounting had been less than perfect. In November 1994, at the same time as it was facing its battles with CARE International, CARE Australia had trouble at home. The Minister for Development Cooperation Gordon Bilney had ordered an audit of CARE Australia's government funding. All was not as it should have been. In one case, funding awarded for one project had been transferred to another. There were also disputes about the extent to which CARE Australia was entitled to claim its overheads. The organisation was ordered to repay amounts relating to two projects: $208 700 from funding for food aid in Mozambique in 1988–89, and another $30 000 relating to an aid project in Sudan. Potentially more damaging were findings that some funds raised from the public had not been used in the ways that had been promised. There had been a 'Trucks for Bosnia' fundraising campaign when there was an urgent need to get food supplies deep into that country. By the time the money was raised, however, the plans had changed. The trucks on offer were found not to be suitable. No trucks were purchased, but the money was spent on other means of transportation.

There was no suggestion that the money had gone astray in the sense of being improperly used by individuals. The audits of CARE Australia's accounts found that since its inception, 95 per cent of funding had gone directly to projects in the field. The average for similar organisations in Australia was 89 per cent.[9] CARE Australia's administrative costs were unusually low. Despite this, officials within AusAID encouraged the auditor to include a recommendation that some matters be referred to the federal police for further investigation. Fraser recalls, 'The auditor didn't think it was necessary. It was that one official in AusAID that insisted'. For the next eighteen months, Fraser was pleading with the police and the federal government to speed up the investigation. 'Of course, it wasn't a high priority for the police, but while it was unresolved, we weren't eligible for federal funding.' When the police finally turned their attention to the issue, they quickly found that there were no grounds for an investigation, but in the meantime CARE Australia's reputation had been badly damaged.

Today, Fraser puts the problems down to the speed of CARE Australia's growth, and the nature of emergency work. 'You know, you are not just sitting down behind a nice desk. In emergency situations, certainly you've got to look after the books—you've got to account for all the funding—but it is not doing normal commercial business in a normal, quiet, peaceful environment. There were lessons for us in the audit, but at the same time what are you going to do in a situation like Somalia? You are not going to say, "Oh, I could save a life here, but I'm not going to because I have to hire another accountant first".'

CARE Australia had repaid the money to the Australian Government and was moving towards 'compliance' with CARE International's rules when it was hit by another disaster. On 26 May 1995, Channel Nine's *Sunday* program devoted an episode to CARE Australia in which all the troubles were cast in the worst possible light. It was said that CARE Australia had 'mismanaged vital aid projects ... misused funds and ... deceived the Australian public, the Australian Government and the United Nations'.[10] The Harare censure motion was canvassed, as were the findings of the audit. Added to this were entirely fictitious allegations that rice had been used to pay bribes and that CARE Australia had 'double dipped' by applying for funding for the same project from two sources. The damage was immense. Partly because of Fraser's profile, the rest of the media were quick to follow up on the *Sunday* allegations. Donations plummeted. By the middle of 1995, the CARE Australia board was considering a list of options, including winding up the organisation.[11] Fraser says today, 'I was not prepared to wind it up. So far as I was concerned that was not an option'. Instead, he threw himself into a special fundraising effort, using his connections. Within a few weeks he had raised more than $1 million for a special reserve fund. This was not to be used without an express decision of the board. Never again would CARE Australia be so vulnerable to a breach in its relationships with government, or to a crisis in public confidence.

Ian Harris resigned in the middle of the year. Today, Fraser says he went of his own accord. 'He realised he had to go. I still don't know anyone else who could have begun an organisation like CARE, and got it up and running and made it a viable operation. None of the other national directors could have done that. They didn't have the get up and go, or drive. So in that sense Ian and I were alike, and our personalities probably suited each other, because I would have lost patience with an organisation that just dribbled along. But Ian had a few powerful enemies, including the one in AusAID. I think that he was nearly always right, but perhaps, a bit like me, he thought that the right should prevail, when sometimes size and power prevail'. In 1995, CARE Australia had to make peace in order to survive.

* * *

Tony Eggleton, Secretary-General of CARE International, was in the Brussels office in mid 1995 when he took the latest life-changing telephone call from Malcolm Fraser. Would he come back and run CARE Australia? Eggleton agreed to return to take over from Ian Harris on one condition: that the organisation committed itself to rebuilding and developing cooperative relationships with CARE International, other aid agencies and the Australian Government. One of the first things Eggleton did was negotiate the dropping of a defamation action by Fraser and the board against the *Sunday* program. Eggleton dealt personally with Kerry Packer, owner of Channel Nine, and struck a deal in which CARE

Australia dropped its action and Channel Nine agreed not to pursue legal costs. Meanwhile, both Eggleton and Fraser visited Labor government ministers and found them mostly sympathetic. Eggleton remembers, 'There was a strong feeling that they were glad things were going to be sorted out because they would hate to lose CARE Australia'. Within a few weeks of Harris's departure, Gordon Bilney announced that government funding was being restored to CARE Australia, despite the fact that the federal police had not yet come to a conclusion on whether or not to investigate the matters raised by the audit. Bilney told parliament that he had every confidence in the organisation. The problems discovered by the audit had all dated from its very early days, and everyone accepted that better systems were now in place.[12] Fraser comments, 'Eggleton was the peacemaker. He is much better at that kind of thing than me'.

When Eggleton sat down in December 1995 to write his end-of-year message for CARE Australia staff, he was able to report that the organisation had come through 'the worst of the storm' in what had been 'a pretty rugged year'. Research had shown 'an encouraging trend' in public perceptions of CARE Australia. Direct mail campaigns were again attracting a good level of donations. The new Governor-General Sir William Deane had agreed to be CARE Australia's patron. Thanks to Kerry Packer, Channel Nine was running CARE Australia community service announcements, and Eggleton said, 'We are enjoying fruitful and cordial relationships with AusAID and we have the friendship and good will of the whole CARE International network'.[13]

So far as CARE International was concerned, new rules had been set up governing emergency operations, and there were new guidelines on lead members and country directors. Heads had been pulled in all round. Eggleton stayed as Secretary-General for just one year, and then moved to the board. He had never wanted to run the organisation long-term. He was replaced in mid 1996 by Charles Tapp, formerly of CARE UK.

The changes to CARE Australia came at a cost. It became more bureaucratic—a mature organisation. Fraser says, 'It had to be so, I suppose. But if CARE Australia had been bureaucratic in its early days, it would not exist. We had to try to be best, try to be fastest, try to be quickest, especially in emergencies. How else could we have gotten in front of the Australian public, and raised the money and done the work?' The organisation settled down. The swagger had gone. But the dramas were not over.

* * *

As Fraser had feared, the collapse of communism in eastern Europe had not brought a new golden age. It was not the end of history. Instead, in the last years of the millennium, the world watched as the former socialist federal republic of Yugoslavia was racked by the deadliest conflicts since World War II, characterised by mass war crimes and a new euphemism for genocide: 'ethnic cleansing'. The West's policy towards Yugoslavia had helped to exacerbate the conflict. Germany had declared that it would support the independence of Croatia and Slovenia if they wished to secede; this guaranteed the break-up of Yugoslavia. There had been slaughter in Bosnia, with human rights abuses on all sides. More than half a million Serbs had been driven from their homes, and hundreds were murdered by the Croats, who abused human rights as viciously as the Serbs had done elsewhere. CARE Australia was one of the main aid agencies helping the resulting refugees, most of whom were Serbs.

In 1998, it seemed there was to be another catastrophe in the Yugoslav region of Kosovo, as Serbs and the Muslim Albanian majority fought over the future of the province. For the Serbs, Kosovo was heartland, as vital to national identity as Jerusalem to the Jews. But for several years the Albanian Kosovo Liberation Army had waged a guerrilla war to 'liberate' Kosovo. The United States' approach, in Fraser's view, was partisan, interpreting the conflict as Serbian persecution of Albanians, when the truth was something closer to civil war. Fraser later said: 'There are no saints in the Balkans, but likewise I do not believe any one race or group should be demonised and made responsible for all the sins of the region'.[14] The United States, in his view, was all too ready to act against the Serbs, when the Albanians were equal aggressors. Meanwhile, thousands of people had been driven out of their homes and into the hills as winter descended.

In February 1999, there was an attempt by the United States and its North Atlantic Treaty Organisation (NATO) allies to impose a settlement in talks at the French castle of Rambouillet. Henry Kissinger later described the settlement as 'a provocation, an excuse to start bombing. Rambouillet was not a document that an angelic Serb could have accepted. It was a terrible diplomatic document that should not have been presented in that form'.[15] Fraser agreed. 'I am not sure there were any angelic Serbs, but no Serb leader would or could have signed that agreement.' Yet NATO was threatening to bomb Serbia unless President Slobodan Milosevic agreed to arrangements that would effectively encourage the secession of Kosovo and allow NATO troops free access to any part of Yugoslavia. The NATO powers were depicting the intervention as humanitarian. Fraser thought this clearly false: the United States was being 'partisan and spurious', ignoring the human rights abuses perpetrated against the Serbs and exaggerating those perpetrated by them. The US Secretary of State Madeleine Albright was apparently determined that NATO should act.

On 23 March 1999, NATO began to bomb Yugoslavia. It was, as Fraser argued publically at the time, a clear breach of international law. There was no United Nations Security Council resolution authorising the action, and NATO was perverting its own charter, which forbade it from going to war unless it was to defend a member state under attack. The British Prime Minister Tony Blair described this as a new kind of 'progressive' war, aimed at preventing barbarism within Europe and preserving the principle of freedom from persecution. US President Bill Clinton described the bombing as a 'moral imperative'. This, Fraser thought, was another example of the dangerous thinking he had detected in the post–Cold War US mindset. The United States saw itself as having a unique moral duty that justified unilateral action outside the rule of international law. The US state department had once regarded the Kosovo Liberation Army as a terrorist organisation, but had now rebadged its members as freedom fighters against Serb oppression. As Fraser said later: 'The only thing that had changed was state department policy'.[16]

Even on pragmatic grounds, Fraser thought the bombing was wrong. The NATO leaders believed that a few days of bombing would bring Milosevic to the negotiating table. They were wrong. Fraser says today, 'If there hadn't been any bombing, Milosevic would have been removed by his own people within six months. I met dozens of Serbs who hated him and had been ready to act against him. But the Serb mentality was: "Everyone is against us, so when we are under attack—seven hundred million of the world's richest people against eleven million Serbs—what can we do but unite?"'

CARE Australia had been feeding tens of thousands of refugees in Yugoslavia. When the bombing began, the aid workers were forced to retreat. Locally employed workers were sent on leave, and most of the foreigners were evacuated, but the Country Director Steve Pratt and his colleague Peter Wallace remained in Belgrade, hoping that the war would not last long and they would be able to resume work. Pratt, a former army Major, was a logistics expert. For weeks before the bombing began, he had been sending regular situation reports back to CARE in Australia, detailing the military action of both Serbs and Albanians and trying to calculate its impact on his work. CARE Australia had to know which roads and bridges were open, and where there was conflict, in order to be able to deliver supplies to the refugees safely. Such information was vital to its mission. Pratt had a high profile with the media covering the war. The CARE workers were well placed to bear witness to the gap between Blair and Clinton's rhetoric of 'moral war' and the reality.

When NATO bombed two refugee centres in Serbia, it was Pratt who brought it to international attention.

After the seventh night in a row of NATO bombing and with no end in sight, Pratt and Wallace decided it was time to leave the country. Early on the morning of 31 March, in the car park of the Hotel Intercontinental in Belgrade, they loaded two vehicles with reports, laptop computers and satellite telephones, and then headed for the Hungarian border, about five hours away. Along the drive they changed their minds and decided to take the shorter route to the Croatian border. As they drove, they were using their mobile phones to stay in touch with CARE Australia and their families. Then they reached the border, and disappeared.

Fraser found out that the two CARE Australia workers were missing within hours of their disappearance. The Australian Ambassador to Yugoslavia Chris Lamb was in Australia and on leave at the time. He got on a plane straightaway with Charles Tapp. Meanwhile, Fraser began to make his own plans to travel to Europe. 'I thought that I ought to go and be near the scene of action. I was the only one in CARE International with the contacts and the knowledge and the capacity to get other governments supporting us.'

The Yugoslav authorities denied any knowledge of the two men. It seemed likely that they were dead—perhaps picked up and killed by one of the paramilitary groups that obeyed nobody's rules but their own. Brian Doolan, by this time working in the CARE Australia headquarters, remembers, 'It was horrible. I had worked with both Steve and Peter in the Iraq operation, and so it was a bad period. The whole organisation was in shock'. If there was any hope, it seemed to lie in gaining a lot of media attention to try to convince anyone holding the men captive that they were an asset, and should not be killed out of hand.

Then, on 11 April, Serbian television broadcast a grainy video of Pratt supposedly 'confessing' to being a spy. By then, one of CARE's Yugoslav workers, Branko Jelen, had also been arrested. At least the Yugoslav authorities were now admitting that Pratt and

Wallace were in custody. Within days, Fraser was in Yugoslavia and by the end of the following week the Minister for Foreign Affairs Alexander Downer had appointed him the Australian Government's 'special envoy' with responsibility for negotiating the prisoners' release. The idea had come from Fraser, although Downer willingly agreed. Fraser wanted as much official clout as he could muster to negotiate with the Milosevic regime. So began five of the most extraordinary months of his life, during which he, Tapp and Doolan crisscrossed the globe in their efforts to free the three men.

* * *

Bombs were still falling when Fraser made the first of his five trips into Belgrade. Tamie, who remained in Australia, remembers ringing Fraser at his hotel. 'I'd hear these enormous bangs, and I'd say, "What's that?"

'"Oh", he'd say, "there's bombs dropping down the street. Don't worry: all the press are in this hotel. They never bomb the hotels the press are in".'

Doolan was with Fraser on his second trip, having had to wait in Zagreb for a visa to be issued. He remembers, 'We sat for a long time at the border crossing. There was no other traffic into Yugoslavia. I remember listening to the sounds of birds at the border crossing because it was so quiet. It was the same crossing at which Pratt and Wallace had been arrested. It was a very strange experience. After a long period we were across the border. We were met on the Yugoslav side by Chris Lamb and one of his staff, and the trip into Belgrade was very slow because there was bombing in front of us. And then when the bombing finished we went so fast that it was really equally frightening'. That night, they met the Chinese Ambassador. NATO had managed to put a bomb through the Chinese embassy, and was claiming it was a mistake. Doolan says, 'Malcolm made a point of giving his very sincere condolences, and he was very firmly of the view that it was not an accident, that there was plenty of information about the location of the Chinese embassy, and he saw that as an incredibly provocative act and he was deeply angry about it'.

Fraser says that travelling to Belgrade taught him in a direct and visceral way what he had known in theory: that in a war, one's own 'side' can lie as comprehensively as any enemy. The Chinese embassy had been clearly marked on maps. Fraser believes that NATO was targeting communications equipment in the belief that it was being used to help the Yugoslavs. In the days that followed he saw other examples of NATO's lies. The Belgrade Central Hospital was bombed, and the claim was made by NATO's spokesman that it was the Serbs' fault because a command centre and tanks squadron had been located next door. Fraser remembers, 'So I said, "I want to cancel my appointments this morning and go to the Belgrade Central Hospital". They showed me the children's ward with a smart bomb through the middle of it, and all around the building I looked for tank tracks. There were none. There was no sign of any command centre, no scar marks in the bark of any of the trees in the park. The idea that there was a command centre behind it was absolute bloody nonsense'.

On another occasion, Fraser heard the NATO spokesman say that a factory that built aircraft for the Serbian airforce had been destroyed. Later that day he was passing the building, and went to investigate. 'We walked through the building. It was making windows and structural components for low-cost housing. In one corner of it there were a few aircraft fuel tanks, but nothing was being made for the airforce. The Serbs realised their airforce wouldn't survive five seconds against NATO forces, so they never used them. No parts for aircraft were being made at that factory at that time.'

One day, he was due to have dinner with the United Nations' High Commissioner for Human Rights Mary Robinson, who had been touring the southern town of Nis, where civilians had been killed by NATO cluster bombs. 'She arrived late, looking terribly pale. She had been walking through suburbs of flattened houses.' Later, Robinson put out an extraordinary and brave statement criticising NATO for killing civilians, and questioning the legality of the bombings. She told the United Nations Human Rights Commission in Geneva that both sides could be accused of war crimes.[17]

Meanwhile, Fraser, Doolan, Tapp and the CARE team were putting all their effort into persuading the Yugoslav authorities to release the CARE workers, walking both the dark side and the light side of international diplomacy. Doolan remembers, 'It was a time of extraordinary adrenalin. We were prepared to try anything. Charles Tapp and Malcolm and I would have spoken on the phone perhaps ten times a day, no matter where we were on the globe. And there were times, with the emotion of it, that I remember having to talk to the staff back in Australia, and you would find everyone getting choked up. It is hard to describe what it was like'.

During the first few days of his captivity, Pratt had been beaten. The so-called 'confession' that had been broadcast on Serbian television had been extracted when he was in fear for his life. Now, though, he was in the hands of the Yugoslav prison system and things were improving. By mid April, Chris Lamb had been granted consular access to the men, and a week later Fraser was allowed to see them for the first time. Pratt later described the scene:

> I am stunned to look up and see that with the Australian Ambassador … is the looming and massive figure of Malcolm Fraser. He is dressed in a dark blue pinstriped suit. Absurdly, I notice at first how large his bloody feet are! It is tremendous to see him, and for a fleeting second I fantasise that he is here to collect me and take me away. More than anything else in the world right now, I just want to get up and walk out that door with Malcolm Fraser. Malcolm is forcing a brave smile and I will be damned if I can't see just a small quivering at the corner of his mouth and a little moisture in one of his eyes … He is as big as an oak tree and his presence for me that minute is very, very important.[18]

Milosevic's regime was surrounded by a Mafia-style network of state-sanctioned criminal activity that extended over the borders of Yugoslavia and through Albania, Italy, Macedonia and beyond. Doolan says, 'To exercise any influence with Milosevic, it was necessary for us to map that network as much as we could. We were trying to seek the patronage or the favour of powerful individuals in that network to intervene and to say to Milosevic, "These guys are a distraction; your fight is with NATO. You've got a couple of Australian aid workers. Your image is not looking good. Just throw them out". That was the strategy'. Many dubious characters 'came out of the woodwork' and claimed to have the ear of Milosevic. Some of them had information. They were able to give Fraser and the team precise information about meetings that had been held between the senior figures of government. Fraser resolved to speak to anyone who might be able to bring influence to bear, but he knew there were risks and barriers. He would not, he made it clear to the team, talk about money. The men were prisoners, and they were innocent; they were not hostages.

Meanwhile, Fraser and Lamb were calling on all the official representatives of government in Yugoslavia who would agree to see them. Fraser was travelling all over Europe and beyond, drumming up support. Kenneth Kaunda of Zambia made a statement advocating the CARE workers' release. Olusegun Obasanjo, newly elected for a second term as President of Nigeria, rang and offered to help in any way he could. By now it was clear that Pratt, Wallace and Jelen would be charged, and there would have to be a trial. The CARE workers would be allowed a defence. There would be the opportunity for an appeal. Fraser remembers, 'But we were also told that the result was never in doubt. One way or another they would be found guilty. The process would be fair, but the result would be political'. The main hope was an appeal to Milosevic for clemency, combined with international pressure.

One night, Fraser encountered the notorious Serbian career criminal Zeljko Raznatovic, better known as Arkan. He was an untouchable figure, operating with Milosevic's blessing. Arkan headed one of the most notorious paramilitary forces in the Yugoslav wars. Even before the war, he had been on Interpol's most-wanted list for robberies and murders. During the chaos and paranoia that were Belgrade under the bombing, Arkan seemed to be making a point of being visible in the international hotels, including the Hyatt, where Fraser was staying. Arkan's henchman approached Fraser and Doolan and invited them to meet his boss.

'Should we speak to him?' Doolan asked.

'Certainly', said Fraser. 'He has influence.'

They sat down together. Arkan drank no alcohol, but quaffed numerous cups of tea. Fraser remembers, 'He had one of the toughest army men I had ever seen with him. I could believe that he might do anything, but Arkan himself had quite a baby face'. Arkan told Fraser that he was convinced Pratt and Wallace were innocent, and he said he would help to get them released.

In April and May, Fraser visited President Ahtisaari of Finland, who was one of the few European leaders still talking to Milosevic. He secured statements in the men's support from Nelson Mandela, Reverend Jesse Jackson and United Nations Secretary-General Kofi Anan. Meanwhile, CARE asked other aid agencies working in Yugoslavia to let it be known that their operations might not continue if the men remained in captivity. Particularly helpful were the International Committee of the Red Cross and the United Nations Office for the Coordination of Humanitarian Affairs. The strategy, worked out between Fraser, Doolan and Tapp, was to emphasise Yugoslavia's need of humanitarian aid along with the risk that aid agencies would pack up shop if the CARE workers were not released. Doolan remembers, 'Malcolm left absolutely no stone unturned. He harassed Downer's office; he harassed Howard's office; he harassed the Department of Foreign Affairs and Trade; he stayed on the back of all the embassies. He did media interviews. Those three men could easily have been forgotten, but he kept them in the media and on the international agenda, purely through extending and using his international networks. It was extraordinary to watch'.

The Department of Foreign Affairs and Trade provided help. Murray Cobban was the CARE group's main point of contact, and he was, Fraser remembers, 'enormously helpful'. The minister's office was not always so helpful. Doolan says, 'I think there was a bit of jealousy, really, that there we were, with a former Australian Prime Minister, getting all the profile. There were certainly times when it was tense'.

In early May, Fraser and Doolan were in Belgrade, and wondering how long they should stay. Doolan had organised legal representation for the men and had talked to the remaining CARE staff, all locals who particularly appreciated the cartons of cigarettes he carried with him. Fraser had a commitment to give a Commonwealth speech in London the next day. Doolan and Fraser retired to their rooms, having agreed to reassess in the morning. If there was nothing left for them to do, they might as well leave. In the middle of the night, Doolan heard a knock on his hotel room door. 'I opened it and there was somebody from the embassy, and Malcolm in his dressing gown. Malcolm said, "Oh, Brian, we will be leaving early in the morning".

'"What's the problem?"

'"Well, the charges have been released. You have been named in the indictment as being one of the spy masters."'

Doolan, along with Tapp, had received Pratt's detailed situation reports, and was therefore cast as being at the centre of the alleged spy ring. Doolan remembers, 'So here I am sitting in a country at war, and named as being a spy master. So we decided that we would make a strategic withdrawal very early in the morning, and I breathed a sigh of relief when we crossed the border the next day'. Doolan did not return to Yugoslavia until after the official end of the war, in late June.

On his sixty-ninth birthday, on 21 May 1999, Fraser was attending a meeting of the Interaction Council in Cairo. Heather Barwick, his personal assistant, was travelling with him. She remembers that there was a dinner held on a boat on the Nile. While they were waiting to board, Fraser was spending every minute on a mobile phone trying to reach his international contacts. 'He was frantic to get in touch with people, then once we were on board, he discovered the phone was out of range. By this time we were mid river, the party was going, and there were security speedboats alongside, and he was demanding to be let off the boat so he could finish his calls.' Then, as he protested, he was presented with a cake. A belly dancer began to gyrate in front of the group. His fellow council members were trying to celebrate his birthday. Barwick remembers, 'He just sat there and fumed'. Reminded of this today, Fraser looks surprised. 'Was it my birthday?' he says. 'I didn't realise that.'

Fraser had been working at understanding the Milosevic regime. 'I don't exactly have a reputation for being diplomatic', he says, 'but I understand negotiation. You have to understand the other person's view. You have to understand what it is possible for them to give you, and both of those things may be less than what you want, but that is the place that you start. And you must not let yourself get provoked. I said to the team, "No matter what these people say to us, we will not be provoked. We will talk calmly and rationally to them"'. In one meeting with a Yugoslav Government minister, Fraser had to deal with the effect of a statement by Downer that the Serbians were behaving like barbarians. 'I pretended I hadn't seen Downer's statement, but I had. They were saying, "So, if we are barbarians, why don't we kill these men straightaway? Why don't we cut off their ears and their fingers and their tongues, if we are barbarians?" It took two hours to get that off the table and begin to be able to talk about real things.'

Fraser asked the Australian Department of Foreign Affairs and Trade to do some research on Milosevic's wife, Mirjana Markovic, who was influential with her husband. He was told that the research department no longer existed. 'I wanted to try to see if there was any avenue or argument that I could use that would appeal to her.

I needed insight into how she thought. So I asked the department if there was anyone who could do some research, and they gave me 100 pages of research off the computer which was about the wrong political party and the wrong woman.' Fraser organised his own research. 'I got a lot of stuff she had written. She was saying, "Everybody wants our country. It is so beautiful. It is so wonderful, the most wonderful country in the world, and that is why we are always under attack, and that is why Serbs must stick together, to defend what we have; otherwise, we will lose it forever". That was the thinking, and there was a historical strand through it. And you could see there was some truth at the basis of it, and understand how it would feel to be under the bombs. It helped me to understand the thinking.'

Even before the CARE workers had been captured, Fraser had been on the record as opposing the NATO bombing. He continued to publish columns and articles condemning it, and drawing attention to the damage done to civilians. These were his genuine views, but he was also aware that with Howard and Downer in lock-step with NATO, his preparedness to speak out might operate in the CARE workers' favour.

Back in Australia, Doolan had found a woman who had had contact with Milosevic's wife through the Communist Party. He rang her and asked if she would speak to Fraser to help him gain some insights. The woman agreed, and a telephone conference was arranged, but by the time Fraser made the call, the woman had changed her mind. Doolan recalls, 'We were sitting round the table with the phone on loudspeaker, and the woman said to Malcolm, "Look, I've thought about this and I am not prepared to deal with you, Mr Fraser. I have no respect for you". And she was really very strong about that, talking about the dismissal and so on, and I saw him flinch. He was so focussed on getting these guys out, and I think he was really hurt by the idea that here was an Australian who would put the politics of what he had done in front of helping these two Australian guys who were caught in a war zone and in a jail. But he was very good. He just said something like, "I respect your views, and if you want to reconsider and talk to us at a later stage, I'd be very keen to learn of your experience"'.

Meanwhile, Fraser had made an alarming discovery. While in London, he was told that during the lead-up to the NATO bombing, CARE Canada had signed a contract with the Government of Canada—a NATO member—to recruit people to help monitor events in Yugoslavia. The monitoring had been done for the Organization for Security and Co-operation in Europe (OSCE). It was not for the purposes of war, but rather to monitor the peace. Nevertheless, the Belgrade CARE office had been used to provide the monitors with administrative support. In the eyes of the Yugoslavs, the OSCE and NATO were close to one and the same thing. Fraser says, 'It was an honourable program, but in the context of a paranoid country about to be bombed it was a reckless decision to involve CARE'. The contract meant that CARE had, in fact, been involved in what amounted to an intelligence operation—no matter how innocent the purpose. Pratt, as Country Director, had objected to the arrangement and had put his objections in writing. Nevertheless, the contract had gone ahead with the agreement of Tapp, and without Fraser's knowledge. 'There I was trying to get these men out of jail on spy charges, and then I find this out.'

It was a bad moment for Fraser, and possibly a worse one for Charles Tapp and CARE Australia's Director of International Operations Robert Yallop, who had to admit to Fraser that they had been aware all along of CARE Canada's involvement with the OSCE. 'After I had finished speaking to Yallop he said he was going to walk round the block and that he might not come back', Fraser recalls. Doolan felt the reverberations from Australia. 'Malcolm was absolutely furious', he says. 'He tore strips off him.' Fraser says today that Yallop was a very good CARE development officer. He valued him highly. But CARE should never have agreed to the OSCE arrangement, particularly when it was opposed by the Country Director. Opposing such arrangements was one of the things that had earned Ian Harris enemies within CARE International. After the Yugoslav experience, CARE International made a formal declaration that the organisation should no longer be involved in such programs. 'It's not that the program was bad', Fraser says. 'It is just an inappropriate thing for an aid organisation to do.'

The CARE team had no idea whether the Yugoslavs knew about the OSCE contract or planned to raise it in court. The defence team had to be prepared, but they didn't want to tip off the authorities. In the utmost secrecy, the team compiled the evidence for the defence. Depositions were collected from people in the Canadian Government. The letter in which Pratt had objected to the contract was dug up. Rather than carry all this material into Belgrade, where hotel rooms had already been searched and little was secure, the documents were kept in Budapest until the day before the trial, then brought to Belgrade in the diplomatic pouch. Thankfully, they were not needed. No mention of the OSCE was made in the trial.

The trial began on 26 May. Nine of Pratt's detailed situation reports formed the evidence for the spying allegations. No mention was made of the so-called 'confession'. The evidence fell a long way short of proof that there was a spy ring. The men were found not guilty, but, on the last day of the trial, the judge made use of a common provision of European law in which a new charge can be added to the indictment, providing the penalty is less than that for the original charge. The new charge, of which the men were declared guilty, was providing secret information to a foreign organisation. Any aid worker, and all of the journalists operating out of the war zone, would have been guilty of the same thing. An appeal was lodged, but it was clear that the men's main hopes lay in Milosevic granting clemency. Although the result was never in doubt, Fraser likes to comment today that the trial process in Yugoslavia at war was more just than the US military courts used against terrorist suspects during the time of George W Bush's presidency.

In the meantime, faced with the possibility of a NATO ground attack, Milosevic began peace negotiations. By late June, the war was over. The conditions of the peace were considerably fairer to Serbia than the conditions that had been offered at Rambouillet. At Rambouillet, the occupying force was to be NATO; at the end of the war, it was agreed that it should be the United Nations. At Rambouillet, it had been insisted that NATO should have free access to any part of Yugoslavia; at the end of the war, it was agreed that the United Nations force should be restricted to Kosovo. As well, it was agreed that Kosovo would be recognised by the international community as an integral part of Yugoslavia. Fraser says today, 'If those conditions had been offered to Milosevic at Rambouillet, there would have been no excuse for the war. The USA has never explained why that wasn't done'.

With the ending of the war, there was much less political motivation for keeping the CARE men in jail. Fraser and the CARE team was being told by contacts in the Yugoslav military that Milosevic's senior army officers had advised him to release the workers. They were told that there was 'paranoia' in the Milosevic household that made it difficult to predict what he would do. The international pressure continued. The Victorian Labor backbencher Dimitri Dollis arrived in Europe to garner support in the Greek community. Australian Serbs organised to intervene directly with Milosevic, and were highly effective. In fact, this intervention was one of the most effective actions of all.

Meanwhile, work continued in the shadows. Charles Tapp, operating out of Vienna, was introduced to a man who called himself simply George. He claimed to be representing the Milosevic regime. Eventually it emerged that George was the Yugoslav Ambassador in Vienna, with the full name of Djordje Eugenisevic. Tapp was also introduced to Tomislav Vesovic, the Manager of Yugoslav Airlines in Vienna. As Tapp mentioned in his briefing notes to Fraser, it was some time since the airline had flown out of Vienna, which raised a question 'I wonder what he really does?' The message from these men was clear: Yugoslavia wanted something in return for the CARE workers' release. The Yugoslavs, Tapp was told, did not want to negotiate with the Australian Government, because 'Downer is viewed as a fool and American puppet'. The Australian Ambassador Chris Lamb was 'much liked and respected' but was 'unconventional, and he and his staff are unable to keep their mouths shut'. Fraser, on the other hand, was respected because he had spoken in opposition to the bombings. The meetings with CARE had to be kept quiet, Tapp was warned, or, 'The keys would be thrown away'. The proposal advanced by Eugenisevic was that Fraser should enter into a 'gentlemen's agreement, like the Mafia, whereby the other side could be trusted to do the right thing'. There would be two parts: first, a guarantee of humanitarian assistance from CARE, together with funding from the Australian Government; second, help with reconstruction, particularly the electricity supply. The gentlemen's agreement would commit Fraser to using his contacts in China and Japan to help the Yugoslavs gain finance for infrastructure reconstruction.[19]

It was not clear to Fraser and the team whether the men talking to Tapp could really deliver the CARE workers' release, but the CARE team continued its policy of talking to anyone who might be able to exert influence. A gentlemen's agreement was drafted. This was ticklish territory. The agreement committed Fraser to no more than he might have been prepared to do in any case: giving humanitarian aid, and lobbying. Yet the process was murky. Tapp, Doolan and Fraser discussed whether, in effect, the men were now hostages being held to ransom. 'No money terms can be discussed', Fraser told Tapp. The meetings continued but came to nothing. The agreement was never signed or endorsed in any way, and today Fraser and Doolan believe that the dealings in Vienna were irrelevant to the final outcome of the crisis. In the meantime, Downer visited Belgrade but was snubbed by Milosevic and his request for the men's release was turned down.

The controversial Italian lawyer Giovanni di Stefano got in touch with Downer, who passed the contact to Fraser. Di Stefano was a notorious lawyer known for representing undesirable clients. Soon he was writing letters to the CARE team in which he claimed to be able to have the men released. Fraser agreed to meet him, but insisted on doing so in the embassy in Brussels, with the Ambassador present. Di Stefano revealed that he knew the flamboyant Sydney solicitor John Marsden, who was then fighting a defamation case against Channel Seven. Di Stefano asked for Marsden's phone number. Doolan tracked it down through friends. Doolan remembers, 'Marsden was going through a terrible period in his life. He was in a fragile emotional state, but he was saying things like, "Look, I am going to go over and meet with Giovanni and Milosevic and I will negotiate the release".

'And I said, "That is absolutely crazy; don't get involved in it".

'Well, of course he did, without us knowing. He turned up over there and made all these mad phone calls in the middle of the night, saying, "Oh, I can negotiate their release. I am going into Belgrade". And I was begging him to stop, and telling him he was involved with very dangerous people'. The Marsden intervention was an extra worry for Doolan, and a distraction. Once again, it had no other impact on the negotiations that CARE was conducting, or on the outcome.

In fact, none of the shadowy dealings with people claiming to have influence came to anything. Fraser remembers asking the Yugoslav Foreign Minister for some advice. 'I said, "Look, there are all these people who claim to have influence, and we want our people out. What should we do? Do they have influence?"

'Well, there was a long silence, and then he said, 'In an ideal world such people would not exist, but they are a fact of life. They are mostly crooks and evil men. I would like to say they have no influence on government and by and large they do not". Despite everything, the government was operating as a government.'

In July, the men's appeal was rejected. This was no surprise. Negotiations continued, and the team was led to believe that it was likely Milosevic would grant clemency. Then, in mid July, Fraser became aware that cables were being sent back to Canberra from the

Australian embassy in which there was discussion of money being paid in return for the men's release. Fraser spoke to Murray Cobban to tell him that a clear message should be given that this was not how Australia did business. Sadly, the message that was authorised was more equivocal. 'They said that money would only be given for project aid. That was stupid, because of course the answer came back from the Yugoslavs "Oh, well we have plenty of projects you can fund", but of course it was basically the same thing. And who knows where the money would have ended up?'

By late August, there was an expectation that the men would be released. Fraser asked Downer if he would go to Yugoslavia for the occasion. Downer said he would not—there was no need: it was a done deal. Fraser wasn't so sure, and because he was aware of the cables mentioning money, he wanted someone with him who could act as a witness to anything that might occur. He asked for Cobban. He was not available, and instead Fraser was accompanied by the Deputy High Commissioner in London David Ritchie. 'I was very happy with that, because he was a good traditional diplomat and an honourable man', Fraser remembers. Fraser and Ritchie arrived in Belgrade on 31 August, expecting to have a meeting with Milosevic the following day, prior to the men's release. Fraser recalls, 'We arrived at the Australian embassy, and I said, "Where is the Ambassador?" I was told that he was in the office of the Minister for Refugees Bratislava "Buba" Morina, negotiating an agreement. I spoke to him on the phone, and he told me there was an agreement being drafted with money amounts in it, but it was in terms that were not acceptable to the Australian Government. He was redrafting it in terms that would be acceptable. Well, I told him to get out of there as quickly as possible. I said, "Tell them I have arrived and you have to see me urgently. I don't know, make some excuse, but get out of there"'.

The draft agreement presented by the Yugoslavs was headed 'Memorandum of Understanding', and was made out for Fraser's signature on behalf of 'the Australian side' and Buba Morina for 'the Yugoslav side'. This memorandum was a strange document. It committed Australia to 'cooperate in preparing and implementing the projects to be financed by the Australian side'. Five projects were listed with price tags attached. The total bill came to almost ninety-three million Deutschmarks (AU$64 million). There was another clause in the agreement that read: 'Immediately upon signing this memorandum and not later than within two days, the Australian side shall with a view to urgently addressing the problems associated with providing for refugees and displaced persons, pay the amount of US$4 million … to Yugoslavia for buying 20 000 tons of fuel oil'. The name and number of the account into which the money was to be paid were included in the agreement, which went on to commit 'the Australian side' to take 'appropriate steps within the Council of Former Prime Ministers, the Yugoslav diaspora in Australia and international financial institutions to help the Federal Republic of Yugoslavia to obtain financial resources for the reconstruction of destroyed infrastructure'. (The 'Council of Former Prime Ministers' was apparently a reference to the Interaction Council.)

The redraft prepared by the Australian Ambassador was not much better, in Fraser's view. It made similar commitments, but without the specific dollar amounts. This version referred to 'discussions which took place on 25 June 1999 between the Australian Ambassador in Belgrade' and Morina. Australia was prepared to make 'a significant contribution' towards humanitarian needs, and this was to be channelled through CARE Australia.[20]

Fraser rang Downer. It was mid afternoon in Belgrade, and about one o'clock in the morning in Canberra. 'I told him this wasn't the sort of document I was prepared to sign or CARE was prepared to sign, and I didn't think he should be contemplating it either. And I told him I wasn't sure that we were going to get the men out after all. Well, there was a lot of silence on the line, and I said, "Look, I can't be ringing you up every five minutes. You should trust me, or if you don't trust me you should trust Ritchie. You are going to have to trust our judgement of how to handle it". And you could almost hear the relief on the other end of the line. He was probably thinking, "Thank God. If the men aren't released, it will be Fraser's fault".'

Fraser asked for an urgent meeting with Morina. It was arranged at short notice at about seven-thirty that night. Fraser's aim was to have the dubious document withdrawn without jeopardising the men's release. 'Clearly I was trying to soft-soap them, to say basically "no" without ruining everything.' Over several hours, Fraser assured Morina that once the men were released, CARE wanted to expand its operations in Yugoslavia, and he, Fraser, would be prepared to lobby for more humanitarian aid, but a formal agreement would be 'very difficult'. Once the men were released, he would pursue other options. CARE would work towards a country agreement with Yugoslavia to govern the ongoing relationship. (CARE normally had country agreements in all the places it operated. The absence of one in Yugoslavia was an oversight.) If the CARE workers were released, this should lead to better funding from the United Nations High Commissioner for Refugees, and there would be contributions from Australia as well. The notes of the discussion show Fraser telling Morina that he hoped she could understand that he could not persuade the Australian Government to sign a formal document at this point, while the CARE workers were held captive. 'The perception of a precedent alone was enough to make it impossible.'

Fraser promised that if the men were released, he would accompany them to the United Kingdom and then return immediately so he could spend 'a few days examining at first hand the effects of the bombing'. He promised to raise Yugoslavia's humanitarian crisis with the Interaction Council and his overseas contacts. Morina was not easily dissuaded. Did this mean Fraser would sign the document after his return from the United Kingdom? she asked. 'It is the wrong kind of document', Fraser responded. What was needed was a proper, conventional country agreement with CARE. Morina was cross. Too many countries had promised assistance, she said, and nothing had happened. Yugoslavs had heard about the evidence against Pratt and his fellows 'with a heavy heart'. Their release would be a hard thing for the man in the street to swallow. The Yugoslav public required a document. They wanted a new relationship with Australia. There was nothing explicit in the document to link the money to the release of the men. Why couldn't Fraser sign it? It was not logical for Fraser to 'reject' the document, yet be prepared to inspect bomb damage and discuss projects two days later. The clemency gesture by Milosevic was based on an understanding that the document would be signed. How could it proceed if the document was retracted?[21]

The release of the men seemed to be in the balance, but at the same time it was clear to Fraser that the international pressure had worked. The government actually wanted to release the men. 'I think someone had just said, "Let's see what we can get", and they were trying it on.' Finally, at the end of a long evening of negotiation, one of the Yugoslav officials left the room, then came back to whisper in Morina's ear. 'Probably he had gone to ring Milosevic and say that Buba wasn't going to get anything out of Australia', Fraser says today. After the whispered conversation, Morina's attitude completely changed. She told Fraser that she accepted him as an honourable man. The document was off the table—null and void. Fraser had committed Australia to nothing, and the men were still to be released.

The next day, Fraser met Milosevic. Fraser remembers, 'He came over to me bright-eyed and smiling. He said, "I hear you dealt with our Buba Morina rather well yesterday". So she had probably told him that she thought she could get money out of us, and he had said, "Okay, well give it a go"'. Milosevic insisted that Morina saw refugees as 'her children' and was therefore likely to promote ideas that were 'unusual'. They went on, chatting about China and Taiwan and the Australian economy. Milosevic assured Fraser that he would always be welcome in Yugoslavia.[22]

Pratt and Wallace were released the next day, 2 September. Pratt later wrote:

> We emerge through the towering front doors into brilliant sunlight. We see four cars and a gaggle of people waiting. Most prominent among them … is the towering figure of Malcolm Fraser. He is as pleased as punch, warmly shaking our hands and patting our shoulders. He is a bloody sight for sore eyes.

Soon after, they were at the Croatian border.[23]

In his media release announcing the good news, on 2 September, Downer named the international leaders who had brought pressure to bear on Milosevic. The list included President Ahtisaari of Finland, the Greek Foreign Minister George Papandreou and the Greek Government, the United Nations High Commissioner for Refugees Sadako Ogata, the United Nations High Commissioner for Human Rights Mary Robinson, Russian Envoy Victor Chernomyrdin, Reverend Jesse Jackson, former US President Jimmy Carter, former US Secretary of State Henry Kissinger, Kenneth Kaunda of Zambia and Nelson Mandela. It was rare indeed for such a prominent international coalition to come together to lobby on behalf of Australian interests.

Pratt and Wallace went for trauma counselling in London, although Wallace walked out, claiming he didn't need it. Then the two men returned to Canberra for a party. The Governor-General Sir William Deane, who was also a patron of CARE, had tied three yellow ribbons to his balcony in Yarralumla for the entire period the men had been in prison. Now he cut two of them. One remained. Branko Jelen, who as a Yugoslav national was in an even more vulnerable position than Pratt and Wallace had been, was still in jail.

Fraser and Doolan were given access to Jelen, then serving his sentence in jail in Pozarevac. Doolan remembers Fraser being feted by the jail authorities. 'He knew what he was doing. Branko was brought into the room and sat next to me. Malcolm engaged the jailers in conversation. He charmed them. I leaned over and said quietly to Branko, "Are you OK?"

'He replied, "No. Get me out of here or I am dead. I promise you, I will not last much longer in this place".'

Jelen was seriously depressed by his situation, but in fact, Fraser says, the jail treated him well. He was allowed more visits than most prisoners. Fraser arranged for the prison to be given extra blankets and medical supplies, 'partly to get cooperation, but in fact the cooperation was there anyway'.

Fraser kept up the diplomacy and the international pressure. As promised, he returned and reviewed the results of the NATO bombing. As promised, he used his influence to lobby for more humanitarian aid. He continued to speak out in strong terms about the awful impact of the NATO bombs.

Meanwhile, CARE Australia had to make a difficult decision. Its work in Yugoslavia had been suspended while Pratt and Wallace had been in jail. Should it now be resumed, even though Jelen was still detained? The decision was made to resume operations, both on humanitarian grounds and because it would give CARE leverage in the campaign for his release. A new and, in Fraser's view, 'first-class' Country Director was appointed: Bernard Barron. His was an even more than usually demanding post.

In November 1999, CARE Australia's Belgrade-based staff wrote a memorandum to put on the record a suspicious course of events. They had invited tenders for winter deliveries of food and fuel, in a project funded by the United Nations High Commissioner for Refugees. A day or two before the tenders were to be opened, they had received a call from an official in the Australian Department of Foreign Affairs and Trade, saying that a friend of his, 'Jack', had submitted a tender, and wanted to know about its progress. Soon, Jack—who was one of the shadowy people who had claimed to have influence when Pratt and Wallace were in jail—was exerting considerable pressure. The CARE staff were told that their phones were bugged, and that if Jack's company did not get the contract, Jelen would never be released. Jack's tender, however, had already been ruled out. He had quoted for a 25 per cent commission;

most other tenders had quoted commission of between 7 and 10 per cent. Jack met the CARE staff and made 'Mafia-like threats, saying things like Branko would never be released, that CARE was a crooked and fraudulent organisation, that it would soon blow up in our faces and the banner headlines in the daily newspaper would be 8 centimetres high'. CARE did not cave in, instead sending all the tender documents to Ernst & Young and asking for a report verifying the integrity of the tender process. The threats died away, but CARE was told that three different intelligence agencies were bugging their telephone lines.[24]

Fraser, Tapp and Doolan do not believe that Jack was really in a position to exercise influence. It was another case of the semi-criminal network surrounding the regime trying to gain advantage by pretending to have more power than it did. Nevertheless, the pressure CARE was under showed how easy it could be for things to go wrong. Had CARE been less careful, and had Fraser not been involved, it is possible that the Australian Government, CARE and the United Nations could have been seriously compromised in their dealings in Yugoslavia.

Jelen was released to the Australian Ambassador on the last day of 1999. The final yellow ribbon at Yarralumla was cut. Jelen and his family later came to live in Australia. In the end, says Fraser, it was diplomacy and negotiation combined with unprecedented international pressure that freed the CARE workers.

There were a few side effects from the affair. The relationship between Tapp and Fraser was broken. Shortly after Jelen was released, Tapp left CARE Australia for a job with AusAID.

* * *

Fraser retired as Chairman of CARE Australia in 2002. 'I thought it was time they got along without me', he says today. He was replaced by Sir William Deane, who had recently retired as Governor-General. At the gala dinner held to mark Fraser's stepping-down, he spoke about his pride in 'enormously competent young Australians' working all over the world in dedication to 'the intrinsic quality and dignity of all people, regardless of race, ethnicity or religion … If we had a world where CARE was no longer needed, we would all be happy, but the reality is that where poverty exists, CARE will exist'.[25]

After Fraser had stepped down as Chairman, there was a tragic sequel to the Yugoslav drama. On 19 October 2004, CARE Australia's Country Director in Iraq Margaret Hassan was kidnapped in Baghdad. Many CARE workers are heroic, but even in their company Hassan was special. She was both an Iraqi and a British citizen, married to an Iraqi and popular in the country. She had worked in Palestinian refugee camps and fought tirelessly for the thousands of Iraqis in her care. She was also a vocal critic of United Nations sanctions and the US invasion. After her capture, Iraqis demonstrated in the streets to support her release. Even Abu Musab al-Zarqawi, the al-Qaeda leader in Iraq who was later killed by the Americans, joined in the appeal.

Meanwhile, British Prime Minister Tony Blair made exactly the kinds of statements that are least likely to help in a hostage situation, saying that Hassan's kidnap showed 'the type of people we are up against'.[26] Fraser recalls using his contacts to get in touch with Blair's people to 'tell him to shut up'. Today, Fraser comments, 'No government is going to place the interests of an individual above the perceived national interest. Blair was part of the coalition of the willing. It was in his interests to use Hassan's kidnap to argue how terrible these people were. He used her to make the government's case with scant regard for her safety'.

At this time, Tony Eggleton was in the act of taking over the chairmanship of CARE Australia from Deane, but the former Governor-General agreed to stay on to manage a crisis coordination committee.[27] Fraser offered to help CARE to negotiate Hassan's release. He wrote to Deane the day after her kidnap, urging him to make sure that CARE Australia and Hassan's Iraqi husband remained in control of the campaign. Only they would have Hassan's best interests at heart, free from political considerations. 'Margaret Hassan's wellbeing should be placed over and above all other considerations, including relationships with Britain, US, CARE International or with our own government', he wrote. He warned that the United States–dominated CARE International, the British Government and the Australian Department of Foreign Affairs would be compromised by the coalition of the willing's invasion force in Iraq. He urged an approach to Islamic groups in Australia, and he offered to contact Prince Hassan of Jordan, who was a personal friend. Approaches should be made through anyone who was in good standing in Iraq. Time, he warned, was of the essence, and he could be of help.

CARE Australia rejected Fraser's offers of help. Deane wrote saying that while he respected Fraser's views, they were being advised to let CARE International take the lead. Britain became the key player in handling the crisis. Today, Eggleton says that the British and Australian governments warned CARE International against paying a ransom, but nevertheless plans were laid to deal with any and all demands from the kidnappers. In the end, Eggleton says, money was not what the kidnappers were after; their demands were for British withdrawal. 'Bill Deane and I gave serious consideration to packing our bags and heading for Baghdad, but this was quickly vetoed by the Australian and British governments.'

On his own initiative, Fraser contacted his friend James Wolfensohn, President of the World Bank. An arrangement was made for Nigel Roberts, the bank's man in the Middle East, to talk to Yasser Arafat, because he would have had contacts with the terrorist groups. A meeting between Arafat and Roberts was scheduled, but it was later cancelled because, on 25 October, Arafat fell ill. He never recovered, and died shortly afterwards.

At this stage, there was reason to believe that Hassan's release could be secured in return for money. It appeared that she was not a political prisoner, but a hostage held by criminals. Eighty per cent of abductions were undertaken by criminals as money-making operations. Hassan's situation was different from that of Pratt, Wallace and Jelen, who had been in the hands of a government. Fraser says today, 'Everyone pays money in these situations, but nobody talks about it'. He was prepared to raise the funds, but CARE Australia was worried about the effect of the Howard government's legislation making it illegal to pay terrorist organisations. CARE Australia acquired a legal opinion from Mallesons Stephen Jaques that Fraser regarded as 'pathetic': it did little more than recount the law. Fraser on his own initiative arranged another opinion, from Julian Burnside, QC, who advised that prosecution was unlikely, and in any case because it was an emergency a defence would be available under the law. Fraser says today, 'I was prepared to try to raise money from a behind-the-scenes, totally unknown benefactor, not associated with CARE or the Australian Government. I believe that we could have found such a benefactor, and I think there was a chance that we could have got her out'.

Margaret Hassan was not saved. Instead, the world saw a succession of video tapes in which she begged for Blair to withdraw troops from Iraq. On 16 November, Hassan was murdered with a shotgun to the head. The video of her death was given to the media. CARE was devastated, as was everyone associated with the organisation. Eggleton says today, 'The callous and senseless killing of Margaret Hassan was one of the bleakest episodes in the sixty-year history of CARE. A lifetime of humanitarian service was no guarantee of personal safety'.

In the years since, two men have been convicted of Hassan's murder. Mustafa Salam al-Jubouri was convicted and sentenced to life imprisonment in 2006. On appeal, his sentence was reduced to eighteen months. Ali Lutifi Jassar al-Rawi was convicted in June 2009 and at the time of writing is awaiting an appeal hearing. These men, though, were not the ringleaders.

Could Fraser have made a difference? Doolan thinks he might have. 'I think that CARE made a bad mistake in not going to him and using his influence. I still think it is an indictment that they didn't use someone with his experience and proven track record of bringing international pressure to bear.' Why was he not used? Doolan says, 'I think at the time there was a concerted effort to change CARE away from what it had been, and Fraser was seen as part of the past'. Meanwhile, Fraser remains angry that he wasn't used, and that his advice was rejected.

* * *

Nevertheless, Fraser looks back on his time with CARE with great satisfaction. His vision of an organisation carrying Australian help to the world has been fulfilled. CARE Australia remains a fully operational international aid and development agency, managing programs in twenty countries. It is recognised as having particularly low administrative overheads, with over 90 per cent of all funds raised going to programs on the ground. At the time of writing, CARE Australia workers are in Afghanistan, Bangladesh, Cambodia, Ethiopia, India, Indonesia, Jordan, Kenya, Laos, Malawi, Mozambique, Myanmar, Pakistan, the Palestinian territories, Papua New Guinea, South Africa, Sri Lanka, Timor-Leste, Vanuatu, Vietnam and Yemen. CARE Australia's education programs have helped nine million students. Its economic development programs have helped ten million people to save money, gain access to credit and start small businesses. CARE Australia's sanitation programs have given eleven million people access to safe water and improved health.

'There is no doubt', Fraser says, 'that helping to found it was one of the very best things that I have done'. Fraser believes the great strength of CARE is that it is non-political and non-religious, giving help where it is needed, as and when it can. And what about the politics, the disappointments and the betrayals? He shrugs. 'Well, that's people. We are imperfect creatures.' And there were good people too. His board members were astonishingly supportive, and CARE Australia has been served by many dedicated and skilled staff over the years. Tony Eggleton was invaluable in reforming CARE International and bringing CARE Australia back from the brink in 1995.

After these events, Brian Doolan went back to his work in Vietnam and then on to become the Chief Executive Officer of the Fred Hollows Foundation. He maintains a firm friendship with Fraser. Charles Tapp worked for AusAID, and is now a consultant on international aid. Robert Yallop still works for CARE. Today, Fraser says, CARE Australia is in the hands of 'an absolutely first-class management team'.

Phoebe Fraser came home in 1995 and married one of her fellow CARE workers, Rhodri Wynn-Pope. Today, she lives next to her parents on the Mornington Peninsula. She is on the verge of completing a doctorate in international law and human rights—a project which, not surprisingly, she discusses frequently with her father.

This is as good a place as any to say what has become of the Frasers' other children—although none of them welcome publicity. Mark lives with his family north of Mansfield, and breeds horses. Hugh lives with his family east of Armidale, where he farms and runs a knitwear business, Frasers of Arran. Angela lives in Sydney with her husband and twin children, and works as an interior designer and decorator. Phoebe's two children are in and out of their grandparents' house. Together with the Frasers' eight other grandchildren, they light up their grandparents' lives.

In the comfort and elegance of Malcolm and Tamie Fraser's home, it seems hard to believe that armed men will steal blankets from children. The world contains such horrors. Yet Fraser remains an optimist, a believer in the efficacy of good people. In recent years, he has taken to recasting the saying that made him famous, that 'Life wasn't meant to be easy'. He says that the original quotation comes from George Bernard Shaw. It reads: 'Life wasn't meant to be easy, my child. But take courage. It can be delightful'.

22

Enduringly Liberal

In the spring of 2007, as Australia stood on the verge of political change, Malcolm Fraser became a Professorial Fellow of the University of Melbourne, attached to the Asia Pacific Centre for Military Law. He gave an inaugural lecture to mark the occasion. The title was 'Finding Security in Terrorism's Shadow: The Importance of the Rule of Law'.[1] The lecture had been through many drafts. Tamie had run the red pen over it. Fraser had written, re-written, and re-written again. Perhaps partly because of the interviews he was doing for this book, the lecture pulled together the threads of his personal political history to illuminate the present—a world supposedly locked in a war against terror. There were references—so oblique that many people would have missed them—to his disputes with John Gorton over the call-out of troops in the Gazelle Peninsula affair, and to his involvement with the F-111 negotiations. These were used to illustrate the importance of civil rights, of proper limitations on the power of the Prime Minister, and the true nature of the US alliance. Yet in its cadence, its questions, its bristling with ideas and urgency, the lecture was reminiscent of the Deakin lecture of 1971 and of the other speeches of Fraser's youth and early middle age. There could be no doubt that this was the same man—though older and perhaps sadder. The difference was that in the early 1970s, Fraser had been speaking both as a liberal and as a prospective leader of the Liberal Party. In those days, despite its problems, the Liberal Party was the political organisation that best reflected his own ideals. Now he was one of its leading critics. He remained a party member by the skin of his teeth, and only because he thought resigning would let down other party members who were still fighting for true liberal values.

Fraser began his lecture by talking about the post–World War II period, in which he had come to political awareness. In those days the United States had been a force for good in the world, supporting the growth of a global architecture based on mutual respect, due process and the rule of law. 'This by and large was the world inherited by the second President Bush', said Fraser. But the United States had now halted and reversed the progress of previous decades. America had always tended to be careless of its allies; now, it acted unilaterally. The neo-conservatives had seized on terrorism and the 2001 attack on the World Trade Center to cast off the restraints of international law 'like so many unwanted shackles'. The current aim of the United States was not to live and let live, but to 'live and make like us'. In its prosecution of the Iraq war, in the establishment of the detention camp at Guantanamo Bay and of military commissions to try terrorism suspects—'victors' courts, doing justice to a tyranny, but not to a law-based country like the United States'—Bush had set aside the principles vital to the maintenance of civil democracy. And in all this, the Howard government had been complicit, when the role of a friendly ally should have been to speak frankly, as Robert Menzies had to Eisenhower, and (although Fraser did not say so) as Fraser had to Ford, Carter and Reagan.

Fraser turned to talking about the human rights abuses in Australia—the children behind razor wire, the Australian citizens illegally deported and detained. The experience of the Howard government had made him an advocate of a Bill of Rights in the Australian constitution, whereas many years before he had believed that parliament and the common law were sufficient protectors of citizens' rights. This was one way in which Fraser had changed from the young man who first sought political office. Yet in most other ways, there was a clear connecting thread leading from the Fraser who had entered politics half a century before to the man who stood—tall, grey-suited and waistcoated—before an audience largely made up of law students. These young people had not been born when Fraser forced the supply crisis of 1975. They had no memories of his prime ministership. They knew him as an advocate for the rule of law, and a critic of the Howard government's record on human rights.

At the end of the lecture, Fraser took questions. A young woman stood and addressed him as Professor Fraser. He dismissed the new title with a wave. 'Okay,' she said, 'I'll call you Mal', and he smiled and everyone laughed. It must have been hard for this group of young people to believe what some of their parents said—that Fraser had been an austere politician, aloof and hard to like. To them, he was speaking to the very ideals that might lead young people to study law.

Fraser had done many things over the previous seventeen years. There had been his work for CARE Australia and CARE International, and his continued advocacy for the world's poorest people. He was deeply involved in commentary on the role of the United Nations in responding to international crises. He continued his work with the Interaction Council, including helping to develop and promote a Declaration of Human Responsibilities, intended as a companion document to the Declaration of Human Rights. He was always active on the international stage. Yet, at the same time, he was making a difficult journey at home in Australia, and in his relationship with the Liberal Party.

In the period during which this book was being written, he was often subjected to personal abuse by members of the Liberal Party. The shadow minister Sophie Mirabella described him as a 'frothing at the mouth lefty' guilty of 'nauseating acts of political sycophancy' and 'hypocrisy'.[2] About the nicest thing Liberals were saying about Fraser was that he was 'misguided'. Fraser never mentioned this attack, or others like it, during the interviews for this book. He seemed not to notice them, or to regard them as irrelevant. The things that bothered him were the attacks on his record, particularly those that misstated the facts. Personal abuse had to be drawn to his attention, and even then he normally didn't want to comment. 'But if it is just personal, then it doesn't really matter, does it?' he said at one stage. Meanwhile, he hung on to his Liberal Party membership out of a mixture of hope and conviction that, one day soon, being a member of the Liberal Party would once again equate with being a liberal.

In the eight years following his defeat in the election of 1983, Fraser commented only sparingly on domestic politics. His abstinence came to an end in August 1991, when Australia was deep in recession and unemployment was in double digits. Fraser began a regular column in *The Sunday Age* newspaper. He wrote in the first instalment that he had previously turned down invitations to contribute articles on the state of Australia. 'I did not want to be partisan; perhaps I wanted to avoid controversy! That is changed. I am too concerned about Australia's future to stay silent.'[3] Fraser saw a new threat that was in many ways communism's reverse image: an unreasoning faith in free markets as an organising principle in human affairs.

Labor had been in power for eight years, yet despite recession and double-digit unemployment, the Liberal Party was still a long way from forming government. The party had not recovered from years of division as Andrew Peacock and John Howard fought over the spoils of defeat. John Hewson's offering to the electorate was 'Fightback'—a policy prescription even more rigidly economically rationalist than that of the Hawke–Keating Labor government.

Fraser's first column revisited the concept on which Robert Menzies had founded the Liberal Party as representative of the forgotten people.

> No country can be well governed in the interests of ordinary people unless the authorities, government and the Reserve Bank manage the growth of credit with discretion and caution ... Neither party [has been] prepared to question any aspect of deregulation, or the abdication of government responsibility, which pervades current attitudes.

The following week he expanded his critique, painting economic rationalism as the new aggressive threat in the world now that socialism was dead. The Australian Labor Party, he noted, currently talked about privatisation rather than nationalisation.

> The changes in the ALP have removed much of the ideology from the political debate, which is now more about competence than contradiction. It would have been more so had the Liberal Party maintained its traditional, essentially liberal approach to policies and not believed it necessary to dramatically change its philosophy.

It had become almost blasphemous to speak critically of floating the dollar, of deregulating the capital markets, of 'free trade'. But these, coupled with weak corporate supervision, 'had contributed significantly to our present problems'.[4]

Fraser was not against everything in Hewson's Fightback package. He argued in favour of a goods and services tax: such a tax would not solve all the tax problems, he said, but it would enable income tax to be lowered, which was essential for individual incentive.[5] But the rest of the economic rationalist agenda, he argued, was based not on reason, but on dogma. Those who had characterised Fraser as a conservative who had resisted deregulation while in government would have found material here to confirm their views. Fraser expressed himself with characteristic vigour, but he was not arguing against all deregulation.

> Deregulation has become a religion, and its cause does not need to be supported by rational argument ... While there can be much good in many aspects of deregulation, the mood has been so strong that the deregulators have not had to prove their case ... Deregulation, whatever it means, has become to its proponents more important than good government ... deregulation has become mythology. The good and the bad are hopelessly mixed. Deregulation is often good, but it is not a good in itself. It depends on circumstances.[6]

Fraser asserted that at the very beginning of the deregulation debate, during his time in government, there had been a 'significant conceptual confusion'. It had been wrong to try to control the financial markets as closely as had been the case before the Campbell Inquiry, but, 'It was certainly not wrong to influence, indeed to determine, the overall quantum of ... lending or borrowing'.[7]

Politics, Fraser said, had become largely a matter of who could manage things best. What, then, distinguished or should distinguish the Liberal Party? He answered by reverting to Menzies's forgotten people—those who did not have powerful friends or interest groups to represent them. These people became victims if governments abandoned responsibility and left the population at the mercy of the rule of the jungle.

> Is there no sense of pride, of national obligation, of shared destiny and of common purpose? What indeed have we become? Economic rationalism will leave a wasteland as barren and empty as the moon. We ordinary Australians do not live for a corrupt theory, for an economist's dream. We bleed and we hurt. If we work and try hard to help build a better Australia, we owe each other. What else does Australian mateship mean? When needed, if we can, we lend a helping hand.[8]

By 1992 Fraser had become recognised as one of the main critics of economic rationalism. This position had brought him back into the orbit of a man who had never really let Fraser out of his sight, or out of his sphere of influence—Bob Santamaria. Santamaria shared Fraser's views about unrestrained capitalism. He had long wanted to establish a third force in Australian politics. Now he wrote to Fraser saying he thought Hewson would lose the forthcoming election. The Liberal Party had taken a wrong turn. Instead, it should be trying to 'build the coalition which Reagan built, and which Bush is attempting to reassemble'. By this, Santamaria meant a broad-based alliance of voters from the middle ground of politics. Reagan had cultivated the middle ground 'because it was recognised that the Republicans alone did not have the voting force to win. Especially after a dose of Hewson economics, I think it will be the same with the Liberals'.[9]

A series of meetings followed in which Santamaria explored whether Fraser would be prepared to lead a new political group to challenge economic rationalism. Others were involved, including Fraser's biographer, Philip Ayres, the sociologist John Carroll and academic Robert Manne, who was at that time the editor of *Quadrant* magazine. Ayres wrote to Fraser advising on the 'philosophical thrust' of a statement that Fraser might make to launch the group, and 'how it could maximise your advantages, appeal to as wide a cross section as possible, and weaken any charge that you're out to hurt the Liberal Party'. Ayres was urging an explicitly conservative appeal. 'With the things ordinary people most want to *conserve* (prosperity, jobs, social and family fabric) being eroded by economic forces and theories, people should respond, as they did with Menzies, to a strong *conservative* voice with experience behind it that asserts concern for ordinary people' (emphasis in original).[10] Whatever Santamaria was trying to achieve, Fraser did not conceive of the group as a new political party, but as a think tank, dedicated to putting forward ideas and forcing the discussion of policy; but he says today that there never was a clear proposal or plan. 'We talked, we explored ideas, but there was never anything really on the table for me to consider and say yes or no to.' Unlike Ayres, Fraser did not think the appeal to the people should be about conservatism. 'I have never been a conservative. Always a progressive.' In any case, the discussions came to nothing.

As the March 1993 federal election approached, Fraser was still enough of a loyal Liberal Party member to put the best face on things. Hewson had softened Fightback after poor public opinion polls, and was widely criticised for it. Fraser congratulated him. The most important message, he said, was that the opposition had listened. 'If the opposition gets into government, as it now has a reasonable chance of doing, it is very important that message be carried through into government and that never again does it give the appearance of being ideological, remote and uncaring.'[11] But after Hewson lost the election, giving Paul Keating his 'sweetest victory of all', Fraser made his views clear: 'Australians voted the way they did not out of attachment to the Keating government and the policies which brought the country to this pass, but from a deep distrust of what they perceived as a reckless and ideologically blinkered alternative'.[12] Hewson had been given extraordinary loyalty, Fraser said, but loyalty should not imply blind acceptance of policy, which in this case had been prepared by specialist commercial advisers and foisted on the party. 'The intellectual strength of the party rests on its capacity to analyse, to question, to probe. Vigorous debate is a sign of health.' The Liberal Party should have asserted its claim to be able to manage better by standing on its record of understanding middle Australia. Instead, it had been guided by ideology, 'rules without deviation which would be applied to all circumstances, and more often than not the rules did not fit the circumstances of real life'.[13]

⋆ ⋆ ⋆

Shortly after he wrote these words, Fraser's commentary on domestic politics went into recess. There was a reason: he had announced that he would seek the federal presidency of the Liberal Party. Fraser was offering his party himself, his experience and his abilities. He might have been critical, but he was still a deeply engaged and hopeful member.

Tamie thought that seeking the presidency was a bad idea. She says today, 'I think he shouldn't have even thought about that. I tried to put him off it, quite honestly. I didn't see that he could possibly do it, from where he'd been, but he so passionately wanted to contribute, to be part of things. I understood where it came from'. Tamie was not alone in her reservations. Fraser promised to be 'just a quietly unobtrusive person in the back room'.[14] Not surprisingly, many in his own party did not believe him. If Fraser was successful, he would be the first former Prime Minister to hold the post. Was it reasonable to expect him to be seen and not heard in the back room of party politics? He had already been so outspoken that a vote for him could be seen only as a vote against John Hewson, who was still hanging on to the party leadership. Fraser countered that he, at least, had 'some experience in winning elections ... My record in winning elections is rather better than the current parliamentary party'.[15] Fraser's main opponent was Tony Staley—the man who had, almost twenty years before, engineered Fraser becoming Leader of the Opposition. After months of controversy within the party, the aversion to Fraser's candidacy was so strong that on the eve of the ballot he decided to withdraw. He made a speech saying he was doing so because there was a risk that he would become the issue, rather than the necessary reforms to the party. The presidency went to Staley.

Was Fraser hurt by the rejection by so many of his fellow party members? He claims today not to remember how he felt. 'I have never been someone to reflect on what is past and done with.' At the time, he used his newspaper column, now appearing in *The Australian*, to congratulate Staley. 'I hope very much he can revive the basic strength of the party. The task ahead is formidable.' Membership had fallen by one-third. Fraser believed the party should reform itself to make sure that it represented 'today's Australia'. Candidates for federal elections should be pre-selected only by people from within their own electorate. The role of the state organisation should be reduced. Candidates should be independent of the party machine, able to speak out without fear of retribution, as he had done all those years ago as a junior candidate in Wannon.

> If the Liberal banner is to be carried with pride right around Australia, the average member needs to feel a sense of involvement in relation to policy and to the selection of his representatives in the parliament. There is much to be done. Everyone will wish Tony Staley well. The results will be watched with great interest.[16]

For those in the know, Fraser's remarks were pointed. Staley did not agree with Fraser's views on party reform. Fraser says today, 'Certainly I would have tried to make the party machine relevant and useful, but the real issue was whether the machine was going to dominate the membership, or the membership dominate the machine. I thought the membership should be dominant'.

* * *

In May 1994, John Hewson brought months of speculation to a head by announcing a ballot for the leadership. John Howard would be a contender, as would a team of Alexander Downer as leader and Peter Costello as deputy. Fraser urged the party to move back to the middle ground.

> We should have won in 1987, 1990 should have been easy and 1993 should not even have been a race … Burying Fightback is one thing. Re-establishing a sense of direction, a sense of purpose, is quite another. At the moment people do not know what the party stands for. They do not know whether it responds to their concerns.

Fraser did not comment directly on the various candidates for the leadership, but his opinion was clear. Howard and Peacock had had their chance, and should not be chosen. Once again, Fraser was arguing for a flexible, pragmatic party in which individual members could exercise independence and express their views without being accused of disloyalty.

> There are a number of people in the Liberal Party with a proven and demonstrated record of failure. Their seniority has maintained for them an influence over the party's affairs which inhibits younger members of the party and prevents them from exercising their judgements to the full extent. [The party] must look for new faces.[17]

Fraser says today that he was not so much enthused by the Downer–Costello team as eager that the party should move on from the division and failure of Peacock and Howard and the hard-line economic rationalism of Hewson. Fraser had been close to Downer's father, who had been 'a conservative in the best sense of the word'. The son he regarded as largely untried. Yet when Downer was elected leader of the party, Fraser buried his doubts in yet another display of party loyalty.

> Alexander Downer and Peter Costello will give the party direction, conviction, enthusiasm and victory. They will give Australia dignity and decent government. I am delighted at the result of Monday's election and that Australia will once again have a valid and challenging political choice ... For the first time in several years I am enthusiastic about the prospects for the future of the party ... The problems the party has faced will now be overcome.[18]

Fraser was wrong. Within months, Downer had become an embarrassment as he floundered in a mess of his own inexperience, an inability to tackle the intricacy of policy across the spectrum, and a tendency to crack jokes that only he thought funny.

John Howard had been a candidate for the leadership in the ballot that immediately followed the 1993 election loss. He had offered himself again when Downer got the job. He had been comprehensively rejected on both occasions. Now, though, there were very few choices, and Howard was claiming to have reinvented himself. He described himself as a 'tolerant conservative' and said he had rethought his views on Asian immigration. All this made him more acceptable to the moderates that remained in the party. On 30 January 1995, Downer stepped down and Howard was unanimously elected as leader.

Fraser chose to be hopeful. He wrote that Howard had 'broadened his vision and understanding of the requirements of office since the 1980s' and that he had started well. 'His role is all the more important because this may well be the last opportunity for the Liberal Party to achieve credibility in federal politics … His experience and years in politics equip him well to respond to it.' But there were other messages between the lines for those who knew the history of Howard's relentless undermining of Peacock. Fraser wrote:

> Downer is now guaranteeing that John Howard will be given the unity necessary to achieve victory … In this sense, Howard is an extraordinarily fortunate leader, because it is something that the party lacked through the 1980s, and most of the 1990s. This needs to be more than a temporary lesson. A party divided can't govern Australia because it can't govern itself.[19]

* * *

John Howard led the Liberal Party out of the political wilderness and back into power in March 1996. Fraser was more than pleased. Today, he says, 'I might have had reservations about Howard, but I wanted him to succeed, and of course in a way he did'. Yet the

1996 election also contained the seeds of Fraser's final alienation from the party. The seat of Oxley, held by the Labor Party, was one of the safest in Queensland. The Liberal Party candidate, Pauline Hanson, was expected to put up a token showing. Nobody expected her to be in the news, let alone become a transforming force in Australian politics. On the eve of the campaign, she spoke against Asian immigration and aid for Aboriginals. The Liberal Party had lost many of its moderates, but Hanson's views were nevertheless too obnoxious to be tolerated. She was dropped as Liberal Party candidate, and contested the election as an independent. The result took everyone by surprise: Hanson won a swing of 19 per cent—the highest in the country and enough for her to take the seat from Labor. This alone would have guaranteed her media attention, but when she followed it up, in September 1996, with a maiden speech attacking multiculturalism, she was carried to the frontline of political debate.[20] The reaction of both the mainstream political parties was overwhelmingly negative. Parliament passed a resolution condemning her views on immigration, yet John Howard refused to criticise her. Instead, he said her views were shared by many Australians. He didn't agree with them, but they were evidence that the 'pall of political correctness' nurtured by Labor had been lifted.

Fraser was appalled. His worst fears about Howard had been confirmed. To Howard's line about free speech, Fraser responded that of course Australians could speak as they chose, but,

> It is a question of what is or is not acceptable, what will or will not, if somebody utters certain words, contribute to their own good character or to their own credit … and one of the things that has happened is that people who utter the kinds of words that Pauline Hanson utters now believe that they can utter those things and still regard themselves as respectable. There is a great deal of difference between that and free speech. The views she has, the thoughts she expresses, are not respectable in a civilised society.[21]

In the month following Hanson's maiden speech, Fraser was in New York. He had been appointed, in 1996, as Howard's special envoy to Africa to lobby in support of Australia's candidacy for a two-year seat on the United Nations Security Council. The groundwork for the bid—a three-way ballot for two seats, with Portugal and Sweden the other contenders—had been carried out by the Keating government, in particular by Foreign Minister Gareth Evans. This was part of Australia's long and proud history of influence with the United Nations. Australia had helped to draft the United Nations charter. It had held the presidency in 1948, when the Universal Declaration of Human Rights was adopted.

Fraser was proud to be representing Australia once again, but it was clear to him that Howard didn't have his heart in the attempt. Fraser tried to make up for it, travelling around Africa and then to New York, using all his contacts to lobby on Australia's behalf. He was battling against the wind. Australia had largely withdrawn from Africa over the previous two decades. It had only a handful of missions covering the entire continent. Portugal, which was the competing candidate for the post, had more than fifty. On top of this, the Howard government simply didn't have the necessary international respect to carry the day. Portugal and Sweden won the vote.

Fraser wrote a confidential cable to Howard giving reasons why Australia had suffered 'a surprising and considerable defeat, a defeat which Australia should not have suffered'. Fraser said that Australia's strategy had been flawed. Sweden and Australia had been allied against Portugal, but, Fraser said, Sweden had not delivered on 'our mutual support agreement'. There were other factors.

> There was a perception that we have moved more closely to the United States, that recent meetings in Australia and statements made indicate a resurgence in the relationship which would have been more appropriate in the Cold War days. Quite independently, I have evidence of that same assumption from some of my friends in Asia. This has a particularly adverse effect in the UN context …

> [Also, the] current debate in Australia about immigration and race is already doing us damage throughout Asia … It is no longer possible in my view for the government to tackle current exhibitions of ignorance and simplicity which many construe as racism and bigotry indirectly or half-heartedly. Leaving aside implications within Australia, a clear statement at the highest level is needed for our relationships internationally.[22]

Fraser concluded the cable with the hope that Howard would take the points he had made seriously, and as a message for the future. To say that he was disappointed would be to put it mildly.

* * *

Fraser had in the meantime become a leading figure in the debate over whether or not Australia should become a republic. Paul Keating had put the issue on the agenda as early as 1992, and Fraser's views had often been sought. He was, after all, the Prime Minister who had come to power following the dismissal by the Queen's representative of an elected Australian government.

Fraser had for most of his life been a monarchist. In 1992, he was arguing that there was no good reason to alter a system that had worked well for Australia.[23] Over the next seven years, his views changed completely, to the point where he voted for the republic in the referendum of 1999 'with my head and with my heart'.[24]

Today, he says the shift began years before, when he was Prime Minister, during Prince Charles's visit to Australia in 1977. 'I came to think there was not sufficient commitment to this country from the royal family', he says. Fraser declared that he had become a republican in August 1995, in an article in *The Australian*. 'Emotionally, I have been attached to the monarchy because I believe nations should protect their past and build on it for the future. For a variety of reasons … I now accept that a republic is inevitable and right.'[25] In another article, he said:

> The British monarchy made sense for Australia years ago when most Australians felt that they were British as much as they were Australian. That was certainly how my parents' generation felt. But times have changed. We are now a uniquely, proudly Australian nation. We have come from many cultures and many countries. Our links of history and kinship to Britain will endure forever. But our national institutions, our Head of State, should be unambiguously Australian.[26]

Fraser supported the model for the republic that was offered in the referendum of 1999: a President appointed by two-thirds of parliament. This, he said, would be 'safe and workable'. A popularly elected President, on the other hand, would 'establish a second power base that will rival the people we have already elected. We can't have two governments. Government is difficult enough at the best of times. It would be foolish to make it more difficult'.[27] Only the big political parties would be able to afford to finance an election campaign for President, he said, meaning that a popularly elected position was bound to be politicised. But perhaps the most powerful argument for the republic, Fraser said, was that the model on offer would improve 'our already very stable system of government'. He argued by analysing the events of 1975, and the roles of John Kerr and Gough Whitlam in the lead-up to the dismissal. It was Kerr's insecurity, combined with his concern for the position of the Queen, that had helped to create the circumstances of the dismissal, Fraser said.

> In the current debate there are some who argue that Her Majesty can act almost as a backstop, a safety net, and in some way provide protection for the people of Australia against political action that might be taken in Australia at the highest level. This is a great folly and nonsense. It cannot happen. For example, in the circumstances of 1975, if Her Majesty had been asked to dismiss Kerr she would have had no recourse but to act within hours rather than

> days. If she had delayed such a request because she believed that for some reason it was unreasonable, Her Majesty would have immediately become part of the political process and would have been construed in Australia as being partisan ... It would be quite unreasonable to expect a resident in Britain to act in such a way ... Therefore the suggestion that Her Majesty could be a backstop and second guess recommendations from an Australia Prime Minister are nonsense.[28]

Had Kerr been not Governor-General but a President approved by a two-thirds majority of parliament, his position would have been much more secure. He would not have had to fear being sacked and replaced by someone prepared to do Whitlam's bidding. The Prime Minister's power to put in his personal choice without consultation would have been removed. In these circumstances, Fraser said, Kerr would probably have warned Whitlam that if he refused to call an election, he would be dismissed. Whitlam would then almost certainly have agreed to call an election, which he would have contested as Prime Minister. There would have been no dismissal. The republican model proposed, concluded Fraser, was 'a safe and, in this example, better model than the monarchical system that exists today'. Fraser also pointed out that the Queen would remain as Head of the Commonwealth, and Australia would therefore retain strong links with the royal family. All in all, Fraser concluded, 'It is about time that we had an Australian citizen as our Head of State. The republic proposal is a conservative one which enhances and, I believe, improves our current system of parliamentary government'.[29] In the lead-up to the republican referendum in 1999, Fraser issued a joint statement with Whitlam supporting a 'yes' vote, and appeared with him in a television commercial which concluded with Whitlam turning to Fraser and saying, 'Malcolm, it's time', to which Fraser replied, with a crisp nod, 'It is'.[30]

* * *

Meanwhile, Fraser had all but dropped his commentary on economic affairs to speak on issues of human rights. Economics, after all, was a means to an end. What was at threat under the Howard government was far more important: the values that underlay liberalism, human dignity and the hopes for a decent, outward-looking Australia. Fraser says today, 'People said I was disloyal to the party because I spoke out on these things, because I condemned what Howard was doing. What on earth did they expect me to do? What did anyone who knew me expect me to do?'

Howard had faced the people again in October 1998, six months earlier than required, after a campaign dominated by the goods and services tax. For over a year before that, Fraser had been engaged in a battle within the party. In June 1997, he wrote to party President Tony Staley, urging him to use all his influence to prevent the Liberal Party from directing preferences to Pauline Hanson's One Nation ahead of the Labor Party. Fraser wrote:

> I regard Pauline Hanson, the ideas and policies implicit in her statements, as of extraordinary danger to the unity and cohesion of a fair-minded, democratic Australia. She is clearly of the extreme right. I am sure it does not need me to remind you that Australians have always rejected extreme views in their mainline politics and that any party that has flirted with such extremes, whether of the left or the right, has never done well at the polls ... It is vitally important that the Liberal Party remove itself as far as possible from the politics of Pauline Hanson.

Normally, Fraser acknowledged, decisions on preferences were made only close to an election, but in this case he urged the party to make it clear that it would be placing Hanson behind 'any party currently represented in the federal parliament'. Fraser sent a copy of this letter to every party State President, and to Howard as Prime Minister. He was placing Staley and the party on notice. If the Liberal Party gave 'any comfort to Pauline Hanson and One Nation ... it is something

I would oppose, not only privately but publically with whatever vigour I can command'.[31]

Fraser did not get what he wanted. No statement was made, and by mid 1998 it was clear that the Queensland branch of the Liberal Party, at least, was considering giving preferences to One Nation ahead of Labor. Fraser rang all the state presidents, again appealing for the party to take a public position. Finally, he issued a public statement to the Liberal Party. One Nation's policies, he said, were racist.

> All our experiences in this and other centuries indicate that racism is one of the most evil scourges ... It is not an ancient evil; it is a present evil. Where major political parties compromise their basic principles with a racist political party, experience more often than not has shown that the influence of the racists' party has grown and, in far too many cases, become dominant ... I appeal to you all to put decency and principle before the most base political expediency.[32]

Again, Fraser was unsuccessful. Although most state branches agreed to place One Nation last, the Queensland coalition parties preferenced it ahead of Labor in the state election. One Nation became the third largest party in the Queensland parliament, with more seats than the Liberals. The consensus that had governed politics since 1945—that no party would seek political advantage by playing racist politics—was broken.

Fraser analysed the causes of One Nation's support as being of apiece with the neglect of ordinary people by all mainstream political parties during the years of economic rationalism.

> We should not be surprised that when an alternative appeared, however irrational, however far-fetched, people decided to give that alternative their support. The important question is what should be done. No political party can afford to go ahead as though nothing has happened ... Governments must recognise that they cannot govern for

> the economic bottom line as though there were no other issues. Much of our lives depends on things that are not economic. Rural and regional Australia need to be brought back within the ambit of mainstream politics.

If One Nation won the balance of power in the Senate, he said, it would 'make good government impossible'.[33]

In the 1998 federal election, One Nation attracted one million votes for the Senate and slightly fewer than that for the House of Representatives. It had become the most successful party in Australian history to campaign on a program of limiting immigration and abolishing multiculturalism. This was the pinnacle of One Nation's success. From that point on, it began to collapse under the weight of policy incoherence and fallings-out between its leading figures. In the meantime, though, Howard had moved to claim Hanson's voters for the Liberal Party. A new kind of debate began, in which the views of a supposed army of 'battlers' were said to be opposed to an 'elite' of liberal thinkers out of touch with mainstream Australia. Fraser had thought that Australia had advanced so far that it would never return to the politics of fear, race and sectarianism. Now, all the advances that had been made since the 1960s had to be argued for again. In his attitude to refugees, in his treatment of Aboriginal Australia, in all the other issues that had been so central to the Fraser government, Howard had proved himself assimilationist and reactionary.

As a result of his battle over the preferencing of Hanson, Fraser's relationship with the Liberal Party was under extreme strain after the 1998 election. Things got worse. Over the next three years came Howard's failure to apologise to the stolen generation, the *Tampa* crisis and the increasingly evident inhumanity of the immigration detention camps. In September 2001, Howard invoked the ANZUS treaty after terrorists destroyed the twin towers of the World Trade Center in New York. Fraser reflected on the decades of his political experience—the times when Australia had been told, in no uncertain terms, that it could not rely on US support unless America's own interests were directly involved.

Fraser opposed the second gulf war. There was nothing new or inconsistent in this. For those who had been paying attention, he had opposed NATO's bombing of Yugoslavia on the same principle. Without the United Nations' authorisation, war was a breach of international law. Invading Iraq was wrong in principle, and politically short-sighted. The United States was creating a wellspring of discontent, Fraser said, that would help the terrorists' recruiting efforts for years to come. The role of an ally such as Australia should be to speak openly, to advise the United States against unilateral action. Instead, Howard was in lock-step with the Bush regime and the neo-conservatives. Meanwhile, fear of terrorism was used to push through Australian legislation more draconian than the Communist Party Dissolution Bill proposed by the Menzies Liberal Party decades before, which had been rejected by the people at a time when Australia faced a much more potent threat.

* * *

After the 2001 federal election, with Howard once again victorious, Fraser accused both main political parties of failing to lead the nation. They had ceased to believe in, let alone practise, moral leadership.

> Why did we allow discrimination to become so rife, so blatant? Australia's current policies offend international agreements, but, more importantly, they offend every decent fibre of our being as Australians. Every idea of a fair go, the basic principle that we should do to others what we would like done to us … Who would have thought that Australia in the year 2002 could hold some thousands of men, women and children in prison without charge and without trial? … The government and opposition did not fall into these policies blindly; they planned for it and prepared for it. The boat people have been demonised.[34]

By that time, Fraser and Tamie had sold Nareen. They had sold up, not without regrets, because none of the children wished to take over the property. Meanwhile, they were spending huge amounts of time driving back and forth to Melbourne. In 2001, they were sitting up at night in their new home on the Mornington Peninsula discussing whether they should resign from the party. Their relationship with it was all but broken. For the first time since Billy Hughes, Australia had a Prime Minister who was prepared to use issues of ethnicity and religion for political advantage.

Nothing draws the attention of the news media like conflict. Fraser's open opposition to Howard on issues of race and the Iraq war brought him more media attention than he had had for years. Suddenly, views that Fraser had been expressing since at least the end of the Cold War were noticed and reported as though they were new. Fraser was calling for a reassessment of the US alliance, and for a renewed focus on relationships with the countries of South-East Asia. The media fell on this as fresh evidence that Fraser had really changed, yet there was a clear connecting thread between Fraser in the first years of the new century and the views he had been expressing since the mid 1980s and even earlier, as Prime Minister.

Fraser believed that the end of the Cold War should have been the dawn of a new age of enlightenment. With no apparent enemy, the West had had an opportunity to advance human rights across the globe, and to act with new vigour to solve the problems of trade that condemned the Third World to continued poverty. Fraser says today, 'This could have been an extraordinary century, if only the opportunities had been seized'. Instead, the election of George W Bush as US President in 2001 brought an end to that sense of possibility. The ideas of the neo-conservatives gained a stranglehold over US policy. When terrorists attacked the World Trade Center, eight months after Bush's term had begun, the United States, supported by the Blair government in the United Kingdom and the Howard government in Australia, went to war against Iraq on the basis of the spurious claim that the Western world was threatened by weapons of mass destruction. Howard declared that he would accept the United Nations Security Council's adjudication on the invasion only if it legitimised the US war plan. 'It was a tragedy', Fraser says today. The Howard government had subverted the rules and principles of international conduct to which Fraser had devoted much of his life.

By now, Fraser was taking every opportunity to be heard. There was an air of urgency, even desperation, to his attempts to persuade, as both main political parties supported the abandonment of human rights. He had dropped his commentary on economics to devote himself to the more fundamental battle: advocacy for liberal values. In 2002 he published a collection of his speeches—most of them made in the years since he had ceased to be Prime Minister—under the title *Common Ground: Issues That Should Bind and Not Divide Us*. His appeal was to all Australians, no matter how they voted. He was no longer addressing the country mainly as a member of the Liberal Party, but as an Australian who cared about freedom. He wrote in the foreword: 'The sharp, right-wing, conservative reputation I [had] has dissipated over time, but it was never accurate. Throughout my political life I have had a constant view of many social issues'. What had changed, he asserted, was that the policy differences between socialists and conservatives had disappeared, market-based economies had been embraced by all political parties, and the political spectrum had moved 'leagues to the right'. Fraser argued for increased immigration, for a renewed commitment to human rights, for an optimistic, outward-looking country playing its role in the world.[35] It was while he travelled the country promoting this book that Fraser took to saying that there were, despite appearances, still some liberals within the Liberal Party. It was to them that he owed his loyalty. They were the reason he remained a member. At literary festivals, Fraser was applauded by the same kinds of people who had once reviled him for his role in the dismissal of Whitlam.

In 2006, Fraser founded Australians All, a website dedicated to opposing all forms of racism and discrimination. He had gathered together over forty sponsors for the site, including, as he said in his first post, 'followers of Islam, members of the Jewish faith, of Christian churches and of lay people from across society'. The aim was to

> address issues that are beginning to define the essential nature of the country we live in. In the name of the so-called 'war on terror' legislative change and the politics of fear are beginning to undermine a hard-won pride in an Australia which supports openness, tolerance and diversity and shuns racism, bigotry and discrimination.[36]

Ever the progressive, at the age of seventy-six Fraser was enthusiastic about the possibilities of the internet. He thought the communications revolution had, to a small extent, helped to reduce the problems of concentration of media ownership. He toyed with models for political parties that could be internet-based, in which people could engage in debate without having to turn out to draughty meeting rooms to attend branch functions where their views would be ignored by the party machines. The Australians All website was conceived as the beginnings of a think tank, if not a movement. It publishes Fraser's articles, but also commentary by other leading thinkers on Aboriginal Australia, foreign policy and human rights.

In early 2007, Fraser began work on this book. This, too, was born out of his desire to be heard. He had rejected earlier suggestions that he write his memoirs. Now he wanted a different kind of memoir, one that spoke to a new generation about the true nature of liberalism: its rationality, resilience, beauty, pragmatism and importance. He wanted to use his experience to address the present and the future.

Fraser had begun his political career with his radio addresses to the people of Wannon. Through them, he had tried to bring all the hope and idealism of the postwar world home to the Western District of Victoria. He argued for vision, ambition and determination in the shadow of the communist threat. Now, at the other end of his political career, his columns and speeches formed the bookend to the Wannon radio addresses. So it was that in October 2007, when he gave his inaugural professorial lecture to the Melbourne University Law School, the things he said were part of a consistent line of argument and advocacy. The threats he spoke about were not communism, but the lack of a law-based world. He was still struggling for hope, but at times he did little more than ask anguished questions:

> How do our leaders come to the view that terrorism is so different and so new that we cannot live by our own standards? How do we come to overthrow the principles so necessary for a just and stable society? How do we overturn international obligations designed to limit an arms race between the superpowers? How do we set aside international conventions against torture? How do we embrace a unilateralism that is bound to lead to conflict and instability? How do we emerge from the darker age which has emerged during the war on terror? … How do rule of law countries so demean themselves that they allow these processes to occur? How is it that even more people have not been enraged? Does it rest on the age-old but narrow proposition that the people against whom these acts are directed are not like us? 'They belong to them, not to us.' Haven't we learned time and time again that, if we stand aside and allow somebody's rights to be pushed aside, if we allow arbitrary, injudicious acts of government to destroy the life of one person, don't we understand that that creates a virus that spreads through the body politic?[37]

After the lecture there was a dinner in Fraser's honour. Around the tables were faces from the past and present. Several of his former advisers were there—John Rose, Petro Georgiou and Ian Renard.

So too were some of his new friends and allies—lawyers working for human rights around the world.

The evening ended early. Fraser descended to the street, Phoebe and Tamie at his side. He was stooped, clearly a little tired. 'Ah well', he said. 'It seemed to go okay.' He knew an extract of his speech was appearing in *The Age* the next day. Once again, Fraser was in the headlines.

Four weeks later, the Howard government was defeated in the federal election of November 2007. Fraser had urged a vote for whichever party would best protect human rights.[38] To his great sadness, the Liberal Party could no longer claim that ground as indisputably its own.

23

Hope

Late afternoon in the winter of 2009, and Malcolm Fraser is sitting behind his desk in a straight-backed chair in his office high above Melbourne's Collins Street. He has been submitting himself to the interviews for this book for over two years. They have varied in tone, often interrupted by telephone calls or by Fraser checking a fact. Once, in the middle of a sentence, Fraser called out to his personal assistant, 'Julie, bring me the ANZUS treaty'. And she did. They keep a copy handy.

The conversation has been quiet and slow. This will be the last interview. The subject is the future, and the end of this book. Asked what he wants for himself in the years remaining, Fraser's eyebrows rise. 'Oh, to get my golf handicap down to twelve. But that's not likely for an eighty year old.'

'You're not eighty yet.'

'Nearly.'

There is a pause. Then he says, 'I don't think this book should have stuff in it about what I want for myself'.

It is said that biographers come to know their subject better than the subject knows themself. It can't be true in this case. There are so many parts of Malcolm Fraser that are private. He has never sought to be known, or loved, by the Australian people. He has wanted only respect, and that in the cool political sense. And yet, when one talks about the future with a man nearing eighty, the awareness that he will not be with us forever hangs over the conversation. He is aware of it too. 'This will be the most difficult chapter to write', he says. There are so many things to say to the next generation. So much that he has learned, and thought, and experienced.

* * *

Sixty years before this interview—almost to the day—the nineteen-year-old Malcolm Fraser arrived at Oxford University and began his study of politics, economics and philosophy. The men who taught him had seen two world wars in their lifetime. They were determined that the next generation should build a better world, and for a while it seemed that this would certainly be done. In the postwar years, the United Nations was established; the Universal Declaration of Human Rights was adopted and proclaimed; the International Monetary Fund and the World Bank began their work. Despite the threat of the Cold War, and all the hostility, mistakes, lost opportunities and tragedies that flowed from it, Fraser began his adult life at a time of hope and renewal in human affairs. He remembers, 'People understood that the world simply had to do better, that we couldn't continue in the way the century had begun'. He wanted to be part of building that better world.

This desire and idealism propelled Fraser into politics and public life. He came home to Victoria's Western District and began his radio addresses on the issues of the day. He was elected, served his political apprenticeship, became a minister and then led his party and his country. He achieved a great deal, if not all that he had hoped. Australia played a constructive role in the world. Australia's views were heard, and our country made the most of its influence and position. At home, there was sensible and progressive reform.

Government was prudent, pragmatic and honest. On key issues, such as immigration and Aboriginal affairs, there was leadership. Fraser formed alliances and friendships and also made mistakes and enemies. He carried the lessons he learned into his post-political career, always seeking 'basically to be useful, I suppose'. Experience tempered his idealism and qualified his optimism, but the hope for a better world is with him still.

Today there are new threats, and new, seemingly intractable, problems. The possibility that human beings could alter the weather was nowhere on the political agenda during Fraser's time in power. While he believes in the reality of human-caused climate change, it has not been one of the issues he has made his own. Yet, while the threat is new, he believes the imperatives it imposes are not. Like every other major problem facing the human race at a time of globalisation, climate change can be solved only through international action and cooperation. To play our part in combating the threat, Fraser says, Australia needs to come of age, to show independence of mind and spirit. We need to forge our own path within the community of nations. On climate change as with security, trade and the Third World, Australia as a middle power can have significant influence, acting in concert with others. As with so many other issues, the solution depends on justice—on the rich nations recognising their obligations to the poor. In this way, Fraser says, the problems of climate change are of a piece with the foreign policy challenges of the postwar world, and with the foreign policy preoccupations of his career.

Fraser believes that there is plenty of room for hope, though none for complacency. If the community of nations, against the odds, manages to tackle global warming, then it can mean only that we have reached understandings and cooperative arrangements unlike any the world has ever seen before. In the crisis that threatens the future of the planet, Fraser says, 'There just might be a bigger hope than any I have seen in my lifetime'. There is an opportunity to redraw, modernise and strengthen the architecture established in the wake of the two world wars. The imperative is stronger than ever. The better world remains within our grasp.

So how can Australia play its part? Sometimes, Fraser is tempted to say that Australia is lost. 'Well, I wonder if we are ever going to grow up. If we are ever going to stand on our own two feet.' From Federation to 1939 we relied on the United Kingdom for defence and foreign policy. But when we needed help, the United Kingdom was beleaguered and we turned to the United States. Fraser says, 'Since then, too many Australians have looked to the United States as the country which would secure our future for all time. The result is that too much of our policy has sought to please the United States. Have we asked enough what really is in the Australian interest? Have we shown independence of mind and spirit?' He fears that we will not now be able to make the necessary leap into the present, to true independence, bringing the best of Australian values to our region and the world. The end of the Cold War makes this possible. We no longer need to move in lock-step with superpowers. 'Our leaders tend to underestimate the influence that a middle-ranking power like Australia can have in the world', Fraser says. Such influence, whether it is on climate change or on any other issue, comes from the ability to act with other like-minded countries, particularly the low- and middle-ranking powers of our region. Influence does not come from unquestioning associations with the United States or other great powers; it comes from building relationships founded on integrity and independence. 'The USA has been part of almost every positive development in world affairs, but it has also been a negative influence', Fraser says. 'The Vietnam War. The Iraq War. You don't have to hunt too hard for examples.' For Australia, the best guarantee of future security is to be enmeshed and respected in our region. That implies having a foreign policy that is clearly independent of that of the United States. 'A good ally should speak forthrightly and critically if the best outcomes are to be achieved. We can be a strong ally of the USA without having to agree with them on everything. How long is it since Australia has had a leader who clearly understood that? Certainly not since the end of the Cold War, and it is since then that all the big opportunities have presented themselves.'

More than ever, Fraser believes, it is time for Australia to achieve its potential in world affairs. He wants to see Australia once again arguing what used to be called North–South issues: justice for the developing world. Globalisation is inevitable. It can be a force for good, but only if we make sure it benefits all humankind, not solely the wealthy nations. 'Australia shouldn't be frightened to be in the forefront of international action on climate change', he says. 'We should be asking in international forums what alternatives have been put to developing countries. We should be arguing for justice between countries, and developing our own solutions and getting them heard internationally.'

During his time as Prime Minister, Fraser was not afraid to make a nuisance of himself in the United States, in Europe and in Japan, arguing for trade justice and making common cause with the Third World. He placed Australia in the frontline of the fight for justice in South Africa. As this book was nearing completion, Prime Minister Kevin Rudd was active on the international stage advocating a new nuclear disarmament body and action on climate change. Fraser hopes that these initiatives will be pursued with determination and vigour. Meanwhile, the relationships with the countries of our region are a mixed bag. Fraser has been talking to his Chinese friends. He is told that China is 'perplexed' about Australia's foreign policy. Why has the Rudd government approved a white paper that paints China as a potential enemy? Is this a considered policy, or an accident? 'Nobody really knows what Australia stands for in our region.'

We need, Fraser says, to be part of the effort to build a law-based world. This—the role of law in making freedom possible—has been one of the central preoccupations of his life. He has seen significant advances. When British Prime Minister Tony Blair ordered the defence forces to invade Iraq, the Chief of the Defence

Staff Sir Michael Boyce said he would refuse to issue the order unless he was assured that the war was legal. It was significant that a Commander-in-Chief of the British forces could and would make such a demand of his Prime Minister. Even generals are now concerned for the rule of law. Even generals don't wish to be war criminals. In this way, the world has advanced.

Yet there is plenty of room for pessimism, thanks to the mendacity of some governments. In response to his request, Boyce was given a brief statement of just a few hundred words. The same words were sent to John Howard and were tabled in the Australian Parliament. The statement that Boyce and Howard were given was short and unequivocal. It was not a true legal opinion. The British Attorney-General's real opinion had been given to Blair weeks earlier. It was nothing if not equivocal, stating that the case for the war's legality was no more than reasonably arguable, and asserting that the safest course would be to seek another Security Council resolution. This opinion was suppressed, not even being presented to cabinet, until after the decision had been made to go to war.[1]

In Australia the decision to go to war was made by John Howard alone, before any discussion in cabinet and without the involvement of Australian military or intelligence advisers. Fraser believes that, in the future, no government should be able to take Australia to war unless the decision is sanctioned by both Houses of Parliament.

Australia should be part of building a world in which the great powers will respect the principle that war is illegal, unless authorised by the United Nations Security Council or when conducted in self-defence. 'People criticise the United Nations, and, God knows, it's far from perfect. But it is no more and no less than its members. Countries like Australia should refuse to be part of anything that weakens the United Nations, and they should be arguing for moves to strengthen it. How to establish an international system of law that all countries, even the most powerful, will respect may be the greatest challenge to be faced in this century, but we have to meet it if we are to get a civilised community of nations. I would like to think the record of my government suggests that a middle-ranking power like Australia can play a part in these issues.' Instead, in the last few decades Australia has moved with the United States in undermining the role of international law. 'We have done anything other than think for ourselves and act for ourselves', says Fraser. 'Is that going to change? I hope so.'

Globalisation, 'a cold and technical word, not yet adequately related to human needs', has limited the power of governments to manage their own countries. Globalisation has created great wealth, but has also increased inequalities. The World Trade Organization has largely failed to promote true competition between equal partners. The International Monetary Fund can pick up the pieces after a collapse, but can't seem to prevent the collapse in the first place. Neither are adequate for today's world. Can liberal democracy survive in a world in which corporations can transcend national borders and avoid or overwhelm national attempts at regulation? Fraser says, 'These are challenges that should be met. They are challenges that would have been willingly accepted in the 1950s, but today's world is sadly different. We have to change that. I have no doubt that we can'.

* * *

Rain hammers on the floor-to-ceiling windows. The clouds have closed over the city. It feels as though we are floating, removed from our surrounds. Sometimes, though, the mist lifts and we glimpse reminders of where and when we are. The city picked out in yellow light. The loop of the Yarra, the hills in the distance and other people in neighbouring office buildings. Red tail-lights of cars head out of town in the evening rush hour, making their stop-start journey away from the world of work and towards private spaces and private lives. Then the rain closes in again.

Fraser says, 'Now there is reason for hope. The century is young. We can turn it around'. The United States has elected a new President, Barack Obama, who represents 'all that is best in America'. Obama, says Fraser, is giving exactly the kind of message that the world wants to hear from the most important and powerful country. 'It is very much in our interests and I believe in the interests of the entire world that Obama be re-elected for his second term. No election can be taken for granted.' Australia could be offering support on international issues, and in particular on issues concerning the Middle East, 'a region that has so often been the fount of all terrorism. The United Nations has passed resolution after resolution which we and most other countries have supported, saying that the growth of settlements on the West Bank and east Jerusalem should stop. Israel moves on regardless. Obama, from all reports, is trying to haul the Israelis back'. Fraser asks, 'Do we have the courage to be part of the solution? Obama is pushing for what is right, for justice. We remain silent on such issues. We should support him and persuade others to do so'. Australia should be voicing its support for people such as the former Secretary of State James Baker and the head of the International Crisis Group Gareth Evans, who have asserted that Hamas should be brought in from the cold and become part of the peace process. 'As an ally of the United States, as a country that fervently believes in justice and peace, we should be doing whatever we can do to support President Obama in his major objective. If we moved, others might well follow. That would alter the impetus of the struggle.' Obama has explicitly rejected a future of war between different ideas of civilisation. So too should Australia. 'If we want to be a real ally to the US, if we want justice and peace, we have an opportunity.'

Fraser also believes that Australia should be 'a voice for sanity in Afghanistan'. He listens to the statements of generals, and hears in them the same words that were spoken about the Vietnam War. Change of strategy, more troops, then we will win. 'It's nonsense, of course. When will we recognise the limits of military power and the real efficacy of diplomacy in achieving peaceful outcomes?'

One of the things that prevents Australia from playing a constructive role in the Middle East, Fraser says, is fear of the Israel lobby and its power in Australian politics. Yet he believes that the lobby is of decreasing relevance, not representative of the majority of Jewish opinion. 'But it takes leadership—not just poll-driven stuff, but real leadership—to stand up to them. Where is it?'

And so we move to talking about the nature of leadership, and the things that only well-led governments can do. When Fraser was a young man, he said he hoped to live to see a population of twenty-five million in Australia. At the time it seemed a huge ambition, but today it is clear that he may well see it fulfilled. Now he wants Australia to think big—to aim for significant population increase before the end of this century. Increasing the population is an ethical obligation. 'There is no other country in the world where there is such opportunity reserved for so few. Some say we can't support so many people—that our environment would be damaged—but it can be managed. If we started now, a big national program, imagine how the country would look in a few decades.' Such a change implies big immigration programs, with the preparedness to change and be changed by the new arrivals. It also implies first-class environmental management. Both of these require visionary government and optimistic, powerful leadership. Both require a recognition of the role of government. Fraser says, 'These things can only be done by governments. The free market cannot deliver everything, and political leaders can't abrogate their responsibility to the free market'.

Government, Fraser says, should be tackling the challenges of water scarcity and land degradation with concentrated will. Twenty-six years after the drought that helped to push him out of power, Australia is again in the grip of 'a terrible bloody dry', probably made worse by climate change. Melbourne, the city that lies at our feet, is running out of water. State governments are spending billions on desalination plants and plans to pump water from country to city, yet the federal government has no comprehensive water policy to embrace the nation—country and city alike. 'It might take twenty or thirty years to implement such a policy, but if you started now with a proper plan and government commitment, it could be done. Nobody seems to be thinking with that kind of vision and scope.'

Our other major domestic challenge has been with us since the first days of European settlement: 'how to embrace Indigenous Australians within our society, maintaining respect for their culture and ancient ways; how to work cooperatively together in partnership; how to make sure that Indigenous Australians have ownership of programs designed to assist them'. The Fraser government was considered ahead of its time in the action it took in the 1970s and 1980s. Now, Fraser regrets that he didn't do more. In the present-day attempts to tackle the problems, paternalism is far from dead, he says. He has met Aboriginal people who say that programs are worked out in Canberra: consultation means no more than informing people in remote places what has already been decided. 'We need to think outside traditional ways of delivering services. Special processes are needed so Indigenous Australians can bypass the institutions that have failed them in the past. We have been too slow, by far, to move on these issues, and we have fallen well behind other countries with Indigenous minorities.' Some good things have been done, but more courage is needed, and more bold thinking.

Again, what is needed is leadership. Some Australians will oppose a new and determined focus on Aboriginal Australia. Leaders should have the capacity to argue for policies, Fraser says. When he began his radio addresses to Wannon all those years ago, he deliberately founded them in the belief that his electors were interested, intelligent participants in the political process, with a stake in the outcomes. These days, politics is so often conducted as though it were a spectator sport. The emphasis is on the political game rather than the values and policies. Fraser says, 'Leaders should have faith that Australians can be persuaded by rational argument. Australians can accept difficult decisions if they understand the reasons for them'. This faith in rationality lies at the heart of liberalism. Without a faith in reason, there can be no hope for human advancement, or for justice.

Which political party offers the best hope for Australia? Fraser believes that today, politics is less about ideology than about the ability 'to do it better'. Where should Australia look for the leaders of the future? There are no formulas, he says. 'All we can do is encourage high-minded young people to go into parliament.'

'Like you were?'

'Oh, no, more experienced than I was. Really, when I went into it, I didn't know much at all. I just felt I had something to say, that I had something to offer. I learned as I went along.' There is a long pause, and he smiles. 'I suppose I learned a few things.'

When Fraser entered parliament, the Labor Party included former shearers such as Clyde Cameron. Who in the present-day federal parliament can claim to represent blue-collar workers from the perspective of lived experience? Instead, both the main parties have become heavily influenced by similar kinds of people: political operatives who owe their positions to factions and subservience. The power of the party machine was always significant in the Labor Party. Now it has also become dominant in the Liberal Party, Fraser says. The loss of independence, particularly in the Senate, damages governance. The Howard years, with both sides of politics quiescent as human rights were abused, were possible only because of the victory of machine politics, in which debating ideas was positively discouraged, and disagreement could be understood only as disloyalty. Fraser believes that political parties should recruit people who have experience in business, the workplace, academia or the arts. The best, most independently minded politicians will be those who have achieved something in their own right before they seek public office.

The end of socialism as a political option, Fraser says, has created opportunities for a new kind of thinking. The old categories of 'left' and 'right' no longer carry the same weight of meaning. We have the potential to find new ways of connection, new solutions to old problems. Yet any politician who thinks boldly is soon attacked as being aberrant, or as being 'off message'.

We need renewal, Fraser says, and a clear political philosophy fitted to our times. 'Perhaps we need a new generation of philosophers, a new John Locke, a new Rousseau. We need an idea of how our society will develop and how people will relate to each other in a new, more global, society. We need a philosophical framework.' That framework can be grounded only in liberalism, Fraser believes, however it might be reinvented to fit the times. Liberalism is flexible, able to adapt to changing circumstances, always offering solutions to problems that are pragmatic, based on human beings with all their vulnerabilities and weaknesses, rather than arising from dogma, or counsels of perfection. At the unchanging core, there is respect for the individual, a commitment to individual liberty under the law and the principle that the strong should protect the weak. 'Those are the imperatives for a decent country, and a civilised world', he says.

There is a long silence. Night has fallen. The windows reflect us back at ourselves. 'These are the things I have believed in', says Fraser. 'Was I always right? Of course not. What did I do wrong?' He pauses. 'That will be for the reader to judge.'

The interview is over. We rise. We shake hands. The lift makes its controlled drop to the street. Outside it is cold. It would be too neat to say there is a promise of spring.

Appendix

Military Civic Action Plan 1971–72

CONFIDENTIAL

CONFIDENTIAL

50

R1761-84

HQ AFV
Army Component

3 Feb 71

See Distribution List

MILITARY CIVIC ACTION PLAN 1971/72

1. The following paragraphs contain guidelines to assist 1 Aust CA Unit in planning future activities - particularly the AFV Civic Action Plan 1971/72.

2. Project 399 is to be expedited with a view to completing all work no later than Oct 71.

3. 1 Aust CA Unit is to vacate the medical and educational fields. The unit is also to withdraw from social service type activities such as Youth and Sports since the Vietnamese are now able to develop these functions to the point that the Vietnamese themselves would wish to sustain.

4. HQ AFV will negotiate the gradual transfer of agricultural activities to the Australian Embassy, Saigon. This is expected to take some time, particularly as many of those activities have not yet reached a satisfactory level of development.

5. 1 Aust CA Unit is not to enter into new areas of military civic action.

6. The unit is to aim to be clear of military civic action involvement by the end of 1971.

J. Salmon
(J.R. SALMON)
Col
C of S

Distribution

1 ATF
1 ALSG
1 Aust CA Unit

For Information

HQ RAAF

CONFIDENTIAL

CONFIDENTIAL

Acknowledgements

A book like this owes debts to many people and organisations. Many of these debts are acknowledged in the footnotes and bibliography, but the authors would like to particularly thank some of the people whose assistance has been vital.

Dr Caitlin Stone, formerly the curator of the Malcolm Fraser Collection at the University of Melbourne Archives, acted as research assistant for this book. Her careful work, extensive knowledge of the collection and useful suggestions made an enormous difference to the authors. She became much more than a research assistant, but also a collaborator and friend.

Malcolm Fraser's personal assistants, Heather Barwick and Julie Gleeson, dug up documents, fielded queries, chased up contacts and provided invaluable support well beyond the call of duty.

Particular thanks are due to those authors who have tackled aspects of Fraser's life and career before. Many examples are noted in the bibliography, but Philip Ayres' *Malcolm Fraser: A Biography* and Patrick Weller's *Malcolm Fraser PM: A Study in Prime Ministerial Power in Australia* deserve particular mention. A debt is also owed to Tamie's sister, Christina Hindhaugh, for the very human glimpses of what life was like for Tamie in her book *It Wasn't Meant to Be Easy: Tamie Fraser in Canberra.*

Margaret Simons received a research fellowship from the Australian Prime Ministers' Centre. This was invaluable in funding the costs of many trips to the National Archives of Australia in Canberra, and other aspects of the research. Our thanks to all involved.

Staff at the National Archives of Australia, particularly Carolyn Connor, did their best to make what could have been an impossibly difficult procedure as smooth as possible. Thanks are also due to people at the National Library of Australia, the University of Melbourne Archives, the Australian War Memorial, the Deniliquin Historical Society and the State Library of Victoria.

A number of people consented to be interviewed and provided their insights and recollections for this book. Our thanks to Jim

Begg, Dale Budd, Fred Chaney, Brian Doolan, Alister Drysdale, Tony Eggleton, Robert Ellicott QC, Phoebe Fraser, Petro Georgiou, Owen Harries, Brian Johns, Ian Macphee, Spiro Moraitis, Peter Nixon, John Rose, John Salmon, Tony Staley, Ian Viner and Lorri Whiting.

Particular thanks are due to John Rose, who worked in Malcolm Fraser's office during his time as Prime Minister. Rose devoted hours to assisting with material on the economy and the moves towards financial deregulation, issues with which he was closely involved.

The authors were brought together for this project by the publisher. The idea was Sybil Nolan's and it was enthusiastically put into action by Louise Adler. We thank them for introducing us. Penny Mansley provided close, careful and empathetic copyediting, Tracy O'Shaughnessy and Eugenie Baulch steered us through the process of publication with skill and understanding. The University of Melbourne Vice Chancellor, Glyn Davis, was unfailingly supportive.

Thanks to Philip Ayres for allowing Margaret Simons access to his tape-recorded interviews with Una Fraser, and to Lady Lynch for allowing access to the Lynch Papers at the University of Melbourne Archives.

A number of people read sections of this manuscript and provided the authors with advice and help. Professor Brian Costar read the entire manuscript, as did Diana Gribble. Both were enormously helpful with suggestions and perspectives. Diana Gribble helped us to resolve a number of issues as the book neared completion. Her advice and excellent judgement were invaluable. Margaret Simons would like to thank her other colleagues at the Institute for Social Research, Swinburne University of Technology, particularly Peter Browne and Klaus Neumann for support and advice on particular chapters.

Thanks to the Dickerson family for their hospitality to Margaret Simons and her family when they toured Nareen.

Lastly, we would like to thank our families for their unfailing love and support. Tamie Fraser has been a subject, a source and a support for this book. She has read every word and has been crucial to the project.

Margaret Simons' husband John Wright and children Lachlan and Clare deserve special mention for their understanding during the many months in which every conversation was about Malcolm Fraser.

The faults of this publication are, of course, the responsibility of the authors.

Malcolm Fraser and Margaret Simons

Additional Note by Malcolm Fraser:
While I join with Margaret Simons in thanking all of those mentioned in the acknowledgements for their time, effort and support, Margaret Simons herself deserves a special mention.

I was always reluctant to write, or to be involved in writing a book of this kind because it would have meant many hours and days, even weeks, trawling through archives of the life that I had led. So many contemporary histories are written too much from memory and without sufficient reference to the raw facts of what occurred at the time. Memories can be, as I know of myself, notoriously fallible.

Apart from being an author whom both Tamie and I believe has brought the pages of this book alive, Margaret has done not only the writing but also the assiduous research that the book required. She has done this with unfailing care to make sure the facts are right. This regard for detail is especially important since the book turns some current myths about my public life on their head.

The collaboration with Margaret has been enjoyable and I thank her for the way in which she has devoted herself to bringing the book to finality.

Malcolm Fraser
12 October 2009

Notes

All unsourced quotes throughout the book are from interviews with Margaret Simons conducted between April 2007 and June 2009.

Abbreviations used in Notes and Bibliography

AWM	Australian War Memorial Collection
CD	Cabinet decision
CS	Cabinet submission
DPMC	Department of Prime Minister and Cabinet
FAD	Foreign Affairs and Defence Committee of Cabinet
HR	House of Representatives
MF	Malcolm Fraser
MFC	Malcolm Fraser Collection at the University of Melbourne
MFH	Malcolm Fraser, Hansard, House of Representatives
MFR	Malcolm Fraser, radio addresses (typescripts), originally broadcast on 3HA Hamilton & 3YB Warrnambool
MPCC	Monetary Policy Committee of Cabinet
NAA	National Archives of Australia

A Note from the Narrator

1 MF, 'Towards 2000: Challenge to Australia', fifth Alfred Deakin Lecture, 20 July 1971.

Prelude

1 MF, diary, trip through New South Wales with Gavin Casey, 2–31 March 1949, MFC 108/63.

1 Roots

1 MF, photograph album, handwritten note regarding Balpool-Nyang, [n.d.], MFC 105/36, album PA/123.
2 Una Fraser, interview with Philip Ayres, audio recording, [n.d.], in possession of Ayres. For Una's recollections included in this chapter, see also 'My Son Malcolm', *The Sun*, 19 December 1977; Una Fraser, 'A Letter for You All', letter written for her grandchildren, 1980, in possession of the Fraser family.
3 Details of the Fraser, Woolf and Booth family histories have been drawn from *Australian Dictionary of Biography: Online Edition*, Australian National University, 2006, www.adb.online.anu.edu.au, viewed May

2009; 'Grandpa Simon Fraser: Quite Napoleonic', *The Australian*, 23 July 1978; Fraser family records, various dates, MFC 105/35.

4 Simon Fraser, *The True Story of the Beginning of the Artesian Water Supply of Australia*, George Robertson, Melbourne, [n.d.], p. 5.

5 *The Bulletin*, 2 August 1919.

6 Monica Starke, *The Alexandra Club: A Narrative 1903–1983*, Alexandra Club & Elm Grove Press, Melbourne, 1986.

7 *Table Talk*, 13 September 1889.

8 'Obituary of Sir Simon Fraser', *The Age*, 31 April 1919; *The Bulletin*, 2 August 1919.

9 'Una Fraser (nee Woolf)', photographs, MFC 107/53, BWP/24607.

10 Philip Jones, 'A Woman for the Times in an Age of Constant Change', *The Australian*, 3 June 1998.

11 Unless otherwise noted, details of Woolf's life are drawn from Una Fraser, 'A Letter for You All'.

12 'Will of Louis Arnold Woolf', Probate Jurisdiction, Supreme Court of Western Australia, 13 October 1938, copy in MFC 105/35.

13 *Nulladulla,* Milton Ulladulla District Historical Society, 1972.

14 Accounts of Woolf's campaign appearances can be found in the *Perth Morning Herald*, 6 & 28 February; 2, 4, 6, 11 & 15 March 1901.

15 *Perth Morning Herald*, 19 March 1901.

16 'Truthful Thomas', *Through the Spy-Glass: Short Sketches of Well-Known Westralians as Others See Them*, Praagh & Lloyd, Perth, 1905, p. 32.

17 *Perth Morning Herald*, 8 July 1908.

18 'Will of Louis Arnold Woolf'; 'Funeral of Mr Louis Arnold Woolf at Chapel of Wood, Coppill Ltd in Bathurst Road, Katoomba', *The Sydney Morning Herald*, 14 February 1938.

19 Neville Fraser, diary, various dates, MFC 107/69.

20 MF, letter to *The Sun*, 5 June 1954.

21 Jones.

22 David Marr, *Patrick White: A Life*, Random House, North Sydney, 1991.

23 Tudor House, www.tudorhouse.nsw.edu.au, viewed May 2008.

24 Una Fraser, 'Malcolm', unpublished essay, 1980, in possession of the Fraser family.

25 MF, letters to Neville & Una Fraser, various dates, MFC 108/58.

26 Tudor House reports, Lent & Michaelmas terms 1943, MFC 108/58.

27 Una Fraser, 'Malcolm'.
28 MF, 'These I Have Loved', 1942, MFC 107/53, file 1/1.
29 MF, letter to Neville & Una Fraser, 1 April 1941, MFC 108/58.
30 MF, letter to Neville & Una Fraser, 18 July 1943, MFC 108/58.
31 'Herring' was almost certainly Sir Edmund Herring, who served in both world wars and later became the longest serving Chief Justice and Lieutenant Governor of Victoria. He was known to the Fraser family, and his role in groups such as the White Army has been documented by his biographer: Stuart Sayers, *Ned Herring: A Life of Lieutenant-General the Honourable Sir Edmund Herring*, Hyland House, Melbourne, 1980.
32 'Aims, Objects and Beliefs', in 'Top Secret: General Details of Organisation', *The Association (Post War) and the New Guard (Pre War) Vol 1*, 1931–49, NAA A6122. Histories of the Association and other anti-communist groups include Michael Cathcart, *Defending the National Tuckshop: Australia's Secret Army Intrigue of 1931*, McPhee Gribble, Fitzroy, 1988; Tim Rowse, *Australian Liberalism and the National Character*, Kibble Books, Melbourne, 1978.

2 Learning to Think

1 MF, university notes and essays, [n.d.], MFC 105/82.
2 MF, *Common Ground: Issues That Should Bind and Not Divide Us*, Viking, Melbourne, 2002, pp. 4–5.
3 MF, 'Australians: What Are We? How Do We See Ourselves? How Do Others See Us?', Commonwealth Lecture, 30 April 2007.
4 Mark J Schofield, 'Weldon, Thomas Dewar (1896–1958)', *Oxford Dictionary of National Biography: From the Earliest Times to the Year 2000*, vol. 57, ed. HCG Matthew & B Harrison, Oxford University Press, Oxford & New York, 2004, pp. 987–8.
5 ibid.
6 Anthony King, 'How Many Lives Was It Worth?', *Times Higher Education Supplement*, 25 November 1994.
7 MF, cited in Philip Ayres, *Malcolm Fraser: A Biography*, William Heinemann, Richmond, 1987, p. 53.
8 Imre Salusinszky, 'Two at Oxford', *The Age*, 24 July 1979.
9 Ayres, pp. 48–9.
10 ibid.
11 Una Fraser, interview with Philip Ayres, audio recording, [n.d.], in possession of Ayres.

3 The Candidate Must Have a Voice

1 MF, 'Human Rights and Responsibilities in the Age of Terror', Chancellor's Human Rights Lecture, University of Melbourne, 29 November 2005.
2 Philip Ayres, *Malcolm Fraser: A Biography*, William Heinemann, Richmond, 1987, p. 52.
3 MF, pre-selection speech, draft and final notes, 1953, MFC 105/82 [1].
4 Newspaper articles relating to MF's election, 1953, copies in scrapbook, MFC 108/58.
5 BA Santamaria, *Against the Tide*, Oxford University Press, Melbourne, 1981, p. 142. See also Brian Costar, Peter Love & Paul Strangio (eds), *The Great Labor Schism: A Retrospective*, Scribe, Carlton North, 2005.
6 Santamaria, p. 142.
7 Patrick Morgan (ed.), *BA Santamaria: Your Most Obedient Servant, Selected Letters 1938–1996*, Miegunyah Press, Melbourne, 2007, p. 537.
8 Robert Menzies, *The Measure of the Years*, Cassell, London, 1970, p. 98.
9 Liberal Party, campaign leaflets, 1954, MFC 105/73, box 4.
10 MFR, 24 January 1954, MFC 107/23 [231].
11 MFR, 9 September 1962, MFC 107/24 [2].
12 MFR, 14 February 1954, MFC 107/23 [231].
13 MFR, 21 February 1954, MFC 107/23 [231].
14 MFR, 21 March 1954, MFC 107/23 [231].
15 MFR, 11 April 1954, MFC 107/23 [231].
16 NAA, 'Fact Sheet 130: The Royal Commission on Espionage, 1954–55', NAA, 2006, www.naa.gov.au/about-us/publications/fact-sheets/fs130.aspx, viewed May 2009.
17 Menzies, p. 166.
18 MFR, May 1954, MFC 107/23 [231].
19 ibid.
20 'Close Fight at Polls for Them', *The Sun*, 13 May 1954, copy in scrapbook, MFC 108/58.
21 'All Eyes on Wannon: Liberal "Baby" Fights Way to the Front', *The Argus*, 3 June 1954, copy in scrapbook, MFC 108/58.
22 'Youngest Ever?', *The Sun*, 3 June 1954, copy in scrapbook, MFC 108/58.
23 'A Young Man Brings Hope', editorial, *The Argus*, 5 June 1954, copy in scrapbook, MFC 108/58.

24 MF, speech, republished as 'Liberals Endorse Fraser Again for Wannon Fight', *Horsham Times*, 19 August 1955, copy in scrapbook, MFC 108/58.
25 Quotations from MFR in 1955 are drawn from published transcripts from the *Horsham Times*, copies in scrapbook, MFC 108/58.
26 MF was the youngest member of parliament at the time, but not the youngest ever: that record is held by the Tasmanian Charles William Jackson Falkinder, who was elected in 1946 at the age of twenty-four—a few months younger than Fraser was when he was elected.
27 MF, remarks at launch of *A Thinking Reed* by Barry Jones, 5 October 2006.
28 Santamaria, pp. 120–3.
29 MFH, maiden speech, 22 February 1956, pp. 149–52.

4 Love, Danger and Privilege

1 *Sun* [Melbourne], 25 May 1956. In fact, he was neither the youngest ever, nor the tallest at the time.
2 *Portland Guardian*, 2 February 1956.
3 Dwight D Eisenhower, press statement, 7 April 1954.
4 'The Week in Canberra', *The Age*, 26 March 1956.
5 MFH, 15 March 1956, pp. 860–3.
6 MFH, 10 April 1956, pp. 1135–9; 13 September 1956, pp. 505–11.
7 Zara & Harold Holt, letter to MF, [n.d.], MFC 105/3, box 7 [53].
8 For example, 'Malcolm Fraser Is Sworn In as Member for Wannon', *Hamilton Spectator*, 23 February 1956.
9 MFH, 5 September 1957, pp. 371–3.
10 MFR, [n.d.], MFC 107/24 [1], copy in scrapbook, MFC 108/58.
11 MFH, 25 February 1958, pp. 23–31.
12 MFH, 27 March 1958, pp. 825–9.
13 MFH, 7 August 1958, p. 215.
14 MFR, 24 May 1959, MFC 107/23 [234].
15 MFR, 10 May 1959, MFC 107/23 [235].
16 MFR, 12 April 1959, MFC 107/23 [234].
17 MFR, September 1959, MFC 107/23 [235].
18 MFR, 10 April 1960, MFC 107/23 [235].
19 MFR, 24 April 1960, MFC 107/23 [235].
20 MFR, 26 March 1961, MFC 107/23 [236].
21 MFR, 24 April 1960.

22 MFH, 12 April 1961, pp. 769–72.
23 MFH, 17 August 1961, pp. 270–4.
24 MFR, 4 March 1962, MFC 107/23 [213]; MFH, 6 August 1961, pp. 128–31.
25 Una Fraser, 'A Letter for You All', letter written for her grandchildren, 1980, in possession of the Fraser family.
26 MFR, 12 & 22 November 1963, MFC 107/23 [214].
27 MFR, 12 March 1961, MFC 107/23 [236].
28 MFR, 25 November 1962, MFC 107/23 [213].
29 MFR, 9 September 1962, MFC 107/24 [2].
30 MF, letter, 1963, MFC 105/78, box 2 [24].
31 Alexander Downer (senior), letter to MF, 6 May 1965, MFC 105/78, box 2 [25].
32 MFR, 3 May 1959, MFC 107/23 [234].

5 Vietnam, Act I

1 MFR, 18 April 1965, MFC 107/23 [218].
2 MF, letter to *The Age*, 22 June 1965, copy in MFC 105/73, box 2 [18].
3 Robert McNamara, *In Retrospect: The Tragedy and Lessons of Vietnam*, Vintage, New York, 1996, pp. xx–xxi.
4 Dean Rusk as told to Richard Rusk, in Daniel S Papp (ed.), *As I Saw It*, WW Norton, New York, 1990, p. 492.
5 MF used the phrase a number of times between 1971 and 1973. The most famous occasion was in his Alfred Deakin Lecture, 20 July 1971, but he had used it before. See ch. 8 for other references.
6 MFR, 13 April 1967, NAA M13692 [38].
7 MF, 'Liberalism: As a Liberal MHR Sees It', *Today Ad Lib* (University of Melbourne Liberal journal), vol. 1, no. 1, March 1967, copy in MFC 107/23 [392].
8 John F Kennedy, inaugural address, 20 January 1961.
9 McNamara, pp. 95–7.
10 MF, tape-recorded notes made on trip to Washington, 5 May – 21 July 1964, MFC 105/78 [59] (transcript). The relevant radio addresses: MFR, 17, 20 & 30 May; 1, 5, 18, 22, 26 & 27 June; 1, 6 & 21 July 1964, all at MFC 107/23 [217].
11 MF, 'A Visit to the United States, Canada, South Vietnam and Malaysia from 5th May to July 21st 1964', formal report, 22 July 1964, MFC 107/23 [124].

12 MF, letters to CAH Thomson & Guy Pauker, 29 & 31 March 1965, MFC 107/23 [130]; MFR, official report of trip to Indonesia, March 1965, MFC 107/24 [1].
13 MF, letter to Alan Renouf, 9 March 1965, MFC 105/78, box 2 [25].
14 Correspondence between MF, Richard Krygier & Alan Fairhall, June 1966, MFC 105/73, box 4 [Defence].
15 MF, letter to Harold Holt, 17 February 1966; Holt, letter to MF, 10 June 1966, both at NAA A1209/45.
16 Paul Ham, *Vietnam: The Australian War*, HarperCollins, Sydney, 2007, ch. 15.
17 Photographs of MF taken during trip to Vietnam, 6 July 1966, AWM FOR/66/0530/VN; FOR/66/0532/VN; CAM/67/0616/VN; CAM/67/0618/VN.
18 MF, letters to Harold Holt, 19 & 24 January 1967, NAA A1209/45.
19 MFH, 24 August 1967, pp. 465–71.
20 Clark Clifford, 'A Vietnam Reappraisal', *Foreign Affairs*, vol. 47, 4 July 1969, p. 607, cited in Geoffrey Pemberton, *All the Way: Australia's Road to Vietnam*, Allen & Unwin, Sydney, 1987, p. 327.
21 Tet report received by MF, February 1968, NAA M1369 [64, part 1].

6 Too Near the Sun

1 Alan Trengove, *John Grey Gorton: An Informal Biography*, Cassell Australia, Melbourne, 1969.
2 Gough Whitlam, speech at the Australian Labor Party Victorian Branch annual conference, June 1967, cited in Jenny Hocking, *Gough Whitlam: A Moment in History*, Miegunyah Press, Melbourne, 2008, p. 289.
3 MFR, 11 January 1968, NAA M1369 [241].
4 MF, speech at a seminar arranged by the South Australian zone of the Australian Jaycees, 30 March 1968, NAA M1369 [155].
5 MFH, 20 March 1969, pp. 738–40.
6 MF, speech at the State Zionist Council of New South Wales, 16 November 1969, NAA M1374 [29]. Most attribute the first use of the word 'multiculturalism' in politics to a speech by Gough Whitlam's immigration minster Al Grassby in 1973. This is not correct. See Mark Lopez, *The Origins of Multiculturalism in Australian Politics 1945–1975*, Melbourne University Press, 2000.
7 MFR, 14 & 17 April 1968, NAA M1369 [240].
8 ibid.

9 ibid.
10 Gough Whitlam, at the Gurindji Land Ceremony, 16 August 1975.
11 MFR, 30 August 1968, NAA M1369 [240].
12 ibid.
13 The story of Gorton's nuclear plans is contained in Richard Broinowski, *Fact or Fission: The Truth about Australia's Nuclear Ambitions*, Scribe, Melbourne, 2003.
14 *The Australian Financial Review*, editorial, 30 May 1968, cited in Paul Ham, *Vietnam: The Australian War*, HarperCollins, Sydney, 2007, p. 439.
15 MF, speech at the tenth annual conference of the Australian Colleges of Education, 16 May 1969, NAA M1369 [155].
16 MF, speech at the Lord Mayor's Dinner, Melbourne Town Hall, 10 November 1969, NAA M1369 [155].
17 MF, speech at the Conference on Planning in Higher Education, 11 August 1969, NAA M1369 [80].
18 MFH, 13 August 1969, pp. 185–93.
19 Defence of Government Schools, leaflet, [n.d.], NAA M1369 [80] DOGS.
20 MF, correspondence with Garfield Barwick, 3 October 1968, NAA M1369 [368].
21 MF, correspondence with Frederick White & Peter Nixon, October 1968, NAA M1369 [368].
22 MF, opening speech at the Symposium on the Great Barrier Reef, 3 May 1969, NAA M1369 [155].
23 *The Sydney Morning Herald*, 21 August 1969.
24 *Herald* [Melbourne], August 1969, copy in scrapbook, MFC 108/58.
25 MF, speech at the Lord Mayor's Dinner.

7 Victory and Withdrawal

1 Peter Cook, *Australia and Vietnam 1965–1972*, La Trobe University, Melbourne, 1991, p. 39.
2 Richard Nixon, press statement, 25 July 1969.
3 MF, speech to delegates from university governing bodies, 22 May 1969, NAA M1369 [301].
4 MF, notes on moratorium marches, [n.d.], NAA M1369 [163] Moratorium.
5 MFR, 6 & 10 September 1970, NAA M1369 [163].
6 Evan Williams, 'A Born Winner', *The West Australian*, 5 December 1969.

7 MF, letter to John Gorton, 20 May 1970, copy in possession of MF.
8 MF, record of conversation with Billy McMahon, 6 March 1970, in possession of MF.
9 MFH, 10 March 1970, pp. 232–47.
10 MF, in Philip Ayres, *Malcolm Fraser: A Biography*, William Heinemann, Richmond, 1987, p. 147.
11 Arthur Tange, minute to MF, 20 May 1970, in possession of MF.
12 Arthur Tange, 'Defence Policy-Making: A Close-Up View 1950–1980', *Canberra Papers on Strategy and Defence No. 169*, ed. Peter Edwards, Australian National University E Press, 2008, http://epress.anu.edu.au/sdsc/dpm/html/frames.php, viewed May 2009.
13 Arthur Tange, in Ayres, p. 146.
14 Tange, 'Defence Policy-Making'.
15 Documents regarding Henry Bland's trip to the United States and the cabinet meeting afterwards, 1969, NAA A5619/1 [part 2].
16 MF, CS, 27 February 1970, NAA A5882 CO10 [part 3].
17 Lenox Hewitt, note to John Gorton, 5 March 1970, NAA A5882 CO 10 [part 3].
18 Cablegram, 7 April 1970, NAA A5882 CO 10 [part 2] F111 Discussions.
19 Memorandum agreed between MF & Melvin R Laird, 14 April 1970, NAA A5619 C 40 [part 3].
20 'Compromise Solution', *The Age*, 16 April 1970.
21 Cablegrams, 1970, NAA A5882/2 CO 10 [part 2] & [part 3].
22 Tony Street, letter to MF, [n.d.], NAA M63 [58].
23 MF, draft letter to John Gorton (not sent), July 1970, copy in possession of MF.
24 CD 484, 19 July 1970, copy in possession of MF. See also Elizabeth Ward, 'Call Out the Troops: An Examination of the Legal Basis for Australian Defence Force Involvement in Non-Defence Matters', *Australian Parliamentary Research Paper No. 8*, Commonwealth Parliamentary Library, Canberra, 1997–98.
25 Sir Thomas Daly, unpublished account of the civic action crisis, July 1985. This account is held within the Australian War Memorial archives, AWM 263, folder D/1/7, but is not available for public access. A copy was shown to Margaret Simons by another source. The account of Daly's dealings with Gorton during the civic action crisis is drawn from this document.

26 The account of the circumstances under which the civic action order was drafted is drawn from a transcript of an interview conducted as part of the Army Historical Program with Colonel (later Brigadier) JR Salmon, Chief of Staff, HQ AFV, 27 March 1972, AWM 107/1, and from a personal interview between Margaret Simons and Salmon, 30 April 2009.
27 MF, press statements, 19 & 21 February 1971, NAA M1369 [30] 1971.
28 MF, in *This Day Tonight*, television program, ABC, 23 February 1971, transcript in NAA M1369 [305].
29 *The Australian*, editorial, 23 February 1971.
30 Alan Ramsey, 'Canberra's Warriors Fight for Supremacy', *The Sunday Australian*, 28 February 1971.
31 The account of Gorton's dealings with Baudino is taken from Alan Reid, *The Gorton Experiment*, Shakespeare Head Press, Sydney, 1971; John Gorton, 'I Did It My Way: The Fraser Affair and How I Was Deposed', *The Sunday Australian*, 29 August 1971.
32 Reid, *Gorton Experiment*, p. 421.
33 Peter Samuel, 'The Australian Army's "Revolt" in Vietnam', *The Bulletin*, 6 March 1971 (available from 2 March), pp. 11–12; 'Mr Fraser and *The Bulletin*', *The Bulletin*, 19 March 1971.
34 Reid, *Gorton Experiment*, p. 420.
35 Alan Ramsey, 'General Says Fraser Is Disloyal to Service', *The Australian*, 4 March 1971.
36 Reid, *Gorton Experiment*, p. 425.
37 Alan Reid, in *Meet the Press*, television program, Channel Nine, 7 March 1971.
38 Richard Carleton, in *This Day Tonight*, television program, ABC, 9 March 1971, transcript in NAA M1369 [305].
39 MFH, 9 March 1971, p. 679.
40 Carleton.
41 MFR, 28 March 1971, NAA M1369 [30].
42 For some mentions of Kerr's continued meetings with MF, see Committee of Inquiry into Services Pay (Kerr Review), minutes, various months 1970–71, NAA A3209.

8 Life Wasn't Meant to Be Easy

1 Dr TB Miller, letter to MF, 13 May 1971, MFC 107/3 [3].
2 Patrick Morgan (ed.), *BA Santamaria: Your Most Obedient Servant, Selected Letters 1938–1996*, Miegunyah Press, Melbourne, 2007, p. 266.

3 Dick Casey, letter to MF, 24 November 1969; MF, letter to Casey, March 1970, both at NAA M64 [5].
4 MF, correspondence with BA Santamaria, various dates, NAA M1274 [62]; MFC 106/20 [14]; MFC 106/24 [12].
5 Morgan, p. 327.
6 MFH, 22 April 1971, pp. 1929–31.
7 ibid.
8 MFR, 9 July 1972, MFC 105/72 [2].
9 ibid.
10 MFR, 25 April 1972, MFC 105/72 [2].
11 MF, letters to Don Chipp, 27 April & 31 May 1972; Chipp, letters to MF, 1 May & 8 June 1972, all at MFC 105/73, box 42 [1584].
12 MFR, 6 September 1969, NAA M1369 [163].
13 MF, 'Towards 2000: Challenge to Australia', fifth Alfred Deakin Lecture, 20 July 1971.
14 MF, letter to Billy McMahon, 29 July 1971, copy in possession of MF.
15 Alan Reid, *The Gorton Experiment*, Shakespeare Head Press, Sydney, 1971; John Gorton, 'I Did It My Way: The Fraser Affair and How I Was Deposed', *The Sunday Australian*, 29 August 1971.
16 MFH, 5 October 1971, pp. 1848–9.
17 MF, letter to Lorri Whiting, 20 December 1971, MFC 106/17, box 7 [52].
18 MFH, 22 August 1972, pp. 475–92.
19 MFR, 26 November 1972, MFC 105/72 [4].
20 MFR, 11 March 1973, MFC 105/72 [7].
21 MF, standard response to public correspondence following the Liberal defeat, 1972, MFC 106/12 [5].
22 MF, letter to William Battle, 30 March 1973, NAA M1353 [11].
23 MFR, 29 April 1973, MFC 105/72 [6].
24 MF, letter to Lorri Whiting, 30 March 1973, MFC 106/17, box 7 [52].
25 MFR, 17 December 1973, MFC 105/73 [6].
26 David Kemp, 'A Leader and a Philosophy', *Australian Journal of Political Science* (previously published as *Politics*), vol. 8, no. 1, May 1973, extract in *Checkpoint*, no. 13, January 1973.
27 Women's Electoral Lobby, survey, 1972, NAA MS3683, series 7, boxes 18–19.

28 Beatrice Faust, in 'The Women's Electoral Lobby (WEL)—1972', Social Justice Almanac, CBOnline Project, 2004, www.cbonline.org au/Media/asja/ASJA_WEL_Feature_Article.doc, viewed May 2009.
29 Reg Withers, Hansard, Senate, 27 February 1973, p. 291.
30 MFR, 7 April 1974, MFC 105/72 [8].
31 MFR, 16 September 1973, MFC 105/72 [6].
32 Liberal Party & Country Party, *Employment and Industrial Relations Policy*, leaflet, Porter Print, Prahran, April 1974.
33 MFR, 14 April 1974, MFC 105/72 [8].
34 MF, letter to Lorri Whiting, 18 September 1974, MFC 106/17, box 7 [52].
35 MF, 'We Stand as Liberals 1945–1974 and Beyond', *Herald* [Melbourne], 1 August 1974.

9 Extremis

1 MF, 'What Do We Want to Be?', Walter Murdoch Lecture, 2002.
2 MF, speech notes, [21 March 1975], MFC 107/8 [146].
3 Mike Steketee, 'A Full Throated Roar of Protest'; Michael Gawenda, 'Reeling in the Aisles', both in Sybil Nolan (ed.), *The Dismissal*, Melbourne University Press, 2005.
4 MF, speech notes.
5 MFR, 30 March 1975, MFC 105/72 [9].
6 Letters to MF from: Kerry Packer, 21 March 1975, MFC 106/13, box 2 [10]; James Fairfax, 24 March 1975, MFC 106/15, box 3 [6, part 1]; John Valder, 24 March 1975, MFC 106/13, box 2 [10]; Isi Leibler, 20 May 1975, MFC 106/15, box 4 [12, part 2]; Gilles T Kryger, 24 March 1975, MFC 106/13, box 2 [10]; Alexander Downer (senior), 10 April 1975, MFC 106/15, box 3 [4, part 2]; Alan Jones, [n.d.], MFC 106/15, box 5 [10]; Sir Howard Beale, 1 April 1975, MFC 106/13, box 2 [10]; Ian Spicer, 24 March 1975, MFC 106/13, box 2 [10]; Peter Abeles, 11 May 1975, MFC 106/15, box 1 [1, part 1]; Roy Morgan, 25 March 1975, MFC 106/15, box 7 [19, part 2]; Henry Bland, 21 April 1975, MFC 106/13, box 2 [10]. BA Santamaria, 'Point of View', *News Weekly*, 26 March 1975, p. 16, copy in MFC 106/3, box 2 [10].
7 Harry B Turner, letter to MF, 23 March 1975; MF, letter to Turner, 12 May 1975, both at MFC 106/15, box 8 [21, part 2].
8 Nancy MacPherson, letter to MF, 25 March 1975; MF, letter to MacPherson, [n.d.], both at MFC 106/15, box 6 [13, part 2].

9 Elsa Staley, letter to MF, 25 March 1975; MF, letter to Staley, 11 July 1975, both at MFC 106/15, box 7 [20, part 3].
10 Marlene Stephens, letter to MF, 2 April 1975, MFC 106/15, box 8 [20, part 4].
11 Alan Lambert, letter to MF; MF, letter to Lambert, both 3 May 1975, MFC 106/15, box 5 [12, part 2].
12 MF, in *Catholic Weekly*, 12 June 1975, p. 1, copy in MFC 106/15, box 7 [20, part 1].
13 Correspondence concerning *Alvin Purple*, July 1975, MFC 106/15 [13, part 1].
14 MFH, 28 February 1975, pp. 953–5; 20 May 1975, pp. 2501–23.
15 MFH, 5 June 1975, p. 3460.
16 MFH, 17 April 1975, p. 1808.
17 MFH, 5 June 1975, pp. 3460–3.
18 MF, press statement, 1 April 1975, MFC 105/72 [9].
19 MFR, 13 April 1975, MFC 105/72 [9].
20 Gough Whitlam, Hansard, HR, 22 April 1976, p. 1948.
21 Department of Foreign Affairs, to all posts, 6 May 1975, NAA A1209 1975/1144. See also Community Affairs Branch, 'Vietnamese Refugees', 13 August 1975, NAA A1209 1976/242 [part 1]. Some of those approved for immigration to Australia were subsequently evacuated by the US military. Information drawn from Klaus Neumann & Gwenda Tavan (eds), 'Does History Matter? Making and Debating Citizenship, Immigration and Refugee Policy in Australia and New Zealand', monograph, Australia & New Zealand School of Government, Australian National University E Press, 2009.
22 'Meanness and Despicable Nature of Assistance for South Vietnamese Refugees', *The Age*, 30 April 1975.
23 MF, in *The Australian*, 28 April 1975.
24 MF, correspondence with Gough Whitlam, July–September 1975, MFC 107/5 [1976, part 1].
25 MF, correspondence with Tom Crombie & others, MFC 106/15, box 3.
26 Cited in Nancy Viviani & Joanna Lawe-Davies, 'Australian Government Policy on the Entry of Vietnamese Refugees 1976 to 1978', *Research Paper No. 2*, School of Modern Asian Studies, Griffith University, Brisbane, February 1980.
27 Neumann & Tavan.

28 Peter Wilenski, draft submission to minister, May 1975, NAA A446 1974/77554, cited in Neumann & Tavan.
29 RU Metcalfe, to minister, 4 July 1975, NAA A446 1974/77554, cited in Neumann & Tavan.
30 MFR, 10 July 1975, MFC 105/72 [9].
31 Shadow cabinet minutes, various dates, MFC 106/22 [7].
32 Treasury briefing, July 1975, MFC 106/24 [12].
33 MFR, 17 August 1975, MFC 107/3 [22, part 1].
34 BA Santamaria, letter to MF, 22 August 1975, MFC 106/24 [12].
35 MFH, 26 August 1975, pp. 519–27.
36 MF, foreign policy statement, October 1975, MFC 106/22, box 4 [50].
37 MF, joint party meeting minutes, 30 September 1975, MFC 106/22, box 3 [46].
38 The account of those events in the loans affair and constitutional crisis where MF was not directly involved has, unless otherwise noted, been drawn from Paul Kelly, *November 1975: The Inside Story of Australia's Greatest Political Crisis*, Allen & Unwin, Sydney, 1995.
39 'Statement 10: Historical Australian Government Data', *Budget Paper No. 1: Budget Strategy and Outlook 2009–10*, Commonwealth of Australia, 2009, www.budget.gov.au/2009-10/content/bp1/html/bp1_bst10.htm, viewed June 2009.
40 John Kerr, *Matters for Judgment*, Macmillan, Melbourne, 1978, pp. 238 ff.
41 Rex Connor, Hansard, HR, 9 July 1975, p. 3611.
42 Treasury documents, 1975, MFC 106/22 [13] & [14]; MFC 106/24 [12].
43 MFR, 20 July 1975, MFC 105/72 [9].
44 ibid.
45 MFH, 9 July 1975, pp. 3605–11.
46 Kerr, p. 240.
47 Philip Ayres, *Malcolm Fraser: A Biography*, William Heinemann, Richmond, 1987, p. 258.
48 Four issues went to this referendum: Senate casual vacancies, simultaneous elections, the retiring age of judges and a national song plebiscite.
49 Shadow cabinet minutes, 29 September 1975, MFC 106/2 [44].
50 BA Santamaria, draft speech for MF, cited in Denis Shanahan, 'Santamaria's Secret Dismissal Role', *The Australian*, 6 January 2007. According to Shanahan, the original is held in Santamaria's papers in

the State Library of Victoria, Melbourne, to which the authors have not had access.

51 Peter Baume, 'A Soldier Regrets', in Nolan, p. 62.
52 Tony Eggleton, briefing note to MF, 29 September 1975, MFC 106/22 [45].
53 Shadow cabinet minutes; MF, joint party meeting minutes, both 30 September 1975, MFC 106/22 [44].
54 Shadow cabinet minutes, 6 October 1975, MFC 106/22.
55 MF, cited in Ayres, p. 273.
56 Baume, p. 62.
57 Shadow ministry minutes, 15 October 1975, MFC 106/22 [47].
58 Shadow cabinet minutes, 19 & 21 October 1975, both at MFC 106/22, box 3 [49].
59 Kelly, p. 237.
60 MF, correspondence with Thomas Playford & Don Jessop, 1975, MFC 106/20 [9].
61 MF, correspondence with Dick & April Hamer, 1975, copies in possession of MF.
62 Robert Menzies, press statement, 22 October 1975, MFC 106/24 [28].
63 Shadow cabinet minutes, October 1975, MFC 106/22, box 4 [50].
64 Commissioner of Taxation, memorandum to Deputy Commissioner of Taxation, October 1975, MFC 106/22 [14].
65 MFH, 11 November 1975, p. 2913.
66 Ian Macphee, letter to MF, 2 November 1975; MF, letter to Macphee, 7 November 1975, both at MFC 106/20 [12].
67 Budd, Nolan, p. 48.
68 Tony Eggleton, briefing notes to MF; Joint party meeting minutes, both 11 November 1975, NAA M1360 [52].
69 Kerr, pp. 358 ff.; Gough Whitlam, *The Truth of the Matter*, Melbourne University Press, 2005, p. 110.
70 Kerr, p. 367.
71 Nolan, p. 43.

10 How to Govern

1 Bob Hawke, in Sybil Nolan (ed.), *The Dismissal*, Melbourne University Press, 2005, p. 67.
2 Joint party meeting minutes, 12 November 1975, NAA M1360 [52].
3 Paul Kelly, *The Unmaking of Gough*, Angus & Robertson, Sydney, 1976, p. 375.

4 MF, 'Turn on the Lights', policy speech (pamphlet), 27 November 1975, MFC 107/8 [171].
5 Robert Menzies, letter to MF, 2 December 1975, NAA M1268 [138].
6 Robert Menzies, letter to Tamie Fraser, 10 December 1975, copy in possession of the Fraser family.
7 Shadow cabinet meeting working papers, November 1975, MFC 106/22 [54]; *Public Service Amendment (First Division Officers) Act 1976*; Hansard, HR, 9 May 1984, p. 2152.
8 Cabinet minutes, 14 January 1976, NAA A10756 LC 55.
9 Cabinet minutes, 6 January 1976, NAA A10756 LC 91 [part 1].
10 Tony Eggleton, memorandum to MF, 29 March 1976; John Kerr, handwritten letter to MF, 14 April 1976; MF, letter to Kerr, 14 May 1976; Kerr, letter to MF, 10 June 1977; Eggleton, confidential briefing note to MF, 29 March 1976, all in possession of MF.
11 The documents on which this account is based include: David N Reid, note for file, 21 November 1975; John Menadue, letter to CW Harders, 21 November 1975; Harders, memorandum to Ivor Greenwood, 5 December 1975; Greenwood, letter to MF, 16 December 1975, all at NAA M1356 [36].
12 The account of the Bjelke-Petersen–Fancher allegations is taken from Robert Ellicott, memorandum to MF and enclosures, 1 January 1976, NAA M1268 [304].
13 Hansard, HR, 19 May 1976, pp. 2053–185.
14 Robert Ellicott, Hansard, HR, 6 September 1977, pp. 721–7.
15 For a discussion on the history of the principle and commentary on the Ellicott–Sankey case, see LJ King, 'The Attorney General, Politics and the Judiciary', paper delivered to the fourth annual colloquium of the Judicial Conference of Australia, November 1999. King is a former Attorney-General of South Australia.
16 Sir Maurice Byers, legal opinion, 8 August 1977, NAA 76/02739 [part 2].
17 MFH, 6 September 1977, pp. 721–8.
18 Stephen Foley & Marshall Wilson, *Anatomy of a Coup: The Sinister Intrigue behind the Dismissal*, Canterbury Press, Melbourne, 1990.

11 Balance

1 MF, letter to ministers, 23 December 1975, NAA A10756 LC 94 [part 1].

2 Peter Bowers, 'Quietly, Fraser Is Setting the Scene', *The Sydney Morning Herald*, 9 January 1976.
3 Extracts from budgetary planning documents; MF, note for file, 2 February 1976, both at NAA A10756 LC 52 [part 3].
4 MF, 'The World Economic Crisis: Its History and Solutions', speech at the World Economic and Investment Conference, 20 March 1984.
5 Margaret Thatcher, interview with *Women's Own*, 31 October 1987.
6 MF, 'Towards 2000: Challenge to Australia', fifth Alfred Deakin Lecture, 20 July 1971.
7 Edmund Burke, speech to the electors of Bristol, 3 November 1774, cited in MF, 'Sir Robert Menzies: In Search of Balance', Daniel Mannix Memorial Lecture, 30 July 1987.
8 David Kemp, notes to MF, NAA M1276 [108]. The notes referred to Milton Friedman, 'The Line We Dare Not Cross', *Encounter*, vol. 47, no. 5, November 1976. The Chipman article is not in the archive, so a reference cannot be given.
9 MF, 'Sir Robert Menzies'.
10 CS, May 1976, NAA M1276 [123, part 2].
11 Patrick Weller, *Malcolm Fraser PM: A Study of Prime Ministerial Power in Australia*, Penguin, Melbourne, 1989, p. 223.
12 MF, letter to ministers.
13 *The Age*, 21 May 1976, cited in Weller, p. 228.
14 Phillip Lynch, letter to MF, 14 May 1976, NAA A10756 LC 476.
15 David Kemp, 'The 1976 Cabinet Papers: A Reply to John Stone', *Quadrant*, vol. 51, no. 12, December 2007.
16 Phillip Lynch, Hansard, HR, 20 May 1976, pp. 2329–45.
17 Phillip Lynch, CS 532, 13 July 1976; Ed Visbord, DPMC, commentary, 13 July 1976, both at NAA A10756 LC 869.
18 Correspondence regarding acquisition of information from Treasury, 1976, is drawn from MFC 107/4.
19 MF, record of conversation with Mr Witteveen, 12 October 1976, NAA M1356 [61].
20 CD 1931, 28 November 1976, NAA A13075. For more on the briefings that led up to the decision, see ch. 16.
21 MFH, 30 November 1976, p. 2962.
22 Harold Knight, Hansard, HR, 7 December 1976, pp. 3363–4.
23 MFH, 9 December 1976, pp. 3623–5.

24 Milton Friedman, *The Australian*, 2 December 1976, in 'Adviser's Research Materials', NAA M1276 [78].
25 John Stone, 'The Dismal Beginning to the Fraser Years', *Quadrant*, vol. 51, nos 7–8, July–August 2007.
26 MF, 'Australia and Some World Economic Issues', speech to the Economic Club of New York, 4 January 1979.
27 George Polities, spokesman for national employers, cited in Hansard, HR, 5 May 1981, p. 1941.
28 MF, 'Australia and Some World Economic Issues'.
29 The details of the decisions on the levy are in CD 6465 (Ad Hoc Committee of Cabinet), 28 July 1978, in which cabinet authorised MF and John Howard to settle the final package of budget revenue measures; and in MF, letter to Howard (setting out what they had agreed), 3 August 1978, which became CD 6491 (Ad Hoc Committee of Cabinet), 7 August 1978, all at NAA A13075.
30 John Howard, Hansard, HR, 17 August 1982, p. 61.
31 John Howard, briefing to cabinet; DPMC, commentary, both June 1982, NAA A10756 LC 94 [part 7].
32 David Richardson, 'Official Economic Forecasts—How Good Are They?', *Parliamentary Library Current Issues Brief 17, 2000–2001*, Parliament of Australia, Canberra, 26 June 2001.
33 Treasury statement no. 5, budget papers 1983–84, 1983.
34 Christina Hindhaugh, *It Wasn't Meant to Be Easy: Tamie Fraser in Canberra*, Lothian, Melbourne, 1986.
35 MF, press statement, 16 November 1982.
36 MF, premiers' conference agenda brief, 7 December 1982, NAA M1352 [14].
37 MF, policy speech, 15 February 1983.
38 See 'Statement 10: Historical Australian Government Data', *Budget Paper No. 1: Budget Strategy and Outlook 2009–10*, Commonwealth of Australia, 2009, www.budget.gov.au/2009-10/content/bp1/html/bp1_bst10.htm, viewed June 2009.
39 For Joe Hockey's comments, see David Uren, 'Don't Lose Your Nerve on Reform, Warns Treasury Head Ken Henry', *The Australian*, 20 May 2009. For Ken Henry's remarks, see Henry, 'Post-Budget Address to the Australian Business Economists', 19 May 2009, Commonwealth of Australia, www.treasury.gov.au/documents/1546/

HTML/docshell.asp?URL=Contemporary%20Challenges%20in%20 Fiscal%20Policy.html, viewed June 2009.

12 The Difficulties of Freedom: Aboriginal Australia and Human Rights

1 Photographs of trip to the Northern Territory, 1978, in '1978—Northern Territory', album, MFC 105/104.
2 MF, letter to Ian Viner, 3 May 1978, NAA A10756 LC 793 Aboriginal Policy [part 1].
3 Ralph Hunt, letter to MF, 17 May 1978, NAA M1268 [3, part 2].
4 Documents regarding Aboriginal affairs, 1978, NAA A10756 LC 793 Aboriginal Policy.
5 Peter Sutton, *The Politics of Suffering: Indigenous Australia and the End of Liberal Consensus*, Melbourne University Press, 2009.
6 MFH, 20 April 1961, pp. 1085–8.
7 MF, letter to CE Barnes, 9 March 1965; Barnes, letter to MF, 7 April 1965, both at NAA A452 NT1965/1955.
8 MF, inaugural address to the Institute of Multicultural Affairs, 30 November 1981.
9 Senior advisers' research material, 26 March 1975, NAA M1276 [1] Aboriginal Affairs.
10 Draft Aboriginal Affairs policy, [August 1975], MFC 106/22 [54].
11 CD 1564, 23 September 1976, NAA A10756 LC 793 [part 1].
12 David Hay, *The Delivery of Services Financed by the Department of Aboriginal Affairs*, Australian Government Publishing Service, Canberra, 1976.
13 CS 265 & 287, 25 May 1976, NAA A12909.
14 For the background to why Aboriginals opposed the department and Killoran, see Raymond Evans, *A History of Queensland*, Cambridge University Press, Melbourne, 2007, pp. 235–7.
15 Ian Viner, letter to MF, 2 February 1976, NAA A10756 LC 180.
16 MF, letter to Joh Bjelke-Petersen, 5 March 1976, NAA A10756 LC 180.
17 MF, speech to the National Aboriginal Conference, 3 April 1978.
18 CS 2046, 21 March 1978; CS 2097, 9 April 1978; CS 2538, 24 July 1978; CS 2562, 13 August 1978, all at NAA A12909. See also Jackie Huggins & Peter Read, interview with Ian Viner, Council for Aboriginal Reconciliation Collection, Oral History Collection, National Library of Australia, Canberra, 8 May 2006.

19 Charles Court, letter to MF, August 1980, NAA M1268 [4, part 1].
20 Charles Perkins, interview with Robin Hughes, 6 May 1998, Australian Biography, www.australianbiography.gov.au/subjects/perkins/intertext1.html (transcript), viewed June 2009.
21 Correspondence regarding positive discrimination in the Commonwealth public service, MF, letters to Tony Street, 21 October 1977 & 3 July 1978; John Carrick, letter to MF, 8 November 1978; DPMC, briefing note, September 1977; AJ Ayres, letter to MF, 21 October 1977; CS 2580, 29 August 1978, all at NAA A10756 LC 1381 [part 1].
22 Coordination Committee, CD 12884, 3 November 1980; CS 4511, 15 January 1981; DPMC, briefings to MF, 22 January 1981 & 28 January 1983; CD 13658, 29 January 1981, all at NAA A10756 LC 793 [part 2].
23 Perkins.
24 Peter Sutton, 'The Politics of Suffering: Indigenous Policy in Australia since the 1970s', *Anthropological Forum*, vol. 11, no. 2, 2001, pp. 125–73.
25 Fred Chaney, Lowitja O'Donoghue Oration, 28 May 2009.
26 MF, speech at the forty-sixth ANZAAS Congress, 22 January 1975.
27 CD 1994, 8 December 1976, NAA A10756 LC 1151.
28 Geoffrey Yeend, notes to MF, 16 & 20 May 1977, both at NAA A10756 LC 1151 [part 1].
29 Geoffrey Yeend, note to MF, 21 October 1977, NAA A10756 LC 1151 [part 2].
30 Geoffrey Yeend, note to MF, 14 April 1980, NAA A10756 LC 1151 [part 2].
31 Matthew Franklin, 'John Faulkner in Call for Disclosure', *The Australian*, 6 May 2009; John Faulkner, press statement, 12 May 2009.
32 *Ahmed Ali Al-Kateb v. Philippa Godwin (Deputy Secretary, Department of Immigration and Multicultural and Indigenous Affairs), Julie Helen Keenan (Acting Director of the Unauthorised Arrivals Section) & Minister for Immigration and Multicultural and Indigenous Affairs* (2004) 219 CLR 562; *Minister for Immigration and Multicultural and Indigenous Affairs v. Abbas Mohammad Hasan Al Khafaji* (2004) 219 CLR 6.
33 Northern Territory of Australia, Ordinance No. 16, 1911, published in *Commonwealth of Australia Gazette*, 8 January 1912; F Wise, letter to Secretary of Department of Territories, 28 February 1952;

Paul Hasluck, handwritten notes, all cited in Malcolm Fraser, *Common Ground: Issues That Should Bind and Not Divide Us*, Viking, Melbourne, 2002, pp. 197–201.

34 MF, in *7.30 Report*, television program, ABC, 29 May 2000.

35 MF, 'The Past We Need to Understand', Vincent Lingiari Memorial Lecture, 24 August 2000.

36 MF, 'National Sorry Day: Journey of Healing', speech, 26 May 2004.

37 Rex Wild & Patricia Anderson, *Little Children Are Sacred*, report of the Board of Inquiry into the Protection of Aboriginal Children from Sexual Abuse, Northern Territory Government, Darwin, 30 April 2007.

13 Leadership: Immigration and Refugees

1 Michael MacKellar, CS 2771, 20 November 1978, NAA A10756 LC 1366 [part 2].

2 Nancy Viviani & Joanna Lawe-Davies, 'Australian Government Policy on the Entry of Vietnamese Refugees 1976 to 1978', *Research Paper No. 2*, School of Modern Asian Studies, Griffith University, Brisbane, February 1980, p. 18.

3 LWB Engeldow, discussion paper, 1978, NAA A10756 LC 1366 [part 1].

4 Michael MacKellar & Andrew Peacock, CS 2173, 4 May 1978 and Michael MacKellar, letter to MF, 3 May 1978, NAA A10756 LC 1366 [part 1].

5 Moss Cass, 'Stop This Unjust Queue Jumping', *The Australian*, 29 June 1978, cited in Barry York, 'Australia and Refugees 1901–2002: An Annotated Chronology Based on Official Sources', Parliament of Australia, 2003, www.aph.gov.au/library/pubs/online/Refugees_s2.htm, viewed June 2009.

6 Cabinet Memorandum 380, 11 July 1979, NAA A10756 LC 1366 [part 3].

7 DPMC, notes to MF, AT Griffith 8 February, KS Hutchings 3 May & 11 May, Roger Holdich 21 November 1978; 8 July 1979, all at NAA A10756 LC 1366 [parts 1–3].

8 United Nations Convention Relating to the Status of Refugees, article 31, 28 July 1951.

9 FAD, CD 6716, 14 September 1978, NAA A1076 LC 1366 [part 2].

10 CD 8569, 15 May 1979; CD 9149, 10 July 1979; CD 11759 (ad hoc), 27 May 1980, all at NAA A10756 LC 1366 [parts 2–3].

11 Gwenda Tavan, *The Long Slow Death of White Australia*, Scribe, Melbourne, 2005, p. 216.
12 The figures for countries other than Australia are United Nations High Commissioner for Refugees (UNHCR) statistics to the end of 1981, cited in Nancy Viviani, *The Long Journey: Vietnamese Migration and Settlement in Australia*, Melbourne University Press, 1984, p. 50. It should be noted that the UNHCR statistics for Australia do not correspond exactly with those of the Department of Immigration and Ethnic Affairs.
13 Nancy Viviani, *From Burnt Boats to Barbecues: The Indochinese in Australia 1975–1995*, Oxford University Press, Sydney, 1996, p. 47.
14 Constitution of Nauru, clause 5 (1); Constitution of the Independent State of Papua New Guinea, division 3, s. 32.
15 Human Rights and Equal Opportunities Commission, *A Last Resort? The National Inquiry into Children in Immigration Detention*, Human Rights and Equal Opportunities Commission, Sydney, 2004.
16 Refugee Council of Australia, 'Australia's Refugee and Humanitarian Program', submission to the federal government, Refugee Council of Australia, January 2008, pp. 12, 14, www.refugeecouncil.org.au/docs/resources/submissions/2009-10_intakesub.pdf, viewed June 2009.
17 Howard's denial of the conversation is in Mike Steketee, 'Howard in War Refugee Snub: Fraser', *The Australian*, 1 January 2008. In Howard's recent biography, he claims instead not to remember the exchange, but does not deny it: Wayne Errington & Peter Van Onselen, *John Winston Howard: The Biography*, Melbourne University Press, 2007, p. 77. The cabinet attendance registers are in 'Attendance Sheets 14/1/77–20/12/77', NAA A12575 [1]. The refugee policy was brought to cabinet on 3 May 1977 as CS 1160, and after-discussion was deferred (CD 2855). The policy was adopted by cabinet on 23 May 1977 at a meeting of the FAD: CD 2977, all at NAA A10756 LC 1366 [part 1]. Howard was present at the meeting on 3 May, but not at the FAD meeting on 23 May. These cabinet records are now open to the public.
18 Errington & Van Onselen, pp. 157–8.
19 MF, speech to State Zionist Council of New South Wales, 16 November 1969, NAA M1374 [29].
20 Australian Ethnic Affairs Council, report, 1977, cited in James Jupp, *From White Australia to Woomera*, Cambridge University Press, Melbourne, 2002, p. 85.

21 MF, speech to the inaugural meeting of the Institute of Multicultural Affairs, 30 November 1981.
22 Australian Population and Immigration Council, *Immigration Policies and Australia's Population: A Green Paper*, Australian Government Publishing Service, Canberra, 1977.
23 Department of Immigration and Ethnic Affairs, *Australia's Immigration Policy*, prepared by Michael MacKellar, Australian Government Publishing Service, Canberra, 1978.
24 Department of Foreign Affairs, file note, 24 October 1975, NAA A1838 1634/70/2 [part 8].
25 Department of Foreign Affairs, 'Undertakings by Vietnamese', memorandum, 1 September 1975, NAA A1838 3014/10/15/4 [part 10].
26 CS, 22 September 1976; DPMC, comments, [22 September 1976], both at NAA A10756 LC 1013.
27 CS, 22 November 1976, NAA A10756 LC 1013.
28 Matthew Franklin, 'Fraser Was Warned on Lebanese Migrants', *The Australian*, 1 January 2007.
29 See Katherine Betts & Ernest Healy, 'Lebanese Muslims in Australia and Social Disadvantage', *People and Place* (Centre for Population and Urban Research, Monash University, Melbourne), vol. 14, no. 1, 2006, pp. 38–40.
30 For more comment on the statistics, see George Megalogenis, 'The Threat from Within', *The Weekend Australian*, 8 April 2006.
31 Senate Standing Committee on Foreign Affairs and Defence, *Australia and the Refugee Problem: The Plight and Circumstances of Vietnamese and Other Refugees*, Australian Government Publishing Service, Canberra, 1976, pp. 77, 89.
32 MF, letter to Michael MacKellar, 1 November 1976, mentioned in DPMC, advice on CS 1160, both 7 April 1977, all at NAA A10756 LC 1366 [part 1].
33 MF, speech to the Institute of Multicultural Affairs.
34 Andrew Rule, 'Galbally's Lore', *The Age*, 13 October 2005.
35 Frank Galbally, *Galbally! The Autobiography of Australia's Leading Criminal Lawyer*, Viking, Ringwood, 1989, pp. 166–7.
36 MF, correspondence with Frank Galbally, including letter of 29 September 1977 on administrative arrangements, NAA M1268 [88, part 1].

37 MFH, 30 May 1978, pp. 2727–33.
38 Australian Institute of Multicultural Affairs, *Evaluation of Post Arrival Programs and Services*, Australian Institute of Multicultural Affairs, Melbourne, May 1982, cited in Freda Hawkins, *Critical Years in Immigration: Canada and Australia Compared*, McGill-Queen's University Press, Sydney & Quebec, 1989, ch. 3.
39 Viviani, p. 31.
40 Frank Galbally, Interview for Making Multicultural Australia, 1994, www.multiculturalaustralia.edu.au/library/media/Audio/id/566. Australian-Institute-of-Multicultural-Affairs, viewed May 2009.
41 John Button, Hansard, Senate, 22 May 1980, pp. 2664–7.
42 MF, speech to the Institute of Multicultural Affairs.
43 Pauline Hanson, Hansard, HR, 10 September 1996, p. 3859.
44 Dan Harrison, 'African Refugees Face Integration Issues: Andrews', *The Age*, 3 October 2007.

14 The World

1 Department of Defence, *Defending Australia in the Asia Pacific Century: Force 2030*, white paper, Commonwealth of Australia, Canberra, 2009.
2 Australia, New Zealand and the United States Security Treaty, 1951, articles 3 & 4.
3 Arthur Tange, 'A Memoir on Garfield Barwick, the Man, the Minister', unpublished, February 1999, n.p., copy in possession of the authors. See also David Marr, *Barwick*, Allen & Unwin, Sydney, 1980, pp. 207–9.
4 MFH, 1 June 1976, pp. 2734–44.
5 MF, speech to the Zionist Council of Victoria, 3 May 1981.
6 MFH, 11 September 1980, p. 1199.
7 Senate Foreign Affairs, Defence and Trade References Committee, *East Timor: Final Report of the Senate Foreign Affairs, Defence and Trade References Committee*, Parliament of the Commonwealth of Australia, Canberra, December 2000.
8 Cablegram to Richard Woolcott, 20 November 1975, NAA A11443 [14]; Woolcott, cablegram to MF, 25 November 1975, NAA A11443 [11], both also published in Department of Foreign Affairs and Trade, *Australia and the Indonesian Incorporation of Portuguese Timor*, Melbourne University Press, 2000, p. 579.
9 Andrew Peacock, CS FAD/1, 9 February 1976, NAA A10756 LC 209 [part 1].
10 Senate Foreign Affairs, Defence and Trade References Committee.

11 ibid.
12 MFH, 1 June 1976, pp. 2734–44.
13 Gough Whitlam, Hansard, HR, 1 June 1976, p. 2744.
14 The account of the drafts of this speech and the comments on them is drawn from NAA M1276 [225, parts 1–6].
15 Fred Chaney, notes, [n.d.], NAA M1276 [204].
16 MF, letter to Gerald Ford, March 1976; Andrew Peacock, notes on draft, 6 March 1976, both at NAA M1356 [18].
17 Tamie Fraser, cited in Christine Hindhaugh, *It Wasn't Meant to Be Easy: Tamie Fraser in Canberra*, Lothian, Melbourne, 1986, pp. 31–2.
18 Gary Woodard, Moreen Dee & Max Suich, 'Negotiating the Australia–Japan Basic Treaty of Friendship and Cooperation: Reflections and Afterthoughts', *Asia Pacific Economic Paper No. 362,* Australia–Japan Research Centre, Australian National University College of Asia and the Pacific, Canberra, 2007.
19 *Peking People's Daily*, cited in Philip Ayres, *Malcolm Fraser: A Biography,* William Heinemann, Richmond, 1987, p. 332.
20 Cited in Hindhaugh, p. 38.
21 Record of conversation between MF & President Gerald Ford (also present, Secretary of State Henry Kissinger), 27 July 1976, NAA M1356 [59].
22 Record of conversation between MF & Henry Kissinger, 28 July 1976, NAA M1356 [22].
23 Owen Harries, report of a conversation with Jimmy Carter during eight days on the east coast of the United States, 24 September – 1 October 1976, 5 November 1976, NAA M1276 [105, part 3].
24 Department of Foreign Affairs and Defence, 'Paper on Jimmy Carter's Foreign Policy and Its Implications for Australia', 9 November 1976, NAA A10756 LC 1101 [part 1].
25 Jimmy Carter, press statement, 24 March 1977.
26 Andrew Peacock, report to cabinet, 1 November 1977, NAA A10756 LC 1735.
27 Tange.
28 ibid.
29 Wayne Errington & Peter Van Onselen, *John Winston Howard: The Biography*, Melbourne University Press, 2007, pp. 72–3.
30 MFR, cited in *The Age* (Business section), 27 November 1978.

31 Owen Harries (ed.), *Australia and the Third World: Report of the Committee on Australia's Relations with the Third World*, Australian Government Publishing Service, Canberra, 1979.
32 JDB Miller, 'Encountering a New World', *Australian Journal of International Affairs*, vol. 34, no. 1, April 1980, pp. 100–9.
33 MFH, 19 February 1980, p. 17.
34 CD 10546, 19 December 1979, NAA A10756 LC 1735.
35 MFH, 28 February 1980, pp. 487–9.
36 Andrew Peacock, CS 3748, 8 January 1980, A10756 LC 2773.
37 ibid.
38 Jimmy Carter, letter to MF, 12 December 1979, NAA M1333 [6].
39 Jimmy Carter, *Meeting with Prime Minister J Malcolm Fraser of Australia: Remarks to Reporters on the Prime Minister's Departure*, 7 February 1980, American Presidency Project, 2009, www.presidency.ucsb.edu/ws/index.php?pid=32901&st=malcolm+fraser&st1=, viewed May 2009.
40 MF, draft letters to Jimmy Carter, Pierre Trudeau, Margaret Thatcher, Robert Muldoon & Helmut Schmidt, 21 April 1980, NAA A10756 LC 2773.
41 Mike Safe, 'I Just Wanted to Swim', *The Australian Magazine*, 8–9 March 2008.
42 MFH, 28 August 1980, p. 976.
43 MF, letter to Pierre Trudeau, 10 February 1979, NAA M1333 [1].
44 CD 12130, 15 July 1980, NAA M1268 [300].
45 CD 1239, 23 September 1980, NAA M1268 [300].
46 Andrew Peacock, memorandum to cabinet, 22 August 1980, LC 1101 [part 2].
47 The National Security Council meeting and its result were reported in Bernard Gwertzman, 'US Sides with Britain in Falkland Crisis', *The New York Times*, 1 May 1982.
48 Cabinet memorandum, December 1982, NAA A10756 LC 1101 [part 2].
49 Helmut Schmidt, letter to MF, 1 October 1982, NAA M1333 [2] Correspondence with Heads of Government.
50 MF, 'The World Economic Crisis: Its History and Solutions', speech delivered at the World Economic and Investment Conference, 20 March 1984.
51 MFH, 1 June 1976, pp. 2734–44.

15 Commonwealth

1 Geoffrey Howe, letter to Margaret Thatcher, 2 June 1977, Margaret Thatcher Foundation, 2009, www.margaretthatcher.org/document/BE70125BBE7C43BF980A41A15120799A.pdf, viewed July 2009.
2 Margaret Thatcher, telegram to MF, 15 December 1975, Margaret Thatcher Foundation, 2009, www.margaretthatcher.org/speeches/displaydocument.asp?docid=102470, viewed July 2009.
3 MFH, 1 June 1976, pp. 2734–44.
4 MFH, 15 March 1956, pp. 860–3.
5 MFH, 12 April 1961, pp. 769–72.
6 Information on the history of the Commonwealth of Nations is taken from The Commonwealth, www.thecommonwealth.org, viewed July 2009. See also 'Singapore Declaration of Commonwealth Principles 1971', The Commonwealth, 2004, www.thecommonwealth.org/shared_asp_files/GFSR.asp?NodeID=141097, viewed July 2009.
7 MF, CS 1220; FAD, CD 2882, both 5 May 1977, NAA A10756 LC 1363.
8 Linda Freeman, 'All but One: Britain, the Commonwealth and Sanctions', in Mark Orkin (ed.), *Sanctions against Apartheid*, New Africa Books, Cape Town, 1989, p. 152.
9 MF, speech to the Royal Commonwealth Society, 3 June 1977, cited in Philip Ayres, *Malcolm Fraser: A Biography*, William Heinemann, Richmond, 1987, p. 346.
10 Michelle Grattan, 'Muldoon Upsets the Apple Cart', *The Age*, 5 October 1981.
11 Gleneagles Agreement, Commonwealth Heads of Government Meeting, London, 15 June 1977.
12 The account of the Frasers' experience of the Hilton Hotel bombing is drawn from Christina Hindhaugh, *It Wasn't Meant to Be Easy: Tamie Fraser in Canberra*, Lothian, Melbourne, 1986.
13 MF, speech at the opening of the Commonwealth Heads of Government Regional Meeting, 13 February 1978.
14 Tamie Fraser, cited in Hindhaugh, p. 82.
15 'Hope Protective Security Review', *Parliament Paper 397 (1979)*, Commonwealth of Australia, 1979. Appendix 16, 'The History of Military Involvement in Civilian Security in Britain and Australia'; Appendix 3, 'Commonwealth Heads of Government Regional

Meeting, Sydney, 13–17 February 1978', pp. 257–62, cited in Cameron Moore, 'To Execute and Maintain the Laws of the Commonwealth: The ADF and Internal Security—Some Old Issues with New Relevance', *University of New South Wales Law Journal*, vol. 28, no. 2, 2005.

16 CS 2747, 16 November 1978, NAA A12909.

17 Commonwealth Secretariat, 'From the Archive, Sydney Regional Conference, February 1978', The Commonwealth, 19 May 2009, www.thecommonwealth.org/news/34580/34581/200569/190509archivesydney.htm, viewed July 2009.

18 MFH, 29 May 1978, pp. 2653–5.

19 '1979: End of White Rule in Rhodesia', On This Day 1950–2005, BBC, 2008, http://news.bbc.co.uk/onthisday/hi/dates/stories/june/1/newsid_2492000/2492915.stm, viewed July 2009.

20 Kenneth Kaunda, letter to MF, [1979], NAA M1356.

21 Situation report on Zimbabwe received by MF, 30 July 1979, NAA M1356 [11].

22 Correspondence regarding Zimbabwe, 1979, MFC 106/15 box 3.

23 Margaret Thatcher, speech to the Canberra Press Club, 1 July 1979.

24 Ayres, pp. 382–3.

25 Situation report on Zimbabwe.

26 Tamie Fraser, cited in Hindhaugh, p. 105.

27 MF, at the Commonwealth Heads of Government Meeting, 1 August 1979, cited in Hindhaugh, pp. 108–9.

28 Margaret Thatcher, speech at the Commonwealth Heads of Government Meeting, 3 August 1979.

29 Record of conversation between MF, Andrew Peacock, Margaret Thatcher & Peter Carrington, 4 August 1979, NAA A10756 M1356 [11].

30 Clause 15, final communiqué, Commonwealth Heads of Government Meeting, Lusaka, 1979. The nine points in full read: In relation to the situation in Rhodesia, heads of government:

> a) confirmed that they were wholly committed to genuine black majority rule for the people of Zimbabwe; b) recognised, in this context, that the internal settlement constitution is defective in certain important respects; c) fully accepted that it is the constitutional responsibility of the British Government to grant legal independence to Zimbabwe on the basis of majority

rule; d) recognised that the search for a lasting settlement must involve all parties to the conflict; e) were deeply conscious of the urgent need to achieve such a settlement and bring peace to the people of Zimbabwe and their neighbours; f) accepted that independence on the basis of majority rule requires the adoption of a democratic constitution including appropriate safeguards for minorities; g) acknowledged that the government formed under such an independence constitution must be chosen through free and fair elections properly supervised under British Government authority and with Commonwealth observers; h) welcomed the British Government's indication that an appropriate procedure for advancing towards these objectives would be for them to call a constitutional conference to which all the parties would be invited; and i) consequently, accepted that it must be a major objective to bring about a cessation of hostilities and an end to sanctions as part of the process of implementation of a lasting settlement.

31 Margaret Thatcher, interview with Peter Snow, ITN, 6 August 1979.
32 MFH, 23 August 1979, pp. 577–80.
33 Robert Mugabe, cited in Ayres, p. 392.
34 'Zimbabwe Country Economic Memorandum: Achieving Shared Growth', Report No. 13540-ZIM, World Bank, Washington, DC, 21 April 1995.
35 PM, radio program, ABC, 22 December 2008.
36 Hal Colebatch, 'You Got Him In So Help Kick Him Out', *The Australian*, 16 April 2008.
37 Hindhaugh, p. 157.
38 MF, opening address at the Commonwealth Heads of Government Meeting, 1 October 1981.
39 Margaret Thatcher, letter to MF, 20 August 1981, NAA M1333 [5].
40 Cited in Hindhaugh, p. 162.
41 The Melbourne Declaration, Commonwealth of Nations, Canberra, 3 October 1981.
42 Margaret Thatcher, press statement, 7 October 1981.
43 Michael Foot, Hansard, House of Commons, United Kingdom, 26 October 1981, vol. 10/557–66.

16 Foundations: Fraser and Financial Deregulation

1 John Howard, 'Rudd Demeans Himself over History', *The Australian*, 11 September 2009.

2 'Too Much Politics, Not Enough Policy', *The Weekend Australian*, 16–17 May 2009; Michelle Grattan, 'Turnbull Needs to Find His Reform Mojo to Win this History War', *The Sydney Morning Herald*, 11 September 2009; 'Education: Malcolm Fraser', National Museum of Australia, [n.d.], www.nma.gov.au/education/school_resources/websites_and_interactives/primeministers/malcolm_fraser, viewed May 2009.
3 Paul Kelly, *The End of Certainty*, Allen & Unwin, Sydney, 1992, p. 76.
4 Philip Ayres, *Malcolm Fraser: A Biography*, William Heinemann, Richmond, 1987; Patrick Weller, *Malcolm Fraser PM: A Study in Prime Ministerial Power in Australia*, Penguin, Melbourne, 1989. Both Ayres and Weller had access to the relevant archival records.
5 Christine Wallace, *Hewson: A Portrait*, Sun Australia, Sydney, 1993, p. 122.
6 ibid., p. 125.
7 Wayne Errington & Peter Van Onselen, *John Winston Howard: The Biography*, Melbourne University Press, 2007, p. 88.
8 Wallace, ch. 5.
9 Margaret Simons was granted access to cabinet documents held in the National Archives of Australia under s. 56 of the *Archives Act 1983*, as MF's authorised biographer. Similar special access was given to Philip Ayres and Patrick Weller, whose accounts of events are similar, though less detailed, than the one given here. Sadly, most of the documents are not yet available to the public: cabinet records are closed for thirty years. In the account given, comprehensive endnotes have been used so that accuracy can be checked by future scholars as, year by year, the records become available for public viewing. The desire is to set the record straight.
10 MF, policy launch speech, 27 November 1975.
11 MF, note to Secretary, Treasury, 22 March 1977; Ed Visbord, letter to Secretary of Treasury [n.d.]; CD 2413, 24 March 1977; Reserve Bank of Australia, paper to MF, March 1977; DPMC, note to MF, 30 March 1977, all at NAA A10756 LC 1792 [part 1].
12 Briefing to MF, 14 October 1976; Ian Castles, memorandum to MF, 2 November 1976, both at NAA A10756 LC 1791 [part 1].
13 CD 4487 (MPCC), 17 January 1978; CD 4702 (MPCC), 24 February 1978; CD 4811 (MPCC), 1 March 1978, all at NAA A13075 [vol. 15].
14 Alan Carmody, note to MF, 16 March 1978, NAA A10756 LC 1791 [part 2].

15 Treasury & Reserve Bank of Australia, Cabinet Paper 275, 31 March 1978, presented to cabinet by 3 April 1978, NAA A10756 LC 1791 [part 2].
16 John Howard, paper described as factual update of Treasury & Reserve Bank of Australia, Cabinet Paper 320, 1 May 1978, NAA A10756 LC 1791.
17 KL Mahar, note to MF, 6 April 1978; Mahar, memorandum to MF with attached paper by Ian Castles & John Rose, 14 April 1978, both at NAA A10756 LC 1791 [part 2]; ST Sedgwick, note to MF, 1 May 1978, NAA M2218 [38].
18 CD 5548 & 5549 (MPCC), 26 May 1978, NAA A10756 LC 1791 [part 2].
19 Cabinet Paper 673, 2 August 1978; CD 6630 (MPCC), 24 August 1978, both at NAA A10756 LC 1791 [part 2].
20 CD 11893 (MPCC), 17 June 1980, NAA A10756 LC 1791.
21 John Howard, Memorandum 960, 26 August 1980; CD 12651 (MPCC), 26 August 1980, both at NAA A10756 LC 1792 [part 7].
22 Ed Visbord, memorandum to MF with attached paper by John Rose & John Hewson, 16 January 1978; Rose & Hewson, memorandum to MF, [16 January 1978]; CD 4488 (MPCC), 17 January 1978, all at NAA A10756 LC 1792.
23 Geoffrey Yeend, note for file, 19 January 1978, NAA A10756 LC 1792 [part 1], also at NAA M2218 [35].
24 KL Mahar, note for file, 24 January 1978, NAA A10756 LC 1792 [part 1].
25 Treasury & Reserve Bank of Australia, paper number 234 prepared in response to CD 4488, 9 February 1978, NAA A10756 LC 1792 [part 1].
26 DPMC, KL Mahar, briefing note to MF, 23 February 1978, NAA A10756 LC 1792 [part 1].
27 CD 4703 (MPCC), 24 February 1978, NAA A10756 LC 1792 [part 2].
28 CD 5415 (MPCC), 17 May 1978, NAA A10756 LC 1792 [part 2].
29 Treasury & Reserve Bank of Australia, Cabinet Papers 426 & 427, 17 May 1978, NAA A10756 LC 1792 [part 2].
30 KL Mahar, briefing note to MF, May 1978, NAA A10756 LC 1792 [part 2].
31 CD 6749 (MPCC), 28 July 1978, NAA A10756 LC 1792 [part 2].

32 John Rose, memorandum to MF with attached paper; Ed Visbord, memorandum to MF, both 9 October 1978, NAA A10756 LC 1792 [part 3]; CD 6860 (MPCC), 10 October 1978; Visbord, note to MF, 24 October 1978, both at NAA A10756 LC 1792 [part 3].
33 ST Sedgwick, note to MF, 11 December 1978, NAA A10756 LC 1792 [part 4].
34 KL Mahar, note to MF, 19 January 1979, NAA A10756 LC 1792 [part 4].
35 John Rose & John Hewson, Cabinet Papers 844 & 855; CD 7448 (MPCC) & 7449 (MPCC), all 22 January 1979, NAA A10756 LC 1792 .
36 File note, 5 February 1979, NAA A10756 LC 1792 [part 4].
37 ST Sedgwick, note for file, 13 February 1979, in possession of the authors.
38 John Howard, Cabinet Paper 836, 19 January 1979; Ed Visbord, note to Fraser, 19 January 1979, both at NAA A10756 LC 1792.
39 Howard's submissions and the related decisions include: CS 658 & CD 11108 (MPCC), 14 April 1980; CS, 17 April 1980, with consideration 24 April 1980; cabinet paper, 20 May 1978, all at NAA A10756 LC 1792. Howard's change of mind on the need to wait for Campbell is in cabinet memorandum, 17 November 1980. An initial decision went against him on 19 November 1980, but this decision was set aside and altered in his favour on 2 December 1980. See also CS 4963, 13 July 1981, in which Howard argued for deregulation of controlled bank interest rates, and was supported by the DPMC, but agreed to wait until after the Campbell Inquiry reports. All these at NAA A10756 LC 1792 [part 7]. See also CS 5577, 1982 (after the Campbell Inquiry), NAA A10756 LC 2525 [part 1], in which Howard recommends that no further changes be made to interest rates and maturity controls at that time, but notes that the issue will arise again.
40 MF, correspondence with John Howard, 27 January 1981, in possession of the authors.
41 Ed Visbord, memorandum to MF, 7 July 1981, NAA A10756 LC 1792 [part 8].
42 CD 16390 (MPCC), 15 July 1981, NAA A10756 LC 1792 [part 8].
43 John Howard, CS 1611, 21 July 1981; CD 16462 (MPCC), 23 July 1981, both at NAA A10756 LC 1792 [part 8].

44 MF, letter John Howard, 25 August 1981, in possession of the authors.
45 Treasury & Reserve Bank of Australia, Cabinet Memorandum 1700, 22 October 1981; CD 17038 (MPCC), 26 October 1981, both at NAA A10756 LC 1792 [part 9].
46 John Howard, CS 5299, 22 January 1982, NAA A10756 LC 2525 [part 1].
47 MF, letter to John Howard, 3 February 1982; Howard, letter to MF, 15 February 1982, both at NAA A10756 LC 1792 [part 9].
48 CD 4612 (MPCC), 9 February 1978, NAA A10756 LC 1792 [part 1] & LC 2525 [part 1]. Also CD 4709 (MPCC), 24 February 1978, NAA A10756 LC 2525 [part 1].
49 John Howard, letter to MF, 1 March 1978, NAA A10756 LC 1792 [part 2].
50 CD 5271, 5 May 1978, NAA A10756 LC 1792 [part 2].
51 Cabinet Paper 654; CD 6480 (MPCC), both 28 July 1978, NAA A10756 LC 1792 [part 2].
52 John Howard, letter to MF, 26 October 1978; Ian Castles, memorandum to MF, 26 October 1978; CD 7014 (MPCC), 26 October 1978; Howard, memorandum to (Acting Prime Minister) Doug Anthony, 4 January 1979; CD 7425 (MPCC), 9 January 1979, all at NAA A10756 LC 1792 [part 3] & NAA A1076 LC 2525 [part 1].
53 John Howard, memorandum to MF (forwarding copy of interim report), 12 August 1980; MF, memorandum to Howard, [n.d.], both at NAA A10756 LC 1792 [part 4]; CD 12651, 26 August 1980, NAA A10756 LC 1792 [part 7].
54 Errington & Van Onselen, p. 90.
55 John Howard, memorandum to MF, 12 June 1981; MF, memorandum to Howard, 22 June 1981, both at NAA M2218 [15].
56 John Rose, diary note, 5 November 1981, in possession of Rose.
57 John Howard, letter to MF, 5 November 1981, NAA M2218 [15].
58 CD 17086, 9 November 1981, NAA A10756 LC 2525 [part 1].
59 Stuart Simson, 'Where Howard Can Move on Campbell', *Business Review*, 21–27 November 1981, p. 9.
60 John Howard, memorandum to MF, 15 December 1981, NAA M2218 [15].
61 John Howard, memorandum to MF, 21 January 1982, NAA M2218 [15].

62 Australian Financial System Inquiry task force, paper; John Howard, CS 5328, both 8 February 1982, NAA A10756 LC 2525 [part 1].
63 John Howard, CS 5577, 17 June 1982, NAA A10756 LC 2525 [part 1].
64 Ed Visbord, memorandums to MF, 11 May, 14 & 18 June 1982; John Howard, CS 5577, 17 June 1982, all at NAA A10756 LC 2525 [part 1].
65 CS 5589, 2 July 1982, NAA A10756 LC 2525 [part 1]; VW Fitzgerald, memorandum to MF, 22 July 1982, NAA A10756 LC 2525 [part 2].
66 DPMC, Treasury & Reserve Bank of Australia, paper, 1 July 1982, NAA M2218 [38].
67 CD 18309 (MPCC), 5 July 1982, NAA M2218 [31].
68 CD 18644–7 (MPCC), 28 July 1982, NAA A10756 LC 2525 [part 2].
69 CS 5589, 1 July 1982; CD 18646 (MPCC), 20 July 1982; Ed Visbord, Memorandum 2183 to MF, 27 October 1982; CS 5892, 5 December 1982; Visbord, note on CS 5892, 7 January 1983, all at NAA A10756 LC 2525 [part 2].
70 Ed Visbord, memorandum to MF, 27 October 1982; MF, memorandum to John Howard, 1 November 1982; RG Hawkins, note for file, 4 November 1982; MF, letter to Howard, 9 December 1982, all at NAA M2218 [15]. See also Howard, letter to Fraser, 23 December 1982, NAA A10756 LC 5036 [part 1].
71 CS 5589 (foreign bank entry), 13 July 1982; CD 19530, 19536 & 19537, 13 January 1983; CS 5892, considered by cabinet 13 January 1983, all at NAA A10756 LC 5036 [part 1].
72 CS 5556, 13 January 1983, NAA A10756 LC 5036 [part 1]; CD 19572 (MPCC), 13 January 1983, NAA A10756 LC 5036 [part 1].
73 MF, 'The World Economic Crisis: Its History and Solutions', speech delivered at the World Economic and Investment Conference, 20 March 1984.

17 Land and Sea

1 William EH Stanner, *White Man Got No Dreaming: Essays, 1938–1973*, Australian National University Press, Canberra, 1979, p. 230.
2 MF, speech at the opening of the World Heritage Committee Meeting, 26 October 1981, cited in Denis M White & David A Kemp (eds), *Malcolm Fraser on Australia*, Hill of Content, Melbourne, 1986, pp. 215–16.

3 Doug Lowe, *The Price of Power*, Macmillan, Melbourne, 1984, p. 63.
4 MF, letter to RO Desailly, 17 September 1973, MFC 106/17 [35, part 2].
5 Bob Brown, cited in Rachel Evans, 'Bob Brown and the Rise of the Greens', review of *Bob Brown, Gentle Revolutionary* by James Norman, Green Left Online, 9 March 2005, www.greenleft.org.au/2005/618/35219, viewed July 2009.
6 Queensland CD 23560, 1 December 1975, cited in Jonathan Richards, 'Queensland Cabinet Minutes (1975): A Report for Queensland State Archives', November 2005, Queensland State Archives, 2006, www.archives.qld.gov.au/downloads/1975HistoriansReport.pdf, viewed July 2009.
7 CD 1750 & 1794, 9 November 1976; CD 2094, 17 December 1976, all at NAA A12909.
8 Jonathan West, 'Liquid Fuel Alternatives', in Alan Manning (comp.), *Uranium, a Fair Trial: Both Sides of the Uranium Debate as Presented in the ALP Discussion Kit*, Australian Labor Party, Canberra, 1976, pp. 60–3.
9 MFR, 4 September 1977, cited in White & Kemp, p. 213.
10 CD 144, 30 January 1976; CS 63, 30 January 1976; CS 165, 11 March 1976, all at NAA A12909. See also Patrick Weller, *Malcolm Fraser PM: A Study of Prime Ministerial Power in Australia*, Penguin, Melbourne, 1989, p. 357.
11 CD 1790, 9 November 1976, NAA A13075.
12 *Ranger Uranium Environmental Inquiry*, second report, (RW Fox, chair), Australian Government Publishing Service, Canberra, May 1977, p. 9.
13 MFH, 24 May 1977, p. 1701.
14 MFH, 25 August 1977, pp. 645–51, cited in White & Kemp, p. 212.
15 David Combe, 'Preface', in Manning, p. vi.
16 *Northern Territory Chronicle*, Northern Territory government, 1978.
17 Gerry Blitner, cited in Environment Australia, *Australia's Kakadu: Protecting World Heritage—Response by the Government of Australia to the UNESCO World Heritage Committee Regarding Kakadu National Park*, Commonwealth of Australia, Canberra, April 1999, p. 87.
18 Environment Australia.
19 Fred Chaney, Lowitja O'Donoghue Oration, 28 May 2009.
20 Senate Select Committee on Uranium Mining and Milling, *Uranium Mining and Milling in Australia*, Senate Information Services Section, Canberra, May 1997, ch. 5.

21 MFH, 4 April 1979, pp. 1481–2.
22 Joh Bjelke-Petersen, letter to MF, 19 December 1975; MF, letter to Bjelke-Petersen, 21 December 1975, both at NAA M1268 [158].
23 For more details, see Weller, pp. 279–80.
24 MFH, 21 February 1979, pp. 261–75, cited in White & Kemp, p. 216.
25 Ross Fitzgerald, *From 1915 to the Early 1980s: A History of Queensland*, University of Queensland Press, Brisbane, 1984, p. 373.
26 MFH, 4 June 1979, pp. 2825–6.
27 MF, letter to Joh Bjelke-Petersen, 26 March 1980; Bjelke-Petersen, letter to MF, 2 April 1980, copies in the possession of the authors.
28 Joh Bjelke-Petersen, cited in Fitzgerald, p. 373.
29 ibid., p. 375.
30 MFR, 15 November 1981, MFC 105/72 [10].
31 MF, letter to Doug Lowe, [n.d.], cited in Weller, p. 306.
32 *Stateline* (Tasmania), television program, ABC, 8 December 2006.
33 Cited in Symon Lyster, *International Wildlife Law: An Analysis of International Treaties Concerned with the Conservation of Wildlife*, Cambridge University Press, 1993, p. 223.
34 MF, press statement, 19 January 1983, cited in White & Kemp, p. 218.
35 *Stateline* (Tasmania), television program, ABC, 27 June 2003.
36 Owen Dixon was Chief Justice of the High Court between 1952 and 1964.

18 Loyalty and Loss

1 CD 11101, 14 April 1980, NAA A10756 LC 2855 [part 1].
2 Peter Durack, memorandum to MF, 29 August 1980, NAA A10756 LC 2855 [part 1].
3 Peter Durack, Cabinet Memorandum 2080, 3 September 1982, NAA A10756 LC 2855 [part 2].
4 CD 18858, August 1982; and weekly reports thereafter at NAA A10756 LC 2855 [part 2].
5 MF, press statement, 30 August 1982, NAA M1229.
6 Michelle Grattan, *The Age*, 3 September 1982.
7 MFR, 12 September 1982, MFC 105/72 [10].
8 Liberal Party of Australia, 'Fund Raising Code Adopted by Federal Executive', April 1975, endorsed October 1975, copy in possession of MF; Bob Crichton Brown, letters to MF, 5 April & 10 August 1982, in possession of MF.

9 Cabinet minutes, 12 November 1975 & 2 December 1976; 'Report on Joint Committee on Pecuniary Interests', 30 September 1975, all at NAA A10756 LC 4 [part 1].
10 Phillip Lynch, letter to MF, 12 December 1977, Lynch Papers, University of Melbourne Archives.
11 MF, draft statement, 14 December 1977, Lynch Papers, University of Melbourne Archives.
12 'Royal Commission of Inquiry into Matters in Relation to Electoral Redistribution', *Commonwealth Parliamentary Paper No. 263/1978*, (Commissioner, Mr Justice DG McGregor), Australian Government Publishing Service, Canberra, 1978.
13 MF, letter to Reg Withers, 21 March 1983; Withers, letter to MF, 31 March 1983, MFC 107/29 [18].
14 MFH, 21 September 1982, p. 1621.
15 Justice Edward Woodward, *Report of the Royal Commission into the Australian Meat Industry*, Australian Government Publishing Service, Canberra, 1982.
16 JF Landos, departmental minute, 21 February 1980, NAA M1268 [part 1].
17 MFH, 21 September 1982, p. 1621.
18 Peter Nixon, Hansard, HR, 21 September 1982, p. 1670.
19 'Zanetti's View', *Daily Telegraph* (Sydney), 15 April 1981.
20 Barry Simon, speech, 10 April 1981, NAA M1268 [301] (transcript).
21 Andrew Peacock, cited in media reports, 16 April 1981, NAA M1268 [301] (transcript).
22 Andrew Peacock, Hansard, HR, 28 April 1981, p. 1607.
23 Doug Anthony & Phillip Lynch, press statement, 16 April 1981, NAA M1268 [301].
24 MFH, 28 April 1981, p. 1614.
25 Wayne Errington & Peter Van Onselen, *John Winston Howard: The Biography*, Melbourne University Press, 2007, p. 91.
26 Phillip Lynch, resignation letter to MF, 11 October 1982, Lynch Papers, University of Melbourne Archives.
27 Tony Eggleton, '1983 Election Report', memorandum to Federal Executive of the Liberal Party, 23 March 1983, MFC 107/29 [12].
28 MF, press statement, 3 February 1983, partial transcript published in *The Age*, 4 February 1983.

29 For comparison, the 2009 Black Saturday bushfires in Victoria resulted in a death toll of 173, and 2200 homes lost. Total property damage figures were not available at the time of writing.
30 MF, policy launch speech; Bob Hawke, policy launch speech, both 15 February 1983.
31 Eggleton.
32 Stephen Downes, *The Age*, 7 March 1983.
33 MF, concession speech, 6 March 1983.

19 Change

1 MF, policy speech, 15 February 1983.
2 Garfield Barwick, letter to MF, 22 March 1983; MF, letter to Barwick, 30 March 1983, both at MFC 107/29 [1] A–C.
3 MF, letter to Dot Grimshaw, 27 March 1983, MFC 107/29 [3] G–H.
4 Letters to MF from: Talbot Duckmanton, [n.d.], MFC 107/29 [2]; John B Fairfax, 16 March 1983, MFC 107/29 [2]; Keith Macpherson, 10 March 1983, MFC 107/29 [3]; Paul Hasluck, [n.d.], MFC 107/29 [3]; Gustav Nossal, 7 March 1983, MFC 107/29 [3]; Kerry Stokes, 14 March 1983, MFC 107/29 [7]; Ron Walker, 15 March 1983, MFC 107/29 [8]; Clyde Packer, 5 March 1983, MFC 107/29 [9]; Clyde Cameron, 6 March 1983, MFC 107/29 [1]; Richard Krygier, 7 March 1983, MFC 107/29 [3].
5 For Howard's reaction, see Wayne Errington & Peter Van Onselen, *John Winston Howard: The Biography*, Melbourne University Press, 2007, p. 100.
6 MF, letter to John Howard, 9 March 1983; MF, telegram to Howard, [n.d.]; MF, telegram to Andrew Peacock, [n.d.], all at MFC 107/29 [18].
7 This account of the conversation was sent to Fred Whittemore in July 2009, with a request that he correct it if MF's memory was faulty. The authors have confirmed that Whittemore received the communication, but nothing has been heard in response.
8 MF, speech at Kevin Newman's retirement dinner, [March or April 1985].
9 Errington & Van Onselen, p. 118.
10 MF, 'Liberal Beliefs', speech delivered at a dinner in honour of Malcolm & Tamie Fraser, 7 June 1983.
11 MF, 'The World We Live In: 1984', speech at the University of Tasmania, 12 July 1984. Similar ideas can be found in MF, 'A Conversation with J Malcolm Fraser', speech to the American

Enterprise Institute, 16 January 1984, MFC 105/83 (transcript); MF, 'Liberal Democracies: Challenge and Response', speech delivered at 'Beyond '84', Conference on Communism and Liberal Democracy, 20 March 1985.

12 For example, MF, draft letter to *Business Review Weekly*, 20 May 1985; draft letter to various newspaper editors, 10 June 1987, both at MFC 105/83, box 1 [1].

13 Neil Brown, speech, 12 March 1985, reported in Tess Livingstone, 'Reagan, Thatcher Ideal Models: Top Liberal', *The Courier Mail*, 13 March 1985; John Hodges, letter to Neil Brown & MF, 13 March 1985; MF, letter to Hodges, 10 April 1985, both at MFC 105/83 [box 6].

14 For MF's remarks in this section, see MF, remarks at the launch of *Malcolm Fraser on Australia* by Denis M White & David A Kemp (eds), 17 June 1986; MF, 'How Australia Can Return to the Good Times', speech, 11 December 1986; MF, 'Australia: Fighting for a Future', inaugural Downer Lecture, 30 September 1986; MF, 'Australia 2000', speech, 22 January 1988.

15 Geoffrey Blainey, speech, March 1984, cited in Lois Foster & David Stockley, *Australian Multiculturalism: A Documentary History and Critique*, Multilingual Matters, Clevedon, UK, 1988, p. 225.

16 MF, notes for the Liberal Party, 14 June 1987; Denis White & David Kemp, comments, 15 July 1987, both at MFC 105/83.

17 John Howard, cited in Paul Kelly, *The End of Certainty*, Allen & Unwin, Sydney, 1992, p. 475.

18 Jane Cadzow, 'Life Wasn't Meant to Be This Easy', *Good Weekend*, 30 November 1991, pp. 15–21.

19 MF, in House of Representatives Select Committee on the Print Media, transcripts, vol. 2, 22 October 1991, pp. 829–1630.

20 MF, speech at Interaction Council Meeting, 26 May 1989.

21 Francis Fukuyama, 'The End of History', *National Interest*, no. 16, 1989.

22 MF, 'A World in Transition', B'nai B'rith Oration, 29 October 1989.

20 Mission to South Africa

1 Among other places, the photograph was published in *The Age*, 24 February 1986.

2 The Commonwealth Accord on Southern Africa (The Nassau Accord), Lyford Cay, Nassau, 20 October 1985, reprinted in the

Commonwealth Group of Eminent Persons, *Mission to South Africa: The Commonwealth Report*, Penguin, Harmondsworth, 1986.

3 Bob Hawke, letter to MF, 28 October 1985, MFC 105/71 Consignment 2 [15]
4 MF, press statement, 7 September 1985, MFC 105/83, box 2.
5 MF, statement to the Second Committee of the General Assembly of the United Nations on 'Report and Recommendations of the Panel of Eminent Persons on the Activities of Transnational Corporations in South Africa and Namibia' (typewritten report, 12 October 1985), 22 November 1985, MFC 105/83, box 2.
6 MF, press statement, 7 September 1985.
7 Shridath Ramphal, foreword to *Mission to South Africa*, p. 13.
8 MF, correspondence with Pieter Botha, cited in *Mission to South Africa*, appendices 1 & 2.
9 Unless otherwise referenced, all quotes from the Commonwealth Group of Eminent Persons, and the account of its doings in South Africa, are drawn from *Mission to South Africa.*
10 Ramphal, foreword to *Mission to South Africa*, p. 12.
11 This incident and the two following are recounted by Fraser's previous biographer, Philip Ayres, *Malcolm Fraser: A Biography*, William Heinemann, Richmond, 1987.
12 'Home Truths from South Africa', *Financial Times*, 14 June 1986, copy in MFC 105/71.
13 The account of the meeting with Mandela is drawn from MF's recollection; *Mission to South Africa*; Nelson Mandela, *Long Walk to Freedom*, Little Brown & Co., London, 1994.
14 'Home Truths from South Africa'.
15 MF, article for *Los Angeles Times*, typescript, [n.d.], MFC 105/71 Consignment 1 [7].
16 MF & Olusegun Obasanjo, 'What to Do about South Africa', 24 July 1986, copy in MFC 105/71.
17 ibid. Copies of MF's newspaper articles are in MFC 105/71.
18 MF & Olusegun Obasanjo, letter to Ronald Reagan, 21 July 1986, MFC 105/71, box 3.
19 MF, in *The Gainesville Sun*, 29 July 1986.
20 Richard Stengel, 'Falling Short', *Time*, 24 June 2001.
21 Ronald Reagan, 'Ending Apartheid in South Africa', address to members of the World Affairs Council and Foreign Policy

Association, 22 July 1986, transcript in *US Department of State Bulletin*, 1 September 1986.

22 Desmond Tutu and James Reston, cited in Stengel.

23 Kenneth Kaunda, cited in Stengel.

24 Commonwealth of Nations, Commonwealth Heads of Government Review Meeting communiqué, London, 3–5 August 1986.

25 Running sheets for the Commonwealth Secretary-General election, 1989, MFC 105/83.

26 MF, letter to Bob Hawke, 14 November 1989, MFC 105/83.

27 Lindsay Olney, 'Mal Misses Top Job', *The Sun*, 19 October 1989.

21 CARE

1 The account of the telephone calls and Phoebe Fraser's work in Somalia is drawn from Phoebe Fraser, *A Single Seed*, William Heinemann Australia, Port Melbourne, 1996, pp. 85–132.

2 MF, speech at CARE gala dinner, 2 May 2002.

3 P Fraser, p. 113.

4 ibid., p. 6.

5 'Role and Influence of CARE USA', aide memoir, 8 February 1995, MFC 105/87, box 1.

6 'Care International Executive Review', September 1995, MFC 105/87, box 1.

7 'Motion to Return CARE Australia to Compliance in Kenya and Rwanda', 6 November 1994, MFC 105/87, box 4.

8 Ian Harris, memorandum to Tony Eggleton, 14 November 1994, in possession of the authors.

9 Alexander Downer, Hansard, HR, 11 May 1995, p. 371.

10 *Sunday*, television program, Channel Nine, 26 February 1995, transcript in MFC 105/87.

11 'Strategy for CARE Australia', paper presented to the board, May 1995, copy in possession of the authors.

12 Gordon Bilney, Hansard, HR, 11 May 1995, p. 371.

13 Tony Eggleton, 'End-of-Year Situation Report' (for CARE Australia), 18 December 1995, MFC 105/87, box 6 [33].

14 MF, 'The Current Situation of the World', speech given at the Interaction Council's eighteenth plenary session, 17–20 June 2000.

15 Henry Kissinger, cited in William Shawcross, *Deliver Us from Evil: Warlords and Peacekeepers in a World of Endless Conflict*, Bloomsbury, London, 2000, p. 329.

16 MF, 'The Current Situation of the World'.
17 Mary Robinson, remarks to the United Nations Human Rights Commission, 30 April 1999, reported in 'World: Europe UN Rights Chief Slams NATO Bombings', BBC News, 30 April 1999, http://news.bbc.co.uk/2/hi/europe/332745.stm, viewed August 2009.
18 Steve Pratt, *Duty of Care*, Simon & Schuster, Sydney, 2000, pp. 271–2.
19 Charles Tapp, notes, Vienna, various dates in July & August 1999, copy in possession of the authors.
20 'Memorandum of Understanding', drafts, [n.d.], copies in possession of the authors.
21 Record of conversation between MF & Bratislava Morina, 31 August 1999, copy in possession of the authors.
22 Record of conversation between MF & Slobodan Milosevic, 1 September 1999, copy in possession of the authors.
23 Pratt, p. 300.
24 Bernard Barron & Michael Emery, letter to Robert Yallop, 12 November 1999, copy in possession of the authors.
25 MF, speech at CARE gala dinner.
26 Tony Blair, cited in 'Video Shows Kidnapped Aid Worker', BBC News, 20 October 2004, http://news.bbc.co.uk/2/hi/uk_news/3756192.stm, viewed August 2009, also cited in MF, notes, 24 November 2004, in possession of MF.
27 This account is drawn from the following documents: MF, letter to William Deane, 20 October 2004; Deane, letter to MF, 24 October 2004; Record of telephone conversation between Deane & Fraser, 25 October 2004; Julian Burnside, legal opinion, 8 November 2004; MF, letter to James Wolfensohn, 26 October 2004; Mallesons Stephen Jaques, legal opinion, 11 November 2004, all in possession of MF.

22 Enduring Liberal

1 MF, 'Finding Security in Terrorism's Shadow: The Importance of the Rule of Law', inaugural professorial lecture, Asia Pacific Centre for Military Law, University of Melbourne, 25 October 2007.
2 Sophie Mirabella, 'Fraser's Flawed World View: A Study in Hypocrisy', *The Age*, 6 January 2008.
3 MF, 'The Ordinary People Have Been Forgotten', *The Sunday Age*, 18 August 1991.

4 MF, 'Ideology Out as Parties Embrace the Law of the Jungle', *The Sunday Age*, 28 August 1991.
5 MF, 'Balanced GST Good for the Country', *The Sunday Age*, 13 October 1991.
6 MF, 'Deregulation Dogma Is No Substitute for Common Sense', *The Sunday Age*, 17 November 1991.
7 MF, 'Politics, Banks and the Failure of Deregulation', *The Sunday Age*, 1 September 1991.
8 MF, 'Be Rational, Yes, But Life Was Not Meant to Be a Nightmare', *The Sunday Age*, 3 November 1991.
9 BA Santamaria, letter to MF, 21 August 1992, MFC 105/83 [25].
10 Philip Ayres, letter to MF, 31 August 1992, MFC 105/83 [25].
11 MF, 'Opposition Pricks Up Its Ears', *The Sunday Age*, 10 January 1993.
12 MF, 'Going Nowhere, with Nowhere to Go', *The Sunday Age*, 21 March 1993.
13 MF, 'Party Must Get Off the Straight and Narrow', *The Sunday Age*, 28 March 1993.
14 David Elias, 'Fraser Faces Fight', *The Age*, 6 August 1993.
15 Lindsay Olney, 'Fraser in Lib Presidency Row', *The Advertiser* [Adelaide], 6 April 1993.
16 MF, 'Party's Hopes Rest with New President', *The Australian*, 1 September 1993.
17 MF, 'New Leader Needed to Revive Ailing Libs', *The Australian*, 19 May 1994.
18 MF, 'Enthusiastic Team Can Inspire Renewal', *The Australian*, 25 May 1994.
19 MF, 'Crucial Test for Howard', *The Australian*, 1 February 1995.
20 Pauline Hanson, Hansard, HR, 10 September 1996, p. 3859.
21 MF, speech at the twenty-second anniversary dinner, Ethnic Communities Council of New South Wales, 26 July 1997, copy in possession of the authors.
22 MF, cable to the Prime Minister, Foreign Minister and Secretary of Department of Foreign Affairs and Trade, 21 October 1996, copy in possession of the authors.
23 MF, 'The Historical Facts Are Clear, but a Republic Is Not the Answer', *The Sunday Age*, 8 March 1992.
24 MF, *Weekly Times*, 29 October 1999.
25 MF, 'The Republic: An Idea Whose Time Will Come', *The Australian*, 30 August 1995.

26 MF, *Weekly Times*, 29 October 1999.
27 MF, 'A House Divided against Itself Cannot Stand', *The Australian*, 19 February 1998.
28 MF, 'A Crisis Prevention Model', *The Australian*, 21 October 1999; MF, *Weekly Times*, 29 October 1999.
29 MF, *Weekly Times*, 29 October 1999.
30 The advertisement can be viewed at 'Gough Whitlam and Malcolm Fraser—Yes Ad', YouTube, 2006, www.youtube.com/watch?v=RjqtuUXnm2g, viewed September 2009.
31 MF, letter to Tony Staley, 19 June 1997, copy in possession of the authors.
32 MF, public statement to the Liberal Party, 28 May 1998, copy in possession of the authors.
33 MF, 'This Obscenity Must Be Repelled', *The Australian*, 22 June 1998.
34 MF, 'B'nai B'rith Anti-Defamation Commission. Multicultural Tolerance: The Truth about Lies', speech, 26 May 2002.
35 MF, *Common Ground: Issues That Should Bind and Not Divide Us*, Viking, Melbourne, 2002.
36 MF, 'Why AustraliansAll.com.au, and Why Right Now', Australians All, 14 November 2006, http://australiansall.com.au/archive/post/why-australiansall-com-au-and-why-right-now, viewed September 2009.
37 MF, 'Finding Security in Terrorism's Shadow'.
38 MF, 'Voting to Restore the Decent Values Australia Once Held Dear', *The Age*, 20 November 2007.

23 Hope

1 The British Attorney-General's opinion, dated 7 March 2003, can be read at http://news.bbc.co.uk/2/shared/bsp/hi/pdfs/28_04_05_attorney_general.pdf. The statement given to Howard and Boyce was tabled in federal parliament by Howard on 18 March 2003 (Hansard, HR, p. 12510).

Bibliography

Manuscript Sources

Many of the manuscript sources used in compiling this book are not available for public access. In particular, Margaret Simons was granted special access under the Archives Act to documents held by the National Archives of Australia, including cabinet records less than thirty years old. Applications for access to Malcolm Fraser's personal records held in the Malcolm Fraser Collection at the University of Melbourne should be addressed to the reference archivist; contact details are on the University of Melbourne Archives website at www.lib.unimelb.edu.au/collections/archives. Information about and a selection of speeches and articles contained in the collection are available at www.unimelb.edu.au/malcolmfraser

Malcolm Fraser's Unpublished Papers

Balpool-Nyang, handwritten note in photograph album regarding, [n.d.], MFC 105/36, album PA/123.

Blair, Tony, notes of comments by, 24 November 2004, in possession of MF.

Business Review Weekly, draft letter to, 20 May 1985, MFC 105/83, box 1 [1].

Draft statement, 14 December 1977, Lynch Papers, University of Melbourne Archives.

Gorton, John, draft letter to (not sent), July 1970, copy in possession of MF.

Los Angeles Times, typescript of article for, [n.d.], MFC 105/71 Consignment 1 [7].

McMahon, Billy, notes on conversation with, 6 March 1970, in possession of MF.

New South Wales trip with Gavin Casey, diary, 2–31 March 1949, MFC 108/63.

Newspaper articles relating to MF's election, 1953, copies in scrapbook, MFC 108/58.

Newspaper editors (various), draft letter to, 10 June 1987, MFC 105/83, box 1 [1].

Northern Territory trip, photographs, 1978, in '1978—Northern Territory', album, MFC 105/104.

Pre-selection speech, draft and final notes, [n.d.], MFC 105/82 [1].

Prime Minister, Foreign Minister and Secretary of Department of Foreign Affairs and Trade, cable to, 21 October 1996, copy in possession of the authors.

Record of conversation with Mr Witteveen, 12 October 1976, NAA M1356 [61].
Record of telephone conversation with William Deane, 25 October 2004, in possession of MF.
Speech notes, [21 March 1975], MFC 107/8 [146].
'State of the World' speech, drafts and comments on them, 1976, NAA M1276 [225, parts 1–6].
'These I Have Loved', 1942, MFC 107/53, file 1/1.
Tudor House reports, Lent and Michaelmas terms 1943, MFC 108/58.
University notes and essays, [n.d.], MFC 105/82.
Victory declaration, 1956, brown scrapbook, MFC 108/58.
Vietnam trip, photographs of MF, 6 July 1966, AWM, Canberra, FOR/66/0530/VN; FOR/66/0532/VN; CAM/67/0616/VN; CAM/67/0618/VN.
Washington trip, tape-recorded notes, 5 May – 21 July 1964, MFC 105/78 [59] (transcript).

Correspondence

With Malcolm Fraser

Full details are given in the Notes.

Abeles, Peter, MFC 106/15, box 1 [1, part 1].
Alvin Purple, concerning, MFC 106/15 [13, part 1].
Ayres, AJ, NAA A10756 LC 1381 [part 1].
Ayres, Philip, MFC 105/83 [25].
Barnes, CE, NAA A452 NT1965/1955.
Barwick, Garfield, MFC 107/29 [1] A–C, NAA M1369 [368].
Battle, William, NAA M1353 [11].
Beale, Sir Howard, MFC 106/13, box 2 [10].
Bjelke-Petersen, Joh, NAA A10756 LC 180; NAA M1268 [158]; some in possession of the authors.
Bland, Henry, MFC 106/13, box 2 [10].
Botha, Pieter, cited in The Commonwealth Group of Eminent Persons, *Mission to South Africa*, appendices 1 & 2.
Cameron, Clyde, MFC 107/29 [1].
Carrick, John, NAA A10756 LC 1381 [part 1].
Carter, Jimmy, NAA A10756 LC 2773; NAA M1333 [6].
Casey, Dick, NAA M64 [5].
Chipp, Don, MFC 105/73, box 42 [1584].

Court, Charles, NAA M1268 [4, part 1].
Crichton Brown, Bob, in possession of MF.
Crombie, Tom & others, MFC 106/15, box 3.
Deane, William, in possession of MF.
Desailly, RO, MFC 106/17 [35, part 2].
Downer, Alexander (senior), MFC 105/78, box 2 [25]; MFC 106/15, box 3 [4, part 2].
Duckmanton, Talbot, MFC 107/29 [2].
Eggleton, Tony, MFC 106/22 [45]; NAA M1360 [52]; some in possession of MF.
Ellicott, Robert, NAA M1268 [304].
Fairfax, James, MFC 106/15, box 3 [6, part 1].
Fairfax, John B, MFC 107/29 [2].
Ford, Gerald, NAA M1356 [18].
Fraser, Neville & Una, MFC 108/58.
Galbally, Frank, NAA M1268 [88, part 1].
Gorton, John, NAA A5882 CO 10 [part 2] F111 Discussions; some in possession of MF.
Greenwood, Ivor, NAA M1356 [36].
Grimshaw, Dot, MFC 107/29 [3] G–H.
Hamer, Dick & April, in possession of MF.
Hasluck, Paul, MFC 107/29 [3].
Hawke, Bob, MFC 105/71 Consignment 2 [15]; MFC 105/83.
Hodges, John, MFC 105/83 [box 6].
Holt, Harold, NAA A1209/45.
Holt, Zara & Harold, MFC 105/3, box 7 [53].
Howard, John, MFC 107/29 [18]; NAA A10756 LC 1792 [part 2], [part 3] & [part 9]; NAA A10756 LC 5036 [part 1]; NAA A1076 LC 2525 [part 1]; NAA A13075; NAA M2218 [15]; some in possession of the authors.
Hunt, Ralph, NAA M1268 [3, part 2].
Jones, Alan, MFC 106/15, box 5 [10].
Kaunda, Kenneth, NAA M1356.
Kerr, John, in possession of MF.
Kryger, Gilles T, MFC 106/13, box 2 [10].
Krygier, Richard, MFC 107/29 [3].
——& Alan Fairhall, MFC 105/73, box 4 [Defence].
Lambert, Alan, MFC 106/15, box 5 [12, part 2].

Leibler, Isi, MFC 106/15, box 4 [12, part 2].
Liberal defeat 1972, MF's standard response to public correspondence regarding, MFC 106/12 [5].
Lowe, Doug, cited in Weller, p. 306.
Lynch, Phillip, Lynch Papers, University of Melbourne Archives; NAA A10756 LC 476.
MacKellar, Michael, NAA A10756 LC 1366 [part 1].
McMahon, Billy, in possession of MF.
Macphee, Ian, MFC 106/20 [12].
Macpherson, Keith, MFC 107/29 [3].
MacPherson, Nancy, MFC 106/15, box 6 [13, part 2].
Menzies, Robert, NAA M1268 [138].
Miller, TB, MFC 107/3 [3].
to ministers, NAA A10756 LC 94 [part 1].
Morgan, Roy, MFC 106/15, box 7 [19, part 2].
Muldoon, Robert, NAA A10756 LC 2773.
Nossal, Gustav, MFC 107/29 [3].
Packer, Clyde, MFC 107/29 [9].
Packer, Kerry, MFC 106/13, box 2 [10].
Peacock, Andrew, MFC 107/29 [18].
Playford, Thomas & Don Jessop, MFC 106/20 [9].
Reagan, Ronald, (with Olusegun Obasanjo), MFC 105/71, box 3.
Renouf, Alan, MFC 105/78, box 2 [25].
Santamaria, BA, MFC 105/83 [25]; MFC 106/20 [14]; MFC 106/24 [12]; NAA M1274 [62].
Schmidt, Helmut, NAA A10756 LC 2773; NAA M1333 [2] Correspondence with Heads of Government.
Spicer, Ian, MFC 106/13, box 2 [10].
Staley, Elsa, MFC 106/15, box 7 [20, part 3].
Staley, Tony, in possession of the authors.
Stephens, Marlene, MFC 106/15, box 8 [20, part 4].
Stokes, Kerry, MFC 107/29 [7].
Street, Tony, NAA A10756 LC 1381 [part 1]; NAA M63 [58].
Thatcher, Margaret, www.margaretthatcher.org/speeches/displaydocument.asp?docid=102470; NAA A10756 LC 2773; NAA M1333 [5].
Thomson, CAH & Guy Pauker, MFC 107/23 [130].
Treasury, regarding acquisition of information from, MFC 107/4.
Trudeau, Pierre, NAA A10756 LC 2773; NAA M1333 [1].

Turner, Harry B, MFC 106/15, box 8 [21, part 2].
US embassy friends, MFC 105/78, box 2 [24].
Valder, John, MFC 106/13, box 2 [10].
Viner, Ian, NAA A10756 LC 180; NAA A10756 LC 793 Aboriginal Policy [part 1].
Walker, Ron, MFC 107/29 [8].
White, Frederick & Peter Nixon, NAA M1369 [368].
Whiting, Lorri, MFC 106/17, box 7 [52].
Whitlam, Gough, MFC 107/5 [1976, part 1].
Withers, Reg, MFC 107/29 [18].
Wolfensohn, James, in possession of MF.
Zimbabwe, regarding, MFC 106/15, box 3.

Others

Barron, Bernard & Michael Emery, letter to Robert Yallop, 12 November 1999, copy in possession of the authors.
Fraser, Una, 'A Letter for You All', letter written for her grandchildren, 1980, in possession of the Fraser family.
Harris, Ian, memorandum to Tony Eggleton, 14 November 1994, copy in possession of the authors.
Howe, Geoffrey, letter to Margaret Thatcher, 2 June 1977, www.margaretthatcher.org/document/BE70125BBE7C43BF980A41A15120799A.pdf.
Menzies, Robert, letter to Tamie Fraser, 10 December 1975, copy in possession of the Fraser family.
Wise, F, letter to Secretary of Department of Territories, 28 February 1952, cited in M Fraser, *Common Ground*.

Other Manuscript Sources Cited in the Notes

'Adviser's Research Materials', NAA M1276 [78].
'Aims, Objects and Beliefs', in 'Top Secret: General Details of Organisation', *The Association (Post War) and the New Guard (Pre War) Vol 1*, 1931–49, NAA A6122.
Burnside, Julian, legal opinion, 8 November 2004, in possession of MF.
'Care International Executive Review', September 1995, MFC 105/87, box 1.
Commonwealth Secretary-General election, running sheets, 1989, MFC 105/83.

Daly, Sir Thomas, unpublished account of the civic action crisis, July 1985, AWM 263, folder D/1/7 (not available for public access).

Eggleton, Tony, 'End-of-Year Situation Report' (for CARE Australia), 18 December 1995, MFC 105/87, box 6 [33].

Fraser family records, various dates, MFC 105/35.

Fraser, Neville, diary, various dates, MFC 107/69.

Fraser, Una, interview with Philip Ayres, audio recording, [n.d.], in possession of Ayres.

——'Malcolm', unpublished essay, 1980, in possession of the Fraser family.

'Fraser, Una (nee Woolf)', photographs, MFC 107/53, BWP/24607.

Mallesons Stephen Jaques, legal opinion, 11 November 2004, in possession of MF.

Memorandum agreed between MF & Melvin R Laird, 14 April 1970, NAA A5619 C 40 [part 3].

'Memorandum of Understanding', drafts, [n.d.], copies in possession of the authors.

'Motion to Return CARE Australia to Compliance in Kenya and Rwanda', 6 November 1994, MFC 105/87, box 4.

Record of conversation between MF & Bratislava Morina, 31 August 1999, copy in possession of the authors.

Record of conversation between MF & Slobodan Milosevic, 1 September 1999, copy in possession of the authors.

'Role and Influence of CARE USA', aide memoir, 8 February 1995, MFC 105/87, box 1.

Rose, John, diary note, 5 November 1981, in possession of Rose.

Salmon, JR, interview, Army Historical Program, 27 March 1972, AWM 107/1 (transcript).

'Strategy for CARE Australia', paper presented to the board, May 1995, copy in possession of the authors.

Tange, Arthur, 'A Memoir on Garfield Barwick, the Man, the Minister', February 1999, n.p., copy in possession of the authors.

Tapp, Charles, notes, Vienna, various dates in July & August 1999, copy in possession of the authors.

'Will of Louis Arnold Woolf', Probate Jurisdiction, Supreme Court of Western Australia, 13 October 1938, copy in MFC 105/35.

Women's Electoral Lobby, survey, 1972, NAA MS3683, series 7, boxes 18–19.

Malcolm Fraser's Radio Addresses

The addresses are listed in chronological order. They were originally broadcast on 3HA Hamilton and 3YB Warrnambool.

1950s

24 January 1954, MFC 107/23 [231].
14 & 21 February 1954, MFC 107/23 [231].
21 March 1954, MFC 107/23 [231].
11 April 1954, MFC 107/23 [231].
1955 addresses published as transcripts in *Horsham Times*, copies in scrapbook, MFC 108/58.
12 April 1959, MFC 107/23 [234].
3 May 1959, MFC 107/23 [234].
10 May 1959, MFC 107/23 [235].
24 May 1959, MFC 107/23 [234].
September 1959, MFC 107/23 [235].

1960s

10 & 24 April 1960, MFC 107/23 [235].
12 & 26 March 1961, MFC 107/23 [236].
4 March 1962, MFC 107/23 [213].
9 September 1962, MFC 107/24 [2].
25 November 1962, MFC 107/23 [213].
12 & 22 November 1963, MFC 107/23 [214].
17, 20 & 30 May 1964, MFC 107/23 [217].
1, 5, 18, 22, 26 & 27 June 1964, MFC 107/23 [217].
1, 6 & 21 July 1964, MFC 107/23 [217].
18 April 1965, MFC 107/23 [218].
13 April 1967, NAA M13692 [38].
11 January 1968, NAA M1369 [241].
14 & 17 April 1968, NAA M1369 [240].
30 August 1968, NAA M1369 [240].
6 September 1969, NAA M1369 [163] Moratorium.

1970s

6 & 10 September 1970, NAA M1369 [163].
28 March 1971, NAA M1369 [30].
25 April 1972, MFC 105/72 [2].
9 July 1972, MFC 105/72 [2].

26 November 1972, MFC 105/72 [4].
11 March 1973, MFC 105/72 [7].
29 April 1973, MFC 105/72 [6].
16 September 1973, MFC 105/72 [6].
17 December 1973, MFC 105/73 [6].
7 & 14 April 1974, MFC 105/72 [8].
30 March 1975, MFC 105/72 [9].
13 April 1975, MFC 105/72 [9].
10 & 20 July 1975, MFC 105/72 [9].
17 August 1975, MFC 107/3 [22, part 1].
4 September 1977, cited in White & Kemp, p. 213.
27 November 1978, cited in *The Age* (Business section).

1980s
15 November 1981, MFC 105/72 [10].
12 September 1982, MFC 105/72 [10].

Undated
MFC 107/24 [1], copy in scrapbook, MFC 108/58.

Parliamentary Speeches
Unless otherwise noted, speeches can be found in Hansard, House of Representatives, Australia.

Malcolm Fraser
MF's speeches are listed in chronological order.

1950s
22 February 1956 [maiden speech], pp. 149–52.
15 March 1956, pp. 860–3.
10 April 1956, pp. 1135–9.
13 September 1956, pp. 505–11.
5 September 1957, pp. 371–3.
25 February 1958, pp. 23–31.
27 March 1958, pp. 825–9.
7 August 1958, p. 215.

1960s
12 April 1961, pp. 769–72.
20 April 1961, pp. 1085–8.
6 August 1961, pp. 128–31.

16 August 1961, pp. 128–31.
17 August 1961, pp. 270–4.
24 August 1967, pp. 465–71.
20 March 1969, pp. 738–40.
13 August 1969, pp. 185–93.

1970s
10 March 1970, pp. 232–47.
9 March 1971, p. 679.
22 April 1971, pp. 1929–31.
5 October 1971, pp. 1848–9.
22 August 1972, pp. 475–92.
28 February 1975, pp. 953–5.
17 April 1975, p. 1808.
20 May 1975, pp. 2501–23.
5 June 1975, pp. 3460–3.
9 July 1975, pp. 3605–11.
26 August 1975, pp. 519–27.
11 November 1975, p. 2913.
1 June 1976 ['State of the World' speech], pp. 2734–44.
30 November 1976, p. 2962.
9 December 1976, pp. 3623–5.
24 May 1977, p. 1701.
25 August 1977, pp. 645–51.
6 September 1977, pp. 721–8.
29 May 1978, pp. 2653–5.
30 May 1978, pp. 2727–33.
21 February 1979, pp. 261–75.
4 April 1979, pp. 1481–2.
4 June 1979, pp. 2825–6.
23 August 1979, pp. 577–80.

1980s
19 February 1980, p. 17.
28 February 1980, pp. 487–9.
28 August 1980, p. 976.
11 September 1980, p. 1199.
28 April 1981, p. 1614.
21 September 1982, p. 1621.

Others
Bilney, Gordon, 11 May 1995, p. 371.
Button, John, Hansard, Senate, 22 May 1980, pp. 2664–7.
Connor, Rex, 9 July 1975, p. 3611.
Downer, Alexander, 11 May 1995, p. 371.
Ellicott, Robert, 6 September 1977, pp. 721–7.
Foot, Michael, Hansard, House of Commons, United Kingdom, 26 October 1981, vol. 10/557–66.
Hanson, Pauline, 10 September 1996, p. 3859.
Howard, John, 17 August 1982, p. 61.
Knight, Harold, 7 December 1976, pp. 3363–4.
Lynch, Phillip, 20 May 1976, pp. 2329–45.
Nixon, Peter, 21 September 1982, p. 1670.
Peacock, Andrew, 28 April 1981, p. 1607.
Whitlam, Gough, 22 April 1976, p. 1948; 1 June 1976, p. 2744.
Withers, Reg, 27 February 1973, p. 291.

No Specified Speaker
19 May 1976, pp. 2053–185.
5 May 1981, p. 1941 (citing George Polites).
9 May 1984, p. 2152.

Non-Parliamentary Speeches

Malcolm Fraser
MF's speeches are listed in chronological order.

1960s
30 March 1968, seminar, South Australian zone of the Australian Jaycees, NAA M1369 [155].
3 May 1969, Symposium on the Great Barrier Reef, NAA M1369 [155].
16 May 1969, tenth annual conference of the Australian Colleges of Education, NAA M1369 [155].
22 May 1969, to delegates from university governing bodies, NAA M1369 [301] Universities.
11 August 1969, Conference on Planning in Higher Education, NAA M1369 [80].
10 November 1969, Lord Mayor's Dinner, Melbourne Town Hall, NAA M1369 [155].
16 November 1969, State Zionist Council of New South Wales, NAA M1374 [29].

1970s

20 July 1971, 'Towards 2000: Challenge to Australia', fifth Alfred Deakin Lecture.

22 January 1975, at the forty-sixth ANZAAS Congress.

27 November 1975, policy launch speech.

——'Turn on the Lights', policy speech (pamphlet), MFC 107/8 [174].

3 June 1977, to the Royal Commonwealth Society.

13 February 1978, opening of the Commonwealth Heads of Government Regional Meeting.

3 April 1978, to the National Aboriginal Conference.

4 January 1979, 'Australia and Some World Economic Issues', Economic Club of New York.

1 August 1979, at the Commonwealth Heads of Government Meeting.

1980s

3 May 1981, to the Zionist Council of Victoria.

1 October 1981, opening address at the Commonwealth Heads of Government Meeting.

26 October 1981, opening of the World Heritage Committee Meeting.

30 November 1981, inaugural address to the Institute of Multicultural Affairs.

1983, policy speech.

15 February 1983, policy speech.

6 March 1983, concession speech.

7 June 1983, 'Liberal Beliefs', at a dinner in honour of Malcolm & Tamie Fraser.

16 January 1984, 'A Conversation with J Malcolm Fraser', American Enterprise Institute, MFC 105/83 (transcript).

20 March 1984, 'The World Economic Crisis: Its History and Solutions', World Economic and Investment Conference.

12 July 1984, 'The World We Live In: 1984', University of Tasmania.

[March or April 1985], at Kevin Newman's retirement dinner.

20 March 1985, 'Liberal Democracies: Challenge and Response', at 'Beyond '84', Conference on Communism and Liberal Democracy.

22 November 1985, statement to the Second Committee of the General Assembly of the United Nations on 'Report and Recommendations of the Panel of Eminent Persons on the Activities of Transnational Corporations in South Africa and Namibia' (typewritten report, 12 October 1985), MFC 105/83, box 2.

17 June 1986, at the launch of *Malcolm Fraser on Australia* by Denis M White & David A Kemp (eds).

30 September 1986, 'Australia: Fighting for a Future', inaugural Downer Lecture.

11 December 1986, 'How Australia Can Return to the Good Times'.

30 July 1987, 'Sir Robert Menzies: In Search of Balance', Daniel Mannix Memorial Lecture.

22 January 1988, 'Australia 2000'.

26 May 1989, at Interaction Council Meeting.

29 October 1989, 'A World in Transition', B'nai B'rith Oration.

1990s

26 July 1997, at the twenty-second anniversary dinner, Ethnic Communities Council of New South Wales, copy in possession of the authors.

28 May 1998, public statement to the Liberal Party, copy in possession of the authors.

2000s

17–20 June 2000, 'The Current Situation of the World', Interaction Council's eighteenth plenary session.

24 August 2000, 'The Past We Need to Understand', Vincent Lingiari Memorial Lecture.

2002, 'What Do We Want to Be?', Walter Murdoch Lecture.

2 May 2002, at CARE gala dinner.

26 May 2002, 'B'nai B'rith Anti-Defamation Commission. Multicultural Tolerance: The Truth about Lies'.

26 May 2004, 'National Sorry Day: Journey of Healing'.

29 November 2005, 'Human Rights and Responsibilities in the Age of Terror', Chancellor's Human Rights Lecture, University of Melbourne.

5 October 2006, at launch of *A Thinking Reed* by Barry Jones.

30 April 2007, 'Australians: What Are We? How Do We See Ourselves? How Do Others See Us?', Commonwealth Lecture.

25 October 2007, 'Finding Security in Terrorism's Shadow: The Importance of the Rule of Law', inaugural professorial lecture, Asia Pacific Centre for Military Law, University of Melbourne.

Others

Blainey, Geoffrey, March 1984, cited in Foster & Stockley, p. 225.

Brown, Neil, reported in Livingstone.

Burke, Edmund, to the electors of Bristol, 3 November 1774.

Chaney, Fred, Lowitja O'Donoghue Oration, 28 May 2009.

Hawke, Bob, policy launch speech, 15 February 1983.

Kennedy, John F, inaugural address, 20 January 1961.

King, LJ, 'The Attorney General, Politics and the Judiciary', paper delivered to the fourth annual colloquium of the Judicial Conference of Australia, November 1999.

Peacock, Andrew, cited in media reports, 16 April 1981, NAA M1268 [301].

Reagan, Ronald, 'Ending Apartheid in South Africa', to members of the World Affairs Council and Foreign Policy Association, 22 July 1986, transcript in *US Department of State Bulletin*, 1 September 1986.

Simon, Barry, 10 April 1981, NAA M1268 [301].

Thatcher, Margaret, Canberra Press Club, 1 July 1979.

——Commonwealth Heads of Government Meeting, 3 August 1979.

Whitlam, Gough, Australian Labor Party Victorian Branch annual conference, June 1967.

——Gurindji Land Ceremony, 16 August 1975.

Press Statements

Malcolm Fraser

MF's statements are listed in chronological order.

12 March 1961, MFC 107/23 [236].

25 November 1962, MFC 107/23 [213].

19 & 21 February 1971, NAA M1369 [30] 1971.

1 April 1975, MFC 105/72 [9].

30 August 1982, NAA M1229.

16 November 1982.

19 January 1983, cited in White & Kemp, p. 218.

3 February 1983, partial transcript published in *The Age*, 4 February 1983.

7 September 1985, MFC 105/83, box 2.

Others

Anthony, Doug & Phillip Lynch, 16 April 1981, NAA M1268 [301].

Carter, Jimmy, 24 March 1977.

Eisenhower, Dwight D, 7 April 1954.
Faulkner, John, 12 May 2009.
Menzies, Robert, 22 October 1975, MFC 106/24 [28].
Nixon, Richard, 25 July 1969.
Thatcher, Margaret, 7 October 1981.

Government Papers and Documents

Papers and documents are listed in chronological order.

Malcolm Fraser

22 July 1964, 'A Visit to the United States, Canada, South Vietnam and Malaysia from 5th May to July 21st 1964', formal report, MFC 107/23 [124].
March 1965, Indonesia trip, official report, MFC 107/24 [1].
27 February 1970, CS, NAA A5882 CO 10 [part 3].
2 February 1976, note for file, NAA A10756 LC 52 [part 3].
July 1976, economic commentary, MFC 106/24 [12].
22 March 1977, note to Secretary, Treasury, NAA A10756 LC 1792.
5 May 1977, CS, NAA A10756 LC 1363.
4 August 1979, record of conversation between MF, Andrew Peacock, Margaret Thatcher & Peter Carrington, NAA A10756 M1356 [11].
22 June 1981, memorandum to John Howard, NAA M2218 [15].
1 November 1982, memorandum to John Howard, NAA M2218 [15].
7 December 1982, premiers' conference agenda brief, NAA M1352 [14].
14 June 1987, notes for the Liberal Party, MFC 105/83.
22 October 1991, cited in House of Representatives Select Committee on the Print Media, transcripts, vol. 2, pp. 829–1630.

Undated

Memorandum to John Howard, NAA A10756 LC 1792 [part 4].
Moratorium marches, notes, NAA M1369 [163] Moratorium.

Others

1968–71

February 1968, Tet report received by MF, NAA M1369 [64, part 1].
1969, Henry Bland, documents regarding trip to the United States and the cabinet meeting afterwards, NAA A5619/1 [part 2].
1970, cablegrams, NAA A5882/2 CO 10 [part 2] & [part 3].
1970–71 (various months), Committee of Inquiry into Services Pay (Kerr Review), minutes, NAA A3209.

5 March 1970, Lenox Hewitt, note to John Gorton, NAA A5882 CO 10 [part 3].
7 April 1970, cablegrams, NAA A5882 CO 10 [part 2] F111 Discussions.
20 May 1970, Arthur Tange, minute to MF, in possession of MF.
19 July 1970, CD 484, copy in possession of MF.

1975
Shadow cabinet minutes, MFC 106/22 [7].
Shadow cabinet working papers, NAA M1360 [54].
Treasury documents, MFC 106/22 [13] & [14]; MFC 106/24 [12].
26 March, senior advisers' research material, NAA M1276 [1] Aboriginal Affairs.
April, Liberal Party of Australia, 'Fund Raising Code Adopted by Federal Executive', endorsed October 1975, copy in possession of MF.
May, Peter Wilenski, draft submission to minister, NAA A446 1974/77554.
6 May, Department of Foreign Affairs, to all posts, NAA A1209 1975/1144.
July, Treasury briefing, MFC 106/24 [12].
4 July, RU Metcalfe, to minister, NAA A446 1974/77554.
[August], draft Aboriginal Affairs policy, MFC 106/22 [54].
13 August, Community Affairs Branch, 'Vietnamese Refugees', NAA A1209 1976/242, part 1.
1 September, Department of Foreign Affairs, 'Undertakings by Vietnamese', memorandum, NAA A1838 3014/10/15/4 [part 10].
29 September, shadow cabinet minutes, MFC 106/2 [44].
30 September, joint party minutes, MFC 106/22, box 3 [46].
——'Report on Joint Committee on Pecuniary Interests', NAA A10756 LC 4 [part 1].
——shadow cabinet minutes, MFC 106/22 [44].
October, Commissioner of Taxation, memorandum to Deputy Commissioner of Taxation, MFC 106/22 [14].
——Liberal Party, foreign policy statement, MFC 106/22, box 4 [50].
——shadow cabinet minutes, MFC 106/22, box 4 [50].
6 October, shadow cabinet minutes, MFC 106/22.
15 October, shadow ministry minutes, MFC 106/22 [47].
19 & 21 October, shadow cabinet minutes, MFC 106/22, box 3 [49].
24 October, Department of Foreign Affairs, file note, NAA A1838 1634/70/2 [part 8].

November, shadow cabinet working paper, MFC 106/22 [54].
11 & 12 November, joint party minutes, NAA M1360 [52].
12 November, cabinet minutes, NAA A10756 LC 4 [part 1].
20 November, cablegram to Richard Woolcott, NAA A11443 [14].
21 November, David N Reid, note for file, NAA M1356 [36].
——John Menadue, letter to CW Harders, NAA M1356 [36].
25 November, Richard Woolcott, cablegram to MF, NAA A11443 [11].
5 December, CW Harders, memorandum to Ivor Greenwood, NAA M1356 [36].

1976

6 January, cabinet minutes, NAA A10756 LC 91 [part 1].
14 January, cabinet minutes, NAA A10756 LC 55.
30 January, CD 144, NAA A12909.
——CS 63, NAA A12909.
9 February, Andrew Peacock, CS FAD/1, NAA A10756 LC 209 [part 1].
6 March, Andrew Peacock, notes on draft, NAA M1356 [18].
11 March, CS 165, NAA A12909.
May, CS, NAA M1276 [123, part 2].
25 May, CS 265 & 287, NAA A12909.
13 July, Phillip Lynch, CS 532, NAA A10756 LC 869.
——Ed Visbord, DPMC, commentary, NAA A10756 LC 869.
27 July, record of conversation between MF & President Gerald Ford (also present, Secretary of State Henry Kissinger), NAA M1356 [59].
28 July, record of conversation between MF & Henry Kissinger, NAA M1356 [22].
22 September, CS, NAA A10756 LC 1013.
[22 September], DPMC, comments, NAA A10756 LC 1013.
23 September, CD 1564, NAA A10756 LC 793 [part 1].
14 October, briefing to MF, NAA A10756 LC 1791 [part 1].
2 November, Ian Castles, memorandum to MF, NAA A10756 LC 1791 [part 1].
5 November, Owen Harries, report of a conversation with Jimmy Carter during eight days on the east coast of the United States, 24 September – 1 October 1976, NAA M1276 [105, part 3].
9 November, Department of Foreign Affairs and Defence, 'Paper on Jimmy Carter's Foreign Policy and Its Implications for Australia', NAA A10756 LC 1101 [part 1].
——CD 1750 & 1794, NAA A12909.

——CD 1790, NAA A13075.
22 November, CS, NAA A10756 LC 1013.
28 November, CD 1931, NAA A13075.
2 December, cabinet minutes, NAA A10756 LC 4 [part 1].
8 December, CD 1994, NAA A10756 LC 1151.
17 December, CD 2094, NAA A12909.

1977
March, Reserve Bank of Australia, paper to MF, NAA A10756 LC 1792 [part 1].
24 March, CD 2413, NAA A10756 LC 1792.
30 March, DPMC, note to MF, NAA A10756 LC 1792 [part 1].
7 April, DPMC, advice on CS 1160, NAA A10756 LC 1366 [part 1].
3 May, CS 1160, NAA A10756 LC 1366 [part 1].
5 May, FAD, CD 2882, NAA A10756 LC 1363.
——CS 1220, NAA A10756 LC 1363.
16 & 20 May, Geoffrey Yeend, notes to MF, NAA A10756 LC 1151 [part 1].
23 May, FAD, CD 2977, NAA A10756 LC 1366 [part 1].
8 August, Maurice Byers, legal opinion, NAA 76/02739 [part 2].
September, DPMC, briefing note, NAA A10756 LC 1381 [part 1].
21 October, Geoffrey Yeend, note to MF, NAA A10756 LC 1151 [part 2].
1 November, Andrew Peacock, report to cabinet, NAA A10756 LC 1735.

1978
Documents regarding Aboriginal affairs, NAA A10756 LC 793 Aboriginal Policy.
Engeldow, LWB, discussion paper, NAA A10756 LC 1366 [part 1].
16 January, Ed Visbord, memorandum to MF with attached paper by John Rose & John Hewson, NAA A10756 LC 1792.
[16 January], John Rose & John Hewson, memorandum to MF, all at NAA A10756 LC 1792.
17 January, CD 4487 (MPCC), NAA A13075 [vol. 15].
——CD 4488 (MPCC), NAA A10756 LC 1792.
19 January, Geoffrey Yeend, note for file, NAA A10756 LC 1792 [part 1]; NAA M2218 [35].
24 January, KL Mahar, note for file, NAA A10756 LC 1792 [part 1].
8 February, AT Griffith, DPMC, notes to MF, NAA A10756 LC 1366 [parts 1–3].

9 February, CD 4612 (MPCC), NAA A10756 LC 1792 [part 1] & LC2525 [part 1].
——Treasury & Reserve Bank of Australia, paper number 234 prepared in response to CD 4488, NAA A10756 LC 1792 [part 1].
23 February, KL Mahar, DPMC, briefing note to MF, NAA A10756 LC 1792 [part 1].
24 February, CD 4702 (MPCC), NAA A13075 [vol. 15].
——CD 4703 (MPCC), NAA A10756 LC 1792 [part 2].
——CD 4709 (MPCC), NAA A10756 LC2525 [part 1].
1 March, CD 4811 (MPCC), NAA A13075 [vol. 15].
16 March, Alan Carmody, note to MF, NAA A10756 LC 1791 [part 2].
21 March, CS 2046, NAA A12909.
31 March, Treasury & Reserve Bank of Australia, Cabinet Paper 275, presented to cabinet by 3 April 1978, NAA A10756 LC 1791 [part 2].
6 April, KL Mahar, note to MF, NAA A10756 LC 1791 [part 2].
9 April, CS 2097, NAA A12909.
14 April, KL Mahar, memorandum to MF with attached paper by Ian Castles & John Rose, NAA A10756 LC 1791 [part 2].
May, KL Mahar, briefing note to MF, NAA A10756 LC 1792 [part 2].
1 May, John Howard, paper described as factual update of Treasury & Reserve Bank of Australia, Cabinet Paper 320, NAA A10756 LC 1791.
——ST Sedgwick, note to MF, NAA M2218 [38].
3 & 11 May, KS Hutchings, DPMC, notes to MF, NAA A10756 LC 1366 [parts 1–3].
4 May, Michael MacKellar & Andrew Peacock, CS 2173, NAA A10756 LC 1366 [part 1].
17 May, CD 5415 (MPCC), NAA A10756 LC 1792 [part 2].
——Treasury & Reserve Bank of Australia, Cabinet Papers 426 & 427, NAA A10756 LC 1792 [part 2].
20 May, John Howard, cabinet paper, NAA A10756 LC 1792.
26 May, CD 5548 & 5549 (MPCC), NAA A10756 LC 1791 [part 2].
24 July, CS 2538, NAA A12909.
28 July, Cabinet Paper 654, NAA A10756 LC 1792 [part 2].
——CD 6465 (Ad Hoc Committee of Cabinet), NAA A13075.
——CD 6480 (MPCC) & 6749 (MPCC), NAA A10756 LC 1792 [part 2].

2 August, Cabinet Paper 673, NAA A10756 LC 1791 [part 2].
7 August, CD 6491 (Ad Hoc Committee of Cabinet), NAA A13075.
13 August, CS 2562, NAA A12909.
24 August, CD 6630 (MPCC), NAA A10756 LC 1791 [part 2].
29 August, CS 2580, NAA A10756 LC 1381 [part 1].
14 September, FAD, CD 6716, NAA A1076 LC 1366 [part 2].
9 October, John Rose, memorandum to MF with attached paper, NAA A10756 LC 1792 [part 3].
——Ed Visbord, memorandum to MF, NAA A10756 LC 1792 [part 3].
10 October, CD 6860 (MPCC), NAA A10756 LC 1792 [part 3].
24 October, Ed Visbord, note to MF, NAA A10756 LC 1792 [part 3].
26 October, CD 7014 (MPCC), NAA A10756 LC 1792 [part 3] & NAA A1076 LC 2525 [part 1].
——Ian Castles, memorandum to MF, NAA A10756 LC 1792 [part 3] & NAA A1076 LC 2525 [part 1].
16 November, CS 2747, NAA A12909.
20 November, Michael MacKellar, CS 2771, NAA A10756 LC 1366 [part 2].
21 November, Roger Holdich, DPMC, notes to MF, NAA A10756 LC 1366 [parts 1–3].
11 December, ST Sedgwick, note to MF, NAA A10756 LC 1792 [part 4].

1979

4 January, John Howard, memorandum to (Acting Prime Minister) Doug Anthony, NAA A10756 LC 1792 [part 3] & NAA A1076 LC 2525 [part 1].
9 January, CD 7425 (MPCC), NAA A10756 LC 1792 [part 3] & NAA A1076 LC 2525 [part 1].
19 January, John Howard, Cabinet Paper 836, NAA A10756 LC 1792.
——KL Mahar, note to MF, NAA A10756 LC 1792 [part 4].
——Ed Visbord, note to Fraser, NAA A10756 LC 1792.
22 January, John Rose & John Hewson, Cabinet Papers 844 & 855, NAA A10756 LC 1792.
——CD 7448 (MPCC) & 7449 (MPCC), NAA A10756 LC 1792.
5 February, file notes, NAA A10756 LC 1792 [part 4].
13 February, ST Sedgwick, note for file, in possession of the authors.
15 May, CD 8569, NAA A10756 LC 1366 [parts 2–3].
8 July, DPMC, notes to MF, NAA A10756 LC 1366 [parts 1–3].

10 July, CD 9149, NAA A10756 LC 1366 [parts 2–3].
11 July, Cabinet Memorandum 380, NAA A10756 LC 1366 [part 3].
30 July, situation report on Zimbabwe received by MF, NAA M1356 [11].
19 December, CD 10546, NAA A10756 LC 1735.

1980

8 January, Andrew Peacock, CS 3748, A10756 LC 2773.
21 February, JF Landos, departmental minute, NAA M1268 [part 1].
14 April, CD 11101, NAA A10756 LC 2855 [part 1].
——CD 11108 (MPCC), NAA A10756 LC 1792.
——John Howard, CS 658, NAA A10756 LC 1792.
——Geoffrey Yeend, note to MF, NAA A10756 LC 1151 [part 2].
17 April, John Howard, CS, with consideration 24 April 1980, NAA A10756 LC 1792.
27 May, CD 11759 (ad hoc), NAA A10756 LC 1366 [parts 2–3].
17 June, CD 11893 (MPCC), NAA A10756 LC 1791.
15 July, CD 12130, NAA M1268 [300].
12 August, John Howard, memorandum to MF, NAA A10756 LC 1792 [part 4].
22 August, Andrew Peacock, memorandum to cabinet, LC 1101 [part 2].
26 August, CD 12651 (MPCC), NAA A10756 LC 1792 [part 7].
——John Howard, Memorandum 960, NAA A10756 LC 1792 [part 7].
29 August, Peter Durack, memorandum to MF, NAA A10756 LC 2855 [part 1].
23 September, CD 1239, NAA M1268 [300].
3 November, Coordination Committee, CD 12884, NAA A10756 LC 793 [part 2].
17 November, John Howard, cabinet memorandum, NAA A10756 LC 1792.
19 November, CD, NAA A10756 LC 1792 [part 7].
2 December, CD, NAA A10756 LC 1792 [part 7].

1981

15 January, CS 4511, NAA A10756 LC 793 [part 2].
22 January, DPMC, briefings to MF, NAA A10756 LC 793 [part 2].
29 January, CD 13658, NAA A10756 LC 793 [part 2].
12 June, John Howard, memorandum to MF, NAA M1352 [15].
7 July, Ed Visbord, memorandum to MF, NAA A10756 LC 1792 [part 8].
13 July, John Howard, CS 4963, NAA A10756 LC 1792.

15 July, CD 16390 (MPCC), NAA A10756 LC 1792 [part 8].
21 July, John Howard, CS 1611, NAA A10756 LC 1792 [part 8].
23 July, CD 16462 (MPCC), NAA A10756 LC 1792 [part 8].
22 October, Treasury & Reserve Bank of Australia, memorandum, NAA A10756 LC 1792 [part 9].
26 October, CD 17038 (MPCC), NAA A10756 LC 1792 [part 9].
9 November, CD 17086, NAA A10756 LC 2525 [part 1].
15 December, John Howard, memorandum to MF, NAA M1352 [15].

1982
21 January, John Howard, memorandum to MF, NAA M2218 [15].
22 January, John Howard, CS 5299, NAA A10756 LC 2525 [part 1].
8 February, Australian Financial System Inquiry task force, paper, NAA A10756 LC 2525 [part 1].
——John Howard, CS 5328, NAA A10756 LC 2525 [part 1].
11 May, Ed Visbord, memorandum to MF, NAA A10756 LC 2525 [part 1].
June, John Howard, briefing to cabinet, NAA A10756 LC 94 [part 7].
——DPMC, commentary, NAA A10756 LC 94 [part 7].
14 June, Ed Visbord, memorandum to MF, NAA A10756 LC 2525 [part 1].
17 June, John Howard, CS 5577, NAA A10756 LC 2525 [part 1].
18 June, Ed Visbord, memorandum to MF, NAA A10756 LC 2525 [part 1].
1 July, CS 5589, NAA A10756 LC 2525 [part 2].
——DPMC, Treasury & Reserve Bank of Australia, paper, NAA M2218 [38].
2 July, CS 5589, NAA A10756 LC 2525 [part 1].
5 July, CD 18309 (MPCC), NAA M2218 [31].
13 July, CS 5589 (foreign bank entry), NAA A10756 LC 5036 [part 1].
20 July, CD 18646 (MPCC), NAA A10756 LC 2525 [part 2].
22 July, VW Fitzgerald, memorandum to MF, NAA A10756 LC 2525 [part 2].
28 July, CD 18644–7 (MPCC), NAA A10756 LC 2525 [part 2].
August, CD 18858 and weekly reports thereafter, NAA A10756 LC 2855 [part 2].
3 September, Peter Durack, Cabinet Memorandum 2080, NAA A10756 LC 2855 [part 2].
27 October, Ed Visbord, Memorandum 2183 to MF, NAA A10756 LC 2525 [part 2].

——Ed Visbord, memorandum to MF, NAA M2218 [15].
4 November, RG Hawkins, note for file, NAA A10756 LC 5036 [part 1]; NAA M2218 [15].
December, cabinet memorandum, NAA A10756 LC 1101 [part 2].
23 December, John Howard, letter to Fraser, NAA A10756 LC 5036 [part 1].

1983

Treasury statement no. 5, budget papers 1983–84.
7 January, Ed Visbord, note on CS 5892, NAA A10756 LC2525 [part 2].
13 January, CD 19530, 19536 & 19537, 19572 (MPCC), NAA A10756 LC 5036 [part 1].
——CS 5556, NAA A10756 LC 5036 [part 1].
——CS 5892, considered by cabinet, NAA A10756 LC 5036 [part 1].
28 January, DPMC, briefings to MF, NAA A10756 LC 793 [part 2].
23 March, Tony Eggleton, '1983 Election Report', memorandum to Federal Executive of the Liberal Party, MFC 107/29 [12].

1987

15 July 1987, Denis White & David Kemp, comments (on MF, notes for the Liberal Party, 14 June 1987), MFC 105/83.

Undated or Various Dates

Budgetary planning documents, NAA A10756 LC 52 [part 3].
Chaney, Fred, notes, NAA M1276 [204].
Attendance Sheets 14/1/77/–20/12/77, NAA A12575 [1].
Kemp, David, notes to MF, NAA M12T6 [108].
Visbord, Ed, letter to Secretary of Treasury, NAA A10756 LC 1792.

Books and Leaflets

Australian Dictionary of Biography: Online Edition, Australian National University, 2006, www.adb.online.anu.edu.au.
Ayres, Philip, *Malcolm Fraser: A Biography*, William Heinemann, Richmond, 1987.
Broinowski, Richard, *Fact or Fission: The Truth about Australia's Nuclear Ambitions*, Scribe, Melbourne, 2003.
Burger, Angela, *Neville Bonner: A Biography*, MacMillan, Melbourne, 1979.
Cathcart, Michael, *Defending the National Tuckshop: Australia's Secret Army Intrigue of 1931*, McPhee Gribble, Fitzroy, 1988.

The Commonwealth Group of Eminent Persons, *Mission to South Africa: The Commonwealth Report*, Penguin, Harmondsworth, 1986. Foreword by Shridath Ramphal.
Cook, Peter, *Australia and Vietnam 1965–1972*, La Trobe University, Melbourne, 1991.
Costar, Brian, Peter Love & Paul Strangio (eds), *The Great Labor Schism: A Retrospective*, Scribe, Carlton North, 2005.
Defence of Government Schools, leaflet, [n.d.], NAA M1369 [80] DOGS.
Errington, Wayne & Peter Van Onselen, *John Winston Howard: The Biography*, Melbourne University Press, 2007.
Evans, Raymond, *A History of Queensland*, Cambridge University Press, Melbourne, 2007.
Fitzgerald, Ross, *From 1915 to the Early 1980s: A History of Queensland*, University of Queensland Press, Brisbane, 1984.
Foley, Stephen & Marshall Wilson, *Anatomy of a Coup: The Sinister Intrigue behind the Dismissal*, Canterbury Press, Melbourne, 1990.
Foster, Lois & David Stockley, *Australian Multiculturalism: A Documentary History and Critique*, Multilingual Matters, Clevedon, 1988.
Fraser, Malcolm, *Common Ground: Issues That Should Bind and Not Divide Us*, Viking, Melbourne, 2002.
Fraser, Phoebe, *A Single Seed*, William Heinemann Australia, Port Melbourne, 1996.
Fraser, Simon, *The True Story of the Beginning of the Artesian Water Supply of Australia*, George Robertson, Melbourne, [n.d.].
Galbally, Frank, *Galbally! The Autobiography of Australia's Leading Criminal Lawyer*, Viking, Ringwood, 1989.
Ham, Paul, *Vietnam: The Australian War*, HarperCollins, Sydney, 2007.
Hawkins, Freda, *Critical Years in Immigration: Canada and Australia Compared*, McGill-Queen's University Press, Quebec, 1989.
Hindhaugh, Christina, *It Wasn't Meant to Be Easy: Tamie Fraser in Canberra*, Lothian, Melbourne, 1986.
Hocking, Jenny, *Gough Whitlam: A Moment in History*, Miegunyah Press, Melbourne, 2008.
Jupp, James, *From White Australia to Woomera*, Cambridge University Press, Melbourne, 2002.
Kelly, Paul, *The Unmaking of Gough*, Angus & Robertson, Sydney, 1976.
——*The End of Certainty*, Allen & Unwin, Sydney, 1992.

——*November 1975: The Inside Story of Australia's Greatest Political Crisis*, Allen & Unwin, Sydney, 1995.

Kerr, John, *Matters for Judgment*, Macmillan, Melbourne, 1978.

Liberal Party & Country Party, *Employment and Industrial Relations Policy*, leaflet, Porter Print, Prahran, April 1974.

Liberal Party Campaign Leaflets, 1954, MFC 105/73, box 4.

Lopez, Mark, *The Origins of Multiculturalism in Australian Politics 1945–1975*, Melbourne University Press, 2000.

Lowe, Doug, *The Price of Power*, Macmillan, Melbourne, 1984.

Lyster, Symon, *International Wildlife Law: An Analysis of International Treaties Concerned with the Conservation of Wildlife*, Cambridge University Press, 1993.

McNamara, Robert, *In Retrospect: The Tragedy and Lessons of Vietnam*, Vintage, New York, 1996.

Mandela, Nelson, *Long Walk to Freedom*, Little, Brown & Co., London, 1994.

Marr, David, *Barwick*, Allen & Unwin, Sydney, 1980.

——*Patrick White: A Life*, Random House, North Sydney, 1991.

Menzies, Robert, *The Measure of the Years*, Cassell, London, 1970.

Morgan, Patrick (ed.), *BA Santamaria: Your Most Obedient Servant, Selected Letters 1938–1996*, Miegunyah Press, Melbourne, 2007.

Nolan, Sybil (ed.), *The Dismissal*, Melbourne University Press, 2005. Peter Baume, 'A Soldier Regrets'; Michael Gawenda, 'Reeling in the Aisles'; Mike Steketee, 'A Full Throated Roar of Protest'.

Nulladulla, Milton Ulladulla District Historical Society, 1972.

Orkin, Mark (ed.), *Sanctions against Apartheid*, New Africa Books, Cape Town, 1989. Linda Freeman, 'All but One: Britain, the Commonwealth and Sanctions'.

Papp, Daniel S (ed.), *As I Saw It*, WW Norton, New York, 1990.

Pemberton, Geoffrey, *All the Way: Australia's Road to Vietnam*, Allen & Unwin, Sydney, 1987.

Pratt, Steve, *Duty of Care*, Simon & Schuster, Sydney, 2000.

Reid, Alan, *The Gorton Experiment*, Shakespeare Head Press, Sydney, 1971.

Rowse, Tim, *Australian Liberalism and the National Character*, Kibble Books, Melbourne, 1978.

Santamaria, BA, *Against the Tide*, Oxford University Press, Melbourne, 1981.

Sayers, Stuart, *Ned Herring: A Life of Lieutenant-General the Honourable Sir Edmund Herring*, Hyland House, Melbourne, 1980.

Schofield, Mark J, 'Weldon, Thomas Dewar (1896–1958)', *Oxford Dictionary of National Biography: From the Earliest Times to the Year 2000*, vol. 57, ed. HCG Matthew & B Harrison, Oxford University Press, Oxford & New York, 2004, pp. 987–8.

Shawcross, William, *Deliver Us from Evil: Warlords and Peacekeepers in a World of Endless Conflict*, Bloomsbury, London, 2000.

Stanner, William EH, *White Man Got No Dreaming: Essays, 1938–1973*, Australian National University Press, Canberra, 1979.

Starke, Monica, *The Alexandra Club: A Narrative 1903–1983*, Alexandra Club & Elm Grove Press, Melbourne, 1986.

Sutton, Peter, *The Politics of Suffering: Indigenous Australia and the End of Liberal Consensus*, Melbourne University Press, 2009.

Tavan, Gwenda, *The Long Slow Death of White Australia*, Scribe, Melbourne, 2005.

Trengove, Alan, *John Grey Gorton: An Informal Biography*, Cassell Australia, Melbourne, 1969.

'Truthful Thomas', *Through the Spy-Glass: Short Sketches of Well-Known Westralians as Others See Them*, Praagh & Lloyd, Perth, 1905.

Viviani, Nancy, *The Long Journey: Vietnamese Migration and Settlement in Australia*, Melbourne University Press, 1984.

——*The Indochinese in Australia 1975–1995: From Burnt Boats to Barbecues*, Oxford University Press, Melbourne, 1996.

Wallace, Christine, *Hewson: A Portrait*, Sun Australia, Sydney, 1993.

Weller, Patrick, *Malcolm Fraser PM: A Study in Prime Ministerial Power in Australia*, Penguin, Melbourne, 1989.

White, Denis M & David A Kemp (eds), *Malcolm Fraser on Australia*, Hill of Content, Melbourne, 1986.

Whitlam, Gough, *The Truth of the Matter*, Melbourne University Press, 2005.

Newspaper and Periodical Articles

Malcolm Fraser

MF's articles are listed in chronological order.

5 June 1954, letter to *The Sun*.

22 June 1965, letter to *The Age*, copy in MFC 105/73, box 2 [18].

March 1967, 'Liberalism: As a Liberal MHR Sees It', *Today Ad Lib* (University of Melbourne Liberal journal), vol. 1, no. 1, copy in MFC 107/23 [392].

1 August 1974, 'We Stand as Liberals 1945–1974 and Beyond', *Herald* [Melbourne].

24 July 1986, MF & Olusegun Obasanjo, 'What to Do about South Africa', copy in MFC 105/71.

29 July 1986, *The Gainesville Sun.*

18 August 1991, 'The Ordinary People Have Been Forgotten', *The Sunday Age.*

28 August 1991, 'Ideology Out as Parties Embrace the Law of the Jungle', *The Sunday Age.*

1 September 1991, 'Politics, Banks and the Failure of Deregulation', *The Sunday Age.*

13 October 1991, 'Balanced GST Good for the Country', *The Sunday Age.*

3 November 1991, 'Be Rational, Yes, But Life Was Not Meant to Be a Nightmare', *The Sunday Age.*

17 November 1991, 'Deregulation Dogma Is No Substitute for Common Sense', *The Sunday Age.*

8 March 1992, 'The Historical Facts Are Clear, but a Republic Is Not the Answer', *The Sunday Age.*

10 January 1993, 'Opposition Pricks Up Its Ears', *The Sunday Age.*

21 March 1993, 'Going Nowhere, with Nowhere to Go', *The Sunday Age.*

28 March 1993, 'Party Must Get Off the Straight and Narrow', *The Sunday Age.*

1 September 1993, 'Party's Hopes Rest with New President', *The Australian.*

19 May 1994, 'New Leader Needed to Revive Ailing Libs', *The Australian.*

25 May 1994, 'Enthusiastic Team Can Inspire Renewal', *The Australian.*

1 February 1995, 'Crucial Test for Howard', *The Australian.*

30 August 1995, 'The Republic: An Idea Whose Time Will Come', *The Australian.*

19 February 1998, 'A House Divided against Itself Cannot Stand', *The Australian.*

22 June 1998, 'This Obscenity Must Be Repelled', *The Australian.*

21 October 1999, 'A Crisis Prevention Model', *The Australian.*

29 October 1999, *Weekly Times.*

20 November 2007, 'Voting to Restore the Decent Values Australia Once Held Dear', *The Age.*

Others

'All Eyes on Wannon: Liberal "Baby" Fights Way to the Front', *The Argus*, 3 June 1954, copy in scrapbook, MFC 108/58.

'The Australian Army's Revolt in Vietnam', *The Bulletin*, 6 March 1971, pp. 11–12.

'A Young Man Brings Hope', editorial, *The Argus*, 5 June 1954, copy in scrapbook, MFC 108/58.

Betts, Katherine & Ernest Healy, 'Lebanese Muslims in Australia and Social Disadvantage', *People and Place* (Centre for Population and Urban Research, Monash University, Melbourne), vol. 14, no. 1, 2006.

Bowers, Peter, 'Quietly, Fraser Is Setting the Scene', *The Sydney Morning Herald*, 9 January 1976.

Cadzow, Jane, 'Life Wasn't Meant to Be This Easy', *Good Weekend*, 30 November 1991, pp. 15–21.

Cass, Moss, 'Stop This Unjust Queue Jumping', *The Australian*, 29 June 1978.

Catholic Weekly, interview with MF, 12 June 1975, p. 1, copy in MFC 106/15, box 7 [20, part 1].

Clifford, Clark, 'A Vietnam Reappraisal', *Foreign Affairs*, vol. 47, 4 July 1969, pp. 601–22.

'Close Fight at Polls for Them', *The Sun*, 13 May 1954, copy in scrapbook, MFC 108/58.

Colebatch, Hal, 'You Got Him In So Help Kick Him Out', *The Australian*, 16 April 2008.

'Compromise Solution', *The Age*, 16 April 1970.

Downes, Stephen, *The Age*, 7 March 1983.

Elias, David, 'Fraser Faces Fight', *The Age*, 6 August 1993.

Franklin, Matthew, 'Fraser Was Warned on Lebanese Migrants', *The Australian*, 1 January 2007.

——'John Faulkner in Call for Disclosure', *The Australian*, 6 May 2009.

Fraser, Una, 'My Son Malcolm', *The Sun*, 19 December 1977.

Friedman, Milton, 'The Line We Dare Not Cross', *Encounter*, vol. 47, no. 5, November 1976.

Fukuyama, Francis, 'The End of History', *National Interest*, no. 16, 1989.

'Funeral of Mr Louis Arnold Woolf at Chapel of Wood, Coppill Ltd in Bathurst Road, Katoomba', *The Sydney Morning Herald*, 14 February 1938.

Gorton, John, 'I Did It My Way: The Fraser Affair and How I Was Deposed', *The Sunday Australian*, 29 August 1971.

'Grandpa Simon Fraser: Quite Napoleonic', *The Australian*, 23 July 1978.

Grattan, Michelle, 'Muldoon Upsets the Apple Cart', *The Age*, 5 October 1981.

——*The Age*, 3 September 1982.

——'Turnbull Needs to Find His Reform Mojo to Win this History War', *The Sydney Morning Herald*, 11 September 2009.

Gwertzman, Bernard, 'US Sides with Britain in Falkland Crisis', *The New York Times*, 1 May 1982.

Harrison, Dan, 'African Refugees Face Integration Issues: Andrews', *The Age*, 3 October 2007.

'Home Truths from South Africa', *Financial Times*, 14 June 1986, copy in MFC 105/71.

Howard, John, 'Rudd Demeans Himself over History', *The Australian*, 11 September 2009.

Jones, Philip, 'A Woman for the Times in an Age of Constant Change', *The Australian*, 3 June 1998.

Kemp, David, 'A Leader and a Philosophy', *Australian Journal of Political Science* (previously published as *Politics*), vol. 8, no. 1, May 1973.

——'The 1976 Cabinet Papers: A Reply to John Stone', *Quadrant*, vol. 51, no. 12, December 2007.

King, Anthony, 'How Many Lives Was It Worth?', *Times Higher Education Supplement*, 25 November 1994.

'Liberals Endorse Fraser Again for Wannon Fight', *Horsham Times*, 19 August 1955, copy in scrapbook, MFC 108/58.

Livingstone, Tess, 'Reagan, Thatcher Ideal Models: Top Liberal', *The Courier Mail*, 13 March 1985.

'Malcolm Fraser Is Sworn In as Member for Wannon', *Hamilton Spectator*, 23 February 1956.

'Meanness and Despicable Nature of Assistance for South Vietnamese Refugees', *The Age*, 30 April 1975.

Megalogenis, George, 'The Threat from Within', *The Weekend Australian*, 8 April 2006.

Miller, JDB, 'Encountering a New World', *Australian Journal of International Affairs*, vol. 34, no. 1, April 1980, pp. 100–9.

Mirabella, Sophie, 'Fraser's Flawed World View: A Study in Hypocrisy', *The Age*, 6 January 2008.

Moore, Cameron, 'To Execute and Maintain the Laws of the Commonwealth: The ADF and Internal Security—Some Old Issues with New Relevance', *University of New South Wales Law Journal*, vol. 28, no. 2, 2005.
'Mr Fraser and *The Bulletin*', *The Bulletin*, 19 March 1971.
'Obituary of Sir Simon Fraser', *The Age*, 31 April 1919.
Olney, Lindsay, 'Mal Misses Top Job', *The Sun*, 19 October 1989.
——'Fraser in Lib Presidency Row', *The Advertiser* [Adelaide], 6 April 1993.
Ramsey, Alan, 'Canberra's Warriors Fight for Supremacy', *The Sunday Australian*, 28 February 1971.
——'General Says Fraser Is Disloyal to Service', *The Australian*, 4 March 1971.
Reagan, Ronald, 'Ending Apartheid in South Africa', *US Department of State Bulletin* (address transcript), 1 September 1986.
Rule, Andrew, 'Galbally's Lore', *The Age*, 13 October 2005.
Safe, Mike, 'I Just Wanted to Swim', *The Australian Magazine*, 8–9 March 2008.
Salusinszky, Imre, 'Two at Oxford', *The Age*, 24 July 1979.
Samuel, Peter, 'The Australian Army's "Revolt" in Vietnam', *The Bulletin*, 6 March 1971, pp. 11–12.
Santamaria, BA, 'Point of View', *News Weekly*, 26 March 1975, p. 16, copy in MFC 106/3, box 2 [10].
Shanahan, Denis, 'Santamaria's Secret Dismissal Role', *The Australian*, 6 January 2007.
Simson, Stuart, 'Where Howard Can Move on Campbell', *Business Review*, 21–27 November 1981.
Steketee, Mike, 'Howard in War Refugee Snub: Fraser', *The Australian*, 1 January 2008.
Stengel, Richard, 'Falling Short', *Time*, 24 June 2001.
Stone, John, 'The Dismal Beginning to the Fraser Years', *Quadrant*, vol. 51, nos 7–8, July–August 2007.
Sutton, Peter, 'The Politics of Suffering: Indigenous Policy in Australia since the 1970s', *Anthropological Forum*, vol. 11, no. 2, 2001, pp. 125–73.
Thatcher, Margaret, interview with *Women's Own*, 31 October 1987.
'The Week in Canberra', *The Age*, 26 March 1956.
'Too Much Politics, Not Enough Policy', *The Weekend Australian*, 16–17 May 2009.

Uren, David, 'Don't Lose Your Nerve on Reform, Warns Treasury Head Ken Henry', *The Australian*, 20 May 2009.

Williams, Evan, 'A Born Winner', *The West Australian*, 5 December 1969.

'Youngest Ever?', *The Sun*, 3 June 1954, copy in scrapbook, MFC 108/58.

'Zanetti's View', *Daily Telegraph* (Sydney), 15 April 1981.

Papers and Reports

Australian Institute of Multicultural Affairs, *Evaluation of Post Arrival Programs and Services*, Australian Institute of Multicultural Affairs, Melbourne, May 1982.

Australian Population and Immigration Council, *Immigration Policies and Australia's Population: A Green Paper*, Australian Government Publishing Service, Canberra, 1977.

Community Affairs Branch, 'Vietnamese Refugees', 13 August 1975, NAA A1209 1976/242 [part 1].

Department of Defence, *Defending Australia in the Asia Pacific Century: Force 2030*, white paper, Commonwealth of Australia, Canberra, 2009.

Department of Foreign Affairs and Trade, *Australia and the Indonesian Incorporation of Portuguese Timor*, Melbourne University Press, 2000.

Department of Immigration and Ethnic Affairs, *Australia's Immigration Policy*, prepared by Michael MacKellar, Australian Government Publishing Service, Canberra, 1978.

Environment Australia, *Australia's Kakadu: Protecting World Heritage—Response by the Government of Australia to the UNESCO World Heritage Committee Regarding Kakadu National Park*, Commonwealth of Australia, Canberra, April 1999.

Fox Inquiry—see *Ranger Uranium Environmental Inquiry*.

Harries, Owen (ed.), *Australia and the Third World: Report of the Committee on Australia's Relations with the Third World*, Australian Government Publishing Service, Canberra, 1979.

Hay, David, *The Delivery of Services Financed by the Department of Aboriginal Affairs*, Australian Government Publishing Service, Canberra, 1976.

'Hope Protective Security Review', *Parliament Paper 397 (1979)*, Commonwealth of Australia, 1979. Appendix 16, 'The History of Military Involvement in Civilian Security in Britain and Australia'; Appendix 3, 'Commonwealth Heads of Government Regional Meeting, Sydney, 13–17 February 1978', pp. 257–62.

Human Rights and Equal Opportunities Commission, *A Last Resort? The National Inquiry into Children in Immigration Detention*, Human Rights and Equal Opportunities Commission, Sydney, 2004.

Manning, Alan (comp.), *Uranium, a Fair Trial: Both Sides of the Uranium Debate as Presented in the ALP Discussion Kit*, Australian Labor Party, Canberra, 1976. David Combe, 'Preface'; Jonathan West, 'Liquid Fuel Alternatives'.

Ranger Uranium Environmental Inquiry (Fox Inquiry), second report, (RW Fox, Chair), Australian Government Publishing Service, Canberra, May 1977.

Richardson, David, 'Official Economic Forecasts—How Good Are They?', *Parliamentary Library Current Issues Brief 17, 2000–2001*, Parliament of Australia, Canberra, 26 June 2001.

'Royal Commission of Inquiry into Matters in Relation to Electoral Redistribution', *Commonwealth Parliamentary Paper No. 263/1978*, (Mr Justice DG McGregor, Commissioner), Australian Government Publishing Service, Canberra, 1978.

Senate Foreign Affairs, Defence and Trade References Committee, *East Timor: Final Report of the Senate Foreign Affairs, Defence and Trade References Committee*, Parliament of the Commonwealth of Australia, Canberra, December 2000.

Senate Select Committee on Uranium Mining and Milling, *Uranium Mining and Milling in Australia*, Senate Information Services Section, Canberra, May 1997.

Senate Standing Committee on Foreign Affairs and Defence, *Australia and the Refugee Problem: The Plight and Circumstances of Vietnamese and Other Refugees*, Australian Government Publishing Service, Canberra, 1976.

Viviani, Nancy & Joanna Lawe-Davies, 'Australian Government Policy on the Entry of Vietnamese Refugees 1976 to 1978', *Research Paper No. 2*, School of Modern Asian Studies, Griffith University, Brisbane, February 1980.

Ward, Elizabeth, 'Call Out the Troops: An Examination of the Legal Basis for Australian Defence Force Involvement in Non-Defence Matters', *Australian Parliamentary Research Paper No. 8*, Commonwealth Parliamentary Library, Canberra, 1997–98.

Wild, Rex & Patricia Anderson, *Little Children Are Sacred*, report of the Board of Inquiry into the Protection of Aboriginal Children from Sexual Abuse, Northern Territory Government, Darwin, 30 April 2007.

Woodard, Gary, Moreen Dee & Max Suich, 'Negotiating the Australia–Japan Basic Treaty of Friendship and Cooperation: Reflections and Afterthoughts', *Asia Pacific Economic Paper No. 362*, Australia–Japan Research Centre, Australian National University College of Asia and the Pacific, Canberra, 2007.

Woodward, Edward, *Report of the Royal Commission into the Australian Meat Industry*, Australian Government Publishing Service, Canberra, 1982.

'Zimbabwe Country Economic Memorandum: Achieving Shared Growth', *Report No. 13540-ZIM*, World Bank, Washington, DC, 21 April 1995.

Internet Sites and Articles

'1979: End of White Rule in Rhodesia', On This Day 1950–2005, BBC, 2008, http://news.bbc.co.uk/onthisday/hi/dates/stories/june/1/newsid_2492000/2492915.stm, viewed July 2009.

Carter, Jimmy, 'Meeting with Prime Minister J Malcolm Fraser of Australia: Remarks to Reporters on the Prime Minister's Departure', 7 February 1980, American Presidency Project, 2009, www.presidency.ucsb.edu/ws/index.php?pid=32901&st=malcolm+fraser&st1=, viewed May 2009.

Commonwealth Secretariat, 'From the Archive, Sydney Regional Conference, February 1978', The Commonwealth, 19 May 2009, www.thecommonwealth.org/news/34580/34581/200569/190509archivesydney.htm, viewed July 2009.

The Commonwealth, www.thecommonwealth.org, viewed July 2009.

'Education: Malcolm Fraser', National Museum of Australia, [n.d.], www.nma.gov.au/education/school_resources/websites_and_interactives/primeministers/malcolm_fraser, viewed May 2009.

Evans, Rachel, 'Bob Brown and the Rise of the Greens', review of *Bob Brown, Gentle Revolutionary* by James Norman, Green Left Online, 9 March 2005, www.greenleft.org.au/2005/618/35219, viewed July 2009.

Fraser, Malcolm, 'Why AustraliansAll.com.au, and Why Right Now', Australians All, 14 November 2006, http://australiansall.com.au/archive/post/why-australiansall-com-au-and-why-right-now, viewed September 2009.

Galbally, Frank, Interview for Making Multicultural Australia, 1994, www.multiculturalaustralia.edu.au/library/media/Audio/id/566. Australian-Institute-of-Multicultural-Affairs, viewed May 2009.

'Gough Whitlam and Malcolm Fraser—Yes Ad', YouTube, 2006, www.youtube.com/watch?v=RjqtuUXnm2g, viewed September 2009.

Henry, Ken, 'Post-Budget Address to the Australian Business Economists', Commonwealth of Australia, 19 May 2009, www.treasury.gov.au/documents/1546/HTML/docshell.asp?URL=Contemporary%20Challenges%20in%20Fiscal%20Policy.html, viewed June 2009.

NAA, 'Fact Sheet 130: The Royal Commission on Espionage, 1954–55', NAA, 2006, www.naa.gov.au/about-us/publications/fact-sheets/fs130.aspx, viewed May 2009.

Neumann, Klaus & Gwenda Tavan (eds), 'Does History Matter? Making and Debating Citizenship, Immigration and Refugee Policy in Australia and New Zealand', monograph, Australia and New Zealand School of Government, Australian National University E Press, 2009.

Perkins, Charles, interview with Robin Hughes, Australian Biography, 6 May 1998, www.australianbiography.gov.au/subjects/perkins/intertext1.html (transcript), viewed June 2009.

Refugee Council of Australia, 'Australia's Refugee and Humanitarian Program', submission to the federal government, Refugee Council of Australia, January 2008, www.refugeecouncil.org.au/docs/resources/submissions/2009-10_intakesub.pdf, viewed June 2009.

Richards, Jonathan, 'Queensland Cabinet Minutes (1975): A Report for Queensland State Archives', November 2005, Queensland State Archives, 2006, www.archives.qld.gov.au/downloads/1975HistoriansReport.pdf, viewed July 2009.

Robinson, Mary, remarks to the United Nations Human Rights Commission, 30 April 1999, reported in 'World: Europe UN Rights Chief Slams NATO Bombings', BBC News, 30 April 1999, http://news.bbc.co.uk/2/hi/europe/332745.stm, viewed August 2009.

'Singapore Declaration of Commonwealth Principles 1971', The Commonwealth, 2004, www.thecommonwealth.org/shared_asp_files/GFSR.asp?NodeID=141097, viewed July 2009.

'Statement 10: Historical Australian Government Data', Budget Paper No. 1: Budget Strategy and Outlook 2009–10, Commonwealth of Australia, 2009, www.budget.gov.au/2009-10/content/bp1/html/bp1_bst10.htm, viewed June 2009.

Tange, Arthur, 'Defence Policy-Making: A Close-Up View 1950–1980', Canberra Papers on Strategy and Defence No. 169, ed. Peter Edwards, Australian National University E Press, 2008, http://epress.anu.edu.au/sdsc/dpm/html/frames.php, viewed May 2009.

Tudor House, www.tudorhouse.nsw.edu.au, viewed May 2009.

'Video Shows Kidnapped Aid Worker', BBC News, 20 October 2004, http://news.bbc.co.uk/2/hi/uk_news/3756192.stm, viewed August 2009.

'The Women's Electoral Lobby (WEL)—1972', Social Justice Almanac, CBOnline Project, 2004, www.cbonline.org.au/Media/asja/ASJA_WEL_Feature_Article.doc, viewed May 2009.

York, Barry, 'Australia and Refugees 1901–2002: An Annotated Chronology Based on Official Sources', Parliament of Australia, 2003, www.aph.gov.au/library/pubs/online/Refugees_s2.htm, viewed June 2009.

Television and Radio Programs

7.30 Report, television program, ABC, 29 May 2000.

Meet the Press, television program, Channel Nine, 7 March 1971.

PM, radio program, ABC, 22 December 2008.

Stateline (Tasmania), television program, ABC, 27 June 2003; 8 December 2006.

Sunday, television program, Channel Nine, 26 February 1995, transcript in MFC 105/87.

Thatcher, Margaret, interview with Peter Snow, television program, ITN, 6 August 1979.

This Day Tonight, television program, ABC, 23 February 1971, transcript in NAA M1369 [305]; 9 March 1971, transcript in NAA M1369 [305].

Other Published Sources

Al-Kateb, Ahmed Ali v. Philippa Godwin (Deputy Secretary, Department of Immigration and Multicultural and Indigenous Affairs), Julie Helen Keenan (Acting Director of the Unauthorised Arrivals Section) & Minister for Immigration and Multicultural and Indigenous Affairs (2004) 219 CLR 562; *Minister for Immigration and Multicultural and Indigenous Affairs v. Abbas Mohammad Hasan Al Khafaji* (2004) 219 CLR 6.

Australia, New Zealand and the United States Security Treaty, 1951.

The Commonwealth Accord on Southern Africa (The Nassau Accord), Lyford Cay, Nassau, 20 October 1985.
Commonwealth Heads of Government Meeting, Gleneagles Agreement, London, 15 June 1977.
——final communiqué, Lusaka, 1979.
Constitution of Nauru.
Constitution of the Independent State of Papua New Guinea.
Huggins, Jackie & Peter Read, interview with Ian Viner, Council for Aboriginal Reconciliation Collection, Oral History Collection, National Library of Australia, Canberra, 8 May 2006.
The Melbourne Declaration, Commonwealth of Nations, Canberra, 3 October 1981.
Northern Territory of Australia, Ordinance No. 16, 1911, published in *Commonwealth of Australia Gazette*, 8 January 1912.
Public Service Amendment (First Division Officers) Act 1976.
United Nations Convention Relating to the Status of Refugees, 28 July 1951.

Index

THE MIEGUNYAH PRESS

The text was typeset by Megan Ellis
The text was set in 12 point Bembo Regular
with 15 points of leading
The text is printed on 80 gsm Offset

This book was edited by Penny Mansley